Lecture Notes in Computer Science

Lecture Notes in Artificial Intelligence   16121

Founding Editor

Jörg Siekmann

The series Lecture Notes in Artificial Intelligence (LNAI) was established in 1988 as a topical subseries of LNCS devoted to artificial intelligence.

The series publishes state-of-the-art research results at a high level. As with the LNCS mother series, the mission of the series is to serve the international R & D community by providing an invaluable service, mainly focused on the publication of conference and workshop proceedings and postproceedings.

José Valente de Oliveira · João Leite ·
João Rodrigues · João Dias · Pedro Cardoso
Editors

Progress in Artificial Intelligence

24th EPIA Conference on Artificial Intelligence, EPIA 2025
Faro, Portugal, October 1–3, 2025
Proceedings, Part I

 Springer

Editors
José Valente de Oliveira 🆔
University of Algarve
Faro, Portugal

João Leite 🆔
NOVA University Lisbon
Costa da Caparica, Portugal

João Rodrigues 🆔
University of Algarve
Faro, Portugal

João Dias 🆔
University of Algarve
Faro, Portugal

Pedro Cardoso 🆔
University of Algarve
Faro, Portugal

ISSN 0302-9743   ISSN 1611-3349 (electronic)
Lecture Notes in Artificial Intelligence
ISBN 978-3-032-05175-2   ISBN 978-3-032-05176-9 (eBook)
https://doi.org/10.1007/978-3-032-05176-9

LNCS Sublibrary: SL7 – Artificial Intelligence

This Springer imprint is published by the registered company Springer Nature Switzerland AG
The registered company address is: Gewerbestrasse 11, 6330 Cham, Switzerland

If disposing of this product, please recycle the paper.

Preface

The EPIA Conference on Artificial Intelligence is a well-established conference in the field of Artificial Intelligence (AI). The 24th edition, EPIA 2025, was held in Faro at the University of Algarve, Campus de Gambelas, October 1–3, 2025 (https://epia2025.ual g.pt/).

Faro is the charming capital of the Algarve region in southern Portugal, renowned for its history, picturesque old town, and vibrant culture. The city features cobbled streets, historic landmarks like the Faro Cathedral, and a scenic waterfront along the Ria Formosa lagoon, which is a protected nature reserve teeming with diverse wildlife. Its welcoming atmosphere, combined with lively markets, traditional cuisine, and cultural festivals, makes Faro a captivating destination for travelers seeking both history and relaxation.

The conference was organized with the patronage of the Portuguese Association for Artificial Intelligence (APPIA – http://www.appia.pt). EPIA covers theoretical, fundamental questions, and applications in Artificial Intelligence, allowing scientific exchange between researchers, engineers, and professionals in related disciplines.

The EPIA 2025 program included 15 thematic tracks dedicated to specific areas in AI:

- AI and Creativity (AIC);
- AI for Architecture, Engineering and Conservation (AI4AES);
- Ambient Intelligence and Affective Environments (AmIA);
- Artificial Intelligence and IoT in Agriculture (AIoTA);
- Artificial Intelligence and Law (AIL);
- Artificial Intelligence for Industry and Societies (AI4IS);
- Artificial Intelligence in Medicine (AIM);
- Artificial Intelligence in Power and Energy Systems (AIPES);
- Artificial Intelligence in Transportation Systems (AITS);
- Ethics and Responsibility in AI (ERAI);
- Fuzzy Data Analysis and Applications (FDA);
- Generative AI – Foundations and Applications (GenAI);
- Knowledge Discovery and Business Intelligence (KDBI);
- Natural Language Processing, Text Mining and Applications (NLP-TeMA);
- Artificial Intelligence - Theory, Methods, and Applications (AITMA).

In this edition, EPIA received 158 submissions from 32 different countries. Each submission was reviewed by at least three Program Committee (PC) members of each thematic track. These volumes contain all 76 accepted papers from the thematic tracks.

The conference also featured three distinguished keynote speakers: Paulo Torroni (University of Bologna, Italy) with a talk on "Argument Mining and Reasoning with Large Language Models"; Frans A. Oliehoek (Delft University of Technology, Netherlands) with a talk on "Model-based reinforcement learning and abstraction"; and Mário Figueiredo (Instituto Superior Técnico, University of Lisbon, Portugal) with a talk on

"The Why of AI: Causal Discovery from Observational Data". The invited talks' abstracts are included in these proceedings' front matter.

The EPIA organizers are thankful to our outstanding keynote speakers, to the EPIA 2025 International Steering Committee members for their guidance regarding the scientific organization, and to the Thematic Track Chairs and their respective Program Committee members. Very special thanks are due to all the student volunteers and the Local Organizing Committee, who did a fantastic job, contributing to a very successful conference. The organization would also like to express its gratitude to our sponsors, Empowered Startups (https://empoweredstartups.com/), Dengun (http://dengun.com/) and STAP, SA (http://www.stap.pt/) and Springer (https://www.springer.com) who sponsored the Best Paper Award. To conclude, a word of thanks to our hosts, Câmara Municipal de Faro, the University of Algarve and its Faculty of Sciences and Technology, and the Faculty of Economics.

October 2025

José Valente de Oliveira
João Leite
João Rodrigues
João Dias
Pedro Cardoso

Organization

Event and Program Chairs

José Valente de Oliveira	University of Algarve, Portugal
João Leite	NOVA University Lisbon, Portugal
João Rodrigues	University of Algarve, Portugal
João Dias	University of Algarve, Portugal
Pedro Cardoso	University of Algarve, Portugal

Organization Chairs

Simão Melo de Sousa	University of Algarve, Portugal
Helder Daniel	University of Algarve, Portugal
José Barateiro	University of Algarve, Portugal
Marielba Zacarias	University of Algarve, Portugal
Paula Ventura Martins	University of Algarve, Portugal
Sofia Vairinho	University of Algarve, Portugal

International Steering Committee

Alípio Jorge	University of Porto, Portugal
Ana Bazzan	Federal University of Rio Grande do Sul, Brazil
Bernadete Ribeiro	University of Coimbra, Portugal
Eugénio Oliveira	University of Porto, Portugal
Goreti Marreiros	Polytechnic Institute of Porto, Portugal
Inês Lynce	University of Lisbon, Portugal
José Júlio Alferes	NOVA University Lisbon, Portugal
Juan Pavón	Complutense University of Madrid, Spain
Luís Correia	University of Lisbon, Portugal
Luís Paulo Reis	University of Porto, Portugal
Paulo Novais	University of Minho, Portugal
Virginia Dignum	Umeå University, Sweden

Thematic Track Chairs

AI and Creativity (AIC)

João Miguel Cunha	University of Coimbra, Portugal
Pedro Martins	University of Coimbra, Portugal
Tiago Martins	University of Coimbra, Portugal
Maria Hedblom	Jönköping University, Sweden
Moritz Schwind	Technische Hochschule Nürnberg Georg Simon Ohm, Germany

AI for Architecture, Engineering and Conservation (AI4AES)

Daniele Corradetti	University of Lisbon, Portugal
Nuno Marques	NOVA University Lisbon, Portugal
José Delgado Rodrigues	Consultant in Heritage Conservation, Portugal
Roberta Spallone	Politecnico di Torino, Italia

Ambient Intelligence and Affective Environments (AmIA)

Manuel Rodrigues	Universidade do Minho, Portugal
Luís Conceição	ISEP, Portugal
Sara Rodríguez	University of Salamanca, Spain
Peter Mikulecky	University of Hradec Králové, Czech Republic
Goreti Marreiros	ISEP, Portugal
Paulo Novais	Universidade do Minho, Portugal

Artificial Intelligence and IoT in Agriculture (AIoTA)

Luís Pádua	UTAD, Portugal
Filipe Neves dos Santos	INESC-TEC, Portugal
José Boaventura Cunha	UTAD, Portugal
Paulo Moura Oliveira	UTAD, Portugal
Raul Morais	UTAD, Portugal

Artificial Intelligence and Law (AIL)

Pedro Miguel Freitas   Universidade Católica Portuguesa, Portugal
Ugo Pagallo   University of Torino, Italy
Massimo Durante   University of Torino, Italy
Paulo Novais   Universidade do Minho, Portugal

Artificial Intelligence for Industry and Societies (AI4IS)

Filipe Portela   University of Minho, Portugal
Sherin M. Moussa   Université Française d'Égypte, Egypt
Teresa Guarda   Universidad Estatal Península de Santa Elena,
                                    Ecuador
Ioan M. Ciumasu   Paris-Saclay University, France

Artificial Intelligence in Medicine (AIM)

Manuel Filipe Santos   University of Minho, Portugal
Manuel Fernandez Delgado   University of Santiago, Spain
Tiago André Guimarães   University of Minho, Portugal

Artificial Intelligence in Power and Energy Systems (AIPES)

Zita Vale   Polytechnic Institute of Porto, Portugal
Tiago Pinto   UTAD and INESC TEC, Portugal
Pedro Faria   Polytechnic Institute of Porto, Portugal
Bo Norregaard Jorgensen   University of Southern Denmark, Denmark

Artificial Intelligence in Transportation Systems (AITS)

Alberto Fernandez   Universidad Rey Juan Carlos, Spain
Tania Fontes   INESC TEC, Portugal
Zafeiris Kokkinogenis   University of Porto, Portugal
Rosaldo Rossetti   University of Porto, Portugal

Ethics and Responsibility in AI (ERAI)

Tânia Carvalho	University of Porto, Portugal
João Vinagre	European Commission, Joint Research Centre, Spain
Catarina Silva	University of Coimbra, Portugal
Nuno Moniz	Lucy Family Institute for Data & Society, USA

Fuzzy Data Analysis and Applications (FDA)

Susana Nascimento	NOVA University Lisbon, Portugal
Gozde Ulutagay	Ege University, Turkey
João Paulo Carvalho	INESC-ID and University of Lisbon, Portugal

Generative AI – Foundations and Applications (GenAI)

Penousal Machado	University of Coimbra, Portugal
José Machado	University of Minho, Portugal
Paulo Moura Oliveira	UTAD and INESC TEC, Portugal

Knowledge Discovery and Business Intelligence (KDBI)

Paulo Cortez	University of Minho, Portugal
Albert Bifet	Université Paris-Saclay, France
Luís Cavique	Universidade Aberta, Portugal
João Gama	University of Porto, Portugal
Nuno Marques	NOVA University Lisbon, Portugal
Manuel Filipe Santos	University of Minho, Portugal
Rita P. Ribeiro	University of Porto, Portugal

Natural Language Processing, Text Mining and Applications (NLP-TeMA)

Joaquim Silva	NOVA University Lisbon, Portugal
Pablo Gamallo	Universidade de Santiago de Compostela, Spain
Paulo Quaresma	Universidade de Évora, Portugal
Irene Rodrigues	Universidade de Évora, Portugal
Alípio Jorge	University of Porto, Portugal

Artificial Intelligence - Theory, Methods, and Applications (AITMA)

José Valente de Oliveira	University of Algarve, Portugal
João Leite	NOVA University Lisbon, Portugal
João Rodrigues	University of Algarve, Portugal
João Dias	University of Algarve, Portugal
Pedro Cardoso	University of Algarve, Portugal

Program Committee

AI and Creativity (AIC)

Ana Rodrigues	University of Coimbra, Portugal
André Fabiano De Moraes	Instituto Federal Catarinense, Brazil
Brad Spendlove	Randolph College, USA
Carlos León	Universidad Complutense de Madrid, Spain
Caterina Moruzzi	University of Edinburgh, UK
Evana Gizzi	Tufts University, USA
F. Amílcar Cardoso	University of Coimbra, Portugal
Ivan Guerrero	UNAM, Mexico
Ivan Miguel Pires	Universidade de Aveiro, Portugal
João Gonçalves	University of Coimbra, Portugal
Kazjon Grace	University of Sydney, Australia
Ludovica Schaerf	University of Zurich, Switzerland
Manex Agirrezabal	University of Copenhagen, Denmark
Max Peeperkorn	University of Kent, UK
Sara González Gutiérrez	Universidad de Salamanca, Spain
Senja Pollak	Jožef Stefan Institute, Slovenia
Sérgio Rebelo	University of Coimbra, Portugal

AI for Architecture, Engineering and Conservation (AI4AES)

Alberto Pugnale	University of Melbourne, Australia
Amaral Gustavo Garcia Do	University of Kansas, USA
Camilla Pezzica	Cardiff University, UK
David Semedo	NOVA University Lisbon, Portugal
Dominik Lengyel	Brandenburg University of Technology, Germany
Enrico Pupi	Politecnico di Torino, Italy
Fátima Batista	LNEC, Portugal

Francesco Carota	University of Kansas, USA
Gabriele Mirra	Delft University of Technology, Netherlands
João Manso	LNEC, Portugal
João Marcelino	LNEC, Portugal
Michele Russo	Sapienza University of Rome, Italy
Nuno Correia	NOVA University Lisbon, Portugal
Pingbo Tang	Carnegie Mellon University, USA
Rui Nóbrega	NOVA University Lisbon, Portugal
Sarah Fakhreddine	Carnegie Mellon University, USA
Susana Nascimento	NOVA University Lisbon, Portugal
Valerio Palma	Politecnico di Torino, Italy

Ambient Intelligence and Affective Environments (AmIA)

Antonio Fernández-Caballero	Universidad de Castilla-La Mancha, Spain
F. Amílcar Cardoso	University of Coimbra, Portugal
Fábio Silva	University of Minho, Portugal
Fernando De La Prieta	University of Salamanca, Spain
Florentino Fdez-Riverola	University of Vigo, Spain
Hoon Ko	Sunmoon University, South Korea
Ichiro Satoh	National Institute of Informatics, Japan
Javier Jaen	Universitat Politècnica de València, Spain
Jean-Michel Ilié	Sorbonne Université, France
José Machado	University of Minho, Portugal
Jose M. Molina	Universidad Carlos III de Madrid, Spain
Lino Figueiredo	ISEP, Portugal
Luis Macedo	University of Coimbra, Portugal
Miguel J. Hornos	University of Granada, Spain
Ricardo Santos	Polytechnic Institute of Porto, Portugal
Ricardo Costa	Polytechnic Institute of Porto, Portugal
Shinichi Konomi	University of Tokyo, Japan
Tatsuo Nakajima	Waseda University, Japan
Vicente Julian	Universitat Politècnica de València, Spain

Artificial Intelligence and IoT in Agriculture (AIoTA)

Anakkallan Subeesh	ICAR, India
Aneesh Chauhan	Wageningen University and Research, Netherlands
Bruno Tisseyre	Institute Agro Montpellier, France

Carlos Serodio	UTAD, Portugal
Dinos Ferentinos	Hellenic Agricultural Organization (Demeter), Greece
Emanuel Peres	UTAD, Portugal
Javier Sanchis Saez	Universitat Politècnica de València, Spain
João Coelho	Instituto Politécnico de Bragança, Portugal
João Valente	Spanish National Research Council, Spain
Joaquim João Sousa	UTAD, Portugal
José Antonio Sanz Delgado	Universidad Pública de Navarra, Spain
Pedro Couto	UTAD, Portugal
Stef Maree	Wageningen University and Research, Netherlands
Tatiana M. Pinho	INESC TEC, Portugal
Telmo Adão	UTAD, Portugal
Vítor Filipe	UTAD, Portugal

Artificial Intelligence and Law (AIL)

Arlindo Oliveira	INESC-ID and University of Lisbon, Portugal
Carlisle George	Middlesex University London, UK
Cesar Analide	University of Minho, Portugal
Cristina Salgado	Universidad de Santiago de Compostela, Spain
Dalila Durães	Universidade do Minho, Portugal
Daniel Braun	University of Twente, Netherlands
Davide Carneiro	Polytechnic Institute of Porto, Portugal
Enrico Francesconi	IGSG-CNR, Italy
Fábio Silva	University of Minho, Portugal
Francisco Andrade	University of Minho, Portugal
Francisco Marcondes	University of Minho, Portugal
Giovanni De Gregorio	Católica Global School of Law, Portugal
Giovanni Sartor	EUI/CIRSFID, Italy
Goreti Marreiros	Polytechnic Institute of Porto, Portugal
Haihua Chen	University of North Texas, USA
José Machado	University of Minho, Portugal
Luís Conceição	Polytechnic Institute of Porto, Portugal
Luis Mendes Gomes	Universidade dos Açores, Portugal
Lurdes Mesquita	Polytechnic Institute of Porto, Portugal
Manuel Masseno	Polytechnic Institute of Beja, Portugal
Manuel Rodrigues	University of Minho, Portugal
Marco Gomes	University of Minho, Portugal
Marco Gonçalves	University of Minho, Portugal

Pedro Rangel Henriques	University of Minho, Portugal
Sérgio Gonçalves	PHD, Portugal
Teresa Coelho Moreira	University of Minho, Portugal
Tomer Libal	University of Luxembourg, Luxembourg
Vasileios Rovilos	Credo AI, USA
Vicente Julian	Universitat Politècnica de València, Spain

Artificial Intelligence for Industry and Societies (AI4IS)

Alfonso González Briones	University of Salamanca, Spain
Ana Azevedo	CEOS.PP and Polytechnic Institute of Porto, Portugal
Antoni Morell	Universitat Autònoma de Barcelona, Spain
Antonio Moreira	IPCA, Portugal
Cihan Tunc	University of North Texas, USA
Daniel Urda	University of Burgos, Spain
Fabrizio Messina	University of Catania, Italy
George Stalidis	International Hellenic University, Greece
Hanmin Jung	KISTI, South Korea
Hatem Mrad	Université du Québec en Abitibi-Témiscamingue, Canada
Inna Skarga-Bandurova	Oxford Brookes University, UK
Jorge Bernardino	Polytechnic Institute of Coimbra, Portugal
Juan-Ignacio Latorre-Biel	Public University of Navarre, Spain
Mahmoud Mounir	Ain Shams University, Egypt
Marco Alfonse	Université Française d'Egypte, Egypt
Mariam Gawich	Université Française d'Égypte, Egypt
Matsatsinis Nikolaos	Technical University of Crete, Greece
Muhammad Younas	Oxford Brookes University, UK
Omid Fatahi Valilai	Constructor University Bremen, Germany
Panos Fitsilis	University of Thessaly, Greece
Roaa Elghondakly	Ain Shams University, Egypt
Sara Paiva	Instituto Politécnico de Viana do Castelo, Portugal
Sergio Ilarri	University of Zaragoza, Spain
Spyros Panagiotakis	Hellenic Mediterranean University, Greece
Vicente Ferreira Lucena Junior	Federal University of Amazonas, Brazil
Waleed Adel	Université Française d'Egypte, Egypt

Artificial Intelligence in Medicine (AIM)

Ailton Moreira	University of Minho, Portugal
António Abelha	University of Minho, Portugal
Beatriz De La Iglesia	University of East Anglia, UK
Filipe Portela	University of Minho, Portugal
Francini Hak	University of Minho, Portugal
Hugo Peixoto	University of Minho, Portugal
Inna Skarga-Bandurova	Oxford Brookes University, UK
João Lopes	University of Minho, Portugal
José Machado	University of Minho, Portugal
Júlio Duarte	University of Minho, Portugal
Luis Mendes Gomes	Universidade dos Açores, Portugal
Panagiotis Bamidis	Aristotle University of Thessaloniki, Greece
Pedro Gago	Polytechnic Institute of Leiria, Portugal
Regina Sousa	University of Minho, Portugal
Rui Camacho	University of Porto, Portugal
Susana Brás	Universidade de Aveiro, Portugal

Artificial Intelligence in Power and Energy Systems (AIPES)

Alfonso Briones	University of Salamanca, Spain
Ana Estanqueiro	LNEG, Portugal
António Couto	LNEG, Portugal
Brígida Teixeira	GECAD, Portugal
Catia Silva	INESC, Portugal
Fernando Lezama	Polytechnic Institute of Porto, Portugal
Fernando Lopes	LNEG, Portugal
Gabriel Santos	Polytechnic Institute of Porto, Portugal
Germano Lambert-Torres	PS Solutions, USA
Hugo Morais	Universidade de Lisboa, Portugal
John Eugenio Peñaloza Morán	INESC TEC, Portugal
José Baptista	UTAD and INESC TEC, Portugal
Jose L. Rueda	Delft University of Technology, Netherlands
Leonardo Pilarski	UTAD, Portugal
Luis Gomes	Instituto Superior de Engenharia do Porto, Portugal
Mohammad Javadi	INESC-TEC, Portugal
Pedro Salomé	INL, Portugal
Philipp Thunshirn	University of Applied Sciences Technikum Wien, Austria

Ricardo Faia   GECAD, Portugal
Rita Teixeira   UTAD, Portugal
Tiago Soares   INESC TEC, Portugal
Zheng Ma   University of Southern Denmark, Denmark
Zia Ullah   UTAD, Portugal

Artificial Intelligence in Transportation Systems (AITS)

Ana L. C. Bazzan   Universidade Federal do Rio Grande do Sul,
                                 Brazil
António Costa   University Rey Juan Carlos, Spain; University of
                                 Porto, Portugal
António Pedro Aguiar   University of Porto, Portugal
Carlos A. Iglesias   Universidad Politécnica de Madrid, Spain
Cristina Olaverri-Monreal   Johannes Kepler University Linz, Austria
Daniel Castro Silva   University of Porto, Portugal
Davide Carneiro   Polytechnic Institute of Porto, Portugal
Eduardo Camponogara   Federal University of Santa Catarina, Brazil
Fabien Leurent   Université Paris-Est, France
Francesco Renna   University of Porto, Portugal
Gonçalo Correia   Delft University of Technology, Netherlands
Hilmi Berk Celikoglu   Technical University of Istanbul, Turkey
Holger Billhardt   Universidad Rey Juan Carlos, Spain
Joaquín Arias   Universidad Rey Juan Carlos, Spain
Joel Ribeiro   INESC TEC, Portugal
Luís Nunes   University Institute of Lisbon, Portugal
Marin Lujak   Rey Juan Carlos University, Spain
Pedro M. D'Orey   University of Porto, Portugal
Sara Ferreira   Universidade do Porto, Portugal
Sascha Ossowski   Rey Juan Carlos University, Spain

Ethics and Responsibility in AI (ERAI)

Ana Madureira   Departamento de Engenharia Informática,
                                 Portugal
Catarina Barata   Instituto Superior Técnico, Portugal
Jaime Cardoso   University of Porto, Portugal
Joana Costa   Polytechnic Institute of Leiria, Portugal
João Manuel R. S. Tavares   University of Porto and INEGI, Portugal
Joerg Osterrieder   University of Twente, Netherlands

Karla Figueiredo   Rio de Janeiro State University, Brazil
Luis F. Teixeira   Fraunhofer Portugal AICOS, Portugal
Marcelo Graglia   Pontifícia Universidade Católica de São Paulo,
                                  Brazil
Mario Figueiredo   Universidade de Lisboa, Portugal
Marley Vellasco   Pontifical Catholic University of Rio de Janeiro,
                                  Brazil
Nuno Lourenço   University of Coimbra, Portugal
Petia Georgieva   University of Aveiro, Portugal
Raquel Sebastião   University of Aveiro, Portugal

Fuzzy Data Analysis and Applications (FDA)

Fernando Gomide   University of Campinas, Brazil
João Sousa   University of Lisbon, Portugal
João Moura-Pires   Universidade NOVA de Lisboa, Portugal
Renato Amorim   University of Essex, UK
Rui Jorge Almeida   Maastricht University, Netherlands
Uzay Kaymak   Eindhoven University of Technology, Netherlands
Vitor Lobo   NOVA IMS, Portugal

Generative AI – Foundations and Applications (GenAI)

António Abelha   University of Minho, Portugal
Cristiana Neto   University of Minho, Portugal
Dalila Durães   Universidade do Minho, Portugal
Deden Witarsyah   Universiti Tun Hussein Onn Malaysia, Malasya
Diana Ferreira   University of Minho, Portugal
F. Amílcar Cardoso   University of Coimbra, Portugal
Francisco Marcondes   University of Minho, Portugal
Hugo Peixoto   University of Minho, Portugal
Ichiro Satoh   National Institute of Informatics, Japan
Jaume Jordán   Universitat Politècnica de València, Spain
João Miguel Cunha   University of Coimbra, Portugal
Jose Luis Calvo-Rolle   University of A Coruña, Spain
Júlio Duarte   University of Minho, Portugal
Manuel Filipe Santos   University of Minho, Portugal
Miguel J. Hornos   University of Granada, Spain
Omar D. Castrillon   Universidad Nacional de Colombia, Colombia
Regina Sousa   University of Minho, Portugal

Tatsuo Nakajima   Waseda University, Japan
Vicente Julian   Universitat Politècnica de València, Spain

Knowledge Discovery and Business Intelligence (KDBI)

Agnès Braud   University of Strasbourg, France
Alberto Bugarín-Diz   Universidade de Santiago de Compostela, Spain
Amilcar Oliveira   Universidade Aberta, Portugal
Andre de Carvalho   University of São Paulo, Brazil
Armando Mendes   University of Azores, Portugal
Carlos Ferreira   University of Porto, Portugal
Catarina Moreira   University of Technology Sydney, Australia
Elaine Faria   Federal University of Uberlândia, Brazil
Fátima Rodrigues   Institute of Engineering of Porto, Portugal
Manuel Fernandez Delgado   University of Santiago de Compostela, Spain
Marcos Aurélio Domingues   State University of Maringá, Brazil
Margarida Cardoso   ISCTE, Portugal
Murat Caner Testik   Hacettepe University, Turkey
Nuno Cruz Garcia   University of Lisbon, Portugal
Orlando Belo   Universidade do Minho, Portugal
Paulo Pombinho   Universidade Aberta and Atlântica - Instituto
                                     Universitário, Portugal
Rui Camacho   University of Porto, Portugal
Susana Nascimento   NOVA University Lisbon

Natural Language Processing, Text Mining and Applications (NLP-TeMA)

Bruno Martins   University of Lisbon and INESC-ID, Portugal
Eric De La Clergerie   INRIA, France
Fernando Batista   INESC-ID and ISCTE-IUL, Portugal
Francisco Couto   University of Lisbon, Portugal
Gaël Dias   University of Caen Normandie, France
Hugo Gonçalo Oliveira   University of Coimbra, Portugal
Isabel Trancoso   INESC-ID and University of Lisbon, Portugal
Jesús Vilares   Universidade da Coruña, Spain
João Dias   University of Algarve, Portugal
Manex Agirrezabal   University of Copenhagen, Denmark
Marcos Garcia   Universidade de Santiago de Compostela, Spain
Mário J. Silva   INESC-ID and University of Lisbon, Portugal

Miguel A. Alonso   Universidade da Coruña, Spain
Nuno C. Marques   NOVA University Lisbon, Portugal
Pavel Brazdil   University of Porto, Portugal
Sérgio Nunes   INESC TEC and University of Porto, Portugal

Artificial Intelligence - Theory, Methods, and Applications (AITMA)

Agnès Braud   University of Strasbourg, France
Alberto Bugarín-Diz   Universidade de Santiago de Compostela, Spain
Amilcar Oliveira   Universidade Aberta, Portugal
Ana Azevedo   CEOS.PP and Polytechnic Institute of Porto,
                          Portugal
Andre de Carvalho   University of São Paulo, Brazil
António Abelha   University of Minho, Portugal
António Costa   Rey Juan Carlos University, Spain; University of
                          Porto, Portugal
António Pedro Aguiar   University of Porto, Portugal
Arlindo Oliveira   INESC-ID and University of Lisbon, Portugal
Bruno Martins   University of Lisbon and INESC-ID, Portugal
Carlos Ferreira   University of Porto, Portugal
Carlos A. Iglesias   Universidad Politécnica de Madrid, Spain
Daniel Castro Silva   University of Porto, Portugal
Daniel Urda   University of Burgos, Spain
Daniele Corradetti   University of Lisbon and Universidade do
                          Algarve, Portugal
Davide Carneiro   CIICESI and Polytechnic Institute of Porto,
                          Portugal
Eduardo Camponogara   Federal University of Santa Catarina, Brazil
Enrico Pupi   Politecnico di Torino, Italy
Eric De La Clergerie   INRIA, France
Fabrizio Messina   University of Catania, Italy
Fátima Rodrigues   Institute of Engineering of Porto, Portugal
Francisco Couto   University of Lisbon, Portugal
Gaël Dias   University of Caen Normandie, France
George Stalidis   International Hellenic University, Greece
Giovanni Sartor   EUI/CIRSFID, Italy
Hanmin Jung   KISTI, South Korea
Hilmi Berk Celikoglu   Technical University of Istanbul, Turkey
Holger Billhardt   Universidad Rey Juan Carlos, Spain
Hoon Ko   Sunmoon University, South Korea
Isabel Trancoso   INESC-ID and University of Lisbon, Portugal

Jaume Jordán	Universitat Politècnica de València, Spain
João Moura-Pires	Universidade NOVA de Lisboa, Portugal
João Paulo Carvalho	University of Lisbon and INESC-ID, Portugal
Joel Ribeiro	INESC TEC, Portugal
Jose Luis Calvo-Rolle	University of A Coruña, Spain
Juan Pavón	Universidad Complutense de Madrid, Spain
Juan-Ignacio Latorre-Biel	Public University of Navarre, Spain
Luis Macedo	University of Coimbra, Portugal
Luís Correia	Universidade de Lisboa, Portugal
Luís Nunes	ISCTE, Portugal
Marin Lujak	Rey Juan Carlos University, Spain
Mário J. Silva	INESC-ID and University of Lisbon, Portugal
Matsatsinis Nikolaos	Technical University of Crete, Greece
Muhammad Younas	Oxford Brookes University, UK
Murat Caner Testik	Hacettepe University, Turkey
Omar D. Castrillon	Universidad Nacional de Colombia, Colombia
Omid Fatahi Valilai	Constructor University Bremen, Germany
Orlando Belo	Universidade do Minho, Portugal
Paulo Novais	University of Minho, Portugal
Paulo Pombinho	Universidade Aberta and Atlântica - Instituto Universitário, Portugal
Paulo Quaresma	Universidade de Évora, Portugal
Pedro M. D'Orey	University of Porto, Portugal
Petia Georgieva	University of Aveiro, Portugal
Sara Ferreira	University of Porto, Portugal
Sara Rodríguez	University of Salamanca, Spain
Spyros Panagiotakis	Hellenic Mediterranean University, Greece
Susana Nascimento	NOVA University Lisbon, Portugal
Tatsuo Nakajima	Waseda University, Japan
Vicente Ferreira Lucena Junior	Federal University of Amazonas, Brazil
Vicente Julian	Universitat Politècnica de València, Spain

Keynotes

Argument Mining and Reasoning with Large Language Models

Paolo Torroni

University of Bologna, Italy

Abstract. The rapid evolution of Large Language Models has sparked discussions about their ability to reason and how they may affect human reasoning. In this talk, we look at LLM reasoning through the lens of argumentation. We will explore how argumentation theories can help investigate the limits of current LLMs and reason about their role in pubic debate.

Model-based Reinforcement Learning and Abstraction

Frans A. Oliehoek

Delft University of Technology, The Netherlands

Abstract. In reinforcement learning (RL), we develop techniques to learn to control complex systems, and over the last decade we have seen impressive successes ranging from beating grandmasters in the game of Go to real-world applications like chip design, power grid control, and drug design. However, nearly all applications of RL require access to an accurate and lightweight simulator from which huge numbers of trials can be sampled. In this talk, I will cover some settings where this is not the case, and where therefore we need to engage in some form of 'model-based RL' to learn an appropriate model. Specifically, I will give an overview of a number of different problem settings (MDPs, POMDPs, and multiagent problems) and various corresponding approaches to learning and using models of the environment (ranging from deep learning, to Bayesian inference, and from planning with MCTS variants to model-free RL), highlighting their strong points as well as limitations. Central to all these approaches is the notion of abstraction: how finely do we represent the world when learning and planning? And what impact might such abstractions actually have on theoretical guarantees of MBRL methods?

The Why of AI: Causal Discovery from Observational Data

Mário Figueiredo

Instituto Superior Técnico, University of Lisbon, Portugal

Abstract. In causal discovery, the aim is to uncover the causal mechanisms that drive the relationships between variables — a critical step beyond the correlational models prevalent in modern machine learning. This pursuit is foundational for the next generation of robust and explainable AI, with applications in most scientific fields. Although, in principle, identifying causal relationships requires interventions (experiments), it is often the case that this is impossible, impractical, or unethical. The challenge of learning cause and effect from purely observational data is therefore central to causal discovery. In this talk, after briefly surveying the field, I will discuss recent advances in causal discovery from data, namely the problem of distinguishing cause from effect on bivariate data.

Contents – Part I

AI for Architecture, Engineering and Conservation (AI4AEC)

Knowledge Discovery and Business Intelligence (KDBI)

Generative AI: Foundations and Applications (GenAI)

Contents – Part II

Artificial Intelligence and IoT in Agriculture (AIoTA)

Artificial Intelligence in Transportation Systems (AITS)

**Natural Language Processing, Text Mining and Applications
(NLP-TeMA)**

Ambient Intelligence and Affective Environments (AmIA)

AI and Creativity (AIC)

Artificial Intelligence in Power and Energy Systems (AIPES)

Fuzzy Data Analysis and Applications (FDA)

Artificial Intelligence in Medicine (AIM)

AI-Driven Mobile Solution for Early Detection and Management of Diabetic Foot Ulcers

António Chaves®, Rúben Ganança®, Tayan Peller®, António Abelha®,
José Machado®, and Hugo Peixoto$^{(\boxtimes)}$®

LASI/Algoritmi Research Centre, Universidade do Minho, Braga 4715, Portugal
`antonio.chaves@algoritmi.uminho.pt`, `{pg54203,pg54451}@alunos.uminho.pt`,
`{abelha,jmac,hpeixoto}@di.uminho.pt`

Abstract. Diabetic Foot Ulcers (DFUs) are one of the most serious and common complications of diabetes mellitus, with an estimated 15% to 25% of people with diabetes developing a DFUs during their lifetime. To combat misinformation and promote treatment adherence, it is proposed to develop an integrated follow-up framework, capable of intelligent treatment monitoring. The application integrates a Deep Learning (DL) approach to analyse images submitted by patients and provide personalized feedback to help adapt and optimize treatment. The proposed tool aims not only to provide educational information but also facilitate remote communication between the patient and the healthcare professional, contributing to the improvement of existing ulcers and the early detection of new lesions. The architecture of a mobile application for this purpose is outlined, and the routing of information in the application via APIs is also explained so that data can be recorded and captured efficiently. The joint implementation of the Deep Learning, YOLO/RetinaNet, and Segment Anything Model (SAM) models to classify and segment, respectively, the images submitted to the application is likewise described. Preliminary results indicate that the YOLOv11n and RetinaNet with resnet50+FPN backbone models achieved mAP@50 of 0.844 and 0.811, respectively.

Keywords: Deep Learning · Personalised Medicine · Computer Vision · Remote Patient Monitoring · Health Information Systems · Diabetic Foot Ulcers

1 Introduction

Diabetic foot ulcers (DFUs) are a serious complication of diabetes mellitus resulting from neuropathy and peripheral vascular disease [8, 11]. They are characterised by loss of sensation, deformity and increased pressure on the plantar surface, favouring the development of hard-to-heal wounds that, if left untreated, can lead to serious infection and amputation [9]. It is estimated that 10% to 15% of people with diabetes develop DFUs, with up to 85% of unhealed ulcers

J. Valente de Oliveira et al. (Eds.): EPIA 2025, LNAI 16121, pp. 3–14, 2026.
https://doi.org/10.1007/978-3-032-05176-9_1

leading to amputation [12], so implementing preventive strategies and effective diagnostic methods is crucial for reducing amputations and improving patients' quality of life [10].

In this context, innovative technologies such as artificial intelligence (AI) and mobile applications have demonstrated potential in addressing the complications associated with DFUs [20]. This article expounds on the architecture and functionality of a mobile application that is founded on deep learning (DL) to monitor and prevent the progression of DFUs. The system employs a two-stage workflow, integrating image detection/classification and segmentation with advanced models such as You Only Look Once (YOLO) and Segment Anything Model (SAM).

2   State of Art

Mobile health (mHealth) can be defined as an innovative approach to remote user monitoring, based on the use of mobile applications to support healthcare provision [17]. The solution facilitates the exchange of information between users and healthcare professionals, thereby promoting closer and more continuous monitoring. This instrument is especially beneficial in circumstances where access to healthcare is restricted, for example in isolated regions or for individuals with impaired mobility, such as those suffering from diabetic foot disease [16].

The most common features in diabetic foot care apps are to facilitate self-care, promote dialogue between patient and healthcare professional, and ensure effective daily monitoring. Other applications provide more specialised functionality, such as orthopaedic footwear recommendations, care checklists and more [13,14]. The MyFootCare application excels at monitoring DFUs, offering audio-assisted image capture for better framing and manual delineation of the ulcer for easier segmentation [15,18]. It also has a gallery for storing images and a notification system to remind you of essential tasks such as changing dressings and booking appointments. However, its interface is not visually appealing, a relevant factor, as intuitive interfaces improve the user experience, reduce costs and increase the quality of care [19].

A notable challenge associated with applications designed for diabetes or diabetic foot monitoring is the limited interaction they offer users, typically confined to the presentation of information. This passive approach compromises day-to-day usability and conveys the feeling that these tools are more orientated towards healthcare professionals than effective user monitoring. The proposed solution fosters enhanced user engagement with the application, thereby fostering greater user commitment to their treatment.

Various studies have explored the use of Deep Learning (DL) models for the detection and segmentation of DFUs, with a focus on mobile-based solutions. Diverse works like [1,2,6] utilise models such as Faster R-CNN and YOLOv3 for real-time detection and classification of DFUs using mobile devices. These models enable smartphones to capture images of the foot and automatically analyse them for diagnosis and monitoring of DFUs. The use of YOLO is also widely explored in other studies, such as [2], which refine the YOLOv3 architecture to detect the Wagner grades of DFUs. The advantage lies in its speed, enabling real-time detection directly on smartphones. Cloud integration plays a crucial role in storing and updating models, ensuring continuous improvements without overburdening mobile devices. The combination of YOLO with segmentation techniques, as explored by [3], offers an integrated solution for precise DFUs diagnosis and segmentation.

For wound segmentation, the work by [1] stands out, where U-Net and MobileNet architectures are employed to segment chronic wounds, including DFUs. Their approach leverages mobile devices for automated segmentation, eliminating the need for user interaction. The generalisation of these models to different wound types further highlights their promise in remote wound monitoring. In all these approaches, cloud integration remains pivotal. It allows for the storage of large datasets, model training, and remote image analysis. The cloud, along with mobile optimization techniques demonstrated by [5], ensures that these solutions can run efficiently on smartphones with limited resources, offering accessible and effective DFUs monitoring solutions.

3   Architecture

The application follows a client-server architecture, structured in three layers: frontend, backend and database, as shown in Fig. 1. The frontend, developed in Flutter (Dart), is responsible for the user interface and communication with the backend via HTTP. It uses Firebase Authentication for authentication, and user data is stored in the Firebase Firestore. It also interacts with the API for registration operations and communication with the Deep Learning (DL) model. The backend is also implemented in Dart and acts as an intermediary between the frontend and the database, managing user registration, data submission and communication with the DL model. It is also responsible for processing the submitted images and generating the feedback that is made available to the user. The Firebase database includes the Firestore for storing information, Authentication for managing access and, potentially, Firebase Storage for storing images. The workflow starts with a POST request from Flutter to the API, which passes the user data stored in the firestore. When an image is submitted, Flutter sends it to the API, which passes it to the DL model for analysis. After processing, the model returns the feedback to the backend, which forwards it to the frontend, making the answer available to the user.

The system follows an optimized flow to process images efficiently, with all inference operations executed in the cloud to ensure scalability and consistent performance across devices. YOLOv11n is reponsible for detecting ulcers by identifying bounding boxes, classes and confidence scores, while SAM receives the image and meta-data performing detailed segmentation, therefore reducing the device's computational consumption [3,7]. This approach guarantees fast response, low impact on the device's battery and high accuracy, as well as allowing future implementation of continuous fine-tuning with new acquired images.

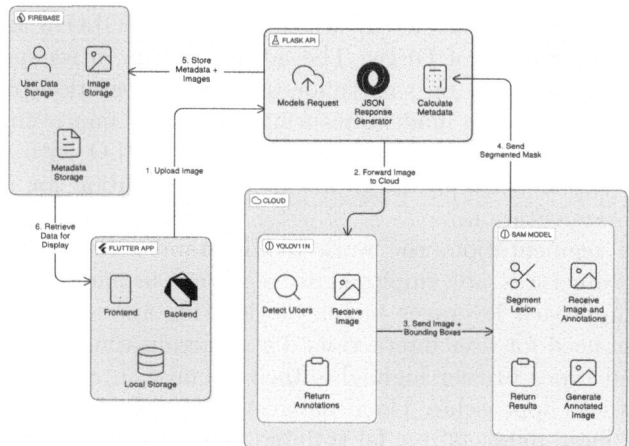

Fig. 1. Diagram showing the architecture and information flow of the application.

The user captures or selects an image via the mobile app, which is then converted to Base64 and sent via HTTP POST request to the backend. On the device, the YOLOv11n model detects the ulcers, returning the bounding boxes, the detected class and the confidence level [2, 3]. To optimise processing, the original image, together with the annotations generated by YOLOv11n (bounding box, confidence and class), is sent to the server for segmentation.

On the cloud, SAM processes the original image and uses the annotations received to restrict segmentation to only the areas identified by YOLOv11n [7]. The model generates a binary mask precisely delimiting the area of the lesion within the identified bounding box. In addition, essential metadata are calculated, such as the centroid, area and perimeter of the segmentation, providing additional data for clinical evaluation [6]. After processing, the server returns to the application a structured JSON containing the extracted information, as well as the annotated image displaying the segmentation and bounding box with the visible confidence level.

4   Implementation

The solution presented in this paper allows users to photograph their feet using their smartphone camera, enabling a deep learning model to detect early signs of ulcers, such as changes in skin texture and pigmentation, that might otherwise go unnoticed. As illustrated in Fig. 2, the capacity to access the camera is implemented for the purpose of capturing images of the foot, and a gallery for the purpose of viewing previously taken photographs. By selecting the button that is designated by the camera icon, the user is redirected to the image capture interface. Following confirmation, the photograph is displayed on the main screen. In order to view previous images or to make a comparison between them and the most recent one, the user can access the gallery by selecting the corresponding button. Furthermore, this mock-up illustrates the integration of Deep Learning models that are capable of detecting and segmenting an ulcer from a captured image and returning a segmented image and its prediction with associated confidence levels. The interface also displays the metadata associated with the segmentation, including the centroid coordinate, as well as the area and perimeter of the lesion. Figure 2 illustrates this functionality.

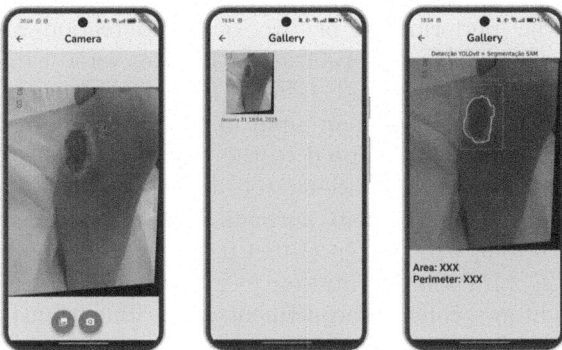

Fig. 2. Camera page, gallery page and mock-up of photo page already analised.

The primary dataset used in this study is DFUC-2024 [22], available on the Roboflow Universe platform. Originally intended for image classification tasks, this dataset lacks object detection annotations such as bounding boxes. Its structure consists of splits folders like training, validation, and test subsets each containing class-separated directories. Due to the lack of bounding boxes, an automatic annotation strategy was adopted using a YOLOv8n model previously trained on DFUs images. Inference was performed on each class directory, respecting the original splits (train, validation, test). Since the pretrained model only recognised the generic class "ulcer", final labels were inferred based on the source directory of each image. A class mapping was defined as: class 0 corresponds to Ischaemia, class 1 to Infected, class 2 to non-Ischaemia, and class 3 to not-Infected. All annotated images were consolidated into a single images directory, and YOLO-format labels were stored in the labels directory. The non_Ischaemia and not_Infected classes were removed, leaving only the Ischaemia (0) and Infected (1) classes.

To include the Healthy class (2), the foot ulcers dataset [23]-also available on Roboflow-was used. This dataset included diabetic foot ulcer and healthy foot classes, which only healthy foot was used (over 500 images of healthy feet). To improve class balance and representation, data augmentation techniques were applied to this subset. After merging and normalising all valid images and annotations, a new integrated dataset was created shifting the labels by +1, considering the background label used in PyTorch native models. This dataset was then split in a stratified manner: 70% for training, 20% for validation, and 10% for testing, ensuring that the model has sufficient data for training while maintaining separate validation and test sets for performance evaluation [2,4]. Furthermore, YOLO-format annotations were used to generate JSON files for each subset with a personalized script, converting in COCO format, to facilitate usage with PyTorch-based models. Although initial balancing was done at the image level, the final dataset design considered the total number of bounding boxes, acknowledging that multiple lesions can appear in a single image. This approach provides a more realistic instance-level distribution for model training.

To evaluate the performance of two object detection architectures for DFUs classification, we trained RetinaNet with a ResNet50-FPN backbone and YOLOv11-nano on the constructed dataset. Both models were trained for 30 epochs with a batch size of 16 and an input image resolution of 640×640 pixels. The preprocessing steps were adapted to the requirements of each framework. For RetinaNet, images and annotations were loaded in COCO format. Preprocessing included resizing to 640×640, normalization to zero mean and unit variance (mean = (0.0, 0.0, 0.0), std = (1.0, 1.0, 1.0)), and conversion to tensors using ToTensorV2(). Data augmentation techniques, including horizontal flipping, random brightness/contrast adjustments, and affine transformations, were applied. Although their impact on mAP was limited, training with these augmentations allowed for longer sessions without overfitting, ultimately improving the model's generalization. The model was optimised using the AdamW optimizer with a learning rate of 1e-4 and weight decay of 1e-4. A cosine annealing learning rate scheduler was applied on a per-batch basis to facilitate convergence. Validation used the same resizing and normalisation pipeline without augmentation. Evaluation metrics included per-class mean Average Precision (mAP) at IoU thresholds 0.5 and 0.5:0.95.

For YOLOv11-nano, the dataset was provided in YOLO format. Preprocessing and augmentation were handled internally by the Ultralytics training framework, which standardizes bounding box format, resizes images to 640×640, and applies built-in augmentations (including flipping, color jittering, and scaling). Training was conducted on GPU with a learning rate of 1e-4 and weight decay of 1e-4. In addition to object detection, SAM was employed as part of the segmentation pipeline. SAM was used to segment lesion regions based on bounding boxes predicted by YOLOv11n. This integration enables high-quality segmentation by leveraging accurate object localisation, enhancing the extraction of lesion contours and morphological metadata [3,7]. Although the SAM model is not directly compared in the performance results, it plays a complementary role in the broader annotation and segmentation workflow.

5   Results

This section presents a comprehensive analysis of the training and evaluation performance of two object detection architectures–YOLOv11 nano and RetinaNet with a ResNet50+FPN backbone–for the task of DFUs detection. The evaluation is based on standard object detection metrics: Precision (P), Recall (R), mean Average Precision at IoU threshold 0.5 (mAP@0.5), and mean Average Precision across IoU thresholds from 0.5 to 0.95 (mAP@0.5:0.95). Results were obtained using a validation set comprising 1,650 images and 2,180 annotated instances. The YOLO model categorize the loss plots into three types: box_loss, cls_loss, and dfl_loss. The box_loss measures errors in bounding box placement, quantifying how far predicted boxes deviate from the actual object boundaries. The cls_loss reflects errors in object classification, indicating how well the model distinguishes between DFUs and healthy feet. The dfl_loss (Distribution Focal Loss) represents errors in refining bounding box predictions, focusing on the fine-tuning of box placement.

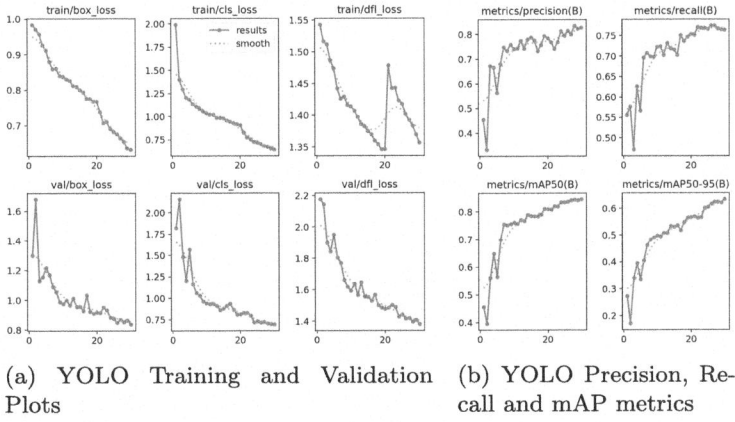

(a) YOLO Training and Validation Plots

(b) YOLO Precision, Recall and mAP metrics

Fig. 3. Evaluation of the model: (a) Loss Plots, (b) Metrics

The Fig. 3a reveals consistent improvement across all metrics as the number of epochs increases. Both train/box_loss and val/box_loss show a steady decline, indicating that the model is becoming more accurate in predicting bounding box placements without signs of overfitting. Similarly, train/cls_loss and val/cls_loss exhibit a decreasing trend, suggesting that the model is improving its classification accuracy and generalizing well to unseen data. The train/dfl_loss also decreases steadily, reflecting better refinement of bounding box predictions, while the val/dfl_loss follows a similar trend, although with minor fluctuations, which may indicate slight inconsistencies in generalising to the validation set. Precision measures the proportion of correctly identified positive cases among all predicted positives, with higher values indicating fewer false positives. In Fig. 3b, the YOLOv11 nano model achieves a precision around 0.828, suggesting reliable classification with limited misidentification of healthy tissue as ulcers. Recall, which quantifies the proportion of actual ulcers correctly detected, reaches 0.763– demonstrating effective sensitivity, essential for clinical diagnostics where missing a true case can have severe consequences. The model's detection accuracy is further reflected in the mAP@0.5 metric, which evaluates how well predicted bounding boxes align with ground truth at a 50% IoU threshold. YOLOv11 nano attains a high mAP@0.5 of 0.844, indicating strong performance in object localisation. Meanwhile, mAP@0.5:0.95, a stricter metric that averages precision across IoUs from 0.5 to 0.95, reaches 0.633. Although lower, this score still reflects solid robustness in bounding box precision under varied localisation demands, confirming the model's overall consistency and generalisation ability.

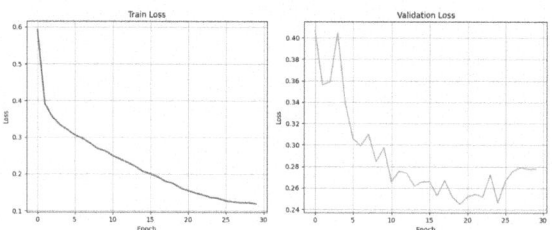

Fig. 4. Training and Validation Plots

Unlike YOLOv11 nano, the RetinaNet architecture does not explicitly report separate loss components such as bounding box regression, classification, or refinement losses. Therefore, the analysis of its performance is based on the overall training and validation loss curves. The training loss measures how well the model fits the training data, while the validation loss evaluates how effectively the model generalizes to previously unseen data. Figure 4 illustrates the evolution of training and validation losses throughout the epochs. Initially, both losses decrease, indicating that the model is learning representative features from the dataset and generalising effectively. However, beginning around epoch 20, a divergence is observed: the training loss continues to decline, while the validation loss plateaus and begins to rise slightly, a common indication of overfitting. From this point onward, the results were considered irrelevant for analysis.

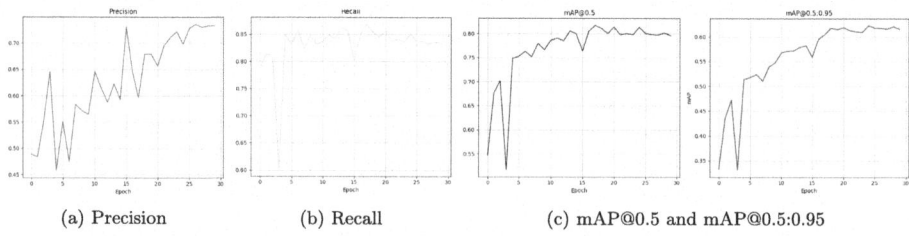

(a) Precision   (b) Recall   (c) mAP@0.5 and mAP@0.5:0.95

Fig. 5. Evaluation metrics of the model: (a) Precision, (b) Recall, and (c) mean Average Precision (mAP).

In terms of evaluation metrics, Fig. 5, precision refers to the proportion of predicted ulcer cases that are actually correct, while recall measures the proportion of true ulcer cases that the model successfully detects. In the case of RetinaNet, the high recall value of 0.855 indicates strong sensitivity to actual ulcer regions, making it particularly useful in medical applications where minimising false negatives is critical. However, the lower precision of 0.679 suggests that the model is prone to generating false positives, which may lead to unnecessary concern or additional medical evaluation. The model reaches a mAP@0.5 of 0.811, indicating reliable detection at a standard IoU threshold and good localization of ulcer regions in most cases. Its mAP@0.5:0.95, however, is slightly lower at 0.617, suggesting less robustness when evaluated across stricter localisation criteria.

6   Discussion

Table 1 summarizes key metrics and datasets used in recent studies on DFUs detection, including our results with YOLOv11 nano and RetinaNet. The models show varying strengths across precision, recall, F1-score, and mean Average Precision (mAP@0.5), reflecting different trade-offs in detection performance. YOLOv11 nano model achieved a high precision and a good recall on the created dataset, resulting in a mAP@0.5 of 0.844. These results indicate the model's robustness in accurately localising ulcers while minimising false positives, essential in clinical settings to reduce unnecessary interventions. In comparison, the RetinaNet with ResNet50+FPN backbone demonstrated a higher recall of 0.855, which is critical for maximising ulcer detection and minimising missed cases. However, this came at the cost of a lower precision (0.679), suggesting more false positives.

Table 1. Summary of models and evaluation metrics used in recent DFU detection studies.

Model/Study	Prec.	Rec.	F1	mAP@0.5	mAP@0.5:0.95
YOLOv11 nano (this work)	**0.828**	0.763	–	0.844	**0.633**
RetinaNet ResNet50+FPN (this work)	0.679	**0.855**	–	0.811	0.617
SSD + MobileNetv2 [2]	–	–	–	0.894	–
Faster R-CNN + ResNet101 [2]	–	–	–	0.904	–
YOLOv3 refinements [2]	–	–	–	**0.919**	–
Faster R-CNN (Def.) [6]	0.720	0.769	0.743	0.694	0.472
EfficientDet (Post) [6]	0.728	0.760	**0.744**	0.569	–
YOLOv5 (E60 SELF90) [6]	0.760	0.717	0.738	0.627	–
YOLOv3 (B50 Overlap) [6]	0.732	0.736	0.734	0.648	–
YOLOv5 (SELF100 TTA) [6]	0.752	0.719	0.735	0.629	–
YOLOv3 (B50) [6]	0.699	0.750	0.724	0.656	–
CA-DetNet [6]	0.664	0.741	0.700	0.639	–
Ensemble (FRCNN+EffDet) [6]	0.813	0.716	0.762	0.643	–

Han et al. [2] evaluated several object detection models on the DF dataset, including SSD with MobileNetv2, Faster R-CNN with ResNet101, and refined versions of YOLOv3. Their results showed high mAP@0.5 values, particularly 0.919 for refined YOLOv3 and 0.904 for Faster R-CNN. However, key metrics such as precision, recall, and F1-score were not reported, limiting insight into detection balance and model sensitivity. In contrast, our YOLOv11 nano and RetinaNet models–evaluated on the DFUC2024 + Foot2 dataset–provide a more complete metric profile, including a mAP@0.5 of 0.844 and recall of 0.855, respectively. When comparing similar architectures, our models demonstrate competitive or improved performance despite the difference in datasets.

Yap et al. [6] conducted a broad evaluation of models on the DFUC2020 dataset, including YOLOv3, YOLOv5, EfficientNet, and a deformable Faster R-CNN. Their best-performing models achieved balanced precision and recall, such as 0.720 and 0.769 for the deformable Faster R-CNN, with mAP@0.5 values generally below 0.70. YOLO-based models in their study also showed F1-scores around 0.735, with mAP results ranging from 0.627 to 0.656. In our work, RetinaNet and YOLOv11 nano achieved higher values across similar metrics, with RetinaNet reaching a recall of 0.855 and YOLOv11 nano achieving a precision of 0.828 and mAP@0.5 of 0.844. While the datasets differ, the performance of our models highlights architectural improvements and robustness in recent approaches.

Beyond model performance, these results have important practical implications. An effective ulcer detection model can assist healthcare providers in automating initial screenings, reducing the manual workload and enabling earlier interventions [21]. This, in turn, could help prevent severe complications such as infections or amputations. Additionally, integrating the model into a mobile application for patient use could facilitate remote monitoring, promoting timely medical attention and improving treatment adherence.

This project is therefore deemed feasible for the early detection and treatment of DFUs, with the aim of improving the health of users without the necessity of a consultation. It is evident that a primary benefit of this application is the reduction in consultations provided by health professionals, consequently leading to a decrease in waiting lists. Despite the efforts to construct a functional and coherent dataset, several limitations must be acknowledged. The lesion bounding boxes were generated using a pre-trained YOLOv8n model, with class divisions inherited from the original dataset. Although this strategy enabled the creation of a detection dataset from classification-based data, it introduces potential annotation noise. Integration of the Healthy class involved external images from a different dataset [23]. This raises concerns regarding visual and contextual homogeneity between the image domains of ulcerated and healthy feet, which could impact model generalisation.

7   Conclusion

In summary, the application under discussion enables continuous monitoring of DFUs. Symptoms and images are analysed to provide personalised feedback to the user, facilitating more effective treatment. The architecture of the application is based on a client-server model, ensuring scalability and efficient integration between its components. The frontend, developed in Flutter, communicates with the API, which intermediates the exchange of data between the user, the Firebase database and the deep learning model. The future direction of this research is to enhance the models for improved detection and segmentation accuracy, optimise the calibration of hyper parameters, and investigate pre and post-processing techniques to enhance the reliability of predictions.

Acknowledgments. This work has been supported by *FCT – Fundação para a Ciência e Tecnologia* within the R&D Units Project Scope of the Unit 00319

Disclosure of Interests. The authors have no competing interests to declare that are relevant to the content of this article.

References

1. Scebba, G., et al.: Detect-and-segment: a deep learning approach to automate wound image segmentation. Inform. Med. Unlocked. **29**, 100884 (2022). https://doi.org/10.1016/j.imu.2022.100884
2. Han, A., Zhang, Y., Li, A., Li, C., Zhao, F., Dong, Q., et al.: Deep learning methods for real-time detection and analysis of wagner ulcer classification system. In: Proceedings of the 2022 International Conference on Computer Applications Technology (CCAT 2022), pp. 11–21 (2022). https://doi.org/10.1109/CCAT56798.2022.00010
3. Pandey, S., Chen, K.F., Dam, E.B.: Comprehensive multimodal segmentation in medical imaging: combining YOLOv8 with SAM and HQ-SAM models. In: 2023 IEEE/CVF International Conference on Computer Vision Workshops (ICCVW), pp. 2584–2590 (2023). https://doi.org/10.1109/ICCVW60793.2023.00273
4. Goyal, M., Hassanpour, S.: A refined deep learning architecture for diabetic foot ulcers detection. arXiv [Preprint] (2020). http://arxiv.org/abs/2007.07922
5. Ignatov, A., Timofte, R., Chou, W., Wang, K., Wu, M., Hartley, T., et al.: AI benchmark: running deep neural networks on android smartphones. In: Lecture Notes in Computer Science **11133**, 288–314 (2019). https://doi.org/10.1007/978-3-030-11021-5_19
6. Yap, M.H., Hachiuma, R., Alavi, A., Brüngel, R., Cassidy, B., Goyal, M., et al.: Deep learning in diabetic foot ulcers detection: a comprehensive evaluation. Comput. Biol. Med. **135**, 104596 (2021). https://doi.org/10.1016/j.compbiomed.2021.104596
7. Kirillov, A., Mintun, E., Ravi, N., Mao, H., Rolland, C., Gustafson, L., et al.: Segment anything. In: 2023 IEEE/CVF International Conference on Computer Vision (ICCV), pp. 3992–4003 (2023). https://doi.org/10.1109/ICCV51070.2023.00371
8. Zhang, Y., et al.: Global epidemiology of diabetic foot ulceration: a systematic review and meta-analysis. Ann. Med. (2017). https://doi.org/10.1080/07853890.2017.1310813
9. Boulton, A., Armstrong, D., Albert, S., Frykberg, R., Hellman, R., Kirkman, M., et al.: Comprehensive foot examination and risk assessment. Diabetes Care **31**(8), 1679–85 (2008). https://doi.org/10.2337/dc08-9021

10. Ahmad, J.: The diabetic foot. Diabetes and Metabolic Syndrome: Clinical Research and Reviews **10**(1), 48–60 (2016). https://doi.org/10.1016/j.dsx.2015.04.002
11. Khanolkar, M.P., Bain, S.C., Stephens, J.W.: The diabetic foot. QJM Int. J. Med. **101**(9), 685–695 (2008). https://doi.org/10.1093/qjmed/hcn027
12. Sanders, L.J.: Preventive foot care in people with diabetes. J. Am. Podiatric Med. Association **84**(7), 322–328 (1994). https://doi.org/10.7547/87507315-84-7-322
13. Mourão, L.F., Marques, A.D.B., Moreira, T.M.M., Oliveira, S.K.P.: Mobile applications to promote diabetic foot care: Scoping review. Revista Eletrônica de Enfermagem, 24 (2022). https://doi.org/10.5216/ree.v24.69625
14. Yap, M.H., et al.: A new mobile application for standardizing diabetic foot images. J. Diabetes Sci. Technol. **12**(1), 169–173 (2018). https://doi.org/10.1177/1932296817713761
15. Ploderer, B., Brown, R., Seng, L.S.D., Lazzarini, P.A., Van Netten, J.J.: Promoting self-care of diabetic foot ulcers through a mobile phone app: User-centered design and evaluation. JMIR Diabetes **20**(10) (2018). https://doi.org/10.2196/10105
16. Sadler, S., et al.: The use of mHealth apps for the assessment and management of diabetes-related foot health outcomes: systematic review. J. Med. Internet Res. **25**(1) (2023). https://doi.org/10.2196/47608
17. Rowland, S.P., Fitzgerald, J.E., Holme, T., Powell, J., McGregor, A.: What is the clinical value of mHealth for patients? NPJ Digit. Med. **3**(1) (2020). https://doi.org/10.1038/s41746-019-0206-x
18. Brown, R., Ploderer, B., Seng, L.S.D., Lazzarini, P., Van Netten, J.: MyFootCare: A mobile self-tracking tool to promote self-care amongst people with diabetic foot ulcers. In: Proceedings of the ACM International Conference, pp. 462–466. ACM (2017). https://doi.org/10.1145/3152771.3156158
19. Peixoto, H., Machado, J., Neves, J., Abelha, A.: Semantic interoperability and health records. IFIP Adv. Inf. Commun. Technol. **335**, 236–237 (2010). https://doi.org/10.1007/978-3-642-15515-4_30
20. Chaves, A., Sousa, R., Machado, J., Abelha, A., Peixoto, H.: Collaborative platform for intelligent monitoring of diabetic foot patients – Colab4IMDF. In: Rocha, Á., Ferrás, C., Hochstetter Diez, J., Diéguez Rebolledo, M. (Eds.), Information Technology and Systems, pp. 195–204 (2024).
21. Chaves, A., Sousa, R., Abelha, A., Peixoto, H.: Steps towards intelligent diabetic foot ulcer follow-up based on deep learning. In: Machado, J.M., Peixoto, H. (eds.) AI-assisted solutions for COVID-19 and biomedical applications in smart cities, pp. 81–90. Springer (2023)
22. wed. DFUC 2024 Classification Dataset and Pre-Trained Model 2025. https://universe.roboflow.com/wed-axnxx/dfuc-2024. Accessed: 22 May 2025
23. SLIIT Kajanan. Diabetic Infection Detection Object Detection Dataset (2024). https://universe.roboflow.com/sliit-kajanan/foot-ulcers. Accessed: 22 May 2025

Deep Neural Networks to the Detection of Lumbar Hernias: Methodology and Preliminary Results

António Fernandes[1], João Rodriguez[1], Susana Moleirinho[1], Irina Trofimenko[1], Ekaterina Guseva[1], Alexander Martinovich[1], Ilzane Morais[1], Louise Bisolo[1], Luis M. Gomes[2(✉)] 📷, and José M. Machado[3] 📷

[1] SliceD Group Research Center, Lisbon, Portugal
[2] Centro ALGORITMI/LASI, University of Azores, Ponta Delgada, Portugal
`luis.mp.gomes@uac.pt`
[3] Centro ALGORITMI/LASI, University of Minho, Braga, Portugal
`jmac@di.uminho.pt`

Abstract. The growing demand for lumbar spine MRI exams, coupled with a shortage of radiologists, highlights the need for automated diagnostic tools for spinal conditions. Despite advancements in AI across radiology, no CE or FDA-approved solutions currently target lumbar spine pathologies. This paper introduces a deep learning pipeline designed to automatically detect intervertebral disc herniation, aiming to support faster and more accurate clinical decisions. A dataset of 165 lumbar spine MRI exams, totalling 5,200 sagittal slices from four manufacturers, was annotated by radiologists. The experiment includes a multi-stage approach. MA-Net with EfficientNet-B2 achieved the best segmentation results, reaching a Dice Score of 0.898. For herniation classification, the ViT model outperformed others, achieving an F1-Score of 0.905 and accuracy of 0.826. Simplifying the segmentation task to three classes enhanced robustness, and anatomical labelling enabled precise disc-level classification. The pipeline demonstrates the feasibility of automated herniation detection in lumbar MRI, supporting improved diagnostic consistency and reduced radiologist burden.

Keywords: Deep Learning · Radiology Automation · Spine MRI

1 Introduction

Accurate identification of the pain source in spinal pathologies remains a complex clinical challenge due to the presence of multiple degenerative changes observable in lumbar spine imaging. Determining which of these changes corresponds to the symptoms of the patient is critical for effective treatment planning. Radiology stands as a cornerstone of modern medicine, offering critical insights into human anatomy and pathology through advanced imaging modalities. Yet, the exponential rise in imaging demands continues to outpace the availability of radiologists. This imbalance has led to increased workloads,

J. Valente de Oliveira et al. (Eds.): EPIA 2025, LNAI 16121, pp. 15–25, 2026.
https://doi.org/10.1007/978-3-032-05176-9_2

diagnostic delays, and decreased accuracy, impacting patient outcomes and placing significant strain on healthcare systems [1, 2]. Automation, particularly through Artificial Intelligence (AI), is increasingly recognized as a necessary evolution in radiological practice to enhance efficiency and diagnostic quality [3].

In this paper we introduce an innovative AI-based diagnostic interface that supports radiologists in pinpointing the origin of lumbosacral root compression, commonly associated with sciatic pain, through an advanced MRI image analysis. We consider a deep learning-powered algorithm designed to automatically detect and classify lumbar disc herniation, a key compressive mechanism in radicular pain. The study explores the following research question: *which deep learning architecture most reliably detects disc herniation in lumbar MRI scans?* To answer this, a rigorous comparison of several models was conducted, evaluated against standard performance metrics.

We begin by framing the clinical background and relevance of lumbar disc herniation and the role of imaging in its diagnosis. The methodology section outlines the construction of an automated pipeline involving segmentation of lumbar structures and classification of disc pathology. The models were trained, validated, and tested on annotated MRI datasets to assess their practical utility.

The results demonstrate that advanced architectures, especially transformer-based models, offer improved diagnostic performance. And then we discuss clinical implications, identify current limitations such as data diversity and class imbalance, and propose future research directions to further enhance the clinical integration of AI in spine radiology.

2 Background

AI technologies have made remarkable progress across medical domains. As of the latest data from Grand Challenge, 223 AI tools have been CE- or FDA-approved in radiology, with 46 dedicated to neuroradiology [4]. However, a notable gap persists none of these address pathologies within the lumbar spine, a region critically implicated in one of the most widespread and disabling conditions, known as low back pain [4].

Magnetic resonance imaging (MRI) of the lumbar spine is among the most requested diagnostic tools for assessing back pain [5, 6]. A typical scan requires comprehensive evaluation of five intervertebral disc levels, each with five critical zones (central, bilateral paracentral, and foraminal regions), as well as the spinal canal, nerve roots, facet joints, ligamentum flavum, and bony structures. In degenerative cases, multiple abnormalities often co-exist, complicating diagnosis and demanding time-intensive analysis from radiologists. These assessments are highly subjective and suffer from low reproducibility [7].

This context reveals an urgent need for automated tools capable of standardizing and quantifying lumbar spine findings. AI applications that can rapidly and reproducibly identify structures and pathologies, such as disc herniation or nerve root compression, would relieve radiologists of repetitive tasks and allow their expertise to be directed toward more complex diagnoses. Moreover, such tools could help correlate image phenotypes with patient-reported symptoms, a longstanding challenge in spinal diagnostics [8, 9]. By targeting these needs, we had been focused on building a pipeline for automated lumbar spine MRI interpretation. It aims to bridge the gap in current AI applications, offering a novel solution to stratify pain sources and improve both diagnostic accuracy and treatment planning.

Recent advances in spinal imaging AI have demonstrated increasing sophistication in both model architecture and diagnostic scope. For example, the SpineNet++, a multi-view transformer-based model for comprehensive spine pathology detection, achieving strong performance through cross-plane feature integration. Similarly, Deep Disc-Net, a multitask convolutional neural network designed to jointly detect disc degeneration features including herniation, bulging, and Modic changes, leveraging task-specific branches to enhance performance.

3   Experiment Design

We did not follow a methodology commonly used in machine learning studies (e.g. CRISP-DM). We prefer to describe the sequence of steps we took in transposing our medical practice to the application of machine learning models and then observing their results. We developed an automated pipeline for detecting lumbar disc herniation using deep learning models, following two steps, namely: dataset construction and pre-processing procedures, including annotation and segmentation.

To ensure diversity and generalizability, 165 lumbar spine Magnetic Resonance Images (MRI) cases were collected from four different scanner manufacturers: Siemens (64 cases), Philips (48), Toshiba (27), and GE Healthcare (26). The dataset includes 325 sagittal MRI sequences (T1, T2, and STIR) amounting to 5,200 sagittal plane images. The inclusion of different manufacturers was intentional, aiming to ensure diversity and generalizability in the dataset by capturing variations in acquisition protocols and scanner characteristics. The images with severe artifacts, non-degenerative pathologies, or scoliosis were excluded. All considered images were stored in DICOM format, with significant heterogeneity in file structures, necessitating custom routines for reading, standardizing, and volumetric reconstruction. Compatibility with 3D Slicer was achieved via.nrrd export, enabling both algorithm validation and manual corrections. The demographic analysis revealed an average patient age of 51.54 ± 16.2 years (range: 19–82), with 60.3% male representation. The average patient height and weight were 1.76 ± 0.07 m and 84.2 ± 11.7 kg, respectively. Image resolution averaged 487.1×486.4 pixels. Only sagittal plane images were included for model training and validation.

Annotation was performed by five radiologists, with 2–15 years of experience, using standardized sagittal T1/T2 TSE and axial T2 TSE sequences. These sequences provide high diagnostic value for detecting disc pathology and nerve root compression. Each case was examined at five lumbar levels (L1–L2 through L5–S1) for disc herniation using a structured classification: Absent (Negative), Bulging, Protrusion, Extrusion, and Sequestration. All abnormal morphologies were labelled as "Present" to ensure diagnostic consistency. Radiologists underwent training with sample cases and feedback sessions to standardize the annotation process. Manual segmentation was conducted using 3D Slicer's "Segment Editor," where each vertebral body (L1–S1) and intervertebral disc was annotated across ~11 sagittal slices per disc level. This generated a detailed labelled dataset essential for training segmentation models to detect spinal structures and associated pathologies.

Vertebral body segmentation encompassed identification of the endplates, osteophytes, and both anterior and posterior cortices. This segmentation also included intervertebral disc features such as protrusions, hernias, sequestrations, and Schmorl's nodes. The vertebral canal was segmented to include the dural sac (cerebrospinal fluid space) and surrounding epidural fat. The cranial boundary was defined at the superior vertebral body of L1, while the caudal boundary extended to the inferior endplate of S1. Lateral recesses were included in the canal region. Manual segmentation for each case took approximately 90 min, applied to a total dataset of 5,200 MRI, which results from multiplying the number of sequences by the average number of slices per sequence.

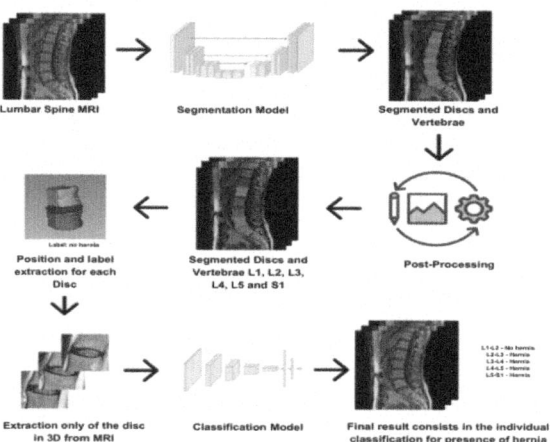

Fig. 1. The pipeline applied for hernia detection.

We have divided the pipeline represented in Fig. 1 into 3 phases, namely: (i) segmentation phase; (ii) post-processing; (iii) classification phase. In (i), a deep segmentation model was trained to classify each voxel into background, vertebra, or intervertebral disc classes, but the differentiate between individual discs or vertebrae (e.g., L1–L2 vs. L2–L3) was not identified. While in (ii), a rule-based and morphological analysis pipeline refined these masks, removing artifacts and assigning anatomical labels to individual discs and vertebrae, ensuring spatial consistency and anatomical accuracy. And, finally, in (iii), from the refined masks, 3D patches of each intervertebral disc were extracted, and a binary classification model was then applied to predict the presence or absence of herniation.

While SpineNet++ and Deep DiscNet mentioned above reflect the progression of the field toward integrative solutions, the present pipeline introduces several key innovations. First, it achieves end-to-end integration of segmentation and structured classification, enabling anatomically grounded, interpretable predictions at the level of individual intervertebral discs. Second, it employs explicit disc-level labelling, producing rich outputs aligned with radiological practice. Third, and critically, it is trained on a heterogeneous, real-world dataset comprising MRIs from four different manufacturers and diverse acquisition protocols, which enhances its potential for generalization. This combination of architectural coherence, clinical granularity, and data diversity distinguishes the proposed pipeline from prior approaches and positions it as a robust foundation for prospective multicentre validation and clinical translation.

For segmentation, multiple encoder-decoder architectures were tested. Encoders included ResNet34, EfficientNet-B2, VGG16, and Mix Vision Transformer (ViT) as backbone feature extractors in segmentation to leverage their powerful representation learning. ResNet50 offers deep residual learning for stable training [10]. EfficientNet-B2 balances accuracy and efficiency via compound scaling [11]. SENet enhances channel-wise feature recalibration for better discriminative power [12]. ViT introduces global self-attention, capturing long-range dependencies beyond CNNs [13]. Integrating these backbones improves segmentation accuracy by providing rich, multi-scale, and context-aware features, enabling precise and robust delineation in complex anatomical regions like the lumbar spine. This stage boosts overall model performance and adaptability to diverse image variations. Decoders comprised UNet, UNet++, DeepLabV3+, Seg-Former, and MANet. Their proven strengths. U-Net [14] and U-Net++ [15] offer strong encoder-decoder structures with skip connections, particularly in medical image segmentation. DeepLabV3+ captures multiscale context with atrous convolutions and an efficient decoder [16]. SegFormer leverages transformers for global context and efficient feature extraction [17]. And MA-Net introduces multi-attention modules that refine spatial and channel features, enhancing precision [18]. Comparing them involves evaluating segmentation accuracy, boundary delineation, computational cost, and robustness to spinal anatomical variability, achieving the best trade-off between performance and efficiency for clinical use. We notice that most of these deep learning architectures have open-source implementations available on PyTorch through torchvision.models and timm.

Images were resized to 256×256 pixels. All models were trained using the Adam optimizer [19] with a learning rate of 1e−4, a batch size of 4, and Dice Loss to mitigate class imbalance. Each architecture was trained for 30 epochs with a ReduceLROn-Plateau scheduler. Evaluation was based on the Dice Coefficient, due to its suitability for imbalanced segmentation tasks in medical imaging.

The dataset consisted of sagittal lumbar spine MRIs, manually annotated by expert radiologists. Each image had a corresponding segmentation mask with three categories: background, vertebrae (classes 1–6), and intervertebral discs (classes 7–11). Due to limited labelled cases, the segmentation network was trained only to separate vertebrae and discs, with fine anatomical labels later recovered via post-processing.

An 80/20 training-validation split was used. Input preprocessing included grayscale normalization and resizing. To maintain fair comparisons across architectures, all models were trained with identical hyperparameters and optimizer settings.

Although segmentation predicted general anatomical structures, a custom post-processing system was employed to assign specific anatomical labels. This involved: noise reduction using morphological operations; connectivity analysis to identify individual discs and vertebrae; anatomical label assignment based on spatial ordering and disc-vertebra relationships. This ensured the segmented outputs aligned with radiological ground truth. The post-processing involved the following steps (Fig. 2):

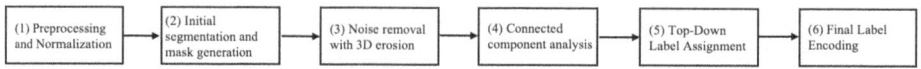

Fig. 2. Steps of the post-processing system applied.

In (1), we resize and normalize MRI to ensure consistency in scale and intensity. Create segmentation masks with three distinct classes, namely background, vertebra, and intervertebral disc, is made on (2). Then we eliminate small irrelevant structures with preserving key anatomical regions in (3). In (4), we identify and label vertebrae and intervertebral discs as distinct structures. Then we label uniquely each structure based on its vertical positioning along the spine. And, finally, we generate a segmented output with distinct identifiers for each vertebra and intervertebral disc.

Using the refined segmentation masks, 3D patches centred on each disc were extracted from the MRI volumes. Each patch had fixed dimensions of $(20, 80, 80)$ (depth $\times$ height $\times$ width). Zero-padding was applied when necessary. Each disc was labelled as herniated or non-herniated based on manual expert annotations. Data Augmentation, implemented via TorchIO, improved generalizability, namely: Gaussian noise, brightness/contrast variations, random motion artifacts, elastic deformations, and affine transformations.

A range of 3D deep learning models were evaluated, namely: 3D ResNet-50, 3D EfficientNet-B2, 3D SEResNet-50, 3D SEResNeXt-50, and 3D Vision Transformer (ViT). These models were implemented using MONAI, and trained using Adam optimizer with BCEWithLogitsLoss, suitable for binary classification. The batch size was fixed at 4 to accommodate 3D memory requirements. A threshold of 0.5 on the output logits was used for classification. To ensure fair benchmarking, these models were trained on the same dataset split and preprocessed inputs. Evaluation metrics included Precision and F1-Score, with the F1-Score selected as the primary metric due to dataset class imbalance.

4 Results

This section presents the outcomes from the three main phases of the proposed pipeline: segmentation, post-processing, and classification.

The experiments were conducted on the following hardware: AMD Ryzen Threadripper PRO 3975WX @ 3.5 GHz with 256 GB DDR4 of RAM to which we add a GPU NVIDIA RTX A6000 with 48 GB VRAM. And the software used was PyTorch 2.0 (via MONAI 1.3) running over Ubuntu 22.04 LTS. Training times ranged from 30 min to 1 hour per model, depending on architecture and input volume, and were GPU-accelerated using mixed-precision training.

In the initial phase, 51 spine MRI exams were annotated across 18 classes: 17 anatomical structures and one background class. A U-Net model with an EfficientNet-B2 encoder was trained on sagittal slices using these annotations, achieving a Dice Score of 0.734. The model was used to pre-annotate an additional 114 exams, which were subsequently reviewed by radiologists, yielding a finalized dataset of 165 exams and over 5,200 annotated sagittal images.

Attempts to train segmentation models on the full 18-class dataset did not exceed an F1-Score of 0.765, with underrepresented structures (e.g., foramina) yielding poor performance. Moreover, multiclass pathology annotation (up to 65 classes per patient) proved infeasible due to data sparsity.

To overcome these limitations, the task was reformulated to segment only three classes: background, vertebrae, and discs. This approach increased class density, reduced variability, and enabled the training of simpler, more robust 2D models. Several architectures were evaluated using consistent training parameters (30 epochs, fixed learning rate, <2 h per model).

The Table 1 summarizes the comparative performance (Mean Dice Score) in which each decoder was trained with an encoder to achieve the best possible model for the task. The metric used was the Mean Dice Score (Macro Dice Score) across all model classes.

Table 1. Results for the Segmentation Model.

Architecture	ResNet34	EfficientNet-B2	VGG16	MixViT
U-Net	0.776	0.897	0.895	0.769
U-Net++	0.883	0.892	0.771	*
DeepLabV3+	0.878	0.890	*	0.875
SegFormer	0.887	0.889	0.885	0.757
MAnet	0.876	0.898	0.768	*

The asterisks (*) denote the encoders that were not compatible with the decoders used in these scenarios.

EfficientNet-B2 [11] consistently performed well across all decoders, with MAnet + EfficientNet-B2 achieving the highest score (0.898). These results emphasize the advantage of hybrid architectures combining convolutional and attention mechanisms in medical image segmentation. Using this selected model, all 5,200 images were re-labelled with predicted masks (three-class), replacing manual annotations. The Fig. 3 illustrates an example of a mask generated on a sagittal slice, comparing it to the original manual segmentation consisting of 18 classes.

These predictions formed the basis for the classification task, simulating a fully automated diagnostic pipeline. Validation data from the segmentation step was reused in classification to avoid data leakage. While the three-class segmentation improved volumetric precision, it lacked anatomical granularity, failing to differentiate individual vertebrae (e.g., L1, L2) or discs (e.g., L2–L3). To address this, a post-processing pipeline was introduced to individualize these structures. This process includes Z-axis separation of vertebral and disc volumes, morphological filtering to remove noise and refine boundaries, and labelling of segmented units based on spatial positioning. The Fig. 4 illustrates the mask improvement post-processing. This step enabled anatomical alignment and extraction of disc-specific sub volumes required for classification.

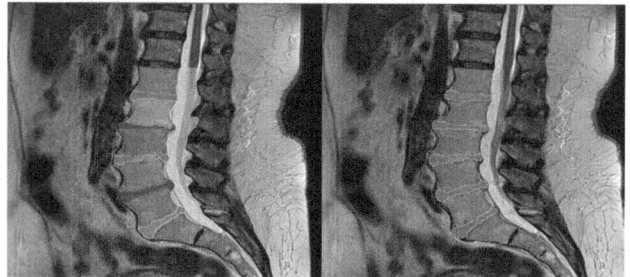

Fig. 3. Segmented mask created by radiologists with 18 classes (left) compared to the mask segmented by the trained model with 3 classes (right).

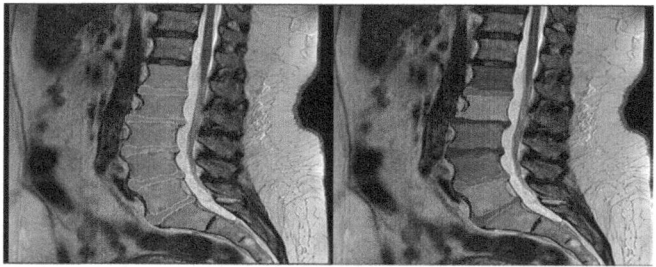

Fig. 4. Mask generated by the three-class segmentation model (left) and the same mask post-processed to independently extract each disc and vertebra (right).

Following post-processing, the geometric centres of each identified disc were used to extract fixed-size volumetric patches centred on the intervertebral discs. These patches served as inputs for classification models trained to detect pathological changes. Four 3D models were trained and evaluated on 30 epochs using identical hyperparameters. Training durations ranged from 30 min to 1 hour per model. The Table 2 presents validation performance using F1-Score and Accuracy, in which each decoder was trained with one encoder to identify the optimal architecture for the task. The evaluation metric employed was the Mean Dice Score (Macro Dice Score) [20], calculated across all model classes.

Table 2. Results for the Segmentation Model.

Model	F1-Score	Accuracy
ResNet50	0.793	0.680
EfficientNet-B2	0.897	0.814
SENet (ResNet50)	0.839	0.738
ViT	**0.905**	**0.826**

The ViT model achieved the best F1-Score with the value of 0.905, and Accuracy with the value of 0.826. The F1-Score was prioritized due to dataset imbalance, as it balances precision and recall, ensuring better identification of altered discs. The loss function combined Binary Cross-Entropy (BCE) (c.f., [21]) with F1 Loss. Models trained with only BCE yielded higher accuracy but lower F1-Scores, failing to detect rarer positive cases effectively. Despite overall success in binary classification, the sample size could be insufficient for reliable multiclass classification of subtypes (e.g., bulging, protrusion).

5 Conclusions and Further Research

This paper proposed a multi-stage deep learning pipeline tailored for the detection of lumbar disc pathologies, tackling the limitations imposed by small sample sizes, anatomical complexity, and the need for precise spatial localization. By strategically decomposing the problem into segmentation, post-processing, and classification, the approach effectively isolated intervertebral discs, reduced input noise, and enhanced model interpretability. The segmentation phase, simplified to three classes, achieved a robust Dice Score of 0.898, enabling a fully automated pre-processing stage that greatly reduces radiologist workload.

The critical methodological insight was the decision to first segment and localize each disc before classification, avoiding ambiguity introduced by multi-disc input volumes. This architectural decoupling increased classification performance (F1-Score of 0.902) and laid the groundwork for scalable dataset growth. Moreover, the pipeline's ability to automatically extract disc centres supports annotation refinement and dataset reuse, emphasizing reproducibility and clinical relevance.

A systematic comparison of deep learning architectures demonstrated the high performance of hybrid models like MA-Net with EfficientNet-B2, suggesting that combining convolutional precision with attention mechanisms is particularly advantageous in medical imaging. These insights are instrumental for guiding architecture selection in related biomedical tasks.

Regarding our initially research question, namely: *which deep learning architecture most reliably detects disc herniation in lumbar MRI scans?* The study demonstrates a scalable, interpretable, and clinically applicable AI pipeline for spinal imaging, marking a step toward intelligent, semi-automated radiological workflows in real-world healthcare environments. Nonetheless, limitations remain. Chief among them are class imbalances among disc alteration types and the absence of external test datasets, which restrict the broader generalizability of the results. Additionally, the labour-intensive nature of multilayered annotations constrained full dataset utilization. Despite this, the depth and quality of the annotations confer enduring value to the dataset and provide a rich foundation for future work.

This study should be interpreted as a single-center validation, conducted using retrospective data acquired from a single institutional imaging network encompassing scanners from four major manufacturers. While this design allowed for controlled annotation quality, consistent acquisition protocols, and in-depth model evaluation, it inherently limits the immediate generalizability of the findings to broader clinical environments with heterogeneous imaging protocols, demographic variability, and disease prevalence.

As such, the current results reflect internal validity rather than external robustness. To address this limitation, future work will focus on prospective multicenter testing, involving datasets from geographically and institutionally diverse sources. This next phase will aim to evaluate the performance of the pipeline under real-world deployment conditions, assess its interoperability with varied Picture Archiving and Communication Systems (PACS), and determine its resilience to domain shift. Such multicenter validation is essential for establishing the model's clinical generalizability, regulatory readiness, and translational applicability at scale.

Future directions include the expansion of the dataset through multi-institutional collaboration and the integration of multimodal data (clinical, radiological, biomechanical) to build comprehensive, personalized diagnostic models. There is also significant potential in incorporating temporal analysis using spatiotemporal models or transformers for progression tracking. Equally important is the development of explainable AI tools to bridge the translational gap between algorithmic performance and clinical adoption.

Disclosure of Interests. The authors have no competing interests to declare that are relevant to the content of this article.

References

1. Radiology ES of Radiology staffing and workload in Europe: a growing crisis (2023)
2. Brady, A.P., et al.: Developing, purchasing, implementing and monitoring AI tools in radiology: practical considerations. A multi-society statement from the ACR, CAR, ESR, RANZCR & RSNA. Can. Assoc. Radiol. J. **75**(2), 226–244 (2024)
3. Erickson, B.J., Korfiatis, P., Akkus, Z., Kline, T.L.: Machine learning for medical imaging. Radiographics **37**(2), 505–515 (2017)
4. Grand Challenge AI Database (2024)
5. Hartvigsen, J., et al.: What low back pain is and why we need to pay attention. Lancet **391**(10137), 2356–2367 (2018)
6. Wu, A., et al.: Global low back pain prevalence and years lived with disability from 1990 to 2017: estimates from the Global Burden of Disease Study 2017. Ann. Transl. Med. **8**(6), 299 (2020)
7. Awadalla, A.M., et al.: Management of lumbar disc herniation: a systematic review. Cureus **15**(10) (2023)
8. Galbusera, F., Cina, A.: Image annotation and curation in radiology: an overview for machine learning practitioners. Eur. Radiol. Exp. **8**(1), 11 (2024)
9. Foster, N.E., et al.: Prevention and treatment of low back pain: evidence, challenges, and promising directions. Lancet **391**(10137), 2368–2383 (2018)
10. He, K., Zhang, X., Ren, S., Sun, J.: Deep residual learning for image recognition. In: Proceedings of the IEEE Conference on Computer Vision and Pattern Recognition, pp. 770–778 (2016)
11. Tan, M., Le, Q.: Efficientnet: rethinking model scaling for convolutional neural networks. In: International Conference on Machine Learning, pp. 6105–6114. PMLR (2019)
12. Hu, J., Shen, L., Sun, G.: Squeeze-and-excitation networks. In: Proceedings of the IEEE Conference on Computer Vision and Pattern Recognition, pp. 7132–7141 (2018)
13. Dosovitskiy, A., et al.: An image is worth 16×16 words: transformers for image recognition at scale. arXiv preprint arXiv:2010.11929 (2020)

14. Ronneberger, O., Fischer, P., Brox, T.: U-net: convolutional networks for biomedical image segmentation. In: Medical Image Computing and Computer-Assisted Intervention–MICCAI 2015: 18th International Conference, Munich, Germany, 5–9 October 2015, Proceedings, Part III 18, pp. 234–241. Springer, Cham (2015)
15. Zhou, Z., Rahman Siddiquee, M.M., Tajbakhsh, N., Liang, J.: UNet++: a nested u-net architecture for medical image segmentation. In: Deep Learning in Medical Image Analysis and Multimodal Learning for Clinical Decision Support: 4th International Workshop, DLMIA 2018, and 8th International Workshop, ML-CDS 2018, Held in Conjunction with MICCAI 2018, Granada, Spain, 20 September 20, Proceedings 4, pp. 3–11. Springer, Cham (2018)
16. Chen, L.C., Zhu, Y., Papandreou, G., Schroff, F., Adam, H.: Encoder-decoder with atrous separable convolution for semantic image segmentation. In: Proceedings of the European Conference on Computer Vision (ECCV), pp. 801–818 (2018)
17. Xie, E., Wang, W., Yu, Z., Anandkumar, A., Alvarez, J.M., Luo, P.: SegFormer: simple and efficient design for semantic segmentation with transformers. In: Advances in Neural Information Processing Systems, vol. 34, 12077–12090 (2021)
18. Hettihewa, K., Kobchaisawat, T., Tanpowpong, N., Chalidabhongse, T.H.: MANet: a multi-attention network for automatic liver tumor segmentation in computed tomography (CT) imaging. Sci. Rep. 13(1), 20098 (2023)
19. Kingma, D.P., Ba, J.: Adam: a method for stochastic optimization. arXiv preprint arXiv:1412. 6980 (2014)
20. Dice, L.R.: Measures of the amount of ecologic association between species. Ecology 26(3), 297–302 (1945)
21. Shannon, C.E.: A mathematical theory of communication. ACM SIGMOBILE Mob. Comput. Commun. Rev. 5(1), 3–55 (2001)

Knowledge-Aware Clinical Narrative Extraction Using Ontologies and Knowledge Graphs

Maria Leite[1] , Rita Rb-Silva[4,5] , Nuno Guimarães[1,2] , Lise Stork[3] ,
and Alípio Jorge[1,2(✉)]

[1] INESC TEC, Porto, Portugal
nuno.r.guimaraes@inesctec.pt
[2] Faculdade de Ciências, Universidade do Porto, Porto, Portugal
amjorge@fc.up.pt
[3] University of Amsterdam, Amsterdam, The Netherlands
l.stork@uva.nl
[4] Research Centre of the Portuguese Institute of Oncology of Porto (CI-IPOP),
Porto, Portugal
[5] RISE-Health, Departamento de Medicina da Comunidade, Informação e Decisão
em Saúde, Faculdade de Medicina, Universidade do Porto, Porto, Portugal
rrsilva@med.up.pt

Abstract. Providing healthcare professionals with quick access to structured standardized information enables comprehensive analysis and improves clinical decision-making. However, an important part of the records in health institutions is in the form of free text. This paper proposes a pipeline that automatically extracts medical information from Electronic Medical Records (EMRs), based on large language models (LLMs) and a domain ontology defined and validated in collaboration with a medical expert. The output is a knowledge graph of clinical narratives that can be used to search through repositories of EMRs or discover new facts. To promote the standardization of the extracted medical terms, we link them to existing international coding systems using biomedical repositories (UMLS - Unified Medical Language System and BioPortal - Biomedical Ontology Repository). We showcase our approach on a set of Portuguese clinical texts of cases of Acute Myeloid Leukemia (AML) guided by one medical expert. We evaluate the quality of the extraction and of the knowledge graph.

Keywords: Electronic Medical Records · Clinical Narratives · Ontologies · LLMs · Information Extraction

1 Introduction

In contemporary healthcare, Electronic Medical Records (EMRs) play a significant role in providing detailed patient information, including symptoms, exams,

J. Valente de Oliveira et al. (Eds.): EPIA 2025, LNAI 16121, pp. 26–41, 2026.
https://doi.org/10.1007/978-3-032-05176-9_3

diagnoses and treatments. However, the unstructured nature of text and its linguistic complexity makes information extraction challenging. Moreover, the diversity in standards and terminologies used in different institutions creates significant heterogeneity in clinical data, complicating comprehensive analysis. Terms like *non-insulin dependent* and *type 2 diabetes* refer to the same condition as do HTN and chronic hypertension. Thus, they may be used interchangeably. This disparity, compounded by the variety of patients' clinical histories and the extensive range of documents involved, makes it challenging for physicians to attain a comprehensive and holistic view of information. Thus, these challenges call for robust methods for extracting and structuring clinical information.

Ontologies offer a promising approach to defining standards in healthcare and biomedical informatics, by organizing information into structured hierarchies and relationships, thereby enhancing reliable extraction, integration, and interpretation of clinical data for decision-making and interoperability purposes [1]. Ontologies also promote the use of consistent language which helps to improve diagnostic accuracy and reduce medical errors [2]. Additionally, they facilitate large-scale multi-document data integration and research, enabling the identification of trends and correlations for the whole institution or health system [3].

However, despite their potential, challenges persist. Developing specialized ontologies for various medical specialities requires extensive domain knowledge and collaboration with experts to ensure comprehensiveness and relevance. Additionally, integrating data from diverse sources remains a complex task, necessitating robust methods to harmonize disparate data formats and terminologies into a cohesive ontological structure.

To address these challenges, including the extraction and structuring of clinical information (entities and relations), we propose a pipeline that prompts large language models (LLMs) to annotate EMRs with terms from the domain ontology (Fig. 1). To link the vocabulary of the expert to standard terms we use biomedical knowledge repositories like UMLS [3] and BioPortal [4]. This results in a knowledge graph (KG) of clinical narratives that can be used to search through repositories of EMRs or discover new facts. The developed pipeline facilitates the access of healthcare professionals to standardized structured data obtained from EMR, according to their perspective, and producing a knowledge graph. We showcase our approach on real pseudoanonymized EMRs of Acute Myeloid Leukemia (AML). This work has been developed in the context of HfPT project (Health from Portugal) to enhance the capabilities of standardized information extraction methods in a clinical context towards the automatic processing of clinical annotation in free text.

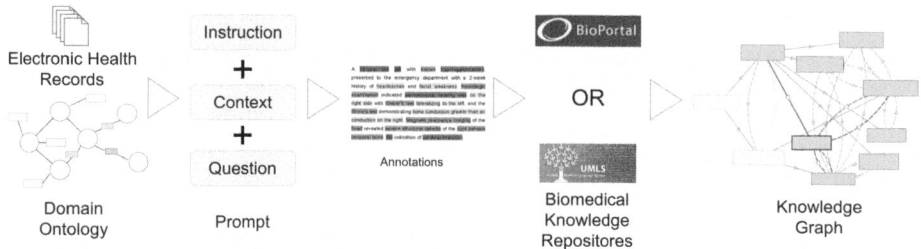

Fig. 1. Pipeline for clinical narrative extraction and standardization using ontologies.

2   Related Work

Ontologies role in healthcare is multifaceted and essential for the advancement of biomedicine. They enable the integration of data from various sources, facilitating interoperability between different systems, contributing significantly to the standardization and normalization of medical terminologies. Ontologies also play an important role in biomedical research, facilitating the annotation of experimental and clinical data, which consequently leads to an easier interpretation of large volumes of medical data. This is important for the development of new treatments and therapies, as it allows researchers to identify patterns and correlations more efficiently. Additionally, ontologies serve as the basis for the development of various computational tools, such as clinical decision support systems and data integration platforms, which use ontological knowledge to provide more accurate and relevant results [5].

Notable ontologies, such as SNOMED-CT[1] and PICO[2], provide structured categorizations, facilitating better data integration and research [6,7]. Two repositories widely used to promote the interoperability of health data are UMLS[3] and BioPortal[4]. UMLS integrates and distributes key terminology, classification and coding standards, and associated resources to promote the development of more effective and interoperable biomedical information systems and services, including electronic health records [6]. BioPortal is a comprehensive repository of biomedical ontologies that facilitates the sharing and reuse of ontological knowledge within the biomedical community. It supports various features, including browsing, searching, visualization and mapping between the different ontologies available [8].

The Ontology-Based Frameworks for Clinical Information Extraction can effectively standardize medical terms and enhance data accuracy. For instance, Jusoh et al. (2020) [9] propose the COBIE framework, which combines information extraction (IE) and ontology techniques to extract clinical concepts from medical records. Using tokenization and named entity recognition (NER),

---

[1] https://www.snomed.org/what-is-snomed-ct.

[2] https://linkeddata.cochrane.org/pico-ontology.

[3] https://www.nlm.nih.gov/research/umls/index.html.

[4] https://bioportal.bioontology.org/.

COBIE identifies entities and relationships from unstructured data and organizes them into a structured ontology. This enhances clinical information extraction, visualization, and supports decision-making. Muhammad Afzal et al. developed the N2K Mapper, a framework that uses natural language processing (NLP), named entity recognition (NER), and biomedical ontologies to transform clinical narratives into KGs. The process includes three steps: narrative preprocessing, RDF triple extraction, and validation. The N2K Mapper identified 1,630 unique entities and generated 4,174 RDF triples, enriching KGs and aiding in disease diagnosis and clinical decision support systems (CDSS).

Concerning information extraction methods used in the literature, these range from rule-based systems to machine learning approaches. For instance, the i2b2 challenge employs a rule-based model to extract medication-related information, using tailored rules for document structure and specific syntax [10]. Conversely, machine learning techniques, such as convolutional neural networks and models like DocR-BERT, focus on extracting relationships between biomedical entities, enhancing tasks like disease prediction [11,12].

Other works mainly focus on the combination of NLP tools with ontologies. For example, MetaMap [13,14] is a computational linguistic tool that identifies words and phrases in free text English (although it was posterior adapted to other languages, with varying degrees of success) and maps them to the UMLS. MetaMap applies various processing steps to the input clinical text, such as tokenization, part-of-speech tagging, and syntactic analysis, to identify relevant concepts to map to a chosen ontology in the UMLS. More recently, the authors in [15] propose the CLEAR pipeline, which uses ontologies and LLMs for data augmentation combined with a RAG approach to retrieve clinical note chunks relevant to a given target entity. Similarly, [16] introduce DR.KNOWS (Diagnostic Reasoning Knowledge Graph System), a system that combines UMLS-based knowledge graphs with LLMs to enhance diagnostic predictions from EHR by retrieving contextually relevant pathways tailored to individual patient information

3   Methodology and Development

In this section, we present the methodology used to develop the pipeline that converts EHR and domain-specific ontologies into a knowledge graph.

Domain Ontology Definition: The first step of the process is to manually define a domain-specific ontology that represents the relevant knowledge of the expert on a specific topic (e.g. a disease) using their custom vocabulary. This is a one-time effort for a specific domain. In our case study, we collaborated with a medical expert experienced in the field of Acute Myeloid Leukemia (AML), a cancer of hematopoietic progenitor and/or stem cells, characterized by the proliferation and accumulation of immature blood cells in the bone marrow, bloodstream, and/or other tissues [17]. Consequently, the medical expert started by annotating a sample of pseudoanonymized oncological EMRs related to AML in order to name relevant categories and relations. Figure 2 shows a fictional annotation example. From the resulting list of categories and relations we defined a patient-centric ontology (Fig. 3) which was then coded in RDF (Resource Description Framework)

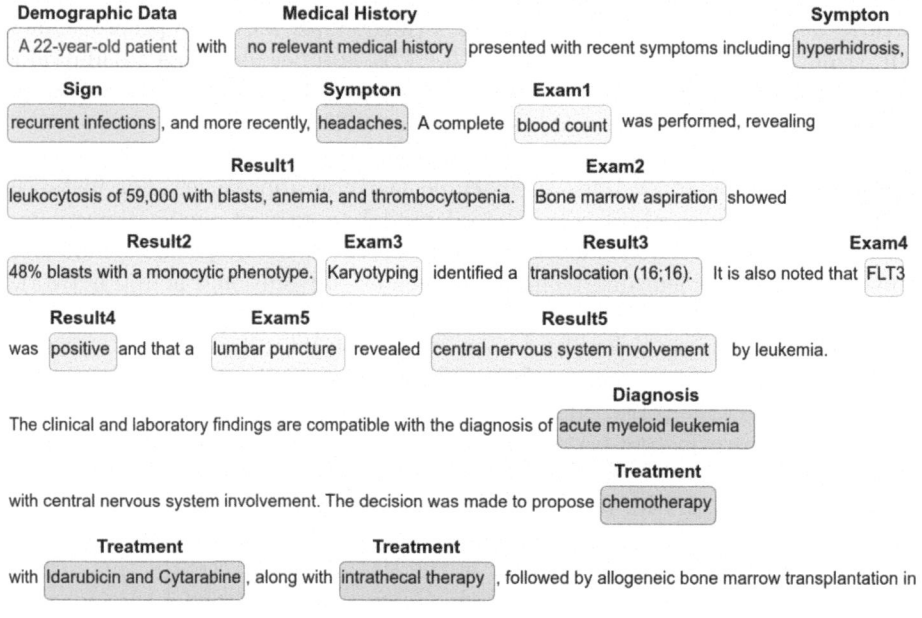

Fig. 2. Example of annotated text (translated to English) showing different categories suggested by the expert.

Information Extraction: The next step is to extract information from the EMR using a Large Language Model (LLM) combined with a prompting strategy to produce automatic annotations, which follow the guidelines given by the medical expert in the domain-specific ontology. For this task, we employed the generative models Med42-70b [18] and Zephyr-7b-beta [19]. The Zephyr-7b-beta is a general-purpose model optimized for a wide range of NLP tasks with 7 billion parameters. It is designed to balance performance and computational efficiency, making it suitable for various applications without requiring excessive computational resources. In contrast, the Med42-70b is a specialized model for the medical domain, with 70 billion parameters, designed to handle complex medical terminology and provide accurate matches in highly specialized contexts.

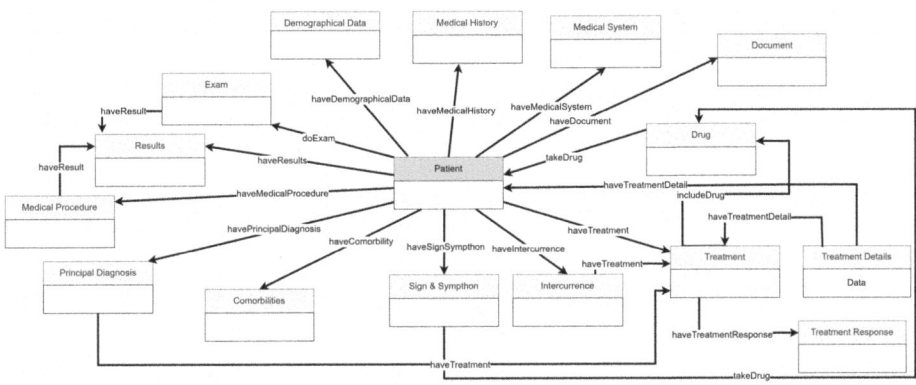

Fig. 3. Local domain ontology created in collaboration with a medical expert.

To ensure consistent extraction of relevant information and produce annotations aligned with the defined ground truth [20], these models require a carefully designed prompt.

The prompt used in our illustrating case was the following:

I am a doctor specializing in leukemia and I want you to annotate clinical texts. Base your annotations on this ontological structure I created:

ontology = {ontology structure}

Use the classes provided in the ontology and apply the suffixes _I, _II, etc., when necessary, based on the relationships between words in the text. The format for annotations should be: [term : class_ suffix]. For example, [Hemogram : Exam_ I], [Anemia : Result_ I]. Now, annotate the following text using the same format I gave you:

Report: {EMR to annotate}

The Prompt has four sections: 1) the context asking the user to act as a leukemia specialist annotating clinical texts; 2) the domain ontology with a list of classes and relationships; 3) output formatting guidelines; 4) the EMR to annotate.

[22 anos : DadoDemografico],

[Sem antecedentes relevantes : HistoriaMedica],

[Hipersudorese : SinaisSintomas],

[Leucocitose : SinaisSintomas - Disease or Syndrome],

[Infecções : HistoriaMedica - Pathologic Function],

[Anemia : SinaisSintomas - Disease or Syndrome],

[Leucemia Mieloide Aguda : DiagnosticoPrincipal_I - Neoplastic Process],

[Quimioterapia : Tratamento_I - Preventive Procedure],

[Idarrubina : Tratamento_I],

[Citarabina : Tratamento_I - Nucleic Acid],

[Tratamento intratecal : Tratamento_I - Preventive Procedure],

[Alotransplante de medula óssea : Tratamento_I - Tissue]

Fig. 4. Representation of an example of the output of the extraction and standardization process. Extracted terms in brown, categories from the domain ontology in green and associated standard categories in blue. (Color figure online)

Entity Linking and Classification: Next, to ensure standardization, we link the category of each automatically annotated term to the categories in the biomedical repository. For this work, we used UMLS and BioPortal. This linking step is done through exact matching using UMLS or BioPortal API. Figure 4 illustrates part of an example output for our Acute Myeloid Leukemia running example. The terms extracted by the LLM are in brown. The categories from the domain ontology assigned by the LLM are in green. The linked categories (standard) from the biomedical ontology (UMLS or BioPortal) are in blue.

Knowledge Graph Construction: Given a set of EMR with cases from the disease of interest, the automatically annotated and classified terms are used to construct a KG. In terms of representation they are transformed into RDF triples [21]. Once the ontology has been instantiated into a knowledge graph, an RDF file is generated, which can then be interpreted by tools like Protégé for consultation [22]. By visualizing the ontology, domain experts can understand its structure and explore the relationships between elements. This also helps to identify inconsistencies which enables data validation. Figure 5 shows a snapshot of Protégé Ontograf visualization with the medical information from one particular patient.

4   Results and Discussion

In this section, we evaluated the different components of the proposed pipeline. First, we assess the quality of the extraction process. Second we evaluate the knowledge graph output based on its information and structure.

4.1   Information Extraction Evaluation

We began the evaluation by analysing how capable is the extraction process of following the provided ontology. Thus, to evaluate the information extraction process by the LLMs, we used 26 texts annotated by experts. These covered 21 classes and relations. We measured *Precision, Recall, F*1 and *Accuracy* for the extraction of the *Classes*, and of *Terms* of interest annotated by the expert. We also assessed the ability of models for extracting simultaneously the pairs $<Term, Class>$, which is a much more demanding task. These aspects were evaluated using both exact match and partial match criteria. The criteria are defined as follows:

Exact Match: This criterion assesses whether there is a perfect match between the expected and actual results. It is a stringent measure that only counts a match as correct if all aspects of the result are identical to what was expected.

Partial Match: This criterion provides flexibility by allowing for variations between expected and actual results. It defines a partial match as correct if a significant portion of the result aligns with the expected outcome, even if it is not an exact match. To implement this, we utilize a function that calculates the Levenshtein distance between the annotated and expected terms. The Levenshtein

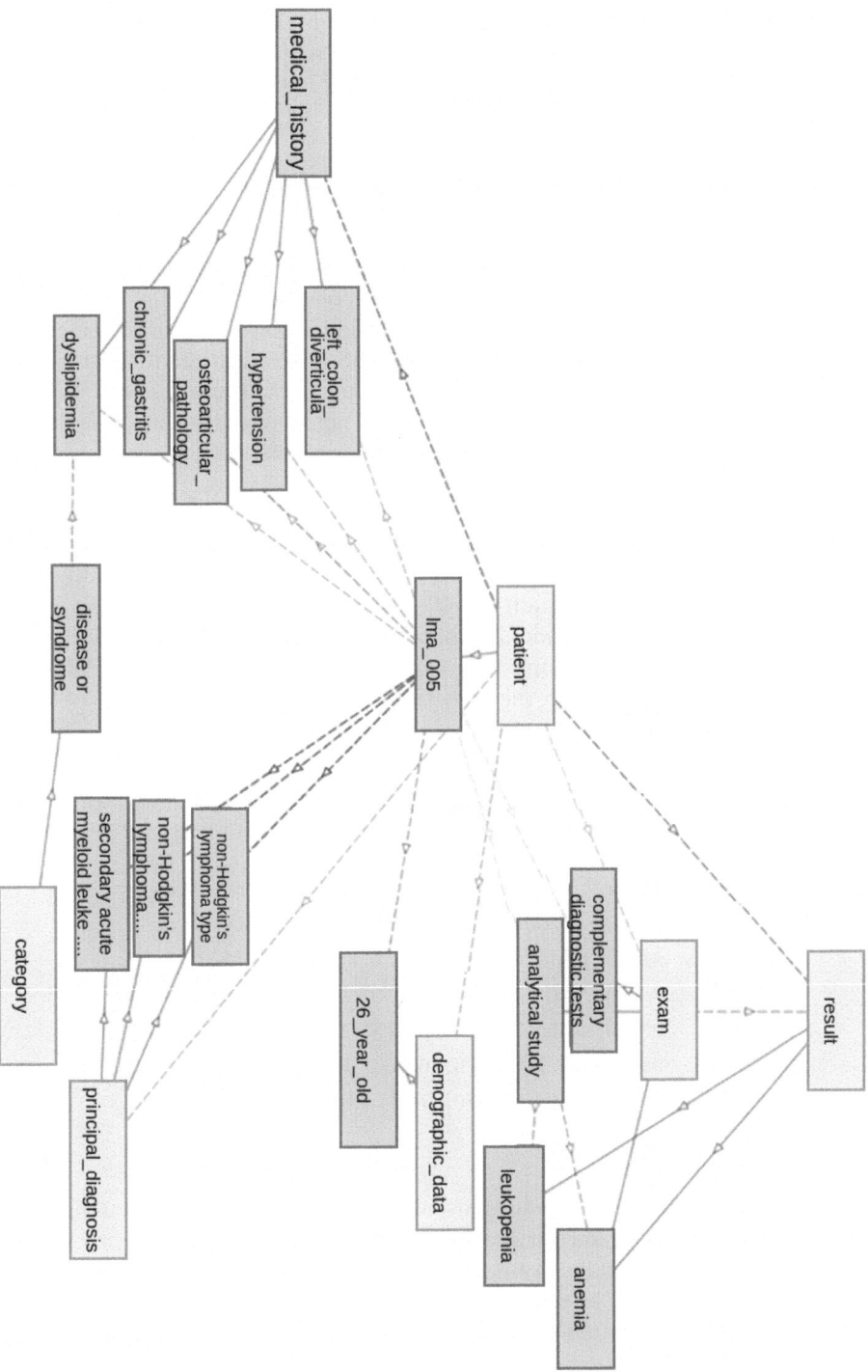

Fig. 5. Part of the knowledge graph as visualized in Protégé (translated to English and improved for better visualization).

distance measures the minimum number of single-character edits (insertions, deletions, or substitutions) required to transform one term into another. We set the threshold at 3, meaning that if the terms differ less than tree single-character operation, they are considered sufficiently similar to qualify as a partial match according to the Levenshtein criterion.

Table 1 presents the performance metrics of two models, zephyr-7b-beta (M1) and med42-70b (M2), for various match types: Class Match, Term Match, and <Term, Class> Match.

In the Class Match task, Model 1 demonstrates exceptional performance in partial matches, indicating its high effectiveness in identifying classes with 99.5% accuracy. Model 2, however, shows slightly lower performance in this category with 97.5% accuracy, suggesting that its specialization in exact medical terminology may limit its flexibility in handling partial information. When it comes to exact matches, both models show a noticeable drop in performance, being less effective under stricter precision requirements, with Model 1 achieving 60% accuracy and Model 2 56.8%.

For the Term Match task, Model 1 performs slightly better with an accuracy of 80.1%, demonstrating its capability to effectively handle various terms. Model 2, although slightly behind with 76.2% accuracy, still shows reasonably good performance, reflecting its domain-specific training. In the <Term, Class> Match task, Model 1 outperforms Model 2 in both partial and exact matches, indicating robust performance in matching terms with their respective classes. Model 2, while effective, does not match the versatility and broader applicability of Model 1 in this scenario.

Table 1. Extraction performance of the two models in Class, Term, and <Term, Class> pairs using partial and exact match. M1 is Zephyr-7b-beta, M2 is Med42-70b.

	Class				Term				<Term, Class>			
	Partial		Exact		Partial		Exact		Partial		Exact	
Metrics	M1	M2	M1	M2	M1	M2	M1	M2	M1	M2	M1	M2
Precision	98.4	98.8	56.8	52.1	76.1	69.2	57.4	58.1	78.6	69.7	38.1	33.4
Recall	98.5	97.2	55.4	53.3	76.1	69.2	55.2	53.9	76.3	68.2	35.7	32.1
F1	98.5	98.0	55.5	52.7	76.1	69.2	55.1	55.5	77.4	68.9	36.9	32.8
Accuracy	99.5	97.5	60.0	56.8	80.1	76.2	54.6	53.5	82.3	75.3	37.3	36.2

In general, partial match values are always higher than exact match values, which is to be expected since it is very difficult to identify exact terms in their entirety. Partial match values range between 70–100%, unlike exact match values, which are between 30–60%. When comparing partial matches with exact matches, Model 1 consistently performs well in partial matches across all categories, indicating strong generalization and flexibility in handling approximate information. Model 2, on the other hand, excels in exact matches, particularly in Class Matches, reflecting its training focus on precise medical terminology. However, it is weaker in partial matches, suggesting limitations in flexibility and handling broader or less precise contexts.

After analyzing the model results, it is important to examine the distribution of the identified classes. In Fig. 6, we have the count for each class comparing the results for Model 1, Model 2, and human annotation.

When comparing human annotations (considered as the ground truth) with the results of Models 1 and 2, we can observe significant differences across various classes. In classes such as *Paciente* and *Exame*, both models show data counts that are quite close to the human annotations, indicating good precision. However, in classes like *História Médica* and *Medicamento*, Model 1 significantly underestimates the occurrences. This discrepancy suggests that Model 1 has difficulties recognizing or correctly classifying these categories.

On the other hand, Model 2 demonstrates a performance closer to human annotations in several categories, such as *Dado Demográfico* and *História Médica*, where its counts are well-aligned or slightly above the human annotations. However, Model 2 also exhibits notable overestimations, especially in classes like *Resultado*, where it exceeds the human annotations. This may indicate a tendency to confuse other classes with this one or to erroneously identify additional instances.

We also highlight that Model 1 performs worse in overrepresented categories such as *Comorbilidade* and *Intercorrência*, where its counts are significantly higher than the human annotations.

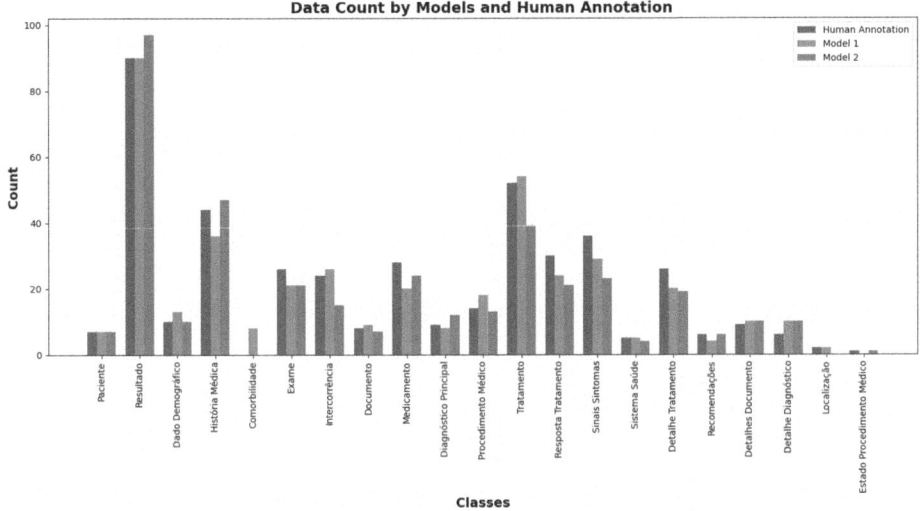

Fig. 6. Class Distribution Counts (class names in Portuguese).

After extracting terms using the LLMs, we combined the annotations with the categories extracted by BioPortal and UMLS. In this process of combining annotations, we introduced a new class: *Categoria*. This is the only class with different results, as this class is only considered after the annotations are generated by the models. This class counts the number of terms with a category identified by UMLS or BioPortal, separately. Figure 7 shows the results for this class.

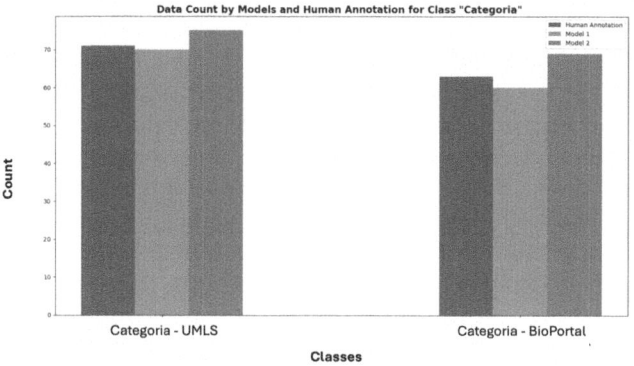

Fig. 7. Comparing Class *Categoria* (Category) with UMLS and BioPortal.

For the *Categoria* class using UMLS, both Model 1 and Model 2 present counts very close to human annotations, with Model 1 being practically identical and Model 2 slightly higher. This means that out of the total 433 annotations defined by human annotation across 26 texts, only 71 have a category according to UMLS and 63 according to BioPortal. Out of the 414 annotations made by Model 1, 70 are categorized by UMLS and 69 by BioPortal. Similarly, of the 386 annotations identified by Model 2, 63 are categorized by UMLS and 60 by BioPortal.

The number of identified categories is low because the category must exactly match the terms in the annotations. For example, UMLS and BioPortal do not have categories for specific terms such as *22 anos* or *Tacrolimus 1.5+1.5mg*.

4.2   Ontology Evaluation

In this second phase, we evaluate how good the produced knowledge graph is. Additionally, we assess how that quality varies with the model and the source of the terms. This is a one-instance evaluation since it requires all the available data. Nevertheless, it illustrates the capabilities of our approach and highlights future research developments. To evaluate the quality of the knowledge graph, we use objective measures and do not rely on more subjective human evaluation. The quality of the generated knowledge graph and the utility of the services UMLS and BioPortal were assessed using *ontology quality dimensions* and *competency questions* (i.e. specific questions that should be answered by the knowledge-graph). The ontology quality measures used are *Coverage* for domain representation, *Cohesion* for logical consistency, *Size* in nodes, *Richness* for information content per concept and *Redundancy* to identify and minimize duplicate or unnecessary elements [23,24]. Table 2 shows the results and compares the use of BioPortal and UMLS for linking to standardized categories. Both these results are compared with the results of human annotation, which serve as the ground-truth in this evaluation. Human annotation was conducted by a medical expert and consisted of manually linking the annotated terms and categories to the standard terms.

Table 2. Summary of Ontology Statistics and Metrics

Metric	Annotation		Model 1		Model 2	
	BioPortal	UMLS	BioPortal	UMLS	BioPortal	UMLS
Classes	22	22	22	22	22	22
Properties	29	29	29	29	29	29
Instances	471	**561**	434	**522**	419	**530**
Axioms	**2,374**	1,848	**2,242**	1,742	**2,120**	1,768
Logical Axioms	**1,469**	679	**1,396**	648	**1,312**	655
Declaration Axioms	22	24	22	24	22	24
Annotation Properties	27	27	26	26	26	26
	Human Annotation		Model 1		Model 2	
Coverage	56.26%	61.09%	55.19%	60.96%	55.33%	60.52%
Cohesion	100%	100%	100%	100%	100%	100%
Size	522	612	485	573	470	581
Richness	4.59	2.84	4.68	2.90	4.57	2.89
Redundancy	0%	0%	0%	0%	0%	0%

The structure of the produced knowledge graph remained consistent across annotation sources (human, models) and standardization sources (BioPortal, UMLS), identifying the same classes and properties. However, UMLS covered a greater number of instances (Coverage) compared to BioPortal. Both model-based approaches showed simplification with respect to human annotations, resulting in fewer instances and axioms. This reduction can be interpreted as a simplification of the ontological structure by the models, which may be eliminating redundant or less relevant axioms. BioPortal enables the identification of more logical axioms[5] than UMLS, but both models captured fewer logical axioms compared to human annotations. Despite this, both BioPortal and UMLS maintained 100% logical consistency, ensuring integrity and navigability in the graph.

---

[5] Specific types of axioms that describe logical rules and constraints within the ontology. These include equivalences (defining when two classes are considered equal) and subsumptions (defining hierarchical relationships where one class is a subset of another).

Regarding the other quality dimensions, BioPortal excelled in Richness, offering more attributes and relationships per concept. UMLS also resulted in larger ontologies (Size), potentially leading to more detailed data representations. No redundancies were found, which simplifies ontology maintenance and inference. The comparison between models and human annotations highlighted that, while the models effectively captured relevant terms and maintained logical integrity, some discrepancies with human annotations were present. This points to both the strengths and limitations of the models in addressing the richness and complexity of medical information. Overall, this analysis provides valuable insights into the advantages and challenges of using UMLS and BioPortal for ontology development, guiding future improvements and applications.

4.3   Competency Questions

Competency questions serve to asses the correctness and domain coverage of a knowledge graph and they basically test whether the ontology is able to provide answers to specific questions [25]. In our experiments, these questions were formulated based on potential user queries, ensuring that the ontology meets information needs. These were validated by the experts and compared with human annotations (ground truth) to ensure accuracy.

To illustrate a competency question, we show one example of one (*Which are the most frequent exams?*) in detail. Figure 8 compares the exams identified by models and human annotations. The analysis highlights that *aspirado medular* and *hemograma* were consistently identified, while *cariótipo* appeared in both Model 2 and human annotations. Although *biópsia de medula óssea* and *biópsia ecoguiada* are exams, they're usually classified as procedures, and *pancitopenia* is wrong as it's an exam result.

The results in general show high consistency with medical expert expectations, indicating that the created knowledge graph effectively addresses clinical inquiries with accurate content. The results also show that models can identify correct terms not recognized by human annotations due to the variations in annotation or due to the lack of occurrences of one item. Overall, the result of this evaluation shows that knowledge graphs can be used to extract useful information aligned with medical knowledge, demonstrating their potential in clinical scenarios.

Which are the most frequent exams?

	Human Annotation	Model 1	Model 2
Green : Correct	Aspirado medular	Aspirado medular	Hemograma
Red : Incorrect	Hemograma	Hemograma	Aspirado medular
Orange : Possibly Correct	Cariótipo	Biópsia de medula óssea	Cariótipo
	Estudo Analítico	Pancitopenia	Biópsia ecoguiada

Fig. 8. Most Frequent Exams by Model and Human Annotation (in Portuguese).

5 Conclusion

This paper explores the automatic extraction and structuring of clinical information from pseudonymized clinical texts, using expert-defined local ontologies. The proposed extraction pipeline goes from clinical texts enriched by a local ontology to a knowledge graph that represents one or more clinical cases. The resulting ontology is represented in RDF and can be visualized and edited in a tool like Protégé, enabling further improvement and exploration by medical staff. With this work we have shown how incorporation of ontology structures with LLMs enables knowledge-aware entity and relation extraction, especially with the Zephyr-7b-beta model for extraction and UMLS for linking.

6 Limitations

Our work is an exploratory study that encourages the inclusion of domain ontologies in LLM prompts for medical information extraction. Due to the laborious pipeline, we did not compare the results with alternative approaches. Despite being a train-free approach (which *per se* does not require a separate test set), due to the reduced number of EMRs and annotations, some of the EMRs used for assessment were also partially used in preliminary explorations. Only two locally installed LLMs were tested which we deem sufficient to raise interest in the approach, but does not guarantee the success of this procedure in general. In particular, no external APIs (e.g. OpenAI, Google Gemini) were used due to the sensitivity of the data. Only one medical expert annotated the EMR, defined the domain ontology and provided qualitative feedback for the approach. Most of the empirical results point in the direction that justifies exploiting this kind of approach. However, some of our results were not fully exploited and are not thoroughly justified.

Acknowledgements. This work is co-financed by Component 5 - Capitalization and Business Innovation, integrated in the Resilience Dimension of the Recovery and Resilience Plan within the scope of the Recovery and Resilience Mechanism (MRR) of the European Union (EU), framed in the Next Generation EU, for the period 2021–2026, within project HfPT, with reference 41. It is also funded by national funds through FCT – Fundação para a Ciência e a Tecnologia, I.P., under the support UID/50014/2023 (https://doi.org/10.54499/UID/50014/2023).

Disclosure of Interests. The authors have no competing interests to declare that are relevant to the content of this article.

References

1. Rector, A.L., Qamar, R., Marley, T.: Binding ontologies and coding systems to electronic health records and messages. Appl. Ontol. 4(1), 51–69 (2009)

2. Arbabi, A., Adams, D.R., Fidler, S., Brudno, M., et al.: Identifying clinical terms in medical text using ontology-guided machine learning. JMIR Med. Inform. **7**(2), e12596 (2019)
3. Liyanage, H., Williams, J., Byford, R., Stergioulas, L., de Lusignan, S.: Ontologies in big health data analytics - application to routine clinical data. Stud. Health Technol. Inform. (255) (2018)
4. National Center for Biomedical Ontology. Bioportal: A web portal for biomedical ontologies. NCBO (2023)
5. Bodenreider, O., Stevens, R.: Bio-ontologies: current trends and future directions. Brief. Bioinform. **7**(3), 256–74 (2006)
6. Bodenreider, O.: The unified medical language system (UMLS): integrating biomedical terminology. Nucleic Acids Res. **32**(suppl_1), D267–D270 (2004)
7. Mavergames, C., Oliver, S., Becker, L.: Systematic reviews as an interface to the web of (trial) data: using PICO as an ontology for knowledge synthesis in evidence-based healthcare research. In: Castro, A.G., Lange, C., Lord, P.W., Stevens, R. (eds.) Proceedings of the 3rd Workshop on Semantic Publishing, Montpellier, France, 26 May 2013. CEUR Workshop Proceedings, vol. 994, pp. 22–26. CEUR-WS.org (2013)
8. Noy, N.F., et al.: Bioportal: ontologies and integrated data resources at the click of a mouse. Nucleic Acids Res. **37**(Web Server issue), W170–W173 (2009)
9. Jusoh, S., Awajan, A., Obeid, N.: The use of ontology in clinical information extraction. In: Journal of Physics: Conference Series, vol. 1529, p. 052083 (2020)
10. Deléger, L., Grouin, C., Zweigenbaum, P.: Extracting medical information from narrative patient records: the case of medication-related information. J. Am. Med. Inform. Assoc. **17**(5), 555–558 (2010)
11. Li, Z., Chen, H., Qi, R., Lin, H., Chen, H.: Docr-BERT: document-level R-BERT for chemical-induced disease relation extraction via Gaussian probability distribution. IEEE J. Biomed. Health Inform. **26**(3), 1341–1352 (2021)
12. Li, Y., et al.: BEHRT: transformer for electronic health records. Sci. Rep. **10**(1), 7155 (2020)
13. Chiaramello, E., Pinciroli, F., Bonalumi, A., Caroli, A., Tognola, G.: Use of "off-the-shelf" information extraction algorithms in clinical informatics: a feasibility study of metamap annotation of Italian medical notes. J. Biomed. Inform. **63**, 22–32 (2016)
14. Aronson, A.R.: Effective mapping of biomedical text to the UMLs metathesaurus: the metamap program. In: Proceedings of the AMIA Symposium, p. 17. American Medical Informatics Association (2001)
15. Lopez, I., et al.: Clinical entity augmented retrieval for clinical information extraction. NPJ Digit. Med. **8**(1), 45 (2025)
16. Gao, Y., et al.: Leveraging medical knowledge graphs into large language models for diagnosis prediction: design and application study. JMIR AI **4**, e58670 (2025)
17. Shimony, S., Stahl, M., Stone, R.M.: Acute myeloid leukemia: 2023 update on diagnosis, risk-stratification, and management. Am. J. Hematol. **98**(3), 502–526 (2023)
18. Christophe, C., et al.: Med42–evaluating fine-tuning strategies for medical LLMs: Full-parameter vs. parameter-efficient approaches. arXiv preprint arXiv:2404.14779 (2024)
19. Tunstall, L., et al.: Zephyr: direct distillation of LM alignment. arXiv preprint arXiv:2310.16944 (2023)
20. Balani, R.: Prompt engineering: unlocking the power of generative AI models. LinkedIn Pulse (2023)

21. W3C. RDF 1.1 primer (2014). Accessed 25 June 2024
22. Musen, M.A.: The protégé project: a look back and a look forward. AI Matters **1**(4), 4–12 (2015)
23. Reyes-Peña, C., Tovar-Vidal, M.: Ontology: components and evaluation, a review. Res. Comput. Sci. **148**(3), 257–265 (2019)
24. Brank, J., Mladenic, D., Grobelnik, M.: Golden standard based ontology evaluation using instance assignment. In: Vrandecic, D., Suárez-Figueroa, M.C., Gangemi, A., Sure, Y. (eds.) Proceedings of 4th International EON Workshop 2006 Evaluation of Ontologies for the Web Co-located with the WWW2006 Edinburgh, UK, 22 May 2006. CEUR Workshop Proceedings, vol. 179. CEUR-WS.org (2006)
25. Noy, N.F., McGuinness, D.L., et al.: Ontology development 101: a guide to creating your first ontology (2001)

Deep Learning-Based Microbial Colony Detection on Agar Plates

Miguel Silva[1]([✉]) [iD], Diogo Martinho[1,2]([✉]) [iD], and Goreti Marreiros[1,2] [iD]

[1] GECAD – Research Group on Intelligent Engineering and Computing for Advanced Innovation and Development, ISEP, Polytechnic of Porto, Rua DR. António Bernardino de Almeida, 4249-015 Porto, Portugal
{mafda,dep,mgt}@isep.ipp.pt
[2] LASI, School of Engineering, University of Minho, Campus Azurém, 4800-058 Guimarães, Portugal

Abstract. Surgical teams often face delays due to bottlenecks in the sterilization process, where staff handle instruments without assessing actual contamination levels. A deep learning-based method is introduced that detects microbial colonies on agar plates aiming to optimize sterilization workflows. Several state-of-the-art object detection models were trained and evaluated, including Faster R-CNN with ResNet-50 and MobileNet backbones, SSD300 with VGG16, FCOS with ResNet-50-FPN, and YOLOv11 using both nano and small variants. All models were tested on a dataset containing over 9,000 unannotated images captured at 10-minute intervals to provide a dense temporal view of microbial development. Annotations were generated using ColTapp, a colony analysis tool that outputs colony coordinates and radii, and any noise introduced by the automatic process was addressed through prior data preprocessing. Despite this challenge, YOLOv11 consistently delivered the best results in both detection accuracy and computational performance. Its growing adoption in real-time vision applications reinforces its effectiveness, mainly due to its substantial speed-accuracy tradeoff. The top-performing configuration achieved 99.1% precision, a recall of 91.7% and a F1 score of 95.3%. This solution presents a scalable and cost-effective alternative to manual contamination assessment. By integrating this approach into hospital sterilization workflows, healthcare systems could reduce instrument turnaround times, improve resource allocation, and strengthen infection control. Ultimately, this work paves the way toward smarter, AI-driven clinical operations that enhance efficiency and patient safety.

Keywords: Computer Vision · YOLOv11 · Object Detection · Colony Detection · Agar Plate Analysis · Bacterial Growth Analysis

1 Introduction

Hospital-acquired infections (HAIs) represent one of the main public health challenges worldwide, with profound impacts on patients' quality of life, healthcare

J. Valente de Oliveira et al. (Eds.): EPIA 2025, LNAI 16121, pp. 42–54, 2026.
https://doi.org/10.1007/978-3-032-05176-9_4

safety, and the costs associated with the hospital system [14]. HAIs are infections that a patient does not possess before being admitted to a hospital. These infections do not exist during any latency period. Instead, they manifest either upon the patient's arrival at the hospital or after admission [9].

Among the various preventive strategies, ensuring the proper sterilization of surgical instruments plays a critical role in minimizing the risk of HAIs and maintaining procedural efficiency.

Sterilizing surgical instruments is essential for patient safety and the prevention of HAIs. However, poorly sterilized instruments must undergo the sterilization process again, causing delays in clinical decisions, especially during emergencies.

In 2024, there are still reports of failures in sterilizing medical instruments, with residues on sterilized materials and inadequate use of disinfectants. Hospital inspections have revealed recurring problems that compromise the safety and efficiency of processes [18]. These incidents highlight the urgent need for more advanced technologies that reduce human error and make sterilization a proactive process, anticipating contamination risks before they become a problem rather than being reactive to late-detected faults [1].

This problem is exacerbated by the prevalence of older traditional verification methods, where much of the effectiveness evaluation of sterilization is done manually, which is not only time-consuming but also prone to human error [20]. Furthermore, manual verification presents significant challenges, such as inconsistency between operators, difficulty in detecting contamination invisible to the naked eye, and lack of predictability in bacterial growth on inadequately cleaned instruments.

The study of bacterial colony evolution examines how bacterial populations change over time in response to different environmental, genetic, and treatment factors. This is fundamental to understanding the behavior of microorganisms because it challenges the simplistic view that bacteria are just single-celled entities that continually divide and die [15].

In microbiology, a colony is a cluster of bacteria growing together. The Colony Forming Units (CFUs) serve as a metric for assessing the quantity of viable bacteria capable of proliferating on solid media. To measure CFUs, bacterial cultures are added to agar plates (Fig. 1), often by serially diluting the original sample as it might be too concentrated to count [7, 10].

Fig. 1. A visual representation of bacterial colonies, with each colony representing a CFU, grown on a Petri dish.

In the context of surgical instruments, CFUs are particularly useful for evaluating the degree of contamination, and healthcare professionals can assess the extent of viable bacterial contamination by quantifying the colonies developed on an agar plate from a sample collected from a surgical instrument [12]. This technique is essential for determining the efficacy of sterilization and disinfection processes, as even minimal CFU counts may pose potential infection risks if not appropriately managed. The detection of bacteria on surgical instruments, even in small amounts, can result in serious Surgical Site Infections if the tools are not sufficiently sterilized [3].

In current sterilization routines (Fig. 2), surgical instruments are rinsed and then sampled onto agar plates, which must be incubated for at least 72 h to allow any contaminating bacteria to grow. During that time, clinical staff perform a manual visual inspection of the plates to decide whether the instruments are safe for the next procedure or need to be re-sterilized and re-run through the 72 h cycle. This delay not only ties up critical instrumentation, especially in emergencies, but also relies on subjective judgments that can miss early, low-density growth.

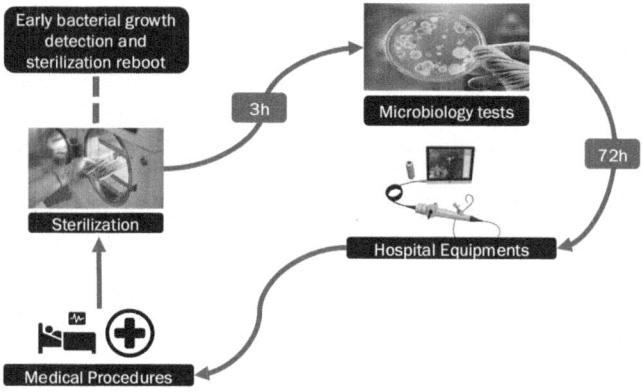

Fig. 2. Sterilization workflow.

This paper presents the development of an object detection pipeline for identifying and counting bacterial colonies on agar plates. Several state-of-the-art models were trained and compared, including Faster R-CNN with ResNet-50 and MobileNet backbones, SSD300 with VGG16, FCOS with ResNet-50-FPN, and YOLOv11 in its nano and small variants. YOLOv11 was verified as the most suitable model, offering an optimal balance between detection accuracy and inference speed, making it ideal for integration into real-time clinical workflows.

The models were trained on a unique and underutilized time-lapse dataset developed initially to study the growth dynamics of Staphylococcus aureus colonies under various conditions. The dataset comprises over 9,000 high-resolution images captured at 10-minute intervals across 22 independent cultures, including untreated controls and samples exposed to antibiotic treatment. This temporal resolution provides a rare opportunity to analyze bacterial development, reflecting real-world variability in contamination progression. ColTapp, a colony analysis tool, was utilized to automatically annotate the dataset by extracting colony coordinates and radii, enabling large-scale supervised training.

The method could addresses critical limitations in current sterilization practices, by inserting an automated colony-detection step into this pipeline, any plate that shows detectable growth, would trigger an immediate "sterilization reboot" without waiting for the full 72 h incubation. As soon as the model flags positive growth, often within the first few hours, the instrument is sent back for cleaning and re-sterilization. This early-warning capability shifts the process from reactive (waiting 72 h and then reacting) to proactive (detecting and stopping contamination as soon as it appears), thereby cutting turnaround times, reducing instrument downtime, and enhancing patient safety by catching low-density growth that might be overlooked in a purely visual check.

The remainder of this paper is structured as follows: Sect. 2 reviews existing work and object detection models applied to microbial colony analysis. Section 3 describes the methodology, including data preparation, model training, and evaluation procedures. Section 4 presents and interprets the quantitative results. Section 5 discusses the findings, limitations, and practical implications. Finally, Sect. 6 concludes and outlines future work: multi-strain, multi-environment benchmarks; standardized evaluation protocols; and enhancements in labeling quality, hardware resources, and deployment readiness.

2   Current Work

The application of deep learning techniques for automated microbial colony analysis has gained substantial momentum in recent years. Several studies have focused on object detection models for colony counting and contamination assessment, demonstrating their effectiveness across diverse settings.

OnePetri, introduced in [13], is a mobile application that leverages a YOLOv5 based model to count bacteriophage plaques on Petri dishes. It achieved notable improvements in accuracy and speed compared to manual counting methods, underscoring the suitability of YOLO architectures for microbiological applications. Building on this, [17] evaluated multiple YOLOv5 variants such as Nano, Small, Medium, and Large, reporting mAP@0.5 scores between 96.1% and 99.1%. Despite facing challenges such as overlapping colonies and background noise, these models consistently delivered fast and precise results, validating YOLO's role in rapid microbial analysis.

Complementing these YOLO based efforts, [6] conducted a comprehensive benchmark study involving two stage detectors like Faster R-CNN, Cascade R-CNN, Libra R-CNN, and CBNetV2, as well as single stage detectors such as YOLOv4 and transformer based models like Deformable DETR and XCiT. Among them, YOLOv4 stood out for its efficiency and accuracy, while two stage detectors maintained their strength in detection quality, albeit with longer inference times.

Further expanding on classification tasks, [8] explored various CNN architectures, including ResNet-18, AlexNet, VGG-16, SqueezeNet, and DenseNet-161 for identifying bacterial species from colony images. While the primary goal was classification rather than detection, this work showcased the effective use of transfer learning in adapting general purpose architectures to microbial imagery.

Low data environments have also inspired innovative approaches. The study in [19] introduced a few shot learning technique using a modified YOLOv3 model and the Random Cover Targets Algorithm (RCTA), achieving over 95% accuracy with only five annotated images. This approach demonstrated the feasibility of training colony detection models even with limited annotated data.

Other research combined classical image processing with deep learning to enhance colony quantification. For example, [11] developed a semi-automated CFU counting system that employed median filtering and watershed segmentation techniques. The system proved effective but highlighted practical issues like image quality and colony overlap that continue challenging automated detection.

Alongside developing detection models, tools have emerged to assist with colony quantification through graphical interfaces and classical image processing techniques. ColTapp, introduced in [2], quantifies bacterial colony growth from time-lapse and endpoint images. With a user-friendly interface, ColTapp allows users to extract and export multiple features of microbial colonies, including size, growth rate, morphological characteristics, and appearance time, enabling detailed analysis of bacterial dynamics. The tool combines top-hat filtering, adaptive thresholding, and binary image processing to detect and track colonies over time. Evaluations using a Staphylococcus aureus dataset [16] demonstrate its ability to effectively estimate colony radii and appearance times. While image quality and colony density can influence ColTapp's performance, it fills a critical gap by making detailed spatial and temporal colony analysis accessible for clinical and environmental microbiology applications.

Finally, [4] presented a real-time colony counting system using YOLOv5 trained on cloud-based GPUs. The system achieved exceptionally low error rates and demonstrated the potential of deploying deep learning models in high-throughput clinical diagnostic environments.

Together, these studies illustrate a clear trend toward adopting deep learning based object detection models, especially YOLO and Faster R-CNN variants, as robust and adaptable tools for automated colony analysis across research and applied microbiology domains.

3   Methodology

This section describes the complete pipeline to develop and evaluate object detection models for microbial colony detection. It covers the dataset preparation and annotation process, including strategies for handling missing or inconsistent label data. It also details the training configurations and evaluation procedures adopted for each model, focusing on ensuring fairness and consistency across all experiments.

3.1 Data Preparation

The dataset consists of 9,000 time-lapse images captured every 10 min across 22 independent cultures, comprising eight control and 14 antibiotic-treated plates. To simplify processing and improve traceability, all photos were moved into a single directory and renamed using a format that identifies the treatment group, the culture plate, and the image sequence. This structure supported streamlined indexing and alignment with the exported annotations. As illustrated in Fig. 3, the number of detected colonies varies significantly between plates and treatment groups, highlighting the biological diversity captured in the dataset.

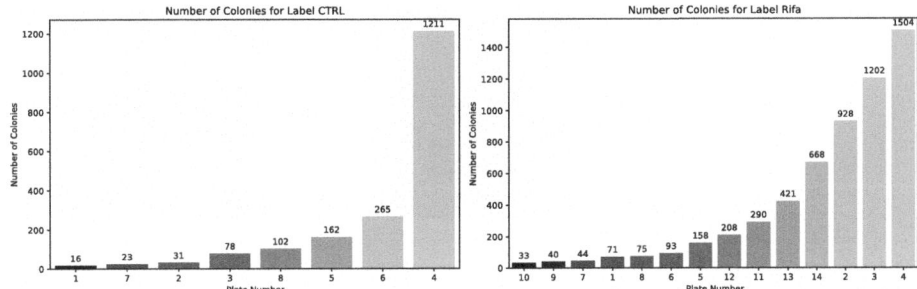

Fig. 3. Number of colonies detected per plate for control (CTRL) and antibiotic-treated (Rifa) groups.

Since the dataset lacks pre-existing labels, colony detection was performed using ColTapp, a tool designed to analyze time-lapse sequences of microbial growth. ColTapp detects individual colonies, estimates their appearance time, and tracks their evolution. The tool exports a CSV file for each plate containing spatial coordinates (X and Y), colony radius per frame, and appearance time.

A preliminary analysis of the exported data revealed several inconsistencies. Some colonies had negative or missing appearance times, while others contained incomplete radius values across frames. These inconsistencies required targeted corrections to ensure label reliability. Radius values appearing before a colony's reported emergence were reset to zero. Post-appearance frames with invalid or missing radius values were filled using the subsequent available valid measurement, as later frames generally exhibited more stable tracking. A median value was estimated for colonies with undefined appearance times based on the overall dataset distribution. These preprocessing steps were crucial in maintaining label integrity for the training pipeline.

Bounding boxes were generated using each colony's X and Y coordinates along with its corresponding radius, forming the final set of annotations used during object detection training.

Following these preprocessing steps, a manual review of the generated bounding boxes was performed to confirm annotation accuracy. Plates containing fewer colonies were particularly straightforward to inspect, allowing rapid identification and correction of any mismatches between box and colony. For higher-density plates, targeted spot checks of representative regions ensured that overall bounding-box placement remained reliable before proceeding to model training.

An initial interface prototype was also developed to facilitate real-time interaction with detection outputs. As illustrated in Fig. 4, this tool allows users to input an agar plate image and visualize detected colonies, laying the groundwork for integration into practical sterilization workflows.

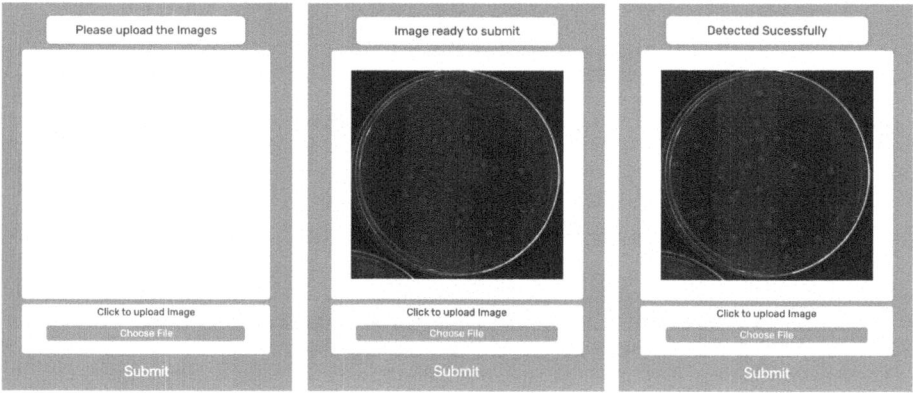

Fig. 4. Prototype interface for visualizing colony detection. The user can input an image of an agar plate and receive bounding box predictions highlighting microbial colonies.

3.2 Training and Evaluation

All models were trained and evaluated using cloud-based environments, specifically Google Colab and Kaggle. The hardware setup included NVIDIA Tesla T4 GPUs on Colab and NVIDIA Tesla P100 GPUs on Kaggle, depending on availability. The training process involved the object detection models previously described, using PyTorch and Torchvision for Faster R-CNN, SSD, and FCOS architectures, and the Ultralytics implementation for YOLOv11 [5].

To provide visual insight into the dataset, Fig. 5 shows an example of a single agar plate captured at three different stages of colony development, illustrating how colonies grow and change over time. The dataset was split into 80% for training, 10% for validation, and 10% for testing. All models were trained on images resized to 512 × 512 pixels. Due to memory limitations on the available hardware, plates containing more than 300 colonies were excluded from training to reduce computational overhead.

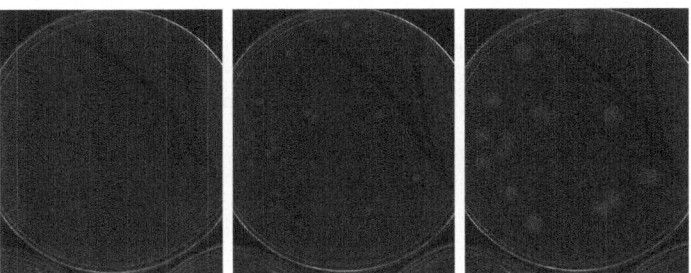

Fig. 5. Example of a single agar plate captured at three different stages of colony development. The image illustrates the temporal progression of bacterial growth across the time-lapse sequence.

The learning rate was set to 0.01, and each model was trained for up to 100 epochs, with an early stopping mechanism triggered by a patience value of 10 epochs to prevent overfitting. Hyperparameters were selected manually to ensure efficient GPU utilization under constrained conditions. Batch size varied between 8, 16, and 32 depending on the memory footprint of each model.

Evaluation focused on precision, and recall, for YOLOv11, all metrics were recorded using its built-in validation tools, while the remaining models were evaluated using standard PyTorch-based implementations for computing precision and recall.

4   Results

Table 1 summarizes the performance of all trained object detection models in terms of precision, recall and the harmonic mean of the two (F1 score). YOLOv11s again leads across all three metrics, with a precision of 99.1%, recall of 91.7% and an F1 score of 95.3%, confirming its excellent balance between accuracy and sensitivity. Its nano variant, YOLOv11n, also remains highly competitive, achieving 97.9% precision, 89.6% recall and a strong F1 of 93.6%.

Among the remaining models, SSD300 with a VGG16 backbone delivers solid performance (91.4% precision, 74.1% recall) and an F1 score of 81.8%, outperforming all Faster R-CNN variants based on ResNet-50 except in pure precision. The original and V2 ResNet-50 FPN versions maintain very high precision (97%+), yet their lower recall (65.1% and 62.4%) yields moderate F1 scores of 78.1% and 76.0%, indicating they miss more colonies despite reliable classification when detections occur.

The lightweight and anchor-free designs, FCOS ResNet-50 FPN and the MobileNet-based Faster R-CNNs, exhibit sharper drops in recall (61.9% down to

17.9%), with corresponding F1 scores of 76.0%, 67.4% and 28.3%. These lower F1 values highlight that, although some models maintain reasonable precision, their sensitivity to dense colony regions is insufficient and calls for further backbone or loss-function optimization.

Table 1. Precision and recall for each trained model.

Model	Precision (%)	Recall (%)	F1 Score (%)
YOLOv11s	**99.1**	**91.7**	**95.3**
YOLOv11n	97.9	89.6	93.6
SSD300 VGG16	91.4	74.1	81.8
Faster R-CNN ResNet-50 FPN	97.5	65.1	78.1
Faster R-CNN ResNet-50 FPN v2	97.3	62.4	76.0
FCOS ResNet-50 FPN	98.3	61.9	76.0
Faster R-CNN MobileNet V3 Large FPN	84.1	56.3	67.4
Faster R-CNN MobileNet V3 Large 320 FPN	67.5	17.9	28.3

Overall, YOLOv11s not only achieves the highest precision and recall but also the top F1 score, underlining its suitability for real-time, high-density colony detection and making it the prime candidate for contamination assessment workflows.

5   Discussion

The results presented in Table 1 highlight significant performance differences between object detection architectures when applied to microbial colony detection. YOLOv11s demonstrated the highest precision (99.1%), recall (91.7%) and F1 score (95.3%), establishing it as the most reliable model for correctly identifying and detecting colonies across diverse images. This strong performance can be attributed to YOLOv11's single-stage design, which enables efficient detection without the latency of region proposal stages, as well as its architectural optimizations that balance inference speed with representational depth.

YOLOv11n also performed remarkably well, achieving 97.9% precision, 89.6% recall and an F1 score of 93.6%, demonstrating that even lighter variants of this architecture can effectively tackle high-density colony detection. SSD300 with a VGG16 backbone delivered 91.4% precision, 74.1% recall and an F1 score of 81.8%, underscoring its continued value as a fast, lightweight alternative for real-time applications.

In contrast, two-stage models like Faster R-CNN with ResNet-50 FPN achieved very high precision (97.5%), lower recall (65.1%) and an F1 score of 78.1%, suggesting these architectures are conservative, producing fewer false positives at the expense of missing many valid colonies. While this may be acceptable when absolute precision is required, it limits applicability in scenarios where overlooking a contaminated instrument carries serious risk. Faster R-CNN variants with MobileNet backbones performed even worse: the standard MobileNet V3 Large FPN reached an F1 of 67.4%, and the 320-pixel variant fell to just 28.3%, underscoring their difficulty generalizing under high-density, small-object conditions.

The FCOS detector, despite its anchor-free design and firm theoretical grounding, achieved high precision (98.3%), but suffered in recall (61.9%) and yielded an F1 score of 76.0%, indicating challenges in accurately localizing numerous small colonies. These limitations may stem from its fixed feature-level resolution and lack of explicit proposal mechanisms, which are critical in dense scenes.

Several factors influenced these results. While diverse and temporally rich, the dataset posed challenges the exclusion of plates with more than 300 colonies reduced the presence of highly complex samples. Furthermore, all models were trained under manually selected hyperparameters due to computational constraints, preventing systematic tuning that might have improved underperforming models.

Despite these constraints, the experiments demonstrate that YOLOv11, particularly in its small variant, offers the best trade-off between accuracy and practicality for real-time microbial contamination screening. Its effectiveness in high-density, small-object detection positions it as a valuable tool for integration into hospital sterilization workflows, where fast, scalable, and consistent colony detection is essential.

6 Conclusion and Future Work

This work proposed a deep learning-based pipeline for the automated detection of bacterial colonies on agar plates, targeting a critical gap in hospital sterilization workflows.

In many clinical settings, delays in surgical procedures stem from inefficient and reactive sterilization processes, where microbial contamination is often only detected after failures occur. By automating colony detection and quantification, the presented approach aims to support proactive sterilization protocols, enabling healthcare professionals to prioritize instrument processing based on actual contamination levels. In future work, the solution is intended to be validated in collaboration with hospital partners, with the goal of assessing its practical impact in real-world clinical environments.

To address this challenge, a comparative evaluation of object detection models was performed, including Faster R-CNN, SSD300, FCOS, and YOLOv11, was conducted on a unique time-lapse dataset comprising over 9,000 images of *Staphylococcus aureus* cultures. The dataset was annotated using ColTapp, with additional preprocessing applied to correct inconsistencies such as missing appearance times and radius values. The training was conducted under resource-constrained environments using cloud-based GPUs, with all models evaluated on precision, recall and F1 score.

The results highlight YOLOv11s as the most suitable model for this task, achieving 99.1% precision, 91.7% recall and F1 score (95.3%). Its single-stage architecture and lightweight design enable accurate and scalable detection of small, densely packed colonies, making it ideal for real-time use in hospital environments. In contrast, while precise, two-stage models struggled with recall, often failing to identify all colonies within an image. The demonstrated performance of YOLOv11s underlines its potential as a practical solution for reducing surgical delays, enhancing infection control, and contributing to a more resilient healthcare infrastructure.

However, several limitations were identified that suggest directions for future work. Although manual review was performed on all plates to correct bounding box placements, some noise in higher-density plates may still have escaped verification. In the context of this work, which used only plates containing fewer than 300 colonies, this residual noise had minimal impact on model performance. Future studies that incorporate the full range of plate densities will require more comprehensive validation procedures, such as additional manual inspections, semi-automated checks or robust ensemble-based labeling pipelines. Hardware constraints also prevented inclusion of the highest-density samples, with greater computational resources and automated hyperparameter tuning, those challenging cases could be incorporated to further improve model robustness.

Another critical avenue involves leveraging the temporal nature of the dataset more directly. While this study treated each frame independently, future models could integrate temporal cues to track colony evolution across time, potentially improving robustness and reducing false positives. Also, deployment considerations such as user interfaces, integration with sterilization record systems, and real-time alerts should be explored to translate this research into a scientifically valuable and operationally impactful tool.

A further limitation arises from the absence of direct baselines: at the time of this study, no previous work had evaluated object-detection models on the dataset used on this study, making quantitative comparison with existing solutions infeasible. Moreover, transferring the trained model to other datasets is nontrivial, since each experimental setup: bacterial strain, lighting conditions, plate background, imaging hardware and protocol, can significantly alter detection performance. As this field continues to grow, future work should therefore prioritize the assembly of multi-strain, multi-environment benchmark datasets and the development of standardized evaluation protocols to enable meaningful comparisons across methods.

A key next step in this research involves moving beyond detection to modeling colony growth dynamics over time. The primary goal is to predict the growth rate of individual bacterial colonies based on early visual cues and temporal sequences. This capability could significantly enhance sterilization workflows by enabling earlier and more informed decisions about the contamination status of surgical instruments. Instead of waiting for colonies to become visually prominent, healthcare staff can anticipate whether microbial growth will likely exceed safety thresholds, allowing for smarter prioritization or even early rejection of instruments at risk. This predictive layer will transform the system from a reactive quality control tool into a proactive contamination assessment platform. To support this vision, the existing prototype interface, which currently accepts input images and displays detected colonies, will extend to visualize predicted growth trends and provide actionable feedback. Such improvements aim to bridge the gap between deep learning models and real-world clinical decision-making.

Acknowledgments. This research was supported by the PROFIT project - Procedure Optimization and Data-driven Operational Efficiency in Healthcare Environments (ITEA 22021), funded by the European Regional Development Fund (ERDF) through the COMPETE 2030 Programme, project number COMPETE30-FEDER-00376900, and by national funds from the Portuguese Foundation for Science and Technology (FCT), under the R&D Units Project Scope UIDB/00760/2020 and UIDP/00760/2020. More information is available at: https://itea4.org/project/profit.html.

Disclosure of Interest. The authors declare no competing interests relevant to the content of this article.

References

1. Alfa, M.J.: Medical instrument reprocessing: current issues with cleaning and cleaning monitoring. Am. J. Infect. Control **47**, A10–A16 (2019). https://doi.org/10.1016/j.ajic.2019.02.029. https://www.sciencedirect.com/science/article/pii/S0196655319301439, disinfection, Sterilization and Antisepsis: Principles, Practices, Current Issues, New Research and New Technologies
2. Bär, J., Boumasmoud, M., Kouyos, R.D., Zinkernagel, A.S., Vulin, C.: Author correction: efficient microbial colony growth dynamics quantification with ColTapp, an automated image analysis application. Sci. Rep. **11**(1), 6050 (2021)
3. Dancer, S., Stewart, M., Coulombe, C., Gregori, A., Virdi, M.: Surgical site infections linked to contaminated surgical instruments. J. Hosp. Infect. **81**(4), 231–238 (2012). https://doi.org/10.1016/j.jhin.2012.04.023. https://www.sciencedirect.com/science/article/pii/S0195670112001442
4. Fathiyah, A.N., Loniza, E., Putra, K.T.: Automatic colony counter using computer vision and artificial intelligence. In: 2023 International Workshop on Artificial Intelligence and Image Processing (IWAIIP), pp. 122–126 (2023). https://doi.org/10.1109/IWAIIP58158.2023.10462747
5. Jocher, G., Qiu, J.: Ultralytics YOLO11 (2024). https://github.com/ultralytics/ultralytics
6. Majchrowska, S., Pawłowski, J., Czerep, N., Górecki, A., Kuciński, J., Golan, T.: Deep neural networks approach to microbial colony detection–a comparative analysis. In: Biele, C., Kacprzyk, J., Kopeć, W., Owsiński, J.W., Romanowski, A., Sikorski, M. (eds.) Digital Interaction and Machine Intelligence, pp. 98–106. Springer, Cham (2022)
7. McVey, D.S., Kennedy, M., Chengappa, M.M., Wilkes, R.: Veterinary Microbiology, 4th edn. Wiley, Hoboken (2022)
8. Nagro, S.A., et al.: Automatic identification of single bacterial colonies using deep and transfer learning. IEEE Access **10**, 120181–120190 (2022). https://doi.org/10.1109/ACCESS.2022.3221958

9. Raoofi, S., et al.: Global prevalence of nosocomial infection: a systematic review and meta-analysis. Plos One **18**(1), 1–17 (2023). https://doi.org/10.1371/journal.pone.0274248

10. Revive: Colony-forming unit (CFU) (2024). https://revive.gardp.org/resource/colony-forming-unit-cfu/?cf=encyclopaedia. Accessed 04 Dec 2024

11. Rodrigues, P.M., Luís, J., Tavaria, F.K.: Image analysis semi-automatic system for colony-forming-unit counting. Bioengineering **9**(7) (2022). https://doi.org/10.3390/bioengineering9070271. https://www.mdpi.com/2306-5354/9/7/271

12. Rutala, W.A., Gergen, M.F., Jones, J.F., Weber, D.J.: Levels of microbial contamination on surgical instruments. Am. J. Infect. Control **26**(2), 143–145 (1998). https://doi.org/10.1016/S0196-6553(98)80034-5. https://www.sciencedirect.com/science/article/pii/S0196655398800345

13. Shamash, M., Maurice, C.F.: Onepetri: accelerating common bacteriophage petri dish assays with computer vision. Phage (New Rochelle) **2**(4), 224–231 (2021). https://doi.org/10.1089/phage.2021.0012

14. Šuljagić, V., et al.: A nationwide assessment of the burden of healthcare-associated infections and antimicrobial use among surgical patients: results from Serbian point prevalence survey, 2017. Antimicrob. Resist. Infect. Control **10**(1), 47 (2021). https://doi.org/10.1186/s13756-021-00889-9

15. Ughy, B., et al.: Reconsidering dogmas about the growth of bacterial populations. Cells **12**(10), 1430 (2023). https://doi.org/10.3390/cells12101430

16. Vulin, C.: Data_ColTapp (2020). https://doi.org/10.6084/m9.figshare.12951152.v1. https://figshare.com/articles/media/Data_ColTapp/12951152

17. Whipp, J., Dong, A.: YOLO-based deep learning to automated bacterial colony counting, pp. 120–124 (2022). https://doi.org/10.1109/BigMM55396.2022.00028

18. Wingerter, M.: Aurora VA hospital stops surgeries due to sterilization concerns. The Denver Post (2024). https://www.denverpost.com/2024/05/19/aurora-va-hospital-stop-surgeries-sterilization/. Accessed 04 Dec 2024

19. Zhang, B., Zhou, Z., Cao, W., Qi, X., Xu, C., Wen, W.: A new few-shot learning method of bacterial colony counting based on the edge computing device. Biology **11**(2) (2022). https://doi.org/10.3390/biology11020156. https://www.mdpi.com/2079-7737/11/2/156

20. Zhang, X., Zhang, D., Zhang, X., Zhang, X.: Artificial intelligence applications in the diagnosis and treatment of bacterial infections. Front. Microbiol. **15**, 1449844 (2024). https://doi.org/10.3389/fmicb.2024.1449844

Towards Intelligent Low-Code Systems:
A Systematic Review

Daniel Sá$^{(\boxtimes)}$ ⓘ, Tiago Guimarães ⓘ, and Manuel Filipe Santos ⓘ

Algoritmi Research Center/LASI, University of Minho, Braga, Portugal
sadaniel@dsi.uminho.pt

Abstract. The growing interest in Low-Code Systems, combined with the evolution of Generative Artificial Intelligence (AI), has driven new ways of creating applications in the field of digital health (eHealth). However, the effective integration of these technologies, particularly in regulated and clinical contexts, has not been widely explored. This systematic review aims to identify the main features assisted by generative AI in low-code systems and to understand what the challenges and limitations of these systems are based on the eHealth context.

We analysed 56 scientific articles published between 2020 and 2025, selected from databases such as Scopus, PubMed and IEEE Xplore. Data extraction and analysis were based on a multidimensional model constructed from the research questions. The results reveal a prevalence of empirical studies with limited methodological transparency. These studies often lack clearly defined research designs or validation processes, and there is a general absence of practical implementations. Furthermore, none of the studies demonstrated the simultaneous integration of generative AI and interoperability standards such as FHIR or OpenEHR. It was also found that the majority of studies represent a fragmented form of the dimensions, i.e. they address critical dimensions (AI, privacy, scalability) but in isolation.

The conclusion is that, although there is great potential, the maturity of these systems is still limited. Future research should focus on the development of Intelligent Low-Code solutions that fulfil the requirements of the health sector, with greater regulatory alignment, integration of generative AI and validation in real clinical environments.

Keywords: Low-Code · Generative AI · eHealth

1 Introduction

Software development has been progressively democratised through the emergence of Low-Code systems, which allow applications to be created with minimal manual coding effort. These systems combine graphical interfaces and pre-built components that facilitate rapid and collaborative development, even by users with little or no programming experience [1].

Despite their effectiveness in specific scenarios, Low-Code systems have structural limitations - they are often oriented towards isolated problems, which makes it difficult to integrate them with broader systems or with the normative standards of certain

J. Valente de Oliveira et al. (Eds.): EPIA 2025, LNAI 16121, pp. 55–67, 2026.
https://doi.org/10.1007/978-3-032-05176-9_5

domains [2, 3]. In the context of eHealth, for example, compliance with standards such as OpenEHR, HL7 or FHIR, which are fundamental to ensuring interoperability and portability of clinical data, is necessary. However, most Low-Code systems do not offer native support for these standards, thus representing an obstacle to their adoption [4, 5].

In this context, the integration of generative AI emerges as a transformative factor. Generative AI, as illustrated by models such as GPT, has demonstrated the ability to generate original content, including text, source code and even complete business logic [6, 7].

Despite its potential, the literature still reveals an incipient and fragmented scenario with regard to convergence between Low-Code systems, generative AI and interoperability standards. Current research focuses mainly on specific cases, with little systematisation of how these technologies can be effectively integrated into critical domains such as health [1].

This fragmentation is particularly problematic in the eHealth context, where development platforms must address technical requirements as well as strict regulations, data privacy concerns and clinical interoperability standards. Integrating generative AI into Low-Code Systems in this domain remains a significant challenge, requiring solutions that are secure, explainable and adaptable to complex healthcare workflows. This review aims to address this issue by analysing the intersection of these technologies and the barriers to their combined adoption in healthcare.

2 Objective of the Systematic Review

To identify the main features assisted by generative AI in Low-Code Systems and to understand the challenges and limitations of these systems based on the eHealth context. To this end, two research questions were defined:

- **RQ1:** "What are the main features, assisted by generative AI, in Low-Code systems in the eHealth domain?"
- **RQ2:** "What are the main challenges and limitations encountered in the application of Low-Code systems assisted by generative AI in the eHealth context?"

3 Methods

The systematic review was conducted based on Preferred Reporting Items for Systematic Reviews and Meta-Analysis (PRISMA) statements [8], followed by a checklist and a flow diagram.

3.1 Information Sources

Seven online data sources were selected. Firstly, a search was carried out on Scimago [9], where it was possible to obtain three Q1 quartile journals relevant to this study: Nature, IEEE Access and Journal of Medical Internet Research. After this and in order to cover as many scientific articles as possible, four public repositories were selected: Scopus, PubMed, AIS eLibrary and WebOfScience. Table 1 provides information on the types of data sources selected.

Table 1. Information of selected data sources. Source: Scimago Journal and Country Rank via www.scimagojr.com, accessed on Jan, 2025

Data Source	Publication Type	Subject Area	Quartile	H-Index
Scopus	Repository	Multidiscipline	-	-
PubMed	Repository	Biomedical	-	-
AIS eLibrary	Repository	Information Systems	-	-
Nature	Journal	Multidiscipline	Q1	1442
IEEE Access	Journal	Computer Science	Q1	242
Journal of Medical Internet Research	Journal	Computer Science	Q1	197
WebOfScience	Repository	Multidiscipline	-	-

3.2 Eligibility Criteria and Search Strategy

In order to select the most relevant studies for this systematic review, some eligibility criteria were defined: (i) open access or free text studies; (ii) written in English; (iii) between 2014 and 2025. To meet these criteria, search filters were created in each of the data sources. In order to identify studies with the desired focus, the following query terms were defined: (ALL ("low-code" OR "low code" OR "no-code" OR "no code") AND ALL ("generative AI" OR "Gen AI" OR "GPT" OR "large language model" OR "LLM" OR "Artificial Intelligence" OR "intelligent systems") AND ALL (eHealth OR "healthcare" OR "health care" OR "medical" OR "medicine" OR "digital health")).

During the research, the analysis and selection strategy began with a reading of the title, abstract and keywords in order to understand whether the study corresponded to what was being sought. The aim was to analyse which scientific articles were related to the defined methodology and research objectives, as well as the defined RQ1 and RQ2. If this point was not met, these articles were removed. However, when these parameters were not sufficient to assess whether they met the requirements, a full reading of the article was carried out.

3.3 Data Extraction and Management

Data extraction was conducted systematically based on a set of previously defined criteria, which supported the qualitative and quantitative analysis of the included studies. To this end, a coding grid was used, structured into 19 columns representing the outcomes that allowed each article to be characterised in a uniform way. These analysis criteria were selected based on the existing literature, making it possible to guarantee that they corresponded to all the important points of the object under study.

Their definition was based on the relevance identified in the literature for dimensions such as the presence of generative AI, the degree of user assistance, compliance with interoperability standards (e.g. HL7, FHIR), and critical aspects such as privacy, scalability and technical limitations [10].

Integration with interoperability standards, such as FHIR or OpenEHR, is widely seen as essential to guarantee secure data exchange and integration with legacy systems in the healthcare sector [5]. In addition, privacy and data security concerns are recurrent in the literature, especially when it comes to applying AI to sensitive clinical data [11]. Finally, criteria such as scalability, generalisation and technical challenges are highlighted as key indicators of the maturity and real applicability of these solutions in regulated contexts [12].

The columns used are shown in Table 2, as well as other generic columns such as article title, year, authors, country and data source.

Table 2. Description and methodology for analysing columns

Analyse Criteria	Standard Format
Study Design	Eg: Case Study, Survey, Experimental Study, Tool Evaluation, Conceptual Framework, Systematic Review, Prototype Design, Mixed Methods, Expert Interviews, Teaching Module, Cross-case Analysis, Other
Type of Low-Code	Eg: Low-Code Platform, No-Code Tool, AutoML, GenAI-Enhanced LCDP, Prompt-based, RPA
Domain Areas	Eg: Education, Healthcare, Enterprise, Industry, Agriculture, Software Engineering, IoT, Public Sector, Other
Low-Code Features	Eg: Drag-and-drop; GUI; Workflow builder; AutoML
IA present?	Eg: Yes – LLM, Yes – AutoML, No
Level of assistance by AI	Eg: Suggestion, Code generation, Model training, Dialogue management, N/A
Observed/Expected Impact	Eg: Faster development, User empowerment, Improved UX, Educational gains, Automation, etc.
Human-AI Interaction	Eg: GUI, Chatbot, Prompt-based, None, Form-based, Voice, etc
Privacy/Security	Eg: GDPR, Federated privacy, Organizational policies, Cloud-based compliance, N/A
Challenges/Limitations	Eg: Bias, Explainability, Integration, Security, Tool immaturity, Lack of control, N/A
Scalability/Generalisation	Eg: Scalable, Adaptable, Limited, Not evaluated, N/A
Interoperability Standards	Eg: openEHR, HL7, FHIR, snomed, loinc, icd9/icd10, dicom
Type of Integration (Standards)	Evaluate whether the article proposes or mentions integration with regulatory frameworks and/or interoperability standards

All the data was extracted manually and recorded in a structured spreadsheet. Where applicable, coding was carried out by more than one reviewer to reinforce the reliability of the categorisation.

4 Results

4.1 Selection Process

The study selection process followed the PRISMA guidelines and is shown in Fig. 1. In the identification phase, 1,014 records were obtained from the scientific databases identified in Sect. 2.1: Scopus (n = 818), IEEE Access (n = 101), AIS eLibrary (n = 64), PubMed (n = 23) and Web of Science (n = 8). Nature and JMIR were also consulted, but did not produce any relevant results in the context of the research.

These 1,014 records were obtained by applying the above-defined query to the different data sources.The titles of all the articles found were then extracted and 15 duplicate records were automatically identified and removed. This resulted in 999 unique articles being available for the filtering phase.

During the first filtering phase, eligibility criteria (i), (ii) and (iii) were applied, resulting in 530 articles (53.1%) being excluded for not meeting these criteria. A total of 469 articles (46.9%) proceeded to full evaluation and analysis, beginning with a complete review to verify their eligibility in relation to the review's objectives. At this stage, 413 articles (88.1% of those read in full) were excluded as they were not considered relevant to the research objectives or RQ1 and RQ2.

After this phase, 56 articles (5.5% of those initially identified) were included in the final synthesis, forming the basis of this research. These articles proceeded to the next phase, enabling the necessary information to be extracted.

4.2 Study Characteristics

This section presents a descriptive analysis of the 56 studies included in the systematic review, with the aim of characterising the general profile of existing research in the area of study.

The articles analysed were published between 2020 and 2025, with a greater concentration from 2021 onwards, highlighting the recent growth of interest in this topic. In geographical terms, the studies come from a variety of countries, with the United States standing out with 14 articles (25%), Germany with 10 articles (17.9%) and the United Kingdom with 7 articles (12.5%). These three countries together account for more than 55% of scientific production in this area.

In methodological terms, the types of study originally identified were standardised and grouped into more homogeneous categories. As shown in Table 3, the most prevalent category is 'Empirical Research (Unspecified)', comprising 16 articles (28.6%). These articles present some form of practical research, such as the development, application, or evaluation of systems; however, they do not clearly specify their methodological design. This category was created for studies with relevant empirical evidence, but without a declared methodological typology. Its prevalence suggests a strong focus on applied

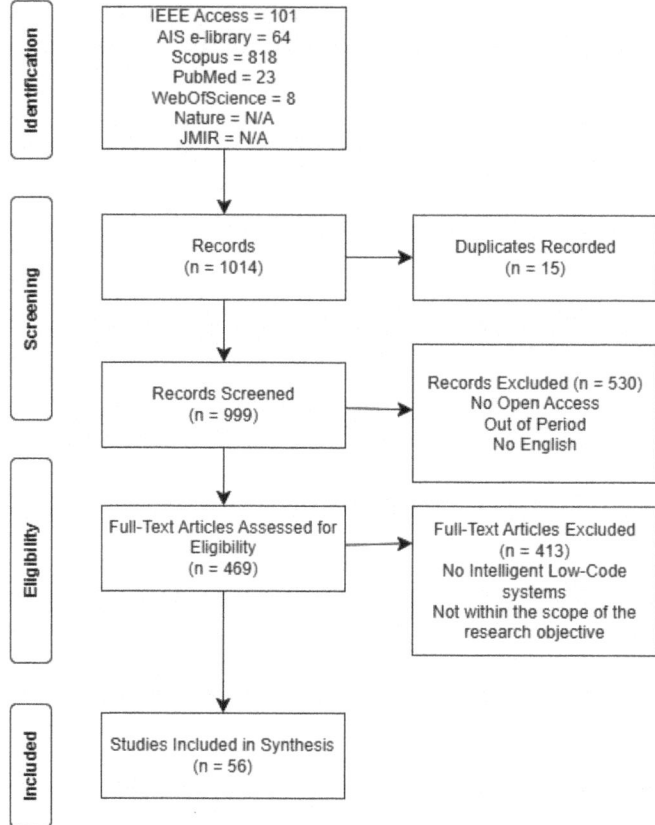

Fig. 1. Flow diagram of study selection for systematic review

experimentation in the field of low-code systems. However, it may also reflect limitations in the systematisation and scientific communication of the approaches adopted.

This is followed by the categories "Case Study" (7 articles; 12.5%), "Systematic Review" (7 articles; 12.5%) and "Experimental Study" (7 articles; 12.5%), showing a relatively even distribution between applied empirical approaches and systematic literature reviews. Design Science Research" came in with 4 articles (7.1%). This methodological diversity demonstrates the emerging and multidisciplinary nature of research on Low-Code systems, with room for future consolidation of more robust and standardised approaches.

4.3 Outcomes

Based on the research questions and in order to answer them, a multidimensional analysis model was developed which made it possible to systematically map the presence, absence and level of detail of critical elements for understanding the maturity of the systems under study. This model was structured based on grouping the results of applying the

Table 3. Distribution by Study Design

Standardised Study Type	Number of Articles
Empirical Research (Unspecified)	16
Case Study	7
Systematic Review	7
Experimental Study	7
Design Science Research	4
Prototype/Tool Evaluation	4
Conceptual/Theoretical	3
Mixed Methods	3
Survey	3
Teaching/Tutorial	2

previously defined data analysis criteria Table 2, applied systematically to each of the articles included.

The six dimensions are shown in Table 4, along with the respective extraction criteria and the key parameters considered in their identification.

Figure 2 shows the frequency with which each of these dimensions was identified in the studies analysed. Although a proportion of the articles analysed are in the healthcare field (11 articles), there is a low incidence of advanced components such as generative AI and integration with interoperability standards, critical dimensions for viability in real healthcare contexts. In addition, aspects such as privacy, scalability and explicit reporting of limitations are also under-represented.

Figure 3 shows the time distribution of the dimensions analysed in this study, based on the year of publication. There is a clear concentration of studies from 2021 onwards, reflecting the increased interest in low-code systems assisted by generative AI, as well as low-code systems in eHealth context.

The 'Health Domain' dimension remains constant between 2021 and 2023, with an increase in 2024, while 'Reported Challenges', 'Scalability' and 'Privacy/Security' have emerged more strongly, reflecting growing concerns about regulation, scalability and adaptability of systems and data security. The use of generative AI and the adoption of interoperability standards remain sporadic, with very occasional mentions and a lack of sustained growth. This time gap suggests that these areas are still in an exploratory phase, not yet significantly absorbed by consolidated eHealth practices.

The time analysis reinforces the evidence that Low-Code systems with application potential in healthcare contexts still need more robust integration with standards, scalability and AI-assisted capabilities to reach a greater degree of maturity.

Table 4. Multidimensional Analysis Model

Dimension	Description	Analyse Criteria	Research key parameters
Use of Generative AI	Evaluates if the paper describes the use of Generative AI techniques	Level of assistance by AI	code generation, program synthesis, prompt-based, instruction revision
Health Domain Context	Check if it applies to the eHealth domain	Domain Areas	health, healthcare, eHealth
Reference to Interoperability Standards	Check for reference to standards	Interoperability Standards	=/=N/A
Privacy and Security Considerations	Identify whether the study refers to GDPR, anonymisation, compliance	Privacy/Security	gdpr, anonymization, data protection, blockchain, local processing
Scalability/Generalisation Mentioned	Evaluates if the system is described as scalable, adaptable or generalisable	Scalability/Generalisation	scalable, adaptable, generalizable
Challenges or Limitations Reported	Check if the article points out technical, ethical or normative limitations	Challenges/Limitations	=/=N/A

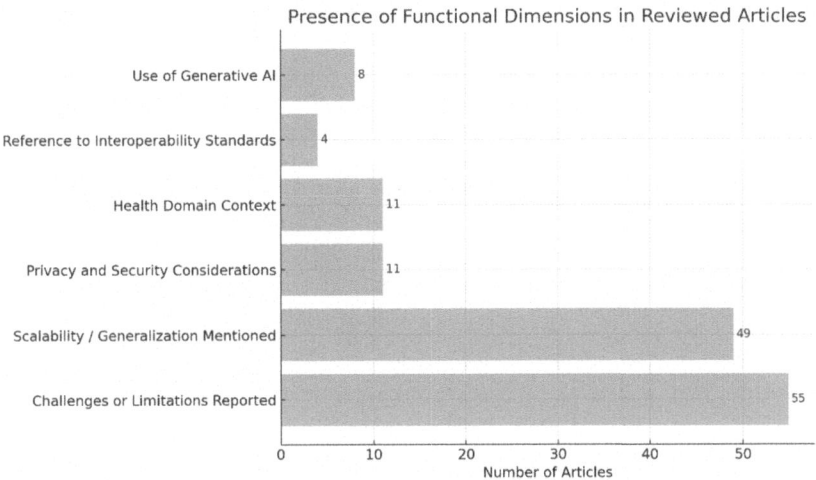

Fig. 2. Presence of Functional Dimensions in Reviewed Articles

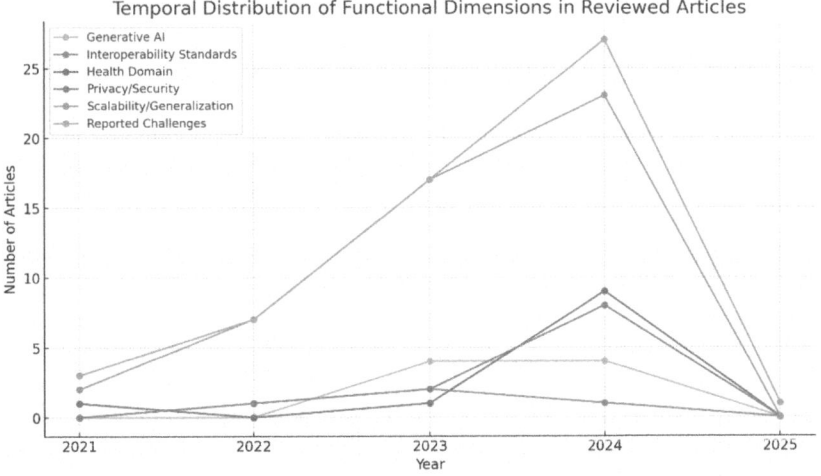

Fig. 3. Temporal Distribution of Functional Dimensions in Reviewed Articles

5 Cross-Analysis of Functional Dimensions

This section aims to summarise the results of the multidimensional analysis applied to the articles included in this study, with a focus on identifying relevant combinations and intersections between the different dimensions considered. This analysis aims to highlight the degree of articulation between capabilities considered relevant to the construction of Intelligent Low-Code Systems, assisted by generative AI, with special attention to the eHealth context.

Figure 4 shows a heatmap of co-occurrence between the functional dimensions analysed. Each cell indicates the number of articles in which two specific dimensions occur

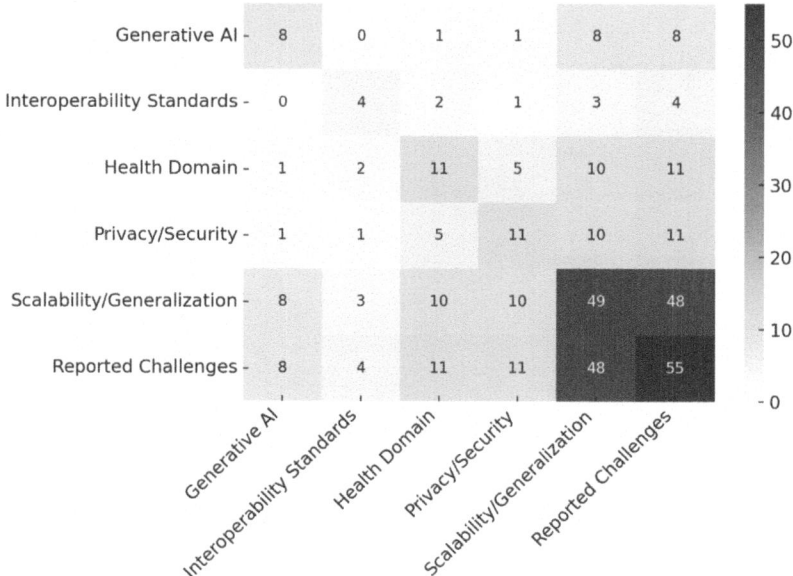

Fig. 4. Cross-analysis of Functional Dimensions Across Articles

simultaneously. It can be seen that the most common combination occurs between the fields 'Reported Challenges' and 'Scalability', corresponding to 85.71% (48 articles), showing that studies with practical application tend to recognise relevant limitations or barriers. However, combinations that are more critical and relevant to the object of study, such as 'Generative AI' and 'Interoperability Standards' do not show results, indicating that to date there have been no studies identified that combine these two dimensions. Similarly, only 1.79% (1 article) combines 'Generative AI' with 'Privacy and Security' concerns and 14.29% (8 articles) combine 'Generative AI' with 'Scalability'.

This data indicates that, although some dimensions are discussed in isolation, there is a clear lack of convergence between AI-assisted capabilities and critical regulatory and operational requirements, such as interoperability standards and data privacy.

6 Discussion

The results of this systematic review reveal a growing interest in Low-Code systems, reflected both in the number of recent publications and in the diversity of methodological approaches identified. However, when critically analysing the studies included, a significant gap becomes evident between the potential of these approaches and their practical application in real eHealth contexts, most of which need to meet certain standards.

Despite the technological evolution and enthusiasm surrounding generative AI, the data from this review indicates that its integration with Low-Code systems in the health sector remains limited and fragmented. The multidimensional analysis model developed made it possible to identify that none of the articles analysed simultaneously combines generative AI with integration with interoperability standards such as FHIR or OpenEHR

- a fundamental requirement for the adoption of these technologies in hospital environments. This lack of convergence between innovation and regulatory compliance reinforces the perception that the practical application of Intelligent Low-Code Systems in the eHealth context is still in its early stages.

The co-occurrence analysis between the dimensions also revealed that although concepts such as "generative AI", "privacy" or "scalability" appear with some frequency, their intersections are scarce, demonstrating an isolated and rarely integrated approach to the main technical requirements in the context of eHealth. In addition, the results of the mapping of study types show that the majority of articles fall into the category of 'Empirical Research (Unspecified)' (28.6%), followed by case studies and systematic reviews. This predominance of descriptive and exploratory approaches, often without validation in real-life scenarios, indicates that much of the research remains conceptual or limited to prototypes, without reaching the stages of implementation or practical evaluation. This reality limits the transfer of the knowledge produced to applied contexts, hindering the adoption of these tools.

Although some studies demonstrate the technical feasibility of building clinical models using no-code platforms (as in automatic medical imaging diagnosis), these cases continue to represent one-off exceptions rather than a consolidated trend. The lack of longitudinal studies or in-depth field studies on the adoption of these technologies also prevents us from understanding the real impacts, risks and training needs of the healthcare professionals involved.

7 Conclusion and Future Work

The results of this systematic review highlight the high potential of Low-Code platforms supported by generative AI in the healthcare sector, although their practical application remains underdeveloped. While a considerable number of studies with empirical characteristics were identified, they often lacked methodological transparency and formal validation, as well as the direct involvement of end users. The absence of user-centred validation limits our understanding of the real-world impact of such systems, as well as the barriers to adoption and associated learning curves.

A key finding is the complete absence of studies that integrate generative AI and clinical interoperability standards, such as FHIR or OpenEHR, simultaneously. This shortcoming compromises the applicability of these approaches in regulated clinical environments, revealing a critical gap between technological potential and the concrete requirements of the healthcare domain. While many studies address important issues such as privacy, scalability and AI, they tend to do so in isolation rather than in an integrated way. This results in limited technological maturity, generally corresponding to Technology Readiness Levels (TRL) 1 to 3 according to the framework by Bayrak [13].

A significant geographic bias was also observed, with more than 55% of analysed articles originating from the USA, the UK or Germany, and very limited representation from developing countries. This pattern may be partly related to the use of English-language sources, but it also indicates the need to explore how these systems can be adapted for use in low-resource settings to promote broader inclusion, digital equity, and long-term sustainability.

Regarding generative AI-assisted features, the following approaches were identified: code generation; workflow automation; natural language interface creation; and AutoML-assisted modelling. However, these functionalities are found in isolation and not in combination with interoperability standards or systematic clinical validations.

Future work should focus on developing a categorisation model for Intelligent Low-Code Systems based on their primary function, such as administrative automation, data integration and clinical decision support. Additionally, there is a critical need to design solutions that are more closely aligned with regulations and that have been validated in real clinical environments, with the involvement of end users from the outset and throughout the process. These technologies must achieve higher levels of technological maturity and clinical readiness if they are to contribute effectively and safely to the sustainable digital transformation of the healthcare sector.

Acknowledgements. This work has been supported by FCT – Fundação para a Ciência e Tecnologia within the R&D Unit Project Scope UID/00319/Centro ALGORITMI (ALGORITMI/UM).

Disclosure of Interests. The authors have no competing interests to declare that are relevant to the content of this article.

References

1. Sá, D., Lobo, A., Cunha, J., Duarte, R., Guimarães, T., Santos, M.F.: A state-of-the-art of intelligent problem-oriented low-code systems. Procedia Comput. Sci. **257**, 1122–1127 (2025). https://doi.org/10.1016/J.PROCS.2025.03.148
2. Rokis, K., Kirikova, M.: Challenges of low-code/no-code software development: a literature review. Lecture Notes in Business Information Processing, LNBIP. vol. 462, pp. 3–17 (2022). https://doi.org/10.1007/978-3-031-16947-2_1
3. Phalake, V.S., Joshi, S.D.: Optimized low code platform for application development. Int. J. Contemp. Archit. **8**(2) (2021). https://www.researchgate.net/publication/362519472
4. Kryszyn, J., Smolik, W.T., Wanta, D., Midura, M., Wróblewski, P.: Comparison of OpenEHR and HL7 FHIR Standards. Int. J. Electron. Telecommun. **69**(1), 47–52 (2023). https://doi.org/10.24425/IJET.2023.144330
5. Benson, T., Grieve, G.: Why interoperability is hard, pp. 19–35 (2016). https://doi.org/10.1007/978-3-319-30370-3_2
6. Stokel-Walker, C., Van Noorden, R.: What ChatGPT and generative AI mean for science. Nature **614**(7947), 214–216 (2023). https://doi.org/10.1038/D41586-023-00340-6
7. Bengesi, S., El-Sayed, H., Sarker, K., Houkpati, Y., Irungu, J., Oladunni, T.: Advancements in Generative AI: A Comprehensive Review of GANs, GPT, Autoencoders, Diffusion Model, and Transformers. https://towardsdatascience.com/applied-deep-learning-part-3. Accessed 14 May 2024
8. Moher, D., et al.: Preferred reporting items for systematic reviews and meta-analyses: the PRISMA statement. PLoS Med. **6**(7), e1000097 (2009). https://doi.org/10.1371/JOURNAL.PMED.1000097
9. Scimago Journal & Country Rank. https://www.scimagojr.com/
10. Templin, T., Perez, M.W., Sylvia, S., Leek, J., Sinnott-Armstrong, N.: Addressing 6 challenges in generative AI for digital health: a scoping review. PLOS Digit. Health **3**(5), e0000503 (2024). https://doi.org/10.1371/JOURNAL.PDIG.0000503
11. Murdoch, B.: Privacy and artificial intelligence: challenges for protecting health information in a new era. BMC Med. Ethics **22**(1), 1–5 (2021). https://doi.org/10.1186/S12910-021-00687-3/PEER-REVIEW
12. Kelly, C.J., Karthikesalingam, A., Suleyman, M., Corrado, G., King, D.: Key challenges for delivering clinical impact with artificial intelligence. BMC Med. **17**(1), 1–9 (2019). https://doi.org/10.1186/S12916-019-1426-2/PEER-REVIEW
13. Hak, F., Guimaraes, T., Santos, M.: Towards effective clinical decision support systems: a systematic review. PLoS ONE **17**(8), e0272846 (2022). https://doi.org/10.1371/JOURNAL.PONE.0272846

Unveiling MicroRNA Biomarkers for Breast Cancer Sub-typing Using Discriminative Models

João Mota[1], José Romano[1], Ana Rita Grosso[2], João Conde[3],
Bárbara Mendes[3], and David Semedo[1]

[1] NOVA LINCS, NOVA School of Science and Technology, Universidade NOVA de Lisboa, Lisbon, Portugal
jn.mota@campus.fct.unl.pt, df.semedo@fct.unl.pt
[2] Applied Molecular Biosciences Unit - NOVA School of Science and Technology, Universidade NOVA de Lisboa, Lisbon, Portugal
j.romano@campus.fct.unl.pt, ar.grosso@fct.unl.pt
[3] Comprehensive Health Research Centre (CHRC), NOVA Medical School, Universidade NOVA de Lisboa, Lisbon, Portugal
{joao.conde,barbara.mendes}@nms.unl.pt

Abstract. Breast cancer is a heterogeneous disease comprising multiple molecular subtypes, each with distinct clinical outcomes and therapeutic challenges. MicroRNAs (miRNAs), as key regulators of gene expression, hold great promise as biomarkers for cancer subtyping and developing personalized treatments. In this paper, we propose a machine-learning discriminative modeling framework to uncover subtype-specific miRNA biomarkers for breast cancer. Our approach jointly integrates miRNA expression data with patient clinical data, to identify miRNA signatures that differentiate between luminal A, luminal B, HER2-enriched, and Basal-like subtypes. We conduct extensive validation across multiple discriminative models and provide evidence that microRNAs are strong discriminators within breast cancer subtypes, achieving up to 90% F1. Furthermore, we contrast our findings against state-of-the-art multi-omics integration and biomarker discovery, and provide a reassessment of its predicted miRNA signatures. To this end, a model explainability approach is employed to analyze and pinpoint subtype-specific miRNA profiles. These potentially highlight subtype-specific biologically meaningful and functionally relevant miRNAs, that can now be therapeutically validated through in vitro and in vivo experiments.

Keywords: breast cancer · microRNA · biomarker discovery · machine learning

1 Introduction

Breast cancer is one of the most prevalent and challenging malignancies in women worldwide, with complex molecular mechanisms driving its progression

© The Author(s), under exclusive license to Springer Nature Switzerland AG 2026
J. Valente de Oliveira et al. (Eds.): EPIA 2025, LNAI 16121, pp. 68–80, 2026.
https://doi.org/10.1007/978-3-032-05176-9_6

and treatment resistance. It affects millions of women and causes thousands of deaths annually. It's natural heterogeneity presents a clinical challenge, by being categorized according to the expression of hormone receptors, namely estrogen receptor (ER) and progesterone receptor (PR), and human epidermal growth factor receptor 2 (HER2). These molecular subtypes, Luminal A, Luminal B, HER2-enriched, and Basal-like (also referred as Triple Negative), differ significantly in prognosis, response to treatment and chance of metastasis. Identifying new biomarkers and personalized therapeutics is urgently necessary to reduce mortality and address the critical lack of targeted treatment options.

Recent studies have demonstrated that microRNAs (miRNAs), non-coding RNAs involved in gene regulation, play a significant role in breast cancer development [15,16]. With miRNAs expression levels demonstrating unique signatures across breast cancer molecular subtypes, the necessity of systematically pinpointing a restricted set of relevant microRNAs for each subtype, that can posteriorly be analysed through in-vitro and in-vivo analyses, is paramount, towards the design of gene-based nanotherapies. Machine learning-based approaches have demonstrated great potential in cancer profiling [4,6,10]. These have demonstrated to be capable of leveraging high-dimensional multi-omics data, and either uncover latent microRNA, genes and proteins interactions [14] or cancer diagnosis [4].

In this work we introduce a multi-source breast cancer biomarker identification framework, combining individuals' microRNAs expression levels and clinical attributes (e.g., age, disease progression indicators, among others). We follow related work, applied to gastric cancer biomarker identification [4], and follow an approach where discriminative classification tasks are used as a proxy to assess multi-source feature relevance. In particular, we leverage well-established but explainable discriminative classification models to robustly conduct breast cancer subtyping in two fundamental settings: 1) miRNA-only expression-levels, and 2) hybrid miRNA and patient clinical data.

Our systematic evaluation demonstrates that not only breast cancer subtypes can be robustly predicted with high effectiveness solely from miRNA expression levels (up to 87% precision), but that integrating patient clinical features positively improves performance. From these high-performing models, we further conduct a model explainability study where we systematically identify key responsible miRNA biomarkers per subtype, drawing key insights to both subtype-specific and shared microRNA biomarkers.

2   Related Work

Recent advances have positioned miRNAs as highly promising biomarkers in breast cancer research. Their stability in biological fluids and specificity for tumor subtypes make them particularly suitable for non-invasive diagnostics such as liquid biopsies [15,16]. Panels of miRNAs have demonstrated strong discriminatory power across breast cancer subtypes, aiding early detection and patient stratification for tailored therapies [11,17]. Simultaneously, machine learning (ML) techniques have proven to be powerful tools for cancer subtype classification. Supervised classifiers outperform traditional methods like immunohistochemistry by effectively leveraging high-dimensional datasets, including miRNA expression profiles [7]. Moreover, these facilitate the identification of the most predictive features through embedded techniques like regularization and recursive feature elimination, enhancing both classification accuracy and biological interpretability.

However, key challenges remain. Class imbalance- particularly for rare subtypes like Basal-like- continues to hinder generalizability, requiring strategies such as resampling and synthetic data generation (e.g., SMOTE) [2]. Moreover, while complex models often offer improved performance, their opacity limits clinical trust. This has spurred the adoption of explainable AI (XAI) methods like SHAP [8] and LIME [13], which attribute model predictions to input features, increasing transparency and biological credibility [5]. Research in adjacent domains reinforces these trends. Azari et al. extended this methodology using multiple ML models to detect 29 miRNAs linked to gastric cancer prognosis, yielding 93% accuracy and 88,5% AUC with SVM [1]. These studies illustrate the potential of ML-driven miRNA biomarker discovery, which is now being translated into breast cancer research with increasing success.

Therapeutically, miRNAs are gaining traction beyond diagnostics. Approaches such as AntagomiRs and miRNA mimics are under clinical investigation for restoring tumor-suppressive miRNA activity or inhibiting oncogenic miRNAs [9,12]. Additionally, nanocarrier systems are being developed to deliver these molecules with high specificity, offering promising routes for RNA-based personalized therapies [3].

Together, these advances suggest that ML-enabled miRNA analysis holds transformative potential for breast cancer subtype classification, early detection, and individualized treatment design.

3   A Multi-source Breast Cancer Biomarker Identification Framework

In this work, we introduce a general-purpose framework for identifying microRNA biomarkers relevant to breast cancer subtyping using discriminative machine learning models. Rather than relying on latent variable methods or integration through component extraction, our approach focuses on a direct supervised learning strategy, leveraging both miRNA and clinical data as sources of predictive signal.

Our pipeline is composed of three core stages: data preparation, discriminative modeling, and biomarker evaluation. As illustrated in Fig. 1, we process miRNA expression and clinical data independently, cleaning each source before concatenating the features into a unified input space for posterior split and normalization. This integration enables the models to access multi-source information directly, without the need for explicit projection into a shared latent space.

Once the data is prepared, we train classification models to predict breast cancer subtypes using two configurations: homogeneous (miRNA only) and heterogeneous (miRNA + clinical). The goal is not only to optimize subtype classification performance, but also to uncover which features - especially miRNAs -

are most indicative of each subtype. We later employ explainability techniques, such as SHAP and coefficient analysis, to extract and rank relevant microRNAs from our top-performing model.

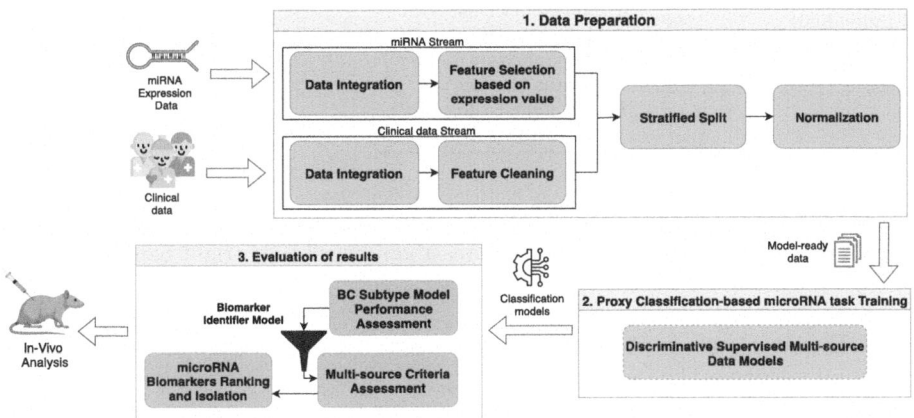

Fig. 1. Unified framework for miRNA biomarker identification and subtyping in Breast Cancer, using discriminative models.

The entire workflow can be summarized in five key steps:

1. **Data curation and preprocessing**, including filtering of redundant miR-NAs and cleaning of clinical records.
2. **Feature integration** by concatenating miRNA and clinical data into a single matrix.
3. **Model training** under homogeneous (miRNA-only) and heterogeneous (miRNA + clinical) settings.
4. **Model evaluation** using accuracy, precision, recall and F1-score.
5. **Feature importance analysis** to identify subtype-specific biomarkers.

Discriminative Models. Considering the limited size of our dataset (244 individuals/samples with an aggregate set of 462 features - more details in Sect. 4.1), we opt for classical discriminative models that are well-suited to high-dimensional, low-sample-size scenarios, offering a more robust and interpretable foundation for biomarker identification. Larger models, with higher number of parameters to tune, would pose a severe risk of overfitting. Therefore, to support our framework, we selected three discriminative models that balance performance and interpretability:

- **Decision Tree**: A decision tree classifier, using the Gini impurity as classification criteria, offering fully interpretable decision rules.
- **Logistic Regression**: A linear multinomial logistic regression classifier, with ℓ_2 regularization.

Statistic	Total
# Samples	244
# Individuals	244
# microRNAs	442
# Clinical Attributes	20

Sample Clinical Attrs.
Age (*numeric*)
ER Status (*boolean*)
Metastasis (*boolean*)
Lymph Nodes (*numeric*)
Mutations (*numeric*)
Overall Survival (*numeric*)
PR Status (*boolean*)
Tumor Stage (*categorical*)
...

Fig. 2. Descriptive statistics of the TCGA full dataset (left table), sample clinical features (right table) and histogram per breast cancer subtype (right figure).

- **XGBoost**: A gradient-boosted decision tree model, optimized with a multinomial negative likelihood.

This combination of tree-like and regression models, including simpler (Decision Tree) to boosted models (XGBoost), enable us to understand how discriminative models of different complexities, can leverage microRNAs to conduct breast cancer profiling.

4 Evaluation

4.1 Dataset

The primary dataset utilized in this study is a curated subset of the publicly available TCGA (The Cancer Genome Atlas) database, specifically comprising miRNA expression profiles from breast cancer patients. Initially, the dataset included expression levels for 888 distinct miRNAs across 251 patients.

Upon detailed examination, it was observed that several miRNAs with the same base identifier- for example, *MIR-758*, *MIR-758/3P*, and *MIR-758/5P* - exhibited identical expression values across all samples. This redundancy is likely due to limitations in the measurement technique, which may lack the sensitivity required to distinguish between these closely related variants. Consequently, to reduce redundancy and eliminate features that do not contribute additional variance or informative signal to the model, all such miRNAs sharing the same base and expression profile were removed. This preprocessing step reduced the number of miRNA features from 888 to 464, eliminating 446 non-informative miRNAs.

In addition to the miRNA expression data, clinical details from the same dataset, containing complementary patient information was incorporated. As shown in Fig. 2, it comprises features such as age, cancer stage, presence of metastasis, number of lymph nodes, among others. These clinical variables are particularly valuable as they are often readily accessible without the need for costly procedures and may provide significant predictive power for subtype classification.

Features with more than 90% missing values were excluded to ensure data integrity. Additionally, six patients were discarded due to incomplete clinical attributes. Given the intrinsic biological heterogeneity among individuals- where similar diagnoses can result in divergent outcomes- it was deemed inappropriate to impute missing values. All features were appropriately encoded and normalized. In particular, to mitigate the risk of data leakage, z-score normalization was applied exclusively based on the training set: the scaling parameters were computed from the training data and then used to transform both the training and testing sets. This normalization was applied to all continuous numerical features, including miRNA expression values and clinical variables.

In overall, we obtain a final dataset of 244 patients (samples), comprising a total of 462 features (microRNAs and clinical attributes), annotated with the corresponding breast cancer subtype.

4.2   Protocol

To establish a solid evaluation benchmark, we trained three classical machine learning models: **Decision Tree**, **Logistic Regression** and **XGBoost**. These were selected due to their proven performance on high-dimensional biological datasets and their interpretability [4,10].

To benchmark the effectiveness of our discriminative pipeline, we compare against **DIABLO** [14][1], a leading multi-omics integration method based on latent variable modeling. While DIABLO aims to capture correlated structures across modalities, our pipeline aims purely at optimizing discriminative performance. We applied the recommended cross-validation and hyperparameter tuning steps.

The combined dataset of miRNA expression values and clinical features (see Sect. 4.1) was randomly split into training (80%) and testing (20%) subsets using stratified sampling to preserve class distribution. This resulted in 195 training and 49 testing samples (see Fig. 2).

Scaling parameters (mean and standard deviation) were computed from the training data and applied to both training and testing subsets. This normalization was applied to all continuous variables, including miRNA expression levels and clinical features. All models were evaluated using well-established classification metrics: *accuracy, precision, recall* and *F1-score*.

4.3   Results

To evaluate the performance of discriminative models in breast cancer subtype profiling, we conducted experiments using both homogeneous data (with miR-NAs expression values only) and heterogeneous data (miRNA + clinical features

---

[1] Available in the `mixOmics` R package.

Table 1. Homogeneous classifiers (<u>miRNAs</u> only). Results are shown in percentage.

Model	Overall				Basal	HER-2	Lum A	Lum B
	P	R	F1	Acc	F1			
DIABLO Single Block	75.27	67.26	67.69	73.47	**100.00**	40.00	80.77	50.00
Decision Tree	57.35	56.40	56.79	57.14	87.50	36.36	61.90	41.38
Logistic Regression	80.26	**75.60**	73.50	**77.55**	94.12	61.54	**85.71**	**52.63**
XGBoost	**86.96**	74.40	**76.73**	75.51	**100.00**	**80.00**	76.92	50.00

Table 2. Heterogeneous models (<u>miRNAs + Clinical Data</u>). Results are shown in percentage.

Model	Overall				Basal	HER-2	Lum A	Lum B
	P	R	F1	Acc	F1			
DIABLO All Blocks	78.47	72.62	73.82	79.59	**100.00**	40.00	85.71	69.57
Decision Tree	62.01	63.69	62.45	61.22	88.89	54.55	61.90	44.44
Logistic Regression	77.22	75.60	75.57	79.59	94.12	54.55	**86.96**	66.67
XGBoost	**90.06**	**79.17**	**82.17**	**83.67**	**100.00**	**66.67**	85.11	**76.92**

from the patient). This section presents a comparative analysis of model performance across different metrics and class distributions, succeeded by a discussion on the various advantages of discriminative models over the latent representation approach used in DIABLO.

Performance of Discriminative Models Using MiRNAs Only. In this first segment, we assessed the predictive performance of three discriminative models - Decision Trees, XGBoost, Logistic Regression - trained solely on microRNA expression values. Table 1 presents their results in comparison with DIABLO using a single omics block (in DIABLO, datasets of different natures are called omics blocks - in this case, the single omics block that was used to classify the subtype of BC was miRNA).

XGBoost stood out with the highest overall F1-score (76.73%) and precision (86.96%), followed closely by Logistic Regression (F1 = 73.50%, precision = 80.26%). The findings of this experiment corroborate the initial suppositions that a dataset solely with microRNA (miRNA) values can serve as a resource to distinguish breast cancer subtypes, achieving up to 87% precision. In contrast, the Decision Tree showed lower performance across all metrics, suggesting limited generalization.

When analyzing subtype-specific results reveal perfect classification (F1 = 100%) for the Basal-like subtype, and this results is sustained by multiple models. However, performance drops for less distinct subtypes such as HER2-enriched and Luminal B. For instance, DIABLO's F1-score on HER2 was only 40.00%, where XGBoost doubled that score with 80.00%. Logistic Regression also performed well in these conditions across all classes, achieving the highest F1-score for Luminal A (85.71%) and Luminal B (52.63%).

These results indicates that discriminative models trained solely on miR-NAs can produce clinically relevant predictions, reinforcing the value of miRNA expression patterns alone.

Impact of Adding Clinical Data. In the second phase, we incorporated patient clinical features along with miRNA features to evaluate whether this multimodal integration could enhance model performance. Table 2 shows a consistent performance boost across all models.

When we analyzed the performance of the models, XGBoost showed the most substantial improvement, with the F1-score increasing from 76.73% to 82.17% and accuracy from 75.51% to 83.67%. Logistic Regression also benefited from the aggregation of clinical data (F1-score from 73.50% to 75.57% and accuracy from 77.55% to 79.59%), but being dethroned by XGBoost across all general metrics. These improvements suggest that clinical features provided complementary information that helped refine the subtype decision boundaries, particularly for overlapping classes.

At the subtype level, overall, the models exhibited enhanced classification of previously ambiguous groups. XGBoost's F1 for Luminal B rose from 50.00% to 76.92%, and Logistic Regression increased from 52.63% to 66.67%. This came with the cost of reducing XGBoost's F1 on HER2-enriched (which can be attributed to class imbalances or sensitivity to the integration process), but maintaining the top performance versus other models. This cost is seen as worth it, especially when we consider the rise of the other metrics for the other classes and the improvement in the model's classification ability.

To better understand the contribution of the clinical data, we analyzed the relative feature importance of each dataset as a whole using XGBoost model (the model that performed the best in this heterogeneous environment). As shown in Fig. 3, miRNAs accounted for the vast majority of total feature importance across all subtypes (often above 90%). Yet, the small contribution from clinical features still had a measurable impact on the model performance, especially for the more ambiguous subtypes (Luminal B and HER2-enriched). This underscores the high informational density of clinical data, which helps resolve cases where miRNA profiles alone are ambiguous.

Discriminative vs. Latent Representation Approaches. A direct comparison between DIABLO and discriminative models underscores the advantages of our approach. While DIABLO (All Blocks) improved its performance over its single-block version (F1: 73.82% vs. 67.69%), it still fell behind both XGBoost (F1: 82.17%) and Logistic Regression (F1: 75.57%) under the same multimodal setup.

Confusion matrices (Fig. 7) offer additional insights into the strengths of the discriminative models. Both XGBoost and Logistic Regression made fewer misclassifications in difficult subtypes such as HER2-enriched and Luminal B.

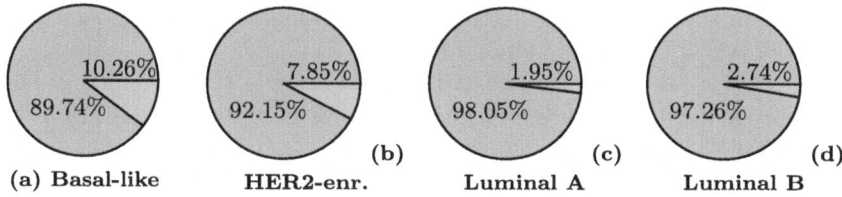

Fig. 3. XGBoost-Based Feature Group Importance per Breast Cancer Subtype. (blue represents miRNA features while pink represent clinical features) (Color figure online)

DIABLO, on the other hand, often confused HER2-enriched with Luminal A or Luminal B, suggesting that its latent space did not adequately disentangle these phenotypically close subtypes.

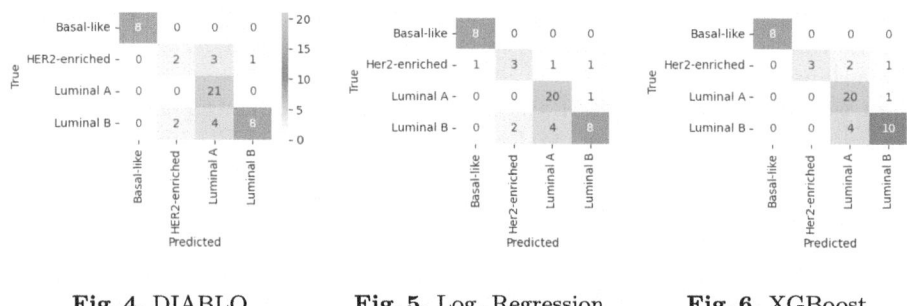

Fig. 4. DIABLO   **Fig. 5.** Log. Regression   **Fig. 6.** XGBoost

Fig. 7. Confusion matrices for each model using miRNA + clinical data.

In addition to that, the interpretability of discriminative models such as XGBoost further supports their applicability in clinical settings. Their coefficients can be directly linked to miRNA or clinical features, enabling biomarker identification and validation (more on that in Sect. 4.4. In contrast, DIABLO's latent components are harder to interpret and require additional steps to trace back to the original features.

In summary, discriminative models not only achieved higher predictive performance but also offered clearer insights into feature importance and subtype boundaries. These attributes are essential in biomedical contexts where transparency and traceability are paramount.

4.4   Identifying MicroRNA Biomarkers Candidates

To derive the final set of candidate miRNA biomarkers, we applied an intersecting strategy across multiple machine learning models and explainability methods (shown in Table 3). We computed feature importance using both model-specific

Table 3. Top 10 most important miRNA features, and corresponding score ($\times 10^{-1}$ scale), per breast cancer subtype, using XGBoost. Common top miRNAs across subtypes are colored with red, green and blue. The prefix "MIR" is omitted for presentation purposes.

Basal-like		HER2-enriched		Luminal A		Luminal B	
Feature	Score	Feature	Score	Feature	Score	Feature	Score
135B/135B*	1.487	192/192*	0.814	105-1/105	0.456	135B/135B*	0.231
934/934	1.026	187/187	0.523	205/205*	0.423	934/934	0.188
190B/190B	0.974	34C/5P	0.436	25/25	0.342	125A/3P	0.173
455/5P	0.615	30C-2/2*	0.436	19A/19A	0.326	205/205*	0.159
577/577	0.564	148/148A	0.407	1301/1301	0.293	320B-2/320B	0.144
455/3P	0.410	497/497*	0.378	942/942	0.261	339/3P	0.144
18A/18A*	0.359	30C/3P	0.349	3200/3P	0.244	187/187	0.130
99A/99A*	0.205	2115/2115*	0.262	342/5P	0.195	148/148A	0.115
140/3P	0.205	3150B/3P	0.233	1270/1270	0.147	744/744*	0.115
9-1/9*	0.154	210/210	0.203	26A/26A	0.130	125B-2/2*	0.115

techniques (e.g., coefficients) and model-agnostic methods like SHAP. For each subtype, we ranked features according to their contribution and retained the top features per method. The final set was obtained by selecting miRNAs that consistently appeared among the top-ranked features across different models and explanation techniques. This cross-validation across interpretability sources ensured that only robust, repeatable signals were considered, increasing confidence in their potential as true subtype-discriminative biomarkers. We take it that the top three miRNAs distinguish themselves highly from the rest. These miRNAs often, in the individual analyses, revealed high importance across different models. The MIR-934/934 ranked first half of the subtypes, it alone has great distinction capabilities.

We leveraged SHAP [8] as an explainability technique to understanding which features were most influential. The spread and direction of SHAP values offer insight into how consistently each feature contributes across samples. Narrow distributions indicated potential subtype patterns, while large spreads, though still insightful, not as it's own biomarker alone. Overall, the SHAP analysis improved model transparency and provided biological understanding of miRNAs' role in separation supporting it's promise as potential biomarkers.

The plots (Fig. 8) display the results for the SHAP analysis on the XGBoost model. It shows the top 10 features influencing predictions for each breast cancer subtype. miRNA expression features were consistently among the most impactful, suggesting their strong discriminative power. Clinical variables such as HER2

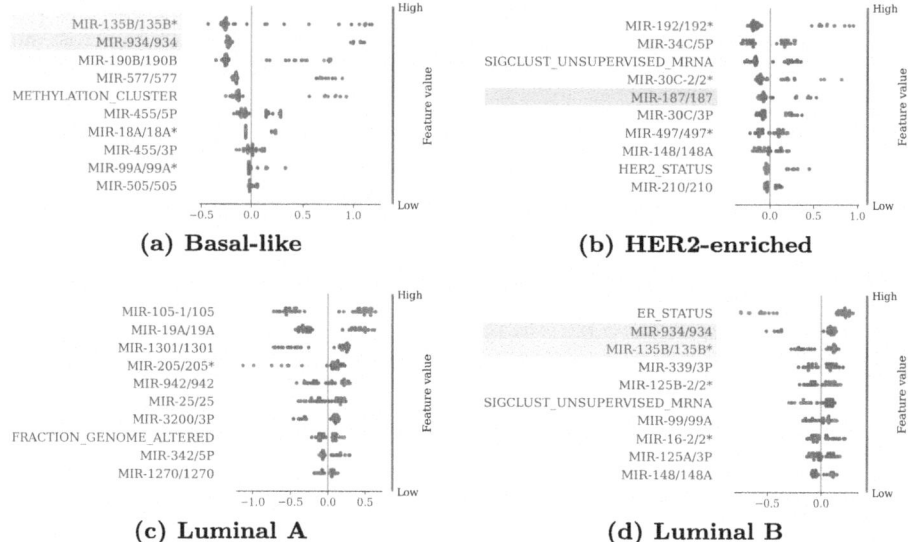

Fig. 8. SHAP summary plots for the top 10 features for each BC subtype (XGBoost model) - same color scheme used in Table 3.

Status and ER status also appeared with high importance in relevant subtypes, aligning with established clinical markers. These plots unveil what impact each miRNA has towards the individual predictions per breast cancer subtype. For example, low expression of the MIR-190B/190B, indicates an increase in the chance of a classification of the Basal-like subtype. Another relevant distinction is how the ER status feature strongly influences the classification of the Luminal B subtype, where a positive label is associated with the subtype. These results provide strong evidence regarding potential biomarkers to further explore and study with in laboratorial in-vitro and in-vivo settings.

5 Conclusion

In this paper, we introduce a multi-source breast cancer biomarker identification framework that integrates individuals' microRNA expression profiles with clinical attributes to enhance subtype classification. We provide compelling evidence that microRNA expression profiles alone offer strong discriminative power for accurately classifying breast cancer subtypes. Furthermore, our findings reveal that integrating clinical features further boosts predictive performance, highlighting the value of multimodal data in subtype assessment. Through a model explainability approach, we isolate a focused set of subtype-specific potential microRNA biomarkers. The next step consists of conducting in-vitro and in-vivo laboratory validation, towards further validating their potential to develop targeted therapeutics, for each breast cancer subtype.

Acknowledgements. This work has been partially funded by the FCT project NOVA LINCS Ref. UIDP/04516/2020, by the FCT Grant LISBOA2030-FEDER-00862500-14998 – OncoNanoAI, and by Liga Portuguesa contra o cancro - project BECAME.

Disclosure of Interests. The authors have no competing interests to declare that are relevant to the content of this article.

J.C. is a co-founder and shareholder of TargTex S.A.-Targeted Therapeutics for Glioblastoma Multiforme. J.C. is a member of the Global Burden Disease (GBD) consortium of the Institute for Health Metrics and Evaluation (IHME), University of Washington (US), and the Scientific Advisory Board of Vector Bioscience, Cambridge.

References

1. Azari, H., et al.: Machine learning algorithms reveal potential miRNAs biomarkers in gastric cancer. Sci. Rep. **13**(1), 6147 (2023)
2. Blagus, R., Lusa, L.: SMOTE for high-dimensional class-imbalanced data. BMC Bioinform. **14**(1), 106 (2013)
3. Bravo-Vázquez, L.A., et al.: Applications of nanotechnologies for miRNA-based cancer therapeutics: current advances and future perspectives. Front. Bioeng. Biotechnol. **11**, 1208547 (2023)
4. Gilani, N., Arabi Belaghi, R., Aftabi, Y., Faramarzi, E., Edgünlü, T., Somi, M.H.: Identifying potential miRNA biomarkers for gastric cancer diagnosis using machine learning variable selection approach. Front. Genet. **12**, 779455 (2021)
5. Hrinivich, W.T., Wang, T., Wang, C.: Editorial: interpretable and explainable machine learning models in oncology. Front. Oncol. **13**, 1184428 (2023)
6. Hu, Z., et al.: Identification and validation of screening models for breast cancer with 3 serum miRNAs in an 11,349 samples mixed cohort. Breast Cancer **31**(6), 1046–1058 (2024)
7. Li, J., Zhang, H., Gao, F.: Identification of miRNA biomarkers for breast cancer by combining ensemble regularized multinomial logistic regression and cox regression. BMC Bioinform. **23**(1), 434 (2022)
8. Lundberg, S.M., Lee, S.I.: A unified approach to interpreting model predictions. In: Guyon, I., et al. (eds.) Advances in Neural Information Processing Systems, vol. 30. Curran Associates, Inc. (2017)
9. Mendes, B.B., et al.: Nanodelivery of nucleic acids. Nat. Rev. Methods Primers **2**(1) (2022)
10. Mendes, B.B., et al.: A large-scale machine learning analysis of inorganic nanoparticles in preclinical cancer research. Nat. Nanotechnol. **19**(6), 867–878 (2024)
11. Muñoz, J.P., Pérez-Moreno, P., Pérez, Y., Calaf, G.M.: The role of MicroRNAs in breast cancer and the challenges of their clinical application. Diagnostics (Basel) **13**(19) (2023)
12. Pagoni, M., et al.: MiRNA-based technologies in cancer therapy. J. Pers. Med. **13**(11), 1586 (2023)
13. Ribeiro, M., Singh, S., Guestrin, C.: "Why should I trust you?": explaining the predictions of any classifier. In: DeNero, J., Finlayson, M., Reddy, S. (eds.) Proceedings of the 2016 Conference of the North American Chapter of the Association for Computational Linguistics: Demonstrations, pp. 97–101. Association for Computational Linguistics, San Diego, California (2016)

14. Singh, A., et al.: Diablo: an integrative approach for identifying key molecular drivers from multi-omics assays. Bioinformatics **35**(17), 3055–3062 (2019)
15. Valihrach, L., Androvic, P., Kubista, M.: Circulating miRNA analysis for cancer diagnostics and therapy. Mol. Aspects Med. (2020)
16. Wang, W.T., Chen, Y.Q.: Circulating miRNAs in cancer: from detection to therapy. J. Hematol. Oncol. **7**(1), 86 (2014)
17. Wang, Z., et al.: miRNA-205 affects infiltration and metastasis of breast cancer. Biochem. Biophys. Res. Commun. **441**(1), 139–143 (2013)

Smartphone Keyboard Typing for Rheumatic Disease Identification: A Machine Learning Approach

Pedro Matias[1(✉)], Pedro Afonseca[1,2], Francisco Nunes[1,3],
Ana Rita Henriques[4], Cátia Gonçalves[4], Ana Rodrigues[4], and Inês Sousa[1,3]

[1] Fraunhofer Portugal AICOS, Rua Alfredo Allen 455/461, 4200-135 Porto, Portugal
pedro.matias@fraunhofer.pt
[2] Faculdade de Ciências, Universidade do Porto, Porto, Portugal
[3] Comprehensive Health Research Center, Fraunhofer AICOS, Porto, Portugal
[4] Comprehensive Health Research Center, NOVA Medical School, Universidade NOVA de Lisboa, Lisbon, Portugal

Abstract. Hand function impairment is among the most common symptoms of several Rheumatic and Musculoskeletal Diseases (RMD), making its timely assessment essential for diagnosis and disease management. However, standard clinical evaluations are often subjective, irregular, and inconclusive. In this study, we explore the potential of keyboard-derived features, such as inter-key flight and hold times, as digital biomarkers of fine-motor skill impairment in individuals with RMDs. Data from 59 participants (31 patients, 28 controls) was retrieved from the COTIDIANA dataset. Each participant completed a transcription task on a smartphone, from which keyboard typing dynamics were retrieved. We defined a binary classification task to distinguish (i) RMD patients with and (ii) healthy controls without hand joint pain. We applied multiple Machine Learning (ML) pipelines using keyboard features, functional tests, and Patient-Reported Outcome Measures (PROM), comparing their predictive performance via balanced accuracy, F1-score, and AUROC. Our best keyboard-based ML predictive model achieved a test AUROC of 0.87 and F1-score of 0.83, outperforming most traditional PROM-based assessments such as EQ-5D-5L, HADS, and functional tests (MPUT). Feature importances revealed that RMD patients exhibited longer typing latency than controls, which is consistent with previous Parkinson's and Multiple Sclerosis research. Findings suggest fine-motor impairments can be effectively captured through typing dynamics, supporting the generalization of this approach across motor-related conditions. Integrating digital assessment tools into rheumatology care could promote more objective, data-driven strategies to improve patient identification and referral. This would enable the fast-screening of individuals exhibiting early fine-motor signs of decline, fostering efficient access to clinical care.

Keywords: machine learning · fine-motor skills · keyboard typing · rheumatology · disease identification

J. Valente de Oliveira et al. (Eds.): EPIA 2025, LNAI 16121, pp. 81–92, 2026.
https://doi.org/10.1007/978-3-032-05176-9_7

1   Introduction

1.1   Background and Motivation

Rheumatic and Musculoskeletal Diseases (RMDs) affect over 1.7 billion people worldwide, imposing substantial physical, psychological, and economic burdens [18]. A progressive loss of finger dexterity is a commonly reported symptom in some RMDs that impacts patients' daily life activities. The loss of fine-motor skills becomes also reflected in the biomarker patterns raised by their interaction with everyday digital devices, in particular smartphones [17]. Actually, digital biomarkers are defined as physiological and behavioral metrics captured by digital devices, having increasingly been recognized for their potential to complement traditional clinical assessment scores in RMDs [14]. For assessing finger dexterity, Patient-Reported Outcome Measures (PROMs) [6,18], grip strength tests [20], and dexterity timed tests (e.g., Moberg Pick-Up Test, MPUT) [19] are some of the traditional approaches applied in clinical practice. On the other hand, keyboard typing dynamics (flight and hold times) captured during keyboard typing have raised promise as non-invasive, effortless indicators of hand function in neurologic and RMD populations [8]. In fact, very few studies have compared the disease identification power of keystroke typing dynamics with that of validated self-report instruments, such as the Health Assessment Questionnaire (HAQ), the EuroQoL-5 Dimensions-5 Levels (EQ-5D-5L), and the Hospital Anxiety and Depression Scale (HADS), as well as validated timed assessments, such as the MPUT. Most of these strategies are based on self-reported answers (questionnaires) or do not capture all the dimensions of the hand function, failing to address the demand of tracking fine-motor function for diagnosis, monitoring, and prognosis purposes. Alternatively, keyboard typing metrics may help fill this gap as it gathers granular dynamics of typing in a continuous fashion. This helps track both speed and pressing patterns of any individuals, which can potentially be associated with their hand function. Integrating sensor-driven features with machine learning (ML) techniques can enhance disease classification and stratification, distinguishing between different levels of RMD severity. Once validated, such metrics may integrate the standard clinical practice, with proved efficacy in disease diagnosis and monitoring.

1.2   Related Work

Literature of the last decade has focused on applying smartphone keyboard typing dynamics to study fine-motor skills in multiple chronic diseases, such as Parkinson's disease (PD) [2,3,9,11], Multiple Sclerosis (MS) [10,12], and Amyotrophic Lateral Sclerosis (ALS) [1]. For example, in PD disease, Tat et al. demonstrated that flight time (FT) and hold time (HT) metrics can distinguish early-stage Parkinson's Disease (PD) patients from healthy controls with notable accuracy (~0.98) using passive touchscreen typing data [21]. Despite that, the pipeline still requires further validation as it was only tested in three subjects. In MS disease, a longitudinal analysis of keystroke dynamics (FTs and HTs) revealed a strong association with clinical disability measures such as the Nine-Hole Peg Test and Symbol Digit Modalities Test, indicating their sensitivity to changes in motor and cognitive function over time [12]. Severity classification within MS cohorts using passively collected smartphone keystrokes achieved AUROC scores above 70% for fine motor skill estimation, underscoring their potential as unobtrusive monitoring tools [10]. Keystroke features have also been leveraged to detect depressive tendencies. By extracting HT and FT sequences during natural typing, recent studies achieved Sensitivity and Specificity scores greater than 80% in classifying individuals with depressive symptoms versus healthy controls [7]. In ALS condition, a recent study explored the predictive power of FT and HT dynamics in discerning ALS from healthy controls, having reached an AUC score of 89%. Slow vs. fast ALS progression was also performed, achieving AUC scores within [65, 80]% [1]. Comprehensive reviews also highlight the broad applicability of smartphone keystroke dynamics as digital biomarkers for disorders affecting fine motor skills, and call for further exploration of these metrics across diverse clinical populations [8]. In rheumatology, studies of typing dynamics are still scarce. Recently, the COTIDIANA dataset [16] collected FT and HT sequences during transcription tasks in age-matched RMD patients and healthy subjects, providing a unique resource to study digital biomarkers of fine-motor function.

1.3 Main Objectives

In this study, we processed and investigated hand function data retrieved from COTIDIANA dataset [16]. By using Artificial Intelligence (AI) and data mining techniques, we investigated their predictive power in distinguishing painless healthy controls and RMD patients who reported hand joint pain and stiffness. Regarding hand function, keyboard typing dynamics data were collected during a transcription test where each subject wrote ten consecutive sentences of growing complexity on a smartphone keyboard. In this study, insights from these sequences are compared against validated PROMs and a timed test, using an automated ML pipelines for classification. In this scope, we focused on a binary classification task: Healthy controls (HC) versus RMD patients (RMD). The results helped us address the following research questions: *Can keyboard typing dynamics serve as a viable alternative to replace or complement standard PROMs for identifying and prioritizing RMD patient subgroups?* (**RQ1**); *Can keyboard typing metrics help characterize RMD signs of fine-motor impairment?* (**RQ2**) This study, thus, explores how using keyboard-driven metrics can improve the identification and diagnosis of RMD patient groups and strengthen patient prioritization guidelines in clinical practice. By quantifying the trade-off between typing effort and predictive accuracy, we also establish practical guidelines for deploying lightweight, patient-centric digital assessments, ultimately leading to better clinical decision support in rheumatology.

2 Methods

2.1 Dataset

The COTIDIANA dataset [15] is a publicly available multimodal collection of mobility and fine motor skill data from 59 adult participants (31 diagnosed with RMDs) recorded under standardized conditions. Smartphone inertial sensors and keyboard touch-screen events were used to capture both gross and fine-motor measures, while validated self-report instruments and sociodemographic questions provided complementary clinical and lifestyle information. Data are accessible on Zenodo [16]. Table 1 summarizes the demographic and clinical characteristics of the cohort. Since this work focuses on the study of the hand function in RMDs, and there were few RMD patients not reporting pain in hand joints, we excluded (a) any RMD patients without self-reported hand joints affected and (b) any healthy controls who did report hand joints impacted. This approach ensures clearer group distinctions and strengthens the likelihood that any observed differences result from hand joints involvement rather than other unrelated factors.

Table 1. Characterization of participant subjects from COTIDIANA Dataset under demographic and clinical dimensions.

Demographics		Dataset (N = 59)		p-value*
		Patients (N)	Controls (N)	
Age	<40	2	8	>0.05
	40–60	18	12	
	>60	11	8	
Sex	Female	25	19	>0.05
	Male	6	9	
Country	Portugal	24	20	>0.05
	Austria	7	8	
Condition	OA	14	-	**<.001**
	PsA	9	-	
	RA	7	-	
	IJA	1	-	
	Control	-	28	
Total Subjects (N)		31	28	-

OA - Osteoarthritis; PsA - Psoriatic Arthritis;
RA - Rheumatoid Arthritis; IJA - Idiopathic Juvenile Arthritis.
* - Patients vs. Controls, chi-squared test applied (significance at 5%).

Questionnaires. Participants completed four sets of paper-based self-reports during each session, namely, *HAQ*, which assesses functional ability in activities of daily living across domains such as dressing, arising, eating and grip/reach tasks; *EQ-5D-5L*, a five-dimension, five-level instrument measuring health-related quality of life in mobility, self-care, usual activities, pain/discomfort and anxiety/depression; *HADS*, that screens for symptoms of anxiety and depression to account for psychological factors that may influence motor performance; and *Custom Questions*, which collect sociodemographics (age, sex), pain and stiffness locations, and familiarity with mobile technologies.

Functional Test Data. To assess finger dexterity using a timed test, participants performed the MPUT twice (once with each hand). Subjects were asked to move a set of small, unevenly shaped objects from a flat surface into a container as fast as possible. The completion time provides a measure of fine motor dexterity and has been shown to discriminate impairments in RMD populations.

Keyboard Typing Data. Keyboard typing dynamics were captured during a keyboard sentence transcription task in which participants transcribed ten pre-selected sentences of progressively increasing complexity. Using the smartphone, both *flight times* (intervals between releasing one key and pressing the next) and *hold times* (duration of each key press) were retrieved at a millisecond resolution. Sentences were drawn from language-agnostic corpora to ensure consistent linguistic complexity. Figure 1 helps illustrate some of these metrics.

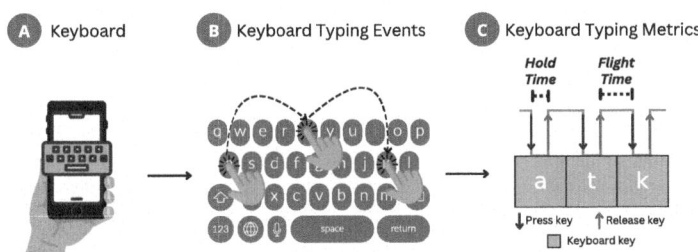

Fig. 1. Generic illustration of the keystroke dynamics captured during the sentence transcription sessions.

2.2 Definition of Machine Learning Tasks

Five binary classification ML tasks were defined, having the common goal of distinguishing RMD patients with from healthy controls without hand joints affected. The tasks differed regarding the input data, ranging from the responses to the HAQ, EQ-5D, and HADS questionnaires, the execution times on the MPUT test, and numerical features retrieved from keyboard typing dynamics.

2.3   Data Processing

The processing stage of the keystroke typing logs was carried out in multiple sequential stages. As illustrated by Fig. 2, typing logs are first turned into two time series for each of the ten sentences: flight times and hold times. Next, each series is cropped into N evenly-sized windows, which we call phases. Within every window we compute a set of statistical and temporal features using TSFEL library [4]. Stacking those window-derived feature vectors yields a compact feature matrix that characterizes the typing dynamics of each subject. In this work, the number of features extracted from keystroke sequences was set to 88, between statistical and temporal. We established the number of windows as $N \in \{1, 3, 5\}$.

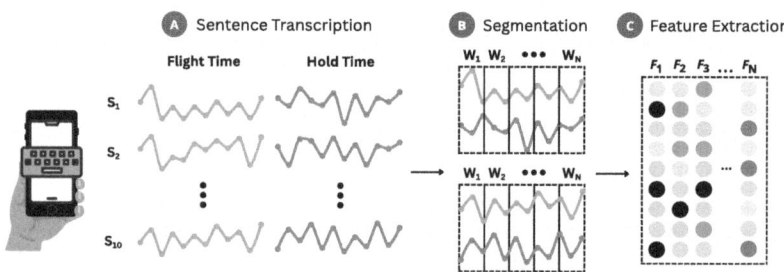

Fig. 2. Generic illustration of the keystroke dynamics captured during the sentence transcription sessions.

2.4   Model Training

Data was first split into 80% for training and 20% held out for final testing. From the 80% training set, we employed a 5-fold *StratifiedGroupKFold* cross-validation (stratified by class and grouped by subject) to select the best hyperparameters and model. Once the optimal configuration was identified, that model was retrained on the full 80% training data and then evaluated on the 20% test set. For the classification pipeline, classical ML algorithms were used to predict each sample into two classes. The training pipeline consisted of three sequential steps: (i) Scaler, where features were normalized using the interquartile range, (ii) Feature selector, where *SelectKBest* was applied to reduce dimensionality of the feature set (applies only to keyboard dynamics data, as questionnaire and functional tests data already had a reduced dimensionality); and (iii) Classification model, which includes Support Vector Machine (SVM), Random Forest (RF), K-Nearest Neighbor (KNN), and Light Gradient Boost Machine (LGBM) algorithms. Hyperparameter tuning was performed for each classifier using a randomized search on pre-defined grids, as detailed in Table 2.

2.5   Evaluation

Classification performance was assessed using (i) macro F1-score, to ensure equal weighting across all classes, (ii) balanced accuracy (BA), to account for any class imbalance, and (iii) the area under the ROC curve (AUROC), to capture the trade-off between sensitivity and specificity. Regarding keyboard-based models, probabilities of each sentence were aggregated using the median values of the model confidence scores (see Fig. 3). Confusion matrices also helped visually inspect patterns of misclassification. To interpret the contribution of features from keystroke dynamics, we analysed the results from *Shapley* values (SHAP) [13] displayed on a beeswarm chart.

Table 2. Hyperparameter search of the pre-defined classification models.

Algorithm	Parameter	Search Range
SVM	*C*	[0.1, 10]
	gamma	[0.001, 1]
	kernel	{linear, rbf, poly, sigmoid}
	degree	[2, 3, 4, 5]
RF	*n_ estimators*	[50, 200]
	max_ depth	[10, 50]
	min_ samples_ split	[2, 20]
	min_ samples_ leaf	[1, 20]
	max_ features	{sqrt, log2}
	criterion	{gini, entropy}
	max_ samples	[0.1, 1.0]
KNN	*n_ neighbors*	[1, 6]
	weights	{uniform, distance}
	metric	{euclidean, manhattan, chebyshev}
LGBM	*n_ estimators*	[50, 200]
	max_ depth	[10, 50]
	learning_ rate	[0.01, 0.3]
	num_ leaves	[20, 150]
	min_ child_ samples	[5, 100]
	reg_ alpha	[0.0, 1.0]
	reg_ lambda	[0.0, 1.0]

SVM – Support Vector Machine; **RF** – Random Forest; **KNN** – K-Nearest Neighbors; **LGBM** – Light Gradient Boosting Machine

3   Results

From a total of 59 participants, we excluded 4 subjects as 3 were patients without hand joints affected and 1 healthy control with joints affected. Considering we are drawing on insights taken from keystroke dynamics, we ensured patients did have

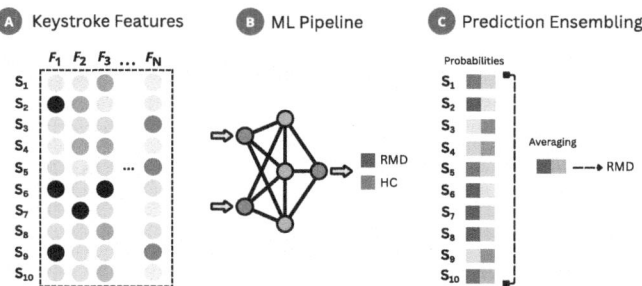

Fig. 3. Generic illustration of how the sentence-level predictions were combined and resulted in a subject-level prediction.

upper-level joint complaints and controls didn't, as it could corrupt our analysis. For the binary classification task, the distribution of classes was: 27 healthy controls without hand joints affected (HC) and 28 RMD patients with hand joints affected (RMD). The obtained results were meant to compare the efficiency of the keyboard-extracted metrics against (i) questionnaires and (ii) functional tests. During cross-validation, pipelines were optimized to maximize BA score for classification. For the keyboard-derived features, the training set was larger as each subject transcribed 10 sentences, totaling 430 samples from 42 subjects to train (HC - 210; RMD - 220). For testing, 110 samples from 11 individuals (HC - 50, RMD - 60) were available. This way, predictive performances were comparable between all data modalities. Table 3 describes the validation and testing performance obtained by the best obtained pipeline for each approach.

Table 3. Description of the main results for the binary classification task. Validation scores result from a 5-fold average. Best results are bolded and second best are underscored.

Data Modality	Best Algorithm	Performance Scores					
		F1-Score		BA		AUROC	
		Val.*	Test	Val.*	Test	Val.*	Test
Keyboard[a]	SVM	0.65 ± 0.10	0.83	0.65 ± 0.06	0.82	0.68 ± 0.09	0.87
HAQ	LGBM	0.75 ± 0.19	**0.91**	0.78 ± 0.19	**0.92**	0.85 ± 0.22	**0.92**
EQ-5D	KNN	0.75 ± 0.19	0.67	0.79 ± 0.16	0.75	0.81 ± 0.16	0.70
HADS	RF	0.72 ± 0.14	0.60	0.73 ± 0.14	0.65	0.74 ± 0.19	0.63
MPUT	KNN	0.55 ± 0.15	0.55	0.65 ± 0.10	0.55	0.67 ± 0.15	0.55

[a] – best signal split obtained with 3 windows; * – cross-validation

Among the different data modalities evaluated, the keyboard-derived features demonstrated competitive performance in distinguishing between RMD patients and healthy individuals. Despite showing slightly worse results during cross-validation, the performance on the test set improved across all metrics due to the sentence-based aggregation adopted. This strong generalization indicates that keyboard features extracted from touch-event dynamics can capture relevant motor patterns associated with RMD-related impairments. Although the HAQ questionnaire reached the highest overall performance, the confusion matrices showed that keyboard-based algorithms misclassified only one more subject than the HAQ-based models (see Fig. 4). In addition, the keyboard-based approach also outperformed other conventional modalities such as EQ-5D, HADS, and MPUT on the test set.

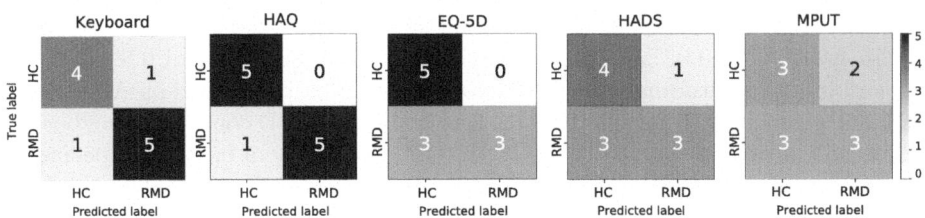

Fig. 4. Confusion matrices of the best models for each data modality evaluated.

Regarding feature importance, the beeswarm plot depicted in Fig. 5 built from computed Shapley values makes it clear that most of the model's decision-making comes from inter-key FT features: the median flight time (*FT_Median*), its minimum (*FT_Min*) and the very low-end quantile (*FT_ECDF_Percentile*) lays at the top of the importance list. In each case, higher values (red points) push the model output toward the RMD patient class, and lower values (blue points) toward healthy controls, i.e., RMD patients tend to pause longer between key presses than controls. With lower strength, the

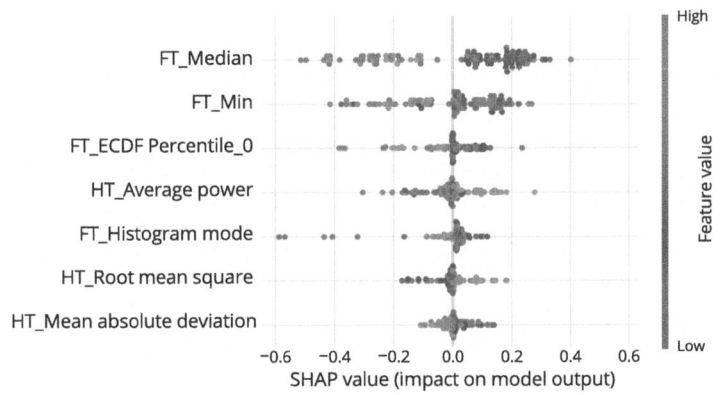

Fig. 5. Beeswarm chart illustrating shapley values (SHAP) computed for the best obtained keyboard-based model. Values presented refer to the RMD patient class. (Color figure online)

root-mean-square of hold times (*HT_Root mean square*) also seemed to reach lower values for RMD patients than controls.

4 Discussion

To the best of our knowledge, we found no studies specifically targeting RMD diagnosis using keyboard features. Nevertheless, for example, Giancardo et al. [9] used routine computer-keyboard hold times to distinguish early PD patients from controls with an AUROC of 0.81. Iakovakis et al. [11] leveraged touchscreen keystroke flight and hold times to detect fine-motor decline in early PD, achieving an AUROC of 0.92, and a specificity/sensitivity/specificity of 0.82/0.81. In an similar but longitudinal study, Arroyo-Gallego et al. [2] reached an AUROC of 0.83, and a sensitivity/specificity of 0.77/0.72. In our RMD cohort, the keyboard-derived SVM achieved a test AUROC of 0.87, sensitivity of 0.83, and specificity of 0.80, essentially identical to those reported in PD studies. Notably, the keyboard modality benefits from a larger training set due to multiple sentence-level samples per subject, and subject-level predictions were stabilized through aggregation of model confidences. These findings support the viability of passive, unobtrusive digital assessments as complementary tools for monitoring motor function in individuals with RMDs. Respecting feature importance, in fact, several previous work have suggested that declining upper-limb function reflects as longer keystroke latencies in MS patients. Lam et al. also reported that worse arm function correlates with longer typing latencies [12]. Chen et al. revealed MS patients typed slower ($p < .001$) and more variably ($p = .032$) than healthy controls [5]. The conclusions retrieved from our SHAP-derived feature importance patterns are in line with previous MS and PD literature, which adds consistency to the fact that keystroke dynamics capture shared motor impairments (slowed and inconsistent keystrokes) that are transversal to multiple diagnoses.

Despite the promising results, our work has several limitations. Our binary labels relied on self-reported hand complaints rather than objective clinical hand-function scores, and all RMD subjects happened to report hand complaints, which may have simplified the problem. A larger cohort with clinically validated hand-function indicators would strengthen phenotype definitions, enable multiclass distinctions, and provide a more rigorous test of keyboard biomarkers. This would also help investigate and stress test the model, in more detail, not only for different RMD phenotypes but also against sub-group minorities (e.g., young males, people from non-western countries or lower technological literacy).

5 Conclusion

In this work, we have demonstrated that passive keyboard-derived metrics can discriminate RMD patients with hand joint pain from HCs without affected joints with a promising performance, outperforming most validated PROMs and functional tests. These findings mirror prior studies investigating fine-motor impairment with Parkinson's and MS patients, confirming that slowed typing keystroke patterns are a shared motor-impairment signature across diverse patient populations. By drawing insights from open data, our work also contributes to open-science and encourages other groups to fill the gap of AI research scarcity in rheumatology. Future perspectives should gather efforts to collect data from broader and more diverse RMD populations, integrate standardized hand-function assessments for ground truth labeling, and explore multi-group assessments to distinguish disease subtypes or severity levels. Importantly, incorporating keyboard-derived metrics could also help rheumatologists prioritize patients more objectively according to their hand function. From a clinical perspective, using typing dynamic metrics could enable more severe individuals (e.g., longer typing latency) to be fast-tracked for specialist evaluation, ensuring that those with early or subtle hand-function decline receive timely intervention. Integrating these scalable digital assessments into rheumatology referral procedures will introduce objective, data-driven criteria to complement and (potentially) improve traditional diagnosis and prioritization strategies currently in force.

Acknowledgments. This work was supported by the project RheumaAID (with DOI 10.54499/2024.07650.IACDC) and the project UID/04923, both funded by the national funds of the Foundation for Science and Technology (FCT).

Disclosure of Interests. The authors have no competing interests to declare that are relevant to the content of this article.

References

1. Acien, A., et al.: A novel digital tool for detection and monitoring of amyotrophic lateral sclerosis motor impairment and progression via keystroke dynamics. Sci. Rep. **14**, 16851 (2024). https://doi.org/10.1038/s41598-024-67940-8
2. Arroyo-Gallego, T., et al.: Detecting motor impairment in early Parkinson's disease via natural typing interaction with keyboards: validation of the neuroqwerty approach in an uncontrolled at-home setting. J. Med. Internet Res. **20**(3), e89 (2018). https://doi.org/10.2196/jmir.9462
3. Arroyo-Gallego, T., et al.: Detection of motor impairment in Parkinson's disease via mobile touchscreen typing. IEEE Trans. Biomed. Eng. **64**(9), 1994–2002 (2017). https://doi.org/10.1109/TBME.2017.2664802
4. Barandas, M., et al.: TSFEL: time series feature extraction library. SoftwareX **11**, 100456 (2020). https://doi.org/10.1016/j.softx.2020.100456
5. Chen, M.H., et al.: Associations between smartphone keystroke dynamics and cognition in MS. Digit. Health **8**, 20552076221143230 (2022). https://doi.org/10.1177/20552076221143234
6. Duruöz, M.T., Öz, N., Karabulut, Y., Gürsoy, D.E., Gezer, H.H., Kasman, S.A.: Validity and psychometric characteristics of the Duruöz Hand Index (DHI) in patients with systemic sclerosis. Rheumatol. Int. **45**, 75 (2025). https://doi.org/10.1007/s00296-025-05829-z
7. Fadul, R., AlShehhi, A., Hadjileontiadis, L.: Robust remote detection of depressive tendency based on keystroke dynamics and behavioural characteristics. Sci. Rep. **14**, 28025 (2024). https://doi.org/10.1038/s41598-024-78489-x

8. Fu, Y., et al.: Smartphone-based hand function assessment: systematic review. J. Med. Internet Res. **26**, e51564 (2024). https://doi.org/10.2196/51564

9. Giancardo, L., et al.: Computer keyboard interaction as an indicator of early Parkinson's disease. Sci. Rep. **6**, 34468 (2016). https://doi.org/10.1038/srep34468

10. Hoeijmakers, A., et al.: Disease severity classification using passively collected smartphone-based keystroke dynamics within multiple sclerosis. Sci. Rep. **13**, 1871 (2023). https://doi.org/10.1038/s41598-023-28990-6

11. Iakovakis, D., Hadjidimitriou, S., Charisis, V., Bostantzopoulou, S., Katsarou, Z., Hadjileontiadis, L.J.: Touchscreen typing-pattern analysis for detecting fine motor skills decline in early-stage Parkinson's disease. Sci. Rep. **8**(1), 7663 (2018). https://doi.org/10.1038/s41598-018-25999-0

12. Lam, K.H., et al.: The use of smartphone keystroke dynamics to passively monitor upper limb and cognitive function in multiple sclerosis: longitudinal analysis. J. Med. Internet Res. **24**(11), e37614 (2022). https://doi.org/10.2196/37614

13. Lundberg, S.M., Lee, S.I.: A unified approach to interpreting model predictions. In: Guyon, I., et al. (eds.) Advances in Neural Information Processing Systems, vol. 30, pp. 4765–4774. Curran Associates, Inc. (2017)

14. Macias Alonso, A.K., Hirt, J., Woelfle, T., Janiaud, P., Hemkens, L.G.: Definitions of digital biomarkers: a systematic mapping of the biomedical literature. BMJ Health Care Inform. **31**(1), e100914 (2024). https://doi.org/10.1136/bmjhci-2023-100914

15. Matias, P., et al.: Cotidiana dataset - smartphone-collected data on the mobility, finger dexterity, and mental health of people with rheumatic and musculoskeletal diseases. IEEE J. Biomed. Health Inform. **28**(11), 6538–6547 (2024). https://doi.org/10.1109/JBHI.2024.3456069

16. Matias, P., et al.: Cotidiana dataset (2024). https://doi.org/10.5281/zenodo.13628911

17. Nagel, J., Wegener, F., Grim, C., Hoppe, M.W.: Effects of digital physical health exercises on musculoskeletal diseases: systematic review with best-evidence synthesis. JMIR Mhealth Uhealth **12**, e50616 (2024). https://doi.org/10.2196/50616

18. Nunes, F., Rato Grego, P., Araújo, R., Silva, P.A.: Self-report user interfaces for patients with rheumatic and musculoskeletal diseases: app review and usability experiments with mobile user interface components. Comput. Graph. **117**, 61–72 (2023). https://doi.org/10.1016/j.cag.2023.10.009

19. Silva, P.G., Jones, A., da Rocha Correa Fernandes, A., Natour, J.: Moberg picking-up test in patients with hand osteoarthritis. J. Hand Ther. **30**(4), 522–528 (2017). https://doi.org/10.1016/j.jht.2016.10.005

20. Sobue, Y., et al.: Validation of grip strength as a measure of frailty in rheumatoid arthritis. Sci. Rep. **12**, 21090 (2022). https://doi.org/10.1038/s41598-022-21533-5

21. Tat, T., Chen, G., Xu, J., Zhao, X., Fang, Y., Chen, J.: Diagnosing Parkinson's disease via behavioral biometrics of keystroke dynamics. Sci. Adv. **11**(14), eadt6631 (2025). https://doi.org/10.1126/sciadv.adt6631

Dual Watermarking with Deep Learning for Enhancing Security of Medical Images

Rajat Sood[1], Jyoti Rani[2], and Ashima Anand[1](✉)

[1] CSED, Thapar Institute of Engineering and Technology, Patiala, Punjab, India
{rsood_be21,ashima.anand}@thapar.edu
[2] Department of Artificial Intelligence and Machine Learning, Manipal University,
Jaipur, Rajasthan, India
jyoti.rani@jaipur.manipal.edu

Abstract. The rapid development of deep neural networks has prompted significant research into watermarking techniques for medical imaging based on deep learning. Ensuring copyright protection by watermarking medical images, particularly chest X-ray images is imperative. However, numerous extant methods cannot effectively utilize image characteristics to achieve embedding and extraction. This study introduces a new dual watermarking system that is based on deep learning and utilizes the Redundant Discrete Wavelet Transform (RDWT) to improve both imperceptibility and robustness. The proposed architecture utilizes a normalizing flow technique within the encoder to seamlessly embed a watermark into a medical cover image, resulting in a securely encoded output. Furthermore, the encoded image incorporates a sophisticated security layer to enhance its protection. The system's robustness is further enhanced by adding a noise layer between the encoder and decoder, designed to separate the secret image with minimal loss. Our approach obtains watermark robustness and imperceptibility that are significantly superior to existing methods, as evidenced by extensive evaluations. Pixel loss can often be below 0.1%. Our method separates secret images with indistinguishable visual quality from the original secret image, as proven by experimental studies conducted on a ChestXray dataset obtained from NIH. The superiority of our dual watermarking architecture over contemporary methodologies is further validated by comparative analysis.

Keywords: Security · Encryption · Deep learning · Data Hiding · Medical Images

1 Introduction

In recent years, verifying the truthfulness and security of medical images has grown more crucial in the digital age, since the widespread availability of digital media and the Internet has greatly eased the unauthorized utilization and alteration of these sensitive images [12]. In the past, people used techniques like physical inscriptions or simple digital tagging to establish ownership. However,

J. Valente de Oliveira et al. (Eds.): EPIA 2025, LNAI 16121, pp. 93–105, 2026.
https://doi.org/10.1007/978-3-032-05176-9_8

these approaches were susceptible to tampering or removal. Given the importance of medical images in diagnosis, training, and research, it is essential to prioritize the protection of their accuracy and the verification of their origin. Digital watermarking provides an evident solution to these difficulties. The process entails the integration of a watermark, which contains unique ownership or source details, directly into medical images [11]. The purpose of this embedded data is to be undetectable so as to not affect the quality of the images while still being able to be retrieved to prove authenticity and ownership when necessary. The approach must possess sufficient resilience to withstand a range of potential attacks that seek to modify or eliminate the watermark [1,9]. This highlights the crucial requirement for improved watermarking technologies that preserve both the integrity of the image and the imperceptibility of the watermark [8,10].

Conventional methods for watermarking have mostly depended on deterministic algorithms, utilizing techniques like the Discrete Cosine Transform (DCT), Discrete Wavelet Transform (DWT), Discrete Fourier Transform (DFT), and Quantization Index Modulation and DWT. These techniques include watermarks into an image either in the spatial or frequency domains, and each method has its own unique advantages in terms of durability and imperceptibility [4,6]. An exemplary instance is the hybrid DWT-DFT technique, which distinguishes itself due to its robustness against JPEG compression and geometric modifications. This quality is particularly vital in medical imaging applications, where image compression and transformation are common [11]. Although deterministic algorithms are successful, their inflexibility can lead to the inability to retrieve watermarks from modified images reliably. This is particularly problematic in medical situations, where image modifications may be necessary for legal purposes [4,6,7]. A hybrid combination of deterministic and deep learning-based watermarking has been investigated to utilize digital watermarking. This hybrid technique provides flexible and robust methods for watermarking, enabling the discovery of the best ways to embed and remove watermarks that can withstand different attacks and changes. This guarantees that the integrity and ownership of medical images are consistently preserved. This paper introduces a hybrid combination of wavelet transform and DNN-based medical image steganography to embed and extract the information. Firstly, Redundant DWT (RDWT) is used to preprocess the cover image and then embed the secret image inside the particular component 'LL' of the cover image using deep learning-based Medical Image Watermarking (MIW). The deep learning method uses three separate networks, including the preparation, hiding, and reveal networks, to enhance resilience and imperceptibility. Experiments demonstrate that RDWT serves as a preprocessing strategy that improves the robustness of deep learning networks by maintaining invisibility and simplifying the model. In addition, other attacks are employed to augment the model's adaptability in countering attacks. The experimental and comparative analysis proves that the proposed work gives the best results in terms of imperceptibility, robustness, and security compared to existing works. The major contributions of the paper are as follows:

- **Preprocessing technique/enhancing payload using RDWT:** Unlike DWT, the RDWT technique has a shift-invariance property, which maintains the high payload for efficient information concealment without compromising image quality, making it perfect for medical imaging applications.
- **Encoder-Decoder based embedding and extraction of dual marks:** A sophisticated twelve-layered encoder design is used for the embedding procedure. This specialized deep neural network is created to perfectly include two secret images into a cover image, guaranteeing that the embedded watermark is undetectable and preserves the medical image's usefulness. Further, two 12-layered decoders use the reveal network individually to extract the two secret images with minimal loss.
- **Enhanced security using hybrid encryption:** A 6-D hyperchaotic system is employed in combination with DNA encoding to ensure the security of the encoded cover image.
- **Robustness against Attacks:** In this work, common types of attacks are used to target the encoded cover image to distort or eliminate the embedded watermark. These assaults encompass Gaussian noise, speckle noise, sharpen attack, etc. These attacks are employed to test the resilience of the watermarking approach in a healthcare environment.
- **Experimental and Comparative Analysis-** The proposed work undergoes experimental testing to evaluate its performance using metrics like Peak Signal-to-Noise Ratio (PSNR), Structural Similarity Index (SSIM), and pixel loss. The performance of the proposed approach is also evaluated by comparing it with other cutting-edge watermarking approaches that employ DWT.

2   Proposed Methodology

A dual watermarking technique using Deep Learning is proposed to achieve both invisibility and robustness of the watermarked image. The algorithm for automatically hiding and revealing (through two secret images) within a single cover image is proposed, ensuring invisibility and robustness against different attacks. One characteristic that makes watermarking digitally valuable for health services is integrating medical images enabled by dual watermarking, which is essential for enhancing the availability and privacy of susceptible data such as patient records. The proposed diagram and algorithm of dual medical image watermarking based on images is presented in Fig. 1 and Algorithm 1.

2.1   Proposed Approach

- **Cover Images:** A cover image(grayscale) of pixel size 128×128 is taken after applying the RDWT.
- **Secret Images:** Two secret images (grayscale) of same pixel size 128×128 are embedded in the cover image by the encoder architecture.

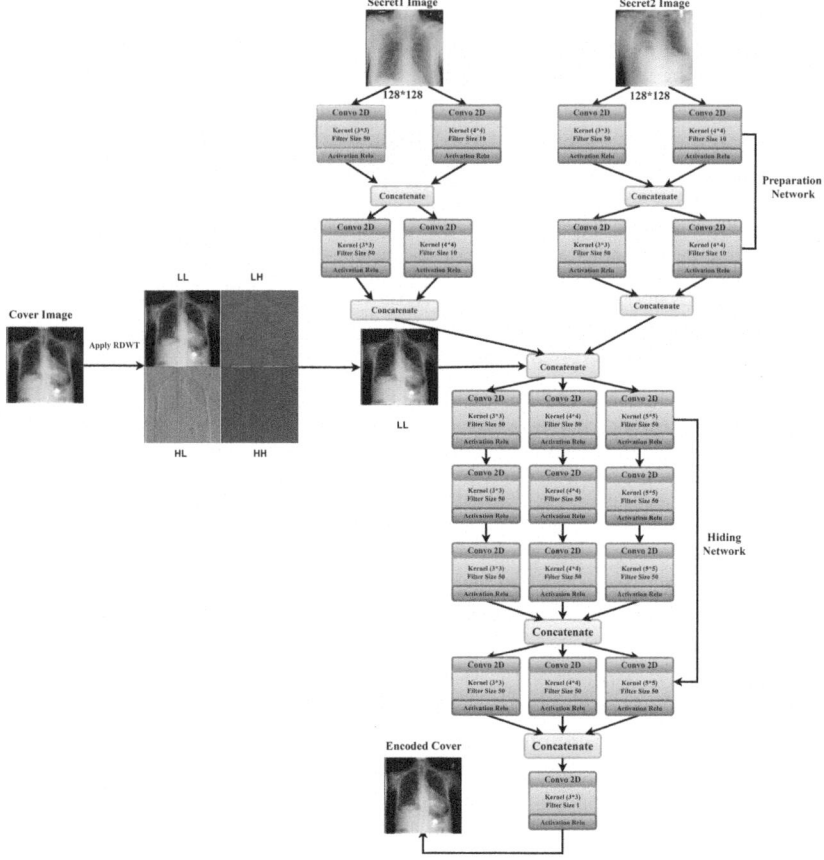

Fig. 1. Proposed diagram

- **Encoder:** The cover image and the two secret images (in grayscale format with dimensions $1 \times H \times W$) are taken by encoder, and a generated image is passed in place of main LL components and applies inverse RDWT to generate the encoded cover image, as shown in Fig. 1.
- **Noises Attack:** Different types of noise distortions are added at random to the watermarked image, creating a noisy version while preserving the original size. The robustness of our model is also evaluated, as demonstrated in the results section.
- **Decoder:** The secret image 1 and secret image 2 are retrieved from the image with noise by the model's two distinct decoders.

2.2   Model Architecture

- **Preparation Network:** Each preparation layer consists of 2 layers with a Relu activation function. Each of the preparation layer is composed of four

---

Algorithm 1: Embedding process using deep learning

Input   : Cover Image (CI), Secret Image1(SI1), Secret Image2(SI2)

Output: Encoded Image (EI), extracted secret images(ext_SI1, ext_SI2)

// Step:1 Use dataset for pre-processing

1    $Resize(CI, SI1, SI2)128 \times 128$;

// Step:2 Apply RDWT on CI of size 128×128

2   [LL,LH,HL,HH] $\leftarrow RDWT(CI)$;

// Step:3 Apply two preparation network for SI1 and SI2 in enocoder

3    $x3, x4 \leftarrow prep\_S1(conv\_layers = 2, channels = 50, 10, Kernelsize = 3, 4, Strides = (1,1), padding\_type =' same', activation =' RELU')(SI1)$;

// Step:4 concatenate x3,x4 layers

4    $x \leftarrow Concat([x3, x4])$;

5    $x3, x4 \leftarrow prep\_S1(conv\_layers = 2, channels = 50, 10, Kernelsize = 3, 4, Strides = (1,1), padding\_type =' same', activation =' RELU')(x)$;

// Step:5 concatenate x3,x4 layers

6    $x1 \leftarrow Concat([x3, x4])$;

7    $x3, x4 \leftarrow prep\_S2(conv\_layers = 2, channels = 50, 10, Kernelsize = 3, 4, Strides = (1,1), padding\_type =' same', activation =' RELU')(SI2)$;

// Step:6 concatenate x3,x4 layers

8    $x \leftarrow Concat([x3, x4])$;

9    $x3, x4 \leftarrow prep\_S2(conv\_layers = 2, channels = 50, 10, Kernelsize = 3, 4, Strides = (1,1), padding\_type =' same', activation =' RELU')(x)$;

// Step:5 concatenate x3,x4 layers

10    $x2 \leftarrow Concat([x3, x4])$;

// Step:6 Concatenate the prep outputs with the 'LL' component

11    $x = concatenate([LL, x1, x2])$;

// Step:7 Apply step 12 convolution layer and then concatenate

12    $x3, x4, x5 \leftarrow preps_S1(conv\_layers \leftarrow 3, channels = 50, Kernelsize = 3, Strides = (1,1), padding\_type =' same', activation =' RELU')(x, x3, x4)$;

// Step:4 Repeat step 7 three times and then concatenate to get encoded LL

13 $EI\_LL \leftarrow Conv2D(1, (3,3), strides = (1,1), padding =' same', activation =' relu', name =' output'_C)(encoded\_img)$;

// Step:8 Apply inverse RDWT to get encoded image(WI of size 128×128

14    $EI \leftarrow IRDWT(EI\_LL, LH, HL, HH)$;

// Step:9 Apply two Decoders for extracting the Secret images.

15    $ext\_SI1, ext\_SI2 \leftarrow Conv2D(1, (3,3), strides = (1,1), padding =' same', activation =' tanh', name =' output\_S')(EI)$;

---

distinct Convolutional 2D (Convo 2D) layers. The secret image is received as input by the first two layers with a kernel size of 3×3 and 4×4 respectively, with a total of 50 and 10 channels. The output of these two layers are concatenated and then used as input to the subsequent layers, which follow the same structure as described above. In each Convo 2D layer padding is same and strides length is remain constant at 1 to ensure that the output retained the same dimensions as input.

- **Hiding Network:** The hiding network aggregates three layers, each consisting of three Convo 2D layers. The hiding network1 consists of separate three Convo 2D layers, each of kernel size is 3×3 and filter size of 50. The output of the preparation layer is passed only to the first layer of the hiding network1, each subsequent layers received the input from the output of its respective preceding layers. Network 1 produces the output denoted as x1. Similarly, Network 2 and 3 consists of 3 Convo 2D layers with kernel sizes of 4×4 and 5×5 respectively, both with a filter size of 50. The output of Networks 1, 2 and 3 are concatenated and passed into the final hiding network, consists of 3 separate Convo 2D layer with kernel sizes of 3×3, 4×4 and 5×5 respectively, and a filter size of 50, The output of the hiding network is concatenated and passed to the final layer of kernel size 3×3 with a total of 1 channel, producing the final watermarked image as illustrated in Fig. 1.
- **Reveal Network:** The revealing network and each individual revealed network, is characterized by three uniformly configured Convo 2D layers. Initially, the watermarked image is processed through a reveal network comprising of three layers with identical kernel sizes and filters as the hiding network. The output of each network is concatenated and then passed to the reveal network consisting of three Convo 2D layers with kernel sizes of 3×3, 4×4 and 5×5 respectively and each have filter size of 50. The output of reveal network is finally passed to the final layer of kernel size 3×3 with a total of 1 channel, to produce the decoded secret image 1. The tanh activation function is used only in the final layer, providing an output range of $[-1, 1]$, which after normalization, aligns with the pixel value range for grayscale images. The same process is repeated for to get the decoded secret image 2.

2.3   6-Dimensional Hyperchaotic System and DNA Encoding Based Image Encryption Algorithm

An image encryption algorithm that utilizes a 6D high-dimensional chaotic system and DNA encoding technique is used to secure the encoded cover image (EI). Initially, a highly complex 6D hyper-chaotic system is utilized as the source of random streams. It produces six distinct chaotic streams with a key and the same features as the EI. Then, it categorizes the six streams into two different categories, one for permutation and the other for diffusion. It also implements pixel-level and DNA-level permutations to ensure the efficiency and security of the permutation process. These permutations weaken the association between the pixels in the EI and the encrypted image. The two permutation operations in the image encryption technique effectively resist shear attacks. This study performs pixel-level and DNA-level diffusion operations on chaotic images following permutation, as the permutation does not alter the distribution and average of pixels. The detailed steps of encryption and decryption are given in Algorithm 2

2.4   Dataset

The dataset of chest X-rays from the NIH is used for dual watermarking. The dataset has high-resolution grayscale medical images. It acts as an important

---

Algorithm 2: Encryption technique based 3D Logistic Map and Improved Chirikov Map

---

    Input   : Encoded Image(c')
    Output: Encrypted Encoded Image(c_e'), Key
    // Stage:1 Generate diffusion and scrambling keys using chaotic
       sequence
1 $[d_k, s_k] \leftarrow C_s(c')$
    // Stage:2 Scramble the original image
2 $Scrambled\_img \leftarrow scramble(c', s_k)$
    // Stage:3 Diffuse the scrambled image
3 $diffused\_img \leftarrow diffuse(Scrambled\_img, d_k)$
    // Stage:4 Encrypt the diffused image with DNA computing
4 $enrypted\_img \leftarrow encrypt(diffused\_img, DCP)$
    // Stage:5 Decrypt the encrypted image
5 $decrypted\_img \leftarrow decrypt(encrypted\_img, DCP)$
    // Stage:6 Dediffuse the diffused image
6 $dediffused\_img \leftarrow dediffuse(diffused\_img, d_k)$
    // Stage:6 Descramble the dediffused image
7 $descrambled\_img \leftarrow descramble\_img(dediffused\_img, s_k)$
8   **return** *Encrypted Encoded Image*

Table 1. Results at different epochs

Epochs	PSNR (in dB)	SSIM	PE_Cover	PE_S1	PE_S2	NC1	NC2
50	84.30	1	3.9617	16.0821	12.5511	0.9669	0.9741
100	86.48	1	3.0820	10.0362	10.7798	0.9733	0.9819
300	87.26	1	2.8177557	8.20569	9.8238	0.9928	0.9843
500	89.01	1	2.3038	6.4287	6.1369	0.9958	0.9944

benchmarking tool to assess the effectiveness and detectability of the model proposed for dual watermarking. The dataset has the extensive pictorial content available; important in assessing any watermarking technology on visual diagnostic data. Pilot studies were conducted to investigate image-guided quality control effects of the method in diagnosis. In addition, the fact that it proved useful in protecting images used for medical purposes (where image integrity is crucial) serves as evidence that our implementation suffices to be applied even within an originally supposed-to-be/frame-described iconoclastic setting like medicine. Moreover, the current approach uses a crackdown on resilient valuation of watermarked solution against various kinds of attacks which is essential from the view point of applications side in medicine.

3   Results and Comparative Analysis

This section assesses the proposed method's efficacy by employing various performance metrics, including PSNR, SSIM, and Normalized Correlation Coeffi-

Table 2. Result analysis of different parameters based on different attacks

Attacks	Intensity	PE_Cover	PE_S1	PE_S2	NC1	NC2
Gaussian	0.05	4.55869331	10.9333819	13.811886	0.98251945	0.98175066
	0.1	4.666524	13.743373	13.435401	0.97435206	0.98896897
Speckle	0.05	3.2508879	10.836102	11.714768	0.97529066	0.9737767
	0.1	4.306153	14.068327	10.960925	0.9622754	0.968244
Salt & Pepper	0.05	3.722591	9.930207	13.000387	0.9890923	0.9775357
	0.1	2.7859776	12.677916	9.507217	0.9595012	0.9882723
Median Noise	0.05	5.5402203	18.631006	17.06291	0.9701962	0.97198945
	0.1	4.55376	17.259918	17.877663	0.97121996	0.9571555
Sharpen Attack	0.05	3.6847718	13.748597	11.123889	0.9823737	0.98124564
	0.1	2.5784552	12.944917	13.227106	0.97735476	0.9880454
Dropout	0.05	2.228641	9.189903	9.562469	0.9777198	0.9894822
	0.1	2.0962167	13.673712	12.363263	0.9824435	0.98996514
Apply Blur	0.05	3.2127206	11.0378275	10.427054	0.9707387	0.98431563
	0.1	3.9685705	11.895489	10.841579	0.96217144	0.9829707
Gaussian Dropout	0.05	6.69157	18.08521	16.224169	0.9629389	0.96988404
	0.1	7.738617	20.117647	19.594662	0.956451	0.95586395
Alpha Dropout	0.05	2.00537	8.0993185	9.886955	0.9932941	0.9872363
	0.1	3.3559496	11.22247	18.50422	0.9874094	0.9599164

cient (NC). PSNR and SSIM have been implemented to guarantee imperceptibility and robustness. On the other hand, the NC score is often used to assess
resilience's effectiveness. This proposed work is implemented using Python 3.9.18
based on TensorFlow 2.10.1, which was trained on an NVIDIA RTX A5000 GPU.
Both of the image's dimensions were given as 128 pixels. During the training
phase, each model passes through many epochs with a batch size of 32. The
Adam algorithm is used for gradient optimization, and the learning rate is set at
0.001. It uses the Rectified Linear Unit (ReLU) as an activation function. The
Adam optimizer, learning rate, and loss function are utilized during model training. The ChestXray images dataset from NIH, which comprises 10,000 images,
is employed to train and evaluate the dual medical image watermarking model
based on deep learning. The model employs cover images that are 128 × 128
pixels in size. Python is utilized to conduct each investigation. Watermarks are
applied to 3000 images, with 1000 images designated as the cover, secret image1,
and secret2. PSNR and SSIM are employed to compute the comparison between
the cover and watermarked images. The difference between the cover and the
watermarked image is demonstrated by pixel error C. The difference between
secret and extracted secret images is measured by pixel error S. The pixel error
closest to 0 is always the best.

Table 3. Average performance analysis of different parameters using 20 images

IMG	PSNR (dB)	SSIM	PE_cover	PE_SE1	PE_SE2	NC1	NC2
IMG1	89.31	1	2.22618	7.36582	4.45949	0.98960114	0.9949733
IMG2	89.01	1	2.30385	6.42877	6.13691	0.99581432	0.99442405
IMG3	87.73	1	2.67008	7.11023	6.92217	0.98942506	0.994757
IMG4	87.27	1	2.81607	7.96285	6.01054	0.9941287	0.99523139
IMG5	88.39	1	2.47417	8.08364	6.65757	0.98032498	0.99286169
IMG6	88.62	1	2.41171	7.23227	7.3892	0.99448699	0.99196678
IMG7	88.33	1	2.49118	7.12234	6.26266	0.99342108	0.99515003
IMG8	88.02	1	2.58163	9.36045	6.53078	0.99190754	0.99315429
IMG9	87.97	1	2.5974	6.4407	3.84893	0.9911207	0.99733186
IMG10	88.36	1	2.48443	7.40761	7.07728	0.99143076	0.99450284
AVERAGE	**88.0015**	**1**	**2.5951045**	**7.6846825**	**6.087505**	**0.99143742**	**0.99463811**

Table 4. Security Analysis of encoded cover image

Sample Image	Entropy	NPCR	UACI
	7.9964	0.996155	0.332
	7.996	0.9961	0.3457
	7.9969	0.9957	0.3229
	7.9963	0.9964	0.3306
Avg of 20 images	**7.9964**	**0.9960**	**0.3191**

Table 5. Comparative analysis of proposed approach in terms of imperceptibility

Parameters	Ref. [13]	Ref. [2]	Ref. [5]	Proposed Work
PSNR (in dB)	47.49	39.592	50.27	89.01
SSIM	0.9965	0.9812	0.99704	1

The results of various assessment parameters as a function of the iterations range from 50 to 500 are presented in Table 1. PSNR and NC values are 89.01 decibels and 0.9958, respectively. The pixel error for the Secret image is 6.4287, whereas the pixel error for the Cover image is 6.1369. Increasing the number of iterations has yielded promising results in terms of pixel error loss, as indicated

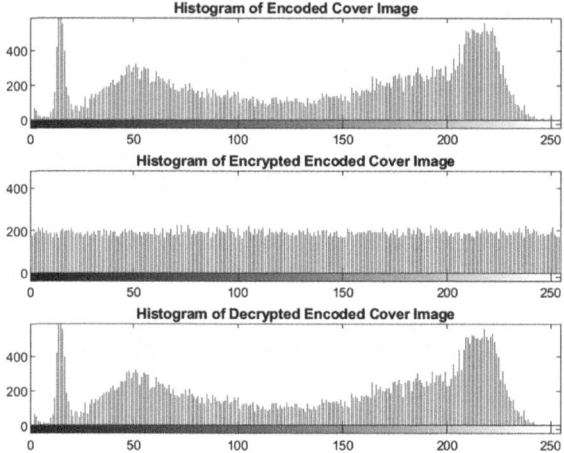

Fig. 2. Histogram of Encoded Image

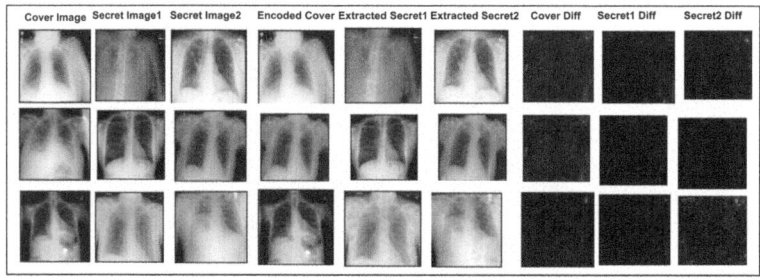

Fig. 3. Sample images of Cover, Secret1 & Secret2 before and after embedding diagram

in Table 1. It additionally offers enhanced resilience for secret image1 and secret image2, with respective values of 0.9958 and 0.9944.

The histogram analysis clearly demonstrates a strong correlation between the cover and encoded cover, as well as the secret and decoded secret images, which suggests a high level of acceptance. This correlation is statistically significant and satisfies the acceptable criteria. The results are illustrated in Figs. 3, which represent the cover and concealed images prior to and following the model's execution for 500 epochs, respectively. It also display the residual difference between cover and encoded cover, Secret1 and Extracted secret1, and secret2 and extracted secret2. Result analysis of different parameters based on different attacks is given in Table 2. All attacks gives acceptable value which proves that the proposed work is robust in all cases. This hybrid framework achieves an average PSNR of 88.0015dB and a SSIM of 1, as shown in Table 3.

The average pixel error values for cover, secret1, and secret2 pixels are 2.595, 7.684, and 6.0875, respectively. In terms of robustness, the average NC values of 'PE_S1' and 'PE_S2' are 0.9914 and 0.9946, respectively.

Table 6. Comparative analysis of proposed approach with existing ones against several attacks

Attacks	Ref. [3]	Ref. [2]		Proposed Work	
	NC	NC1	NC2	NC1	NC2
Median Filter	0.9424	0.944043	0.85577	0.9701	0.9719
Gaussian Noise	0.9983	0.97436	0.991252	0.9825	0.9817
Salt & Pepper	0.9969	0.976195	0.989586	0.98909	0.9775
Speckle (0.001)	0.999	0.98598	0.999418	0.9752	0.9737
Motion Blur	0.9473	0.929237	0.99923	0.9707	0.9843
Sharpening	0.9891	0.9989	0.9998	0.9823	0.9812

The proposed encryption method is robust, as shown by Entropy, NPCR and UACI. The NPCR value is 99.61%, and the UACI value is 33.46%. Table 4 displays the outcomes of the security applications, with the maximum values for NPCR and UACI being 0.9960 and 0.3357, respectively. The entropy value closest to 8 is considered best. Among the 20 images, the highest entropy value achieved is 7.9964. Figure 2 illustrates the histogram of the cover image after it has been encoded, encrypted, and decrypted. NC value shows that our model is resilient against most attacks using intensity values 0.05 and 0.1. A value greater than 0.7 is considered acceptable for robustness. The proposed work produces satisfactory NC outcomes in all cases of attacks. An Alpha Dropout assault achieves a superior maximum PSNR of 90.22 dB and NC is 0.9932, which is best as compared to another attack. Our strategy substantially decreases pixel error loss, approaching less than 0.1% in all cases of attack except Gaussian dropout. The proposed method is compared to various deep learning-based watermarking techniques to see how well it performs. The results can be seen in Table 5. Our proposed methodology not only provides information on the dataset used, but it also exceeds earlier current methods regarding invisibility. Lastly, our technique outperforms other methods with a PSNR of 89.01 dB. Our method achieves better results than previous research, as shown in the Table, even when considering the most exceptional SSIM values. The suggested method has a correlation of 0.9912, which is 0.212% higher than previous research and effectively produces high-quality hidden images. Several attacks are applied on encoded images to verify our method's superiority and assess the results. The nine attacks we developed are listed in Table 6 and include Gaussian, Speckle, S & P, Median, sharpen, Dropout, Blur, Gaussian Blur, and Alpha dropout. The proposed study yields superior outcomes when compared to other existing references, such as Ref [3] and Ref [2],

4   Conclusion

This paper proposes a novel RDWT-based deep learning medical image watermarking (MIW). RDWT has shift-invariance and redundancy qualities that allow for the secure insertion of watermarks without compromising the quality of the cover image, which is essential in healthcare diagnostics. Deep learning models that have a 12×12 encoder-decoder architecture which is a very effective approach in the field of medical image watermarking. Several types of attacks is used to check the robustness of proposed work. The distortion loss has been prevented with little degradation in the quality of the secret information image, which is essential for applications such as POC and E-Healthcare. The method is better suited for preserving utility in digital medical image-sharing applications. Future work will include testing the proposed solution for other medical image dataset applications.

Disclosure of Interests. The authors have no competing interests to declare that are relevant to the content of this article.

References

1. Ambika, Virupakshappa, Uplaonkar, D.S.: Deep learning-based coverless image steganography on medical images shared via cloud. Eng. Proc. **59**(1), 176 (2024)
2. Amrit, P., Baranwal, N., Singh, K.N., Singh, A.K.: Convnet-hide: deep learning-based dual watermarking for healthcare images. IEEE Multimed. (2024)
3. Amrit, P., Singh, A.K., Singh, M.P., Agrawal, A.K.: Embedr-net: using CNN to embed mark with recovery through deep convolutional GAN for secure ehealth systems. IEEE Trans. Consum. Electron. **69**(4), 1017–1022 (2023)
4. Chen, C., Zhang, Y., Xiao, B., Cheng, M., Zhang, J., Li, H.: Deep learning-based image steganography for visual data cybersecurity in construction management. J. Constr. Eng. Manag. **150**(10), 04024125 (2024)
5. Garcia-Nonoal, Z., Mata-Mendoza, D., Cedillo-Hernandez, M., Nakano-Miyatake, M.: Secure management of retinal imaging based on deep learning, zero-watermarking and reversible data hiding. Vis. Comput. **40**(1), 245–260 (2024)
6. Hemalatha, J., Geetha, S., Mohan, S., Nivetha, S.: An efficient steganalysis of medical images by using deep learning based discrete scalable alex net convolutionary neural networks classifier. J. Med. Imaging Health Inform. **11**(10), 2667–2674 (2021)
7. Himthani, V., Dhaka, V.S., Kaur, M., Rani, G., Oza, M., Lee, H.N.: Comparative performance assessment of deep learning based image steganography techniques. Sci. Rep. **12**(1), 16895 (2022)
8. Priya, S., Abirami, S., Arunkumar, B., Mishachandar, B.: Super-resolution deep neural network (SRDNN) based multi-image steganography for highly secured lossless image transmission. Sci. Rep. **14**(1), 6104 (2024)
9. Rajesh Kumar, N., Bala Krishnan, R., Manikandan, G., Subramaniyaswamy, V., Kotecha, K.: Reversible data hiding scheme using deep learning and visual cryptography for medical image communication. J. Electron. Imaging **31**(6), 063028 (2022)
10. Saidi, H., Tibermacine, O., Elhadad, A.: High-capacity data hiding for medical images based on the mask-RCNN model. Sci. Rep. **14**(1), 7166 (2024)
11. Sukumar, A., Subramaniyaswamy, V., Ravi, L., Vijayakumar, V., Indragandhi, V.: Robust image steganography approach based on RIWT-laplacian pyramid and histogram shifting using deep learning. Multimed. Syst. **27**, 651–666 (2021)

12. Sultan, B., Wani, M.A.: Enhancing steganography capacity through multi-stage generator model in generative adversarial network based image concealment. J. Electron. Imaging **33**(3), 033026 (2024)
13. Zhang, J., et al.: Deep model intellectual property protection via deep watermarking. IEEE Trans. Pattern Anal. Mach. Intell. **44**(8), 4005–4020 (2021)

AI for Architecture, Engineering and Conservation (AI4AEC)

.

AI-Driven Adaptive Photogrammetry for Built Heritage Information Modelling

Michele Russo[1]([✉]) [iD], Enrico Pupi[2] [iD], Giulia Flenghi[1] [iD], and Roberta Spallone[2] [iD]

[1] History, Representation and Restauration Department, Sapienza University, Rome, Italy
{m.russo,giulia.flenghi}@uniroma1.it
[2] Architecture and Design Department, Politecnico di Torino, Turin, Italy
{enrico.pupi,roberta.spallone}@polito.it

Abstract. The optimisation of massive data obtained from 3D acquisition methodologies through AI represents an innovative research frontier in 3D data management. It arises from the ever-increasing instruments' capacity to acquire enormous amounts of geometric and radiometric information with a substantial increase in processing times, a demand for computing capacities, and the request to subsample ultra-dense point clouds at the end of the process. On the contrary, a priori intervention on the raw data can mitigate the role of data dimension, reducing processing times while preserving the valuable information to analyse and interpret the artefacts. The research presents a new methodological approach based on integrating photogrammetry and AI. Through AI algorithms, it was possible to optimise the weight of the images, automatically cluster and segment image areas, and assign different resolutions according to the image content. This experimental pipeline significantly reduced calculation times, extracted point clouds with variable resolution according to the elements represented, and preserved the architectural artefacts' geometry.

Keywords: Adaptive Photogrammetry · Image segmentation · Process optimisation

1 Introduction

This research was conducted within the INFORTREAT project, funded by the European Union – Next Generation EU. The study addresses challenges in 3D H-BIM modelling of military architecture. The project aims to create a queryable knowledge tool for fortified heritage conservation, which is increasingly vulnerable to environmental risks.

This contribution focuses on optimising photographic data for photogrammetry by employing AI algorithms to selectively reduce the radiometric resolution of non-critical image elements, primarily vegetation. The core challenge is achieving automated segmentation to streamline data processing and 3D cloud management. This results in adaptive resolution point clouds that preserve detail in primary interest areas while reducing data load from secondary elements.

Experiments were conducted on a section of the Santa Cristina bastion (Citadel of Alessandria), a fortified heritage site characterized by large-scale, significant, often invasive, surrounding greenery.

J. Valente de Oliveira et al. (Eds.): EPIA 2025, LNAI 16121, pp. 109–122, 2026.
https://doi.org/10.1007/978-3-032-05176-9_9

2 Photogrammetric Process and AI Optimisation

The case study presents various problems regarding 3D acquisition and data processing, as well as correct restitution and interpretation. The entire masonry wall of the Santa Cristina baluard was surveyed by integrating geodetic, range-based, and image-based techniques [1], obtaining data oriented in the same reference system. The 3D data redundancy made it possible to plan comparisons to validate their accuracy. The geometric and radiometric data survey showed several bottlenecks related to the scale variation and the complex boundary conditions, characterised by invasive vegetation. The application of different surveying techniques compensated for the first point. The second, on the other hand, represented an insurmountable limitation, generating multiple shadow zones, depth variations and an increase in camera orientation errors (Fig. 1). This complex operating condition resulted in long data processing and the definition of a very heavy point cloud, containing a great density of geometric information of the green portions, secondary in the bastion interpretation and analysis.

Fig. 1. On the left, a digital image acquired by a drone with an evident vegetation component in the scene. On the right is the photogrammetric 3D model with massive geometric and radiometric data related to the vegetation (Acquisition and Editing: MR).

This acquisition condition highlighted a well-known issue in the surveying field, namely the optimisation of the surveyed data, which is now made urgent by introducing cameras capable of capturing 50–100 Mpixel images. If the advancement of data processing systems partly balances instrumental development, managing ultra-dense clouds becomes an issue that cannot be avoided. This is particularly true if part of the acquired data is not helpful or marginal for the analysis and interpretation of the artefact. In this domain, Artificial Intelligence can be of great help. In recent years, some research has been conducted on automatic image masking [2] to optimise the process and reduce data noise by excluding portions of the image [3]. However, this approach is not directly applicable in our case study because geometric information in the green areas, such as the moat or the high portion of the bastion closure, defines the ground attachment and the masonry closure. To solve this problem, we considered a paradigm shift: an innovative approach based on selective subsampling of geometric information (pixels) within the photogrammetric image dataset. The possibility of reducing the number of pixels in some regions of the image in a homogeneous manner, trying to preserve the recognisability of homologous points and the relative extraction of features, would make it possible to obtain point clouds of varying density, conserving camera orientation. The experiment presented here focuses on the distinction between the walls and the green areas in its surroundings. Such an adaptive photogrammetry approach could lead to optimising the incoming raw data through an automatic reprocessing of the contents in a weighted manner, and the processing step, considerably reducing the time effort to orient the cameras and extract the sparse and dense cloud. Of course, introducing such a modified dataset must not lead to camera orientation errors. Therefore, validating the process by comparing the photogrammetric models produced with the original (gold standard) and evaluating the preservation of the geometry, representation, and interpretation is essential. For the experimental phase, two portions of the bastion with different vegetative configurations were selected to test the algorithm with various boundary conditions, highlighting its limits and potential for application at different scales.

3 Methodologies for AI-Enhanced Photographic Sampling

3.1 Comparative Overview of Methodological Approaches

This study introduces a selective image mosaicization approach to reduce point cloud density from vegetated areas in photogrammetric datasets while preserving artificial structures.

The selection of the core AI architecture considered established CNN-based alternatives, such as U-Net and DeepLabv3+. Still, they were deemed suboptimal for our primary goal of process optimisation, due to limitations in capturing global context and significant computational overhead. In parallel, we also assessed more recent architectures, such as Mask2Former, which is known for its high performance in universal segmentation tasks. However, the complexity of its design introduced a computational load exceeding the needs of our specific objective, which focused on the rapid and reliable semantic separation of vegetation and built structures. Similarly, the Segment Anything Model (SAM), despite its flexibility in zero-shot object segmentation, does not natively provide semantic class labels and would require additional integration steps to fit our fully automated workflow. We therefore selected the Transformer-based SegFormer family [4]. This architecture provides an ideal balance of accuracy and efficiency, leveraging a powerful self-attention mechanism for global context and a lightweight decoder for high-speed processing, making it particularly suitable for large-scale imagery [5].

Two parallel methods were tested: Method I utilises SegFormer B4, which dynamically extracts class IDs for vegetation and artificial structures. After comprehensive segmentation, mosaicization is applied to the vegetation, followed by the restoration of artificial elements. Method II employs the lighter SegFormer B2 with a custom green mask, applying mosaicization conditionally. It first verifies a target vegetation class (e.g., "grass") using SegFormer B2, then uses HSV colorimetric filtering for broader green area identification, applying mosaicization if the green pixel proportion exceeds a threshold.

Both methodologies share a common framework for input/output operations and image iteration (Fig. 2).

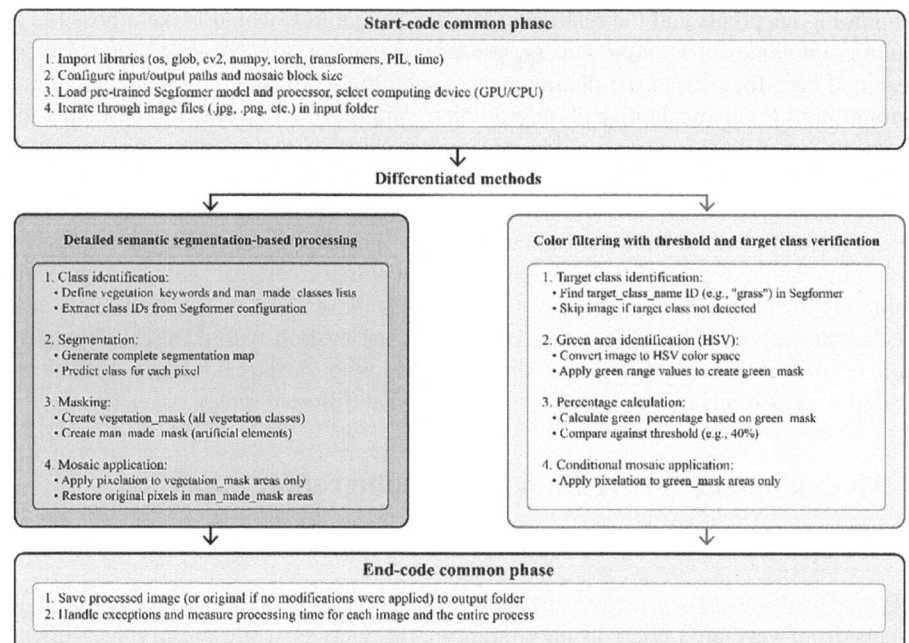

Fig. 2. Overview of the processing pipeline, detailing the typical start/end phases and the two alternative methods for targeted vegetation mosaicization: detailed semantic segmentation-based processing and color filtering with threshold and target class verification. (Editing: EP)

The empirical evaluation utilised two different datasets related to various areas of the Santa Cristina walls: the first is composed of 55 images, the second of 33 images, both acquired by an unmanned aerial vehicle (UAV). The FC7303 camera, mounted on a DJI drone, has a native resolution of 4000×3000 pixels. The setup was a focal length of 4 mm, using ISO 100 and an exposure time of 1/1000.

All computational tasks were performed on a workstation with an Intel(R) Core(TM) i9-14900K CPU, 128 GB of RAM, and an NVIDIA GeForce RTX 4090 GPU with 24 GB GDDR6 VRAM. The software implementation was developed in Python (version 3.14), within the Visual Studio Code environment (version 1.100).

3.2   First Method: Detailed Semantic Segmentation-Based Processing

The first methodology leverages the full inferential power of a sophisticated semantic segmentation model, exemplified in our initial tests by SegFormer B4 [4], to achieve a highly nuanced and precise application of a mosaic process. Central to this approach is a dynamic and comprehensive class identification strategy. Unlike other techniques that rely on a single target class, we interrogate the pre-trained model's configuration, specifically its label2id mapping, a widespread practice in deploying deep learning models for specific downstream tasks [6]. This programmatic interrogation facilitates the extraction of multiple class IDs corresponding to diverse vegetation typologies. This is achieved by matching a predefined list of vegetation keywords (e.g., "grass," "tree," "shrub," "bush," "plant," "forest") against the model's semantic labels. Concurrently, a distinct set of class IDs about pre-specified man-made elements (e.g., "wall," "building," "road") is also identified and extracted.

Following this multi-class identification phase, the SegFormer model performs a comprehensive, pixel-wise semantic segmentation of the input image. This process yields a dense segmentation map, assigning each pixel to its most probable semantic category based on the model's learned features [5]. This detailed map generates two primary binary masks: the vegetation mask is formed by the union of all pixels classified under any of the dynamically identified vegetation categories, and the man-made mask aggregates all pixels recognized as belonging to the predefined artificial elements.

The mosaic process effect is then applied in a carefully controlled, multi-stage manner. Initially, a low-resolution (pixelated) version of the entire original image is generated. The image is selectively transferred only to the regions delineated by the vegetation mask in a copy of the original, high-resolution image. A further step in this pipeline is the subsequent preservation of architectural integrity: original pixel data from the input image is reinstated in all areas covered by the man-made mask. This ensures that even if man-made elements were incidentally located within or adjacent to vegetated regions—and thus potentially affected during the initial broad application of the vegetation mask—their original visual fidelity is fully restored, preventing any unintended quality degradation of these structures.

This process allows for targeted visual quality reduction strictly within vegetated zones while actively safeguarding the integrity of key architectural or infrastructural elements. It offers high control and precision, particularly in complex scenes where vegetation and man-made elements are intricately intermingled (Fig. 3).

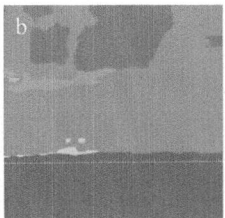

Fig. 3. Illustration of the selective mosaicization process in first dataset: original input image (a); semantic segmentation map generated by the model, identifying the different classes present (b); processed image with mosaic effect applied to vegetated areas using 8 × 8 pixel blocks (c); processed image with mosaic effect and 16 × 16 pixel blocks (d). (Editing: EP)

The primary advantage of this method resides in its robust capacity to distinguish between diverse object categories with high accuracy, significantly mitigating the risk of wrong mosaicization of non-target elements or failing to identify less chromatically distinct vegetation patches that simpler color-based filters might overlook [7]. While this method is potentially more computationally intensive than approaches prioritising computational parsimony, its precision is paramount.

Despite its precision, the methodology described presents certain limitations. The computational overhead associated with comprehensive semantic segmentation, particularly with more complex models, might be substantial [8]. Performance is inherently tied to the pre-trained model's generalisation capacity to the specific visual characteristics of the input dataset; classes (both vegetated and artificial) not well-represented in the model's training data may result in classification inaccuracies. Furthermore, achieving precise delineation at intricate boundaries between vegetation and man-made structures remains a persistent challenge in semantic segmentation, often requiring specialised architectural components or post-processing steps to refine object contours [9], potentially leading to minor inaccuracies in the generated masks. The efficacy of preserving artificial elements also hinges on the exhaustiveness of the predefined man-made classes list.

3.3   Second Method: Color Filtering with Threshold and Target Class Verification

The SegFormer B4 model has proven to be robust and accurate. However, we adopted an alternative approach that combines semantic segmentation using the lighter SegFormer B2 model with a custom green mask to optimise computational resources. Mosaicization is applied exclusively to the vegetated areas of the image, based on a quantitative threshold of detected vegetation.

SegFormer B2 was selected for its ability to deliver faster results while balancing precision and computational efficiency well. This made it possible to process a larger image set in less time, without compromising the semantic integrity of the output. The model was pretrained on the ADE20K [10] dataset, which includes relevant vegetation classes such as grass, trees, and plants.

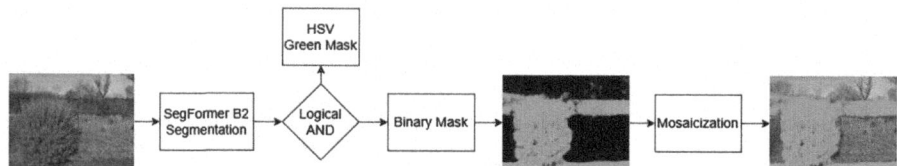

Fig. 4. Hybrid segmentation pipeline combining SegFormer B2 output with an HSV-based green mask. The logical AND produces a final binary mask used to apply mosaicization selectively to vegetated areas, preserving architectural details. (Editing: GF)

Initially, the segmentation process relied exclusively on a green mask generated in the HSV (Hue, Saturation, Value) color space [11–13]. This method isolates green tones by filtering pixels within a predefined hue range. While effective in brightly lit areas or where the vegetation was distinguishable, the green mask approach showed significant limitations in more complex conditions, such as shadows, dry vegetation, or moss on stone surfaces. These factors led to the inclusion of non-vegetated regions and the exclusion of actual vegetation with darker or atypical tones.

To address these shortcomings, a hybrid strategy was implemented. The core of the detection process now relies on semantic segmentation produced by SegFormer B2. The model's output generates a binary mask that identifies regions belonging to predefined vegetation-related classes. This mask is then refined by applying an HSV-based green mask, which serves as a corrective filter. Pixels identified by the model as vegetation but not exhibiting green chromatic characteristics are excluded from the final mask. This decision rule facilitates more accurate discrimination between natural elements and architectural surfaces, particularly in contexts where plant matter overlaps or encroaches on building structures. The two systems work in conjunction: semantic segmentation provides class-based recognition, while the green mask reinforces the visual consistency of the selected regions. Mosaicization is only applied when vegetation covers at least 40% of the image area, a threshold empirically determined through comparative testing with multiple vegetation coverage levels. However, the number of mosaic elements can be adjusted by modifying this threshold according to specific project goals. A value of 40% proved to be the most effective for this dataset, striking a balance between simplification and architectural preservation (Fig. 4).

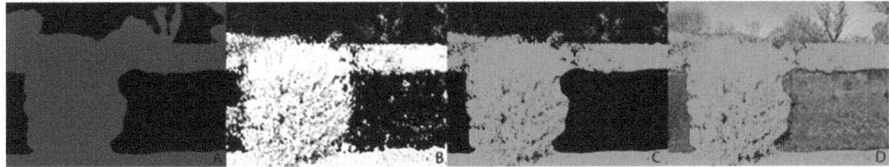

Fig. 5. Visualisation of the hybrid mask generation process. A: Semantic segmentation (AI mask). B: HSV green mask. C: Final mask after logical intersection. D: Final mask overlaid on the original image, indicating areas selected for the mosaic process. (Editing: GF)

The final output is generated by applying a pixelation effect (16 × 16 blocks) exclusively to the validated vegetated areas. This selective resolution reduction decreases the data burden in downstream processes such as photogrammetry or point cloud generation, while preserving the structural definition of architectural elements.

Each processed image is accompanied by a set of diagnostic visualizations, including the original green mask, the AI-generated segmentation mask, the final filtered mask, and the resulting mosaic process (Fig. 5). These outputs enable comprehensive verification of the process and facilitate critical evaluation of segmentation accuracy.

Despite the improvements, the method presents some limitations. Some vegetated areas, particularly those with dry or shaded foliage, may still escape detection. Conversely, certain elements, such as wall-adjacent weeds or moss, may still be mosaiced due to their dual semantic and chromatic profile (Fig. 6). These residual issues highlight areas for future refinement, such as improving the integration between color analysis and class confidence to disambiguate vegetation from architectural context better. Overall, the method has proven effective in generating lighter image datasets while preserving the scene's semantic and architectural fidelity.

Fig. 6. Example of residual mosaic process applied to wall-adjacent vegetation. Due to the overlapping chromatic and semantic profile of moss and weeds, some architectural details are pixelated, illustrating a current limitation of the hybrid masking approach. (Editing: GF)

4   Usability of the Results

The opportunity to have a photogrammetric base that offers segmentation suitable for distinguishing areas of interest, obtained by AI automatic processes, and, at the same time, lighter files as the basis for two- and three-dimensional graphical processing, proves to be very interesting for the research currently being carried out on existing fortified systems and for the foreseeable scalability to other case studies, as will be described in the following paragraphs.

The research object is a sector of the walls of the Citadel in Alessandria, Piedmont. The fortification was built in the 1730s and reflects the new international standards in military construction that were developed following the wars of expansion of Louis XIV of France [14]. Ongoing restoration projects of part of the citadel ensure a strong interest in any further research project on the citadel.

Numerous studies have concerned this fortification work, which is an absolute out-of-scale compared to the urban settlement. This infrastructure links its life to the inseparable relationship with the nearby Tanaro River and the invasive natural environment. In particular, the geometric tracings of the irregular six-sided plan, the subject of the overall project to which this research refers, were developed in the studies of Amelio Fara [15]. Fara's research, however, refers to the reference treatises for Giuseppe Ignazio Bertola, the military engineer to whom the layout of the eighteenth-century citadel is owed. The comparison between the theoretical references identified by Fara and probably applied by Bertola in the planimetric definition of the layout and the actual fortified construction has never been made.

Such a study could take as a basis the horizontal sections of the photogrammetric point cloud to identify the possible rules of plotting on the ground preceding the construction, which, as it is known, can refer to the coeval techniques of Italian, French, and Dutch bastions and their variations. The graphical analysis tools to be employed contemplate geometric and algorithmic drawing software.

As with general research interests, some studies have examined the construction and execution techniques of artefacts and some of their elements, such as vaults and foundations [16–18]. This work was mainly devoted to the reading and interpreting of archival documents, such as the contracts signed by the Azienda generale delle Fabbriche e Fortificazioni (General Company of Buildings and Fortifications).

The construction descriptions and instructions found in such analyses could also be enriched by comparing them with the study of geometric profiles of the actual built consistencies. In that case, Heritage Building Information Modeling (H-BIM) modelling could provide tools to return data at the Level of Geometry (LOG) and Level of Information (LOI).

In both cases, the study of in-ground profiling and vertical profiles reconstruction, generating segmented and lightened a priori images of the photogrammetric process through the AI methodologies described above, would greatly facilitate the generation of the two-dimensional plots and three-dimensional H-BIM models. In addition, a similar result can be obtained using active range techniques. Still, the possibility of applying a photogrammetric approach to all the wall curtains gives the chance to compare reliable geometric and radiometric information. The latter represents a significant source for data interpretation, integrating sections with ortho-images.

5   Foreseeable Applications

5.1   Large-Scale Built Heritage Documentation

The presented class-driven mosaicization paradigm holds considerable potential for advancing built heritage documentation and analysis at the urban scale, addressing persistent challenges in managing and interpreting vast 3D datasets derived from modern survey techniques [19]. The intrinsic flexibility in defining semantic classes, a concept increasingly explored with deep learning for heritage applications, suggests novel avenues for experimental application. Theoretically, one could achieve a highly selective informational focus by designating specific architectural typologies, individual edifices, or even discrete structural components as primary classes of interest and concurrently classifying the surrounding urban matrix as contextual elements. This could enable the generation of 3D datasets where the informational density of the broader context is programmatically attenuated, thereby isolating and emphasising the targeted heritage asset with enhanced clarity and computational efficiency. This approach is particularly relevant for developing interactive and performant digital twin representations of complex urban heritage sites [20]. Further research could explore the efficacy of this methodology in creating multi-layered, semantically rich digital urban environments, potentially streamlining the integration with evolving Heritage Building Information Modelling (H-BIM) frameworks and semantic enrichment processes [21].

5.2   Analysis of Decorative Apparatus and Fine-Scale Features

In the cultural and architectural domains, artificial intelligence techniques can significantly contribute to analysing and managing decorative elements. Deep learning tools applied to image segmentation can, for example, isolate ornamental features such as mosaics, frescoes, or reliefs from the surrounding architectural context, or distinguish between different decorative layers within the same composition. Such approaches can benefit digitisation and restoration processes, allowing for more precise identification of fractures, gaps, or chromatic variations. Automated color-based analysis could enable targeted interventions on specific portions of the image, improving visual readability and supporting the preservation of the most significant elements. In the long term, integrating these tools may facilitate monitoring surface conservation over time and support advanced forms of engagement, such as Augmented Reality, through the selective highlighting of ornamental components.

6 Discussion and Conclusion

The research presented an innovative image transformation process from photogrammetric blocks that were tried for the first time to optimise both the frame orientation process and the extraction of multi-resolution sparse and dense clouds (Fig. 7). The goal is to cope with the ever-increasing information density from current cameras without losing cultural heritage data.

The results obtained are promising. To ensure the validity of our findings, all photogrammetric processing was performed using Agisoft Metashape Professional (version 2.1.2, build 18358, 64-bit). Identical parameters were used across all test cases, including High accuracy for alignment (with a 0-key point limit) and High quality for dense cloud generation (with Mild depth filtering). This consistency ensures that all observed variations in point cloud densities, reported in Tables 1 and 2, are directly attributable to the effects of our AI-driven pre-processing method. Using two different algorithms for segmentation and clustering image areas containing vegetation has shown that these tools, although limited, can reliably detect these portions, albeit with lower resolution. Tables 1 and 2 show a significant reduction in parameters. Regarding the optimisation process, the most promising mosaicization step is 8×8, with a decrease in file size ranging between 32% and 55% and between 55% and 70% in data in the dense cloud.

A noteworthy and counterintuitive result highlighted in the table parameters is the increase in point cloud density observed with the 2×2 mosaic size. Rather than simplifying the image, a small-block mosaic replaces the natural, complex texture of vegetation with high-frequency artificial features. The sharp edges and corners of these microblocks are misinterpreted by feature-detection and dense-matching algorithms as a rich source of valid geometric detail, leading to a denser reconstruction. This effect diminishes as the block size increases (e.g., 8×8), as larger blocks are correctly identified as low-information areas, achieving the intended data reduction. This highlights that for this method to be effective, the mosaic block size must be sufficiently large to remove texture properly, not merely replace it with an artificial pattern.

A comparison of the 3D point clouds extracted from the original and optimised images relative to the rectilinear curtain wall is also interesting (Fig. 8). The geometry of the two models is very similar, with a mean distance of 0.02 m and a standard deviation of 0.036 m, with uniform variation. This means that the image transformation achieved minimal movements of the camera centres during orientation, resulting in insignificant geometry variation (on an architectural scale). The comparison was limited at this stage to the masonry portion, validating this first experimental phase concerning the geometric preservation of the artefact.

However, it is essential to acknowledge that this geometric preservation is most effective on the core structures. At the same time, minor inaccuracies can occur at the immediate boundaries between the original and mosaicized areas. This is an inherent limitation of applying a mask, as the sharp transition can challenge the photogrammetric matching algorithms at the interface zones. The severity of these localized artifacts is directly proportional to the precision of the underlying semantic segmentation, representing an issue for future refinement.

Fig. 7. Comparative dense point clouds from Dataset 1 (left side) and Dataset 2 (right side). Each series displays the original dense point cloud and the results from Methods 1 and 2 using mosaic blocks of 2×2, 4×4, 8×8, and 16×16. (Processing and editing: EP)

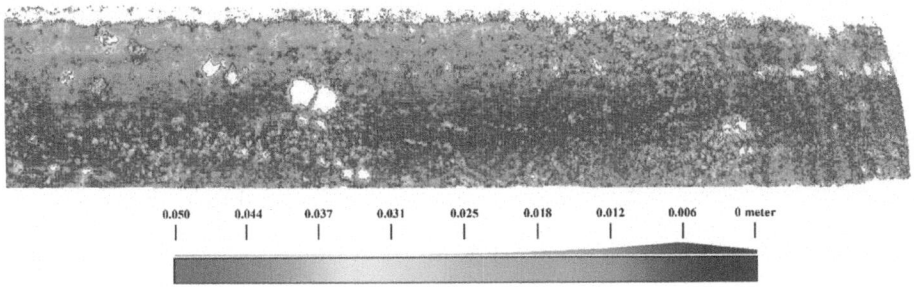

Fig. 8. Comparison map between gold standard data and the new 3D point cloud. (Editing: MR)

Table 1. Dataset 1: Comparative benchmarking (quantitative) of employed methods across varying mosaic block sizes. (Processing and editing: EP)

Parameter / Metric	Original Dataset	Method 1: Detailed semantic segmentation				Method 2: Color filtering and threshold			
Mosaic block size	N/A	2x2	4x4	8x8	16x16	2x2	4x4	8x8	16x16
Output Dataset									
Total size [MB]	289	349	294	129	156	346	305	196	219
Size variation [%]	N/A	+20.76	+1.73	-55.36	-46.02	+19.72	+5.53	-32.17	-24.22
Code Execution									
Time [Seconds]	N/A	148.39	147.44	142.79	138.36	24.72	24.55	24.36	32.71
Metashape Processing									
Sparse Cloud									
Points found	140,283	157,660	95,902	76,843	71,030	158,451	99,842	72,792	50,360
Variation [%]	N/A	+12.38	-31.63	-45.22	-49.36	+12.95	-28.82	-48.11	-64.10
Dense Cloud									
Points found	10,102,740	10,388,199	6,112,076	3,064,846	2,402,605	11,069,114	6,336,773	4,202,992	3,277,923
Variation [%]	N/A	+2.82	-39.50	-69.66	-76.21	+9.56	-37.27	-58.39	-67.55

Table 2. Dataset 2: comparative benchmarking (quantitative) of employed methods across varying mosaic block sizes. (Processing and editing: EP)

Parameter / Metric	Original Dataset	Method 1: Detailed semantic segmentation				Method 2: Color filtering and threshold			
Mosaic block size	N/A	2x2	4x4	8x8	16x16	2x2	4x4	8x8	16x16
Output Dataset									
Total size [MB]	171	200	171	90.8	103	200	175	106	118
Size variation [%]	N/A	+16.95	0	-46.90	-39.76	+16.95	+2.33	-38.01	-30.99
Code Execution									
Time [Seconds]	N/A	93.87	82.35	83.82	90.35	17.21	14.29	14.24	20.56
Metashape Processing									
Sparse Cloud									
Points found	146,118	169,634	97,067	72,801	66,342	169,094	94,225	63,910	49,961
Variation [%]	N/A	+16.09	-33.56	-50.17	-54.59	+15.72	-35.51	-56.26	-65.80
Dense Cloud									
Points found	9,705,419	10,226,273	7,123,433	3,978,737	2,671,726	10,194,668	7,215,008	4,045,841	2,445,300
Variation [%]	N/A	+5.36	-26.60	-59.00	-72.47	+5.04	-25.66	-58.31	-74.80

The limits of optimisation concerning the determination of homologous points and the orientation of the frames are planned to be verified. In addition, it will be essential to evaluate the geometric variation of points related to vegetation. Finally, look for a function that optimises image quality for variations in camera centres, trying to understand if there is a tradeoff and if this depends on the optimised area of the image.

Acknowledgments. The research was conducted within the framework of the PRIN2022 INFORTREAT project, Reconstructing the Early Modern Bastioned Front. INformation models for the fruition of constructive knowledge in FORtified architecture TREATises (16th-18th Century), CUP I53D23005420006, funded by the European Union – Next Generation EU, P.I.: M. G. Bevilacqua, University of Pisa; A.I.: R. Spallone, Politecnico di Torino; A.I.: M. Russo, Sapienza Università di Roma; A.I. A. Giordano, University of Padova. This paper is the result of research jointly carried out by the authors. R. Spallone wrote pars. 1, 4; M. Russo pars. 2, 6; E. Pupi pars. 3.1, 3.2, 5.1; G. Flenghi pars. 3.3, 5.2.

References

1. Russo, M., Asciutti, M., Flenghi, G., Casciola, M., Bertoncini Sabatini, P., Caroti, G.: Survey experiences of city walls of Alessandria and Lucca: an overview. In: Cirillo, V., Zerlenga, O. (eds.) International Conference on Fortification of the Mediterranean Coast 2025, vol. XX, pp. 1189–1196 (2025). ISBN 978-88-85556-37-9

2. Murtiyoso, A., Grussenmeyer, P.: Automatic point cloud noise masking in close range photogrammetry for buildings using AI-based semantic labelling. Int. Arch. Photogramm. Remote Sens. Spatial Inf. Sci. **XLVI-2/W1-2022**, 389–393 (2022)

3. Billi, D., et al.: Machine learning and deep learning for the built heritage analysis: laser scanning and UAV-based surveying applications on a complex spatial grid structure. Remote Sens. **15**(8), 1961, 1–34 (2023). ISSN 2072-4292

4. Xie, E., Wang, W., Yu, Z., Anandkumar, A., Alvarez, J.M., Luo, P.: SegFormer: simple and efficient design for semantic segmentation with transformers. arXiv preprint arXiv:2105. 15203 (2021)

5. Dosovitskiy, A., et al.: An image is worth 16 × 16 words: transformers for image recognition at scale. In: International Conference on Learning Representations (ICLR) (2020)

6. Minaee, S., Boykov, Y., Porikli, F., Plaza, A., Kehtarnavaz, N., Terzopoulos, D.: Image segmentation using deep learning: a survey. IEEE Trans. Pattern Anal. Mach. Intell. **44**(7), 3523–3542 (2022)

7. Sural, S., Qian, G., Pramanik, S.K.: Segmentation and histogram generation using the HSV color space for image retrieval. In: Proceedings. International Conference on Image Processing, vol. 2, pp. II-589–II-592 (2002)

8. Garcia-Garcia, A., Orts-Escolano, S., Oprea, S., Villena-Martinez, V., Garcia-Rodriguez, J.: A review on deep learning techniques applied to semantic segmentation. arXiv preprint arXiv: 1704.06857 (2017)

9. Chen, L.-C., Papandreou, G., Kokkinos, I., Murphy, K., Yuille, A.L.: DeepLab: semantic image segmentation with deep convolutional nets, atrous convolution, and fully connected CRFs. IEEE Trans. Pattern Anal. Mach. Intell. **40**(4), 834–848 (2018)

10. ADE20K Dataset. (n.d.). https://ade20k.csail.mit.edu. Accessed 16 May 2025

11. CVExplained: Color Filtering/Segmentation/Detection – HSV. https://cvexplained.wordpress.com/2020/04/28/color-detection-hsv/. Accessed 16 May 2025

12. Maulion, M.: Color Image Segmentation—Image Processing. https://mattmaulion.medium.com/color-image-segmentation-image-processing-4a04eca25c0. Accessed 16 May 2025

13. Şimşek, G.: Object detection from image and video using HSV color space. https://www.paralect.com/blog/post/object-detection-from-image-and-video-using-hsv-color-space. Accessed 16 May 2025

14. Piccoli, E: The "architecture parlante" of an 18th century fort. In: Vigliocco, E. (ed.) Riuso del patrimonio oversize. Un progetto adattivo per la Cittadella di Alessandria, pp. 68-79. Politecnico di Torino, Torino (2021)

15. Fara, A.: The citadel of Alessandria: Giuseppe Ignazio Bertola's architectural infraction of the hexagon's geometrical regularity. Nexus Netw. J. **16**, 777–793 (2014)

16. Piccoli, E., Tocci, C., Caterino, R., Zanet, E.: Lo Stato entra in cantiere: sviluppo e utilità di una fonte seriale settecentesca. In: Marotta, A., Spallone, R. (eds.) Defensive Architecture of the Mediterranean, VII, pp. 217-224. Politecnico di Torino, Torino (2018)

17. Piccoli, E., Tocci, C., Zanet, E., Caterino, R.: Building on water in the Modern State. Eighteenth century foundation techniques in the fortifications of Alessandria. In: Campbell, J.W.P. (ed.) Proceedings of the Sixth Conference on the Construction History Society CHS, Water, Doors and Buildings. Studies in the History of Construction, Queen's College, Cambridge, pp. 358–373 (2019)

18. Piccoli, E., Tocci, C.: A prova di bomba. Ingegneri, architetti e teorie sulle volte in un cantiere militare di metà Settecento. ARCHISTOR **12**, 212–251 (2019)
19. Adamopoulos, E., Rinaudo, F.: Close-range sensing and data fusion for built heritage inspection and monitoring—a review. Remote Sens. **13**(19), 3936 (2021)
20. Hosamo, H.H., Imran, A., Cardenas-Cartagena, J., Svennevig, P.R., Svidt, K., Nielsen, H.K.: A review of the digital twin technology in the AEC-FM industry. In: Advances in Civil Engineering (2022)
21. Croce, V., Caroti, G., De Luca, L., Jacquot, K., Piemonte, A., Véron, P.: From the semantic point cloud to heritage-building information modeling: a semiautomatic approach exploiting machine learning. Remote Sens. **13**(3), 461 (2021)

From Synthetic Data to Deep Learning Enhancements in Muon Tomography for Cultural Heritage

Davide Cifarelli[1(✉)], Daniele Corradetti[2,3], and Lorenzo Pezzotti[4]

[1] Elementar, Divisione Ricerca e Sviluppo, 10121 Turin, Italy
dcifarelli@elementar.solutions
[2] Grupo de Física Matemática (IST), Av. Rovisco Pais, 1049-001 Lisbon, Portugal
[3] STAP, Rua General Ferreira Martins 8, 1495-137 Algés, Portugal
[4] Istituto Nazionale di Fisica Nucleare, viale Berti Pichat 6/2, 40127 Bologna, Italy

Abstract. Muography provides a non-invasive method for exploring the internal structures of cultural heritage artifacts using cosmic-ray-derived muons. In this work, we present an integrated pipeline combining synthetic data generation via Monte Carlo simulations with advanced deep learning techniques, aiming to overcome traditional limitations in muographic imaging. Utilizing the Geant4 toolkit, muon interactions were simulated within materials such as concrete, limestone, and wood, including concealed metallic elements to replicate realistic structural scenarios. To enhance image quality without requiring prolonged exposure times and to reduce detector costs, our approach employs two neural networks sequentially: an event augmentation network based on a U-Net architecture enriched with residual dense blocks, and a resolution augmentation network designed to improve spatial detail.

Keywords: Muography · Deep Learning · Cultural Heritage · Synthetic Data · Geant4

1 Introduction

Muon tomography, or muography, is an imaging technique that uses natural cosmic-ray muons to probe the internal structure of dense materials. The advantage of muons over other imaging techniques (such as X-rays) lies, on the one hand, in their ability to penetrate thick layers of matter, and on the other, in their widespread natural source [1], namely secondary cosmic rays or athmospheric muons, which makes them logistically available, non-invasive, and environmentally sustainable. These characteristics make muography an ideal method for investigating cultural heritage artifacts and structures, where the need for non-invasive techniques capable of preserving artifacts is of utmost importance, especially when traditional techniques face limitations due to size, density, or accessibility.

The first application of muography dates back to the 1950s when it was used to measure the overburden of a tunnel [2]. Later it was notoriously applied to archeology by physicist Luis Alvarez that employed muon detectors to search

© The Author(s), under exclusive license to Springer Nature Switzerland AG 2026
J. Valente de Oliveira et al. (Eds.): EPIA 2025, LNAI 16121, pp. 123–135, 2026.
https://doi.org/10.1007/978-3-032-05176-9_10

for hidden chambers within the Egyptian pyramids [1]. This work demonstrated the feasibility of using muons for non-destructive imaging, suggesting subsequent applications in archaeology, geophysics, and engineering. In recent decades, advances in detector sensitivity, data processing, and portability have significantly improved muography's applicability to cultural heritage studies [3]. Given that the first applications of muography date back to the 1950s, one might wonder why this technique has not yet become standard practice in the field. The answer lies in two major obstacles to its practical implementation. The first is the logistics of muon detectors: detectors that are easy to transport have only recently become available. The second is the need for a large number of muon events to obtain a sufficiently defined image. Muon events occur at approximately $170 \, \mathrm{Hz/m^2}$, which implies several weeks or months of data collection to achieve acceptable image resolutions. These fundamental limitations of low muon flux rates, combined with the physical constraints of detector hardware, create a dual challenge unique to muography that necessitates a two-stage neural network approach. The first challenge, i.e. insufficient statistical sampling due to low muon rates, requires event augmentation techniques to simulate longer exposure times and reduce data collection periods. The second challenge stems from the physical limitations of detector geometry and cost constraints, for which achieving high spatial resolution would require prohibitively expensive detector arrays. This limitation can be mitigated with resolution-enhancing deep-learning techniques. Additionally, unlike other imaging modalities, muography currently lacks established conventional pipelines that combine Monte Carlo simulations with machine learning approaches and requires specialized methodologies tailored to this unique technology.

This article addresses these issues by presenting a specific pipeline and a method for muography in structural diagnostics and cultural heritage applications. This work is part of an ongoing Portuguese-Italian project involving STAP, S.A., Monumenta S.A., LNEC (Laboratório de Engenheria Civil) and Elementar, s.r.l. aiming to develop a portable muon detector using scintillating optical fibers readout by Silicon PhotoMultipliers (SiPM) that can be effectively used in the field of civil engineering and cultural heritage imaging.

2   Synthetic Data Generation for Muography

To explore the feasibility of reconstructing internal structures within cultural heritage artifacts and to generate related synthetic training data, we performed detailed Monte Carlo simulations of muon interactions with matter using the GEANT4 toolkit [5–7]. This software, widely adopted in high-energy physics, allows for the simulation of radiation-matter interactions with high precision across a broad energy spectrum. Our Monte Carlo simulations were implemented as a C++ code using the GEANT4 library.

The primary goal was to assess the capability of muon tomography to reveal internal metal reinforcements or density anomalies within concrete, stone and wood artifacts. To do it, we modeled a cubic block with dimensions of $30 \times 30 \times 30 \, \mathrm{cm^3}$, composed of concrete-like material with realistic density and

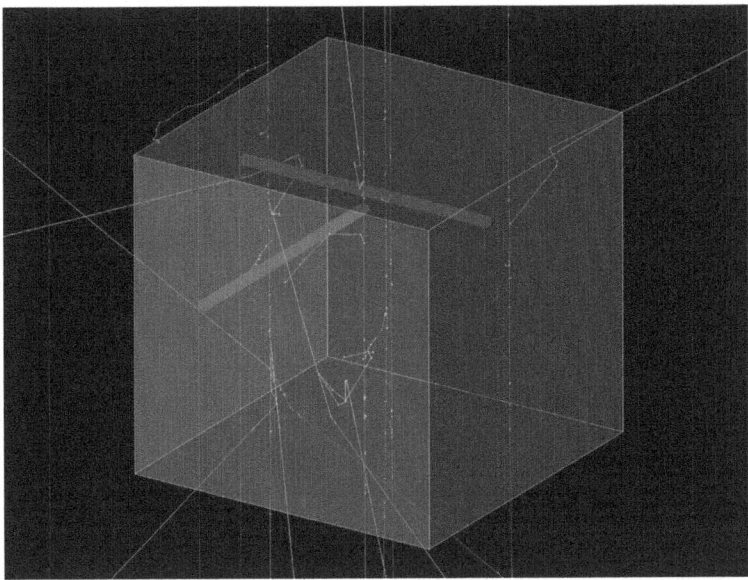

Fig. 1. Muonic events simulated with GEANT4 in a cubic block of concrete-like material with dimensions of $30 \times 30 \times 30\,cm^3$, including 10 mm-thick steel bars. Image from [4].

elemental composition. The simulated composition for concrete was defined by the following mass fractions: H (1.0%), C (0.1%), O (52.91%), Na (1.6%), Mg (0.2%), Al (3.39%), Si (33.70%), K (1.39%), Ca (4.40%), Fe (1.4%). The density was set to 2.3 g/cm^3 and the radiation length amounted to 11.55 cm (Fig. 1).

The simulation included steel rods to mimic potential hidden structures such as reinforcements. Cylindrical rods with a diameter of 1 cm and 25 cm length were inserted inside the cube. The cylindrical rods were randomly positioned within the simulated block, parallel to the x or z axes, while the y axis was the one along which muons travel. The steel density was set to 7.874 g/cm^3 with a radiation length of 1.757 cm. In each simulation, up to 15 rods were placed to evaluate the algorithm's capacity to distinguish multiple hidden elements.

In all simulations, muon tracks were simulated as a uniform flux traveling along the negative y-direction, corresponding to vertical muon incidence. The flux was uniformly distributed over a $28 \times 28\,cm^2$ plane positioned above the block. The muon energy was uniformly distributed between 3 and 4 GeV. Each physical process for muons interacting with such elements was taken into account in the simulation of the passage of muons through the sample under test.

To capture muon positions before and after the material box, four virtual detection planes were included: two upstream and two downstream. These planes recorded the (x, z) coordinates of each muon, providing input data for subsequent image reconstruction. Muons that did not reach the downstream detector, for instance due to nuclear interactions or large scattering angles, were excluded from the dataset.

The dataset comprised 18×10^6 muon events per geometry, ensuring sufficient statistics for image reconstruction. A total of 100 geometries of concrete and steel were simulated, each characterized by different distributions of internal steel rods. The resulting dataset was used to train and validate the deep learning models described in subsequent sections. Extensions of these geometries to the field of cultural heritage assessment will be described in Sect. 5.2.

3 Dataset Analysis and Exploration

The core features chosen for identifying internal structures are the Root Mean Square (RMS) and the Mean of the muon track deflection angle, which predominantly results from multiple scattering within the material. The scattering angle was computed from the vector difference between upstream and downstream hit positions. The angle was obtained by calculating the arc-cosine of the dot product between the normalized track vector and the muon direction vector.

The target image for each geometry was obtained by projecting the material distribution along the y-axis, effectively producing a 2D map of the internal structure. Each map was divided into 1×1 mm^2 pixels, yielding 280×280 pixel images. The mean and the RMS of the scattering angle within each pixel served as the primary features for subsequent deep learning tasks.

4 Deep Learning for Image Enhancement

As previously stated, our pipeline addresses two critical problems of muography: improving spatial resolution to reduce detector costs and decreasing exposure time. Indeed, it is important to underline how, rather than simply enhancing image quality, our approach focuses on augmenting the statistical information extracted from muon events, effectively reducing the exposure time need to resolve the image. It is important to note that while muon detection data is inherently sparse, our neural networks operate on dense statistical representations computed from these sparse events. Rather than attempting to densify the raw sparse muon data, we aggregate statistical moments (such as mean scattering angles) over spatial bins, creating dense feature maps that effectively capture the underlying material properties while preserving the statistical information content of the original sparse measurements.

The process is structured around four key datasets with varying resolution and event counts: High-Resolution Maximum-Events (HRME), Low-Resolution Maximum-Events (LRME), High-Resolution Low-Events (HRLE), and Low-Resolution Low-Events (LRLE) as in Fig. 2. The pipeline operates in two sequential stages. First, an event enhancement neural network transforms a LRLE dataset (representing initial scanner output with limited events and resolution) into an inferred LRME dataset (same resolution but with statistically augmented event data). This step effectively simulates longer exposure times through an "Event Augmentation" neural network. Second, a resolution enhancement neural network converts the LRME dataset into a HRME dataset, significantly improving spatial resolution of the statistical moments without requiring more expensive detector hardware. We called this second neural network as "Resolution Augmentation" network.

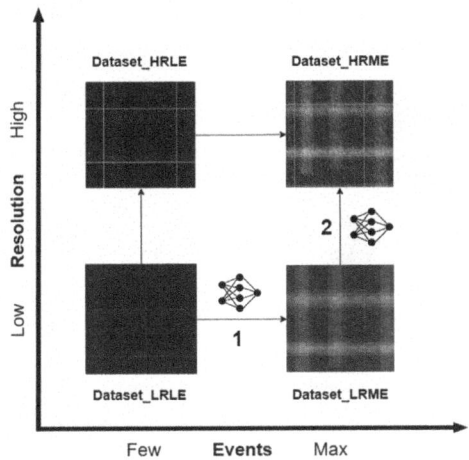

Fig. 2. Diagram of the four datasets: the x-axis denotes the number of muonic events, while the y-axis represents spatial resolution. The transformation follows two main steps: (1) the "event augmentation" neural network enhances event statistics, converting a low-resolution (LR) low-event (LE) dataset into a low-resolution (LR) max-event (ME) dataset; (2) the "resolution augmentation" neural network improves spatial resolution, converting the LRME dataset into a high-resolution (HR) max-event (ME) dataset.

4.1   Data Augmentation

To generate training data efficiently, we implemented a multi-step data augmentation process. Starting with original Geant4 simulations, we applied usual geometric transformations (cropping, rotation, and flipping) to create an augmented dataset. We then subsampled the muon events at different rates to simulate various exposure durations. Elements in the "Low Events" dataset correspond to 100k muonic events while elements in the "Max Events" datasets correspond to 4.5M events, thus separated by a factor of 45. Finally, we aggregated the statistics for both low resolution (94×94 pixels) and high resolution (280×280 pixels) configurations, producing our four distinct datasets (see Fig. 3). High-resolution images are 78.4k pixels, for data augmentation they are divided into 4 images of 19.6k pixel each; while low-resolution images are 8.8k pixels and for data augmentation they were divided into four images of 2.2k pixel each.

4.2   Event Augmentation

For the "Event Augmentation" neural network we implemented a U-Net architecture [8] augmented with residual-in-residual dense blocks (RRDB). This

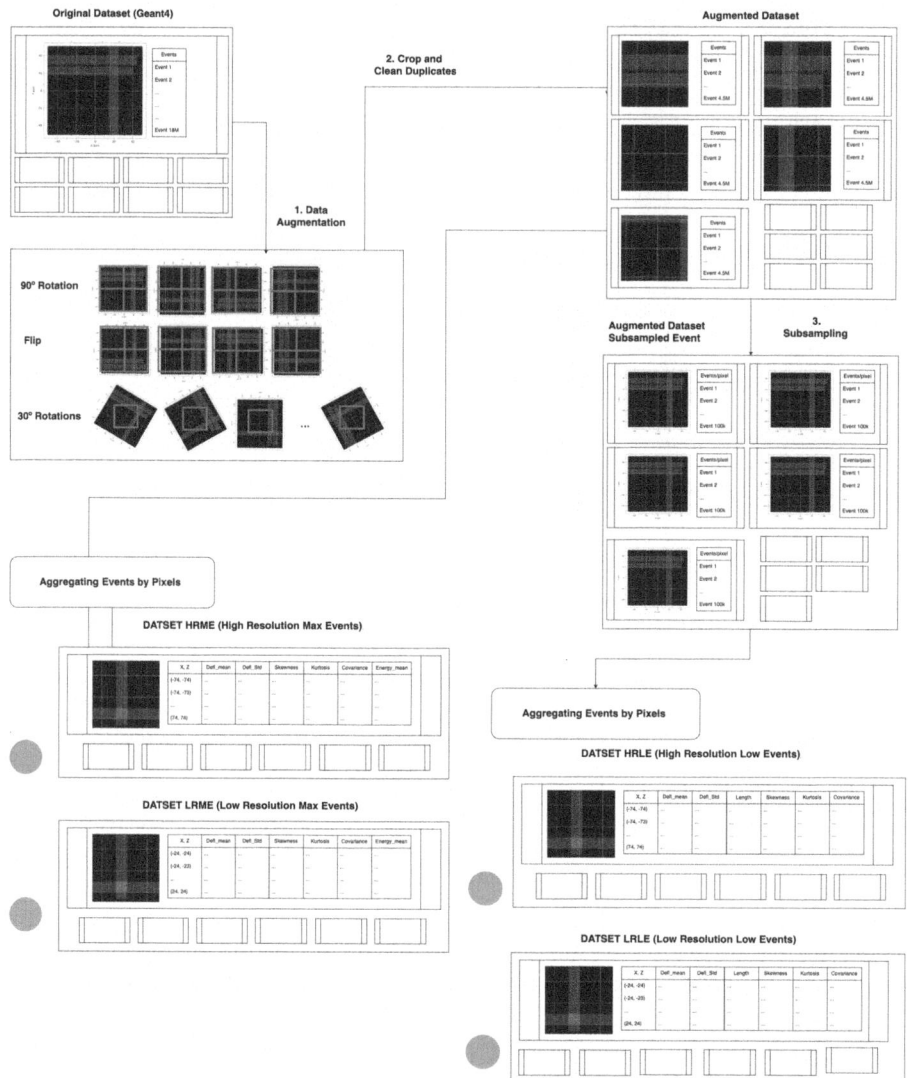

Fig. 3. Overview of the multi-step data augmentation pipeline. Starting with the original dataset produced in Geant4. Then basic geometric transformations (crop, rotate, flip) are operated on the events obtaining the Augmented Dataset. This Dataset is then augmented by subsampling the events. The statistics are then aggregated and computed for two different resolutions (94 × 94 pixels and 280 × 280 pixels) thus obtaining all four datasets HRME, LRME, HRLE, LRLE.

design has proven efficacy in super-resolution and image restoration [9], since its encoder-decoder framework captures multi-scale features: the encoder downsamples inputs via convolutional layers with batch normalization and activation, extracting global context, while the decoder upsamples and integrates these features with skip connections to preserve spatial details. RRDB, embedded in the bottleneck, employ densely connected convolutional layers with residual connections to improve feature extraction and noise suppression, addressing the low signal-to-noise ratio of muographic data. Channel attention modules [10] are integrated throughout to adaptively weight feature channels.

Training Process. The network was trained to map statistical moments from low-resolution low-event dataset (LRLE) to low-resolution max-event datasets (LRME), using 5, 20, and 50 geometries to evaluate performance scalability. Training utilized the L1 loss function for robust convergence and sharp reconstructions, paired with the AdamW optimizer [11] featuring an initial learning rate of 10^{-6}, increased to 5×10^{-4}, and gradient clipping for stability. A learning rate scheduler and early stopping based on validation loss stagnation were employed, with an 80/20 train/validation split ensuring generalization. Conducted on an NVIDIA T4 GPU (16 GB), training times ranged from 1 to 8 h with approximately 30% memory usage. The optimized model (36 MB) performs inference in tens of milliseconds per sample.

4.3   Resolution Augmentation

For the resolution enhancement task, we implemented a specialized architecture which builds upon proven super-resolution methodologies but is specifically tailored to enhance muographic data. Unlike traditional image super-resolution, our goal is not merely to enlarge low-resolution images but to enhance statistical information captured at different spatial resolutions. This architecture consists of several key components. First, an initial feature extraction layer processes the 17 statistical features of the muographic data using a convolutional layer with PReLU activation. Prior to this, a channel attention module weighs the importance of each input feature. This channel attention mechanism, applies both average and max pooling operations followed by a shared fully-connected network to adaptively recalibrate feature responses. The architecture's core consists of four residual blocks, each containing two convolutional layers with PReLU activation and a channel attention module. These residual blocks are connected with a global residual connection, which allows the network to focus on learning the residual information while preserving the low-frequency components of the input signal. For upscaling the spatial resolution from 47×47 to 142×142 (approximately a factor of 3), we employ a PixelShuffle operation preceded by a convolutional layer that increases the feature channels by a factor of 9. This approach efficiently rearranges the feature maps into a higher resolution output without introducing checkerboard artifacts commonly seen in transposed convolutions. We implemented a custom loss function that combines L1 loss (for perceptual quality) and MSE loss (for pixel-wise accuracy), with weights of 0.8 and 0.2 respectively. This balanced approach helps preserve both structural details and statistical accuracy in the super-resolved output.

Training Process: The resolution augmentation network was trained on pairs of LRME (low-resolution maximum-events) and HRME (high-resolution maximum-events) datasets. We conducted training runs with different dataset sizes to evaluate the impact of training data volume on model performance. Specifically, we trained on datasets comprising 5 geometries and 20 geometries respectively, using the same network architecture and hyperparameters. We employed the AdamW optimizer with a weight decay of 0.01, using an initial learning rate of 1e-6 with a warmup period that rapidly increased to 5e-4 within the first few epochs, as shown in Fig. 4. A ReduceLROnPlateau scheduler monitored validation loss and reduced the learning rate when progress plateaued, with a patience of 15 epochs and a reduction factor of 0.1.

The training dynamics, illustrated in Fig. 4, show a rapid initial decrease in both batch and training loss within the first 100 epochs, followed by a more gradual optimization phase. The model trained on 5 geometries (red line) converged faster, reaching its minimum validation loss around epoch 300, while the model trained on 20 geometries (green line) continued to improve gradually over approximately 900 epochs. Both models achieved similar final loss values of approximately 0.6. This suggests that the benefit of additional training data was not in achieving lower final loss values, but rather in the model's ability to generalize better across a wider variety of input geometries. The slight differences in convergence patterns can be attributed to the more varied training signal provided by the larger dataset, requiring more epochs to fully assimilate the diverse geometric patterns. To address the high memory requirements, we implemented gradient accumulation with 8 steps, effectively increasing the batch size while maintaining memory efficiency. Additional regularization techniques included gradient clipping with a maximum norm of 1.0 and proper weight initialization using Kaiming normal initialization. Training was conducted on an NVIDIA T4 GPU with 16 GB of memory, with the 5-geometry model requiring approximately 300 epochs and the 20-geometry model training for about 900 epochs. The final model size was 36 MB, allowing for efficient deployment and inference in tens of milliseconds per sample.

5   Testing and Results

5.1   Evaluating the Models

Neural networks were trained on datasets with 5, 20, and 50 geometries, using the remaining geometries for testing. We assessed image quality using standard metrics (see Fig. 5) such as Peak Signal-to-Noise Ratio (PSNR), Structural Similarity Index Measure (SSIM), and Gradient Magnitude Similarity Deviation (GMSD). Nevertheless the best metric was the visual comparison of the images resulting from the mean (see Fig. 6). Future work will include a comprehensive quantitative evaluation specifically comparing the neural network predictions against the ground truth material budget distributions to assess the physical accuracy of the reconstructed internal structures.

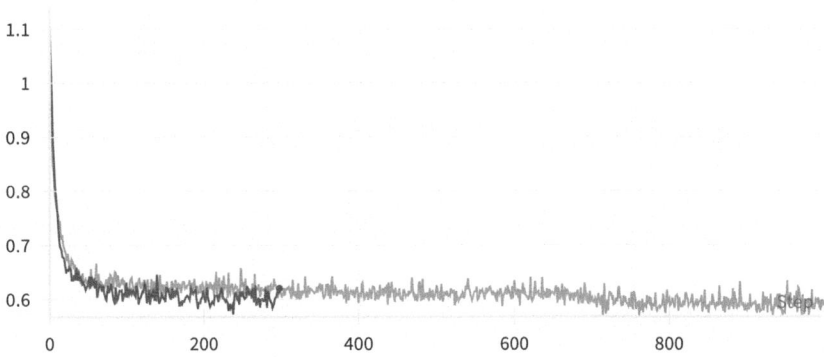

Fig. 4. Training metrics for the resolution augmentation network. The batch loss graph shows the progression of loss values during training, with both models rapidly converging within the first 100 epochs, followed by more gradual optimization. The red line represents the model trained on 5 geometries. The green line shows the model trained on 20 geometries, which continued to improve over approximately 900 epochs. Despite the difference in dataset size, both models achieved similar final loss values, suggesting that the primary benefit of additional training data was improved generalization rather than lower absolute loss. (Color figure online)

5.2   Testing on Limestone and Wood

To evaluate generalization capabilities of our models across different materials, we created additional datasets which use, instead of concrete, limestone and wood. These materials were chosen for their relevance in cultural heritage contexts and their distinct physical properties compared to concrete. The simulated composition for limestone was defined by mass fractions approximating natural stone: Ca (40.05 %), C (12.00 %), and O (47.95 %), with density set to $2.55\,\mathrm{g/cm^3}$. For pine wood, we used a composition of C (50.0 %), O (42.0 %), and H (8.0 %), with a much lower density of $0.5\,\mathrm{g/cm^3}$.

For limestone samples, we embedded cylindrical iron bars with 10 mm diameter, while for the less dense wood, we reduced the diameter to 5 mm to create more subtle detection challenges. Both cases maintained the $30 \times 30 \times 30\,\mathrm{cm^3}$ cube dimensions consistent with our previous simulations using concrete.

The results are visualized in Figs. 7 and 8, and demonstrate the effectiveness of the pipeline across these different material contexts. For the limestone samples, even with limited exposure (100k events), the initial detection showed faint indications of the embedded structures. After applying our event augmentation network, the iron bars became distinctly visible with significantly improved contrast. The subsequent resolution augmentation further refined these details, producing results that closely matched the ground truth distribution. For the wood samples the initial detection showed minimal contrast, with bars barely distinguishable from background noise. However, the event augmentation net-

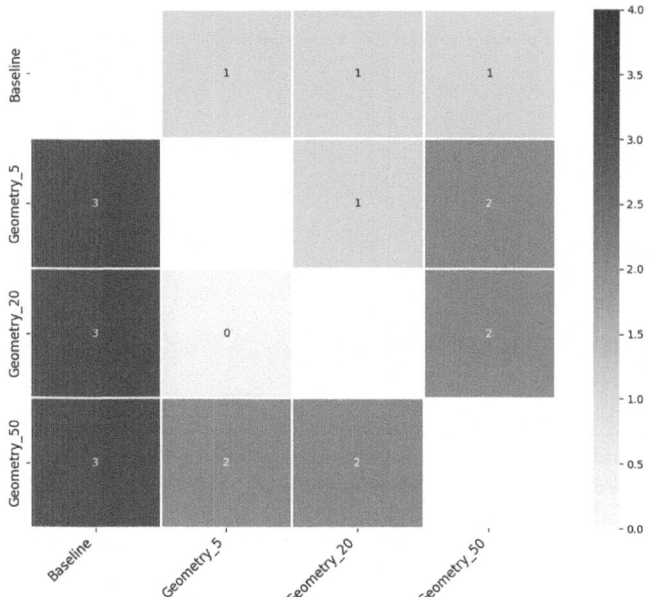

Fig. 5. Confusion matrix comparing Baseline with ML models trained on 5, 20, and 50 geometries across PSNR, SSIM, and GMSD metrics. Each cell shows the number of metrics (0–4) where the row method outperforms the column method. The ML models generally outperform the Baseline on PSNR and SSIM. GMSD initially favored the baseline against HRME because noise was mistaken for detail. However, against ground truth (computed from material budget), the ML models exhibited lower GMSD values, confirming enhanced clarity and noise suppression.

work successfully extracted meaningful patterns from this limited data, with a clear visibility of the embedded structures. Similar images are obtained on all additional limestone and wood datasets. These results validate our approach's adaptability to different material contexts common in cultural heritage applications, from dense stone structures to wooden artifacts with metal components. The consistent performance across these diverse materials indicates that our pipeline could be effectively deployed in various archaeological and conservation scenarios without requiring material-specific retraining.

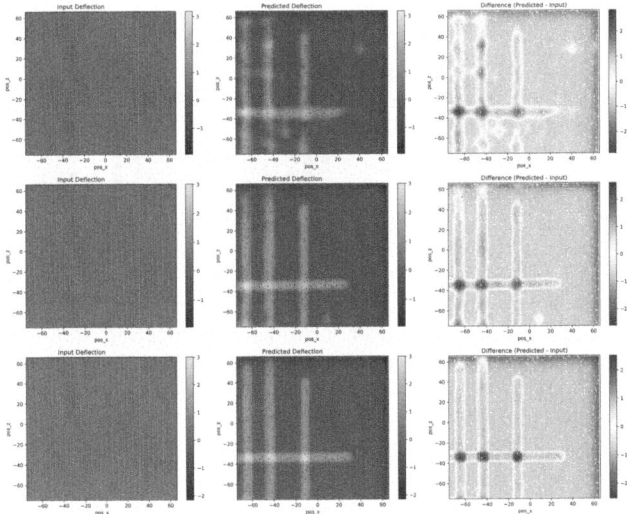

Fig. 6. The first column reports the image obtained from the statistics of the original sample before the event augmentation. On the second column, one can see the image after the event augmentation inferred by models trained on 5, 20 and 50 geometries, respectively. Finally, the third column reports the image resulting from the difference between the input sample and the predicted sample. Image from [4].

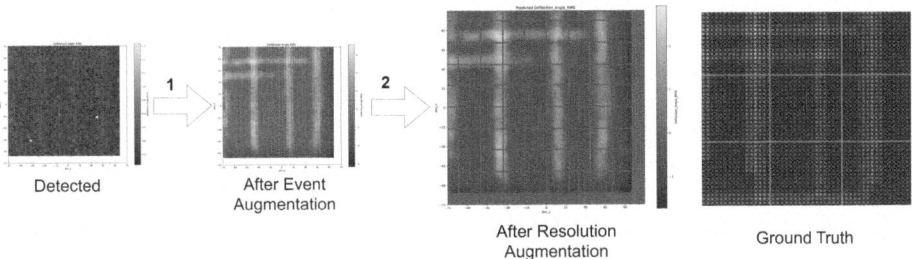

Detected   After Event Augmentation   After Resolution Augmentation   Ground Truth

Fig. 7. Example of the pipeline tested on one element of the dataset 30 cm^3 of limestone and cylindrical iron bars of 10 mm of diameter. The first column ("Detected") shows raw muon-detection data (100k events, 94×94 pixels). The second column ("After Event Augmentation") displays the result of statistically augmenting the number of muon events via a dedicated neural network. The third column ("After Resolution Augmentation") illustrates the enhanced spatial resolution (280×280 pixels). Finally, the fourth column ("Ground Truth") provides a visualization of the known material budget distribution.

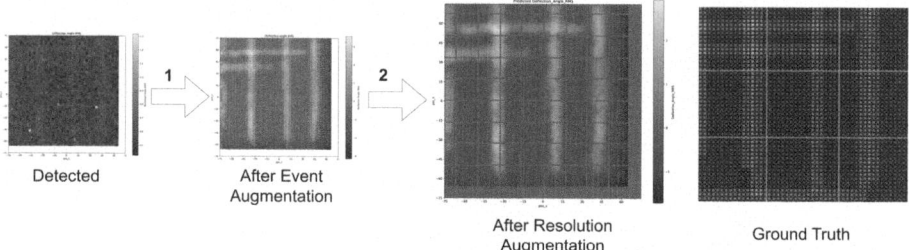

Detected   After Event Augmentation   After Resolution Augmentation   Ground Truth

Fig. 8. Data enhancement pipeline tested on the dataset with 30 cm^3 of wood and cylindrical iron bars of 5 mm of diameter showing the scattering angle: the first column ('Detected') represents the raw muon detection results after 100k muonic events by the four detectors with 94 × 94 pixels of resolution. The second column ('After Event Augmentation') shows the effect of statistical event augmentation through our neural network trained on 50G. The third column ('After Resolution Augmentation') presents the results after applying spatial resolution enhancement techniques. The final column ('Ground Truth') is a visualization of the known material budget distributions.

6   Conclusion

This work describes the first implementation of a pipeline to address the two main limitations in bringing muon tomography to the fields of civil engineering and cultural heritage diagnostics, i.e. the poor resolution of the images showing the internal structures of such samples and the high exposure times that are needed to acquire enough data in order to infer the sample content. Visual analysis of the results, which extends the ones reported in [4], show that it is possible to boost the data acquisition time by a factor of 45 and to improve the pixel resolution by approximately a factor 9 in 2-dimensional images reconstruction. The choice of limestone, wood and concrete as test material is due to the fact that these materials are commonly found in European cultural heritage assets. For example, reinforced concrete is typical of 20th-century architecture while limestone is characteristic of cathedrals and medieval fortifications; finally, wooden structures are commonly found in roofs, wooden naves, and internal frameworks of polychrome sculptures. Beside that, our tests on these material prove that our pipeline achieve consistent performance in such configurations even if not trained on material-specific data, thus delivering promising results towards a generalized, material agnostic, model for muon tomography applications.

Overall, this work chart the path towards machine learning applications in the field of muon tomography and important challenges ahead can be drawn from it. Among them, we stress the need to move from a source of muons traveling parallel to each other along a defined direction, to a realistic source with muons directionality and energy being distributed as naturally occurring at the Earth's surface. This step would require more advanced imaging techniques capable of reconstructing the 3-dimensional content of the samples under study both with analytical and machine-learning based solutions.

Disclosure of Interests. The authors have no competing interests to declare that are relevant to the content of this article.

References

1. Alvarez, L.W., et al.: Search for hidden chambers in the pyramids. Science **167**(3919), 832–839 (1970)
2. George, E.P.: Cosmic rays measure overburden of tunnel. Commonwealth Engineer (1955)
3. Tanaka, H., et al.: Subsurface imaging by cosmic muons. Geophys. Res. Lett. (2013)
4. Pezzotti, L., et al.: A new method for structural diagnostics with muon tomography and deep learning. 2025 JINST 20 P06034. https://doi.org/10.1088/1748-0221/20/06/P06034
5. Agostinelli, S., et al.: Geant4 - a simulation toolkit. Nucl. Instrum. Methods Phys. Res. A **506**(3), 250–303 (2003)
6. Allison, J., et al.: Geant4 developments and applications. IEEE Trans. Nucl. Sci. **53**(1), 270–278 (2006)
7. Allison, J., et al.: Recent developments in Geant4. Nucl. Instrum. Methods Phys. Res. A **835**, 186–225 (2016)
8. Ronneberger, O., Fischer, P., Brox, T.: U-Net: convolutional networks for biomedical image segmentation. In: Navab, N., Hornegger, J., Wells, W.M., Frangi, A.F. (eds.) MICCAI 2015. LNCS, vol. 9351, pp. 234–241. Springer, Cham (2015). https://doi.org/10.1007/978-3-319-24574-4_28
9. Wang, X., et al.: ESRGAN: enhanced super-resolution generative adversarial networks. In: Leal-Taixé, L., Roth, S. (eds.) ECCV 2018. LNCS, vol. 11133, pp. 63–79. Springer, Cham (2019). https://doi.org/10.1007/978-3-030-11021-5_5
10. Hu, J., Shen, L., Sun, G.: Squeeze-and-excitation networks. In: Proceedings of the IEEE Conference on Computer Vision and Pattern Recognition, pp. 7132–7141 (2018)
11. Loshchilov, I., Hutter, F.: Decoupled weight decay regularization. In: 7th International Conference on Learning Representations. OpenReview.net (2019)

Crack Detection in Pavement Imagery: Evaluating U-Net Variants

Gonçalo Silva[1] , Oraib Almegdadi[1] , Fátima Batista[2] , João Marcelino[2] , and Nuno C. Marques[1]($\boxtimes$)

[1] NOVA LINCS, NOVA School of Science and Technology,
Caparica, Portugal
{gab.silva,o.almegdadi}@campus.fct.unl.pt, nmm@fct.unl.pt
[2] National Laboratory for Civil Engineering (LNEC), Lisbon, Portugal
{fabatista,marcelino}@lnec.pt

Abstract. Accurate detection of thin cracks in road surfaces remains a significant challenge with pixel-level precision. In this work, we evaluate the performance of U-Net variants including ThinCrack U-Net and a pretrained VGG-16 encoder. Models are trained using different loss functions and different optimizers like Stochastic Gradient Descent with learning rate reduction on plateau. Experiments on the CrackTree260 dataset (260 annotated road images) assess precision, recall, F1-score and mean Intersection over Union, using both exact-match and some pixel dilation tolerance. While ThinCrack U-Net was designed to enhance narrow crack detection, results show it underperforms the baseline models across several metrics. Notably, U-Net with a combination of Binary Cross Entropy and Dice loss functions yields the best F1-score for exact-match evaluation. We discuss how these results reflect on the limitations of current architectures in capturing true crack width, and propose directions for model refinement and loss design in future work.

Keywords: Road Pavement Cracking · U-Net Parameterization · Crack Detection · Model Trustworthiness · Image Segmentation Datasets

1 Introduction

Road pavements are engineering structures exposed to a wide range of traffic loads and environmental conditions throughout their service life. If no maintenance actions are undertaken, these factors lead to progressive surface deterioration and reduced serviceability, making regular inspection essential to ensure safety and functionality. Among the various indicators of degradation, surface cracking plays a central role in condition assessment and supports risk-based maintenance planning. In recent years, convolutional segmentation models—particularly U-Net variants—have become widely adopted for this task due to their accessibility, extensibility, and relatively low computational cost.

© The Author(s), under exclusive license to Springer Nature Switzerland AG 2026
J. Valente de Oliveira et al. (Eds.): EPIA 2025, LNAI 16121, pp. 136–148, 2026.
https://doi.org/10.1007/978-3-032-05176-9_11

However, these models are not always trustworthy when it comes to accurately estimating crack widths, especially in the presence of fine cracks. Low contrast and the severe foreground–background imbalance present a fundamental challenge to all road-crack detection techniques, often compromising both the consistency and the geometric accuracy of estimated crack widths. Moreover, we show that even minor changes in ground-truth annotations can significantly alter performance metrics and shift the apparent advantage between standard and specialized architectures.

U-Net remains a pragmatic choice in applied AI domains such as infrastructure monitoring due to its simplicity and interpretability. In this study, we revisit the evaluation protocol of a specialized variant—ThinCrack U-Net [14]—using a publicly available dataset to assess whether architectural modifications such as enhanced encoders or atrous convolutions yield tangible improvements in width estimation. While previous studies often report strong F1 scores under relaxed matching conditions (e.g., dilation radius d = 5), such metrics may obscure width-related inaccuracies that are critical in downstream engineering applications. We therefore focus on more rigorous evaluation criteria, emphasizing how architectural decisions affect the reliability of thin-crack delineation at the pixel level.

2 Background and Motivation

Crack detection and characterization are essential for assessing the condition of road pavements, as cracking is one of the earliest and most relevant indicators of surface deterioration. While isolated narrow cracks – such as longitudinal or transverse ones – do not immediately compromise user safety and comfort, they often represent the onset of structural degradation and may allow water infiltration into the pavement layers (Fig. 1), thereby accelerating deterioration. In more severe cases, such as alligator cracking, the impact on the ride quality can be significant and, in certain cases, can even pose direct safety risks. Early crack detection, combined with effective and timely monitoring is therefore essential to support maintenance actions and optimize resource allocation within the broader framework of asset management. To support these goals, infrastructure managers—such as Infraestruturas de Portugal and BRISA—have increasingly adopted automated inspection systems like Laser Crack Measurement System (LCMS) [8] and RoadAI [7]. These platforms enhance inspection efficiency, reduce the subjectivity of manual surveys, and promote standardization in severity classification.

Despite their advantages, such systems require substantial investment in specialized equipment and operational infrastructure. As a cost-effective alternative, image processing techniques using standard photographs and open-source convolutional neural networks (CNNs) have gained relevance. These approaches, often deployed with off-the-shelf cameras or smartphones, enable hybrid detection pipelines that combine traditional edge detection with deep learning for classification and quantification. Building on these developments, this work explores a semi-automatic crack detection methodology based on low-cost image analysis and a web-based submission platform with georeferencing capabilities [10]. Rather than replacing advanced systems, the proposed approach is intended as a complementary tool—especially valuable for early-stage assessments or in regions lacking systematic inspection infrastructure. Central to its effectiveness is a trustworthy classifier that maintains geometric accuracy across diverse image sources and challenging acquisition conditions.

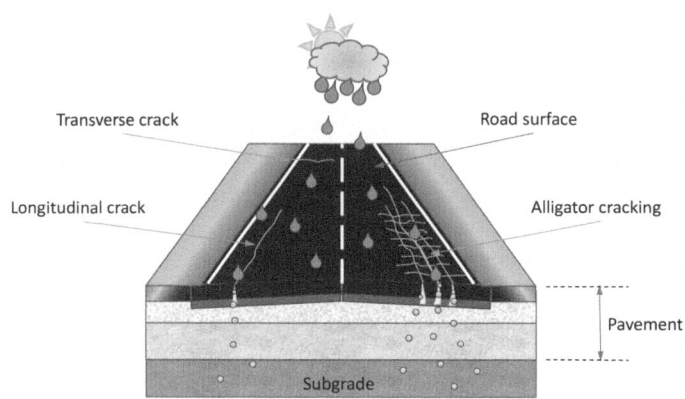

Fig. 1. Schematic illustration of typical surface cracking in flexible pavements (longitudinal cracks, transverse cracks, and alligator cracking).

3   Related Work

U-Net has been widely adopted across domains for segmentation tasks, with initial applications in biomedical imaging [12,20]. Due to U-Net's balance of localization accuracy, computational efficiency, and architectural simplicity, it has become a foundational model in pavement crack detection. For instance, DeepCrack [5,24] introduces multi-scale feature fusion and class imbalance-aware loss functions, improving robustness but often prioritizing crack presence over precise geometry. ThinCrack U-Net [14] specifically targets thin crack segmentation under severe class imbalance, using memory-efficient downsampling and atrous convolutions. While it reports improved F1 scores on CrackTree260 using relaxed evaluation, it offers limited insight into crack width accuracy. Beyond U-Net derivatives, architectures like CrackSeg [15], DeepLabv3+ [16], and VGG16-based SegNet [24] have been applied to low-contrast or noisy imagery. Earlier edge-based methods such as HED [18], RCF [6], and CrackTree [23] show limited geometric precision in comparison.

Recent approaches emphasize lightweight and modular U-Net variants—e.g., CrackUnet [21], Tiny-Crack-Net [1]—as well as hybrid pipelines that combine detection and segmentation stages [3,4,19]. Even in Transformer-inspired models such as CrackFormer [17] and RepCrack [9], U-Net's encoder-decoder structure remains central due to its interpretability, extensibility, and ease of integration. Transformers have emerged as a dominant framework in computer vision, widely recognized for their scalability and ability to model global context. However, recent studies have highlighted that the self-attention mechanism can result in unreliable performance, particularly in tasks requiring precise spatial localization. For example, attention modules may overemphasize irrelevant features or background regions, leading to inaccurate predictions [22]. Moreover, Transformers have shown limitations in balancing global and local dependencies, which can hinder tasks demanding detailed structural understanding [13].

4   Methodology

This section details the design and implementation of the twelve deep learning models evaluated in our experiments. These include seven U-Net variants developed through targeted architectural and training modifications (Table 1), four variants of the ThinCrack U-Net [14] architecture (Table 2), and a pre-trained U-Net_VGG16 model [2,10]. All models were trained and tested on the same dataset and evaluated by same metrics. For further details, the model architecture can be consulted in the ThinCrack U-Net paper or in the experimental documentation [14]. The implementation code, pretrained models, extended documentation and relevant examples to this study are available in the GitHub repository[1].

Implementation Environment and Dataset Preparation: All models, except the pre-trained U-Net_VGG16, were implemented in PyTorch using a publicly available U-Net baseline by Aladdin Persson [2,11]. The pre-trained U-Net_VGG16 was sourced from previous work on pavement crack detection [10]. Custom loss functions, including BCE_Dice and BF1, were implemented to support architectural and training variations. Training was conducted on Kaggle Notebooks using dual NVIDIA T4 GPUs (2×16 GB VRAM), with the code adapted for multi-GPU support via PyTorch's Distributed Data Parallel (DDP) framework. Metric computation and validation loss calculation were refined to ensure equal sample weighting across variable batch sizes.

We used the CrackTree260 dataset, which contains 260 manually annotated images of asphalt pavement at a resolution of 800×600 pixels, each with pixelwise crack masks. Due to the sparse and fine-grained nature of cracks, the dataset exhibits strong class imbalance. To address this, a high positive class weight `pos_weight = 15` was applied when using Binary Cross Entropy (BCEWithLogitsLoss). All images were center- cropped to 512×512 pixels to ensure compatibility with the U-Net architecture, which requires input dimensions divisible by powers of two.

Although the original ThinCrack U-Net [14] paper provides a preprocessing pipeline, it lacks specifics on dataset partitioning. We applied a consistent preprocessing approach but excluded augmentation steps that did not align with our experimental design. Training was limited to 100 epochs, as convergence was typically achieved before epoch 50.

---

[1] https://github.com/GoncaloABdaSilva/Crack-Detection-in-Pavement-Imagery.

U-Net Variations: To analyze the effect of individual modifications, we implemented seven U-Net variants, summarized in Table 1. These include changes in optimizer, loss function, normalization, feature map depth, and architectural design. We use the term "variant" broadly to cover both architectural changes and training strategy choices, as all represent design decisions that influence segmentation performance.

Table 1. Summary of U-Net Variants

Model Name	Optimizer	Loss Function	Normalization	Feature Maps	Additional Modifications
U-Net	Adam	BCEWithLogits	Batch	Default	—
U-Net (SGD, scheduler)	SGD	BCEWithLogits	Batch	Default	ReduceLROnPlateau scheduler
U-Net (SGD, scheduler, Bf1)	SGD	BF1	Batch	Default	—
U-Net (SGD, scheduler, BCE_Dice)	SGD	BCE_Dice	Batch	Default	—
U-Net (SGD, scheduler, BCE_Dice,IN)	SGD	BCE_Dice	Instance	Default	—
U-Net (SGD, scheduler, BCE_Dice, less feature maps)	SGD	BF1	Batch	Âij of default	Matches ThinCrack feature scaling
U-Net (SGD, scheduler, BCE_Dice, Dilated Double-Conv)	SGD	BCE_Dice	Batch	Default	Dilated convolutions in encoder and decoder
U-Net_VGG16 (Pre-trained)	Pre-trained	—	—	Default	—

ThinCrack U-Net Architecture and Variants: The original ThinCrack U-Net [14] follows an encoder-decoder structure starting with tile padding (interpreted as zero padding), followed by MaxPooling, two DoubleConv blocks, and two dilated convolutions in the encoder. The decoder uses convolutional upsampling, followed by two dilated and two regular DoubleConv blocks, with skip connections. It ends with a Transposed Convolution, a 1×1 Convolution, and a Sigmoid activation. The model is trained using Stochastic Gradient Descent (SGD) optimizer with a learning rate of 0.01, momentum of 0.9, weight decay of 0.0005, and a ReduceLROnPlateau scheduler.

Table 2 summarizes the ThinCrack U-Net variants used in our study, highlighting variations in normalization type, feature map depth, and loss functions, as well as architectural modifications such as dilated convolutions and the removal of intermediate pooling layers.

Evaluation Metrics: To enable consistent comparison across all twelve models, we evaluated performance using four standard metrics on the test set: precision, recall, F1-score, and mean Intersection over Union (mIoU). Precision measures the proportion of correctly predicted crack pixels, while recall captures the proportion of actual crack pixels successfully detected. The F1-score balances these two, reflecting both sensitivity and specificity. The mIoU quantifies the average overlap between predicted and ground-truth crack regions.

Table 2. ThinCrack U-Net Architecture and Variants

Model Name	Loss Function	Normalization	Feature Maps	Architectural Features
ThinCrack U-Net	BF1	Batch	Reduced by 4×	Tile padding, dilated convolutions, no intermediate pooling
ThinCrack U-Net (IN)	BF1	Instance	Reduced by 4×	Replaced Batch Normalization with Instance Normalization
ThinCrack U-Net (more features maps)	BF1	Batch	Reduced by 2×	Increased number of feature maps produced in each layer
ThinCrack U-Net (BCE_Dice)	BCE_Dice	Batch	Reduced by 4×	Same as original

5 Results

We evaluated ThinCrack U-Net [14] and several U-Net variants on the Crack-Tree260 dataset, including a pre-trained U-Net_VGG16, targeting pixel-level segmentation of pavement cracks. Contrary to expectations, ThinCrack U-Net yielded significantly lower performance (Precision = 27.2%, F1-score = 37.5%, mIoU = 61.0%) compared to the standard U-Net and its variants. It produced a high number of False Positives (background pixels predicted as crack), resulting in poor scores across Precision, F1-score, and mIoU. In particular, pairing ThinCrack U-Net with BCE_Dice loss led to complete prediction failure during training—no True Positives (correct crack pixel predictions) were made over 100 epochs. In contrast, standard U-Net variants using either BF1 or BCE_Dice loss showed substantial performance improvements. The best-performing configuration—standard U-Net with SGD, learning rate scheduling, and BCE_Dice loss—achieved the highest scores in Precision (77.9%), F1-score (72.4%), and mIoU (78.2%).

Table 3. Performance on CrackTree260 with standard evaluation (Regular) and 5-pixel dilation (d = 5)

Model (Variation)	Regular				Dilated (d=5)			
	Prec.	Recall	F1	mIoU	Prec.	Recall	F1	mIoU
U-Net	34.9%	**88.1%**	50.0%	66.2%	97.3%	**95.4%**	96.3%	96.4%
U-Net (SGD, scheduler)	53.2%	65.8%	58.8%	70.6%	96.3%	77.7%	86.0%	87.6%
U-Net (SGD, scheduler, BF1)	57.7%	80.8%	67.3%	75.2%	98.8%	87.8%	93.0%	93.4%
U-Net (SGD, scheduler, BCE-Dice)	**77.9%**	67.5%	**72.4%**	**78.2%**	97.2%	72.2%	82.9%	85.3%
U-Net (SGD, scheduler, BCE-Dice, IN)	68.1%	73.7%	70.8%	77.2%	92.1%	79.1%	85.1%	86.9%
U-Net (SGD, scheduler, BF1, less feature maps)	49.7%	81.8%	61.8%	72.1%	96.6%	89.7%	93.0%	93.4%
U-Net (SGD, scheduler, BCE-Dice, Dilated DoubleConv)	71.5%	64.4%	67.8%	75.5%	93.0%	70.2%	80.0%	83.2%
ThinCrack U-Net	27.2%	60.4%	37.5%	61.0%	88.9%	83.3%	86.0%	87.6%
ThinCrack U-Net (IN)	24.1%	68.1%	35.6%	60.2%	94.0%	89.3%	91.6%	92.1%
ThinCrack U-Net (more feature maps)	28.0%	66.1%	39.3%	61.7%	91.2%	86.4%	88.7%	89.7%
ThinCrack U-Net (BCE-Dice)	Training failed				Training failed			
U-Net_VGG16	22.0%	20.6%	21.3%	55.6%	**99.9%**	54.2%	70.3%	76.9%

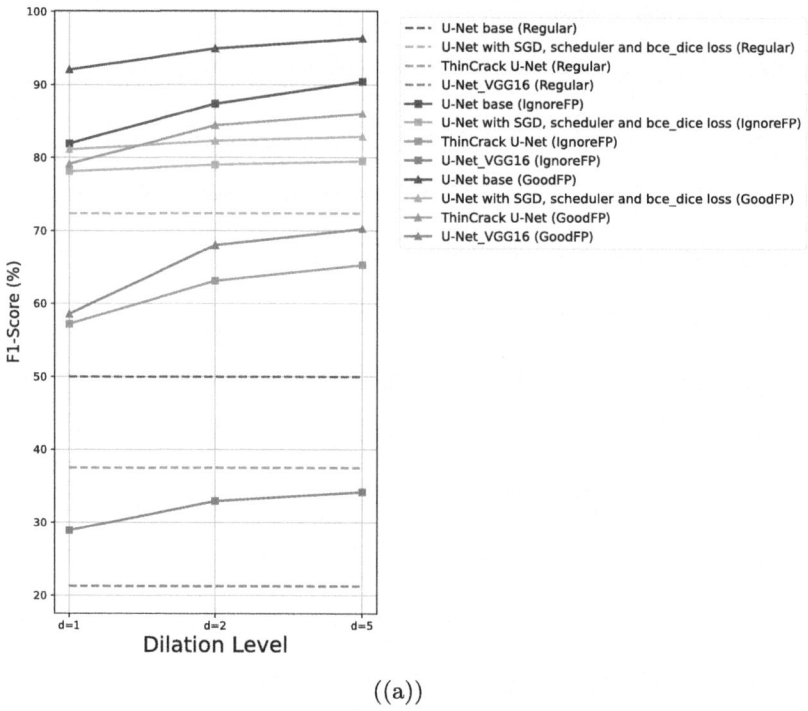

Fig. 2. F1-scores of different models, with different types of dilation and different dilation rates.

Table 3 summarizes the full performance landscape across twelve model configurations and two evaluation settings. While several models achieve competitive scores under relaxed conditions, only a few maintain consistent accuracy across both regimes. Notably, the BCE_Dice-trained U-Net balances high recall and precision under strict evaluation, while ThinCrack U-Net (IN) [14] and U-Net_VGG16 show limited generalization. The table also highlights the influence of secondary factors like normalization type and feature map depth, with minimal gains observed from architectural variants using dilated convolutions or instance normalization.

To investigate spatial tolerance, we applied dilation-based evaluations with radius/dilation rate d = 1, d = 2 and d = 5 pixels. As expected, increasing the dilation rate led to higher metric scores, especially for models with high False Positive rates. This reflects the models' difficulty in achieving precise, one-pixel-wide crack delineation. When comparing with the original ThinCrack U-Net [14] paper—which reported an F1-score of 94.48% at d = 5—our best-performing ThinCrack U-Net implementation achieved a F1-score of 91.6%, a comparable result. The model that most benefited with this evaluation method was the base U-net implementation, achieving the top Recall (95.4%) F1-score (96.3%) and mIoU (96.4%).

We also tested a different approach of applying dilation-ignoring False Positive predictions within the dilation radius (i.e., excluding them from both True Positives and False Positives counts). Figure 2 illustrates how different evaluation protocols affect F1-score, comparing Regular (exact match), IgnoreFP (excluding near-boundary False Positives), and GoodFP (counting them as correct). These delineation tracks reveal the extent to which each model benefits from spatial tolerance around ground truth. For example, at $d = 5$, the base U-net implementation went from 50.0% to 90.4%; U-Net with SGD, scheduler and BCE_Dice loss went from 72.4% to 79.5%; ThinCrack U-Net went from 37.5% to 65.3%; U-Net_VGG16 went from 21.3% to 34.2%. The models that still remain with a lower F1-score indicate greater reliance on relaxed metrics, and suggesting a larger number of False Negative predictions (predicting a crack pixel as background).

The F1-score gap between GoodFP (triangle lines) and IgnoreFP (square lines) provides further insight into boundary precision. Models like the BCE_Dice-trained U-Net display minimal drops, implying that most predictions within the tolerance zone are indeed accurate. Contrarily, ThinCrack U-Net and U-Net_VGG16 exhibit larger discrepancies, indicating that a substantial portion of their GoodFP gains is attributable to spatial leniency rather than precise detection. These discrepancies highlight variability in model robustness: smaller GoodFP–IgnoreFP gaps reflect stronger geometric fidelity, while larger ones reveal over-reliance on buffer-based correction. This trend is also visually evident in Fig. 3, where U-Net variants produce more continuous and accurately aligned crack maps compared to the fragmented or incomplete outputs of Thin-Crack U-Net and U-Net_VGG16.

6 Discussion

As highlighted in Table 3 and Fig. 2, dilation-based evaluation significantly impacts perceived model performance in pavement crack segmentation. While metrics such as F1-score improve with increasing tolerance (e.g., $d = 5$), they often obscure the model's ability to precisely localize narrow cracks. Contrary to its design goal, ThinCrack U-Net [14] consistently underperformed relative to standard U-Net variants, even under relaxed conditions. This raises concerns about its generalization ability and suggests that its architectural modifications may not adequately compensate for the severe class imbalance and low contrast present in CrackTree260. Furthermore, the large gains observed between IgnoreFP and GoodFP metrics in models like ThinCrack U-Net and U-Net_VGG16 indicate high false negative rates and a reliance on proximity-based evaluation to recover performance.

In contrast, models trained with BCE_Dice loss function exhibited more robust behavior, maintaining high F1-scores across strict and relaxed settings. The small performance gap between their GoodFP and IgnoreFP curves indicates better geometric alignment with ground truth boundaries and fewer spurious activations. These observations suggest that architectural parsimony, when paired with well-calibrated loss design, can outperform more specialized variants.

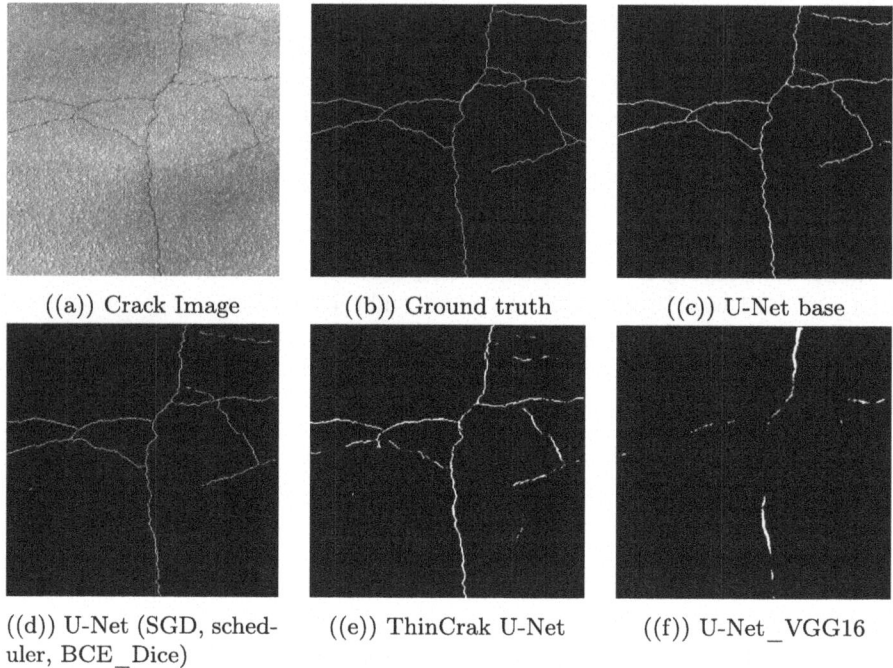

((a)) Crack Image   ((b)) Ground truth   ((c)) U-Net base

((d)) U-Net (SGD, sched-   ((e)) ThinCrak U-Net   ((f)) U-Net_VGG16
uler, BCE_Dice)

Fig. 3. (a) Sample image from the CrackTree260 dataset; (b) Corresponding ground truth annotation; (c-f) Crack predictions generated by various models.

The choice of evaluation protocol emerges as a critical factor in comparing models. Metrics that include false positives within a buffer zone may be suitable for rough damage localization, but they fail to penalize width distortion—undermining their utility in maintenance planning or quantitative condition assessment. In particular, the widespread reliance on relaxed metrics such as dilation-based F1-score (e.g., $d = 5$) can obscure true model limitations and create a false sense of accuracy. Models that perform well under IgnoreFP conditions, with minimal reliance on spatial leniency, should be favored in applications requiring structural fidelity. This calls for more rigorous benchmarking protocols that prioritise exact pixel alignment over inflated performance metrics.

7   Additional Experiment: Multi-class U-Net with Crack Neighborhood Supervision

To further investigate the spatial ambiguity often leading to false positive predictions near crack boundaries, we conducted an auxiliary experiment using a multi-class formulation. In this setup, the standard U-Net architecture was adapted to segment three classes: Background, Crack, and Crack Neighborhood. The goal was to explicitly model the transitional region around cracks that typically causes misclassification. We constructed a modified version of the CrackTree260 dataset by applying morphological dilation (elliptical kernel, 11 × 11) around annotated cracks, labeling the resulting buffer as a distinct Crack Neighborhood class. The model output was adjusted to predict three channels, and training was performed using `CrossEntropyLoss` with class weights of 15 (Crack), 5 (Neighborhood), and 1 (Background).

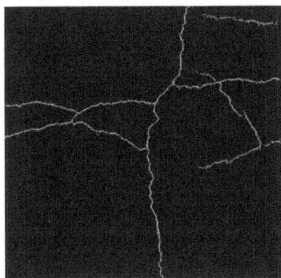

Fig. 4. Crack prediction generated by new experiment.

Evaluation was performed per class using argmax selection. Results for the Crack class were: Precision = 62.7%, Recall = 74.9%, F1-score = 68.3%, and mIoU = 75.7%. The Crack Neighborhood class achieved Precision = 85.5%, Recall = 83.6%, F1-score = 84.5%, and mIoU = 85.7%. These results were comparable to the U-Net configuration with SGD, scheduler and BF1 loss, which had a similar F1-score and mIoU, lower precision and higher recall. Regarding the prediction of the Crack class with dilation (d = 5), it scored: Precision = 97.1%, Recall = 82.2%, F1-score = 89.0% and mIoU = 90.0%. Figure 4 presents the crack prediction outputs generated by our models, corresponding to the same input image used in Fig. 3.

Preliminary feedback from two domain experts suggested that the multiclass model produced more visually complete crack maps. While informal, these observations are consistent with the model's improved F1-score and boundary coverage. This experiment highlights the potential of boundary-aware supervision to reduce misclassification in crack-adjacent regions, while also revealing trade-offs in visual quality due to some artifacts—motivating future work on refinement or regularization strategies.

8   Conclusion

Our experiments show that ThinCrack U-Net [14] does not outperform the standard U-Net or its loss-enhanced variants when evaluated on thin crack segmentation using the CrackTree260 dataset. When relaxed evaluation methods (e.g., dilation with d = 5) are used, performance increases notably, but this masks key issues in precise width prediction. Given that our objective is to extract accurate crack width measurements, high False Positive rates—especially near actual cracks—undermine model utility. This insight is particularly critical in real-world scenarios, where small deviations in predicted crack width can impact maintenance decisions, cost estimation, and safety prioritisation. These findings reaffirm that true geometric fidelity, not just overlap-based metrics, should guide evaluation.

Future directions include integrating width-aware losses, improving pixel-level precision through boundary refinement modules, and considering dataset re-annotation or synthetic augmentation to better capture sub-pixel crack geometry. Evaluation frameworks must align with practical requirements—particularly in engineering applications where physical measurements derived from segmentation matter. Ultimately, we advocate for more realistic and stringent evaluation protocols to prevent overestimation of model robustness and ensure reliability in real-world deployment contexts.

As a complementary step, we explored a multi-class formulation using a newly constructed multi-class dataset to explicitly model transitional regions around cracks. The experiment showed comparable F1-score and mIoU to the third best binary model, while improving precision—but at the cost of more visual artifacts. This trade-off highlights the importance of balancing boundary refinement with structural clarity. Future work should focus on integrating width-aware losses, boundary regularization modules, and context-guided refinement strategies. Moreover, evaluation frameworks must align with engineering needs—especially in tasks requiring accurate physical measurements derived from segmentation outputs—and should be complemented by higher-quality ground truth, further refined through expert annotation and human-in-the-loop validation.

Acknowledgments. This work was supported by UID/04516/NOVA Laboratory for Computer Science and Informatics (NOVA LINCS), with financial support from FCT.IP. The second author also acknowledges funding from the Foundation for Science and Technology (FCT) under the CMU Portugal Affiliated Ph.D. Programs, through the fellowship grant PRT/BD/155062/2024.

Disclosure of Interests. The authors have no competing interests to declare that are relevant to the content of this article.

References

1. Chu, H., Wang, W., Deng, L.: Tiny-crack-net: a multiscale feature fusion network with attention mechanisms for segmentation of tiny cracks. Comput.-Aided Civil Infrastruct. Eng. **37**, 1914–1931 (2022)
2. Ha, K.: crack_segmentation. https://github.com/khanhha/crack_segmentation
3. Jiang, Y., Pang, D., Li, C., Yu, Y., Cao, Y.: Two-step deep learning approach for pavement crack damage detection and segmentation. Int. J. Pavement Eng. **24**, 2065488 (2023). https://doi.org/10.1080/10298436.2022.2065488

4. Liu, J., et al.: Automated pavement crack detection and segmentation based on two-step convolutional neural network. Comput.-Aided Civil Infrastruct. Eng. **35**, 1291–1305 (2020). https://doi.org/10.1111/mice.12622

5. Liu, Y., Yao, J., Lu, X., Xie, R., Li, L.: Deepcrack: a deep hierarchical feature learning architecture for crack segmentation. Neurocomputing **338**, 139–153 (2019). https://doi.org/10.1016/j.neucom.2019.01.036

6. Liu, Y., Cheng, M.M., Hu, X., Wang, K., Bai, X.: Richer convolutional features for edge detection. In: Proceedings of the IEEE Conference on Computer Vision and Pattern Recognition (CVPR) (2017)

7. Menezes, B., Rato, M.J., Matos, A.R.: A inteligência artificial na monitorização do estado superficial de pavimentos. In: Proceedings of the 11th Portuguese Road and Railway Congress (CRP), Portugal (2025), Submission No. 101, 7 pages (in Portuguese)

8. Morgado, J., et al.: Desenvolvimento de uma metodologia para o cálculo da área fendilhada com base na recolha automática do fendilhamento em pavimentos rodoviários. In: Proceedings of the 11th Portuguese Road and Railway Congress (CRP), Portugal (2025), Submission No. 108, 10 pages (in Portuguese)

9. Ni, M., Chen, L., Shi, P., Ren, R.: Repcrack: an efficient pavement crack segmentation method based on structural re-parameterization. Eng. Appl. Artif. Intell. **141**, 109791 (2025). https://doi.org/10.1016/j.engappai.2024.109791

10. Pena, R., Marques, N., Batista, F., Manso, J., Marcelino, J.: Efficient pavement crack monitoring for road life cycle management. In: Proceedings of the 10th Transport Research Arena (TRA), Dublin, Ireland (2024). Paper No. 707, 6 pages

11. Persson, A.: Semantic segmentation using u-net (n.d.). https://github.com/aladdinpersson/Machine-Learning-Collection/tree/master/ML/Pytorch/image_segmentation/semantic_segmentation_unet

12. Ronneberger, O., Fischer, P., Brox, T.: U-net: convolutional networks for biomedical image segmentation. In: Navab, N., Hornegger, J., Wells, W.M., Frangi, A.F. (eds.) MICCAI 2015. LNCS, vol. 9351, pp. 234–241. Springer, Cham (2015). https://doi.org/10.1007/978-3-319-24574-4_28

13. Sanford, C., Hsu, D.J., Telgarsky, M.: Representational strengths and limitations of transformers. In: Advances in Neural Information Processing Systems, vol. 36, pp. 36677–36707 (2023)

14. Siriborvornratanakul, T.: Pixel-level thin crack detection on road surface using convolutional neural network for severely imbalanced data. Comput.-Aided Civil Infrastruct. Eng. **38**, 2300–2316 (2023). https://doi.org/10.1111/mice.13010

15. Song, W., Jia, G., Zhu, H., Jia, D., Gao, L.: Automated pavement crack damage detection using deep multiscale convolutional features. J. Adv. Transp. **2020**, 6412562 (2020)

16. Wang, X., Wang, T., Li, J.: Advanced crack detection and quantification strategy based on clahe enhanced deeplabv3+. Eng. Appl. Artif. Intell. **126**, 106880 (2023). https://doi.org/10.1016/j.engappai.2023.106880

17. Xiao, S., Shang, K., Lin, K., Wu, Q., Gu, H., Zhang, Z.: Pavement crack detection with hybrid-window attentive vision transformers. Int. J. Appl. Earth Obs. Geoinf. **116**, 103172 (2023). https://doi.org/10.1016/j.jag.2022.103172

18. Xie, S., Tu, Z.: Holistically-nested edge detection. In: Proceedings of the IEEE International Conference on Computer Vision (ICCV) (2015)

19. Yang, Q., Ji, X.: Automatic pixel-level crack detection for civil infrastructure using unet++ and deep transfer learning. IEEE Sens. J. **21**, 19165–19175 (2021). https://doi.org/10.1109/JSEN.2021.3089718

20. Zeiser, F.A., et al.: Segmentation of masses on mammograms using data augmentation and deep learning. J. Digit. Imaging **33**, 858–868 (2020)
21. Zhang, L., Shen, J., Zhu, B.: A research on an improved unet-based concrete crack detection algorithm. Struct. Health Monit. **20**, 1864–1879 (2021). https://doi.org/10.1177/1475921720940068
22. Zhou, P., et al.: Attention calibration for transformer-based sequential recommendation. In: Proceedings of the 32nd ACM International Conference on Information and Knowledge Management, pp. 3595–3605 (2023)
23. Zou, Q., Cao, Y., Li, Q., Mao, Q., Wang, S.: Cracktree: automatic crack detection from pavement images. Pattern Recogn. Lett. **33**, 227–238 (2012). https://doi.org/10.1016/j.patrec.2011.11.004
24. Zou, Q., Zhang, Z., Li, Q., Qi, X., Wang, Q., Wang, S.: Deepcrack: learning hierarchical convolutional features for crack detection. IEEE Trans. Image Process. **28**, 1498–1512 (2019). https://doi.org/10.1109/TIP.2018.2878966

Coral and Fish Segmentation Enhanced by Image Restoration and Assisted Labeling via a Foundation Model

Fernando Duarte[1]([✉]) [iD], Nuno Lau[1] [iD], Eurico Pedrosa[1] [iD], Paulo Lopes[1] [iD],
and Pramod Kumar Maurya[2] [iD]

[1] IEETA/DETI/LASI, University of Aveiro, Aveiro, Portugal
{fjosefradique,nunolau,efp}@ua.pt
[2] CSIR-NIO, Dona Paula, India

Abstract. Coral reefs are reported to support up to a quarter of all marine life on Earth. Coral reefs are also reported to be undergoing a severe decline in the last decades worldwide. It is therefore very important to continuously monitor the health of coral reefs. However, this is a challenging task. On the one hand the quality of underwater images can be affected by the physical and chemical characteristics of underwater conditions. On the other hand, it is unfeasible for human scientists to manually review and analyze hundreds or even thousands of underwater images and videos. Recently, Deep Learning methods have been used to facilitate this task. Deep Learning methods, however, pose challenges of their own, namely the need to derive good quality training datasets from new unlabeled data. This work proposes an end-to-end pipeline that receives as input new unlabeled data and outputs a fully trained model capable of performing coral and fish segmentation in underwater videos, with as little human intervention as possible. An important characteristic of this pipeline is its ability to derive a good quality training dataset in an easier, faster and interactive way via assisted labeling with a foundation model. The use of image restoration techniques to improve the quality of the images and computer vision techniques to refine the annotations are also contributing factors to the good quality of the derived training dataset. The promising results achieved seem to validate the quality of the pipeline proposed.

Keywords: Instance Segmentation · Model Distillation · Assisted Labeling

1 Introduction

Coral reefs are very important as they are reported to support up to two million species and a quarter of all marine life on Earth [1]. Coral reefs are also reported to be undergoing a severe decline worldwide [2]. It is therefore very important to monitor coral reefs. However, this presents several challenges. On the one hand the quality of underwater images can be affected by the physical and chemical characteristics of underwater conditions [3], thus hindering the monitorization process. On the other hand, it is very time consuming for human marine biologists to manually inspect and analyze hundreds

J. Valente de Oliveira et al. (Eds.): EPIA 2025, LNAI 16121, pp. 149–161, 2026.
https://doi.org/10.1007/978-3-032-05176-9_12

or even thousands of videos and images. Recently, Deep Learning (DL) methods have started to be employed for the purpose of coral reef monitorization, and specifically to detect coral and fish [2]. However, the use of DL methods presents its own challenges. One such challenge concerns the need for DL methods to be trained on a suitable training dataset. This gives rise to the need to derive good quality training datasets from unlabeled data in an easy and fast way [4].

The goal of this work is to propose an end-to-end processing pipeline that receives as input new unlabeled data, underwater videos in this case, and outputs a fully trained model capable of performing segmentation of coral and fish in these videos. An important characteristic of this pipeline is its ability to derive a good quality training dataset in an easier, faster and interactive way via assisted labeling with a foundation model. The main contributions of this work are as follows:

- The assessment of the importance of choosing a suitable image restoration technique when dealing with low quality images, to obtain a model with good performance.
- The use of assisted labeling to ease and speed up the annotation of new unlabeled data without sacrificing the quality of the derived annotations. This is achieved by integrating Label Studio, as the user interface, with the Segment Anything Model 2 (SAM2) [5] as the labeling assistant, thus creating an interactive annotation environment where the human annotator specifies bounding boxes around regions of interest and SAM2 proposes an annotation, which the human annotator can then review.
- The assessment of the importance of applying a refinement step to the annotations derived via assisted labeling, to obtain a model with good performance.
- A performance assessment of Autodistill [6], a framework that allows the auto-generation of training datasets without human intervention.

The results obtained are very promising and validate the quality of the end-to-end processing pipeline proposed. The remainder of this paper is structured as follows. Section 2 presents a brief overview of the related literature, and a high-level presentation of the tools and methods used. Section 3 presents a detailed discussion of the method proposed. Finally, Sect. 4 presents the conclusions and future work.

2   Technical Background

This section presents previous work related to coral detection as well as the technical background relevant to this work, including the frameworks, models and methods used.

2.1   Coral Detection

Recently, DL methods have been used to monitor coral reefs. Some of this work focuses on coral recognition, where the goal is to localize the coral on the image and specify its species. Some examples of this type of research include the work proposed in [1, 2]. This type of research usually leverages common DL techniques such as convolutional neural networks (CNNs) which are then optimized via supervised learning to derive a coral recognition model.

In cases where simply locating the coral on the image via a bounding box is not sufficient (e.g. accurately calculating the area of coral) a different approach is required. The work proposed in [4] is an example of this type of research. In this work the authors used SAM to perform dense coral segmentation, allowing them to achieve a more reliable and in-depth coral analysis. The work proposed in this paper can be cataloged into this type of research.

2.2 Knowledge Distillation

Knowledge distillation [7] is a technique used to compress a complex and large neural network (referred to as the teacher network), into a smaller and simpler neural network (referred to as the student network), while retaining the performance of the original larger model. The rationale behind knowledge distillation stems from the observation that complex neural networks learn to capture meaningful representations of the data. These representations, which can be thought of as 'knowledge' acquired by the neural network during the training process, can then be transferred to, or distilled into, a student network via supervised learning, for example.

Similarly to knowledge distillation, Autodistill [6] leverages large and complex foundation models, trained on datasets with millions of images, to train simpler and faster models via supervised learning. In this case the 'knowledge' of the foundation model is used to automatically label the training dataset of the simpler model. This distillation process has several advantages: 1) the model derived is simpler, less hardware-demanding and can potentially be used to tackle real-time tasks, 2) this training procedure allows for the model to be fine-tuned to the specificities of the target task and 3) this process can speed up the development phase considerably, even when dealing with unlabeled data, given that no human annotation or labeling is required to derive the necessary training datasets.

2.3 Segment Anything Model

The Segment Anything Model (SAM) [8], a large foundation model developed by Meta AI, is designed as a promptable segmentation system with zero-shot capabilities. Due to its promptable design, SAM can be easily integrated with other systems. For example, Autodistill takes advantage of this to integrate SAM with other foundation models, such as Grounding DINO [9]. In this case, Grounding DINO provides bounding box prompts to SAM. SAM also allows interactive segmentation with human annotators via bounding box or point prompts and can therefore be used as an image labeling assistant.

Furthermore, SAM's zero-shot capabilities mean that it can perform well when presented with unfamiliar images, without the need for additional training or fine-tuning. Finally, the output masks generated by SAM can be leveraged by other AI systems, such as in 3D reconstruction [10]. The newest updated release of SAM, the Segment Anything Model 2 (SAM2) [5] extends the previous release by offering a unified solution for real-time promptable object segmentation and tracking for both images and videos.

2.4 YOLO

YOLO [11, 12] models are a collection of state-of-the-art models designed for performance and flexibility and can be used to tackle a variety of tasks including object detection, tracking, instance segmentation, image classification and pose estimation. Due to their focus on performance, YOLO models are less hardware-demanding and can be used in real-time tasks. Autodistill leverages this fact and uses YOLO as the target model (or student network) of its distillation process. YOLO can also be integrated with other tools. One such use case concerns data labeling tools, where YOLO can be integrated as an image labeling assistant. Finally, in its latest release YOLO can also be used stand-alone to perform auto-annotation without human intervention.

2.5 Label Studio

Label Studio [13] is an open-source data labeling tool that supports different types of labeling with many data formats such as text, image, video and audio. Furthermore, Label Studio can be integrated with several Machine Learning (ML) models via the Label Studio ML Backend. The possible usage scenarios supported by Label Studio include: 1) manual data labeling, 2) the possibility to load pre-existing data annotations and 3) support for interactive data labeling using labeling assistants such as SAM and YOLO. In its Enterprise edition Label Studio also supports continuous active learning.

3 Proposed Method

This section details the method proposed to train a model to perform instance segmentation of coral and fish in underwater videos. The section starts by presenting the results of a benchmark to assess the impact of various image restoration techniques on model performance. The next point of discussion concerns the first 3 steps of the processing pipeline depicted in Fig. 1. More specifically, how to leverage assisted labeling via a foundation model to convert a set of unlabeled data into a good quality candidate training dataset suitable for instance segmentation.

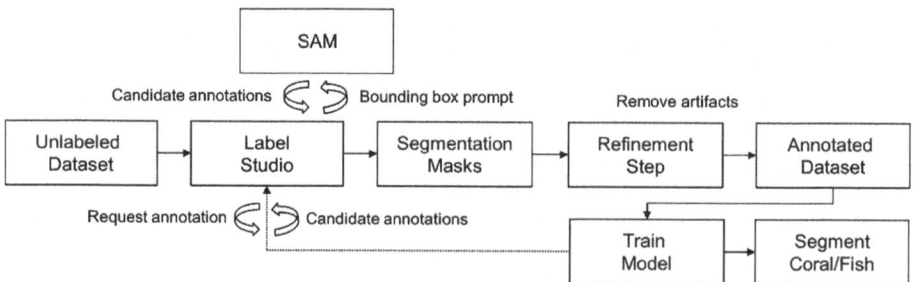

Fig. 1. High-level depiction of the main phases of the pipeline implemented to obtain the final trained detection model, starting from new unlabeled data.

The refinement step is discussed next. The discussion highlights some of the issues inherent to assisted labeling and the need to apply refinement techniques to the annotations obtained to improve the quality of the final annotated dataset. Finally, the section presents and discusses the results obtained by the trained model on the task of coral and fish segmentation. As depicted in Fig. 1, the final trained model can also be leveraged to perform assisted labeling. This step is not discussed in this work.

3.1 Image Restoration

The original dataset provided consisted of 12 unlabeled short videos (less than 45 s each) of shallow underwater video footage. After extracting and inspecting the resulting images using OpenCV [14], it was observed that the images suffered from low contrast. Furthermore, the quality of these images was further degraded by the presence of suspended particles and the occurrence of blur and haze in some regions, see Fig. 2. Given that image quality can have a negative impact on model performance, a comparative benchmark was carried out to try to assess the impact of various image restoration techniques on the performance of several foundation models on the task of object detection.

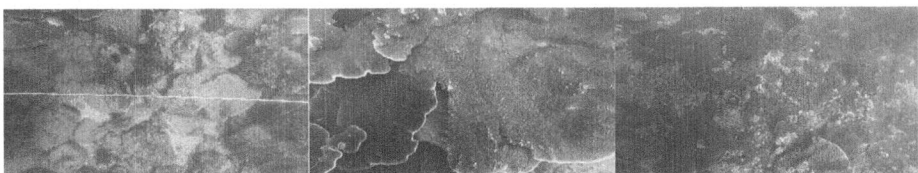

Fig. 2. Examples of some of the images extracted from the original dataset showcasing the sources of quality degradation mentioned above.

The image restoration techniques tested are described in [3], namely: Histogram Equalization (HE) [15], Contrast Limited Adaptive Histogram Equalization (CLAHE) [16], Gamma Correction (GC), Integrated Color Model (ICM) [17], Unsupervised Color Correction Method (UCM) [18], Relative Global Histogram Stretching (RGHS) [19], Rayleigh distribution-based (RD) [20], Single Image Removal (SIR) [21], Underwater Dark Channel Prior (UDCP) [22], Initial Underwater Image Dehazing (IUID) [23], Image Blurring and Light Absorption (IBLA) [24], Underwater Light Attenuation Prior (ULAP) [25], DCP-based rapid image restoration (RIR) [26], underwater image restoration based on the new optical model (NOM) [27], Green Blue Dehazing and Red Correction (BGD + RC) [28] and RoWS [29].

The foundation models tested were: Detic [30], a transformer-based object detection and segmentation model, Florence-2 [31], a multimodal vision model, Grounding-Dino [8], a zero-shot object detection model, Kosmos-2 [32], a multimodal language model that can be used for zero-shot object detection, OWLv2 [33], a zero-shot object detection model that follows from the OWL-ViT architecture and LlaVA [34], a multi-modal language model with object detection capabilities. For ease of implementation, the Autodistill wrappers provided for these foundation models were used. Table 1 presents the F1 score results for coral and fish detection. All annotations with an Intersection over Union (IoU) less than 0.50 or a confidence level below 0.7 were discarded.

From the analysis of the results, it can be concluded that most restoration techniques cause performance degradation. From the few that improve the performance of the model, some provide a considerable boost in performance, such as in the case of Kosmos-2 and OWLv2. It is also noteworthy to point out that the best image restoration techniques vary depending on the model and the task. As an example, for OWLv2 the best restoration techniques for the detection of fish are CLAHE and RoWS, but RD performs better for the detection of coral. Overall, the benchmark results seem to suggest that some models may be more sensitive to image quality than others and this sensitivity may also depend on the task.

Also, regarding the performance results achieved in the coral object detection task. Overall, the models were unable to detect most corals. In the case of Florence-2, Grounding Dino and OWLv2 the models consistently labeled the whole image as coral. For Grounding Dino and WOLv2 most of these predictions had a low confidence level and were discarded. In the case of Florence-2, some of these annotations had a high confidence level and were accepted, contributing to its lower F1 score when compared to the other 2. Llava produced very few annotations for both detection tasks (all false positives) and its performance results were omitted from the table.

Table 1. Benchmark results for the detection of fish (left column) and coral (right column). The best scores are highlighted in bold. The row (Raw) stands for the original unprocessed images.

	Detic		Florence-2		Grounding-Dino		Kosmos-2		OWLv2	
Raw	0.50	0.18	0.21	0.01	0.69	0.02	0.23	0.02	0.29	0.02
HE	0.25	0.0	0.13	0.01	0.38	0.02	0.19	0.0	0.27	0.02
CLAHE	0.40	0.04	0.21	0.01	0.57	0.02	0.26	**0.05**	**0.40**	0.0
ICM	0.51	0.13	**0.25**	0.01	**0.70**	**0.03**	**0.33**	0.01	0.39	0.02
UCM	0.45	0.10	0.19	0.01	0.32	**0.03**	0.11	0.0	0.11	0.01
RD	0.23	0.0	0.09	0.01	0.25	0.02	0.05	0.0	0.25	**0.17**
RGHS	0.38	0.13	0.19	0.01	0.59	0.02	0.25	0.01	0.27	0.02
GC	0.45	0.07	0.19	0.01	0.68	0.02	0.27	0.02	0.20	0.0
SIR	**0.53**	**0.21**	0.16	0.01	0.62	0.02	0.16	0.0	0.34	0.02
IUID	0.51	**0.21**	0.20	0.01	0.64	0.02	0.31	0.0	0.39	0.01
RIR	0.0	0.0	0.0	**0.02**	0.0	0.02	0.0	0.0	0.0	0.0
NOM	0.05	0.0	0.0	0.01	0.04	0.02	0.0	0.0	0.0	0.0
IBLA	0.11	0.0	0.08	0.01	0.42	0.02	0.0	0.0	0.27	0.11
ULAP	0.27	0.0	0.14	0.01	0.35	0.02	0.21	0.01	0.02	0.0
BGD + RC	0.39	0.0	0.13	0.01	0.21	0.02	0.02	0.0	0.02	0.0
RoWS	0.50	**0.21**	0.19	0.01	0.61	0.02	0.19	0.0	**0.40**	0.02
UDCP	0.45	**0.21**	0.17	0.01	0.49	0.02	0.11	0.01	0.23	0.02

3.2   Assisted Labeling via a Foundation Model

Given the difficulties inherent to manual annotation, assisted labeling via a foundation model was used instead. For the annotation procedure, Label Studio Community edition was used as the user interface and SAM2 was leveraged as a labeling assistant. As a first approach SAM2 was used in automatic mode to segment the images. After collecting the segmentation results, the masks were converted to Label Studio format and loaded as pre-annotations. Unfortunately, this approach generated an excessive number of annotations for each image (>300), see Fig. 3 for an example. This made the annotation process very hard as the human annotator was forced to reject most of the proposed annotations.

Next, SAM2 was integrated into Label Studio as a labeling assistant, using the Label Studio ML Backend (SAM2 image was used). This allowed for a smoother interactive labeling experience, where the human annotator specifies a bounding box around a region of interest and asks SAM2 for a candidate annotation in the form of a segmentation mask. This was the strategy used to label the whole training dataset. See Fig. 3 for some examples of annotations derived from this interactive labeling process. The histogram equalized images were used for a better viewing experience.

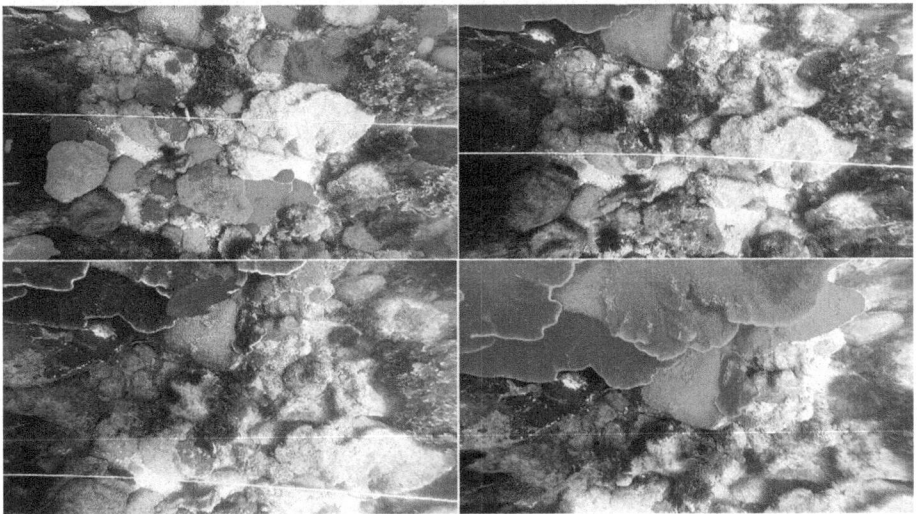

Fig. 3.   Some examples of annotations. (**Top Left**) annotations derived using SAM2 in automatic mode. (**Bottom Left**) annotations derived for fish and (**Top and Bottom Right**) annotations derived for coral using SAM2 in interactive mode using bounding boxes as prompts.

3.3   Annotation Refinement

A final inspection of the quality of the annotations derived via interactive assisted labeling mode, revealed that the quality of the annotations could be further improved. More specifically, some of the annotations presented small holes and/or small disconnected areas resembling noise. These artifacts were introduced by SAM2, since in some cases the segmentation process is not perfect. Therefore, a final refinement step was introduced to address this issue. During this step OpenCV was used to reduce the occurrence of these artifacts on the annotations to further improve their quality. The small, disconnected areas were eliminated with the method *remove_small_areas* (with a threshold of 150), whereas a morphological transformation (closing transformation using the method *morphologyEx*) was used to fill the small gaps inside the masks. See Fig. 4 for some examples of coral segmentation masks before and after this refinement step.

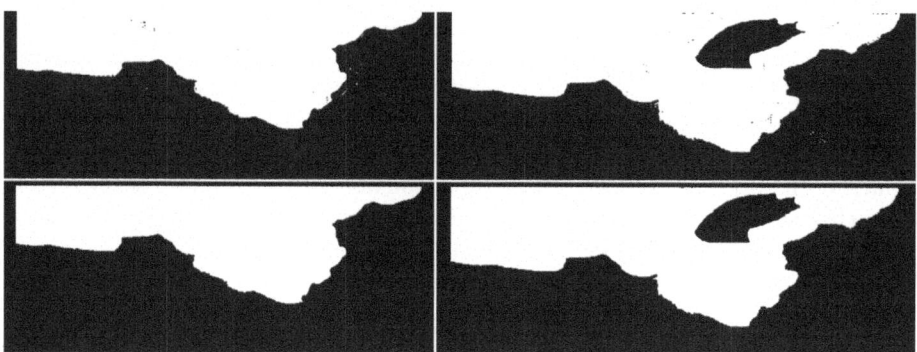

Fig. 4. Some examples of annotations before the refinement step (**top row**), presenting some artifacts introduced during the interactive labeling process, and after the refinement step (**bottom row**), with most artifacts removed.

3.4 Results

The final model derived to perform instance segmentation on coral and fish was obtained by fine-tuning a pre-trained instance of a YOLO model (version 11) for 200 epochs on the training dataset obtained via assisted interactive labeling. Cross-validation was performed using 90% of the data for training and 10% of the data for testing. To validate the impact of the refinement step on model performance, the model was also trained on an unrefined version of the annotations (i.e., the raw annotations without the refinement step). The performance results obtained by this model on the segmentation of coral can be found on the row titled Raw-Unref on the table.

For comparison and given its somewhat interesting results on the task of fish detection, Autodistill GroundedSAM (Grounding Dino + SAM), was also tested on the task of fish segmentation. In this case the whole training process, including the annotation of the training dataset, is automatic and does not involve human intervention. Table 2 and Table 3 depict the validation results obtained for the segmentation of fish and coral, respectively.

As can be shown by the results, namely concerning the MaP50–95 metric, choosing an appropriate image restoration technique can help improve the performance of the model. The results also seem to suggest that skipping the refinement step can cause degradation on the performance of the model. This fact is noticeable in both the segmentation masks and bounding box results. Thess results seem to be intuitive and expected. On the one hand, the small artifacts scattered around the object can contribute to the distortion of the annotation bounding box when compared to the ground truth bounding box. On the other hand, small holes or gaps inside the masks can also contribute to the distortion of the annotation masks when compared to the ground-truth segmentation masks.

Finally, although the results obtained by GroundedSAM on the segmentation of fish are somewhat interesting as a starting point, considering that the whole process was fully automatized, its performance is still very poor when compared to the performance achieved by the model trained with interactive assisted labeling.

Table 2. Validation results obtained for the segmentation of fish. The table depicts the Mean average Precision (MaP) results (MaP50, IoU 0.5 and MaP50–95, IoU 0.5–0.95) for segmentation masks (M) and bounding boxes (B). The best scores for (MaP50–95) are highlighted in bold. The row (Raw) stands for the original unprocessed images.

	MaP50(M)	MaP50–95(M)	MaP50(B)	MaP50–95(B)
Raw	0.995	0.786	0.995	0.888
HE	0.900	0.697	0.900	0.801
CLAHE	0.995	**0.857**	0.995	0.884
ICM	0.950	0.708	0.950	0.793
UCM	0.995	0.771	0.995	0.846
RD	0.995	0.736	0.995	0.803
RGHS	0.995	0.783	0.995	0.819
GC	0.950	0.708	0.950	0.809
SIR	0.995	0.756	0.995	0.891
IUID	0.995	0.779	0.995	0.851
RIR	0.850	0.638	0.850	0.701
NOM	0.950	0.668	0.950	0.693
IBLA	0.950	0.718	0.950	0.789
ULAP	0.950	0.721	0.950	0.797
BGD + RC	0.900	0.666	0.900	0.781
RoWS	0.995	0.736	0.995	**0.899**
UDCP	0.995	0.696	0.995	0.793
GroundedSAM	0.771	0.501	0.771	0.644

3.5 Discussion

Several conclusions can be drawn from the analysis of the performance results obtained. First, applying a suitable image restoration technique to try to improve the quality of the data, images in this case, can provide significant performance improvements to the final trained model. The extent of this improvement depends on the model and the task. This can be more important when dealing with tasks, such as those related to healthcare for example, where accuracy is crucial and the tiniest improvement in model performance is highly desirable.

Second, while using a foundation model as a labeling assistant can ease and speed up the annotation process of new unlabeled data and even improve the accuracy of the annotations compared to human annotation in some cases, there might be times where the quality of the annotation provided by the labeling assistant is not the best. For these cases and as suggested by the results it is important to apply a refinement step to the annotations to improve their quality, since failing to do so may impact the performance of the final segmentation model.

Finally, tools such as Autodistill, which allow the auto-generation of training datasets without human interaction, thus providing a fully automized end-to-end training pipeline from unlabeled data to trained model without the need for human intervention, seem to be more useful as a starting point, than as the end result. Overall, the good results obtained seem to validate the quality of the pipeline proposed, although these results are still somewhat preliminary, given that the dataset provided was relatively small.

Table 3. Validation results obtained for the segmentation of coral. The table depicts the Mean average Precision (MaP) results (MaP50, IoU 0.5 and MaP50–95, IoU 0.5–0.95) for segmentation masks (M) and bounding boxes (B). The best scores for (MaP50–95) are highlighted in bold. The row (Raw) stands for the original unprocessed images.

	MaP50(M)	MaP50–95(M)	MaP50(B)	MaP50–95(B)
Raw	0.964	0.918	0.964	**0.954**
Raw-Unref	0.928	0.876	0.928	0.892
HE	0.964	0.914	0.964	0.933
CLAHE	0.964	0.869	0.964	0.899
ICM	0.964	0.914	0.964	0.932
UCM	0.929	0.872	0.929	0.919
RD	0.929	0.852	0.929	0.879
RGHS	0.964	0.913	0.964	0.913
GC	0.964	0.905	0.964	0.947
SIR	0.964	0.917	0.964	0.900
IUID	0.964	0.890	0.964	0.932
RIR	0.964	**0.919**	0.964	0.947
NOM	0.929	0.878	0.929	0.917
IBLA	0923	0.853	0923	0.887
ULAP	0.964	0.891	0.964	0.921
BGD + RC	0.928	0.865	0.928	0.870
RoWS	0.964	0.896	0.964	0.922
UDCP	0.964	0.880	0.964	0.901

4 Conclusion

This work proposes an end-to-end pipeline from unlabeled new data (underwater videos) to a fully trained model capable of performing instance segmentation of coral and fish. A key component of this pipeline is the ability to derive a good quality training dataset from these unlabeled data in an easier, faster and interactive way via labeling assistance from a foundation model.

Furthermore, this work showed the importance of choosing an appropriate image restoration technique when faced with images of poor quality and the importance of applying a refinement process to the annotations when using a labeling assistant, such as a foundation model, on the performance of the final trained model.

The promising performance results obtained by the trained model on the task of coral and fish instance segmentation seem to indicate that this pipeline offers a good solution to derive both a good quality training dataset and a good segmentation model. In future work, we aim to leverage the model obtained in this phase to calculate several metrics of interest such as coral area and fish density from underwater videos.

Acknowledgments. This work is financed by national funds through FCT - Foundation for Science and Technology, I.P., under project UID/00127 and grant number RAIECO/DRI/INDIA/0688/2020.

Disclosure of Interests. The authors have no competing interests to declare that are relevant to the content of this article.

References

1. Gómez-Rios, A., Tabik, S., Luengo, J., Shihavuddin, A.S.M., Krawczyk, B., Herrera, F.: Towards highly accurate coral texture images classification using deep convolutional neural networks and data augmentation. Expert Syst. Appl. **118**, 315–328 (2019)
2. Raphael, A., Dubinsky, Z., Iluz, D., Benichou, J.I.C., Netanyahu, N.S.: Deep neural network recognition of shallow water corals in the Gulf of Eilat (Aqaba). Sci. Rep. **10**(1), 12959 (2020)
3. Wang, Y., Song, W., Fortino, G., Qi, L., Zhang, W., Liotta, A.: An experimental-based review of image enhancement and image restoration methods for underwater imaging. IEEE Access **7**, 140233–140251 (2019)
4. Ziqiang, Z., Yaofeng, X., Liang, H., Yu, Z., Yeung, S.-K.: CoralVOS: Dataset and benchmark for coral video segmentation. CoRR, vol. abs/2310.01946 (2023)
5. Ravi, N., et al.: SAM 2: segment anything in images and videos. CoRR, vol. abs/2408.00714 (2024)
6. Roboflow: Autodistill (2023). https://github.com/autodistill/autodistill
7. Hinton, G.E., Vinyals, O., Dean, J.: Distilling the knowledge in a neural network. CoRR, vol. abs/1503.02531 (2015)
8. Kirillov, A., et al.: Segment anything. CoRR, vol. abs/2304.02643 (2023)
9. Liu, S., et al.: Grounding DINO: marrying DINO with grounded pre-training for open-set object detection. CoRR, vol. abs/2303.05499 (2024)
10. Wu, C.-Y., Johnson, J., Malik, J., Feichtenhofer, C., Gkioxari, G.: Multiview compressive coding for 3D reconstruction. In: IEEE/CVF Conference on Computer Vision and Pattern Recognition, CVPR 2023, pp. 9065–9075. IEEE, Canada (2023)

11. Redmon, J., Divvala, S.K., Girshick, R.B., Farhadi, A.: You only look once: unified, real-time object detection. In: IEEE Conference on Computer Vision and Pattern Recognition, CVPR 2016, pp. 779–788, IEEE Computer Society, USA (2016)
12. Jocher, G., Qiu, J., Chaurasia, A.: Ultralytics YOLO (2023). https://github.com/ultralytics/ultralytics
13. A.H.N.L. Maxim Tkachenko Mikhail Malyuk: Label Studio: Data labeling software (2025). https://github.com/HumanSignal/label-studio
14. Bradski, G.: The OpenCV Library. Dr. Dobb's J. Softw. Tools (2000)
15. Hummel, R.: Image enhancement by histogram transformation. Comput. Graphics Image Process. **6**(2), 184–195 (1977)
16. Zuiderveld, K.J.: Contrast limited adaptive histogram equalization. In: Heckbert, P.S. (ed.) Graphics Gems, pp. 474–485. Elsevier (1994)
17. Iqbal, K., Abdul Salam, R., Osman, M., Talib, A.: Underwater image enhancement using an integrated colour model. IAENG Int. J. Comput. Sci. **34** (2007)
18. Iqbal, K., Odetayo, M.O., James, A.E., Salam, R.A., Talib, A.Z.: Enhancing the low-quality images using unsupervised colour correction method. In: Proceedings of the International Conference on Systems, Man and Cybernetics, pp. 1703–1709. IEEE, Turkey (2010)
19. Huang, D., Wang, Y., Song, W., Sequeira, J., Mavromatis, S.: Shallow-water image enhancement using relative global histogram stretching based on adaptive parameter acquisition. In: MultiMedia Modeling, pp. 453–465. Springer, Thailand (2018)
20. Ghani, A.S.A., Isa, N.A.M.: Underwater image quality enhancement through composition of dual-intensity images and Rayleigh-stretching. In: IEEE Fourth International Conference on Consumer Electronics, pp. 219–220. IEEE, Germany (2014)
21. He, K., Sun, J., Tang, X.: Single image haze removal using dark channel prior. IEEE Trans. Pattern Anal. Mach. Intell. **33**(12), 2341–2353 (2011)
22. Drews, P., Nascimento, E., Moraes, F., Botelho, S., Campos, M.: Transmission estimation in underwater single images. In 2013 IEEE International Conference on Computer Vision Workshops, pp. 825–830. Computer Society, Australia (2013)
23. Carlevaris-Bianco, N., Mohan, A., Eustice, R.M.: Initial results in underwater single image dehazing. In: OCEANS 2010, MTS/IEEE SEATTLE, pp. 1–8 (2010)
24. Peng, Y.-T., Cosman, P.C.: Underwater image restoration based on image blurriness and light absorption. IEEE Trans. Image Process. **26**(4), 1579–1594 (2017)
25. Song, W., Wang, Y., Huang, D., Tjondronegoro, D.: A rapid scene depth estimation model based on underwater light attenuation prior for underwater image restoration. In: Advances in Multimedia Information Processing - PCM 2018 - 19th Pacific-Rim Conference on Multimedia, vol. 11164, pp. 678–688. Springer, China (2018)
26. Yang, H.-Y., Chen, P.-Y., Huang, C.-C., Chuang, Y.-Z., Shiau, Y.-H.: Low complexity underwater image enhancement based on dark channel prior. In: Second International Conference on Innovations in Bio-inspired Computing and Applications, IBICA 2011, pp. 17–20. IEEE Computer Society, China (2011)
27. Wen, H., Tian, Y., Huang, T., Gao, W.: Single underwater image enhancement with a new optical model. In: 2013 IEEE International Symposium on Circuits and Systems (ISCAS2013), pp. 753–756. IEEE, China (2013)
28. Li, C., Quo, J., Pang, Y., Chen, S., Wang, J.: Single underwater image restoration by blue-green channels dehazing and red channel correction. In 2016 IEEE International Conference on Acoustics, Speech and Signal Processing, pp. 1731–1735. IEEE, China (2016)
29. Chao, L., Wang., M.: Removal of water scattering. In: 2010 2nd International Conference on Computer Engineering and Technology, pp. 35–39 (2010)
30. Zhou, X., Girdhar, R., Joulin, A., Krähenbühl, P., Misra, I.: Detecting twenty-thousand classes using image-level supervision. In: Computer Vision - ECCV 2022 - 17th European Conference, vol. 13669. pp. 350–368. Springer, Israel (2022)

31. Xiao, B., et al.: Florence-2: advancing a unified representation for a variety of vision tasks. In: IEEE/CVF Conference on Computer Vision and Pattern Recognition CVPR 2024, pp. 4818–4829. IEEE, USA (2024)

32. Peng, Z., et al.: Kosmos-2: grounding multimodal large language models to the world. CoRR, vol. abs/2306.14824 (2023)

33. Minderer, M., Gritsenko, A.A., Houlsby, N.: Scaling open-vocabulary object detection. In: Advances in Neural Information Processing Systems 36: Annual Conference on Neural Information Processing Systems 2023, NeurIPS 2023, USA (2023)

34. Liu, H., Li, C., Wu, Q., Lee, Y.J.: Visual instruction tuning. In: Advances in Neural Information Processing Systems 36: Annual Conference on Neural Information Processing Systems 2023, NeurIPS 2023, USA (2023)

Multimodal Pipeline for Underwater Artifact Detection and 3D Reconstruction with VLM and Gaussian Splatting

Niccolò Simonato[1,2](✉), Daniele Corradetti[3,4], and José Bettencourt[5,6]

[1] Dipartimento di Scienze Matematiche, Informatiche e Fisiche (DMIF), Università degli Studi di Udine, Via delle Scienze, 206, 33100 Udine, Italy
nsimonato8@gmail.com
[2] Elementar s.r.l., Divisione Ricerca e Sviluppo, Galleria Enzo Tortora 21, 10121 Turin, Italy
[3] STAP Reabilitação Estrutural, SA Rua General Ferreira Martins 8 - 9B, 1495-137 Algés, Portugal
[4] Grupo de Física Matemática, Instituto Superior Técnico, Av. Rovisco Pais, 1049-001 Lisbon, Portugal
[5] Centro Nacional de Arqueologia Náutica e Subaquática, Rua da Manutenção 5, 1900-440 Lisbon, Portugal
[6] CHAM - Centro de Humanidades, Faculdade de Ciências Sociais e Humanas, Avenida de Berna, 26-C, 1069-061 Lisbon, Portugal

Abstract. In this work, we present a complete pipeline for the detection and three-dimensional reconstruction of archaeological artifacts in underwater environments. Our approach leverages the advantages of Large Multimodal Models (LMMs) that allow for integrating historical, geographical, and contextual data with captured images, a necessary step in the identification and interpretation of objects of possible archaeological interest, otherwise unattainable through unimodal models. In addition to multimodal integration, our pipeline suggests the use of a 3D visualization method (Gaussian Splatting) that has not yet been applied to underwater archaeology but is, in many respects, a natural candidate to replace photogrammetry techniques, which encounter many problems in underwater environments. To demonstrate the effectiveness of the methodology, we have concretely implemented a version of this pipeline and applied it to the study of the wreck of the *SS Main* steamship (1892), located in Porto Pim Bay, Faial Island, Azores.

Keywords: Water Splatting · Gaussian Splatting · Underwater Image Enhancement

1 Introduction

Nowadays, accurate documentation to preserve submerged archaeological sites represents an important challenge in underwater archaeology. In this regard,

© The Author(s), under exclusive license to Springer Nature Switzerland AG 2026
J. Valente de Oliveira et al. (Eds.): EPIA 2025, LNAI 16121, pp. 162–174, 2026.
https://doi.org/10.1007/978-3-032-05176-9_13

digital photogrammetry has recently established itself as a very useful tool for quickly and non-invasive recording of artifacts and structures below sea level, allowing the creation of detailed 3D models of submerged artifacts [11]. At the same time, the development of deep learning algorithms trained on large collections of images is demonstrating the ability to recognize archaeological patterns and objects in underwater photos, helping archaeologists identify artifacts that are difficult to discern with the naked eye on the seabed [16].

Despite these premises, we must note that both photogrammetry and deep learning have significant limitations. Photogrammetry presents many difficulties in underwater environments due to refraction, water turbidity, rapid light attenuation, and camera aberration [4,5]. In addition to these typical underwater environment issues, we must add the need for a large number of images required for the 3D model creation and the high computational capabilities required. In this sense, a new technology (3D Gaussian Splatting) is emerging in the 3D visualization sector for its computational lightness and reduced load of images required for reconstruction [6,8,13]. However, despite the great potential of this technology, experiments with Gaussian Splatting in underwater environments are very experimental [9] and have never been applied in underwater archaeological contexts.

At the same time, classic deep learning algorithms for image recognition and object detection also have profound limitations: while they can help in artifact identification, they do not take into account the historical, geographical, and documentary context of the site under analysis. Moreover, the lack of unique visual features of the underwater artifacts requires context from associated documentation for proper interpretation. In fact, the arrangement of a wreck and its cargo makes full sense only when correlated with ancient trade routes and historical documents about the sinking [10]. A specific case consists of the wreck of the *Main* (see Sect. 4), which oral tradition identified as a local merchant ship, and archaeological study allowed correct and unambiguous identification only in 2016 [1].

In this sense, the possibility offered by new Large Multimodal Models to integrate textual information from sources of diverse natures, such as chronicles and logbooks (textual), geographical maps (visual), and paleo-environmental data (structured data) into the visual identification phase greatly enriches the interpretation process, allowing the contextualization of each artifact already in a first phase, thus overcoming the limitations of unimodal deep learning techniques.

In the next section, we propose a pipeline for processing underwater archaeological data that goes in this direction: on one hand, using the latest generation of multimodal LLMs for the first phase of archaeological artifact identification and, on the other hand, using the Gaussian Splatting technique for the 3D reconstruction of localized artifacts and/or details of archaeological sites.

2   The Proposed Pipeline

The proposed pipeline for underwater archaeological site analysis is structured as follows:

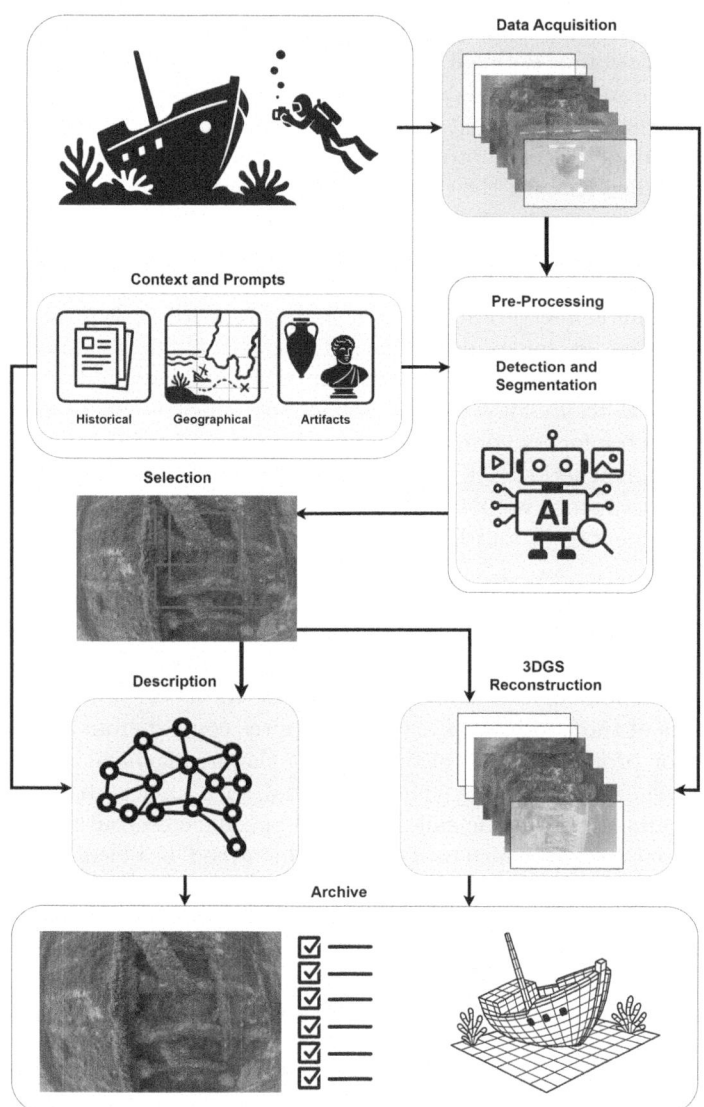

Fig. 1. Pipeline for the detection and 3D reconstruction of underwater artifacts. The workflow begins with the acquisition of video sequences and contextual data (historical, geographical, artifact), followed by frame preprocessing and identification and segmentation of Regions Of Interest (ROIs) through LMM. After a selection of the most relevant frames, the images are sent to an LMM to generate descriptions and classifications according to a predefined schema. In parallel, a selection of contiguous frames is used as a basis for 3D reconstruction through Water Splatting. Finally, original and preprocessed images, masks, textual annotations, and three-dimensional models are archived for subsequent analysis and monitoring.

1. Contextual Data.
2. Image Acquisition.
3. Preprocessing.
4. Object detection and Segmentation.
5. Frame Selection and Captioning.
6. 3D Reconstruction.
7. Archiving Results.

The process begins with the acquisition of high-resolution video and photographic sequences, carried out by divers, possibly accompanied by underwater Remotely Operated Vehicles (ROVs). In this phase, it is important to note that, parallel to image acquisition, a documentary phase is necessary for the production of contextual files (historical, geographical information, and possibly images of interest) to be provided to the LMMs (Fig. 1).

Before proceeding with automatic identification, the frames undergo a preprocessing phase, aimed at correcting color and deformations due to underwater environment lighting.

From these frames, a Visual Language Model (such as Florence 2 or proprietary models from OpenAI, Google, etc.) identifies the structures indicated by archaeologists through a prompt provided as input, extracting the Regions Of Interest (ROI). These are subsequently used by an image segmentation model (in this case, SAM2) that defines their contours.

The processed images obtained at step 3 are then subjected to a frame selection and grouping algorithm, which uses the results from the previous step to gather images related to the same artifact in groups of temporally adjacent frames. For each of these image groups, the one with the best quality is extracted to be subsequently commented on and classified by a dedicated LMM, according to a predefined schema.

The image groups identified at step 5 are subsequently used to generate 3D models of the details to provide archaeologists with a way to check and possibly correct the identification made. The obtained 3D model supports rotation, zoom, and lighting variations in real-time, making it particularly useful for subsequent analysis by the archaeological team.

Finally, all original and preprocessed frames, segmentation masks, textual captions, and 3D models are saved in standard formats and archived in a database, ensuring traceability, chronological searches, and monitoring of degradation over time.

3   Implementation of a Proof of Concept

Based on the guidelines defined in the previous section, we decided to proceed with the creation of a proof of concept accessible at https://github.com/nsimonato8/multimodal_pipeline_underwater. In this implementation, we use the technologies that seemed best to us at the moment, but given the exponential evolution of technologies, we opted for a modular structure that would allow replacing elements and models if they proved to be obsolete (Fig. 2).

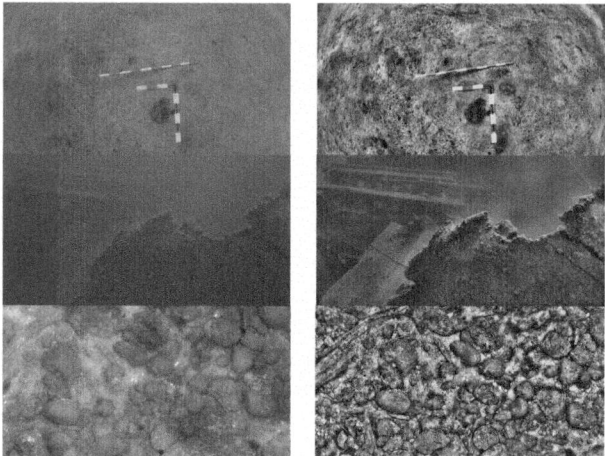

Fig. 2. Examples of unprocessed images (left) and processed images (right). The images come from the archaeological campaign of the *Main* (top), *Bom Rei* (middle) and *Arade* (provided by CHAM).

Contextual Data. For this phase, we decided to prepare four distinct text files, which are subsequently used as contextual input in the LMM prompts:

- `Artifacts.txt`, dedicated to the description of artifacts expected in the site of interest. For simplicity at this stage, we have considered a simple text file, but future versions of the pipeline could integrate images of interest with descriptions of the artifacts to provide a "few shots learning" of the artifacts of interest to the model.
- `Historical.txt`, constitutes a text file, typically in the order of 2000 words containing information on the historical and documentary context of the site.
- `GeographicalEnvironment.txt`, is instead a text file related to the geographical and environmental context in which the site is located (e.g., geographical coordinates, information on marine fauna and flora, environmental information that could alter recognition, etc.).
- `ClassificationSchema.txt`, is a text file in which the data schema necessary for the correct classification of artifacts is described.

Image Acquisition. Parallel to the generation of contextual data, it is necessary to proceed with the collection of visual data. This version is specifically designed for frame sequences, i.e., a collection of JPEG images. In order to make a reliable three-dimensional reconstruction of the object of interest possible, it is necessary to have multiple images that depict the same artifact from different angles and from distinct spatial positions. A wide visual coverage of the various points of the artifact is recommended to optimize the results of the 3D Reconstruction step. The use of underwater ROVs can facilitate this phase, as it reduces the risk posed to human operators in underwater environments.

Preprocessing. In the analysis of aquatic images, the preprocessing part is fundamental and very delicate. In this proof of concept, we have implemented a methodology, illustrated in Fig. 3, consisting of: a local equalization of the image (CLAHE or Contrast Limited Adaptive Histogram Equalization) to take into account the non-uniformity of light in underwater environments; a white balance with the "Gray World" method to counterbalance the general blue dominance given by water; finally, an enhancement of color, saturation, and brightness (HSV or Hue-Saturation-Value).

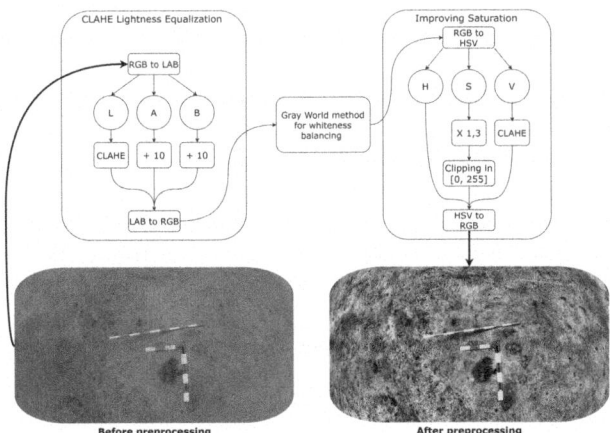

Fig. 3. Illustration of the preprocessing methodology implemented. The complete code is available in the GitHub repository specified in the Data Availability section.

Object Detection and Segmentation. In the current implementation of the pipeline, the object detection and instance segmentation phases are implemented through the integration of Florence-2 [15] and SAM2 [12]. Florence-2, in this step of the pipeline, uses the textual prompt provided by users, contained in `Artifacts.txt`, to identify objects of interest. Specifically, this is done by providing the aforementioned prompt, the image, and specifying the task `<CAPTION_TO_PHRASE_GROUNDING>`. The SAM2 model, on the other hand, uses the output of Florence-2, that is, the segmentation mask in the Florence-2 annotation format, as input for the segmentation of the identified objects.

Frame Selection and Captioning. In this phase, the results derived from object detection are temporally aggregated, grouping the recognized instances of the same object in consecutive frames.

Subsequently, for each identified object, the image with maximum Peak Signal to Noise Ratio (PSNR) compared to the original unprocessed one is chosen, which is then used as input by the LMM model (in this case `gpt-4.1-nano`), instructed with the prompt provided in the `Historical.txt` file and the geographical context defined in `GeographicalContext.txt`, with the aim of generating a description of the identified object. The model is also instructed to produce an output that reflects the schema contained in `ClassificationSchema.txt`.

In subsequent versions of this pipeline, this step will be implemented using a Large Language Model (LLM) which will select the image that presents the clearest representation of the object under examination.

3D Reconstruction. The three-dimensional reconstruction of the artifacts is carried out using 3D Gaussian splatting, a recently developed technique that allows the creation of three-dimensional models of scenes acquired through image sequences [8].

This step of the process is based on the selected image groups of individual artifacts from the previous phase of the pipeline. Currently, the methodology is in an experimental phase and guarantees reliable results only in optimal visibility conditions. Some preliminary examples have also been obtained using Post-Shots, although in future versions of the pipeline, the WaterSplatting method is expected to be adopted for its real-time rendering capability and superior quality compared to traditional NeRF methods [9].

Archiving Results. Following the creation of the 3D model in the PLY format of the identified artifacts of interest, the results are saved in a JavaScript Object Notation (JSON) format file, which ensures uniformity and portability of the data that has been processed.

3.1   Limitations

The limitations of the proposed pipeline lie in its two main components: the use of Large Language Models (LLMs) and the three-dimensional reconstruction phase.

Regarding the former, it is possible that prediction errors from a model may propagate in the pipeline, deteriorating the quality of the process output. Future studies could analyze the performance of the proposed pipeline as a function of the LLM models employed in different tasks, and identify those most suitable.

The most critical component of the pipeline, however, lies in 3D reconstruction, whose effectiveness is substantially constrained by the quality of the acquired video material. The complexity of this phase derives from the high number of variables involved, which make complete automation impractical at the present time. In particular, it is possible to automate the selection of frames related to an interest detection to feed the three-dimensional generation process, however without being able to guarantee the quality or final success of the reconstruction.

Finally, the pipeline has been designed and tested to handle the processing of a single artifact at a time. Evaluations of the system's behavior in the presence of multiple artifacts simultaneously within the same image are not yet available, representing a further area for future development and validation.

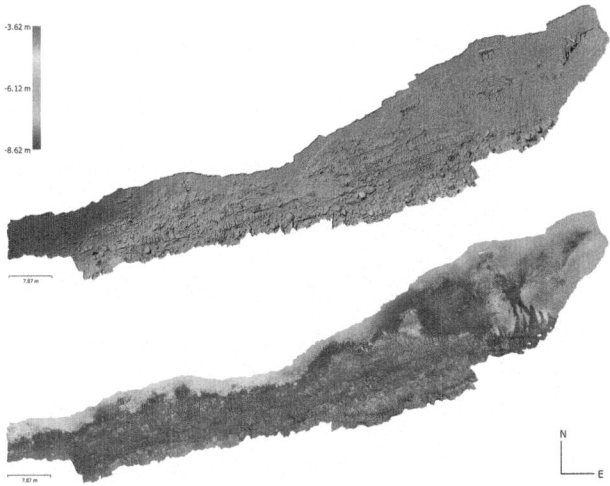

Fig. 4. Digital Elevation Model (top) and Orthomosaic of the *Main* wreck (1892) (images: CHAM).

4   Case Study: The *Main* Wreck

The proposed pipeline has been applied to images of the *Main* wreck, whose technical data and historical context will be provided in the following paragraphs. Below are the specifications relating to the images and textual inputs used for the experiments.

4.1   Context and Site Description

The *SS Main* (I) steamship was built in 1868 for the prestigious German company Norddeutscher Lloyd (NDL) at the Caird & Company shipyards in Greenock [3]. The transatlantic vessel sailed the Atlantic for over twenty years before passing under the British flag and then meeting its tragic fate in the Azores in 1892 in Porto Pim Bay, on the island of Faial [1, 2].

The *Main* was built entirely of iron with original dimensions of about 106.1 × 12.2 m and with a registered gross tonnage (GRT) equal to 3,087 GRT [3]. The design of the steamship followed a clipper bow, a very elegant feature still widespread at the time, designed for speed and to give visual and functional impetus to the hull. It was propelled by a steam engine, which after a modernization carried out in 1878 was capable of developing a power of about 3000 horsepower to obtain a service speed of about 14 knots. It could accommodate about 70 passengers in first class, 100 in second class, and 600 in third class [3].

After its inauguration on November 28, 1868, the *SS Main* faithfully served Norddeutscher Lloyd, mainly on the prestigious transatlantic route between Germany and the United States. However, despite the modernization carried out ten years after the inauguration, already in 1881 the steamship began to lose competitiveness compared to other vessels, to such an extent that it was then sold in 1891 to the Anglo-American Steamship Co.

In November 1892, the *SS Main*, now under the British flag, was navigating in the North Atlantic with a cargo mainly of cotton and livestock headed for Liverpool [1,2]. While navigating aboard the *Main*, a fire broke out that led to diverting to the nearby port of Horta, on the island of Faial. Arriving already engulfed in flames, and representing a serious danger to other vessels, local authorities made the decision to have the *Main* moved to the nearby Porto Pim Bay, which is a smaller and sheltered bay, located south of Horta, at the foot of Monte da Guia. Despite rescue operations that saved the crew, the fire remained uncontrollable. The *Main* burned completely and, consumed by flames, the ship eventually sank in the shallow waters of Porto Pim Bay on November 25, 1892 (for the date see [1]).

Today, the remains of the *SS Main* constitute an important underwater archaeological site, in Porto Pim Bay, on the island of Faial, Azores. The depth of the site is very shallow, situated between 3.5 and 8.5 m (see Fig. 4). The shallow depth, combined with the relative clarity of the bay's waters in favorable conditions, makes the wreck visible even from the surface. The first archaeological survey of the site dates back to 1999 by the Institute of Nautical Archaeology (INA) [7], but only subsequent investigations in 2016 and 2022 allowed a detailed mapping of the site and certainty in identifying the wreck remains with those of the *Main* steamship (contrary to a local oral tradition that identified the wreck remains as those of a merchant ship used for inter-island traffic). Currently, the remains of the *Main* extend for a length exceeding 100 m. The stern section, significant portions of the starboard side planking, and the bow structure have been identified and mapped. It is believed that much of the port side has collapsed to the north and is now buried under the sandy bottom; its position is suggested by an alignment of remains of the beams (the transverse beams that supported the decks) that emerge from the sand. Despite the structural collapse, a significant part of the external planking of the hull is still present and identifiable (see Fig. 4). The current state of the wreck is therefore that of a metal structure collapsed and partially dismantled by natural agents, but which still retains a remarkable extension and planimetric integrity, as well as key structural elements. The partial burial of some sections may have contributed to better preserving them from marine action.

Image Acquisition. Main was documented by photogrammetry twice, in 2015 and in 2022. The images used for this experiment were collected in the 2022 campaign. This included a survey using two different methods. In order to georeference the site, the wreck was partially documented using photographs taken with a CANON EOS 7D camera equipped with a 10 mm Tokina lens (with a resolution of 5184 × 3456 pixels). These photos were then georeferenced by locating them with data obtained with the UWIS navigation system [14], syncing log time with camera time. To refine the model, scale bars were placed throughout the site.

The entire site was then documented with video using the same equipment and the same camera. The frames extracted from the video (1 per second, with a resolution of 1920 × 1080 pixels) were used to produce the 2.5D model that is the basis for the Digital Elevation Model and the orthomosaic in Fig. 4. The site was also documented on video with a Gopro 8.

No data was acquired on parameters such as IMU, inclination and rotation. No data was collected on the environmental conditions but the temperature was around 21 °C and visibility was over 10 m for most of the dive time.

Textual Prompts. The prompts used for generating the results are available in their complete form in the GitHub archive of this project.

Segmentation and Frame Selection. Figure 5 shows the images of objects identified by the model. Specifically, the image of an instrument used for measuring artifacts is shown.

Fig. 5. Example of output from the Object Detection and Segmentation phase. The instrument positioned on the left of the image is first identified through a ROI and subsequently its silhouette is identified.

3D Reconstruction. Below are frames taken from the video generated using the Gaussian Splatting technique. As can be seen from Fig. 6, the results related to 3D visualization are absolutely comparable if not better to those obtainable with photogrammetry.

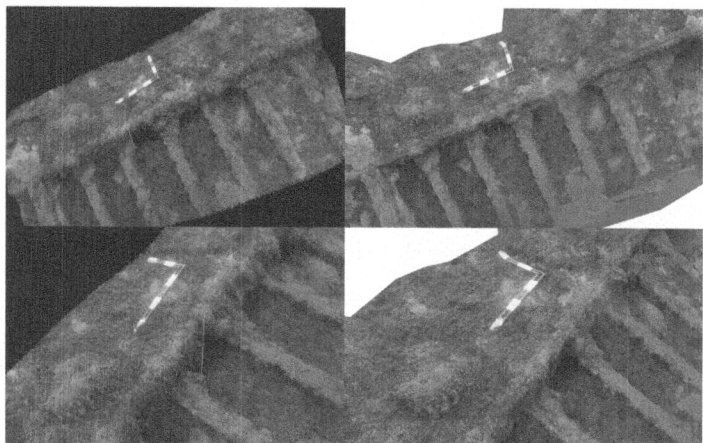

Fig. 6. Reconstruction of the same artifact through Gaussian Splatting (left) and Photogrammetry (right). The 3DGS image was created with `Jawset PostShots v.0.6` default settings while the photogrammetric model with `AgiSoft v.2.1`.

4.2   Conclusions and Future Works

In conclusion, this study realizes the proposal of a pipeline with applications in the field of underwater archaeological exploration, which integrates contextual data with underwater images, allowing to speed up if not automate the process of identification and cataloging of artifacts.

The use of alternative LLMs or the fine-tuning of those used are proposed as the natural continuation of this study. In future versions, the Water Splatting technique will be experimented with in the 3D reconstruction phase as a substitute for Gaussian Splatting, to verify its real applicability to underwater environments. Preliminary results obtained on the photographic material of the *Main*, and which we plan to validate extensively on other concrete cases of marine archaeological sites, suggest the 3DGS technique as an aid to photogrammetry rather than a substitute. Compared to photogrammetry, in fact, 3D visualization seems to be more faithful and agile in the case of Gaussian Splatting, however, the immature state of this technology does not yet allow for automatic correction of the produced 3DGS (which generally need to be cleaned of artifacts), nor to generate orthomosaics (which, instead, are of great utility in underwater archaeological practice).

We therefore consider it necessary to proceed systematically in the evaluation of this pipeline by applying it to various scenarios to highlight its limits and possibly add elements (such as the production of an orthomosaic obtainable via photogrammetry).

Future implementations may include the integration of the proposed pipeline with Retrieval Augmented Generation (RAG) systems, which would allow to further automate the retrieval of the contextual information needed for the detection of the artifacts and the enrichment of the classification output.

Acknowledgments. We would like to thank Cristóvão Fonseca (CHAM - Centro de Humanidades) for providing additional material collected the Arade used for the experimentation of the preprocessing process. Moreover, we would like to thank José Paulo Costa and STAP for promoting this research. We also would like to thank Veira Freitas, Isabel Soares and the DMP - Archaeological Studies of the Câmara Municipal de Portimão for useful suggestions their help in orientation and contacting the CHAM.

Thanks to my brother, Federico, for providing the hardware on which the computations were performed.

Data Availibility Statement. All images have been provided CHAM - Centro de Humanidades. A selection of images and the code to experiment with the pipeline are available on GitHub at https://github.com/nsimonato8/multimodal_pipeline_underwater.

Disclosure of Interests. The authors have no competing interests to declare that are relevant to the content of this article.

References

1. Bettencourt, J.: Os açores na navegação global: o contributo da arqueologia sub-aquática. Boletim do Núcleo Cultural da Horta **XXVI**, pp. 307–342 (2017)
2. Bettencourt, J.: Shipwrecks in the Azores and global navigation (sixteenth to nineteenth centuries): an overview. Int. J. Hist. Archaeol. **28**(4), 895–926 (2024). https://doi.org/10.1007/s10761-024-00737-7
3. Bonsor, N.R.P.: North Atlantic Seaway: An Illustrated History of the Passenger Services Linking the Old World with the New, vol. 2. Brookside Publications (1979)
4. Calantropio, A., Chiabrando, F.: Underwater cultural heritage documentation using photogrammetry. J. Mar. Sci. Eng. **12**(3), 413 (2024)
5. Costa, E.: Survey and photogrammetry in underwater archaeological contexts at low visibility in the Venice lagoon. Digit. Appl. Archaeol. Cultural Heritage **24**, e00215 (2022)
6. Gao, K., Gao, Y., He, H., Lu, D., Xu, L., Li, J.: NeRF: neural radiance field in 3D vision, a comprehensive review (2023). https://arxiv.org/abs/2210.00379
7. Institute of Nautical Archaeology (INA): Field report: survey in the Azores, 1998. INA Q. **26**(1) (1999)
8. Kerbl, B., Kopanas, G., Leimkühler, T., Drettakis, G.: 3D gaussian splatting for real-time radiance field rendering (2023). https://arxiv.org/abs/2308.04079
9. Li, H., Song, W., Xu, T., Elsig, A., Kulhanek, J.: Watersplatting: fast underwater 3D scene reconstruction using gaussian splatting (2024). https://arxiv.org/abs/2408.08206
10. McAllister, M.: The problem with "digital realism" in underwater archaeology: photogrammetric digital 3D visualization and interpretation. J. Marit. Archaeol. **16**(2), 253–275 (2021)
11. Menna, F., Agrafiotis, P., Georgopoulos, A.: State of the art and applications in archaeological underwater 3D recording and mapping. J. Cult. Herit. **33**, 231–248 (2018)
12. Ravi, N., et al.: Sam 2: segment anything in images and videos (2024). https://arxiv.org/abs/2408.00714

13. Tianrun, H.: Gaussian splatting toolkit: a toolkit for gaussian splatting (2024). https://github.com/Gaussian-Splatting-Toolkit/Gaussian-Splatting-Toolkit
14. UWIS: Photogrammetry.   https://uwis.fi/en/references/photogrammetry. Accessed 06 July 2025
15. Xiao, B., et al.: Florence-2: advancing a unified representation for a variety of vision tasks (2023). https://arxiv.org/abs/2311.06242
16. Yang, Y., Liang, W., Zhou, D., Zhang, Y., Xu, G.: Object detection for underwater cultural artifacts based on deep aggregation network with deformation convolution. J. Mar. Sci. Eng. **11**(12), 2228 (2023)

From Facades to 3D Models: Automating Building Reconstruction with Deep Learning and Texture Analysis

Oraib Almegdadi$^{(\boxtimes)}$ (iD), Sofia Monteiro (iD), Rui Nóbrega (iD),
and Nuno C. Marques$^{(\boxtimes)}$ (iD)

NOVA LINCS, NOVA School of Science and Technology, Costa da Caparica, Portugal
{o.almegdadi,scl.monteiro}@campus.fct.unl.pt,
{rui.nobrega,nmm}@fct.unl.pt

Abstract. Urban digitalization requires scalable and interoperable methods for accurate building modelling. Traditional approaches to facade extraction and 3D reconstruction often lack seamless generalisation and adaptability, as well as integration with geospatial systems. This work presents an automated pipeline that transforms street-level imagery into georeferenced 3D building models by combining deep learning with texture-based analysis. The pipeline uses window annotations for visual structure detection and integrates geographic information system (GIS) building footprints from OpenStreetMap (OSM) to ensure spatial alignment. Unlike prior approaches that rely on multi-element semantic annotations, our method reduces labeling costs while preserving geometric accuracy. The window detection model achieves a mean Average Precision of 0.94 at 50% IoU threshold (mAP@50), indicating strong detection performance suitable for large-scale 3D modelling tasks. Our automated pipeline—window detection, texture analysis, GIS alignment, and Unity export—supports generation of georeferenced 3D building models at city scale.

Keywords: Facade detection · 3D Building Reconstruction · Texture Analysis · OpenStreetMap · Urban Digitalization

1 Introduction

The digital transformation of urban environments demands efficient, scalable, and accurate 3D representations of buildings. Traditional methods for building modelling, including manual facade extraction and 3D reconstruction, are labor-intensive and often infeasible for large-scale applications such as smart city planning and urban analytics. High-detail modelling is essential in fields such as architectural preservation. In contrast, domains like structural monitoring, risk assessment, and emergency planning prioritize geometry-based representations over decorative details. In such cases, the ability to generate quick, automated models from limited data becomes essential.

© The Author(s), under exclusive license to Springer Nature Switzerland AG 2026
J. Valente de Oliveira et al. (Eds.): EPIA 2025, LNAI 16121, pp. 175–187, 2026.
https://doi.org/10.1007/978-3-032-05176-9_14

Developing accurate 3D building models from street-level imagery presents numerous technical challenges due to the unstructured and cluttered nature of urban environments. Occlusions caused by streetscape features, pedestrians, and vehicles often hide key architectural elements, reducing the completeness and accuracy of detection-based pipelines [18,33]. The architectural diversity found in real-world cities, which ranges from minimal modernist forms to elaborately decorated baroque facades, further complicates generalization, as building components like windows, balconies, and cornices vary significantly in shape, spacing, and visual hierarchy [6,29]. Additional challenges include the sparse or inconsistent annotations typical in available datasets and the surface ambiguity introduced by repetitive textures or materials such as glass and polished stone, which can confuse detection and segmentation models [8,13]. Moreover, the high-resolution demands of facade imagery and the fine-grained detail required for accurate reconstruction introduce additional processing burdens that limit scalability in real-time or city-scale applications [19]. In response to these challenges, recent advancements in computer vision, particularly deep learning, offer promising solutions for automating facade analysis. Object detection models such as YOLO (You Only Look Once) [21] have demonstrated strong performance in identifying structural elements like windows, which act as anchors for interpreting facade layout. These models are especially attractive for their speed and relatively low annotation requirements. Meanwhile, texture analysis methods, notably Gabor filters, have shown effectiveness in capturing repetitive surface patterns that define architectural boundaries [1,5]. Combining these methods offers a lightweight yet reliable approach to facade interpretation.

To address the above challenges, we propose an automated and modular pipeline that transforms street-level images into 3D building models. The process begins with detecting windows using a YOLOv8-based model trained on urban facade datasets. To estimate facade boundaries, we initialise a convex hull around the detected windows and apply Gabor-based texture analysis within this region. The response is then expanded into the surrounding neighbourhood to refine the full extent of the facade. From the extracted surfaces, we compute geometric and structural statistics—such as facade area, window density, and estimated floor count—which are subsequently used to construct 3D models in Unity. These models are georeferenced using GIS footprints from OSM, ensuring spatial alignment and integration with city-scale systems. Rather than focusing on decorative detail, the resulting models prioritise morphogeometric representation—capturing the essential structural geometry, facade layout, and spatial alignment of buildings. This abstraction supports use cases where geometric fidelity is more critical than ornamentation, such as digital twins, structural assessment, and urban simulations. We validate our method using street-level imagery from Lisbon, Portugal—a city known for its architectural richness and stylistic variation. Experimental results demonstrate robust window detection performance (mAP@50 = 94.2%) and strong visual fidelity in the reconstructed models. The main objectives of this work are:

(a) To develop an automated pipeline capable of detecting windows and estimating facade boundaries through deep learning and texture-based analysis. The pipeline also extracts geometric structure from street-level imagery to support downstream modelling tasks;

(b) To generate georeferenced 3D building models by integrating structural statistics with OSM footprints within the Unity environment;

(c) To produce simplified morphogeometric 3D models from street-level imagery for applications such as digital twins, structural monitoring, and urban planning.

2 Background and Related Work

Recent advances in deep learning—particularly convolutional neural networks (CNNs) and vision transformers (ViTs)—have significantly improved computer vision tasks such as object detection and structural pattern recognition [9,34]. These models have been successfully applied across various domains,including medical imaging [25,32], autonomous driving [3], environmental monitoring [2], and urban analysis [29], showing strong generalization to complex visual scenes.

Supervised learning has been widely adopted and consistently demonstrated effectiveness in structured vision tasks [19]. When trained on accurately annotated and well-curated datasets, these models are capable of performing classification, detection, tracking, and pose estimation with high reliability and accuracy [7,12]. In this work, we adopt a supervised learning approach to detect windows, which serve as key architectural elements in facade images.

Detecting facade elements such as windows has evolved from hand-crafted methods [15,27] to end-to-end deep learning architectures like Faster R-CNN [22] and YOLO [20]. We employ YOLOv8 [10] due to its accuracy–efficiency balance and anchor-free design [24]. Although newer versions like YOLOv10–12 show improvements in real-time applications [23], YOLOv8 offers interpretability and stability for batch processing of high-resolution street-level imagery. Comparative studies [4] also favor YOLO for city-scale detection tasks, supported by its open-source maturity and pretrained model availability. Detected windows are used as structural guide to estimate facade boundaries. The spatial layout of detected windows informs downstream segmentation using Gabor-based texture analysis. Unlike methods such as RTFP [28] that rely on dense pixel-level annotation and heavy transformer backbones, our approach uses only bounding boxes, offering a lightweight alternative for scalable facade modelling. Texture analysis methods—particularly Gabor filtering—have proven effective for extracting directional and repetitive features [13]. Prior work has demonstrated Gabor-based delineation in urban contexts [16,31], and recent extensions integrate texture geometry into deep segmentation networks. These studies validate the use of texture-based refinement when full semantic segmentation is impractical or overly resource-intensive. Finally, integrating facade imagery with GIS data enables the generation of spatially consistent 3D models. Existing frameworks align visual cues with OSM footprints to improve reconstruction accuracy [18,30], while participatory and open-data platforms [11,33] demonstrate

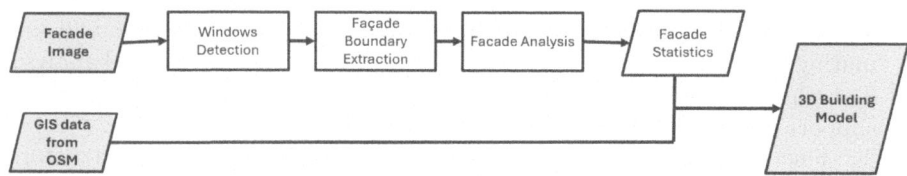

Fig. 1. Pipeline overview: from street-level facades and GIS footprints to 3D models

scalable urban modelling using lightweight inputs. Our pipeline builds on these ideas by combining object detection, texture refinement, and GIS alignment into a modular framework capable of generating detailed yet efficient 3D building representations.

3   Methodology

This section presents our end-to-end pipeline for generating georeferenced 3D building models from facade imagery and GIS data. As illustrated in Fig. 1, the pipeline consists of five main stages: (1) input acquisition, (2) window detection, (3) facade boundary extraction, (4) structural attribute extraction, and (5) 3D model generation. The design emphasizes minimal annotation requirements, architectural fidelity, and spatial accuracy.

Data Inputs. The system operates on two complementary data sources: (i) facade images collected from street-level platforms, which provide visual cues about architectural structures; and (ii) building footprint data obtained from OSM, for geographic alignment of the final 3D models with real-world locations.

Window Dataset Description. We used the publicly available Window Detector dataset from Roboflow Universe [26]. The original dataset includes approximately 5K unique facade images, which were expanded to 13K annotated images through automated augmentations. The final dataset was split into 11K training images (91%), 763 validation images (6%), and 465 testing images (4%). All images were resized to 640×640 and preprocessed with auto-orientation. Augmentations included shearing (±15°), grayscale conversion (applied to 25% of images), Gaussian noise (5%), mosaic composition, and bounding box blur (up to 10px). Each original image contributed multiple augmented variants. The dataset was exported in YOLOv8 format and used without further modification, preserving the original annotation and augmentation structure.

Window Detection Model. We employ a YOLOv8 object detection model to identify windows within each facade image. Windows are selected as the only annotated element due to their structural consistency across architectural styles and their widespread distribution across all floors and building types. This makes them a reliable structural reference for facade interpretation, even in the presence of stylistic or geometric variability.

Facade Boundary Extraction. The resulting bounding boxes from the previous step serve as semantic anchors for estimating facade geometry. We begin by computing the convex hull around the detected windows, providing an initial coarse estimate of the facade region. To refine this boundary, we apply a multi-scale bank of Gabor filters, which capture directional texture features characteristic of facade surfaces. We then extend the region based on the filter responses to better approximate the full facade area. This refinement helps distinguish architectural regions from non-facade elements such as sky, vegetation, or occlusions.

Structural Attribute Extraction. From each refined facade surface, we extract structural attributes such as facade area, window coverage ratio, estimated floor count, and window alignment. The output also includes window and floor statistics, including average dimensions and spacing, in a structured format that supports automated integration with the 3D reconstruction pipeline.

Geospatial 3D Model Generation. The extracted structural attributes are combined with geospatial building footprints from OSM to construct 3D building models in Unity. This integration shows promise in preserving both semantic and spatial fidelity in the generated models. Such integration aligns with prior efforts in interactive AR content insertion for multimedia applications, where visual realism and user interaction were key [17].

4   Experiments

4.1   Window Facade Detection

We trained and evaluated three YOLOv8 model variants—Nano (YOLOv8n), Medium (YOLOv8m), and Large (YOLOv8l)—to identify the optimal balance between performance and training time for window detection. All models were trained using the Ultralytics YOLOv8 framework (v8.3.23) on a system with an NVIDIA GeForce RTX 4080 Laptop GPU (12 GB VRAM), using Python 3.9 and PyTorch 2.5.0.

The training configuration was identical across all runs: 100 epochs, batch size of 16, input image resolution of 640×640 pixels, Adam optimizer, an initial learning rate of 0.01, and a final learning rate fraction of 0.2. Early stopping was applied with a patience of 30 epochs. Table 1 summarizes the evaluation results across the three model variants. Precision reflects the proportion of correctly predicted windows among all predictions, while recall indicates the model's ability to detect all instances of windows present in the image. mAP@50 represents the mean average precision at an intersection-over-union (IoU) threshold of 0.50, offering a measure of performance on relatively easy detections. In contrast, mAP@50–95 averages precision across stricter IoU thresholds from 0.50 to 0.95, providing a more comprehensive assessment across varying detection difficulties [10, 21].

Given the importance of detection accuracy for downstream facade reconstruction, we selected **YOLOv8l** for all subsequent experiments. While the differences in performance metrics between the models were relatively small, YOLOv8l consistently achieved the highest precision, recall, and mAP scores. As our use case prioritizes accuracy over inference speed, the added training time and computational cost were considered acceptable to ensure maximum reliability in window detection.

Discussion. Our best model performance was evaluated using standard object detection metrics, including precision, recall, mAP@50, and mAP@50–95, all computed via the YOLOv8 evaluation framework. Among these, mAP@50 was used as the primary indicator due to its widespread adoption and ease of interpretability, while mAP@50–95 provides a more stringent measure of detection quality. To further characterize the model's behaviour, we present four diagnostic curves in Fig. 2. Subplots (a) and (b) illustrate how precision and recall vary with confidence thresholds, revealing the typical trade-off between minimizing false positives and maximizing detection coverage. The F1-Confidence curve in (c) peaks near a threshold of 0.35, suggesting this value offers the most balanced detection setting. Lastly, the Precision–Recall curve in (d) demonstrates consistently high performance across recall levels, with an area under the curve closely matching the reported mAP@50 score of 0.942. In addition, Fig. 3 shows the evolution of loss and metric values throughout training. The consistent reduction in box, classification, and distribution focal losses across training and validation phases demonstrates stable convergence and effective learning. The synchronized increase in precision, recall, and mAP values highlights the model's ability to capture spatial and semantic patterns, while the alignment between mAP@50 and the stricter mAP@50–95 further confirms localization robustness. Collectively, these results demonstrate the YOLOv8l model's strength in detecting windows across visually and structurally diverse urban scenes.

4.2   From Facade Image to 3D Model

To illustrate the full workflow of the proposed pipeline, Fig. 4 presents a step-by-step transformation of a real-world street-level image into a georeferenced 3D building model. From left to right:

(a) **Input Image:** A standard street-level screenshot of a Lisbon building, captured using Google Street View.
(b) **Window Detection and Initial Segmentation:** Windows are detected using YOLOv8l model, with bounding boxes color-coded by floor. Using

Table 1. Comparison of YOLOv8 model variants

Model	Precision	Recall	mAP@50	mAP@50–95	Time (hrs)
YOLOv8n	0.849	0.877	0.923	0.639	5.52
YOLOv8m	0.858	0.899	0.940	0.674	7.09
YOLOv8l	**0.860**	**0.907**	**0.942**	**0.683**	**10.27**

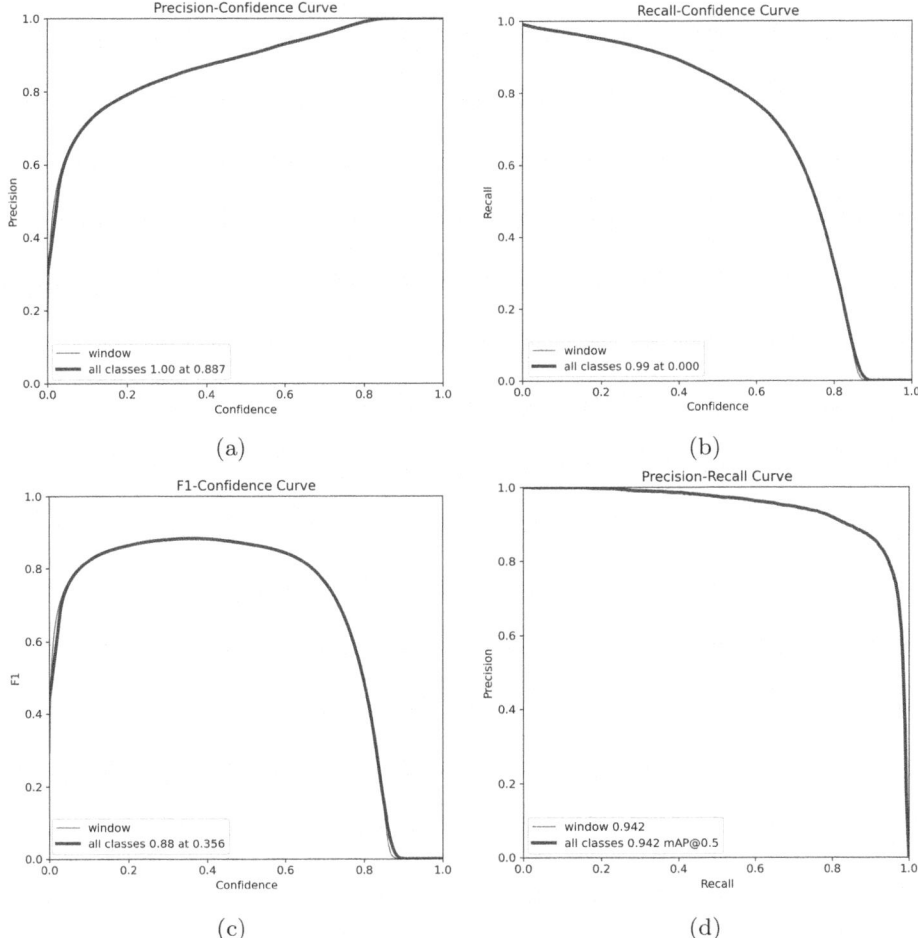

Fig. 2. Detection performance curves for the YOLOv8l window detector: (a) Precision vs. Confidence, (b) Recall vs. Confidence, (c) F1-score vs. Confidence, and (d) Precision–Recall curve.

the convex hull around the windows as a structural guide, Gabor-based texture analysis is applied to estimate the full facade area. The refined region is outlined in purple, and the orange rectangle represents the tightest bounding box enclosing the estimated facade.

(c) **Facade Projection in 3D Space:** The estimated facade boundary and detected windows are used to generate a single vertical face of the 3D model in Unity. This projected facade surface represents the current viewable side of the building and captures structural attributes such as floor divisions and window alignment.

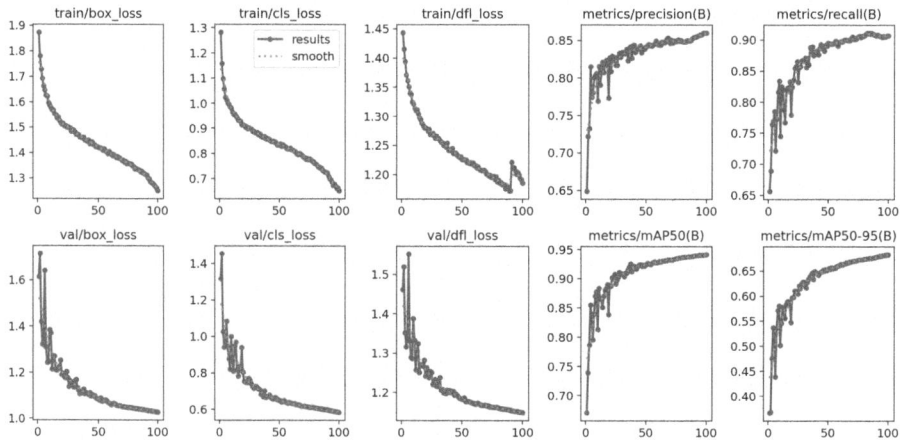

Fig. 3. Training evolution of the YOLOv8l model across epochs. The convergence patterns indicate stable learning dynamics and consistent generalization across training and validation datasets.

(d) **3D Model Construction:** A complete volumetric model is constructed in Unity using the facade statistics derived from the image analysis. The building footprint is retrieved from OSM, ensuring geospatial accuracy and enabling integration into larger-scale urban environments.

4.3   Case Studies Discussion

The three case studies illustrated in Fig. 4 demonstrate the generalizability, robustness, and limitations of the proposed pipeline across diverse architectural settings in Lisbon. Each case exemplifies a complete transformation from street-level imagery to a georeferenced 3D volumetric model, highlighting the pipeline's modular design and real-world applicability.

In the first case study, the number of estimated floors is consistent with the true building structure, validating the accuracy of vertical window alignment and spacing analysis. Several windows on the second and third floors were missed due to occlusions caused by trees and lamp posts, while the doors on the ground floor were not detected. Despite the visual similarity between the building's light-blue facade and the sky, the Gabor-based texture refinement successfully delineated the actual facade surface. The final 3D model preserved realistic proportions and was correctly aligned with the OSM footprint, indicating that the pipeline remained effective even under challenging color and lighting conditions.

In the second case study, the pipeline achieved near-perfect performance. All windows were detected across five floors, including those partially obscured by balconies or decorative frames. The estimated facade boundary closely followed the real structure, excluding adjacent buildings, sidewalk areas, and other visual distractions. The clean geometry and regular spacing of architectural elements

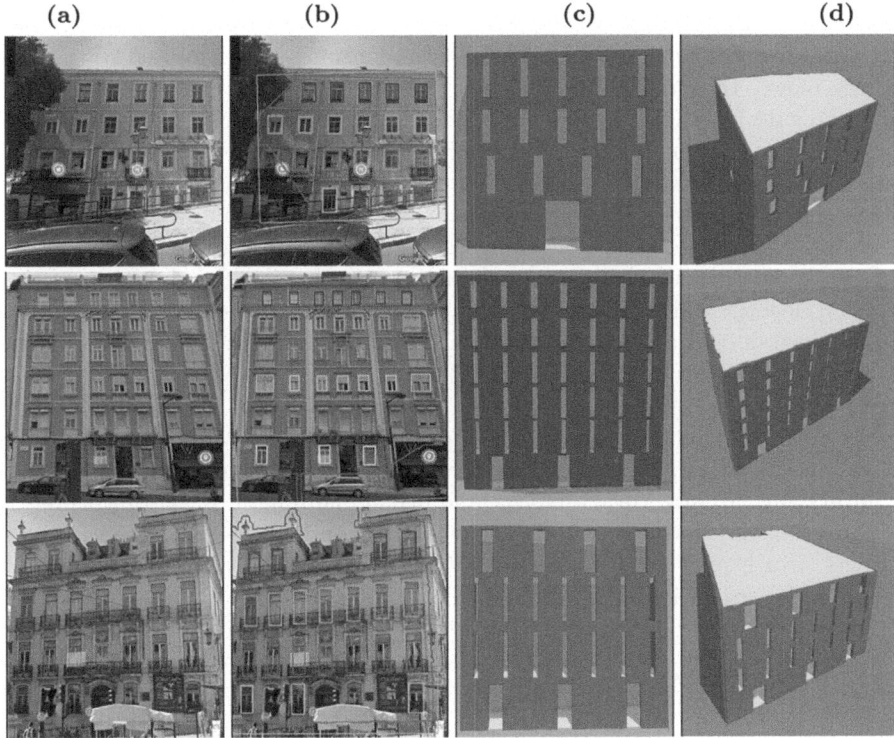

Fig. 4. Three examples illustrate the pipeline overview, showing four main stages: (a) input street-level image, (b) window detection and Gabor-based facade segmentation, (c) facade projection in 3D space, and (d) final volumetric 3D model generated using facade statistics and OSM footprint.

resulted in a highly accurate 3D reconstruction, with facade statistics and OSM integration contributing to strong geospatial alignment and realism.

The third case study involved a more visually complex, decorated building with historic characteristics, including cornices, balconies, and detailed masonry. While most windows were correctly identified, a few ground-floor openings were missed due to occlusions from urban objects such as umbrellas and signage. Nevertheless, the facade extent was effectively captured, with the texture-based segmentation adapting well to the irregular boundary. The final 3D model retained architectural fidelity, demonstrating the method's ability to generalize even under intricate and cluttered conditions. However, due to the lack of semantic labels for decorative features, vertical proportions—especially in the uppermost floor—are approximated and may not fully match the original elevation. This highlights a key limitation of the current approach when applied to buildings with highly articulated or ornamented upper structures.

Beyond individual case-specific challenges, a broader limitation of the pipeline arises when dealing with buildings that feature varying architectural styles and diverse window dimensions, which may lead to less accurate 3D representations. Although individual window dimensions are estimated during the analysis phase, the final 3D models rely on averaged statistics when passed to Unity. This design choice prioritises consistency and simplicity but may reduce geometric accuracy in buildings with highly diverse window sizes or irregular spacing. As a result, while window positions are preserved based on the detection layout, their reconstructed dimensions do not always reflect true variations—particularly in facades with non-uniform window structures.

Overall, the pipeline performs reliably across varying facade complexities, occlusion levels, and stylistic variations. Its modular design—consisting of YOLO-based detection, texture refinement using Gabor filters, and GIS-aligned 3D modelling in Unity—enables adaptation and improvement at individual stages.

The consistent integration of facade geometry with OSM data supports the generation of spatially accurate 3D models suitable for downstream applications in digital twins, architectural analysis, and urban planning. Limitations primarily stem from missed detections under heavy occlusion or non-standard structural elements, which may be addressed in future work through semantic refinement or temporal aggregation using multi-angle views.

5   Future Work

Possible extensions of this work could include expanding the semantic scope of detection to cover additional architectural elements such as balconies and doors. Robustness under occlusion and visual clutter may also be improved by integrating multi-angle imagery or temporal observations. Additionally, future studies could explore quantitative evaluation of the 3D reconstruction accuracy by comparing estimated structural attributes—such as height, floor count, and window alignment—with ground truth data from GIS or architectural plans. Another direction involves exploring clustering facade regions based on Gabor filter responses using Self-Organizing Maps (SOMs) [14] enabling unsupervised grouping of texture-based elements to enhance structural analysis.

6   Conclusions

This paper presents a scalable and annotation-efficient pipeline for 3D building reconstruction using deep learning and texture analysis. By applying the YOLOv8 large model, we achieve high-precision window detection on urban imagery with minimal annotation effort. The integration of Gabor-based texture analysis further enhances facade boundary estimation, allowing for realistic and structurally coherent 3D models to be rapidly generated within the Unity environment.

Despite the limited diversity of window types in our training set, the method generalizes effectively across Lisbon's heterogeneous facades. By anchoring on OpenStreetMap footprints, we achieve precise geospatial alignment, enabling city-scale deployment. The modular pipeline—spanning window detection, Gabor-based texture refinement, GIS alignment, and automated Unity export—supports scalable operation through minimal annotation, batched inference, and headless 3D model generation. This framework lays the foundation for large-scale digital twin creation, structural risk assessment, and urban analytics.

Acknowledgments. This work was supported by the project PR3248 - B0038/2023, in collaboration with the Portuguese Army. It was also supported by UID/04516/NOVA Laboratory for Computer Science and Informatics (NOVA LINCS), with financial support from FCT.IP. The first author further acknowledges funding from the Foundation for Science and Technology (FCT), through the CMU Portugal Affiliated Ph.D. Programs, under the fellowship grant PRT/BD/155062/2024.

Disclosure of Interests. The authors have no competing interests to declare that are relevant to the content of this article.

References

1. Bianconi, F., Fernández, A.: Evaluation of the effects of gabor filter parameters on texture classification. Pattern Recogn. **40**(12), 3325–3335 (2007)
2. Chen, Y., Mancini, M., Zhu, X., Akata, Z.: Semi-supervised and unsupervised deep visual learning: a survey. IEEE Trans. Pattern Anal. Mach. Intell. **46**(3), 1327–1347 (2022)
3. Cunningham, P., Cord, M., Delany, S.J.: Supervised learning. In: Machine learning techniques for multimedia: case studies on organization and retrieval, pp. 21–49. Springer (2008)
4. Ezzeddini, L., et al.: Analysis of the performance of faster r-cnn and yolov8 in detecting fishing vessels and fishes in real time. PeerJ Comput. Sci. **10**, e2033 (2024)
5. Fogel, I., Sagi, D.: Gabor filters as texture discriminator. Biol. Cybern. **61**(2), 103–113 (1989)
6. Georgiou, Y., Loizou, M., Kelly, T., Averkiou, M.: Facadenet: conditional facade synthesis via selective editing. In: Proceedings of the IEEE/CVF Winter Conference on Applications of Computer Vision, pp. 5384–5393 (2024)
7. He, K., Gkioxari, G., Dollár, P., Girshick, R.: Mask r-cnn. In: Proceedings of the IEEE International Conference on Computer Vision, pp. 2961–2969 (2017)
8. Jain, A.K., Farrokhnia, F.: Unsupervised texture segmentation using gabor filters. Pattern Recogn. **24**(12), 1167–1186 (1991)
9. Jamil, S., Jalil Piran, M., Kwon, O.J.: A comprehensive survey of transformers for computer vision. Drones **7**(5), 287 (2023)
10. Jocher, G., Qiu, J., Chaurasia, A.: Ultralytics YOLO (2023). https://github.com/ultralytics/ultralytics
11. Khayyal, H.K., Zeidan, Z.M., Beshr, A.: Creation and spatial analysis of 3d city modeling based on gis data. Civil Eng. J. **8**(1), 105 (2022)
12. Krizhevsky, A., Sutskever, I., Hinton, G.E.: Imagenet classification with deep convolutional neural networks. Adv. Neural Inf. Process. Syst. **25** (2012)
13. Manjunath, B.S., Ma, W.Y.: Texture features for browsing and retrieval of image data. IEEE Trans. Pattern Anal. Mach. Intell. **18**(8), 837–842 (2002)

14. Marques, N.C., Silva, B.: Exploratory cluster analysis using self-organizing maps: algorithms, methodologies, and framework. In: Philosophy of Artificial Intelligence and its Place in Society, pp. 187–213. IGI Global (2023)

15. Mathias, M., Martinović, A., Van Gool, L.: Atlas: a three-layered approach to facade parsing. Int. J. Comput. Vision **118**, 22–48 (2016)

16. Munawar, H.S., Aggarwal, R., Qadir, Z., Khan, S.I., Kouzani, A.Z., Mahmud, M.P.: A gabor filter-based protocol for automated image-based building detection. Buildings **11**(7), 302 (2021)

17. Nóbrega, R., Correia, N.: Interactive 3d content insertion in images for multimedia applications. Multimedia Tools Appl. **76**, 163–197 (2017)

18. Pang, H.E., Biljecki, F.: 3d building reconstruction from single street view images using deep learning. Int. J. Appl. Earth Obs. Geoinf. **112**, 102859 (2022)

19. Rawat, W., Wang, Z.: Deep convolutional neural networks for image classification: a comprehensive review. Neural Comput. **29**(9), 2352–2449 (2017)

20. Redmon, J., Divvala, S., Girshick, R., Farhadi, A.: You only look once: unified, real-time object detection. In: Proceedings of the IEEE Conference on Computer Vision and Pattern Recognition, pp. 779–788 (2016)

21. Redmon, J., Farhadi, A.: Yolov3: an incremental improvement. arXiv preprint arXiv:1804.02767 (2018)

22. Ren, S., He, K., Girshick, R., Sun, J.: Faster r-cnn: towards real-time object detection with region proposal networks. IEEE Trans. Pattern Anal. Mach. Intell. **39**(6), 1137–1149 (2016)

23. Santos Júnior, E.S.d., Paixão, T., Alvarez, A.B.: Comparative performance of yolov8, yolov9, yolov10, and yolov11 for layout analysis of historical documents images. Appl. Sci. **15**(6), 3164 (2025)

24. Sundaresan Geetha, A., Alif, M.A.R., Hussain, M., Allen, P.: Comparative analysis of yolov8 and yolov10 in vehicle detection: performance metrics and model efficacy. Vehicles **6**(3), 1364–1382 (2024)

25. Takahashi, S., et al.: Comparison of vision transformers and convolutional neural networks in medical image analysis: a systematic review. J. Med. Syst. **48**(1), 84 (2024)

26. tau: window detector dataset (2023). https://universe.roboflow.com/tau-bu7eo/window-detector

27. Teboul, O., Simon, L., Koutsourakis, P., Paragios, N.: Segmentation of building facades using procedural shape priors. In: 2010 IEEE Computer Society Conference on Computer Vision and Pattern Recognition, pp. 3105–3112. IEEE (2010)

28. Wang, B., Zhang, J., Zhang, R., Li, Y., Li, L., Nakashima, Y.: Improving facade parsing with vision transformers and line integration. Adv. Eng. Inf. **60**, 102463 (2024)

29. Wang, S., Kang, Q., She, R., Tay, W.P., Navarro, D.N., Hartmannsgruber, A.: Building facade parsing r-cnn. arXiv preprint arXiv:2205.05912 (2022)

30. Wu, C., Yu, X., Ma, C., Zhong, R., Zhou, X.: Integrating geospatial data and street-view imagery to reconstruct large-scale 3d urban building models. Trans. GIS **28**(5), 1326–1352 (2024)

31. Yang, Y., Tang, R., Xia, M., Zhang, C.: A texture integrated deep neural network for semantic segmentation of urban meshes. IEEE J. Sel. Topics Appl. Earth Obs. Remote Sens. **16**, 4670–4684 (2023)

32. Zeiser, F.A., et al.: Segmentation of masses on mammograms using data augmentation and deep learning. J. Digit. Imaging **33**, 858–868 (2020)

33. Zhang, C., Fan, H., Kong, G.: Vgi3d: an interactive and low-cost solution for 3d building modelling from street-level vgi images. J. Geovisualizat. Spatial Anal. **5**(2), 18 (2021)
34. Zhao, X., Wang, L., Zhang, Y., Han, X., Deveci, M., Parmar, M.: A review of convolutional neural networks in computer vision. Artif. Intell. Rev. **57**(4), 99 (2024)

Challenging Fortification Attribution Through AI-Assisted Geometric Analysis

Olha Tikhonova$^{(\boxtimes)}$

Art History Department of Seville University, 41005 Seville, Spain
otikhonova@us.es

Abstract. Despite long-standing claims that the bastion fortification of Zbarazh castle follows the Dutch school of military architecture, this article challenges that assumption through computational AI-assisted analysis. While the layout has traditionally been associated with the Dutch system of fortifications—supported by researchers such as Janusz Bogdanowski and Adam Miłobędzki, who placed Zbarazh within the "Polish manner" derived from Dutch models—no prior study has applied quantitative methods to test this attribution. This study employs a computational workflow that integrates AI-based image segmentation, vectorization of the castle plan, and analysis using Rhino and Grasshopper. Using a scanned plan of Zbarazh castle, automatically converted to editable vector geometry for Rhino, the key geometric features of the bastion outline—specifically, the flanked angles and shoulder angles, critical indicators in bastion classification —were extracted and measured. The analysis reveals that the flanked angles range from 73° to 78°, with an average of around 76.4°, which is significantly higher than the typical Dutch range of 60° to 65°. Similarly, shoulder angles range from 93° to 100°, averaging 96.79°, notably lower than the Dutch standard of 102°30′ to 105°. These findings demonstrate a clear and systematic deviation from Dutch fortification geometry. The results suggest a closer alignment with the Italian school, particularly the New Italian system, which aligns with historical references to Scamozzi's original design. Ultimately, the study not only repositions Zbarazh within a different architectural lineage but also highlights the value of AI-assisted geometric analysis in correcting historical misattributions in architectural heritage research.

Keywords: Computational Architectural Analysis · Bastioned Fortifications · AI

1 Introduction

The bastion fortification of Zbarazh castle, located in present-day Ukraine, has been traditionally associated with the Dutch school of military architecture. Influential researchers, such as Janusz Bogdanowski [1], included Zbarazh in his classification of fortresses within the Polish Crown that exhibit features of the "Polish manner," derived from Dutch fortification principles. Others, including Miłobędzki [2], noted irregularities in the design, attributing them to potential amateur involvement by the patron or builder.

© The Author(s), under exclusive license to Springer Nature Switzerland AG 2026
J. Valente de Oliveira et al. (Eds.): EPIA 2025, LNAI 16121, pp. 188–200, 2026.
https://doi.org/10.1007/978-3-032-05176-9_15

Zbarazh bastion castle is widely regarded as one of the most prominent examples of the *palazzo in fortezza* typology. This fortified palace form represents the apex of residential bastioned architecture in the early modern period. Its significance lies in being one of Europe's few fully integrated fortification-residence complexes, explicitly described in the well-known architectural treatise. The original design, attributed to the Italian architect Vincenzo Scamozzi, was developed specifically for the Duke of Zbarazh and is featured in Scamozzi's treatise (*L'idea dell'architettura universal* [3]). Although the constructed version diverges in certain aspects from the theoretical plan, the conceptual foundation clearly reflects the Italian school of fortification, distinguishing it from the Dutch model to which it is often erroneously attributed.

The authorship of the final design remains unresolved. While Scamozzi is credited with the initial plan, the executed project was changed by an unknown architect. Scholars differ in their views on who may have revised the design. Nicieja [4] suggests that the owner, Jerzy Zbaraski, may have adopted solutions proposed by the Dutch architect Henryk van Peene. Pilarczyk [5], as well as Czołowski and Bogdanowski [6], go further, claiming that van Peene was officially commissioned to design the fortress in the New Dutch manner. Tadeusz Polak [7] cautiously acknowledges van Peene's possible involvement, noting that "some researchers see here the hand of Henry van Peene, an architect from the Netherlands." However, none of these attributions are substantiated by direct documentary evidence, and the identity of the final designer remains speculative.

Despite these scholarly debates, no prior study has undertaken a rigorous, quantitative analysis of the bastion geometry at Zbarazh. This study addresses this gap by applying a computational workflow using Grasshopper and Rhino, supplemented by an AI-based segmentation tool, to evaluate the formal properties of the bastion layout. Focusing on flanked and shoulder angles—key indicators in fortification typology—this research presents empirical findings that challenge the prevailing classification of Zbarazh as a Dutch-style fortress.

2   Methodology

The adoption of AI-assisted segmentation and parametric computation enhances the reproducibility and scalability of fortification analysis. Compared with traditional CAD-based tracing, the automated pipeline enables the rapid processing of large datasets, with consistent extraction of angular and metric relationships. While manual methods offer flexibility, they are often limited by subjective interpretation and time constraints. The proposed approach introduces rule-based geometric recognition, which collectively allows for systematic testing of typological hypotheses, such as the degree of conformity to Dutch fortification canons. However, expert oversight remains essential in interpreting ambiguous features and integrating historical context.

The method has limitations and warrants further testing to assess its robustness across a broader range of historical examples and diverse types of cartographic inputs. The accuracy of quantitative analysis fundamentally hinges on the fidelity of the geometry extracted from archival representations—sources that are often subject to stylization, scale distortions, and material degradation. These conditions introduce ambiguities that demand a cautious, layered strategy. While the method may not yet be universally robust across all types of historical imagery, it performed reliably in the case studies tested, especially with high-resolution scans of clean, well-preserved drawings, where segmentation and vectorization yielded highly accurate geometric data. Repeated extractions consistently yielded accurate results in the tested cases.

Ultimately, while automation enhances consistency and analytical reach, expert oversight remains essential. It is the architectural historian who discerns intent from artifact, interprets irregularities in light of terrain or typological drift, and situates geometry within broader design cultures. The result is a methodological framework (Fig. 6) that does not replace interpretation with computation but rather strengthens it—an interface where precision and historical imagination converge.

2.1 Source Data and Vectorization

A high-resolution raster image of the current floor plan of Zbarazh castle served as the starting point for the analysis (see Fig. 1).

Image Segmentation Using AI. As the first step in processing the floor plan of the bastion castle, AI-based image segmentation was used to isolate the castle outline from the rest of the raster plan. The Segment Anything Model (SAM), developed by Kirillov et al. [8] as part of the Segment Anything project, was employed for this task. SAM is a foundation model for computer vision that enables flexible, promptable segmentation of any object in any image, even without prior exposure to that object class or domain. It is trained on over one billion segmentation masks and can operate in a zero-shot setting, meaning it can perform accurate segmentation without fine-tuning or additional task-specific data. The tool is openly accessible through a web-based interactive demo (https://segment-anything.com/demo), allowing users to experiment with segmentation tasks directly in the browser (see Figs. 1 and 2). Furthermore, the complete source code and pre-trained models are freely available on GitHub, accompanied by detailed documentation. This open-source structure enables the adaptation and customization of the model to meet specific research needs.

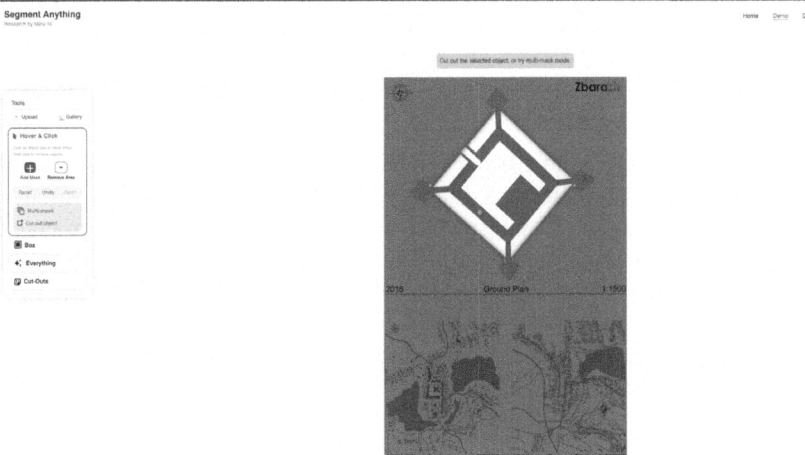

Fig. 1. A screenshot of the Segment Anything Demo with the image of the floor plan of Zbarazh Castle made by the author based on the data collected in 2016.

In this project, SAM was used to extract the outline of the bastion castle from a scanned architectural drawing. While this particular case presented a relatively clean and clearly defined target for segmentation, the model's broader utility was tested on a range of archival map scans containing forts and castles with more complex backgrounds and degraded image quality (see Fig. 2). SAM successfully segmented relevant architectural features in these cases, demonstrating its strong generalization capabilities across different historical representations.

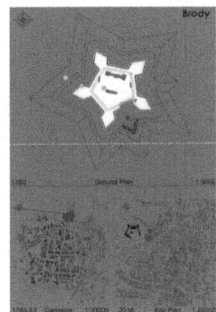
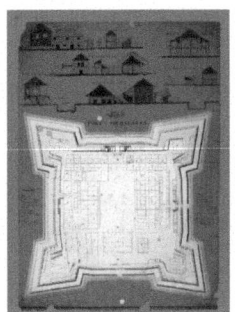

Fig. 2. Screenshot showing the results of multiple AI-based segmentation attempts applied to various bastioned castles. The images include examples following the same layout as the primary case study in the article, as well as segmentation outputs from other scanned historical drawings and archival maps of bastioned fortifications. The comparison illustrates the model's adaptability across different document qualities and graphic styles. Source of documents under analysis: Author's drawing and historical maps of Indonesian forts sourced from the Hague Archives, available in the public domain.

Applying segmentation without training a model or supplying annotated examples significantly reduced the preprocessing burden. The resulting mask, containing only the bastion layout, was then exported and vectorized for further analysis in Rhino and Grasshopper.

Automatic Image Vectorization in Rhino. The Vectorize plugin for Rhino was used to convert the raster plan of the castle into editable vector geometry. This tool is available via Food4Rhino. Once the plugin was installed, the Vectorize command was executed within Rhino's command line interface. The software then prompted the user to select the desired raster image file. Upon selection, the plugin generated a real-time preview of the vectorization process, allowing for basic visual inspection of the curve extraction quality. Optimal results require adjusting parameters such as threshold levels and turn policy settings, which influence the sensitivity of edge detection and the continuity of curves during vectorization.

After confirming the operation, the image was automatically converted into Rhino-native curve geometry, consisting of closed and open curves (see Fig. 3). These vector outputs were then further processed, filtered, and analyzed within Rhino using Grasshopper for geometric evaluation of the fortification layout.

A filtering process was applied in Grasshopper to extract the necessary outline, isolating closed curves and identifying the largest among them, which corresponded to the entire perimeter of the bastion layout.

Fig. 3. Screenshot showing the automatic vectorization results applied to the Zbarazh bastion castle's drawing image.

2.2   Computational Analysis in Grasshopper

A custom geometric analysis script was developed in Grasshopper to extract and evaluate angular relationships within the vectorized outline of the bastioned castle. The script first identifies curtain walls and bastion-flanked angles. Then it calculates two key geometric values: flanked angles, formed between two adjacent faces, and shoulder angles, located at the junction between each bastion face and the adjoining flank. This computational approach enables the precise and reproducible measurement of fortification geometry, which is crucial for comparative analysis against established typological standards.

This analytical workflow aligns with ongoing scholarly work that focuses on parametric modeling of historical fortifications in treatises. Notably, researchers such as Roberta Spallone, Marco Vitali, Fabrizio Natta, and Enrico Pupi at Politecnico di Torino have developed parametric reconstructions of treatise-based fortification systems, including Guarini's *Trattato di Fortificatione*, within the INFORTREAT research framework [9, 10]. Their work uses Grasshopper to encode theoretical rules into parametric design models, enabling variations in fortress configurations based on respective treatise principles. In contrast, the present study adopts a mirrored approach: rather than modeling from prescriptive rules, it analyzes an existing historical fortification to assess whether its geometry aligns with the norms found in Dutch military treatises. This inverse application of parametric tools allows for empirical testing of attribution claims based on geometric evidence.

This analysis begins by converting the vectorized curve into a polyline, followed by the application of the Polygon Topology Point Analysis, a Grasshopper Add-on component designed for closed polylines. The centroid of the outline is then computed; this point corresponds to the geometric and conceptual center of the bastion system as described in 17th-century architectural treatises.

From the center point, lines are drawn to all detected vertices of the polygon. However, due to over-segmentation during the vectorization process, the number of vertices exceeds the actual number of structural edges in the bastion outline. In many cases, additional points were generated at the midpoints of segments. The shortest one, perpendicular to the nearest curtain wall, is identified among these radial lines. A rectangle is then constructed using twice the length of this shortest distance as one side, knowing that the interior polygon of the castle is a perfect square. This rectangle, oriented along the direction of the shortest radial line, is aligned to the outline and functions as the interior polygon—a geometric structure, the base of the bastion castle outline.

To assess each capital (or magistral) line of the outline, the longest radial distance from the center to an outline vertex is recorded. This distance represents the central axis of each bastion projection. The script identifies the furthest point (the bastion apex) and calculates the flanked angles by determining its two nearest neighbors along the polygon. Vectors are drawn from this salient point of the bastion to the neighboring points, and the angle between these vectors is computed to determine the flanked angle.

To compute shoulder angles, the vectors described above are extended as lines until they intersect with the previously constructed interior polygon. This line corresponds to the Razant line of defense (see Fig. 4). The first intersection point helps to define the shoulder angle. Based on standard bastion geometry, where the curtain wall forms a right angle (90°) with the interior polygon, the shoulder angle is calculated using the formula (1):

$$y = 90° + x \tag{1}$$

where x is the angle between the interior polygon edge and the flank vector (see Fig. 5). This process enabled precise, reproducible measurement of relevant angular relationships in the fortress layout.

The use of the 90° curtain wall assumption reflects a geometric ideal rooted in Dutch and early modern fortification theory, as widely disseminated in European military treatises. In the specific context of Polish-Lithuanian bastion castles built from scratch, this assumption is further validated by historical sources that advocated for the use of regular geometric plans—often four- or five-sided—as codified in the proportional tables of Freitag and early Polish manuals [11, 12]. Nevertheless, in practical conditions, slight deviations from orthogonality may occur due to local terrain or construction variability. To address this, the model employs a conservative angular tolerance of ± 3°, based on reconstruction studies and observed discrepancies. Deviations within this range are considered acceptable field adaptations, provided they do not undermine the underlying geometric intent. In future applications, this parameter may be dynamically integrated into the model to generate confidence intervals and tolerance zones, thereby contextualizing the results and distinguishing between design fidelity and local reinterpretation.

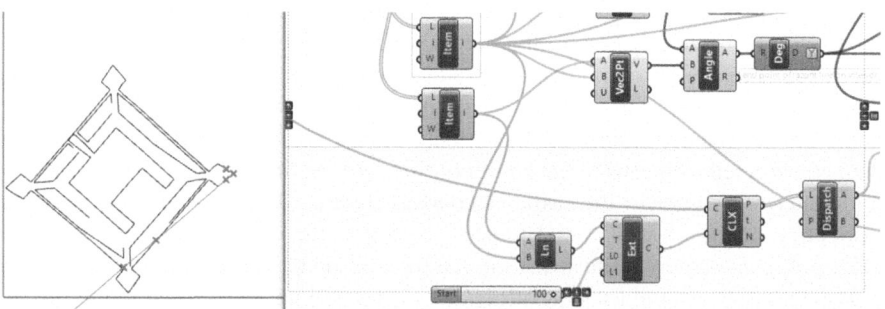

Fig. 4. Screenshot from Rhino showing the Razant line of defense of the Zbarazh bastion castle and intersection points with the interior polygon (curtain walls).

2.3 Benchmark Comparison

To evaluate the geometric characteristics of Zbarazh castle's bastion layout, benchmark values were established based on reference ranges drawn from historical Dutch fortification treatises and validated by prior scholarly studies. These benchmarks provided

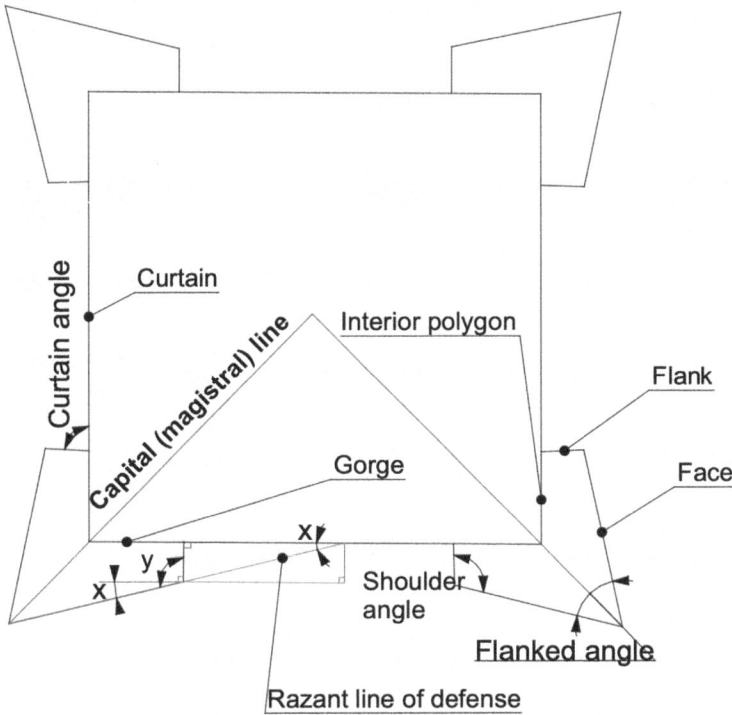

Fig. 5. Author's drawing to explain the terminology and calculation of *y* in the formula.

normative parameters for assessing whether the measured angles at Zbarazh align with those characteristics of the Dutch fortification school.

Specifically, two angular types were used as key indicators:

- Flanked angles (formed between two adjacent faces, also known as salient angles) typically range between 60° and 65° in the Dutch system.
- Shoulder angles (formed between the face of the bastion and the flank) traditionally fall within 102°30′ to 105°.

These values reflect both engineering conventions and tactical principles fundamental to Dutch military architecture [13]. They are documented in the most influential Dutch fortification treatises of the 17th century, including those written by Adam Freitag [14], and were later reiterated in Poland's first native treatise on military architecture by Naronowicz-Naroński [11].

In this study, the measured flanked and shoulder angles of the Zbarazh bastion were directly compared against these benchmarks. Any significant deviations from the reference ranges were interpreted as indicators of design divergence, potentially pointing to alternative fortification systems or adaptations influenced by other architectural traditions. This comparative framework served as the basis for assessing the extent to which Zbarazh conforms to—or fails to conform to—the Dutch model.

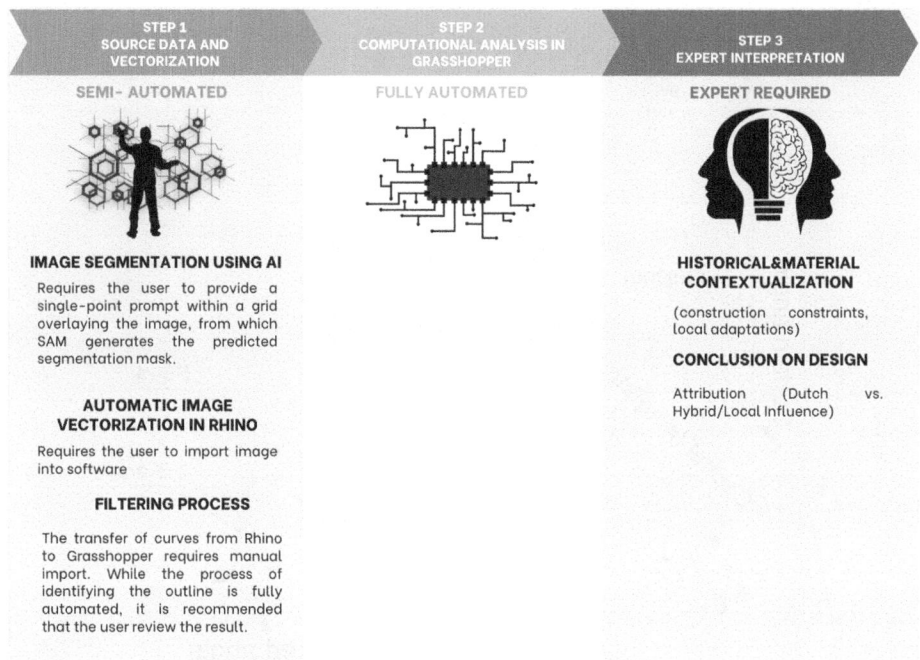

Fig. 6. A flowchart illustrating the methodology's hybrid structure, distinguishing between automated processes and stages requiring expert intervention.

3 Results

The computational analysis of the Zbarazh bastion layout produced both quantitative and qualitative data, enabling a systematic comparison with Dutch fortification benchmarks. The results are organized into three analytical categories: flanked angles, shoulder angles, and general geometric configurations.

Although the benchmark values are grounded in canonical military treatises and widely accepted within the scholarly literature, it must be acknowledged that they were not derived using the same computational methodology presented in this study. This introduces a degree of methodological asymmetry into the comparison. To address this limitation, the interpretation does not rely on strict metric equivalence but instead emphasizes proportional tendencies and misalignment with the core geometric principles of the Dutch fortification school.

To enhance the methodological consistency of future research, it is recommended that the same AI-assisted analytical framework be applied to bastioned fortresses in the Netherlands or other canonical Dutch examples. Such an approach would facilitate the creation of a unified dataset, reduce uncertainty, and improve the robustness of comparative inferences across case studies.

3.1 Flanked Angles

- Measured range: 73°–78°
- Average: 76.4°

The flanked angles measured in the Zbarazh bastions significantly exceed the standard range defined by Dutch fortification treatises, typically between 60° and 65°. In the Dutch system, such angles are deliberately constrained to create acute projections that enhance defensive crossfire along the curtain walls. The consistently larger angles observed at Zbarazh suggest a departure from this logic, resulting in wider, less aggressive flanks that compromise enfilade fire capabilities. This discrepancy alone is sufficient to cast doubt on a strict Dutch attribution of the design.

3.2 Shoulder Angles

- Measured range: 93°–100°
- Average: 96.79°

Shoulder angles—the angles formed at the junction between each bastion face and flank—were also found to deviate substantially from Dutch norms, which are typically within the range of 102°30′ to 105°. The reduced angular values at Zbarazh produce a noticeably tighter geometry, contributing to the appearance of underdeveloped bastions with reduced structural projection. These smaller shoulder angles further distinguish the design from the standardized Dutch system, where broader angles contribute to increased defensive robustness.

3.3 Visual and Geometric Observations

Beyond the angular data, the geometry of the bastion layout reveals qualitative characteristics that reinforce the divergence from Dutch models:

- The bastions are notably small and structurally underdeveloped, lacking the mass and spatial depth commonly found in mature Dutch fortifications.
- Face-to-curtain proportions are imbalanced, suggesting a layout that does not conform to the geometric regularity and proportional logic seen in Dutch treatises.
- The overall design is visually more aligned with early New Italian fortification principles, as seen in the first design by Scamozzi.

Taken together, these findings indicate a systematic deviation from Dutch fortification doctrine. The measured values and spatial relationships suggest a design more consistent with Italian or transitional regional models, possibly shaped by reinterpretation or partial understanding of imported architectural ideas.

4 Conclusions and Discussion

The results presented here challenge the prevailing narrative that Zbarazh bastion castle exemplifies the Dutch school of bastion fortification. Contrary to earlier interpretations, critical angular metrics fall outside the acceptable ranges of Dutch canonical design, and the visual configuration of the bastions—marked by short faces, shallow shoulders, and exaggerated flanked angles—bears a stronger resemblance to the Italian fortification logic articulated by Scamozzi. These deviations are not incidental nor isolated; they form a consistent and measurable pattern across the entire layout. If Dutch influence was indeed present in Zbarazh's conception, it appears to have been misinterpreted, diluted, or deliberately reworked through a lens of local experimentation. This interpretation finds further support in Miłobędzki's hypothesis that the owner of Zbarazh may have played an active role in shaping the castle's layout. Such involvement points toward an architectural process not strictly bound by professional military engineering, but rather mediated by personal agency, regional conventions, and material realities.

The computational framework developed in this study is designed precisely to interrogate such complexities. Tested on the Zbarazh fortress, the methodology integrates AI-assisted segmentation, rule-based geometric recognition, and parametric proportional analysis to produce a scalable and reproducible approach to study early modern fortifications. By balancing automated extraction with expert oversight, the tool allows for systematic testing of typological adherence while acknowledging the interpretive nature of historical evidence.

While the current pipeline is optimized for square-based bastioned outlines, it is also adaptable to other shapes. Applying the method to another base polygon or testing another school rules requires only targeted code modifications or recalibration of benchmark values. Future development will incorporate formal uncertainty margins, based on empirical deviation values measured during repeated vectorization trials of different maps with an imperfect base. This will enable users to evaluate the robustness of attribution hypotheses better.

Crucially, the methodology remains a proof of concept, not a final verdict. The historiography of early modern fortification is deeply layered, shaped by a web of overlapping design traditions, localized practices, evolving artillery technologies, and the logistical constraints of construction. Drawing definitive conclusions from a single case would be premature. However, by offering a replicable and flexible pipeline, this research lays the groundwork for a comparative architectural analysis—one that spans canonical Dutch sites and peripheral or colonial variants across Central Europe and beyond.

Planned applications of this methodology to a broader dataset of over a dozen bastioned fortresses will enable systematic testing of military school attributions across diverse geopolitical and material contexts. This expansion promises a deeper understanding of how proportional logic was transmitted, transformed, and embedded in the geometry of early modern defensive landscapes.

For instance, within the framework of another ongoing project led by the author, the method plans to be applied to the database of the Indonesian Center for Documentation, which catalogs 442 forts, most of which were built under Dutch influence. The aim is to develop an automated classification of fortification layouts using this dataset. While the current algorithm is calibrated for square-based designs, adapting it to such a large and varied corpus will require extending the code to recognize pentagonal, triangular, and irregular plans.

Fortunately, the available plans—provided in JPEG format—are generally of good contrast and feature a consistent representation style, always including a single fort per image, which suggests they are well-suited for automated segmentation. Nonetheless, training the segmentation process specifically on bastioned fortification drawings would significantly improve accuracy and robustness, as the reliability of the method is inherently tied to the fidelity of the input maps. While the hybrid use of different approaches, such as tracing, edge detection, and parametric reconstruction of the external outline, mitigates some of these challenges, certain angular assumptions—such as the orthogonality of curtains—introduce simplifications. Moreover, the semi-automated segmentation process still requires human correction and interpretive judgment, and the current parametric environment may pose accessibility challenges to heritage professionals unfamiliar with computational modeling.

Additional scripting will be required to formalize geometric recognition for regular pentagonal and triangular bases using the same parametric logic developed in this study. In contrast, analyzing irregular plans may necessitate entirely new approaches. Comparing fortification "schools" with a square base, which belong to other architectural traditions, such as those of Italy, France, Poland, Spain, and Portugal, and integrating their known benchmarks into the tool is a technically straightforward process. However, one must account for the internal variability within even each school, where individual engineers often modified canonical ratios in pursuit of improved geometry and defense.

The most rigorous path forward would be to test the methodology on a wide array of well-documented examples attributed to each school. Such comparative analysis could form the backbone of a significant international research initiative. This, in turn, would enable the establishment of reliable geometric benchmarks for use in analyzing overseas examples, many of which exhibit local adaptations due to the availability of materials and environmental constraints. Notably, cases where construction stones were imported from the Netherlands are rare exceptions and merit their focused analysis.

Addressing these challenges will inform future development, including the creation of more user-friendly interfaces. Ultimately, the goal is not to reduce fortification design to numbers, but to expand the interpretive horizon—to bridge the precision of geometry with the nuance of history, and to let the stones speak not only of form, but of intention, adaptation, and identity.

Disclosure of Interests. The author has no competing interests to declare that are relevant to the content of this article.

References

1. Bogdanowski, J.: Wpływ szkoły staroholenderskiej na uformowanie się "polskiej maniery" w sztuce obronnej XVII w. In: Niderlandyzm w sztuce polskiej: materiały Sesji Stowarzyszenia Historyków Sztuki, Toruń, grudzień 1992, 1st edn. Wydawnictwo Naukowe PWN, Warszawa, pp. 327–351 (1995)
2. Miłobędzki, A.: Architektura Polska XVII wieku. Państwowe Wydaw. Naukowe, Warszawa (1980)
3. Scamozzi, V.: Dell'idea della architettura universale di Vicenzo Scamozzi architetto veneto. Parte prima, libro primo [-seconda, libro sesto]... Novamente stampato, ed in quest'ultima edizione accresciuto d'un curioso trattato del sesto ordine dell'architettura.. Alessandro della Via (1615)
4. Nicieja, S.: Twierdze kresowe Rzeczypospolitej: historia, legendy, biografie. Iskry, Warszawa (2006)

5. Pilarczyk, Z.: Fortyfikacje na ziemiach koronnych Rzeczypospolitej w XVII wieku. Instytut Historii UAM, Poznán (1997)
6. Czołowski, A., Janusz, B.: Przeszłość i zabytki województwa tarnopolskiego. Nakład Powiatowej Organizacji Narodowej, Tarnopol (1926)
7. Polak, T.: Zamki na kresach: Białoruś, Litwa, Ukraina, 1st edn. Pagina, Warszawa (1997)
8. Kirillov, A., et al.: Segment anything. ArXiv. https://doi.org/10.48550/arXiv.2304.02643 (2023)
9. Spallone, R., Vitali, M., Natta, F., Pupi, E.: Parametric variations of the "delineationi seconde delle fortezze, e dell'ortografia loro", from the Trattato di Fortificatione by Guarini. In: Proceedings of the International Conference on Fortifications of the Mediterranean Coast FORTMED 2025, vol. 20, pp.1211–1218. edUPV. Editorial Universitat Politècnica de València, València (2025)
10. Rechichi, P., Miele, V., Bevilacqua, M.G.: Modelli informativi digitali di architettura militare della prima età moderna. Il caso del Corno Dogale di Pietro Sardi. In: Angeli, F. (ed.) Misura / Dismisura I Measure/Out of Measure. FrancoAngeli srl, Milano (2024)
11. Gruszecki, A.: Bastionowe zamki w Małopolsce. Ministry of National Defense, Warsaw (1962)
12. Bogdanowski, J.: Sztuka Obronna. Zarząd Zespołu Jurajskich Parków Krajobrazowych w Krakowie, Krakow (1993)
13. Naronowicz-Naroński, J.: Optica lubo perspectiva to iest opisanie nauk widzenia albo przezoru w obaczeniu wszelkich rzeczy wymalowania y własney postaci wyrażenia także osobliwie architectura militaris to iest budownictwo woienne... potem architectura civilis - budownictwo pałaco. Przedmowa do czytelnika narodu sarmackiego o trzecim thomie xiąg nauk mathematycznych, k 1–1 v 146 (1659)

Experimental LINCS Dam for Low-Cost Monitoring

Daniel Eugénio[1] , João Marcelino[2] , Ricardo Santos[2] , Nuno Marques[1] ,
and João Manso[2(✉)]

[1] NOVA LINCS, NOVA School of Science and Technology,
Costa da Caparica, Portugal
d.eugenio@campus.fct.unl.pt, nmm@fct.unl.pt
[2] Laboratório Nacional de Engenharia Civil (LNEC), Geotechnical Department,
Lisbon, Portugal
{marcelino,ricardos,jmanso}@lnec.pt

Abstract. This work presents *LINCS-Dams*, a cost-effective prototype for dynamic monitoring of embankment dams. The experimental setup uses affordable sensors, including micro-electromechanical system (MEMS) in-place inclinometers (IPIs), water-level gauges, and
vibration accelerometers. Sensor outputs are managed by a finite state
machine (FSM) that defines accident driven alert and alarm levels while
dynamically adjusting each sensor's data sampling frequency, optimizing
energy consumption and ensuring timely responses. The main goal of this
work is implementing and validating the proposed system and assessing
its value to small embankment dams, which often lack regular monitoring. Our cost-effective AIoT approach combines sensor networks with
intelligent monitoring for early detection and adaptive response, particularly valuable for embankment dams facing increased climate-driven
risks. Experimental results confirm that the prototype delivers reliable
response and effective dynamic event detection.

Keywords: Sensor networks · State machine · AIoT

1 Introduction

Dams are critical infrastructures whose failure can lead to significant human,
environmental, and economic losses. As such, ensuring dam safety requires a
continuous and adaptive risk management process. Traditionally, dam safety
assessments have been performed under the assumption of stationary climatic
and non-climatic conditions [7]. However, climate change has led to increasingly frequent and intense extreme weather events, raising concerns about the
resilience of these structures under evolving conditions. Despite efforts by various institutions to integrate climate change considerations into decision-making
processes, the application of such guidance to dam safety remains limited due
to a lack of accessible and actionable data. In parallel, conventional dam monitoring relies on instruments such as strain gauges, tiltmeters, and piezometers.

© The Author(s), under exclusive license to Springer Nature Switzerland AG 2026
J. Valente de Oliveira et al. (Eds.): EPIA 2025, LNAI 16121, pp. 201–213, 2026.
https://doi.org/10.1007/978-3-032-05176-9_16

While effective, these systems are typically expensive, require specialised maintenance, and often depend on proprietary platforms. Additionally, the data collected is usually discrete in time and not always available after critical events. These limitations highlight the need for more efficient, affordable, and continuous monitoring solutions.

Recent advancements in the integration of Artificial Intelligence and Internet of Things (AIoT) technologies have opened new opportunities for automated and cost-effective dam monitoring systems [17]. To address this need, the LINCS Dams project proposes the development of a low-cost, IoT-based prototype specifically designed for embankment dam monitoring. While large national databases, such as GestBarragens [15], provide substantial information on major dams, data on smaller embankment dams is often scarce or unavailable. In Portugal, small dams are typically defined as those with a height of less than 15 m and a reservoir capacity under 100,000 cubic metres. Notably, over 50 % of dam incidents occur in structures under 20 m high [12], often due to limited investment in site investigation, construction supervision, and monitoring.

The LINCS Dams system was motivated by the lack of continuous and accessible monitoring data in such smaller structures. A scaled physical model was developed and instrumented with low-cost in-place inclinometers, level sensors, and accelerometers, enabling regular monitoring of dam behaviour. Unlike approaches that rely heavily on advanced machine learning, the LINCS Dams project prioritises instrumentation and consistent data acquisition. The resulting system produces multimodal time series data that can support research in areas such as signal processing, anomaly detection, and state estimation. All software and test procedures developed within the project are publicly available[1], building on previous research efforts [10,11,13–16].

2   Related Work

In-place inclinometer systems have evolved, from using micro-electromechanical system (MEMS) technologies from early triaxial accelerometers that measured three-dimensional ground acceleration and deformation, to sophisticated sensor arrays that deliver real-time, wireless monitoring. Barendse and Machan [4] evaluated early MEMS-based in-place inclinometer strings, highlighting their potential for real-time, cost-effective geotechnical monitoring. Bennett et al. [1] reported designs employing MEMS accelerometers, while later studies introduced integrated systems such as the ShapeAccelArray [2] that combined multi-parameter monitoring with wireless data transmission. Zheng et al. [18] described a flexible inclinometer that achieved angular accuracies of less than 0.04° and displacement accuracies of ±0.4 mm horizontally and ±1.6 mm vertically. Additional studies [5,16] showed that proper calibration and low-cost tilting sensors yielded improved precision and early-warning capabilities in applications ranging from unstable slopes and landslides, to levee systems and tunnels. These findings

---

[1] The data collected, experimental setup, and code are available at https://github.com/dannythe21st/LINCS-Dams.

illustrated a clear trend toward enhanced precision, greater deployment flexibility, and multi-sensor integration in MEMS-based geotechnical applications [13].

Finite-state automata (FSA) are a lightweight and interpretable option to model and manage the behavior of IoT devices, especially in resource-constrained settings. For example, Dargie [6] investigated how to optimize microcontroller energy consumption through various strategies, including the use of finite state automata. Bermudez-Edo et al. [3] proposed an FSM-driven service composition architecture for IoT rapid prototyping, enabling modular and scalable system design suitable for large-scale and budget-constrained infrastructure monitoring projects. Recent work has explored AIoT architectures for real-time assessment using sensor networks [9]. Inspired by these efforts, we developed a dynamic reading monitoring system that follows some of the approaches discussed so far.

3   Finite State Machine for Reservoir Conditions

Dam accidents frequently emerge as a consequence of a combination of technical, environmental, and operational failures. Such failures may include inadequate design, poor maintenance, and, most critically, insufficient or ineffective monitoring.

The Lapão dam, located in Portugal, experienced a rare emergency situation in early 2003 due to an intense and sudden increase in water level caused by exceptional rainfall [11]. Despite the presence of minor anomalies that were identified during the preliminary inspection in December 2001, no major concerns prevented the reservoir from being filled. However, during early 2002, significant displacements were recorded, particularly on the left abutment. Despite ongoing monitoring and a fully open bottom outlet, the reservoir continued to increase rapidly during the particularly wet winter of 2002–2003, reaching critical water levels. On January 2003, the dam operator observed water seeping from the downstream shell and, shortly thereafter, turbid water emerging near the downstream toe, indicating internal erosion. Accelerated deformation rates were detected, prompting immediate emergency measures to avoid the dam failure. The dam remains inoperational to this day.

The Aipim dam operated within normal parameters for the first four years until March 2001, when a sudden flood was triggered by an intense rainfall event [8]. This event had not been preceded by prolonged wet periods. The flood wave resulted in a rise in the reservoir level of over 5 m. This led to overtopping of the dam crest for a period of approximately 20 min. The maximum overtopping depth reached 35 cm at the centre of the crest, decreasing to 8–9 cm at the abutments due to more pronounced post-construction settlement at the dam's centre. Despite all dam structures being affected, the brief duration of the event prevented severe damage.

In both examples, it became evident that a primary concern in dam monitoring is evaluating structural behaviour to enable the timely detection of anomalies. In order for real-time decision-making to be effective, it is essential that the data is reliable, interpretable, and supported by sound numerical models.

In this context, remote sensing technologies are playing an increasingly significant role, enabling the acquisition of consistent, large-scale data necessary to identify early signs of structural deterioration or failure scenarios. Combining with advanced data analysis methods, such as machine learning, remote sensing enhances the ability to validate measurements, interpret dam behaviour, and issue timely alerts, thus contributing significantly to the real-time assessment and safety management of dams. Figure 1 presents a FSM developed to model the operational and safety status of a reservoir system based on sensor inputs. The thresholds were defined based on standard dam operating parameters, such as the normal retention level, maximum flood level and minimum operating level, as well as typical filling and drawdown rates. The FSM consists of the following states:

- **Full (F)**: The full reservoir level is defined as the maximum water level to which the water surface will rise during normal operating conditions. A warning state has been defined in order to indicate when the water level has reached this threshold, and is visually highlighted in orange.
- **Empty (E)**: The minimum pool level is defined as the lowest level up to which the water is withdrawn from the reservoir under normal conditions.
- **Live storage (L)**: This state reflects the volume of water stored, with the quantity ranging between the full reservoir level and the minimum pool level. This value is also referred to as *useful storage*, since it assumes the supply of water for a specific duration to meet the demand. This water level is regarded as the dam's normal capacity.
- **Flood (D)**: The maximum water level is defined as the maximum level to which the water surface will rise, when the design flood passes over the spillway. The occurrence of this critical emergency state is indicated when water level exceeds this limit, or by the presence of a high rate of water level rise (`lim(d)` $\lor$ `isFast(`Δd`, L2)`). This state is represented by the colour red, reflecting its urgency.
- **Stability (S)**: This warning state is triggered by a steep decrease in water level (`isFast(-`Δd`, L1)`), which can potentially lead to destabilization. This is also represented by the colour orange.
- **Alarm (A)**: This critical structural failure state is triggered when inclinometer displacement rate ($\triangle$ I) indicates a potential dangerous movement. Moreover, it can also be activated from the live storage level in the event of extreme seismic activity (`shake()`). This state is similarly identified by a red marker.

Transitions between these states are governed by conditions derived from sensor readings: `isFull(d)`, Triggers a transition from **Live storage** to **Full**, when dam volume threshold is exceeded; $\neg$ `isFull(d)`, Returns to **Live storage** if water level decreases below the threshold; `isFast(-`$\Delta d, L1$`)`, A steep water level change from the live storage state indicates destabilization, moving to **Stability**; `isMoving(`ΔI`)`, High inclinometer displacement rate, while in the **Stability** state causes a transition to **Alarm**; `lim(d)` $\lor$ $isFast(\Delta d, L2)$, Either exceeding a flood limit or a fast increase in water level leads from **Full** to **Flood**; `shake()`, A dashed transition representing an event of extreme vibrations, that can lead

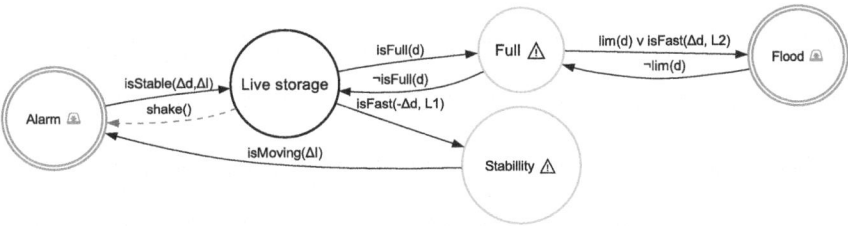

Fig. 1. FSM modelling reservoir safety conditions based on water level and inclinometer displacement rate. The system shifts between states depending on water level rate, volume thresholds, and stability indicators. The colour orange is used to indicate warnings, while red represents critical emergency conditions. (Color figure online)

directly from **Live storage** to **Alarm**. It aims to simulate the implementation of a more complex and costly seismograph, that would be used to detect seismic activity; isStable(Δd, ΔI), This transition allows recovery from **Alarm** to **Live storage**, provided both water and structural stability metrics are within safe bounds.

The state machine developed is deterministic, with transitions defined by customizable thresholds. Its states represent alert and alarm situations that pose significant danger to the structural stability of the dam.

4 System Components, Data Acquisition and FSM Design

The LINCS Dams prototype employs several low-cost components to monitor embankment dams' behaviour over time. In this work, cost-effectiveness refers to the use of consumer-grade sensors and microcontrollers that are readily available and inexpensive. Furthermore, the software infrastructure, which includes Docker, InfluxDB, and Telegraf, is entirely free and open-source. The data collection component set consists of sensors and low-cost, low-energy microcontrollers, namely: **MEMS In-Place Inclinometer node**, one of four nodes that compose the LINCS in-place inclinometer (IPI) prototype [14], measures lateral displacements imposed by changes in water levels inside the reservoir. **TfMini LiDAR Plus**, time-of-flight sensor that measures distance to the surface of the water. This measurement is subsequently used to calculate the water level. **MMA7660FC accelerometer**, triaxial accelerometer used to record vibrations within the dam model. **ESP32 and ESP8266 microcontrollers**, low-cost microcontrollers that connect to the sensors and support data transmission. The IPI system employs three ESP32 boards, while the distance and vibration module makes use of a single ESP8266 microcontroller.

To test the prototype, a reservoir was used and equipped with the system. A complete description of the experimental setup is presented on Sect. 5. To collect sensor data, send instructions to the microcontrollers, and enable real-time data flow, a communication infrastructure is required. This is achieved using Message

Queuing Telemetry Transport (MQTT), a protocol based on a publish-subscribe model, which allows each module to send and receive data asynchronously and efficiently. A Raspberry Pi 5 hosts an instance of the Mosquitto MQTT broker, thereby serving as the system's communications core. To maintain a consistent approach to communication among components, instructions are computed based on that data and published on the broker, updating the system's behaviour.

For data storage, a Docker container stack is deployed on an external server or machine. Containers are managed using a Docker Compose file, and, for this project, the container stack was composed of an InfluxDB instance and Telegraf to fetch and aggregate data published on the broker [14]. Regarding data visualization and analysis, the InfluxDB web interface supports fundamental data visualization methods, and a Grafana container can be included in the stack to build more comprehensive dashboards and to assist during tests, with real-time data visualizations. Finally, Telegraf updates an output file, as new data is published on the broker in a format that can be readily uploaded to Excel, thereby enabling data to be organized in tables for graph creation. Data acquisition is managed by a Python script running on the Raspberry Pi that implements the finite state machine (FSM) using the Transitions library. The script is subscribed to the same topic as Telegraf, receiving readings as they are published and making decisions based on them. This affordable system has limitations, particularly in terms of data precision compared to more advanced systems, however these are mitigated through the use of software-based low-pass filters. For this reason, the system is a viable option on non-critical situations, where high data precision is not required, while maintaining low assembly, operational and maintenance costs. Furthermore, smaller dams with low limited resources and no data collection capabilities can benefit from using such a system, given that more expensive options may not be financially possible.

Current Setup. The system's initial state, live storage, represents the normal operation where the dam's water level is anywhere between the maximum (full reservoir level) and minimum thresholds (minimum pool level). While the situation is structurally stable, data is collected every ten seconds on all sensors and sent to the MQTT broker. Each node in the IPI sends data with a different delay to avoid burdening the broker, so even if only one node is being tested, it will not send data at the same time as the other sensors. Furthermore, the system will not change states even when the dam's current conditions change, so long as the evolution happens gradually, within the state machine's defined parameters.

Three types of event can cause the system to change its behaviour: (i) a high displacement rate in the IPI's profile, (ii) a high rate of water level rise/drop, and (iii) safety thresholds being exceeded. When any of these occur, the state machine increases the data sampling frequency. When the situation stabilizes, data collection moderately decreases over time if the conditions remain secure, eventually returning to the live storage state. Every sensor in the system has a dynamic sampling frequency managed by the state machine, however the system still follows a modular approach by not requiring all sensors to be turned on or actively working for it to work. This allows the system to remain functional, even if one of its components gets damaged or is manually disabled (e.g., for energy-saving purposes).

5   Experiments' Setup and Results

The testing of the LINCS Dams was achieved using a reservoir to simulate the behaviour of the IPI system under dynamic conditions. The experimental apparatus consisted of a single IPI node mounted on a rotating support, influenced by the water level inside a container. As the water level changes, the float mechanism causes the inclinometer to tilt, simulating displacements. The LiDAR sensor, which has been mounted in a position above the reservoir, measures the water level. In addition, the accelerometer measures vibrations. Figure 2 illustrates the experimental setup.

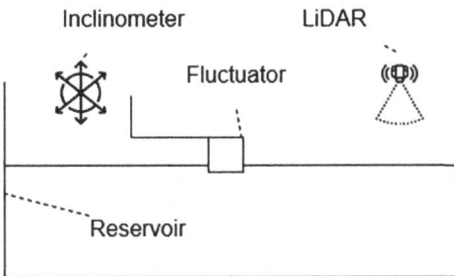

Fig. 2. Experimental Setup Diagram

The test was divided into two scenarios. The first scenario was the filling of the reservoir, which aimed to simulate the effect of water filling a dam. The second scenario was the draining of the reservoir, which accounted for situations where the water level decreases by opening floodgates or the consumption of water by the population. Each test asserts the system's evolution over time, exploring the various states defined in the state machine and leveraging the sensors used in both modules. For these preliminary test runs, only the water level was taken into consideration when setting up the state machine transitions. In addition, the water level in a dam changes the profile of its embankment, justifying the installation of inclinometers.

The two scenarios defined to test the LINCS dams prototype share the same process, differing only in terms of imposing a positive or negative variation in water level. All other tasks required to execute the test are common to both cases and primarily focus on registering before-and-after measurements, namely the initial and final water level, the starting and ending date and time, and the initial and final readings from all sensors.

The activity is recorded and stored in a text file automatically when the script is terminated at the end of a run. The file is formatted to ensure a clear separation of new readings, with each reading accompanied by a timestamp and the identification of the sensor from which it was obtained. Further information includes the previous reading gathered by the same sensor, the system's present state, and the calculations or additional data that were taken into account when determining the state to which the system transitioned. To analyse the data from these tests, the data output from Telegraf was subjected to minor formatting before being uploaded to Excel, where graphs were generated. Additionally, some Python scripts were also developed to create more complex visualizations. Lastly, sensor performance was assessed using criteria such as accuracy and effectiveness. The accuracy was visually validated using a reference scale affixed to the test rig. Monitoring effectiveness was regarded as the system's ability to correctly detect events and adapting its behaviour accordingly. To reduce the influence of using consumer-grade sensors, a low-pass filter was implemented.

To assert the system's correct implementation and to validate that our goals were met, each test scenario was conducted and analysed both during and after each run. To monitor the evolution of the system during each experiment, a Grafana dashboard was built to draw the water level graph in real time. Finally, the data sampling rate was being printed in the terminal by the script as the test went on. Initial trials of the LINCS Dams confirm the system's functionality. The recorded sensor streams exhibit the expected correlations: altering the water level consistently causes gradual inclinometer tilt, extreme conditions cause the system to adapt and the components communicated effectively with each other. The FSM correctly identifies state changes, reacting to considerable environmental differences and maintaining the same behaviour when the situation does not require an increased data sampling rate. As the system was still under development, the dataset was necessarily limited. The ongoing work focuses on extending the monitoring campaign and further assessing energy consumption, with the aim of providing a more comprehensive evaluation in future studies. Table 1 contains LiDAR distance readings used to estimate the water level, both as a continuous value and as a percentage of the total capacity of the LINCS dam. Table 2 outlines how the IPI's sampling frequency evolved over time, reflecting the FSM's response to environmental changes, namely the water level variations. Table 3 contains the angles along the X and Y axes over time. All of these tables are compact representations of the ones created to organize the data collected during testing.

Based on these tables, a series of visualizations were created to assist with data interpretation. These graphs provide a better understanding of system dynamics, depicting key aspects, such as the timing of state transitions and the impact of environmental changes on the sampling frequency. Figures 3 and 4 illustrate the environmental conditions and the system's response to them during a draining and a filling tests. In each pair of graphs, the top plot describes the system's behavioural shifts over time, while the bottom one describes the water level change during a test run.

Table 1. LiDAR Distance and Estimated Water Level at LINCS Dam

Time	Distance	Water Level	
		(cm)	(%)
00:35	15	11	68.7
00:38	15	11	68.7
00:41	14	10	62.5
00:45	14	10	62.5

Table 2. IPI Sampling Frequency Over Time

Time	IPI Frequency (Hz)
00:38	1
00:43	0.2
00:48	0.2
00:53	0.2

Table 3. IPI Inclination Readings per Axis (angle X, angle Y) Over Time

Time	aX	aY
00:36	5.88	−16.90
00:37	5.85	−16.99
00:38	5.93	−17.13
00:43	5.90	−17.23

The draining test (Fig. 3) shows that the LiDAR sensor was able to keep track of the water level steadily and with no misread values. In terms of sampling frequency, the system reacted accordingly, reducing the data collection rate as the water level lowered from a near-flood situation, to a slightly less critical state, and finally returning to the base reading frequency as the water level reaches the top-end of the live storage level. Each sampling rate reduction implies that the system's state changed, therefore the adaptive behaviour is working as expected.

The filling test (Fig. 4) exhibits an overall correct dynamic behaviour in the system. Close to the forty second mark the LiDAR sensor made a wrong measurement, however there was a steady water level rise until the final part of the experiment. These incorrect measurements occur again toward the end of the run, when the water level was kept at the sixteen centimetre mark, yet the sensor had some issues keeping a correct measurement over time. This can be explained due to the sensor's proximity to the water at this point during the test, which exceeded the minimum recommended distance to an object by the sensor's manufacturer. Nonetheless, this run illustrates once more that the system is capable of automatically adapting to changing environmental conditions, autonomously transitioning states and increasing the sampling rate as the water level exceeds the defined thresholds.

Figure 5 illustrates a representative run where a series of steps were defined and executed to simulate the behaviour of a real dam's water level over the years. The process involved translating real water level measurements to the their equivalent in the scale model. Once this planning was finished, the reservoir was manipulated to follow a similar rise and decrease dynamics. The reference dam used as an example follows a seasonal pattern, repeated over the years, where the

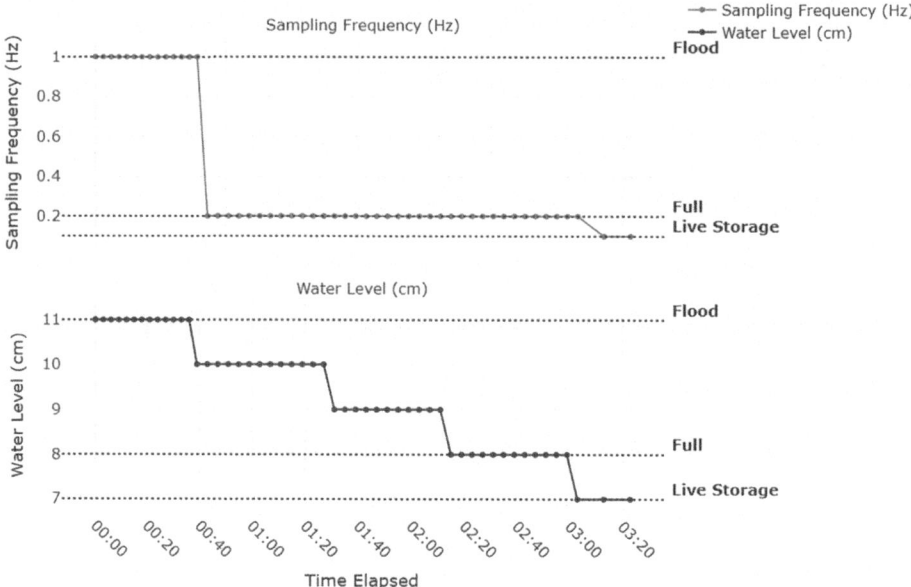

Fig. 3. Dam Draining Test

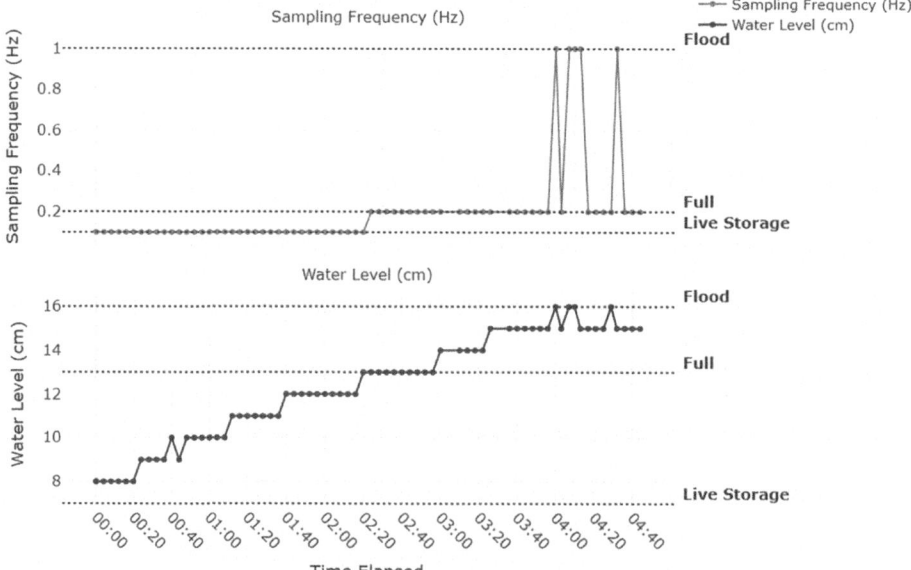

Fig. 4. Dam Filling Test

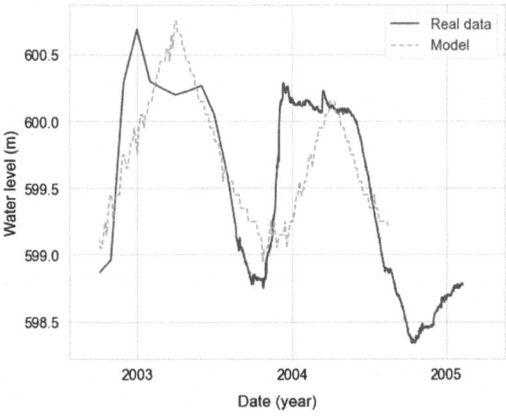

Fig. 5. Model results adjusted to the real data

water level rises during the Winter months and decreases throughout the Summer. The experimental setup was able to successfully resemble the fluctuations of a real dam. The two simulated peaks show a fairly accurate fluctuation. The FSM adjusted the sampling frequency and state transitions correctly based on the water level variations, demonstrating that the prototype can properly adapt to environmental inputs and mirror the temporal patterns of an actual dam. The delay between data acquisition and the system's response has no impact on flood detection, as real world applications' operate on a time scale of days.

Energy consumption was measured on two representative test runs using the KCX-017 USB power meter. The energy test aimed to assert two aspects about the system, the base energy consumption of a microcontroller and the energy-efficient implementation that was not used during the previous tests due to the short time window between readings. The test consisted of gathering data every thirty seconds for ten minutes. The active waiting version consumed 0.037 mAh at 4.97 V (1.8×10^{-4} Wh), while the sleep-based implementation used only 0.017 mAh at 5.09 V (8.7×10^{-5} Wh), saving roughly 50% in energy consumption. These early results validate the system's capacity to consistently observe environmental changes, modify its behaviour through state transitions, and provide accurate sensor communication. This study focused on implementing and validating the LINCS system with regard to sensor integration, data acquisition, and alert thresholds. The experimental setup was used to test the functionality of the system rather than to replicate dam-scale mechanics. Although scale effects were acknowledged, full-scale deployment was planned to address these aspects under real conditions. Overall, the LINCS Dams prototype displays good indicators for scalable and independent dam monitoring in real-world scenarios.

6   Conclusions

This work presented the LINCS Dams, a cost-effective, modular prototype designed to simulate and monitor the behaviour of embankment dams using affordable sensors and a finite state machine (FSM) implemented in Python. Historical cases drove the FSM's design, detecting critical conditions while allowing the environmental variables to evolve naturally without triggering unnecessary alarms. Our simple and efficient implementation addresses shortcomings found in past situations where real-time monitoring systems were missing. Additionally, threshold parameters can be changed to enforce stricter or more permissive alarm criteria, depending on the dam's context.

The system successfully demonstrated the ability to autonomously adapt to environmental changes, such as water level fluctuations, by adjusting the data sampling frequency based on safety thresholds and event triggers. An experimental apparatus was built to test the system's capabilities, enabling the simulation of real dam water level changes. The prototype was tested in different scenarios, through a series of controlled experiments, and confirmed its adaptive response and reliability of component communications. By focusing on data acquisition, modular system design, and dynamic behaviour control rather than on full-scale AI models, the LINCS Dams establishes a solid foundation for future research in intelligent dam monitoring. Although this study focused on other sensors, integrating precipitation monitoring is relevant and will be considered when developing the system further, alongside other external parameters of interest. In future developments, the LINCS Dams monitoring prototype can evolve to an affordable and easy-to-deploy embankment dam monitoring system. Ultimately, the LINCS Dams system aims to support real-world deployments in smaller-scale embankment dams, where cost and accessibility have traditionally limited the implementation of continuous safety monitoring systems.

Acknowledgments. This work was supported by UID/04516/NOVA Laboratory for Computer Science and Informatics (NOVA LINCS), with financial support from FCT.IP.

Competing Interests. The authors have no competing interests to declare that are relevant to the content of this article.

References

1. Bennett, V., Abdoun, T., Barendse, M.: Evaluation of soft clay field consolidation using mems-based in-place inclinometer-accelerometer array. Geotech. Test. J. **38**(3), 1–11 (2015). https://doi.org/10.1520/GTJ20140048
2. Bennett, V., Abdoun, T., O'Meara, K., Barendse, M., Zimmie, T.: Wireless MEMS-based in-place inclinometer-accelerometer array for real-time geotechnical instrumentation. In: Wasowski, J., Giordan, D., Lollino, P. (eds.) GeoMEast 2017. SCI, pp. 90–100. Springer, Cham (2018). https://doi.org/10.1007/978-3-319-61648-3_6

3. Bermudez-Edo, M., Elsaleh, T., Barnaghi, P., Taylor, K.: A finite-state-machine model driven service composition architecture for internet of things rapid prototyping. Futur. Gener. Comput. Syst. **91**, 252–262 (2019)
4. Brian, M.B., Machan, G.: In-place microelectromechanical system inclinometer strings: evaluation of an evolving technology. Geo-Strata **13**(6), 26–29 (2009)
5. Cina, A., Maria, A.M., Horea, I.B.: Improving GNSS landslide monitoring with the use of low-cost mems accelerometers. Appl. Sci. **9**(23), 5075 (2019). https://doi.org/10.3390/app9235075
6. Dargie, W.: Dynamic power management in wireless sensor networks: state-of-the-art. IEEE Sens. J. **12**(5), 1518–1527 (2012)
7. Fluixá-Sanmartín, J., Altarejos-García, L., Morales-Torres, A., Escuder-Bueno, I.: Review article: climate change impacts on dam safety. Nat. Hazard. **18**, 2471–2488 (2018). https://doi.org/10.5194/nhess-18-2471-2018
8. Guidicini, G., Sandroni, S.S., de Mello, F.M.: Lições aprendidas com acidentes e incidentes em barragens e obras anexas no Brasil. Agência Nacional de Águas e Saneamento Básico - ANA (2021)
9. Hariri-Ardebili, M.A., Mahdavi, G., Nuss, L.K., Lall, U.: The role of artificial intelligence and digital technologies in dam engineering: narrative review and outlook. Eng. Appl. Artif. Intell. **126**, 106813 (2023). https://doi.org/10.1016/j.engappai.2023.106813
10. Marcelino, J., Manso, J., Leite, D., Marques, N., Freire, O.: Structural health monitoring and inspection of dams based on Unmanned Aerial Vehicles photogrammetry with image 3D reconstruction, pp. 1807–1810. CRC Press (2024). https://doi.org/10.1201/9781003431749-337
11. Marcelino, J.: Observação da barragem do Lapão. Sua importância na detecção do acidente de Janeiro de 2003. In: II Congresso Luso-Brasileiro de geotecnia. No. January, Aveiro (2004)
12. Marcelino, J.: Projecto, construção e exploração de pequenas barragens de aterro: aspectos geotécnicos. LNEC, Lisboa, Portugal (2008)
13. Palma, J., Marques, N., Santos, R.: Bi-enabled web visualization of in-place inclinometer data for geotechnical applications. Progress in artificial intelligence. In: EPIA 2024. LNCS, vol. 14423, pp. 176–187 (2024). https://doi.org/10.1007/978-3-031-73503-5_15
14. dos Santos, R.C., Marcelino, J.: Development and laboratory testing of a low-cost wireless in-place inclinometer prototype. In: Geotechnical Engineering Challenges to Meet Current and Emerging Needs of Society, pp. 2212–2217. CRC Press (2024)
15. Silva, A., Galhardas, H., Barateiro, J., Portela, E.A.: O sistema de informação gestbarragens (2005). http://repositorio.lnec.pt:8080/jspui/handle/123456789/14087. Accessed 28 May 2025
16. Efthimis, L., Vasiliki, A., Ioannis, L.: Reduction of rockfall risk of the Teleferik Area of Santorini, Greece. In: Lollino, G., et al. (eds.) Engineering Geology for Society and Territory - Volume 2, pp. 183–188. Springer, Cham (2015). https://doi.org/10.1007/978-3-319-09057-3_23
17. Yoo, C., Park, J., Park, J.H., Lee, S.W.: AIoT monitoring technology for optimal fill dam installation and operation. Appl. Sci. **14**(3), 1024 (2024). https://doi.org/10.3390/app14031024
18. Zheng, G., Yuan, B., Lv, F., Shen, Q., Tang, Z., Zheng, S.: Comprehensive calibration and laboratory validation of a micro electromechanical system sensor-based flexible inclinometer. Meas. Sci. Technol. **35**(1), 015101 (2024). https://doi.org/10.1088/1361-6501/acf0f5

Knowledge Discovery and Business Intelligence (KDBI)

Online Data Augmentation for Forecasting with Deep Learning

Vitor Cerqueira[1,2]([✉]), Moisés Santos[1,2], Luis Roque[1,2], Yassine Baghoussi[3], and Carlos Soares[1,2,4]

[1] Faculdade de Engenharia da Universidade do Porto, Porto, Portugal
`vitorc.research@gmail.com`
[2] Laboratory for Artificial Intelligence and Computer Science (LIACC), Porto, Portugal
[3] INESC TEC, Porto, Portugal
[4] Fraunhofer Portugal AICOS, Porto, Portugal

Abstract. Deep learning approaches are increasingly used to tackle forecasting tasks but require substantial training data. When samples are limited, synthetic data generation techniques can effectively augment datasets to improve model performance. Data augmentation is typically applied offline before training a model. However, when training with mini-batches, some batches may contain a disproportionate number of synthetic samples that do not align well with the original data characteristics. This work introduces an online data augmentation framework that generates synthetic samples during the training of neural networks. By creating synthetic samples for each batch alongside their original counterparts, we maintain a balanced representation between real and synthetic data throughout the training process. This approach fits naturally with the iterative nature of neural network training and eliminates the need to store large augmented datasets. We validated the proposed framework using 3797 time series from 6 benchmark datasets, three neural architectures, and seven synthetic data generation techniques. The experiments suggest that online data augmentation leads to better forecasting performance compared to offline data augmentation or no augmentation approaches. The framework and experiments are publicly available.

1 Introduction

Time series forecasting is a relevant problem with vast real-world applications. Increasingly, deep neural networks are emerging as effective alternatives to well-established approaches such as ARIMA or exponential smoothing [11]. Neural architectures such as NHITS [6] or N-BEATS [17], have recently exhibited state-of-the-art forecasting performance in benchmark datasets and competitions.

While deep neural networks excel at forecasting, they require substantial data for effective generalization [3], which is not always available. Time series datasets often suffer from data scarcity, presenting two common limitations: either containing too few time series or including series with insufficient observations. To address these data limitations, synthetic time series generation techniques

J. Valente de Oliveira et al. (Eds.): EPIA 2025, LNAI 16121, pp. 217–229, 2026.
https://doi.org/10.1007/978-3-032-05176-9_17

can be employed to augment sample size. Researchers have developed various approaches for this purpose, ranging from simple methods like jittering to more sophisticated techniques including averaging multiple time series [7] or leveraging advanced generative models [23].

This work addresses univariate time series forecasting problems with datasets containing multiple time series. In these problems, data augmentation processes have been shown to improve forecasting performance of recurrent-based neural networks [3]. In forecasting problems, data augmentation is typically conducted offline before training a model (e.g. [3]). A synthetic dataset is created and combined with the original data, leading to an augmented training set. This augmented dataset is larger and more diverse, thereby improving the performance of models. However, offline data augmentation has limitations. When training with mini-batches, some batches may contain a disproportionate number of synthetic samples that do not align well with the original data characteristics, potentially misleading the learning process.

To address these limitations, we propose an online data augmentation framework that generates synthetic samples during training. This approach fits naturally with the iterative nature of neural network training, where parameters are updated using mini-batches of data. By creating synthetic samples for each batch alongside their original counterparts, we maintain a balanced representation between real and synthetic data throughout the training process. This balanced representation helps prevent the model from overfitting spurious patterns created during the augmentation process, thereby improving forecasting accuracy. The framework is agnostic to both the augmentation method and neural network architecture, making it widely applicable.

While online data augmentation has been explored in speech recognition and computer vision problems [10, 18], time series forecasting presents unique challenges due to its temporal nature and the need to preserve complex patterns such as trends and seasonality. Our work is, to our knowledge, the first application of online data augmentation in this context, showing its effectiveness for forecasting tasks.

We validate the proposed method using 3797 time series from 6 benchmark datasets. The results of the experiments suggest that online data augmentation leads to better forecasting performance relative to several offline data augmentation variants or training models without augmentation. All methods are implemented using the neuralforecast Python library. The experiments are fully reproducible[1] and the framework is available in a Python package[2].

2   Background

2.1   Univariate Time Series Forecasting

A univariate time series is a time-ordered sequence of values $Y = \{y_1, y_2, \ldots, y_t\}$, where $y_i \in \mathbb{R}$ is the value of Y observed at time i and t is the length of

---

[1] https://github.com/vcerqueira/experiments-online_augmentation.
[2] https://github.com/vcerqueira/metaforecast.

Y. Forecasting is the process of predicting the value of upcoming observations $y_{t+1}, \ldots, y_{t+h}$, where h denotes the forecasting horizon. The importance of forecasting spans several domains, including applications in business areas such as inventory management or operations planning.

Machine learning methods tackle forecasting problems using an autoregressive type of modeling. Each observation of a time series is modeled as a function of its past q lags based on time delay embedding [5]. Time delay embedding transforms a time series from a sequence of values into an Euclidean space. In practice, the idea is to apply sliding windows to build a dataset $\mathcal{D} = \{X,y\}_{q+1}^{t}$ where y_i represents the i-th observation and $X_i \in \mathbb{R}^q$ is the i-th corresponding set of q lags: $X_i = \{y_{i-1}, y_{i-2}, \ldots, y_{i-q}\}$. Accordingly, the objective is to train a regression model to learn the dependency $y_i = f(X_i)$.

Forecasting problems often involve datasets with multiple univariate time series. We define a collection of n time series as $\mathcal{Y} = \{Y_1, Y_2, \ldots, Y_n\}$. In these cases, the time delay embedding framework described above is applied to each time series in the collection. In effect, for a collection $\mathcal{Y}$ the dataset $\mathcal{D}$ is composed of a concatenation of the individual datasets: $\mathcal{D} = \{\mathcal{D}_1, \ldots, \mathcal{D}_n\}$, where $\mathcal{D}_j$ is the dataset corresponding to the time series Y_j.

2.2   Forecasting with Deep Learning

In most cases, global forecasting models are trained using deep neural networks. Various types of neural architectures have been recently developed for time series forecasting. Architectures based on recurrent neural networks, such as the LSTM [21], are more common due to their intrinsic capabilities for sequence modeling. However, deep neural networks based on convolutional layers [13], transformers [24], or multi-layer perceptrons (MLPs) [6] have also shown competitive forecasting accuracy.

The MLP is one of the simplest neural network architectures, which is composed of stacks of fully connected layers. Neural networks based on MLPs have been used to tackle forecasting problems for several years [9]. Recently, two particular architectures have shown promising forecasting accuracy and exceptional computational efficiency: N-BEATS [17] and NHITS [6]. Both are based on stacks that contain blocks of MLPs along with residual connections. NHITS [6], short for Neural Hierarchical Interpolation for Time Series Forecasting, extends N-BEATS [17] by including multi-rate input sampling that models data with different scales and hierarchical interpolation for better long-horizon forecasting. NHITS has shown state-of-the-art forecasting performance relative to other deep learning forecasting methods, including several transformers, and recurrent-based neural networks [6]. Challu et al. [6] also provide evidence that NHITS is more computationally efficient than transformer-based methods by a factor of 50.

Kolmogorov-Arnold Network (KAN) [14] have been recently developed as an alternative to MLPs by featuring learnable activation functions on the weights of neural networks. KANs are inspired by the Kolmogorov-Arnold Representation theorem, providing theoretical guarantees regarding function approximation. Concerning time series forecasting, recent works (e.g. [8]) have compared KANs with different neural networks, including transformers, MLPs, or convolutional-based neural networks.

2.3   Time Series Data Augmentation

Flipping or jittering the value of observations are among the simplest approaches to create a synthetic time series from an original one [20]. Jittering involves adding random noise to each data point in the original time series with the goal of making forecasting models robust to such noise. The noise can be defined as $\varepsilon \sim \mathcal{N}(0, \sigma'^2)$, where σ' is the standard deviation of the input time series scaled by some value s ($\sigma' = \sigma \times s$).

Scaling [23] is another time series transformation technique that creates synthetic samples by multiplying each observation by a random factor drawn from a normal distribution centered at 1.0, specifically $\mathcal{N}(1, \sigma^2)$. Scaling affects the magnitude of the time series – a factor below 1 decreases amplitude while a factor above 1 increases it.

Time warping [19] is a technique that distorts the time variable of time series to create synthetic samples. The method works by scaling knot points along the time axis using random factors sampled from a $\mathcal{N}(1, \sigma^2)$, thus creating a smooth warping function using cubic splines. Then, the time series is resampled based on these distortions. Magnitude warping [12] is similar to time warping but applied directly to the values of the time series. The idea is to apply distortions based on a cubic spline to the values of time series. Magnitude warping is also related to scaling. The main difference is that scaling produces local changes that can vary abruptly between consecutive observations, while the changes produced by magnitude warping are smooth due to the spline interpolation.

Jittering, scaling, time warping, and magnitude warping are data generation methods based on applying transformation to the original samples. There are several techniques that aim to mix the patterns of one or more time series to generate new ones. One of these techniques is moving blocks bootstrapping (MBB) coupled with seasonal decomposition. Following Bergmeir et al. [4], the idea is to extract the remainder component of a given log-transformed univariate time series, and resample it using MBB. The resampled remainder is then combined back with the other components, leading to a bootstrapped version of the original series.

DBA [7], short for DTW (dynamic time warping) Barycentric Averaging, is another technique based on pattern mixing that involves averaging multiple time series to create a synthetic one. DBA works by first selecting a subset of time series from a given dataset. Then, these are combined using a weighted averaged based on DTW where the weights are sampled from a Dirichlet distribution.

TSMixup [1] is another time series synthetic generation method that combines the patterns of multiple time series. The method randomly samples a subset of time series of a specified length, and then combines them using weights drawn from a Dirichlet distribution.

3   Methodology

This section describes the methodology for training a univariate time series forecasting model based on artificial neural networks using online data augmentation. We start by describing the data and main preprocessing steps (Sect. 3.1), and then detail the online data augmentation framework (Sect. 3.2).

3.1   Pre-processing Steps

We address univariate time series multi-step forecasting problems using artificial neural networks, focusing on datasets that contain multiple time series. This type of dataset may be composed of individual time series with distinct scales or variances. We pre-process each time series using standardization to stabilize the variance of the dataset and bring the data into a common scale. For forecasting, we first obtain predictions in the standardized scale and then reverse the transformation by multiplying by Y_σ and adding Y_μ.

Having standardized the individual time series, we apply the auto-regressive framework described in Sect. 2.1 to build a global forecasting models using a neural network. Given the training set that contains a collection of time series $\mathcal{Y}$, we first standardize each time series independently. Then, we apply time delay embedding using a window of size q to transform each standardized series into a dataset ready for supervised learning. At each timestep, the following h (forecasting horizon) observations are modeled based on the recent past q values. The resulting samples are concatenated to form a single training set $\mathcal{D}$, which is used to train a neural network. The training procedure follows a multi-input multi-out strategy for multi-step forecasting [22], since neural networks can naturally model multiple output variables.

3.2   Online Data Augmentation

Neural networks are inherently online, with their parameters being updated iteratively based on mini-batches of data. The proposed training framework leverages this property by conducting data augmentation online.

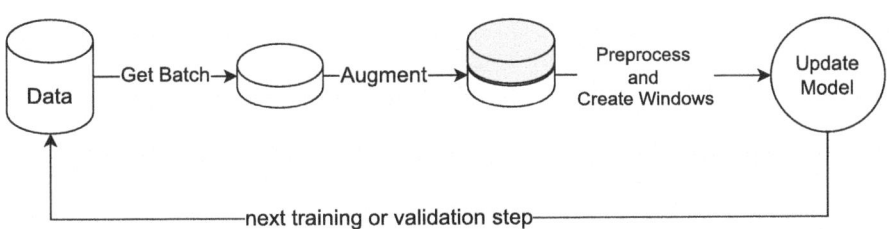

Fig. 1. High-level workflow of the training process of a neural network using the proposed framework for online data augmentation.

Figure 1 shows a high-level diagram that details the workflow in a given training step of a neural network for univariate time series forecasting. First, we get a batch of time series, following the standard mini-batch approach for training neural networks. We augment this batch using some time series synthetic data generation technique. The framework is agnostic to the underlying generation technique, and we test several ones in the experiments. In general, the generation method should be both 1) non-deterministic, so different variations are created at each run on the same time series; and 2) computationally efficient, so it is feasible to apply the method at each training or validation step of a neural network. On top of these, our framework also assumes that the underlying temporal patterns of the original time series are preserved. In other words, the synthetic time series should maintain the essential characteristics of the data while providing useful alternative representations for learning.

For each time series in a given batch, we create a single synthetic variation of it, doubling the number of time series in the batch. We hypothesize that a one-to-one ratio provides a balanced representation between original and synthetic samples. This helps the model learn from real data while benefiting from the additional patterns and variations introduced by data augmentation. Moreover, not creating too many synthetic time series may prevent the model from overfitting to artificial patterns.

After augmentation, data pre-processing is conducted based on the techniques described on the previous section (Sect. 3.1). The processed data is then used to update the model parameters. Note that both original and augmented data are used to compute the loss and update neural network parameters. After this, the synthetic data created for this batch is discarded, and the process is repeated until the training process finishes.

4   Experiments

This section presents the experiments conducted to analyse the performance of online data augmentation. The central research question posed in these experiments is the following: how does online data augmentation perform relative to other training approaches for univariate time series forecasting based on deep learning? This question is addressed based on forecasting accuracy computed from various perspectives.

4.1   Data

We use 6 datasets from four databases and forecasting competitions: M1 [15], M3 [16], and Tourism [2]. M1, and M3 are time series databases that come from the Makridakis competitions. These datasets cover different application domains, including industry, or economics. Tourism is a database focused on the tourism domain. These datasets are summarised in Table 1.

We focus on databases with low-frequency time series, namely monthly and quarterly time series. These are the ones that tend to comprise a lower number

Table 1. Summary of the datasets: average value, number of time series, number of observations, seasonal period, and forecasting horizon.

Dataset	Average value	# time series	# observations	Period	h
M1 Monthly	72.7	617	44892	12	12
M1 Quarterly	40.9	203	8320	4	8
M3 Monthly	117.3	1428	167562	12	12
M3 Quarterly	48.9	756	37004	4	8
Tourism Monthly	298.5	366	109280	12	12
Tourism Quarterly	99.6	427	42544	4	8
Total	-	3797	409602	-	-

of observations, thus where data augmentation can be more useful. Overall, the combined datasets contain 409602 observations across 3797 univariate time series. In terms of forecasting horizon, we set this value to 12 and 8, for monthly and quarterly time series, respectively. The input size (number of lags) is set to 24 for monthly time series and 8 for quarterly ones. These values correspond to two seasonal periods, which provide a robust setup.

4.2 Evaluation

For performance estimation, we leave the last h observations of each time series for testing. The remaining available observations are used for training and validating the model. The validation set is composed of the final h observations of each time series, similarly to the test split. We use the Mean Absolute Scaled Error (MASE) as evaluation metric, which is defined as follows:

$$\text{MASE} = \frac{\frac{1}{n}\sum_{i=1}^{n}|y_i - \hat{y}_i|}{\frac{1}{n-m}\sum_{i=m+1}^{n}|y_i - y_{t-m}|} \tag{1}$$

where $\hat{y}_i$, and y_i are the forecast and actual value for the i-th instance, respectively. MASE is a scale-independent measure of forecast accuracy. The mean absolute error of a given model, computed across n data points, is scaled by the mean absolute error of a seasonal naive forecast with period m.

4.3 Methods

This section describes the methods used in the experiments. First, we present the synthetic time series generation methods used for data augmentation. Then, we described the different approaches used to augment time series datasets based on those time series generation methods. Finally, we also detail the neural networks used to train forecasting models.

Synthetic Time Series Generation Methods. We evaluate the proposed approach using 7 different time series data generation approaches, specifically Seasonal MBB (MBB), Jittering, Scaling, Time Warping (T-Warp), Magnitude Warping (M-Warp), TSMixup, and DBA. These are described in Sect. 2.3. Table 2 shows the parameters of each of these approaches. The parameter values in bold are used by default. In some cases, which will be described in the next section (Sect. 4.3), other configurations are sampled from the list.

Table 2. Parameters of the time series synthetic generation methods.

Method	Parameter	Values
MBB	log	{**True**, False}
Jittering	s	{**0.03**, 0.05, 0.1, 0.15, 0.2, 0.3}
Scaling	σ scaling factor in $\mathcal{N}(1, \sigma^2)$	{0.03, 0.05, **0.1**, 0.15, 0.2, 0.3}
M-Warp	σ scaling factor in $\mathcal{N}(1, \sigma^2)$	{0.05, **0.1**, 0.15}
	# knots	{3, **4**, 5}
T-Warp	σ scaling factor in $\mathcal{N}(1, \sigma^2)$	{0.05, **0.1**, 0.15}
	# knots	{3, **4**, 5}
DBA	Max # time series	{5, 7, **10**, 15}
	Dirichlet concentration	{ **1.0**, 1.5, 2.0}
TSMixup	Max # time series	{5, 7, **10**, 15}
	Dirichlet concentration	{**1.0**, 1.5, 2.0}

Augmentation Approaches. Each of the methods described in the previous section are used for augmenting the training dataset that is used to build a forecasting model. We use the following 6 data augmentation strategies:

- Online: The proposed online data augmentation scheme (c.f. Fig. 1), in which each batch of time series in a given training step is augmented. We use a batch size (for the original set of time series) of 32 and create a synthetic time series for each one of these. This means that, for training, the batch size is 64 where half of them are synthetic. The parameters of the respective synthetic data generation method are fixed based on Table 2.
- Online(E): A variant of Online where the parameters of the synthetic data generation method are randomly sampled in each batch. The possible configurations are described in Table 2;
- Offline(1): An approach that does data augmentation before the fitting process, following Bandara et al. [3]. First, 1 synthetic time series is created for each one available in the original training dataset. Then, a model is trained using the augmented data. The batch size in this case is set to 64 to match the value used in the Online variants;
- Offline(10): A variant of Offline(1), but creating 10 synthetic time series for each one available on the training set, following the heuristic described by Bandara et al. [3];

- `Offline(=)`: Another variant of `Offline(1)`, but creating a number of synthetic time series to match the synthetic sample size created by the `Online` approach. When applying the `Online` data augmentation strategy following the parameters described before, we create a total of 32000 time series (32 batch size times 1000 training steps). To compute the number of synthetic time series required to match the sample size of `Online`, we divide this value (32000) by the number of time series in the dataset.
- `Offline(=, E)`: A variant of `Offline(=)`, but varying the parameters of the time series synthetic data generation method. Specifically, each time a new time series is created, we randomly sample the generation method parameters based on the configuration pool described in Table 2.

Besides these, we also include an `Original` training procedure that does not involve data augmentation.

Neural Network Architectures and Baseline. The time series augmentation approaches described above are tested with three different neural networks: NHITS [6], MLP [9], and KAN [8]. These are briefly described in Sect. 2.2. These particular neural networks have shown competitive forecasting accuracy relative to other deep learning approaches, including several transformers or recurrent-based neural networks [6]. On top of their competitive forecasting accuracy, these methods are also more computational efficient than other popular architectures [6] (c.f. Sect. 2.2). In terms of training protocol, we build one global forecasting model for each dataset listed in Table 1. Besides these neural networks, we also include the seasonal naive method (`Naive`) in the experiments. The baseline technique that uses the last known observation of the same season as the forecast.

We fix the configuration of the architectures for all training procedures to the default values. Following Challu et al. [6], each NHITS model is composed of 3 stacks, each of which with one block of MLPs. Each MLP contains 2 hidden layers, each with 512 units. The activation function is set to the rectified linear unit (ReLU). The initial learning rate is 0.001, which is updated 3 times during training. For the MLP, we use 2 hidden layers, each with 1024 units. The activation function is ReLU and the learning rate is set to 0.001. KAN is trained with a single hidden layers composed of 512 units. The order of the splines is 3. In all three cases, the training process run for a maximum of 1000 steps using the ADAM optimizer. For preprocessing, in all cases the time series are standardized.

4.4 Results

This section presents the results of the experiments. Table 3 shows the average MASE of each data augmentation approach (columns) when applied with different neural networks and time series generation methods (rows), across the 6 datasets listed in Table 1. The bold and underlined result represents the best and second-best score in the respective (neural network, generation method) pair.

Table 3. Average forecasting accuracy (MASE) of each data augmentation approach (columns) when applied with different neural networks and time series generation methods (rows), computed across all 6 datasets. The bold and underlined result represents the best and second-best score in the respective (neural network, synthetic data generation method) pair. To facilitate visual comparison, we repeat the results of `Original` and `Naive` in each row, though no data augmentation is conducted in those cases.

	Online	Online(E)	Offline(1)	Offline(10)	Offline(=)	Offline(=,E)	Original	Naive
KAN								
DBA	**1.0886**	_1.0904_	1.0938	1.0932	1.0977	1.7433	1.1312	1.3427
Jittering	_1.0947_	**1.0739**	1.1179	1.111	1.1065	1.674	1.1312	1.3427
M-Warp	_1.0945_	**1.0922**	1.108	1.1251	1.1258	1.6714	1.1312	1.3427
Scaling	_1.0804_	**1.0778**	1.1	1.1039	1.1304	1.6913	1.1312	1.3427
MBB	_1.0912_	**1.0837**	1.1055	1.1044	1.1097	1.6935	1.1312	1.3427
TSMixup	**1.088**	_1.0926_	1.1239	1.1466	1.1213	1.6829	1.1312	1.3427
T-Warp	**1.1105**	_1.111_	1.1294	1.2637	1.4995	1.736	1.1312	1.3427
MLP								
DBA	_1.0809_	1.0943	**1.0779**	1.3559	1.1	1.8258	1.0997	1.3427
Jittering	**1.0662**	1.0868	_1.0772_	1.0828	1.0928	1.646	1.0997	1.3427
M-Warp	1.0823	_1.0821_	**1.0802**	1.1153	1.1098	1.5976	1.0997	1.3427
Scaling	**1.0571**	1.064	_1.0613_	1.0768	1.1038	1.6913	1.0997	1.3427
MBB	**1.072**	_1.0796_	1.08	1.0943	1.106	1.6498	1.0997	1.3427
TSMixup	_1.071_	**1.0695**	1.0773	1.1189	1.1072	1.6795	1.0997	1.3427
T-Warp	**1.089**	_1.0962_	1.1031	1.2178	1.5132	1.7219	1.0997	1.3427
NHITS								
DBA	**1.0816**	1.1048	_1.0829_	1.0998	1.0919	1.7756	1.1171	1.3427
Jittering	1.0997	**1.0773**	1.1001	1.0964	_1.0927_	1.6883	1.1171	1.3427
M-Warp	1.0889	**1.0856**	_1.0869_	1.118	1.1233	1.6387	1.1171	1.3427
Scaling	_1.0601_	**1.0566**	1.067	1.098	1.1168	1.6839	1.1171	1.3427
MBB	1.0889	_1.0883_	**1.0773**	1.0907	1.1301	1.682	1.1171	1.3427
TSMixup	_1.0827_	**1.0817**	1.0968	1.1131	1.1116	1.6577	1.1171	1.3427
T-Warp	**1.0852**	1.1006	_1.0863_	1.2205	1.5009	1.765	1.1171	1.3427
Average	**1.0835**	_1.0852_	1.0921	1.1355	1.1662	1.695	1.116	1.3427
Avg. Rank	**2.67**	_2.79_	2.97	4.3	4.4	7.5	4.02	7.34

The results suggest that online augmentation using `Online` or `Online(E)` show the best and second-best average MASE and average rank, respectively. The average rank denotes the average relative position of each method (1 being the best) across the 126 variants of dataset, neural network architecture, and time series synthetic generation method.

The benefits of online data augmentation are consistent across the 3 learning algorithms, and 7 time series data generation methods tested. Notwithstanding, `Offline(1)` is more competitive when using `MLP`. When the forecasting models are trained using `KAN`, online augmentation approaches always outperform offline ones across all time series synthetic data generation methods.

Among the offline approaches, `Offline(1)` shows the best performance. This suggests that creating one time series for each one in the dataset leads to better forecast accuracy relative to creating 10, as done by Bandara et al. [3] or matching the number of time series created by `Online` and `Online(E)`.

Varying the parameters of the time series synthetic data generation methods leads to a comparable forecasting accuracy when using online data augmentation. However, this process severely reduces performance in offline approaches (`Offline(=,E)`). Except for `Offline(=,E)`, all approaches outperform `Naive`. This outcome validates the forecast accuracy of the trained neural networks against a standard baseline.

5   Discussion and Final Remarks

The main contribution of this work is a method for applying online data augmentation during the training process of neural networks for univariate time series forecasting. Our extensive empirical analysis provides evidence about the effectiveness of online data augmentation across different datasets, neural network architectures, and synthetic data generation methods.

First, the systematic superiority of online augmentation across different architectures and datasets suggests that the dynamic nature of synthetic sample generation provides an advantage over offline (before training) augmentation. This may be because online augmentation effectively increases the diversity of training samples while maintaining their relevance to the original data distribution since synthetic samples are coupled with real ones at each batch.

The architecture-specific variations in improvement indicate that the benefits of online augmentation may be influenced by model capacity and learning dynamics. This interaction between augmentation strategy and model architecture opens up interesting possibilities for joint optimization of both components. In future work, we will study how to improve the data augmentation process during training. For example, introduce a mechanism that weights time series based on their impact on the training process, akin to boosting. Future work could also explore expanding this approach to multivariate time series and investigating more sophisticated mechanisms for adapting the augmentation process based on model learning dynamics.

Acknowledgements. This work was partially funded by projects AISym4Med (101095387) supported by Horizon Europe Cluster 1: Health, ConnectedHealth (n.o 46858), supported by Competitiveness and Internationalisation Operational Programme (POCI) and Lisbon Regional Operational Programme (LISBOA 2020), under the PORTUGAL 2020 Partnership Agreement, through the European Regional Development Fund (ERDF) and Agenda "Center for Responsible AI", nr. C645008882-

00000055, investment project nr. 62, financed by the Recovery and Resilience Plan (PRR) and by European Union - NextGeneration EU, and also by FCT plurianual funding for 2020-2023 of LIACC (UIDB/00027/2020 UIDP/00027/2020). The computational resources used in this study were made available by the Portuguese National Distributed Computing Infrastructure (INCD) through the FCT Advanced Computing Projects 2024.12160.CPCA.A0.

Declaration. The authors have no competing interests to declare that are relevant to the content of this article.

References

1. Ansari, A.F., et al.: Chronos: learning the language of time series. arXiv preprint arXiv:2403.07815 (2024)
2. Athanasopoulos, G., Hyndman, R.J., Song, H., Wu, D.C.: The tourism forecasting competition. Int. J. Forecast. **27**(3), 822–844 (2011)
3. Bandara, K., Hewamalage, H., Liu, Y.H., Kang, Y., Bergmeir, C.: Improving the accuracy of global forecasting models using time series data augmentation. Pattern Recogn. **120**, 108148 (2021)
4. Bergmeir, C., Hyndman, R.J., Benítez, J.M.: Bagging exponential smoothing methods using STL decomposition and box-cox transformation. Int. J. Forecast. **32**(2), 303–312 (2016)
5. Bontempi, G., Ben Taieb, S., Le Borgne, Y.A.: Machine learning strategies for time series forecasting. Business Intelligence: Second European Summer School, eBISS 2012, Brussels, Belgium, 15–21 July 2012, Tutorial Lectures 2, pp. 62–77 (2013)
6. Challu, C., Olivares, K.G., Oreshkin, B.N., Ramirez, F.G., Canseco, M.M., Dubrawski, A.: Nhits: neural hierarchical interpolation for time series forecasting. In: Proceedings of the AAAI Conference on Artificial Intelligence, vol. 37, pp. 6989–6997 (2023)
7. Forestier, G., Petitjean, F., Dau, H.A., Webb, G.I., Keogh, E.: Generating synthetic time series to augment sparse datasets. In: 2017 IEEE International Conference on Data Mining (ICDM), pp. 865–870. IEEE (2017)
8. Han, X., Zhang, X., Wu, Y., Zhang, Z., Wu, Z.: KAN4TSF: are KAN and KAN-based models effective for time series forecasting? arXiv preprint arXiv:2408.11306 (2024)
9. Hill, T., O'Connor, M., Remus, W.: Neural network models for time series forecasts. Manage. Sci. **42**(7), 1082–1092 (1996)
10. Hou, C., Zhang, J., Zhou, T.: When to learn what: model-adaptive data augmentation curriculum. In: Proceedings of the IEEE/CVF International Conference on Computer Vision, pp. 1717–1728 (2023)
11. Hyndman, R.J., Athanasopoulos, G.: Forecasting: principles and practice. OTexts (2018)
12. Iwana, B.K., Uchida, S.: An empirical survey of data augmentation for time series classification with neural networks. PLoS ONE **16**(7), e0254841 (2021)
13. Koprinska, I., Wu, D., Wang, Z.: Convolutional neural networks for energy time series forecasting. In: 2018 International Joint Conference on Neural Networks (IJCNN), pp. 1–8. IEEE (2018)
14. Liu, Z., et al.: KAN: Kolmogorov-Arnold networks. arXiv preprint arXiv:2404.19756 (2024)

15. Makridakis, S., et al.: The accuracy of extrapolation (time series) methods: results of a forecasting competition. J. Forecast. **1**(2), 111–153 (1982)
16. Makridakis, S., Hibon, M.: The M3-competition: results, conclusions and implications. Int. J. Forecast. **16**(4), 451–476 (2000)
17. Oreshkin, B.N., Carpov, D., Chapados, N., Bengio, Y.: N-beats: neural basis expansion analysis for interpretable time series forecasting. arXiv preprint arXiv:1905.10437 (2019)
18. Park, D.S., et al.: Specaugment: a simple data augmentation method for automatic speech recognition. arXiv preprint arXiv:1904.08779 (2019)
19. Rashid, K.M., Louis, J.: Window-warping: a time series data augmentation of IMU data for construction equipment activity identification. In: ISARC. Proceedings of the International Symposium on Automation and Robotics in Construction, vol. 36, pp. 651–657. IAARC Publications (2019)
20. Roque, L., Soares, C., Torgo, L.: Rhiots: a framework for evaluating hierarchical time series forecasting algorithms. In: Proceedings of the 30th ACM SIGKDD Conference on Knowledge Discovery and Data Mining, pp. 2491–2499 (2024)
21. Siami-Namini, S., Tavakoli, N., Namin, A.S.: A comparison of ARIMA and LSTM in forecasting time series. In: 2018 17th IEEE International Conference on Machine Learning and Applications (ICMLA), pp. 1394–1401. IEEE (2018)
22. Taieb, S.B., Sorjamaa, A., Bontempi, G.: Multiple-output modeling for multi-step-ahead time series forecasting. Neurocomputing **73**(10–12), 1950–1957 (2010)
23. Wen, Q., et al.: Time series data augmentation for deep learning: a survey. arXiv preprint arXiv:2002.12478 (2020)
24. Zhou, H., et al.: Informer: beyond efficient transformer for long sequence time-series forecasting. In: Proceedings of the AAAI Conference on Artificial Intelligence, vol. 35, pp. 11106–11115 (2021)

Time Series Modeling for Smart Energy Consumption in Industry 4.0

Lara Ferreira[1], João Lopes[1]([✉]), Júlio Duarte[1], Daniela Ferreira[2], Rogério Pires[2], Isabel Silva[2], and Manuel Santos[1]

[1] ALGORITMI/LASI Research Centre, University of Minho, Braga, Portugal
`lopesit@outlook.pt`
[2] Bosch Car Multimedia, Braga, Portugal

Abstract. Industry 4.0 has driven a transformation in industrial environments through the adoption of technologies such as Artificial Intelligence (AI), the Internet of Things (IoT), and real-time Big Data analytics. In this context, efficient decision-making becomes essential to address process complexity and operational variability. This work proposes the development of an AI-based system to support informed and adaptive decision-making in industrial processes. By identifying efficiency indicators and applying advanced analytical techniques, the proposed system monitors industrial production processes and continuously adapts to real operating conditions. Adopting the Adaptive Business Intelligence (ABI) paradigm, this work integrates forecasting methods with energy efficiency metrics, pursuing a more effective and dynamic approach to operational management. This project aims to contribute to the advancement of decision support solutions in the Industry 4.0 landscape, promoting a more intelligent and responsive integration of analytical systems into industrial operations.

Keywords: Energy Consumption · Adaptive Business Intelligence · Industry 4.0

1 Introduction

Industry is undergoing a period of profound transformation, driven largely by a technological revolution that aims to enhance flexibility in production and enable mass customization, ultimately improving quality and productivity. Industry 4.0 facilitates the integration of production system technologies into intelligent manufacturing processes, paving the way for a new technological era that promises to fundamentally transform industrial value chains, production systems, and business models [1]. According to Kopeinig et al. (2024), the advent of Industry 4.0 has revolutionized the manufacturing sector by introducing interconnectivity, decentralized decision-making, resource optimization, and automation. The focus has shifted toward production efficiency, real-time transparency, and autonomous management [2].

J. Valente de Oliveira et al. (Eds.): EPIA 2025, LNAI 16121, pp. 230–242, 2026.
https://doi.org/10.1007/978-3-032-05176-9_18

To enable this industrial revolution, it has been essential to integrate a range of advanced technologies, such as the Internet of Things (IoT) and Big Data (BD). Lu (2017) characterizes Industry 4.0 as an integrated, adaptive, optimized, service-oriented, and interoperable manufacturing process that combines algorithms, large volumes of data, and cutting-edge technologies [3]. Digital transformation has significantly impacted industrial processes through the integration of technologies such as Artificial Intelligence (AI), IoT, data analytics, and cloud computing. Within the Industry 4.0 paradigm, these technologies enable process automation, real-time data collection, and seamless communication between systems and equipment [4]. Operating in industrial environments entails dealing with variability, process interdependencies, and resource constraints. These characteristics necessitate data-driven decision-making, influencing key areas such as planning, production, and maintenance. The application of analytical models facilitates such decisions by leveraging data collected during operations. Prescriptive models represent a class of analytical systems that not only predict outcomes but also provide recommendations on the actions to be taken. These models integrate machine learning, optimization, and simulation techniques to propose feasible solutions that account for multiple objectives and operational constraints [5]. However, despite advancements in analytical systems, challenges remain in the deployment of prescriptive solutions within the industrial sector. Existing systems often struggle with knowledge representation, the integration of operational data, and adaptability to dynamic process changes [6].

Building on the challenges identified in industrial process management and the increasing availability of data from interconnected systems in the context of Industry 4.0 (e.g., sensors, production equipment, supervisory systems, operational logs, and maintenance histories), this work aims to enhance decision-making in industrial environments through the application of prescriptive models based on efficiency indicators. Adopting the Adaptive Business Intelligence (ABI) paradigm, this study proposes the development of an AI-based system that integrates forecasting techniques with operational recommendation mechanisms. The focus is on applying AI methods to generate actionable insights that allow processes to be continuously adapted to real operating conditions.

2   Literature Review

2.1   Industry 4.0

Industry 4.0 has the main objective of revolutionizing manufacturing, promising greater flexibility in production, along with mass customization, better quality and greater productivity [1]. It is based on the following 4 design principles [7]:

1. Interconnection of machines, devices, sensors, and people—enabled, for example, by the Internet of Things (IoT)—is a fundamental component, to achieve effective interconnection.
2. Information transparency is a key aspect, as the convergence of physical and virtual environments is intrinsic to Industry 4.0. Transparency enables more informed decision-making.

3. Decentralized decision-making leverages both inter-connectivity among various systems and stakeholders, and the availability of transparent, real-time information.
4. Technical assistance is increasingly important due to the growing complexity of production systems. Advanced support systems aggregate and visualize information in a comprehensible manner, enabling informed decisions.

According to Lasi et al. (2014), Industry 4.0 encompasses a broad range of contemporary concepts, and its classification within a specific discipline, as well as its precise delimitation, is not always possible in individual cases [8]. Some of the main underlying concepts include:

1. Smart Industry, comprising sensors, actuators, and autonomous systems. The integration of advanced technologies with digital representations of factory components and products, along with ubiquitous computing and production environments that operate with a high degree of autonomy.
2. Cyber-Physical Systems, integrating physical and digital layers. For instance, monitoring process parameters such as the production time of mechanical components generates digital records.
3. New Distribution Systems with the coordination of interconnected activities relying on multiple dynamic and adaptive channels.
4. The development of products and services, highlighting open innovation approaches, product intelligence, and digital product memory.
5. Modern production systems must be designed with a focus on human-centric requirements, ensuring usability, safety, and adaptability in the workplace.
6. Corporate social responsibility, resource efficiency, and sustainable production practices are increasingly critical in the design of industrial manufacturing systems.

2.2   Adaptive Business Intelligence

The concept of adaptability is gaining relevance across a wide range of sectors. In modern organizations, data are generated and accumulated at an unprecedented pace, creating an urgent need for advanced intelligent systems capable of extracting meaningful information and supporting accurate, real-time decision making. Adaptive Business Intelligence (ABI) systems address this need by combining predictive components with an optimization layer that explores broader sets of possibilities to each problem [5,15].

Predictive analytics enables the forecasting of future events by addressing key questions such as: What will happen? and Why will it happen? To achieve this, predictive models commonly employ methodologies that include data extraction, Machine Learning (ML), Artificial Intelligence (AI), and simulation techniques [5,11,12]. The application of these techniques enables the prediction of the likelihood of specific events, the identification of patterns that may recur in the future, and the discovery of potential relationships between events. The primary objective is to support planning and decision-making by modeling processes in a way that considers both historical and anticipated future events [9,13].

Prescriptive analytics takes a proactive approach by recommending optimal courses of action based on future forecasts. It enables decision-makers not only to identify problems and opportunities, but also to directly prescribe the most suitable actions in alignment with predefined objectives and expected outcomes. This approach seeks to answer key questions such as: What should a company do to achieve its goals? and How can these goals be achieved? Given that prescriptive analytics is often applied to real-world scenarios characterized by significant uncertainty, the effectiveness of the optimization process is highly dependent on the accuracy of the forecasts [4, 13].

3   Methodologies

This work aims to develop a time series ML model applied to Industry 4.0, based on real data provided by Bosch Car Multimedia.

To this end, two methodologies were followed: Design Science Research (DSR) as a research methodology, providing the necessary guidelines, and the Cross-Industry Standard Process for Data Mining (CRISP-DM). DSR is a problem-solving paradigm that focuses on the creation and evaluation of innovative artifacts intended to address specific, practical problems within a particular domain [14]. The DSR process is typically iterative and involves several key activities [15]:

1. **Problem identification and motivation**, clearly defining the specific research problem and justifying the value of a solution;
2. **Definition of objectives** from the problem definition and knowledge of what is possible and feasible;
3. **Design and development**, creating the artifact. This phase involves exploring design alternatives and defining the artifact's desired functionality and architecture;
4. **Demonstration**, using the artifact to solve one or more instances of the problem;
5. **Evaluation**, observing and measuring how well the artifact supports a solution to the problem. This involves comparing the objectives of a solution to actual observed results from the demonstration;
6. **Communication**, articulating the problem, the artifact, its utility and effectiveness.

For Data Mining (DM) projects, CRISP-DM is a widely adopted methodology that provides a structured framework for DM and ML developments. CRISP-DM is composed of six interconnected phases [16]:

1. **Understanding the business**, starting with an assessment of the current situation, determining objectives and a project plan. It is crucial to understand the problem to be solved and clearly define the project's objectives.
2. **Understanding the data**, focusing on initial data collection, describing and exploring the data, verifying the quality of the data and identifying patterns or initial problems.

3. **Data preparation**, usually the most time-consuming phase, as it involves selecting, cleaning, building, integrating and formatting the data so that it can be used by the modeling tools. The aim is to transform the raw data into a format suitable for analysis.

4. **Modeling**, with the application of various ML techniques. This involves experimenting with different algorithms and building various final models. Often it is necessary to go back to the data preparation phase to make the necessary adjustments.

5. **Evaluation**, determining if the model meets the business success criteria and identifying any important issues that have not been sufficiently considered.

6. **Deployment**, putting the evaluated model into the real business environment. This can range from generating reports to integrating the model into operational decision-making processes. This phase also includes planning for monitoring and maintaining the deployed model.

4   Results

4.1   Theoretical Framework

Efectiveness Efficiency. Evaluating the efficiency of industrial processes necessitates the definition of relevant measures and tools for performance assessment. This evaluation is crucial for leveraging existing infrastructure and achieving company objectives. Key Performance Indicators (KPIs) serve as instruments that enable the measurement of progress towards these objectives [17]. According to Badawy et al. (2016), "KPIs act as a set of measures focused on the aspects of organizational performance that are critical to the success of the organization." Furthermore, the utilization of monitoring data facilitates the optimization of process execution and enables data-driven planning [18].

In the context of Bosch Car Multimedia, enhancing energy efficiency is a key strategic goal. To support this, the main objective is to develop a ML model capable of predicting five critical measures of energy efficiency within their operations: Active Energy consumption, Hours Worked, Units Produced, Humidity and Temperature. Understanding and forecasting these metrics can provide valuable insights for optimizing energy usage and overall operational efficiency through KPIs. Continuous monitoring of these indicators and subsequent KPIs will make it possible to detect deviations from the expected values, allowing for timely interventions and adjustments to the execution of the process as necessary [17].

4.2   Modelling

The ARIMA (AutoRegressive Integrated Moving Average) model is commonly used to model univariate time series that exhibit temporal dependence and potential trends. It comprises three main components: the autoregressive (AR) term, which captures the dependence on past values; the integrated (I) term, which applies differencing to achieve stationarity; and the moving average (MA) term, which models the error as a linear combination of past forecast errors.

The model is parameterized by (p, d, q) corresponding to the orders of the AR, I, and MA components, respectively. ARIMA does not explicitly account for seasonality. For time series that exhibit seasonal patterns, the SARIMA (Seasonal AutoRegressive Integrated Moving Average) model is used. SARIMA extends ARIMA by incorporating seasonal components and is parameterized as $(p, d, q) \times (P, D, Q)s$, which (P, D, Q) denote the seasonal autoregressive, seasonal differencing, and seasonal moving average terms, and s represents the seasonal period. An additional extension, SARIMAX (Seasonal AutoRegressive Integrated Moving Average with eXogenous variables), allows the inclusion of external explanatory variables (Xt) through an additional linear regression term [19]. In summary, ARIMA is suitable for non-seasonal, univariate time series without exogenous influences. SARIMA introduces the ability to model regular seasonal patterns while remaining univariate. SARIMAX further enhances this framework by incorporating exogenous variables, making it more appropriate for scenarios in which external factors influence the time series dynamics.

The LSTM, as an alternative to the models presented, is a recurrent neuronal network developed to deal with sequential data with long-term dependencies. It is effective in predicting time series and its performance depends on the choice of hyperparameters. It has better accuracy and generalization capacity than traditional methods and other neural networks in temporal forecasting tasks [23, 24].

Figure 1 presents the Autocorrelation Function (ACF), indicating that the most appropriate models for the analyzed time series are SARIMA and SARIMAX, due to the presence of a well-defined monthly seasonality. A pronounced autocorrelation peak is observed at *lag 30*, clearly exceeding the confidence bounds. This suggests a recurring pattern approximately every 30 days. The absence of other significant peaks or oscillatory structures at different lags further supports the conclusion that the dominant seasonality is monthly in nature, and that additional cycles with shorter periodicities are unlikely.

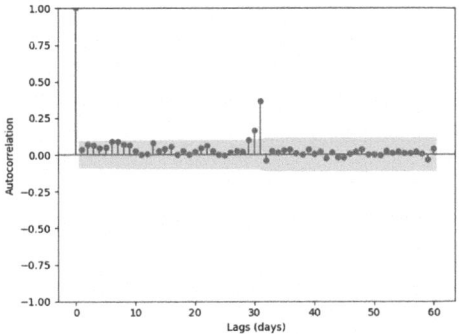

Fig. 1. Autocorrelation Function (ACF).

4.3   Data Analysis and Feature Engineering

The data provided on active energy is organized hierarchically. At the top of the hierarchy is the substation (Level 1), followed by transformer stations (TS) (Level 2), buildings (Level 3) and lines (Level 4). For the substation level, additional variables such as temperature, humidity, number of units produced and number of hours worked are also available.

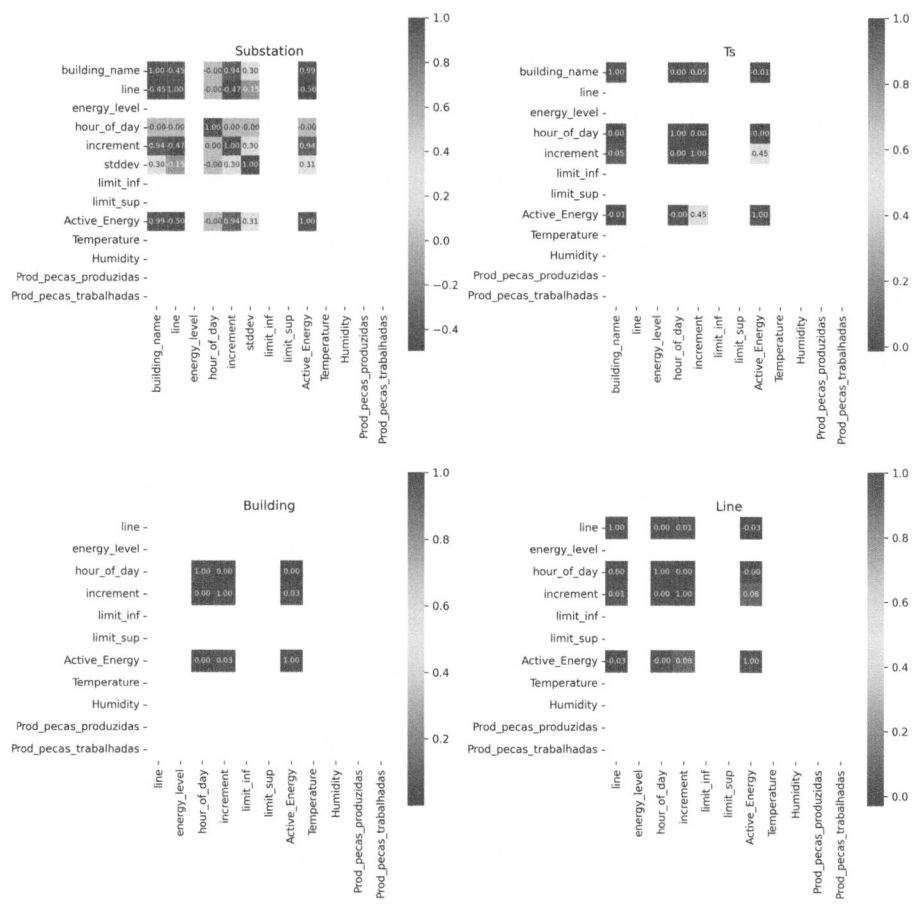

Fig. 2. Correlation with Levels.

As an initial step, the correlations between Active Energy and the remaining variables were computed across each hierarchical level. As illustrated in Fig. 2, the results indicate an absence of significant correlations between active energy and the other variables, suggesting that the inclusion of these exogenous variables may not enhance the predictive performance of the models. However, regarding the substation level information, it is evident that for forecasting the variables presented in the corresponding table, the use of their respective exogenous variables may be relevant. Lastly, the data was resampled to a daily frequency, ensuring an appropriate structure for time series models. To ensure realistic predictions, a treatment was applied to the predicted values, replacing negative values with zero, since energy consumption cannot take on values lower than zero.

4.4   Model Evaluation

Evaluation metrics are used so that the model's performance can be verified [20–22]:

1. **Mean Absolute Error (MAE)** quantifies the average of the absolute differences between the actual values and the values predicted by a model. Formally, it is defined as

$$MAE = \frac{1}{n} \sum_{i=1}^{n} |y_i - \hat{y}_i| \tag{1}$$

in which y_i represents the observed value, $\hat{y}_i$ the predicted value, and n the total number of observations. The MAE provides a clear and direct measure of the average magnitude of forecast errors, being expressed in the same unit as the data.

2. **Mean Squared Error (MSE)**, is one of the most widely used metrics for evaluating regression models. It calculates the average of the squares of the differences between the actual and predicted values, and is given by the following formula.

$$MSE = \frac{1}{n} \sum_{i=1}^{n} (y_i - \hat{y}_i)^2 \tag{2}$$

This metric penalizes larger errors more severely than the MAE, due to the squared elevation. It is therefore particularly sensitive to outliers and large errors. For this reason, the MSE is useful for models that minimize extreme errors.

3. **Root Mean Squared Error (RMSE)**, is the square root of the MSE and is often preferred by analysts because it is on the same scale as the original data. It is calculated using the following formula.

$$RMSE = \sqrt{\frac{1}{n} \sum_{i=1}^{n} (y_i - \hat{y}_i)^2} \tag{3}$$

Similarly to the MSE, the RMSE penalizes larger errors more heavily, which makes it a metric that is sensitive to outliers. In contexts where large errors are particularly undesirable, the RMSE is a robust choice for assessing model quality.

4. **Mean Absolute Percentage Error (MAPE)** measures the average magnitude of the relative error in percentage terms.

$$MAPE = \frac{100\%}{n} \sum_{i=1}^{n} \left| \frac{y_i - \hat{y}_i}{y_i} \right| \tag{4}$$

By normalizing the absolute error by the actual value, MAPE expresses the error as a percentage of the observed value, which facilitates comparisons between different scales of data or variables.

Regarding the definition of the model's hyperparameters, the Grid Search technique was used. This approach consists of an exhaustive search through all possible combinations of a predefined set of values for each relevant hyperparameter. The main goal is to identify the configuration that leads to the best model performance. During this process, for each combination of hyperparameters, the model is trained and then evaluated based on the MAPE metric. This metric, which measures the average absolute percentage error between the predicted and actual values, allows for a consistent comparison of performance across different configurations. After evaluating all possible combinations, the one that yields the lowest MAPE value is selected, as it indicates the highest prediction accuracy. This ensures an effective optimization of the model's parameters, contributing to more robust and reliable results.

Table 1 shows the values of the aforementioned metrics, applying the SARIMA model to forecast energy consumption for each level of the organization.

Table 1. SARIMA Performance

Metrics	Substation	TS	Building	Line
MAE	69.51	3.22	5.49	3.05
MSE	9729.33	25.12	985.73	18.63
RMSE	98.64	5.01	31.40	4.32
MAPE	6.26%	3.93%	7.41%	27.26%

Table 2 shows the same analysis, applying the SARIMAX model to the variables associated with the substation, such as Hours Worked and Parts Produced.

Table 2. SARIMAX Performance

Metrics	Produced Units	Worked Hours
MAE	2.46	1.05
MSE	9.57	1.85
RMSE	3.09	1.36
MAPE	13.34%	9.85%

Table 3 shows the application of the LSTM model to energy levels and the hours and parts associated with the substation.

Table 3. LSTM Performance

Metrics	Substation	TS	Building	Line	Produced Units	Worked Hours
MAE	64.86	6.92	7.33	0.83	3.70	1.54
MSE	6663.44	67.39	1126.67	1.03	29.32	4.55
RMSE	81.63	8.21	33.57	1.02	5.42	2.13
MAPE	5.13%	8.50%	11.58%	6.79%	11.88%	12.65%

4.5 Deployment

The final outcome includes the execution of SARIMA, SARIMAX and LSTM models. The dashboard presented in Fig. 3 enables a comparative analysis between the forecasts generated by both models and the actual observed values for January and February 2025. Additionally, the dashboard provides monitoring of the energy efficiency KPI, allowing users to visualize both the predicted and actual values of this indicator. The energy efficiency KPI is calculated based on the following formula:

$$KPI = \frac{Total\,Active\,Energy}{Total\,Hours\,Worked} \tag{5}$$

The probability of the KPI exceeding a critical value, i.e. the value falling outside the expected range in percentage terms, is calculated based on the distribution generated by Monte Carlo simulations, which propagate the uncertainties in energy and parts forecasts. The Monte Carlo simulation method is particularly useful when variables have associated uncertainties, as is the case with energy and parts forecasts. The central goal is to generate a large number of random samples within a defined confidence interval for each variable. Using these samples, the behavior of the KPI is simulated in all iterations, taking into account the fluctuations in the forecasts. This enables a probabilistic analysis of the KPI under different scenarios, considering the uncertainties in the input forecasts. Based on the point forecasts and their associated confidence intervals, the sampling distributions will be defined using a normal distribution for each variable. Multiple simulations will be conducted to calculate the ratio between energy and parts in each iteration. From this distribution, the confidence interval and the probability of the KPI exceeding a critical value will be determined, providing a probabilistic estimate of the KPI's behavior. Thus, this implementation represents a decisive step toward building an ABI system, in which forecasting, uncertainty management, and the recommendation of operational decisions are integrated into an intelligent decision support system.

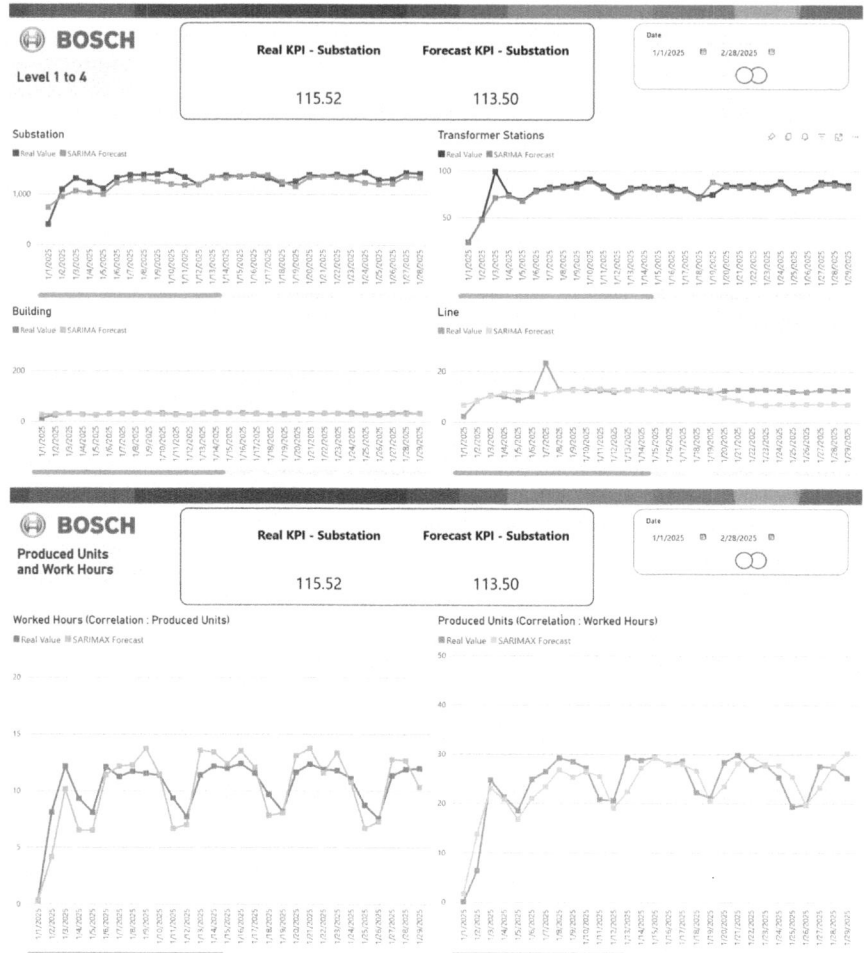

Fig. 3. KPI Monitoring Performance.

5 Conclusion

This work presented the basis of an ABI approach applied to energy consumption and operational variables, in the context of Industry 4.0.

The SARIMA, SARIMAX, and LSTM models were applied using real data, with monthly seasonality confirmed through autocorrelation analysis. It was observed that the SARIMA and SARIMAX models performed better at higher levels of the hierarchy (such as at the Substation level), with SARIMAX being particularly useful when exogenous variables were included. However, the inclusion of these variables in SARIMAX had a limited impact on the forecasting of active energy, although it proved relevant for predicting operational variables such as Produced Parts and Worked Hours. On the other hand, the LSTM model demonstrated competitive performance across all levels analyzed, showing clear improvements in metrics such as MAE and RMSE compared to traditional models. LSTM was especially effective in modeling multivariate time series with nonlinear patterns, making it applicable both at aggregated levels (such as Substation and Line) and for detailed operational variables (such as production and worked hours). Thus, LSTM proved to be a robust and flexible alternative, particularly advantageous when more complex and nonlinear historical data is available.

The results highlighted differences across aggregation levels, underscoring the influence of data structure on the models' predictive capabilities. The developed models were integrated into a final dashboard to enable the visualization of actual and predicted values, as well as the monitoring of the energy efficiency KPI. This KPI was calculated as the ratio between Active Energy and Total Hours Worked, allowing for the analysis of operational performance and the identification of deviations. After analyzing the metrics obtained, the models were approved to move on to the production phase.

Future work includes enhancing hyperparameter optimization, incorporating improved prescriptive analytics components, and extending the historical data period to improve the robustness and reliability of the forecasts.

Acknowledgments. This work is supported by national funds, through the Operational Competitiveness and Internationalization Programme (COMPETE 2020) [Project no 179826; Funding Reference: SIFN-01-9999-FN-179826].

Disclosure of Interests. The authors have no competing interests to declare that are relevant to the content of this article.

References

1. Zhong, R.Y., Xu, X., Klotz, E., Newman, S.T.: Intelligent manufacturing in the context of industry 4.0: a review. Engineering **3**(5), 616–630 (2017). https://doi.org/10.1016/J.ENG.2017.05.015
2. Kopeinig, J., Woschank, M., Olipp, N.: Industry 4.0 technologies and their implications for environmental sustainability in the manufacturing industry. Procedia Comput. Sci. **232**, 2777–2789 (2024). https://doi.org/10.1016/j.procs.2024.02.095
3. Lu, Y.: Industry 4.0: a survey on technologies, applications and open research issues. J. Ind. Inf. Integr. **6**, 1–10 (2017). https://doi.org/10.1016/j.jii.2017.04.005
4. Frazzetto, D., Nielsen, T.D., Pedersen, T.B., Šikšnys, L.: Prescriptive analytics: a survey of emerging trends and technologies. VLDB J. **28**(4), 575–595 (2019). https://doi.org/10.1007/s00778-019-00539-y
5. Lepenioti, K., Bousdekis, A., Apostolou, D., Mentzas, G.: Prescriptive analytics: literature review and research challenges. Int. J. Inf. Manag. **50**, 57–70 (2020). https://doi.org/10.1016/j.ijinfomgt.2019.04.003
6. Bäck, T.: Adaptive business intelligence based on evolution strategies: some application examples of self-adaptive software. Inf. Sci. **148**(1–4), 113–121 (2002). https://doi.org/10.1016/S0020-0255(02)00283-9

7. Hermann, M., Pentek, T., Otto, B.: Design principles for industrie 4.0 scenarios. In: Proceedings of the Annual Hawaii International Conference on System Sciences, pp. 3928–3937 (2016). https://doi.org/10.1109/HICSS.2016.488

8. Lasi, H., Fettke, P., Kemper, H.-G., Feld, T., Hoffmann, M.: Industry 4.0. Bus. Inf. Syst. Eng. **6**(4), 239–242 (2014). https://doi.org/10.1007/s12599-014-0334-4

9. Delen, D.: Prescriptive Analytics: The Final Frontier for Evidence-Based Management and Optimal Decision Making. FT Press (2019)

10. Michalewicz, Z., Schmidt, M., Michalewicz, M., Chiriac, C.: Adaptive Business Intelligence, pp. 37–46. Springer, Heidelberg (2006)

11. Relich, M.: Predictive and prescriptive analytics in identifying opportunities for improving sustainable manufacturing. Sustainability **15**(9) (2023). https://doi.org/10.3390/su15097667

12. Vater, J., Harscheidt, L., Knoll, A.: Smart Manufacturing with Prescriptive Analytics. Institute of Electrical and Electronics Engineers, Inc. (2019)

13. Heldal, R., Pelliccione, P., Eliasson, U., Lantz, J., Derehag, J., Whittle, J.: Descriptive vs Prescriptive Models in Industry (2016). http://www.autosar.org/

14. Hevner, A.R., March, S.T., Park, J., Ram, S.: Design science in information systems research. MIS Q. **28**(1), 75–105 (2004)

15. Peffers, K., Tuunanen, T., Rothenberger, M.A., Chatterjee, S.: A design science research methodology for information systems research. J. Manag. Inf. Syst. **24**(3), 45–77 (2007)

16. Azevedo, A., Santos, M.: Business Intelligence - State of the Art, Trends, and Open Issues. Funchal - Madeira, Portugal (2009)

17. Gackowiec, P., Podobinska-Staniec, M., Brzychczy, E., Kühlbach, C., Özver, T.: Review of key performance indicators for process monitoring in the mining industry. Energies **13**(19) (2020). https://doi.org/10.3390/en13195169

18. Badawy, M., El-Aziz, A.A.A., Idress, A.M., Hefny, H., Hossam, S.: A survey on exploring key performance indicators. Future Comput. Inform. J. **1**(1–2), 47–52 (2016). https://doi.org/10.1016/j.fcij.2016.04.001

19. Banaś, J., Utnik-Banaś, K.: Evaluating a seasonal autoregressive moving average model with an exogenous variable for short-term timber price forecasting. Forest Policy Econ. **131** (2021). https://doi.org/10.1016/j.forpol.2021.102564

20. Chai, T., Draxler, R.R.: Root mean square error (RMSE) or mean absolute error (MAE)? -arguments against avoiding RMSE in the literature. Geosci. Model Dev. **7**(3), 1247–1250 (2014). https://doi.org/10.5194/gmd-7-1247-2014

21. Willmott, C.J., Matsuura, K.: CLIMATE RESEARCH Clim Res (2019). www.int-res.com

22. Hyndman, R.J., Koehler, A.B.: Another look at measures of forecast accuracy. Int. J. Forecast. **22**(4), 679–688 (2006). https://doi.org/10.1016/j.ijforecast.2006.03.001

23. Yadav, A., Jha, C.K., Sharan, A.: Optimizing LSTM for time series prediction in Indian stock market. Procedia Comput. Sci. **167**, 2091–2100 (2020). https://doi.org/10.1016/j.procs.2020.03.257

24. Song, X., et al.: Time-series well performance prediction based on long short-term memory (LSTM) neural network model. J. Pet. Sci. Eng. **186**, 106682 (2019). https://doi.org/10.1016/j.petrol.2019.106682

Towards Smarter Property Recommendations in Complex Housing Market

Ana Rita Nogueira[(✉)], José Pinto, João Silva, Gonçalo Duarte Nunes, Manuel Curral, and Ricardo Sousa

LIAAD, INESC TEC, Rua Dr. Roberto Frias, 4200-465 Porto, Portugal
ana.r.nogueira@inesctec.pt

Abstract. Manual selection of real estate properties can pose considerable challenges for agents since it needs a careful balance of various factors to satisfy client requirements while also manoeuvring through the complexities of the market. Although automated valuation models are widely used to estimate property market values, they are not designed to support property recommendation tasks. To address this gap, filtering-based recommendation methods have been explored, including collaborative and content-based approaches. However, these methods face several limitations in the real estate domain. This paper proposes a recommendation methodology designed to identify houses that closely resemble a given property, allowing agents to select the best matches based on geographical and physical characteristics. To assess the performance of the proposed methodology, we employ a range of evaluation metrics that measure different aspects of the model's effectiveness in ranking and recommending relevant items. The findings suggest that, while geographic features may slightly influence ranking behaviour, the model is capable of producing diverse and relevant recommendations consistently.

Keywords: Real Estate Recommendation · Property Similarity · Gower Distance · Haversine distance

1 Introduction

House prices depend heavily on factors such as location, property size, and market demand [5]. In urban or high-cost areas, prices tend to be higher due to limited supply and strong competition. In addition, proximity to amenities and desirable neighbourhoods also pushes these prices up. In contrast, rural or less populated areas generally have lower prices because of less demand and more available space. Economic factors such as inflation and mortgage rates further influence the market. Buyers should consider these factors and negotiate wisely to obtain the best value [5].

In Portugal, the real estate crisis has made the housing market more complex, as prices fell as a result of the 2008 financial crisis, driven by speculative bubbles, banking concerns, and austerity measures. As many homeowners struggled

© The Author(s), under exclusive license to Springer Nature Switzerland AG 2026
J. Valente de Oliveira et al. (Eds.): EPIA 2025, LNAI 16121, pp. 243–255, 2026.
https://doi.org/10.1007/978-3-032-05176-9_19

financially, foreclosure rates increased and demand turned to rentals. Changes in the country's demographics, such as population growth in urban centres or shifts in household composition, have also contributed to the rise in house prices. In 2014–2015, the market began to revive, driven by foreign investment and programmes such as the Golden Visa. Although urban areas saw price increases, this has resulted in an affordability dilemma for locals, compounded by the increase in short-term rentals. The government must now strike a balance between foreign investment and the access of residents to housing [10].

While buyers want to secure the best deal possible, sellers often aim to maximise their profit by highlighting the property's best features, setting competitive prices, and timing the sale to align with favourable market conditions. Using a real estate agent or company offers numerous advantages for both buyers and sellers. Their expertise in the local market can help buyers find properties that meet their criteria and budget while helping sellers set the right price and effectively market the property. To determine the optimal price, agents perform a Comparative Market Analysis (CMA), which involves identifying comparable properties (recently sold or currently listed homes that closely match the subject property in essential characteristics such as location, year of construction and property type [4]). Agents typically restrict their analysis to properties within the same geographic area to ensure consistency in value and features. This process facilitates smoother transactions and empowers both buyers and sellers to make informed and confident decisions.

To better support real estate agents, a system capable of automatically recommending comparable properties could increase their ability to serve buyers and sellers. For buyers, it would help agents present similar listings, offer a clearer view of market value, and expand their range of options. For sellers, it would help setting a realistic and competitive price by analysing recent sales and comparable properties. Although Automated Valuation Models (AVMs) are widely used for property valuation [1], they are not designed to recommend listings. To bridge this gap, researchers have explored filtering techniques such as collaborative and content-based methods [7,9]. However, these approaches face persistent challenges in the real estate domain: cold start issues for new users and listings, data sparsity that weakens similarity-based recommendations, heavy reliance on high-quality interaction data, and scalability concerns as datasets grow [11]. These limitations highlight the need for a more robust solution that performs well without extensive interaction data, adapts to unseen inputs, and remains competitive in terms of performance.

To address these challenges, this paper proposes a recommendation methodology that closely emulates how real estate agents identify comparable properties. The process begins by selecting listings within a relevant geographic radius, calculated using both Haversine and street distances. Then it filters properties based on postal code similarity to reflect neighbourhood characteristics, followed by a direct comparison of property attributes. Given the mix of continuous and categorical data, the Gower distance is used to compute similarity scores. To explore the trade-off between methodological accuracy and practical efficiency, two variations are evaluated: one that fully replicates the agent's process, including postal code filtering, and another that omits this step to assess its impact on recommendation quality.

This paper is organised as follows: Sect. 2 describes some essential definitions. Section 3 shows some current work in the field. Section 4 illustrates the problem and the data used; Sect. 5 describes the proposed approach, Sect. 6 demonstrates the experimental setup, and Sect. 7 shows the results obtained in the tests.

2   Background

In this section, we introduce some important notations that will be used throughout the document.

2.1   Haversine Formula

The Haversine formula [2] is a formula used to calculate the shortest distance between two points on the surface of a sphere, given their longitudes and latitudes. It is particularly useful in geodesy and navigation for determining distances on the Earth's surface, where the curvature of the Earth must be accounted for. The formula derives its name from the *hav* function, which refers to the half-angle formula for trigonometry. Mathematically, the Haversine formula is expressed as:

$$Haversine = R \cdot c \qquad c = 2 \cdot \text{atan2} \left(\sqrt{a}, \sqrt{1-a} \right)$$
$$a = \sin^2 \left(\frac{\Delta\phi}{2} \right) + \cos(\phi_1) \cdot \cos(\phi_2) \cdot \sin^2 \left(\frac{\Delta\lambda}{2} \right) \tag{1}$$

where ϕ_1 and ϕ_2 are the latitudes of the two points in radians, λ_1 and λ_2 are the longitudes of the two points in radians, R is the radius of the Earth (mean radius = 6,371 km), $\Delta\phi$ and $\Delta\lambda$ are the differences between latitudes and longitudes, respectively.

2.2   Gower Distance

The Gower distance [6] measures the similarity between two data points with mixed attribute types. It is computed as the average contribution of each variable:

$$D_{Gower}(i,j) = \frac{1}{p} \sum_{k=1}^{p} w_k . d_k(i,j), \tag{2}$$

In this context, p is the total number of variables, $d_k(i,j)$ is the distance contribution of the variable k^{th} and w_k is the corresponding weight. For continuous variables, $d_k(i,j)$ is the normalised absolute difference:

$$d_k(i, j) = \frac{|x_k(i) - x_k(j)|}{\text{Range}(x_k)}, \tag{3}$$

In this context, $\text{Range}(x_k)$ is the difference between the maximum and minimum observed values of the variable k. This produces a value between 0 (identical values) and 1 (maximally different). For categorical variables, the contribution is binary:

$$d_k(i, j) = \begin{cases} 0, & \text{if } x_k(i) = x_k(j), \\ 1, & \text{if } x_k(i) \neq x_k(j). \end{cases} \tag{4}$$

This means that for a given categorical variable, the distance contribution is 0 if both datapoints share the same category, indicating no difference; otherwise, it is 1, indicating maximal difference.

3   Related Work

Recent advances in real estate recommendation systems have increasingly emphasised the integration of geographical and contextual data to improve the personalisation and precision of property suggestions. Traditional methods often under-represent the role of spatial proximity, despite its critical influence on buyer preferences. In response, several studies have proposed models that incorporate geographical and spatial characteristics to improve both property recommendations and price predictions. Within this broader context, research in the domain of CMA generally falls into two categories: approaches focused on estimating or recommending property prices and those aimed at identifying comparable properties based on similarity criteria.

For example, a study by Das et al. (2021) [3], which belongs to the first category, proposes a novel framework called Geo-Spatial Network Embedding (GSNE), which improves the prediction of house prices by incorporating geospatial context, such as proximity to essential amenities such as schools, shops and transportation. Using a data set of more than 50,000 house transaction records from Melbourne, Australia, the study shows that GSNE effectively embeds spatial network nodes in a Gaussian feature space, leading to improved predictive accuracy compared to traditional models. Building on the integration of geographical data, Lessani and Li (2024) [8], in the same category, propose a novel regression approach called Similarity and Geographically Weighted Regression (SGWR), which enhances traditional geographically weighted regression (GWR) by incorporating data attribute similarity alongside geographical proximity. These studies underscore the growing importance of geographic data in real estate decision making and highlight the potential of advanced models that integrate spatial information to improve the precision of recommendations and predictive capabilities.

In a different direction (identifying comparable properties based on similarity criteria), Knoll et al. (2018) [7], explored the application of recommendation system techniques within the e-Commerce market of real estate. Their study compared traditional collaborative filtering with more recent approaches, including deep learning and factorisation machines, using real-world user interaction data. The authors demonstrate how incorporating additional property attributes, such as price, living space, and number of rooms, into models can significantly improve the quality of the recommendations. However, they highlight persistent challenges in item cold-start situations, where new listings lack sufficient interaction data. Similarly, Yu et al. (2018) [12], also in the same category, introduced two geoproximity-boosted algorithms tailored for the Chinese real estate market. The research uses the House365 dataset, which includes user click records and Nanjing property details, to capture the influence of geographical factors and property prices on user decisions. Finally, Polohakul et al. (2021) [9], again in the same category, addressed the persistent cold start problem in real estate recommendation systems by proposing a hybrid approach that combines content-based filtering with a modified session-based recommendation model. Evaluated on a large-scale dataset from a Thai real estate platform, the approach demonstrated strong performance in both the cold-start and warm-start scenarios. However, the model does not outperform the specialised methods in either scenario. Additionally, the approach heavily depends on high-quality item metadata and involves a complex architecture that can challenge scalability.

4 Problem

Selecting comparable real estate properties is a complex task that involves balancing location, property features, and market dynamics. Agents typically start within a preferred postal code, using local knowledge to filter by price, size, and amenities. However, even within the same area, properties can differ significantly due to neighbourhood characteristics, proximity to services, and demand trends. When few comparables are found, agents expand their search to nearby regions, each with distinct conditions, making the process even more challenging. Without technological support, this task relies on manual analysis and intuition, which is time-consuming and prone to bias, especially when data are incomplete or nuanced factors like renovations or local taxes are involved. Existing recommendation systems offer limited support: traditional filters and AVMs do not replicate the comparative approach of the agent. Although recent models incorporate spatial and contextual data for the valuation or general recommendations [3,8,12], they do not focus on identifying truly comparable properties. Other methods [7,9], including collaborative filtering and deep learning, often require large datasets and complex architectures that may not scale or generalise well.

This highlights the need for a recommendation approach that (1) mirrors the comparative spatially aware process of the agent, (2) uses structured property data and localised filtering, and (3) provides consistent and interpretable results for both buyers and sellers.

Table 1. Variable Description

Variable Name	Description	Type	Possible Values
Latitude	Property's postal-code latitude	Continuous	Real Number
Longitude	Property's postal-code longitude	Continuous	Real Number
Postal Code	Postal code of the property's location	Other	XXXX-XXX
Rooms	Number of rooms in the property	Continuous	Real number
Area	Total area of the property in square meters	Continuous	Real number
Construction Year	Year the property was constructed	Continuous	Real number
Type	Type of property	Discrete	Apartment, House
CCE	Energy efficiency rating of the property	Discrete	A, B, C, etc.
State	Condition/state of the property	Discrete	New, Used, etc.
Garage	Whether the property has a garage or not	Binary	0 (No), 1 (Yes)
Terrace	Whether the property has a terrace or not	Binary	0 (No), 1 (Yes)
Pool	Whether the property has a pool or not	Binary	0 (No), 1 (Yes)
Public Space	Whether the property has access to public space	Binary	0 (No), 1 (Yes)
User State	User-defined state of the property	Binary	New, Used
Offer	Adjusted the valuation according to the most recent market offer value	Continuous	Real Number (€)

4.1 Data

To address this problem, a Portuguese real estate dataset was used that contains 421 547 transactions from January 2017 to December 2024. The data set comprises 15 variables, including 7 continuous numerical variables and 8 categorical ones. Among the continuous variables are latitude, longitude, number of rooms, area (measured in square metres), construction year, and offer price (Table 1).

The geographical coordinates of the properties exhibit a latitude range of 37.00 to 42.13, with an average latitude of 39.36°. Meanwhile, the longitudinal coordinates extend from -9.49 to -6.23, with a mean longitude of $-8.82°$ (every house in this data set is located in Portugal). The number of rooms ranged from 0 to 20, with an average of 2.48 rooms per property. The area spanned 26 to 1000 square metres, with a mean of 124.93 square metres. The construction year covered a period that spanned more than a century, ranging from 1901 to 2025 with an average construction year of 1992.55. Finally, the offer showed a range from 25356.83 € to 8228882.38 €, with a mean value of 408215.38 € (Table 2).

Categorical variables include binary indicators for the presence of a garage, terrace, pool, and access to public space. Most of the properties did not have these features, 77.48% lacking a garage, 92.19% without a terrace, and 92.89% without a pool. Only 17.38% of the properties had access to public space. The type of property (apartment or house) and state (new, good, used, or bad) provided further classification, with 74.82% classified as apartment and 63.30% in used condition. Furthermore, the state of the user-defined property closely aligned with the actual state variable, where 74.48% of the properties were marked as used by users. Concerning the Energy Efficiency Classification (CCE), a significant portion of properties, specifically 34.30%, were classified under "No information" due to missing detailed data. For properties where data

Table 2. Summary Statistics for latitude, longitude, rooms, area, construction year, and offer

	Rooms	Area	Construction Year	Offer	Latitude	Longitude
mean	2.48	124.93	1993	408215.38	39.36	−8.82
std	1.25	77.43	23	440593.79	1.31	0.45
min	0	26	1901	25356.83	37	−9.49
25%	2	77	1981	183627.05	38.70	−9.16
50%	2	104	1997	278425.14	38.77	−8.96
75%	3	147	2008	461748.56	40.96	−8.56
max	20	1000	2025	8228882.38	42.13	−6.23

were available, the distribution of energy efficiency ratings varied widely: just 1.32% received an A+ rating, 5.67% were rated A, and another 5.63% received a B rating. Lower ratings were more prevalent, with 2.95% classified as B-, 18.67% as C, 17.96% as D, and 9.46% as E. Less efficient properties were classified as F (3.90%) and G (0.14%) (Fig. 1).

5 Methodology

This section introduces a recommendation approach designed to identify comparable properties, those that closely resemble each other. Using geographical data, such as estimated location, incorporates physical attributes such as area, construction year, and number of rooms. The process is structured into three distinct phases: geographical filtering, postal code filtering, and property-level filtering. A visual representation of these phases is provided in Fig. 2.

Before introducing the pipeline, it is important to define how the similarity between comparables is measured. Two properties are considered comparable if they are geographically close and exhibit similar physical characteristics. Geographic proximity ensures that properties share a similar spatial context, including neighbourhood characteristics, accessibility, and local amenities. In addition to location, properties must align in key attributes such as total area and number of rooms, with similarity increasing as these variables match more closely. Given that the variables available for each property are a mixture of continuous and discrete variables, we propose the usage of the Gower distance (Sect. 2.2). The Gower distance is particularly suitable for datasets with mixed data types, as it can handle both types of variables effectively.

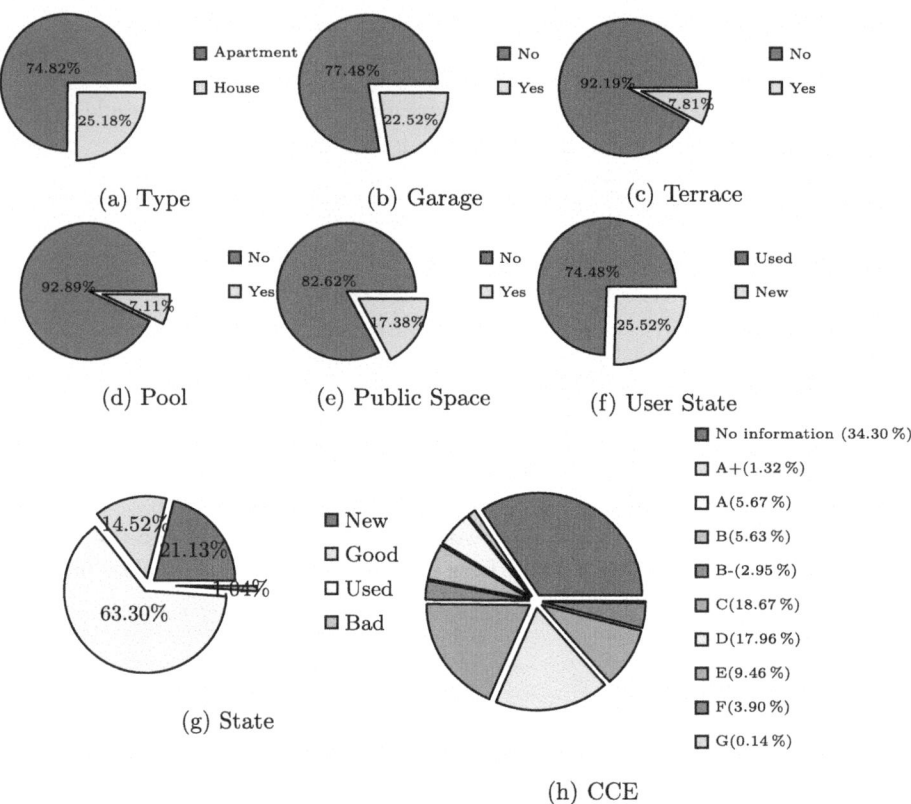

Fig. 1. Frequencies for different variables.

5.1 Geographical Filtering

Since properties with the highest degree of similarity are generally located within proximity, as their contextual conditions and available amenities are usually consistent, the proposed method starts by grouping all properties that are geographically close to each other. To identify these groups, the algorithm follows a two-step approach. First, it defines an n-kilometre radius around the centroid of a target property's postal code. Using the Haversine distance (Sect. 2.1), the proposed methodology calculates the geodesic distance between the centroid of the target property's postal code and those of other postal codes. This step serves as a computationally efficient preprocessing filter, as calculating Haversine distances is significantly less demanding than computing road network distances. By narrowing down the set of candidate postal codes using this method, the algorithm reduces the computational burden in the subsequent step. In the second step, the algorithm refines the selection by calculating the distances of the road network between the centroids within the same n-kilometre radius,

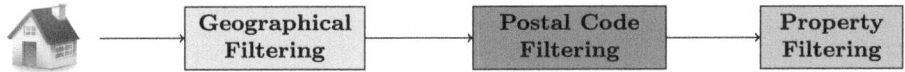

Fig. 2. Pipeline

ID	Garage	Area	...	Construction Year
1	No	122	...	1992
2	Yes	112	...	2010
3	Yes	234	...	2000
4	Yes	395.5	...	1975

ID	Garage	Area	...	Construction Year
5	Yes	100	...	1994
6	No	98	...	2003
7	No	367	...	983
8	Yes	55	...	2021

Target

	5	6	7	8
1	sim(1,5)	sim(1,6)	sim(1,7)	sim(1,8)
2	sim(2,5)	sim(2,6)	sim(2,7)	sim(2,8)
3	sim(3,5)	sim(3,6)	sim(3,7)	sim(3,8)
4	sim(4,5)	sim(4,6)	sim(4,7)	sim(4,8)

$$sim_{pc} = \frac{1}{m \cdot n} \sum_{i=1}^{m} \sum_{j=1}^{n} sim(i,j)$$

Fig. 3. Postal Code Similarities Process ($sim(i,j)$ represents the similarity between houses i and j, and sim_{pc} presents the average similarity between postal codes)

accounting for actual road paths. The result is a list of properties located within an n-kilometre boundary around the target centroid, within which all nearby centroids are selected for further analysis.

5.2   Postal Code Filtering

After reducing the list of properties to the most relevant ones, the proposed framework focusses on comparing postal codes. In this case, we define a postal code as a group of properties within the same geographic area. As mentioned, a property is characterised by a collection of physical traits which can be discrete (e.g. state) and continuous (e.g. property size). To compute the similarity between two postal codes, we compare the properties within each code by evaluating all possible property pairs (one from each postal code). The similarity of each pair is measured using the Gower similarity (see Sect. 2.2). These pairwise scores are stored in a similarity matrix, where each cell represents the similarity between a specific property from the target postal code and a property from a candidate postal code (as illustrated in Fig. 3). The overall similarity between the two postal codes is then calculated as the average of all values in this matrix. Based on this similarity score, a subgroup of postal codes that are most similar to the target is selected for further analysis.

5.3   Property Filtering

With this new subgroup of properties, the proposed method progresses to the last step: compare single properties. This is done by comparing each property with the target, using the Gower distance (Fig. 4). With this, we obtain a list of properties ranked by their similarity to the target. The Gower similarity,

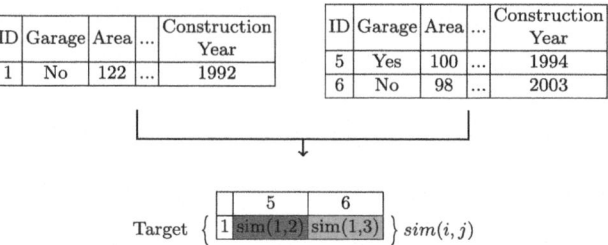

Fig. 4. Properties Similarities Process ($sim(i,j)$ represents the similarity between properties i and j)

which ranges from 0 to 1, is used to measure how similar each property is to the target; lower values indicate greater similarity. Finally, the properties are ranked by minimising both their similarity distance and geographic distance from the target property, and the highest k most comparable properties are returned.

6   Experimental Setup

To evaluate the performance of the proposed methodology, we applied an iterative process throughout the data set, where each property was treated as the reference (or target) in turn, and a group of recommended comparables was generated. Establishing a ground truth for this task was particularly challenging, as real estate agent recommendations are often based on subjective factors such as experience, intuition, and client preferences, which are not systematically recorded. To address this, we defined a method to generate a proxy ground truth: for each property, a set of nearby properties was identified based on geographical proximity (as in the proposed method), and from these, combinations of k properties were evaluated to find the subset that minimised the coefficient of variation between the attributes of the properties. This ensured both spatial and statistical homogeneity. We defined the parameters for the proposed approach based on expert input. The maximum radius of 2km was determined by an expert as the distance at which the properties are affected by the same amenities, and we selected the top 5 properties ($k = 5$) for comparison. Due to the computational complexity of evaluating all combinations, this process was applied to a randomly selected subset of 84 310 instances (20% of the dataset).

To assess the impact of the methodological choices on the quality of the recommendations, we compared two approaches. The first replicates standard real estate practices, including postal code filtering (as described in Sect. 5). The second omits postal code filtering, relying solely on geographical proximity. This comparison evaluates whether postal code filtering significantly influences the quality and consistency of recommendations.

Table 3. Recommendation metrics with and without postal code

Metric	With Postal Code	Without Postal Code
↑ Intra-list Diversity	**4.05** ± 1.31	3.99 ± 1.37
↑ Precision (%)	65.43 ± 47.53	**65.91** ± 47.37
↑ Recall (%)	65.43 ± 47.53	**65.91** ± 47.37
↑ NDCG (%)	17.65 ± 14.47	**17.86** ± 14.49
↑ F1-score (%)	21.87 ± 15.92	**22.03** ± 15.87
↑ Hit Rate (%)	65.50 ± 47.54	**65.98** ± 47.38
↑ MAP (%)	47.37 ± 43.03	**48.00** ± 43.15
↑ MRR (%)	47.43 ± 43.05	**48.06** ± 43.18
↑ PAP (%)	53.96 ± 43.81	**54.49** ± 43.82
↓ Execution Time (s)	0.5385 ± 0.3671	**0.3881** ± 0.3199

We used a variety of evaluation metrics to assess the effectiveness of both approaches in ranking and recommending relevant items. These include: Intra-list diversity, precision @ k, recall @ k, F1 score @ k, Normalized Discounted Cumulative Gain (NDCG), Hit rate, Mean Average Precision (MAP), Mean Reciprocal Rank (MRR), Partial AUC + Precision@k (PAP), and Execution Time (in seconds). In all experiments, unit weights were assigned to each feature, treating all variables as equally important in the similarity calculation. All experiments were carried out using an AMD Ryzen 7 7745HX CPU, 16 GB DDR5 RAM at 5600 MHz, and Python 3.11.4.

7   Results and Discussion

This section presents and discusses the findings obtained from the study conducted using the proposed method. We report results for two configurations: with and without the inclusion of postal code information. Each metric is calculated per property, and the mean and standard deviation are shown to reflect overall performance and its variability between properties. Table 3 presents the performance of the proposed methodology evaluated using the metrics presented in Sect. 6. In addition, we use bold to highlight values in the *Without Postal Code* configuration that are significantly better than the corresponding values in the *With Postal Code* configuration. Statistical significance is determined using the Wilcoxon signed rank test at a significance level 5%.

From these results, we can see that the configuration without postal code information consistently outperforms the alternative on most metrics. In particular, it generates statistically significant improvements in precision, recall, NDCG, F1 score, MAP, MRR, and PAP. These improvements suggest that removing postal code constraints allows the recommendation algorithm to access a broader and more flexible pool of candidate properties, which may lead to the identification of comparables that are more relevant in terms of physical and structural attributes, even if they fall outside strict postal boundaries. In terms of efficiency, the *Without Postal Code* configuration also shows a clear advantage, with a shorter average execution time. This reduction in computational cost is due to the simplified filtering process, which avoids the additional overhead of incorporating postal code processing into the similarity computation. However, this performance gain comes with a minor trade-off in diversity. The *With Postal Code* configuration achieves higher intra-list diversity, indicating that it tends to recommend a more varied set of properties. This could be attributed to the geographic segmentation introduced by postal codes, which can encourage the selection of properties from different microlocations within the same broader area. While diversity is a helpful attribute in recommendation systems, one can argue that, in this case, a smaller intra-list diversity can also represent that the configuration *Without Postal Code* recommends properties that are closely related, meaning that the recommendations are more focused and potentially relevant for the target property.

In summary, the results demonstrate that the proposed recommendation approach is both effective and adaptable across different configurations. By combining geographic filtering with property-level attribute comparison, the method consistently identifies relevant and meaningful comparables. The evaluation shows that the approach performs well under varying conditions (whether or not postal code information is included), highlighting its robustness and flexibility.

8   Conclusion

In an increasingly complex and competitive real estate market, understanding the multifaceted factors that influence property valuation is essential for both buyers and sellers. Real estate agents play a critical role in navigating this landscape, offering not only market expertise but also emotional and strategic support throughout the transaction process. This paper proposes a methodology to support agents by automating the identification of similar properties based on geographic and physical characteristics. By simplifying and accelerating the agents' workflow, the approach contributes to improving the overall efficiency and responsiveness of the real estate market. Furthermore, by evaluating a simplified version of this method, the study explores the trade-offs between computational efficiency and effectiveness. The results show that, while both approaches have satisfactory results, not incorporating postal code information leads to statistically significant improvements in key performance metrics such as precision, recall, and F1 score. Looking ahead, future work could focus on enriching the model with additional contextual data, such as the presence and quality of local amenities, to better characterise postal codes and reflect the qualitative aspects that influence property value. Another potential direction involves applying variable weighting to emphasise features that agents consider most important, such as location or number of bedrooms. Furthermore, establishing a reliable ground truth, ideally curated or validated by domain experts, would be essential to more accurately assess model performance and determine the true similarity between properties.

Acknowledgments. This work is funded by national funds through FCT - Fundação para a Ciência e a Tecnologia, I.P., under the support UID/50014/2023 (https://doi. org/10.54499/UID/50014/2023). We also extend our sincere thanks to Confidencial Imobiliária for providing both the data and valuable insights that contributed to this research.

Disclosure of Interests. The authors have no competing interests to declare that are relevant to the content of this article.

References

1. Batista, P., Marques, J.L.: Automated housing price valuation and spatial data. In: Gervasi, O., et al. (eds.) ICCSA 2021. LNCS, vol. 12952, pp. 366–381. Springer, Cham (2021). https://doi.org/10.1007/978-3-030-86973-1_26
2. Chopde, N.R., Nichat, M.: Landmark based shortest path detection by using A* and haversine formula. Int. J. Innov. Res. Comput. Commun. Eng. (2013)
3. Das, S.S.S., Ali, M.E., Li, Y.-F., Kang, Y.-B., Sellis, T.: Boosting house price predictions using geo-spatial network embedding. Data Min. Knowl. Disc. **35**(6), 2221–2250 (2021). https://doi.org/10.1007/s10618-021-00789-x
4. Diaz III, J.: The process of selecting comparable sales. Apprais. J. (1990)
5. Geng, M.N.: Fundamental drivers of house prices in advanced economies. Technical report WP/18/164, International Monetary Fund (2018)
6. Gower, J.C.: A general coefficient of similarity and some of its properties. Biometrics (1971)
7. Knoll, J., Groß, R., Schwanke, A., Rinn, B., Schreyer, M.: Applying recommender approaches to the real estate e-commerce market. In: Innovations for Community Services (I4CS 2018) (2018)
8. Lessani, M.N., Li, Z.: Sgwr: similarity and geographically weighted regression. Int. J. Geogr. Inf. Sci. (2024)
9. Polohakul, J., Chuangsuwanich, E., Suchato, A., Punyabukkana, P.: Real estate recommendation approach for solving the item cold-start problem. IEEE Access (2021)
10. Ribeiro, R., Poeschl, G., Santos, A.C.: The different sides of the housing crisis in portugal: a contribution to building inclusive, fair, and effective solutions. Polit. Psychol. (2025)
11. Sharma, M., Mann, S.: A survey of recommender systems: approaches and limitations. Int. J. Innov. Eng. Technol. (2013)
12. Yu, Y., Wang, C., Zhang, L., Gao, R., Wang, H.: Geographical proximity boosted recommendation algorithms for real estate. In: Hacid, H., Cellary, W., Wang, H., Paik, H.-Y., Zhou, R. (eds.) WISE 2018. LNCS, vol. 11234, pp. 51–66. Springer, Cham (2018). https://doi.org/10.1007/978-3-030-02925-8_4

Feature Tokeniser-Transformer Autoencoders for Interpretable Tabular Anomaly Detection

J. C. Huskisson[1]($\boxtimes$)(iD), J. Grobler[1](iD), and A. H. Basson[2](iD)

[1] Department of Industrial Engineering, Stellenbosch University,
Stellenbosch, South Africa
20962452@sun.ac.za
[2] Department of Mechanical and Mechatronic Engineering, Stellenbosch University,
Stellenbosch 7602, South Africa

Abstract. This paper presents the feature tokeniser-transformer autoencoder (FT-TAE), a novel adaptation of the FT-Transformer's per-feature tokenisation for inherently interpretable unsupervised tabular anomaly detection. Tailored for mixed-type tabular data, FT-TAE leverages feature-wise token reconstruction. Per-token bottlenecks produce feature-specific error signals, directly linking anomalous predictions to individual features. By reconstructing each feature token independently and maintaining feature dependencies through attention, FT-TAE promotes interpretable anomaly detection while achieving competitive detection performance and statistical gains over state-of-the-art unsupervised anomaly detectors on benchmark datasets. Model interpretability is further demonstrated on a synthetic dataset through comparative analysis with kernel SHAP, a widely adopted industry standard for feature attributions.

Keywords: Anomaly Detection · Unsupervised Learning · Tabular Data

1 Introduction

Anomaly detection (AD) involves the identification of exceptional data across diverse industries such as cybersecurity, healthcare, and finance. These real-world AD efforts face common obstacles, such as highly imbalanced class distributions, complex feature dependencies, mixed-type datasets, and critically, the unavailability of annotated data [16]. Due to the associated time and cost of label annotation, unsupervised AD approaches, which work without label-awareness, are the go-to approach for industry implementations of AD [17]. Unsupervised AD faces fundamental limitations when applied to tabular data which often contain heterogeneous features. Most anomaly detectors, including neural network-based approaches, expect real-valued vectors and thus require encoding or embedding conversions in order to handle categorical columns [8].

© The Author(s), under exclusive license to Springer Nature Switzerland AG 2026
J. Valente de Oliveira et al. (Eds.): EPIA 2025, LNAI 16121, pp. 256–268, 2026.
https://doi.org/10.1007/978-3-032-05176-9_20

One-hot encoding is a commonly used technique for handling mixed-type data in ML, but it risks the creation of sparse and high-dimensional input data in the case of highly cardinal features which distort distance metrics. Manual encoding strategies are diverse and useful on a per-dataset, per-detector basis. For example, histogram-based outlier score (HBOS) and other methods that assume feature independence are incompatible with one-hot but run smoothly under ordinal or frequency encodings [5].

More recent tabular learning approaches, specifically those that use deep learning, have turned to learned embeddings that capture the predictive signal of each feature through dense vector representations [2,6]. Learned embeddings preserve semantic information between categories and solve the issue of sparsity introduced by one-hot encoding. Attention mechanisms create robust feature embeddings that are contextualised by one another. The preservation of semantic feature information between features not only benefits prediction logic, but also improves user feedback by allowing finer-grained prediction attributions [2].

Understandable model predictions are especially useful in AD scenarios where humans have to decide how to deal with flagged anomalies. Intuitive model explanations, or inherently understandable model outputs, can accelerate root cause analysis and reduce time spent on investigating false positives. This benefit is especially evident when working with high-dimensional data, where a single anomaly score must be interpreted across rows containing tens or hundreds of features—as is the case with traditional AEs. Modern approaches to AD often adopt neural network-based architectures, which lack transparency; while these approaches achieve high predictive performance, understanding their decision logic is usually infeasible due to the large number of parameters involved [12].

The field of explainable artificial intelligence (XAI) is concerned with uncovering the decision logic of complex black-box machine learning models [4]. Many different explanation approaches exist and they are either model-specific (intrinsic) or model-agnostic and post-hoc in nature. Model-agnostic approaches work for any detector and are usually more computationally intensive than model-specific approaches. Examples include kernel SHAP's slower, but agnostic, feature attributions compared to the model-specific, speedier, depth-based isolation forest feature importance (Local-DIFFI) and residual explainer (RXP) attributions for the isolation forest (IF) and autoencoder (AE) architectures respectively [4,14,15].

The key contributions of this paper are a novel AE architecture that unifies heterogeneous feature handling with interpretable AD through per-token reconstruction error (RE) signals. Empirical evidence that the proposed architecture can match or exceed traditional methods for unsupervised tabular learning while providing explainability benefits crucial for practical deployment is provided. The rest of this paper comprises a related work section (Sect. 2), a discussion of the proposed FT-TAE architecture (Sect. 3), a description of the evaluation methodology and results (Sect. 4), an interpretability evaluation on a synthetic dataset (Sect. 5), and, finally, a conclusion and future work section (Sect. 6).

2   Related Work

AEs are neural network-based models that are extensively used for deep-learning-based AD. The models consist of an encoder and decoder component with a typically low-dimensional "bottleneck" for added regularisation [17]. The models learn a compressed manifold of the input data by minimising RE. It follows that the model struggles to recreate rare data that are not a part of the normal data generating distribution (anomalies). Thus a higher degree of RE means a higher degree of anomalousness. Figure 1 shows a typical hourglass AE architecture.

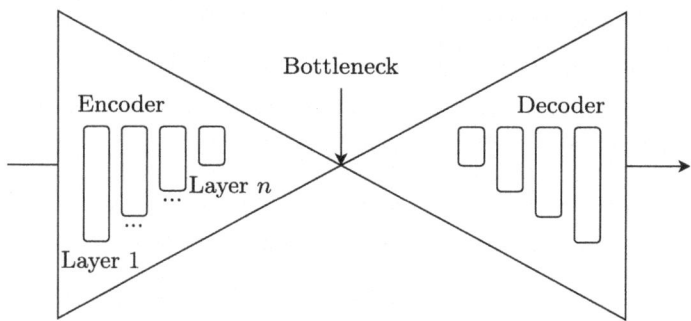

Fig. 1. A typical AE architecture.

Being neural network-based models, AEs are fundamentally designed to consume and reconstruct continuous-valued inputs. To handle discrete features intrinsically, AEs require variational extensions and specialised reparameterisation techniques [10]. The models may also struggle to capture complex inter-feature dependencies due to their compressed dense-vector latent representations and have also been criticised for easily overgeneralising by reconstructing anomalies too accurately [3].

To overcome the lack of feature-feature information inherent to MLP AEs, FT-TAE adopts attention as proposed by Vaswani *et al.* [18]. As previously mentioned, more recent deep tabular learning endeavors have found success by focusing on attention-based embeddings and this research builds on those foundations [6,9]. Attention enables each input token to compute a relevance score with every other token during the forward pass and then combine them to create a context-aware and semantically informed embedding that captures global dependencies in the input data.

Huang *et al.* introduced the TabTransformer, which applies multi-head self-attention to embedded categorical variables to produce contextualised feature representations [9]. The approach was shown to significantly outperform standard multilayer perceptrons (MLPs) for supervised- and semi-supervised learning on tabular data and matched the performance of the state-of-the-art for tabular data modelling, namely gradient-boosted decision trees ensemble algorithms. Gorishniy *et al.* proposed the FT-Transformer, which extends the logic of the TabTransformer to apply attention across every feature whether continuous or categorical [6]. The FT-Transformer's feature tokeniser embeds each input feature as a dense vector token, representing each feature individually. Transformer layers are then applied over the resulting sequence of tokens. For categorical features, the model assigns an integer mapping to each category in every feature. The model then extracts vectors from a shared embedding table to represent the categories.

The FT-Transformer appends a learned [CLS] token to the input sequence, which attends to the other tokens through self-attention and is subsequently used for final predictions. The token aggregates information across input features and provides a global representation of the data. The FT-Transformer achieved strong results, outperforming other deep learning methods in most evaluations. Importantly, the FT-Transformer and TabTransformer were developed for prediction tasks under full supervision and have not been applied in reconstruction-based, unsupervised AD frameworks (Fig. 2).

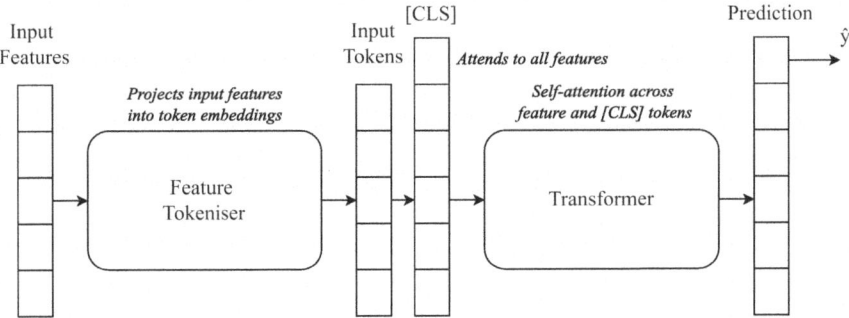

Fig. 2. FT-Transformer tokenisation and prediction logic.

3 FT-Transformer Autoencoders for Unsupervised Anomaly Detection

This section presents the FT-TAE, a reconstruction-based anomaly detector that adapts the FT-Transformer tokenisation logic for tabular data by embedding each column (continuous via a learned linear projection and categorical via learned embeddings indexed by category mappings) into token vectors. FT-Transformer's tokenisation strategy provides FT-TAE with per-feature error signals that drive model interpretability. The FT-TAE consists of transformer layers, and standard multi-layer perceptron layers that are tasked with gradually compressing and reconstructing the embedding size of the feature tokens. The key innovation lies in transforming the classification-oriented FT-Transformer into a reconstruction-based anomaly detector while preserving its elegant handling of heterogeneous features. Figure 3 shows the proposed model architecture where k_{red} represents the number of feed-forward layers and n_{pre} and n_{post} represent the number of transformer layers in the encoder and decoder.

The FT-TAE follows the PreNorm variant of the transformer architecture inherited from the FT-Transformer, where each transformer block applies layer normalisation before the multi-head self-attention and feed-forward network modules, with residual connections bypassing each sub-layer [6]. In the encoder, after the transformer blocks build contextual representations, each token's embedding is passed through a token-wise, rectified gated linear unit (ReGLU)-activated, feed-forward layer that reduces its embedding dimensionality to a lower-dimensional "bottleneck" vector. Every token is compressed independently by the same fraction and number of feed-forward layers between token and bottleneck dimensions—these are tuneable parameters which allow smoother gradual compression ratios. As in the original FT-Transformer, FT-TAE also learns an additive bias vector for each feature token so that the model adjusts each feature's initial embedding independently before attention and bottleneck operations.

Drawing from the [CLS] token logic proposed by Gorishniy *et al.*, FT-TAE appends a learned [CLS] token to capture global feature dependencies, detaches it before dimensionality reduction, and reattaches it afterward to preserve cross-feature information. The [CLS] token guides per-feature reconstruction through a dedicated global reconstruction path that captures global dependencies. Self-attention layers are used before and after the feed-forward bottleneck. Pre-bottleneck attention builds a richer global context before compression, and post-bottleneck attention enables contextualised feature reconstruction. The decoder up-projects each compressed token back toward the original token space before post-bottleneck attention, thereafter separate per-token heads perform feature reconstruction. Each continuous feature is reconstructed by a dedicated linear regressor, while each categorical feature is reconstructed by a dedicated classification head producing logits over its categories.

The model is trained end-to-end by minimising a per-token reconstruction loss i.e. mean-squared error (MSE) for continuous columns and cross-entropy for categorical columns, summing both terms and scaling each by an optional learnable uncertainty weight to accommodate different loss scalings [11]. Both error types are retained in the final anomaly score and cross-entropy is derived from the classification logits produced by the decoder. The two terms capture complementary anomaly behaviour: numerical deviations and low-likelihood categorical values.

Marginally better performance was observed without the uncertainty parameters, perhaps due to a level of intrinsic loss scaling that emerges from two design elements: the standardisation of continuous features to unit variance and the averaging of loss components over their respective feature counts, preventing either continuous or categorical features from dominating the total loss based on quantity rather than reconstruction difficulty. While this study retains equal weighting of continuous and categorical losses, learning uncertainty weights to

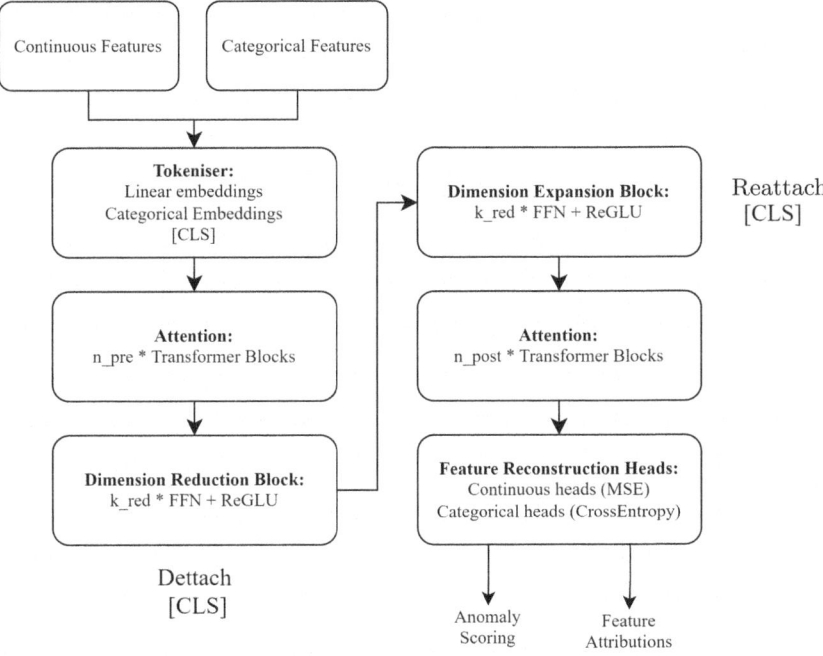

Fig. 3. Feature tokeniser-transformer autoencoder (FT-TAE) architecture.

rebalance them may improve performance on other datasets with strongly imbalanced feature types.

As in the original FT-Transformer paper, linear attention is applied for high-dimensional datasets such as backdoor (196 features, mostly categorical) [7]. Automatic mixed precision (AMP) with gradient scaling is also enabled, which reduces memory needs while maintaining numerical stability. Employing Linformer-style key-value compression, attention complexity is reduced from $O(n^2)$ to $O(n)$ with the "headwise" sharing policy and an embedding size of 128 [6,19].

4   Benchmark Evaluation

The FT-TAE was evaluated against three state-of-the-art anomaly detectors namely, IF, HBOS, and a traditional MLP AE, on three classical AD benchmarks obtained from ADBench, namely Cardiotocography, hepatitis, and backdoor (see Table 1) [7,13]. Notably, the study uses a 2,000 sample subset of the backdoor dataset. The evaluation applied a common heuristic to classify categorical and continuous features. The classification logic was simple and only served as a design choice to provide a consistent and fair comparison between all models when handling heterogeneous data. Non-numeric columns, or numeric columns that are integer-like with a low cardinality were considered to be categorical and features with more than twenty non-integer numeric unique values were considered to be continuous.

Table 1. Dataset characteristics across three AD benchmarks.

Dataset	Samples	Features	% Anomaly	Cat.	Cont.	Domain
Backdoor	2,000	196	2.44%	158	38	Network
Cardiotocography	2,114	21	22.04%	7	14	Healthcare
Hepatitis	80	19	16.25%	13	6	Healthcare

This study adopted the same architectural settings as described by the FT-Transformer paper. FT-TAE implemented 192-dimensional embeddings (128-dimensional on backdoor), 8 attention heads, AdamW optimiser, and feed-forward expansion ratios ranging from $2/3$ to $8/3$ ($5/4$ in the case of backdoor) with a batch size of 256. The evaluation limited transformer depth to 1–4 layers each for encoder and decoder to maintain tractability. The model used gradient clipping, early stopping on validation reconstruction loss, and standard dropout in the attention and feed-forward layers. After creating identical data splits for each model tuner, the models underwent 100 Optuna trials guided by Tree-structure Parzen Estimator (TPE) sampling with 3-fold cross-validation on the training loop to mitigate overfitting [1]. See Table 2 for search ranges.

The final models undergo three rounds of 10-fold cross-validation in the case of Cardiotocography and Backdoor, and 6 rounds of 5-fold cross-validation for the Hepatitis dataset. Analysis across thirty folds enables robust statistical analysis of the results. Importantly, the cross-validation seeds were varied across each run of the final analysis (55–57 and 55–60). A simple assumption was made to further reduce FT-TAE's search space. It was assumed that by first optimising a simple MLP AE, that it was possible to identify a "good enough" compression ratio for the FT-TAE on a given dataset. The MLP AE's bottleneck fraction and number of layers before, and therefore after, the bottleneck were tuned and used to reduce the search space of FT-TAE. These two values were passed onto the feed-forward component of the FT-TAE where parameter values were sampled from that neighbourhood.

Performance was assessed using area under the receiver operating characteristic curve (AUROC) and area under the precision-recall curve (PRAUC), with the latter used as the objective for Optuna tuning due to the imbalanced nature of AD datasets. Reconstruction-based methods compute anomaly scores as the total RE per sample, which applies to the AE and FT-TAE, but the FT-TAE maintains token-wise outputs that can be decomposed into feature-wise errors. HBOS, a statistical, frequency-based approach and the state-of-the-art tree-based method, IF, used their native scoring functions. The average AUROC and PRAUC metrics across 30 folds are reported in Tables 4, 5 and 6.

Statistical analysis using Mann-Whitney U tests (see Table 3) revealed that FT-TAE significantly outperformed traditional AEs across all three

Table 2. Hyperparameter search ranges for each model.

FT-TAE			AE		
Parameters	LB	UB	Parameters	LB	UB
transformer layers (enc.)	1	4	encoder layers	2	6
transformer layers (dec.)	1	4	bottleneck fraction	0.30	0.50
MLP layers	*From AE tuner*		dropout	0.10	0.50
bottleneck fraction	*From AE tuner*		learning rate	1e−05	1e−03
feed-forward ratio	0.667	2.667	weight decay	1e−06	1e−03
feed-forward dropout	0.10	0.50			
attention dropout	0.10	0.50			
learning rate (log-uniform)	1e−05	1e−03			
weight decay (log-uniform)	1e−06	1e−03			
IF			HBOS		
Parameters	LB	UB	Parameters	LB	UB
estimators	100	500	bins	10	50
max samples	0.50	1.00	alpha	0.10	0.90
max features	0.50	1.00	contamination	0.02	0.20

datasets ($p < 0.002$), addressing a key limitation of dense-vector reconstruction approaches. On the Backdoor dataset, FT-TAE also achieved superior AUC performance compared to state-of-the-art IF baseline (mean AUROC: 0.849) and statistically similar performance on Cardiotocography, demonstrating its robustness on high-dimensional mixed-type data. For the Hepatitis dataset, FT-TAE performed comparably to state-of-the-art methods (IF and HBOS), again providing the highest mean AUROC, while providing the additional benefit of feature-level anomaly attributions.

5 Interpretability Evaluation

This section shows how per-feature RE signals, made possible by feature-token embeddings and per-token compression, can be used to perform efficient local anomaly attributions. An FT-TAE is trained to detect anomalies on a synthetic mixed-type dataset. Feature attributions are calculated, timed, and visualised, side-by-side, with the popular kernel SHAP algorithm. Kernel SHAP, being a post-hoc XAI method, relies on expensive perturbation-based sampling. FT-TAE's intrinsic, or model-specific, approach uses per-token RE signals and provides interpretation without performing extra passes or requiring additional training. The synthetic financial dataset simulates transaction records with numerical and categorical features, designed to mimic real-world AD scenarios.

Table 3. Mann-Whitney U test results for model comparisons across datasets.

Metric	Model Comparison	Dataset		
		Hepatitis	Cardiotocography	Backdoor
PRAUC	FTAE vs VanillaAE	U = 667.00, p = 0.0013*	U = 835.00, p < 0.0001*	U = 758.00, p < 0.0001*
	FTAE vs HBOS	U = 467.00, p = 0.8063	U = 733.00, p < 0.0001*	U = 384.00, p = 0.3329
	FTAE vs IF	U = 486.00, p = 0.5978	U = 346.00, p = 0.1260	U = 759.00, p < 0.0001*
	VanillaAE vs HBOS	U = 284.00, p = 0.0143*	U = 333.00, p = 0.0850	U = 133.00, p < 0.0001*
	VanillaAE vs IF	U = 304.50, p = 0.0318*	U = 22.00, p < 0.0001*	U = 408.00, p = 0.5395
	HBOS vs IF	U = 464.00, p = 0.8410	U = 90.00, p < 0.0001*	U = 788.00, p < 0.0001*
AUROC	FTAE vs AE	U = 662.00, p = 0.0017*	U = 862.00, p < 0.0001*	U = 767.00, p < 0.0001*
	FTAE vs HBOS	U = 408.50, p = 0.5418	U = 886.00, p < 0.0001*	U = 590.50, p = 0.0384*
	FTAE vs IF	U = 397.50, p = 0.4388	U = 479.00, p = 0.6735	U = 724.00, p = 0.0001*
	AE vs HBOS	U = 183.50, p = 0.0001*	U = 447.00, p = 0.9705	U = 350.00, p = 0.1412
	AE vs IF	U = 172.00, p < 0.0001*	U = 22.50, p < 0.0001*	U = 400.00, p = 0.4642
	HBOS vs IF	U = 441.00, p = 0.8994	U = 18.00, p < 0.0001*	U = 513.50, p = 0.3516

Note: * indicates statistically significant differences ($p < 0.05$). U represents the Mann-Whitney U statistic.

Table 4. Backdoor dataset results across 30 folds.

Model	Seed:	55	56	57	Mean
FT-TAE	PRAUC:	0.2024	0.1767	0.1984	**0.1925**
	AUROC:	**0.8538**	**0.8488**	**0.8450**	**0.8492**
AE	PRAUC:	0.1012	0.0850	0.0951	0.0938
	AUROC:	0.7315	0.7099	0.6936	0.7117
HBOS	PRAUC:	**0.2088**	**0.2168**	**0.2326**	**0.2194**
	AUROC:	0.7596	0.7575	0.7531	**0.7567**
IF	PRAUC:	0.0850	0.0984	0.0774	0.0870
	AUROC:	0.7355	0.7328	0.7351	0.7345

The dataset contains 5, 000 total samples with 250 known anomalies with four continuous features (*amount, inverse inter-transaction time, user average spend, distance*) and three categorical features (*merchant type, day of week,* and *region*). Three anomaly types are injected into the dataset at a contamination rate of 5% namely, high value perturbations, long-distance transactions, and rapid transactions via controlled multiplicative and additive means. The perturbed features are tracked as ground truth.

Figure 4 shows a side-by-side bar-chart comparison of FT-TAE's normalised RE attributions versus kernel SHAP's normalised attributions on the top three confirmed anomalies. Total attribution runtime was also calculated. Figure 5 shows how the FT-TAE's per-feature REs may be aggregated to form global feature importance (GFI). FT-TAE GFI is plotted against kernel SHAP GFI and, in both figures, the perturbed features are coloured red. For both local and global feature importance, it is clear that both attribution methods accurately

Table 5. Cardiotocography dataset results across 30 folds.

Model	Seed:	55	56	57	Mean
FT-TAE	PRAUC:	0.4772	0.4530	0.4695	0.4666
	AUROC:	**0.7369**	0.7184	**0.7399**	0.7318
AE	PRAUC:	0.3537	0.3367	0.3308	0.3404
	AUROC:	0.5770	0.5820	0.5626	0.5739
HBOS	PRAUC:	0.3792	0.3748	0.3708	0.3749
	AUROC:	0.5638	0.5741	0.5623	0.5667
IF	PRAUC:	**0.4962**	**0.4964**	**0.4900**	**0.4942**
	AUROC:	0.7291	**0.7352**	0.7345	**0.7329**

Table 6. Hepatitis dataset results across 30 folds.

Model	Seed:	55	56	57	58	59	60	Mean
FT-TAE	PRAUC:	**0.6750**	**0.6183**	**0.6482**	**0.5569**	**0.6400**	**0.6433**	**0.6303**
	AUROC:	0.7789	0.7644	0.6900	0.6733	**0.8233**	0.7422	**0.7454**
AE	PRAUC:	0.4058	0.4305	0.4517	0.3662	0.5301	0.3898	0.4290
	AUROC:	0.5489	0.5667	0.5867	0.4722	0.5933	0.5122	0.5467
HBOS	PRAUC:	0.7286	0.4852	0.6186	0.5650	0.5567	0.6186	0.5954
	AUROC:	0.8678	0.7511	0.7900	0.7378	0.7789	0.7889	0.7857
IF	PRAUC:	0.5186	0.5652	0.6133	0.5383	0.5850	0.6126	**0.5722**
	AUROC:	**0.7978**	**0.7911**	**0.8022**	**0.7911**	0.7778	**0.7689**	**0.7881**

identified the features that most contributed to the anomalous predictions. The similarity between FT-TAE and kernel SHAP attributions is encouraging for future FT-TAE attribution endeavours and serves as a validation of the model's ability to identify feature contributions. Notably, leveraging FT-TAE's attention weights could further refine these explanations by exposing inter-feature dependencies.

FT-TAE GFI assigned greater importance to *merchant type* than kernel SHAP did. Interestingly, in the most anomalous sample, FT-TAE's local RE-based attribution correctly ranked *merchant type* as the second-most contributing feature, whereas kernel SHAP did not. For the synthetic dataset, the RE-based attributions of the FT-TAE were computed about eight thousand times faster than post-hoc perturbation-based SHAP (0.12 s and 1020.73 s on L4 GPU with 22.5 GB GPU RAM and 53.0 GB system RAM). This behaviour highlights the benefit of an intrinsically calculated explanation compared to model-agnostic approaches.

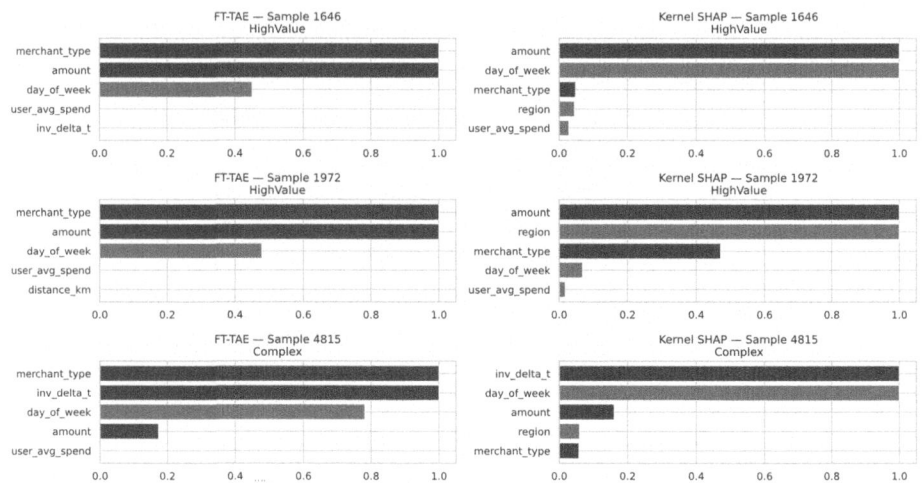

Fig. 4. Attribution comparisons across top 3 anomalous samples (perturbed features are coloured red). (Color figure online)

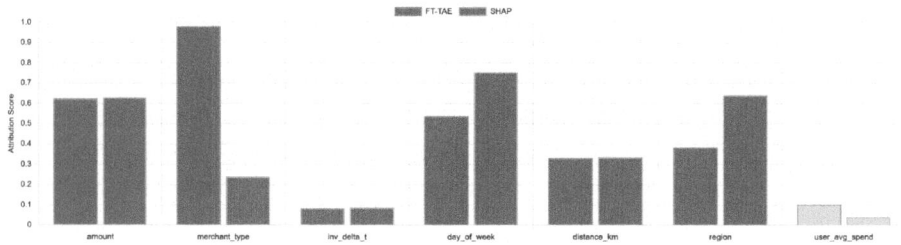

Fig. 5. Global feature importance: FT-TAE versus kernel SHAP (perturbed features are coloured red). (Color figure online)

6   Conclusions

This paper introduced the FT-TAE, a novel transformer-based AE that adapts the FT-Transformer's per-feature tokenisation strategy for scalable interpretable reconstruction-based AD in heterogeneous tabular data. By providing per-feature RE signals, through independent feature-token processing, the FT-TAE maintains interpretability while providing statistically significant gains over baseline models on mixed-type data with many categorical features.

Several limitations of this research warrant consideration. The method's effectiveness on extremely high-dimensional datasets requires further investigation. Additionally, while per-feature REs provide interpretability, more sophisticated attribution methods could further enhance explanation quality by incorporating attention maps. Thus, future work should explore several promising avenues including: extending the proposed FT-TAE architecture to include variational variants and mechanisms such as skip connections; developing methods to more effectively learn from the global [CLS] token; a thorough analysis of the FT-TAE's computational overhead; the exploration of deeper models and model variants. Finally, the integration of attention maps for anomaly attributions could provide an improved view of feature interactions. This research merits comprehensive user studies on real-world datasets to validate its benefits.

The FT-TAE represents a significant step toward unified interpretable AD for heterogeneous tabular data. By leveraging advances in supervised deep tabular learning while addressing specific challenges of unsupervised AD, FT-TAE offers a viable alternative to traditional approaches in situations where both detection performance and explainability are critical requirements. To the authors' best knowledge, this is the first unsupervised AD method that leverages FT-Transformer-style tokenisation for inherently explainable tabular reconstruction.

Acknowledgments. This work was funded by an industry partner that requested to remain anonymous. The sponsor had no involvement in study design, data collection and analysis, decision to publish, or preparation of the manuscript.

Disclosure of Interests. The authors do not have any competing interests to declare that are relevant to the content of this article.

References

1. Akiba, T., Sano, S., Yanase, T., Ohta, T., Koyama, M.: Optuna: a next-generation hyperparameter optimization framework. In: Proceedings of the 25th ACM SIGKDD International Conference on Knowledge Discovery and Data Mining (KDD 2019), Anchorage, AK, USA (2019)
2. Arik, S.Ö., Pfister, T.: TabNet: attentive interpretable tabular learning. In: Proceedings of the AAAI Conference on Artificial Intelligence, vol. 35, no. 8, pp. 6679–6687. AAAI Press, Virtual Event (2021). https://doi.org/10.1609/aaai.v35i8.16826
3. Bouman, R., Heskes, T.: Autoencoders for anomaly detection are unreliable. arXiv preprint arXiv:2501.13864 (2025). https://doi.org/10.48550/arXiv.2501.13864
4. Carletti, M., Terzi, M., Susto, G.A.: Interpretable anomaly detection with DIFFI: depth-based feature importance of isolation forest. Eng. Appl. Artif. Intell. **119**, 105730 (2023). https://doi.org/10.1016/j.engappai.2022.105730
5. Goldstein, M., Dengel, A.: Histogram-based outlier score (HBOS): a fast unsupervised anomaly detection algorithm. In: Poster and Demo Track of the European Conference on Machine Learning and Principles and Practice of Knowledge Discovery in Databases (ECML PKDD), pp. 59–64. University of Kaiserslautern, Kaiserslautern (2012)
6. Gorishniy, Y., Rubachev, I., Khrulkov, V., Babenko, A.: Revisiting deep learning models for tabular data. In: Advances in Neural Information Processing Systems, vol. 34, pp. 18932–18943. Curran Associates, Inc., Virtual Event (2021)
7. Han, S., Hu, X., Huang, H., Jiang, M., Zhao, Y.: ADBench: anomaly detection benchmark. In: Advances in Neural Information Processing Systems, vol. 35, pp. 32142–32159. Curran Associates, Inc., New Orleans (2022)
8. Hancock, J., Khoshgoftaar, T.: Survey on categorical data for neural networks. J. Big Data **7**, 28 (2020). https://doi.org/10.1186/s40537-020-00305-w

9. Huang, X., Khetan, A., Cvitkovic, M., Karnin, Z.: TabTransformer: tabular data modeling using contextual embeddings. In: Proceedings of the 9th International Conference on Learning Representations (ICLR). OpenReview.net, Virtual Event (2021)

10. Jang, E., Gu, S., Poole, B.: Categorical reparameterisation with Gumbel-Softmax. In: Proceedings of the 5th International Conference on Learning Representations (ICLR). OpenReview.net, Toulon (2017)

11. Kendall, A., Gal, Y., Cipolla, R.: Multi-task learning using uncertainty to weigh losses for scene geometry and semantics. In: Proceedings of the IEEE Conference on Computer Vision and Pattern Recognition (CVPR), pp. 7482–7491. IEEE Computer Society, Salt Lake City (2018). https://doi.org/10.1109/CVPR.2018.00781

12. Kim, D., Antariksa, G., Handayani, M.P., Lee, S., Lee, J.: Explainable anomaly detection framework for maritime main engine sensor data. Sensors **21**(15), 5200 (2021). https://doi.org/10.3390/s21155200

13. Liu, F.T., Ting, K.M., Zhou, Z.-H.: Isolation forest. In: Proceedings of the 2008 Eighth IEEE International Conference on Data Mining (ICDM), pp. 413–422. IEEE Computer Society, Washington, DC (2008). https://doi.org/10.1109/ICDM.2008.17

14. Lundberg, S.M., et al.: From local explanations to global understanding with explainable AI for trees. Nat. Mach. Intell. **2**, 56–67 (2020). https://doi.org/10.1038/s42256-019-0138-9

15. Oliveira, D.F.N., et al.: A new interpretable unsupervised anomaly detection method based on residual explanation. IEEE Access **10**, 1401–1409 (2022). https://doi.org/10.1109/ACCESS.2021.3137633

16. Pang, G., Shen, C., Cao, L., Van Den Hengel, A.: Deep learning for anomaly detection: a review. ACM Comput. Surv. **54**(2), 1–38 (2021). https://doi.org/10.1145/3439950

17. Ruff, L., et al.: A unifying review of deep and shallow anomaly detection. Proc. IEEE **109**(5), 756–795 (2021). https://doi.org/10.1109/JPROC.2021.3052449

18. Vaswani, A., et al.: Attention is all you need. In: Advances in Neural Information Processing Systems, vol. 30, pp. 5998–6008. Curran Associates, Inc., Long Beach (2017)

19. Wang, S., Li, B.Z., Khabsa, M., Fang, H., Ma, H.: Linformer: self-attention with linear complexity. arXiv preprint arXiv:2006.04768 (2020). https://doi.org/10.48550/arXiv.2006.04768

Benchmarking Time Series Feature Extraction for Algorithm Selection

Moisés Santos[1]([✉]), Vitor Cerqueira[1], and Carlos Soares[1,2]

[1] LIACC/Faculty of Engineering, University of Porto, Porto, Portugal
{mrsantos,vcerqueira,csoares}@fe.up.pt
[2] Fraunhofer AICOS Portugal, Porto, Portugal

Abstract. Effective selection of forecasting algorithms for time series data is a challenge in machine learning, impacting both predictive accuracy and efficiency. Metalearning, using features extracted from time series, offers a strategic approach to optimize algorithm selection. The utility of this approach depends on the amount of information the features contain about the behavior of the algorithms. Although there are several methods for systematic time series feature extraction, they have never been compared. This paper empirically analyzes the performance of each feature extraction method for algorithm selection and its impact on forecasting accuracy. Our study reveals that TSFRESH, TSFEATURES, and TSFEL exhibit comparable performance at algorithm selection accuracy, adeptly capturing time series characteristics essential for accurate algorithm selection. In contrast, Catch22 is found to be less effective for this purpose. In particular, TSFEL is identified as the most efficient method, balancing dimensionality and predictive performance. These findings provide insights for enhancing forecasting accuracy and efficiency through judicious selection of meta-feature extractors.

Keywords: Forecasting · Algorithm Selection · Feature Extraction · Feature Engineering

1 Introduction

The increasing complexity and diversity of time series data have posed substantial challenges in selecting the most appropriate forecasting algorithm. To address this issue, metalearning has emerged as a promising paradigm [6], using features extracted from time series to guide the algorithm selection process. In recent years, the field of machine learning (ML) has achieved significant advancements, particularly in the area of algorithm selection for time series forecasting [23].

The extraction of time series features is a critical step in the metalearning framework [29]. These features serve as a compact representation of the time series, capturing essential characteristics that influence the performance of the forecasting algorithms [33]. Multiple proposals of methods (and corresponding

© The Author(s), under exclusive license to Springer Nature Switzerland AG 2026
J. Valente de Oliveira et al. (Eds.): EPIA 2025, LNAI 16121, pp. 269–281, 2026.
https://doi.org/10.1007/978-3-032-05176-9_21

software) are available. Despite the growing body of research in this area, there remains a lack of comprehensive empirical studies that compare the effectiveness of different meta-feature extractors for forecasting algorithm selection.

This paper aims to fill this gap by providing an empirical comparison of various meta-feature extractors within the metalearning framework for algorithm selection. Specifically, we evaluate the performance of four prominent meta-feature extraction methods: TSFRESH [9], TSFEATURES [34], TSFEL [4], and Catch22 [17]. Each of these methods has its unique approach to capturing the properties of time series data, and their comparative performance remains under-explored in the context of algorithm selection for forecasting.

We analyze 5000 monthly time series from the M4 competition [21], focusing on the number of attributes generated by different meta-feature extraction methods, as feature space dimensionality directly impacts the efficiency and accuracy of the metalearning process. Our study evaluates the effectiveness of these features in two key aspects: their ability to represent the underlying time series characteristics for algorithm selection and their influence on the predictive performance of various forecasting algorithms.

In the following sections, we will review the existing literature on meta-feature extraction and metalearning, describe the experimental setup and methodologies used in this study, present and discuss the empirical findings, and conclude with recommendations for future research directions.

2 Background

2.1 Time Series Forecasting

Time series analysis is a crucial aspect of understanding temporal data. A univariate time series is one in which only one variable of interest is observed. Formally, a univariate time series can be represented as $y_t = \{y_t\}_{t=1}^{T}$, which is a sequence of observations that are ordered and evenly spaced in time [24]. In contrast, a multivariate time series involves observing two or more related variables over time. The frequency refers to the interval at which observations are recorded, which can be daily, weekly, monthly, or annually, corresponding to each observation representing one day, week, month, or year, respectively [13].

Time series forecasting involves using known observations to predict future values. Given a time series y_t, the goal is to find a function f such that $f(t) = y_{t+h} + \epsilon$ for all $t + h > T$ where ϵ is the forecast error and h denotes the forecast horizon [13]. If $h = 1$, the task is known as one-step ahead forecasting, whereas if $h > 1$, it is referred to as multi-step ahead forecasting. The mapping $\mathcal{A} : y_t \rightarrow f$ represents a forecasting model. These models leverage the relationship between past and future observations to make predictions.

ML models, such as neural networks, support vector machines, and ensemble methods, have shown promise in enhancing the accuracy of time series forecasts by effectively capturing non-linear relationships and interactions within the data [26]. One common approach in ML for time series forecasting is to use regression methods based on autoregressive notation [7]. In an autoregressive model, the future value y_{t+h} is predicted based on a linear combination of past observations. This can be formalized in the Eq. 1.

$$y_{t+h} = \phi_1 y_{t-1} + \phi_2 y_{t-2} + \cdots + \phi_p y_{t-p} + E_t \tag{1}$$

where $\phi_1, \phi_2, \ldots, \phi_p$ are the model parameters, p is the order of the autoregressive model, and E_t is the error term. In the context of ML, this can be generalized by Eq. 2.

$$\hat{y}_{t+h} = f(y_t, y_{t-1}, \ldots, y_{t-p+1}) \tag{2}$$

where f is a function approximated by an ML algorithm. The model is trained on historical time series data to learn the mapping from past observations to future values. This approach allows the model to capture both linear and non-linear dependencies in the data, making it a powerful tool for time series forecasting.

2.2   Metalearning for Algorithm Selection

Let $\mathcal{P}$ represent the space or collection of datasets d relevant to a specific task, such that $d \in \mathcal{P}$. Similarly, let $\mathcal{A}$ denote the space or portfolio of algorithms L applicable to tasks within $\mathcal{P}$, such that $L \in \mathcal{A}$. The mapping $\mathcal{S} : \mathcal{P} \to \mathcal{A}$ applies all algorithms L to all datasets d. From this mapping, we can access the space of performance measures $p : \mathcal{A} \times \mathcal{P} \to \mathbb{R}^n$. The Algorithm Selection Problem (ASP) involves searching within $\mathcal{S}$ for an algorithm L that optimizes a performance measure p for a given dataset d [28].

Given the complexity and the number of algorithms in the portfolio $\mathcal{A}$, finding an algorithm L that meets the desired predictive performance can be computationally expensive. Metalearning offers a way to reduce this cost by leveraging past experience to guide future algorithm selection [27].

Metalearning, or learning to learn, encompasses methods that utilize knowledge extracted from tasks, algorithms, or performance evaluations of algorithms to enhance predictive performance and efficiency in future applications [5,10]. As demonstrated by Hutter et al. (2019) [12], there are various approaches to metalearning. In this study, we focus on metalearning for algorithm recommendation based on meta-features.

Meta-feature-based metalearning uses ML to relate dataset characteristics to the relative performance of algorithms applied to those datasets [5]. For simplicity, we will refer to meta-feature-based metalearning simply as metalearning. This approach involves two main inputs: a set of n tasks, represented by n datasets $D = d_0, d_1, \ldots, d_n$, and a portfolio of m candidate algorithms or base learners $L = l_0, l_1, \ldots, l_m$.

The process begins with the characterization of the datasets, which involves extracting characteristics, known as meta-features, from each dataset. A meta-feature f is formally defined as a function $f : D \to \mathbb{R}^k$, returning a set of k values that describe the dataset d_i [1,29]. Next, the evaluation step applies the base learners L to the datasets D to obtain performance measures $p(L, D)$. The recommendation to be derived for each dataset, based on its meta-features, is termed the meta-target. The meta-target is determined by p and can take various forms: an algorithm, a set of algorithms, a ranking of algorithms, or a performance prediction [5].

The combination of meta-features and the meta-target constitutes the metadata. An ML algorithm is then applied to the metadata to induce a meta-model [5]. When a new dataset, such as a new time series, needs a prediction, the meta-model uses the meta-feature values of this dataset to recommend one of the ML algorithms from the portfolio for this specific task.

2.3   Meta-features for Time Series Data

Several sets of time series features have been proposed for various applications. Although not originally designed for algorithm selection, many feature extractors have been successfully applied for this purpose [23]. Based on the literature, we discuss the main methods.

TSFRESH: TSFRESH (Time Series Feature extraction based on scalable hypothesis tests) [9] is a framework that can extract over 700 features from time series data. These features capture a wide range of properties, including basic statistics (mean, variance), linear trends, and characteristics of the data's distribution and autocorrelation structure. TSFRESH aims to automatically extract these features and select the most relevant ones using hypothesis testing, making it highly effective for identifying important patterns and relationships in time series data.

TSFEL: TSFEL (Time Series Feature Extraction Library) [4] is another Python framework designed to extract a comprehensive set of features from time series data. It provides over 60 features, focusing on the statistical, temporal, and spectral properties of the data. TSFEL features include measures of central tendency, dispersion, and shape, as well as frequency domain characteristics like spectral entropy and dominant frequency components. This diversity of features allows TSFEL to capture both time-domain and frequency-domain characteristics of time series, making it a versatile tool for various applications.

Catch22: Catch22 (Canonical Time-series Characteristics) [17] is a Python package that offers a streamlined set of 22 features. These features are carefully selected to provide a comprehensive summary of the time series, covering properties such as entropy, correlation, and motif statistics. Catch22 is designed to be both computationally efficient and effective in capturing the essential characteristics of time series data. Its features are derived from a broad range of disciplines, ensuring robust performance across different types of time series.

TSFEATURES: TSFEATURES [34] is a feature extraction framework that provides a set of features specifically designed for time series forecasting. It offers a variety of 42 features, including measures of trend, seasonality, autocorrelation, and non-linearity. TSFEATURES focuses on capturing the underlying structure of the time series, making it useful for understanding long-term patterns and periodic behaviors. The features extracted by TSFEATURES are suitable for tasks involving time series decomposition and forecasting.

Each of these frameworks has its strengths and was studied for specific applications, but its effectiveness in algorithm selection has not been benchmarked. One of the objectives of this study is to compare the performance of these methods for the task of algorithm selection, providing information on their relative strengths.

2.4   Metalearning for Forecasting Algorithm Selection

The approaches proposed by Meade and Islam (2000) [22] and Prudêncio and Ludermir (2004) [27] were among the first to utilize metalearning for recommending time series forecasting models. Meade and Islam (2000) [22] investigated the selection of single statistical models and committees, evaluating their metalearning approach using data from the M-Competition (Makridakis et al., 1982) [19] and telecommunication-based time series. Prudêncio and Ludermir (2004) [27] analyzed the use of time series features for recommending rankings of statistical methods for time series forecasting, with experiments conducted on data from the M3 competition (Makridakis and Hibon, 2000) [20]. Both studies yielded promising results, demonstrating the effective application of metalearning in selecting time series forecasting models.

Subsequent research proposed various approaches, characterized by several dimensions. Studies by Meade and Islam (2000) [22], Prudêncio and Ludermir (2004) [27], Lemke and Gabrys (2010) [16], Widodo and Yang (2013) [35], Kück et al. (2016) [15], Ali et al. (2018) [2], and Santos et al. (2024) [32] employed their own sets of meta-features based on descriptive statistics, statistical tests, frequency domain measures (via Discrete Fourier Transform), autocorrelation coefficients, and relative performance of models. Ma et al. (2020) [18] developed a deep learning approach using Convolutional Neural Networks to learn a meta-level representation of time series.

ML models have shown competitive results compared to statistical models (Parmezan et al., 2019) [26]. Despite this, most studies use statistical methods as base learners, although Ma et al. (2020) [18] and Santos et al. (2024) [32] included other ML algorithms as base learners.

3   Experiments

3.1   Data Collection and Preprocessing

This study utilizes a comprehensive dataset of the first 5000 monthly time series from the M4 Competition [21]. The dataset is divided into training and testing sets according to the competition's guidelines, with 18 observations reserved for testing each series. To ensure robust evaluation of the metalearning setup, a k-fold cross-validation approach with 10 folds is applied to the metadata.

3.2 Meta-features Extraction

A diverse set of meta-features is extracted from each time series using previously mentioned methods.

We addressed missing values in the extracted features to ensure the robustness and reliability of the meta-feature datasets. For the TSFEATURES method, any features with missing values were removed from the dataset. For the TSFEL method, we considered only those features that were present across all time series. By including only available features, we ensured consistency and comparability of the meta-features extracted from different time series.

3.3 Base Learners

The base learners evaluated in this study are:

Multi-Layer Perceptron (MLP) [30]: A feedforward artificial neural network model that consists of multiple layers of nodes, with each layer fully connected to the next one. It is capable of capturing complex non-linear relationships in the data.

Neural Hierarchical Interpolation for Time Series (NHITS) [8]: A deep learning model designed for time series forecasting that leverages hierarchical interpolation, allowing it to effectively model time series data with multiple seasonalities and long-term dependencies.

DeepAR [31]: A probabilistic forecasting model based on autoregressive recurrent neural networks. It generates probabilistic forecasts by training on multiple related time series, capturing both temporal patterns and dependencies between series.

Temporal Convolutional Network (TCN) [3]: A deep learning architecture that uses causal convolutions to model temporal dependencies in time series data. TCNs are known for their ability to capture long-term dependencies and produce stable and accurate forecasts.

All the methods employed as base learners in this study are widely recognized and utilized for time series forecasting in research that showcases state-of-the-art results. Given the focus of this study on the empirical comparison of meta-feature extractors, we did not include additional forecasting methods. Instead, we concentrated on a selected set of well-established base learners to maintain clarity and relevance in our evaluation.

The implementations of these base learners are sourced from the `neuralforecast` package [25], which provides robust and efficient tools for time series forecasting. The hyperparameters for each of these base learners are detailed in Table 1. This table provides the specific settings used in our experiments, ensuring transparency and enabling replication of our results.

Table 1. Base-learners hyperparameters.

Model	Hyperparameters
MLP	max_steps = 1000, input_size = 36, scaler_type = 'robust', accelerator = 'cpu', random_seed = 14
NHITS	max_steps = 1000, input_size = 36, scaler_type = 'robust', accelerator = 'cpu', random_seed = 14
DeepAR	max_steps = 1000, input_size = 36, scaler_type = 'robust', accelerator = 'cpu', random_seed = 14
TCN	max_steps = 1000, input_size = 36, scaler_type = 'robust', accelerator = 'cpu', random_seed = 14

3.4 Metalearner

A Random Forest algorithm [11] is employed as the meta-learner, utilizing default hyperparameters except `sample_weight`, which is adjusted for `balanced` to handle the potential class imbalance in the metadata. The Random Forest model is chosen for its robustness and ability to handle high-dimensional data.

3.5 Meta-target

The meta-target is defined by the minimum Mean Absolute Error (MAE) achieved by the forecasting algorithms on each time series. The goal of the meta-learner is to predict the algorithm that yields the lowest MAE for a given set of meta-features.

To justify the use of appropriate performance measures for imbalanced class data in the meta-level evaluation, Table 2 presents the number of examples for each of the base learners. This distribution highlights the need for metrics that can accurately reflect the performance across varying frequencies of different base learners, ensuring a fair and comprehensive assessment of the meta-learner's predictive capabilities.

Table 2. Meta-target class distribution.

Model	Number
MLP	1534
NHITS	1739
DeepAR	946
TCN	781

3.6   Evaluation

Meta-level Evaluation: The performance of the meta-learner is evaluated using balanced accuracy, a metric that accounts for class imbalance by considering both the sensitivity and specificity of the predictions. This ensures a fair assessment of the meta-learner's ability to correctly identify the best forecasting algorithm across different types of time series.

Base Level Evaluation: At the base level, the forecasting algorithms are evaluated independently on the time series data to generate performance benchmarks. The MAE is used as the primary metric for this evaluation, providing a clear measure of the forecasting accuracy of each algorithm.

The Multi-Comparison Matrix (MCM) [14] framework is utilized to extract and compare the statistical performance of the forecasting algorithms. This framework incorporates the Wilcoxon signed-rank test and hierarchical Bayesian testing to ensure robust and reliable statistical comparisons.

Detailed documentation is provided to facilitate the replication of the study and further exploration by the research community[1].

4   Results and Discussion

Figure 1 presents the MCM showcasing the primary statistics from the meta-level evaluation of the different meta-feature extraction methods. The performance of each method is measured by balanced accuracy, ensuring a fair assessment across all classes. The methods evaluated include Catch22, TSFEATURES, TSFRESH, and TSFEL, along with a combined approach denoted as All, which incorporates all the aforementioned meta-feature extraction methods.

Mean-Balanced Accuracy	TSFEATURES 0.3597	All 0.3563	TSFEL 0.3480	TSFRESH 0.3425	Catch22 0.3322
TSFEATURES 0.3597	Mean-Difference / r>c / r=c / r<c / Wilcoxon p-value	0.0034 / 5/0/5 / 0.9219	0.0117 / 7/0/3 / 0.0645	0.0172 / 7/0/3 / 0.1055	0.0275 / 9/0/1 / 0.0098
All 0.3563	-0.0034 / 5/0/5 / 0.9219	-	0.0083 / 6/0/4 / 0.3223	0.0138 / 9/0/1 / 0.0059	0.0242 / 8/0/2 / 0.0195
TSFEL 0.3480	-0.0117 / 3/0/7 / 0.0645	-0.0083 / 4/0/6 / 0.3223	-	0.0055 / 6/0/4 / 0.3750	0.0158 / 8/0/2 / 0.0195
TSFRESH 0.3425	-0.0172 / 3/0/7 / 0.1055	-0.0138 / 1/0/9 / 0.0059	-0.0055 / 4/0/6 / 0.3750	-	0.0103 / 8/0/2 / 0.0488
Catch22 0.3322	-0.0275 / 1/0/9 / 0.0098	-0.0242 / 2/0/8 / 0.0195	-0.0158 / 2/0/8 / 0.0195	-0.0103 / 2/0/8 / 0.0488	If in bold, then p-value < 0.05

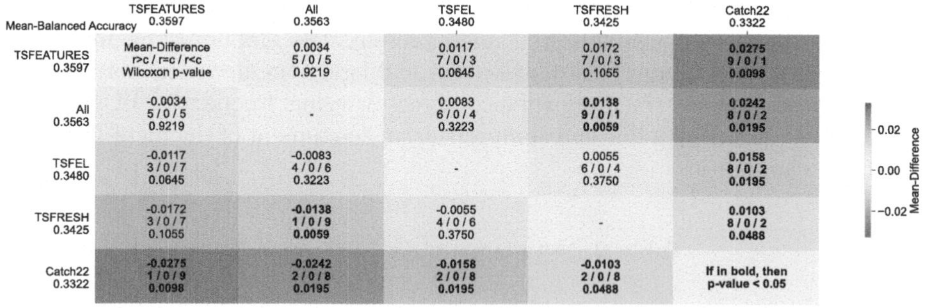

Fig. 1. Multi-Comparison Matrix for Meta-level Results.

Upon analyzing the performance evaluation matrix at the meta-level, we observe that there is no statistically significant difference between the methods

---

[1] https://github.com/moisesrsantos/mfebench.

TSFEATURES, TSFEL, TSFRESH, and the combined approach utilizing all available meta-features. This indicates that these methods perform comparably well in terms of balanced accuracy when predicting the most suitable forecasting algorithm for a given time series.

However, Catch22 demonstrated statistically inferior performance compared to the other methods, except TSFRESH, where the difference was not statistically significant. This suggests that Catch22 may not be as effective in capturing the relevant characteristics necessary for accurate metalearning in this context.

Among the methods evaluated, TSFEATURES exhibited the best average performance at the meta-level, achieving a higher mean balanced accuracy than the other methods and the combined approach. This indicates that TSFEATURES is particularly effective in extracting meta-features that enhance the predictive accuracy of the meta-learner.

In Fig. 2, we present the MCM which shows the main statistics from the base-level evaluation of forecasting algorithms, measured by MAE. This evaluation encompasses the performance of four meta-feature extraction methods: Catch22, TSFEATURES, TSFRESH, and TSFEL, as well as a combined approach denoted as All, which integrates all these meta-feature extraction methods.

	TSFEL 255.6407	All 256.7264	TSFRESH 258.2130	TSFEATURES 260.3895	Catch22 264.6611
Mean-MAE	255.6407	256.7264	258.2130	260.3895	264.6611
TSFEL 255.6407	Mean-Difference / r>c / r=c / r<c / Wilcoxon p-value	-1.0856 / 2500/0/2500 / 0.5589	-2.5722 / 2502/0/2498 / 0.5799	-4.7488 / 2512/0/2488 / 0.9315	-9.0203 / 2531/0/2469 / 0.9518
All 256.7264	1.0856 / 2500/0/2500 / 0.5589	-	-1.4866 / 863/3280/857 / 0.8798	-3.6631 / 1146/2776/1078 / 0.0672	-7.9347 / 1209/2720/1071 / 0.0006
TSFRESH 258.2130	2.5722 / 2498/0/2502 / 0.5799	1.4866 / 857/3280/863 / 0.8798	-	-2.1765 / 1181/2701/1118 / 0.1113	-6.4481 / 1219/2688/1093 / 0.0017
TSFEATURES 260.3895	4.7488 / 2488/0/2512 / 0.9315	3.6631 / 1078/2776/1146 / 0.0672	2.1765 / 1118/2701/1181 / 0.1113	-	-4.2715 / 1139/2804/1057 / 0.0718
Catch22 264.6611	9.0203 / 2469/0/2531 / 0.9518	7.9347 / 1071/2720/1209 / 0.0006	6.4481 / 1093/2688/1219 / 0.0017	4.2715 / 1057/2804/1139 / 0.0718	If in bold, then p-value < 0.05

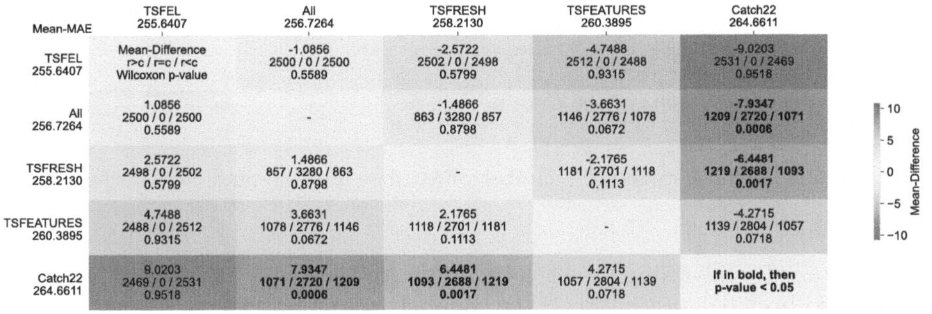

Fig. 2. Multi-Comparison Matrix for Base-level Results.

In the performance analysis matrix at the base level, TSFEL demonstrated the best average performance in terms of MAE. However, this improvement was not statistically significant when compared to the other methods. Catch22, consistent with its meta-level results, exhibited a higher error rate. The difference in performance between Catch22 and the other methods, such as TSFRESH and the combined use of all meta-features, was also not statistically significant.

While the meta-level analysis is crucial for evaluating the meta-learner's ability to recommend the appropriate forecasting algorithm, it is essential to delve deeper into the base-level results. These results are of practical significance as they directly impact the final forecasting performance.

Given this context, it is important to analyze the relationship between the number of features and predictive performance at the base level, as this can provide further insights into the practical applicability and efficiency of each meta-feature extraction method. The subsequent analysis will focus on this aspect, exploring the overall model's effectiveness.

Figure 3 illustrates the relationship between the number of features and the predictive performance, measured by MAE, for the different meta-feature extraction methods. The X-axis represents the number of features, while the Y-axis indicates the predictive performance in terms of MAE. This figure provides a clear visualization of the trade-off between the number of features and the forecasting accuracy. Ideally, a method that achieves a lower MAE with fewer features is considered more efficient.

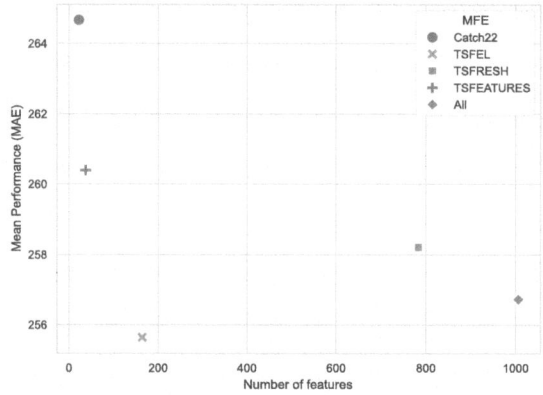

Fig. 3. Relationship between the number of features and the predictive performance.

A detailed analysis of base-level learning reveals that the TSFEL method strikes the best balance between the number of attributes and predictive performance. Catch22, which has the fewest meta-features, shows the worst results at both the meta and base levels, indicating that it lacks sufficient information for effective algorithm selection. On the other hand, TSFRESH, which generates the most meta-features, demonstrates performance closer to that of using all available meta-features.

This analysis leads to the conclusion that there is an equivalence among some of the primary time series feature extraction methods, namely TSFEL, TSFEATURES, and TSFRESH. The combined use of all meta-features does not yield a significant performance gain. Specifically, TSFEL offers the best balance between the quantity of meta-features and predictive performance at the base level. Meanwhile, Catch22 consistently performs worse than the other methods.

The comparable performance of TSFEL, TSFEATURES, and TSFRESH suggests that these methods are robust choices for time series analysis, without the need to combine all meta-features. TSFEL, in particular, stands out for its efficiency and effectiveness in balancing feature count and predictive accuracy.

5 Conclusion

In this study, we have conducted an empirical comparison of various feature extraction methods within the metalearning framework for algorithm selection in time series forecasting. The results of our analyses indicate that the packages TSFEATURES, TSFRESH, and TSFEL are equivalent in terms of performance at the base level. These methods demonstrated robust capability in capturing the essential characteristics of time series data, thus facilitating the selection of effective algorithms. However, Catch22 was found to be a less suitable option for this task, as its performance did not align with the other methods in our comparative evaluation. Regarding efficiency, particularly considering the balance between the number of features generated and predictive performance, TSFEL emerged as the best option.

These findings offer valuable information for researchers and practitioners in selecting appropriate feature extractors to enhance forecasting accuracy and efficiency. Future work could extend this research by exploring different forecasting horizons. Additionally, investigating less commonly used meta-feature extraction methods, as well as feature extraction through embedding learning, could yield further improvements in the metalearning framework.

In conclusion, this study not only highlights the comparative strengths and limitations of current time series feature extraction methods but also paves the way for future research in metalearning for algorithm selection.

Acknowledgments. This work is a result of Agenda "Center for Responsible AI", nr. C645008882-00000055, investment project nr. 62, financed by the Recovery and Resilience Plan (PRR) and by European Union - NextGeneration EU. Funded by the European Union – NextGenerationEU. Funded by the European Union under the Horizon Europe Framework Programme Grant Agreement N°: 101095387. Views and opinions expressed are however those of the author(s) only and do not necessarily reflect those of the European Union or European Commission. Neither the European Union nor the European Health and Digital Executive Agency can be held responsible for them. UID/00027 of the LIACC - Artificial Intelligence and Computer Science Laboratory - funded by Fundação para a Ciência e a Tecnologia, I.P./ MCTES through the national funds. The computational resources of Google Cloud Platform were provided by the project CPCA-IAC/AF/ 594904/2023.

Disclosure of Interests. The authors have no competing interests to declare that are relevant to the content of this article.

References

1. Alcobaça, E., Siqueira, F., Rivolli, A., Garcia, L.P., Oliva, J.T., De Carvalho, A.C.: MFE: towards reproducible meta-feature extraction. J. Mach. Learn. Res. **21**(111), 1–5 (2020)
2. Ali, A.R., Gabrys, B., Budka, M.: Cross-domain meta-learning for time-series forecasting. Procedia Comput. Sci. **126**, 9–18 (2018)

3. Bai, S., Kolter, J.Z., Koltun, V.: An empirical evaluation of generic convolutional and recurrent networks for sequence modeling. arXiv preprint arXiv:1803.01271 (2018)
4. Barandas, M., et al.: TSFEL: time series feature extraction library. SoftwareX **11**, 100456 (2020)
5. Brazdil, P., Carrier, C.G., Soares, C., Vilalta, R.: Metalearning: Applications to Data Mining. Springer (2008)
6. Brazdil, P., van Rijn, J.N., Soares, C., Vanschoren, J.: Metalearning: Applications to Automated Machine Learning and Data Mining. Springer (2022)
7. Cerqueira, V., Torgo, L., Soares, C.: A case study comparing machine learning with statistical methods for time series forecasting: size matters. J. Intell. Inf. Syst. **59**(2), 415–433 (2022)
8. Challu, C., Olivares, K.G., Oreshkin, B.N., Ramirez, F.G., Canseco, M.M., Dubrawski, A.: NHITS: neural hierarchical interpolation for time series forecasting. In: Proceedings of the AAAI Conference on Artificial Intelligence, vol. 37, pp. 6989–6997 (2023)
9. Christ, M., Braun, N., Neuffer, J., Kempa-Liehr, A.W.: Time series feature extraction on basis of scalable hypothesis tests (tsfresh-a python package). Neurocomputing **307**, 72–77 (2018)
10. Finn, C., Abbeel, P., Levine, S.: Model-agnostic meta-learning for fast adaptation of deep networks. In: Proceedings of the 34th International Conference on Machine Learning-Volume 70, pp. 1126–1135. JMLR.org (2017)
11. Ho, T.K.: Random decision forests. In: Proceedings of 3rd International Conference on Document Analysis and Recognition, vol. 1, pp. 278–282. IEEE (1995)
12. Hutter, F., Kotthoff, L., Vanschoren, J.: Automatic machine learning: methods, systems, challenges. Challenges in Machine Learning (2019)
13. Hyndman, R.J., Athanasopoulos, G.: Forecasting: principles and practice. OTexts (2018)
14. Ismail-Fawaz, A., et al.: An approach to multiple comparison benchmark evaluations that is stable under manipulation of the comparate set. arXiv preprint arXiv:2305.11921 (2023)
15. Kuck, M., Crone, S.F., Freitag, M.: Meta-learning with neural networks and landmarking for forecasting model selection an empirical evaluation of different feature sets applied to industry data. In: 2016 International Joint Conference on Neural Networks (IJCNN), pp. 1499–1506 (2016)
16. Lemke, C., Gabrys, B.: Meta-learning for time series forecasting and forecast combination. Neurocomputing **73**(10–12), 2006–2016 (2010)
17. Lubba, C.H., Sethi, S.S., Knaute, P., Schultz, S.R., Fulcher, B.D., Jones, N.S.: catch22: canonical time-series characteristics. Data Min. Knowl. Disc. **33**(6), 1821–1852 (2019)
18. Ma, S., Fildes, R.: Retail sales forecasting with meta-learning. Eur. J. Oper. Res. (2020)
19. Makridakis, S., et al.: The accuracy of extrapolation (time series) methods: results of a forecasting competition. J. Forecast. **1**(2), 111–153 (1982)
20. Makridakis, S., Hibon, M.: The M3-competition: results, conclusions and implications. Int. J. Forecast. **16**(4), 451–476 (2000)
21. Makridakis, S., Spiliotis, E., Assimakopoulos, V.: The M4 competition: 100,000 time series and 61 forecasting methods. Int. J. Forecast. **36**(1), 54–74 (2020)
22. Meade, N.: Evidence for the selection of forecasting methods. J. Forecast. **19**(6), 515–535 (2000)

23. Montero-Manso, P., Athanasopoulos, G., Hyndman, R.J., Talagala, T.S.: FFORMA: feature-based forecast model averaging. Int. J. Forecast. **36**(1), 86–92 (2020)

24. Montgomery, D.C., Jennings, C.L., Kulahci, M.: Introduction to Time Series Analysis and Forecasting. Wiley (2015)

25. Olivares, K.G., Challú, C., Garza, F., Canseco, M.M., Dubrawski, A.: NeuralForecast: user friendly state-of-the-art neural forecasting models. PyCon Salt Lake City, Utah, US 2022 (2022). https://github.com/Nixtla/neuralforecast

26. Parmezan, A.R.S., Souza, V.M.A., Batista, G.E.A.P.A.: Evaluation of statistical and machine learning models for time series prediction: identifying the state-of-the-art and the best conditions for the use of each model. Inf. Sci. **484**, 302–337 (2019)

27. Prudêncio, R.B., Ludermir, T.B.: Meta-learning approaches to selecting time series models. Neurocomputing **61**, 121–137 (2004)

28. Rice, J.R.: The algorithm selection problem. In: Advances in Computers, vol. 15, pp. 65–118. Elsevier (1976)

29. Rivolli, A., Garcia, L.P., Soares, C., Vanschoren, J., de Carvalho, A.C.: Towards reproducible empirical research in meta-learning. arXiv preprint arXiv:1808.10406, pp. 32–52 (2018)

30. Rumelhart, D.E., Hinton, G.E., Williams, R.J.: Learning representations by back-propagating errors. Nature **323**(6088), 533–536 (1986)

31. Salinas, D., Flunkert, V., Gasthaus, J., Januschowski, T.: Deepar: probabilistic forecasting with autoregressive recurrent networks. Int. J. Forecast. **36**(3), 1181–1191 (2020)

32. Santos, M., Carvalho, A.D., Soares, C.: Metafore: algorithm selection for decomposition-based forecasting combinations. Int. J. Data Sci. Anal. 1–14 (2024)

33. Talagala, T.S., Hyndman, R.J., Athanasopoulos, G., et al.: Meta-learning how to forecast time series. Monash Econometrics and Business Statistics Working Papers, vol. 6, no. 18, p. 16 (2018)

34. Wang, X., Smith, K., Hyndman, R.: Characteristic-based clustering for time series data. Data Min. Knowl. Disc. **13**(3), 335–364 (2006)

35. Widodo, A., Budi, I.: Model selection using dimensionality reduction of time series characteristics. In: International Symposium on Forecasting, Seoul, South Korea, pp. 57–118 (2013)

Managing Missing Data and Predictions in Short Time Series

Francisco António[1] 🆔 and Luís Cavique[2(✉)] 🆔

[1] Faculty of Engineering, Lúrio University, Pemba, Mozambique
francisco.araujo@unilurio.ac.mz
[2] Universidade Aberta and Lasige-FCUL, Lisbon, Portugal
luis.cavique@uab.pt

Abstract. Sales forecasting in the presence of Missing Data poses significant challenges, particularly for short time series where limited observations amplify the impact of incomplete records. This study analyzes a real-world transactional dataset (2021–2024) to predict quantities and prices for 2025. We classify missingness patterns and mechanisms (MCAR, MAR, MNAR) to inform the selection of imputation strategies. We evaluate techniques including MICE, Mean, KNN, and Linear Regression under simulated missingness rates, with KNN emerging as the most robust for the MAR mechanism. Regarding very short-term series predictions, the naive forecast Max2 (maximum of the last two observed values) outperformed moving averages. The results highlight the importance of mechanism-aware imputation and domain-tailored forecasting in sparse datasets. This work presents a practical framework for businesses to effectively utilize incomplete sales data.

Keywords: missing data · time series forecasting · imputation techniques · sales prediction · short time series

1 Introduction

Missing or incomplete data frequently hinders accurate forecasting in short time series contexts. These limitations impact the quality and reliability of models, particularly in sales environments where predictions are based on sparse or inconsistent historical records. This paper explores the mechanisms underlying Missing Data (MD), also reported as Missing Values (MVs), assesses their impact on predictive modeling, and evaluates imputation strategies in terms of accuracy and robustness.

Sales forecasting is crucial for optimizing inventory, allocating resources effectively, and informing strategic planning. However, real-world sales data often suffers from incompleteness due to operational gaps, entry errors, or systemic collection issues. Short time series—familiar in niche markets or for seasonal products—are especially vulnerable, as even minor missing data can distort trends and degrade model accuracy. While existing literature offers solutions for large datasets (e.g., ARIMA, LSTM), few address the unique constraints of sparse, incomplete time series.

J. Valente de Oliveira et al. (Eds.): EPIA 2025, LNAI 16121, pp. 282–294, 2026.
https://doi.org/10.1007/978-3-032-05176-9_22

This study bridges this gap by *(i) Diagnosing Missingness*, applying Rubin's framework (MCAR, MAR, MNAR) and Little's test to a real sales dataset (1,402 records, 2021–2024), *(ii) Evaluating Imputation*, comparing Multiple Imputation by Chained Equations (MICE), k-Nearest Neighbors (KNN), Mean and Linear Regression (LReg) under varying missingness rates (1–12%) using RMSE and MAE, and *(iii) Forecasting with Sparsity*, proposing a heuristic Max2 model for short series and validating it against moving averages. Given a real-world transactional dataset (2021–2024) with metadata (MD), the goal is to predict sales for 2025.

Following a review of MD types—patterns, mechanisms, and treatment methods—we apply imputation techniques and predictive models on a real-world sales dataset. The study leverages the Knowledge Discovery in Databases (KDD) methodology to guide data preparation and modeling efforts. Our main contributions include an empirical comparison of multiple imputation methods, and the application of a novel heuristic forecasting technique tailored to short time series with missing data (MD).

The remainder of the paper is structured as follows. Section 2 reviews related work. Section 3 presents the proposed model for managing MD and predicting short-term time series. Sections 4, 5 and 6 outline the methodology, which includes data cleaning, data prediction, and data summarization. Finally, Sect. 7 concludes.

2   Related Work

This section explores key aspects of MD relevant to short-time series forecasting. The discussion is structured around three central questions:

- Patterns: What data is missing?
- Mechanisms: Why is the data missing?
- Techniques: How can missing data be handled?

These elements provide a conceptual framework for understanding and addressing MD in sales and other time series contexts.

2.1   Patterns: What Data is Missing?

According to Newman [1] missing data is a statistical issue that arises when parts of a data matrix are incomplete, typically because respondents fail to provide information for one or more variables. Although the terms are often used interchangeably, MD patterns specifically refer to the structural arrangement of observed and missing data across a dataset. These patterns are essential for diagnosing data quality and guiding appropriate imputation strategies [2].

Newman [1] identifies three distinct levels of missingness: item-level, where MD occur when an individual skips one or more questions within a set of items (e.g., due to confusion or irrelevance); construct-level, where all items related to a specific construct are left blank, omitting entire sections of a survey or dataset; and person-level, where a complete absence of data for an individual results in no variables being filled in at all.

Recognizing these patterns helps determine whether missingness is isolated or systemic, which is crucial for selecting a treatment strategy.

2.2 Mechanisms: Why is the Data Missing?

Rubin's (1976) framework classifies MD mechanisms into three categories [3–5]. Missing Completely at Random (MCAR) is the probability of missingness independent of both observed and unobserved data. In this ideal case, the missingness is purely random. Missing at Random (MAR) is systematically related to other observed variables but not to the MD itself. Missing Not at Random (MNAR). The likelihood of missingness is related to the unobserved value, making the data non-ignorable and more challenging to handle. In practical applications, determining whether data is MNAR is particularly challenging, as it requires knowledge of the values that are not observed [1].

2.3 Techniques: How to Handle MD?

Handling MD involves both preventive strategies (e.g., data validation) and corrective techniques. Three broad approaches are commonly applied: deletion of rows with missing data is removed, which is only advisable when the missingness is Missing Completely at Random (MCAR) and the dataset is sufficiently large. Simple Imputation Methods, such as mean or median imputation, are computationally efficient but can distort variance and reduce model accuracy. Model-based imputation techniques, such as Multiple Imputation by MICE, KNN, Random Forest, and Deep Learning (e.g., GAIN, Autoencoders), provide more robust estimates by leveraging relationships among variables.

3   Proposed Model

This study employs the Knowledge Discovery in Databases (KDD) methodology, as it aligns with the project's objectives. KDD is a well-established framework in machine learning, widely applied in fields such as pattern recognition, statistics, databases, and artificial intelligence. It provides a structured process that culminates in actionable insights, often supported by data visualization [6]. The KDD process in this study is structured into three main steps: *(i) Data Cleaning, (ii) Data Prediction, and (iii) Data Summarization.*

3.1   Data Cleaning

The dataset used in this research originates from a real-world company and comprises approximately 1,402 transactional records spanning the years 2021 to 2024. As sales forecasting depends on historical purchase behavior, this transactional data forms a solid foundation for the prediction model.

Table 1 summarizes the dataset metadata. During the initial data cleaning, duplicate records were removed, which reduced the dataset to 1,370 entries. Records containing missing (*NA*), negative, or outlier values in the *Invoiced_Quant* variable were identified. After excluding all such invalid records, the dataset was reduced to 1,244 clean entries, ensuring data integrity for subsequent analysis.

Table 1. Dataset metadata

Attribute	Type	Description
Year	Int	from September of year X to August of year X + 1
Client	Varchar (5)	client name
Product	Varchar (1)	product name
Unitary Price	Float	invoiced price in monetary units
Budgeted Quantity	Int	budgeted products in units
Invoiced Quantity	Int	invoices for products in units

A pivot table was used to restructure the dataset from a long to a wide format, creating a sub-dataset that aligns better with time-series forecasting needs. The transformation grouped records by *Client*, *Product*, and *Unitary_Price*, while spreading the *Invoiced_Quant* values across four separate columns—one for each year (2021 to 2024). This restructuring resulted in a final sub-dataset of 735 records. The core numerical variables considered for summarization were *Unitary_Price* and *Invoiced_Quant* (see Table 2).

Table 2. Core attributes summary

	Attribute	
	Unitary_Price	*Invoiced_Quant*
Range	1.14 – 8.31	9 – 204,981
Mean	2.68	6,207.3
Median	2.74	1,571
NA	147	–

3.2 Data Prediction: Year 2025

To address MD in *Invoiced_Quant*, an imputation strategy based on the maximum quantity invoiced in the previous two years was employed. For predicting the *Unitary_Price* in 2025, a KNN model was applied. After reversing the transformation to restore the long format, the dataset expanded to 1,623 records.

Given the prevalence of MD, a detailed MD analysis was conducted. MD were classified according to Rubin's framework into: MCAR, MAR, and MNAR [3, 4, 7].

To test for MCAR, Little's test was applied [8]. Based on the classification, a complete dataset was used to simulate various MD scenarios, with missing rates ranging from 1% to 12%. These incomplete datasets were imputed using MICE with a Random Forest model, KNN, Mean, and LReg. This enabled the comparison of imputation techniques under different missingness conditions.

3.3 Data Summarization

After the data cleaning and transformation steps, a comprehensive summarization phase was conducted to explore the structure and key properties of the final dataset. This phase aims to uncover patterns, detect anomalies, and generate insights that can support model design and evaluation.

The cleaned dataset comprises 1,244 transactional records spanning the years 2021 to 2024, covering an average of 578 clients and 4 products.

4 Cleaning Phase

The dataset used in this study comprises 1402 observations, each corresponding to a unique combination of *Year*, *Client*, and *Product*. To ensure analytical integrity, the first step involves removing potential duplicate records based on these three identifiers. This duplication reduced the dataset slightly, ensuring that each row represents a distinct and meaningful observation.

4.1 Patterns

Using the *naniar* package from R, we visualized the pattern of missingness with the *vis_miss()* function. The resulting plot (see Fig. 1) clearly illustrates the proportion and distribution of MD across variables.

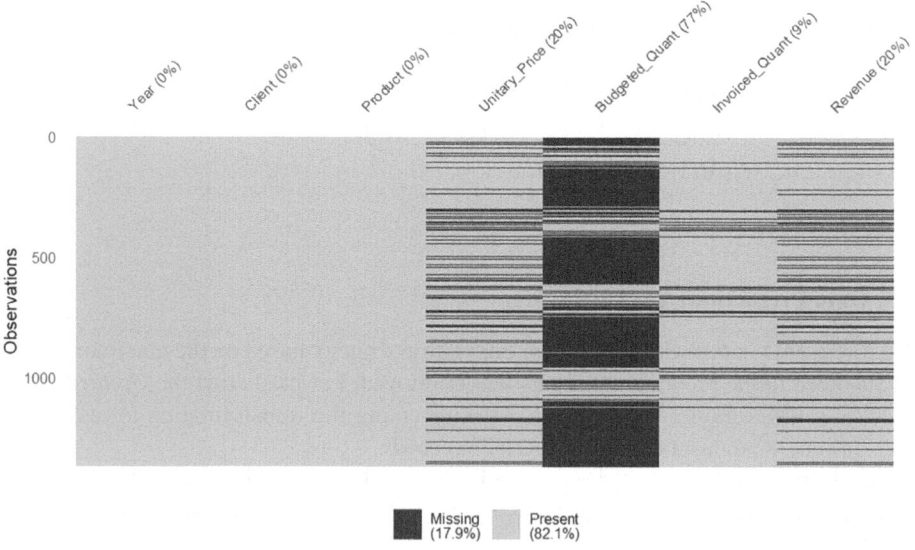

Fig. 1. Dataset MD patterns

This plot (Fig. 1) serves as a crucial diagnostic tool. It shows that while some key variables are complete (e.g., *Client*), others, especially those used in monetary calculations, are highly incomplete. Zero values in financial and quantity fields often indicate either errors in data entry or special conditions such as unavailability. These were replaced by *NA* where appropriate:

These substitutions ensure that later computations and imputations do not treat invalid zeroes as valid values. Where *Revenue* was not recorded directly, it was recomputed as the product of *Unitary_Price* and *Invoiced_Quant*. However, if either component was missing, the result was also replaced by *NA*:

This strategy avoids misleading values and ensures that derived fields are coherent with their inputs. Since time series modeling often requires complete records for the target variable (*Invoiced_Quant*), observations with missing invoiced quantities were excluded: This reduced the dataset from 1370 to a smaller, yet more reliable, subset for forecasting purposes.

4.2 Mechanism

To discover the missing data mechanism present in our dataset, a Little's test [8] was applied to the numeric columns, except for the *Year*, *Client*, and *Product* attributes. The results indicate that the χ^2 statistic equals 308. This large value indicates a significant deviation from MCAR. The Degrees of Freedom (df) = 14 reflects the complexity of the MD patterns, rejecting the MCAR hypothesis. The Little's test also showed *Missing Patterns* = 7, suggesting that there are seven distinct ways for MD to occur in this dataset.

Then, the dataset was analyzed to verify the cases where the missing *Unitary_Price* values were not significant. In this study, the Budgeted Quantity attribute was not considered due to the substantial amount of missing data (MD). Therefore, Invoiced_Quantity was regarded as the dependent variable for the missing *Unitary_Price* (MAR).

4.3 Techniques

Imputation models are a common technique for handling missing data. As noted by Liu and Wu [9], the selection of an appropriate forecasting model depends on the choice of evaluation metrics, although no universal standard exists. Among the most widely accepted metrics are the Mean Absolute Error (MAE) and the Root Mean Square Error (RMSE). These are computed as shown in Eqs. 1 and 2.

$$MAE = \frac{1}{n} \sum_{i=1}^{n} |y_i - \hat{y}_i| \tag{1}$$

$$RMSE = \sqrt{\frac{1}{n} \sum_{i=1}^{n} (y_i - \hat{y}_i)^2} \tag{2}$$

In these formulas, y_i denotes the actual observed value. In contrast, $\hat{y}_i$ represents the predicted value generated by the model. Lower values of the evaluation metrics indicate higher model accuracy and better forecasting performance. To handle MD, we evaluated four algorithms: MICE, KNN, Mean, and LReg. The original dataset contained 1,244 records, with 12% MD in the *Unitary_Price* attribute. We first removed all missing data, resulting in a clean dataset of 1,100 records. Next, we introduced Missing at Random (MAR) MD into the *Unitary_Price* attribute, varying the missing rate from 1% up to 12%. The maximum missing rate (12%) was chosen to match the original percentage of MD in *Unitary_Price* after data cleaning. This approach allowed us to systematically assess the performance of each imputation method under controlled MD conditions (see Table 3 and Fig. 2).

Table 3. Imputations results using RMSE and MAE evaluation metrics

	RMSE				MAE			
%	MICE	KNN	Mean	L.Reg	MICE	KNN	Mean	L.Reg
2	1.19	**0.59**	0.97	0.98	0.99	**0.34**	0.70	0.71
4	1.18	**0.59**	0.78	0.87	0.90	**0.40**	0.65	0.71
6	1.25	**0.49**	0.84	0.92	0.92	**0.30**	0.64	0.75
8	1.01	**0.56**	0.81	0.74	0.81	**0.32**	0.65	0.60
10	1.27	**0.61**	0.94	0.79	0.93	**0.37**	0.74	0.66
12	1.16	**0.72**	0.94	0.83	0.84	**0.41**	0.68	0.61

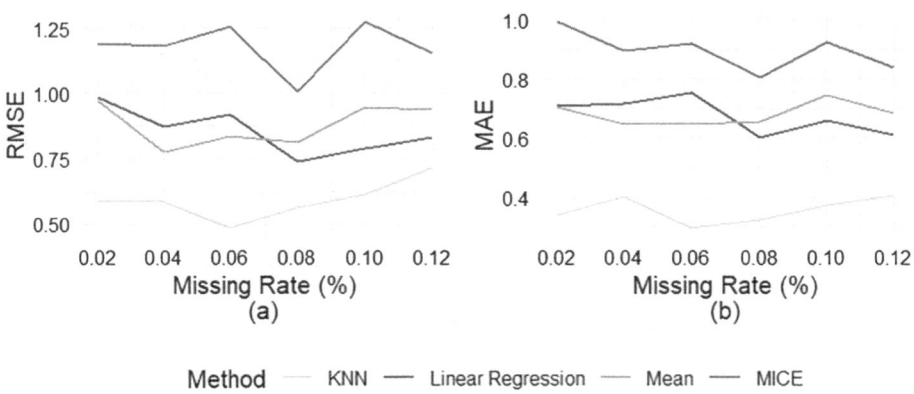

Fig. 2. RMSE and MAE – Imputation methods performance

The RMSE and MAE are consistent, indicating that the KNN algorithm performs best. Then the dataset (n = 1244) with 12% of *Unitary_Price* MD, was completed using the proposed algorithm, resulting in the non-MD dataset.

5   Predicting Phase

5.1   Forecasting Context and the Role of MD

Sales forecasting is the process of predicting future demand based on historical data [10]. Mentzer and Moon [11] define a sales forecast as "a projection into the future of expected demand, given a stated set of environmental conditions."

A variety of classical and modern forecasting methods have been proposed. Statistical models, such as ARIMA, SARIMA, and Exponential Smoothing, remain widely used for univariate time series [12]. Machine Learning techniques, including Random Forests, LSTM networks, and CNNs, have been successfully applied, especially for capturing nonlinear patterns [13–15]. Hybrid approaches combine decomposition techniques with deep learning.

For example, Gao et al. [16] integrated Empirical Mode Decomposition with neural networks to enhance multivariate forecasting performance. Nevertheless, all these approaches are sensitive to MD. Data imputation is thus a critical step, especially in short time series, where even a small number of MD can substantially affect model performance. Traditional methods such as the Single Moving Average and KNN remain effective for straightforward sales environments, as demonstrated in the case of PT.CNC [10].

Despite the wide range of forecasting methods, very short time series often pose challenges where naive models can find feasible solutions.

5.2   Data Transformation and Quantities Prediction

The prediction of quantities for the year 2025 requires a data transformation, as shown in Fig. 3, where the tabular data gives rise to a set of small time series. As exemplified, there are several years during which customers have purchased any product. Training/learning phases from 2021 to 2023, and testing/prediction phase in 2024. After validating the model, it will be applied in 2025.

Year	Client	Product	Price	Quant
2022	1111	B	2.94	1322
2023	1111	B	3.36	1322
2021	1116	A	2.25	1948
2022	1116	A	2.55	28
2024	1116	A	2.22	460
2021	1116	B	2.49	30506
2021	1121	B	2.71	964
2022	1121	B	3.20	1763
2021	1121	C	1.60	2356
2022	1121	C	2.01	7069
2023	1121	C	2.02	6283
2024	1121	C	1.55	7854
2024	1126	B	3.15	823

Product	Client	Year			
		2021	2022	2023	2024
A	1116	1948	28		460
B	1111		1322	1322	
B	1116	30506			
B	1121	964	1763		
B	1126				823
C	1121	2356	7069	6283	7854

Fig. 3. Data transformation to predict invoice quantities

To evaluate the prediction for 2024, two metrics are used. The first is based on the Mean Absolute Error (MAE), and the second is related to the sum of predicted quantities. A final metric combines these two previous ones.

To find the percentage for MAE, the division of the average quantity (Avg) is used, given by MAE% = MAE / Avg * 100. The error of the sum of quantities is provided by the following:

$$SumQuantError\% = \frac{|ActualSumQuant - PredSumQuant|}{ActualSumQuant} *100 \qquad (3)$$

Finally, Mixed Error is given by a convex combination of MAE% and SumQuantError%. In this work, α is set to 0.05, as SumQuantError provides a more accurate representation of the error.

$$MixedError\% = \alpha.MAE\% + (1-\alpha).SumQuantError\% \qquad (4)$$

Two approaches were used to predict the quantities for the year 2024: the classical moving average and a heuristic-based approach. Since the clients do not purchase the same product every year, there are MDs in the short-term series.

Naive models [17], such as using the last period's value as the forecast, are helpful in these conditions with short time series with MD. In this work, the naive model is defined as the maximum of the last two years, referred to as Max2.

The results of the mixed metric are presented in Table 4. The metric MAE% indicates significant errors for both techniques. On the other hand, the error related to the quantities is larger for the moving average technique. When combined in the mixed metric, the Max2 approach yields superior results and will be applied to the year 2025.

Table 4. Mixed metric for predicting techniques

Metrics	Prediction	
	Moving Average 2024	Max2 2024
MAE	2,260	2,422
MAE% = MAE/Avg	69.30%	74.27%
Sum Quant	1,775,018	2,512,861
Sum Quant Error %	25.94%	4.84%
Mixed Error %	47.62%	8.31%

In the next section, the summarizing phases, quantities are predicted using the heuristic Max2, and the price is obtained via the KNN method.

6 Summarizing Phase

The total invoiced quantity shows a steady year-over-year increase from 2021 to 2025.

Product C (cyan) consistently contributes the largest share of invoiced quantities across all years. Product B (green) sees a notable growth starting in 2022, becoming the second-largest contributor from that year forward. Product A (orange) and Product D (purple) contribute relatively small quantities, with slight increases over time. By 2025, the total amount invoiced is expected to surpass 2.5 million units, indicating strong growth (see Fig. 4).

By revenue, we mean the total income generated, calculated as the product of the predicted quantity and the corresponding price.

Like invoiced quantities, total revenue increases steadily from 2021 through 2025. Product B (green) overtakes Product C in revenue starting from 2022, suggesting it has a higher unit price or greater value impact. Product C (cyan) remains a major contributor to revenue but lags Product B slightly from 2023 onward. Product A and Product D contribute less to revenue, although their presence remains consistent. By 2025, revenue is expected to exceed 5 million, reflecting the successful combination of sales volume and pricing (see Figs. 5 and 6).

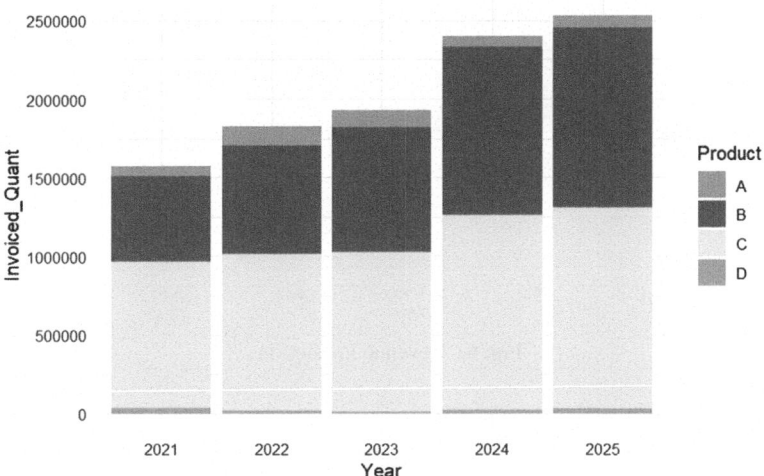

Fig. 4. Invoiced Quantity Prediction

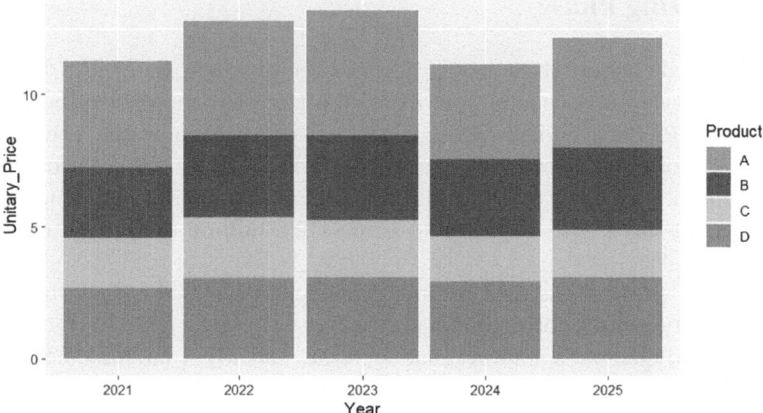

Fig. 5. Unitary Price Prediction

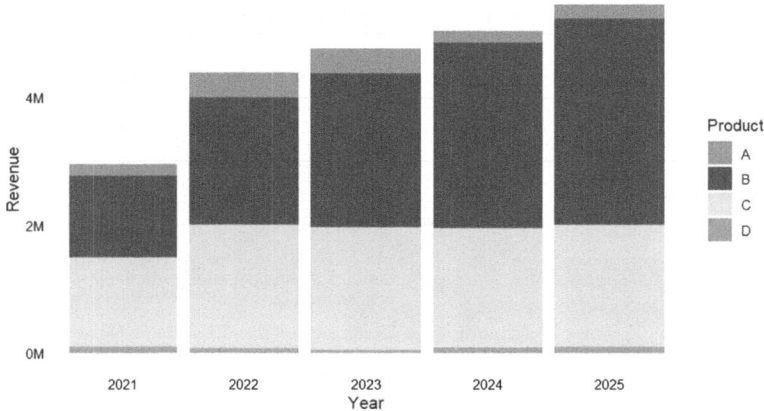

Fig. 6. Revenue Prediction

7   Conclusions

Given a real-world transactional dataset (2021–2024) comprising approximately 1,400 records with missing data (MD), the goal is to predict sales for 2025.

This study reinforces the importance of understanding and addressing MD when dealing with short time series in forecasting contexts. It demonstrates that not all imputation methods are equally effective across different types and rates of missingness.

The predicted price is obtained via KNN, and the quantities forecast use the Max2 naive approach.

In the price prediction, while Mean and Linear Regression perform well in specific scenarios, simpler methods, such as KNN, can still be competitive in environments with low missingness.

Despite the wide range of forecasting methods, very short time series often pose challenges where naive models can find feasible solutions. The Max2 naive approach proposed for forecasting provides an efficient and interpretable alternative to more complex models in settings with frequent data gaps. Mixed error is given by a convex combination that balances a micro vision of MAE with a macro vision of the error given by the sum of the quantities.

The aggregated data for quantity, price, and revenue confirm a reliable and gradual evolution over the 2021–2025 period.

Future work may include expanding the evaluation to multivariate time series models and exploring more robust evaluation schemes, such as growing or rolling window validation, to better reflect real-world scenarios. Furthermore, evaluating recent deep learning-based imputation techniques—such as GAIN and Autoencoders—across multiple datasets could offer deeper insights into their generalizability and effectiveness in time series contexts.

Acknowledgments. This work was supported by the LASIGE Research Unit, reference UID/00408/2025 – LASIGE.

Competing of Interest. The authors have no competing interests to declare that are relevant to the content of this article.

References

1. Newman, D.A.: Missing data: five practical guidelines. Organ. Res. Methods **17**(4), 372–411 (2014). https://doi.org/10.1177/1094428114548590
2. Enders, C.K.: Applied missing data analysis. In: Applied Missing Data Analysis, pp. xv, 377. The Guilford Press, New York (2010)
3. Awan, S.E., Bennamoun, M., Sohel, F., Sanfilippo, F.M., Dwivedi, G.: Imputation of missing data with class imbalance using conditional generative adversarial networks. arXiv:arXiv: 2012.00220 (2020)
4. Hallaji, E., Razavi-Far, R., Saif, M.: DLIN: deep ladder imputation network. IEEE Trans. Cybern. **52**(9), 8629–8641 (2022). https://doi.org/10.1109/TCYB.2021.3054878
5. Little, R.J.A.: A test of missing completely at random for multivariate data with missing values. J. Am. Stat. Assoc. **83**(404), 1198–1202 (1988). https://doi.org/10.2307/2290157
6. Singh, K., Booma, P.M., Eaganathan, U.: E-commerce system for sale prediction using machine learning technique. J. Phys.: Conf. Ser. (2020). https://doi.org/10.1088/1742-6596/1712/1/012042
7. Rubin, D.B.: Inference and missing data. Biometrika **63**(3), 581–592 (1976). https://doi.org/10.2307/2335739
8. Li, C.: Little's test of missing completely at random. Stand. Genomic Sci. **13**(4), 795–809 (2013). https://doi.org/10.1177/1536867X1301300407
9. Liu, Y., Wu, G.: Research on the prediction of short time series based on EMD-LSTM. J. Comput. Methods Sci. Eng. **23**(5), 2511–2524 (2023). https://doi.org/10.3233/JCM-226860
10. Prasetiamaolana, E., Syafrullah, M.: The use of single moving average and linear regression in spare part sales forecasting at PT. CNC, Int. J. Adv. Technol., Eng., Inf. Syst. **4**(1), 1 (2025). https://doi.org/10.55047/ijateis.v4i1.1587
11. Mentzer, J.T., Moon, M.A.: Sales Forecasting Management: A Demand Management Approach, 2nd ed. SAGE Publications, Inc. (2005). https://doi.org/10.4135/9781452204444
12. Eglite, L., Birzniece, I.: Retail sales forecasting using deep learning: systematic literature review. Complex Syst. Inf. Model. Quart. **30**, 53–62 (2022). https://doi.org/10.7250/csimq.2022-30.03

13. Mallik, R.S., Abhiram, R., Reddy, S.R., Jagadish, R.M.: A Comprehensive survey on sales forecasting models using machine learning algorithms. In: 2022 Fourth International Conference on Emerging Research in Electronics, Computer Science and Technology (ICERECT), pp. 1–6 (2022).https://doi.org/10.1109/ICERECT56837.2022.10060168

14. Ensafi, Y., Amin, S.H., Zhang, G., Shah, B.: Time-series forecasting of seasonal items sales using machine learning – a comparative analysis. Int. J. Inf. Manag. Data Insights **2**(1), 100058 (2022). https://doi.org/10.1016/j.jjimei.2022.100058

15. Johnson, M., Prakash, P.A., Saihareesh, V., Rajiv, A., Ananthi, S., Anandakumar, H.: Comparative analysis of future sales prediction using artificial intelligence. In: 2024 9th International Conference on Communication and Electronics Systems (ICCES), pp. 1175–1180 (2024). https://doi.org/10.1109/ICCES63552.2024.10859999

16. Gao, W., Li, C., Dong, S., Zhang, R.: Connector based short time series prediction. Sci. Rep. **15**(1), 7082 (2025). https://doi.org/10.1038/s41598-024-83122-y

17. Makridakis, S.G., Wheelwright, S.C., Hyndman, R.J.: Forecasting: Methods and Applications. John Wiley & Sons Inc., New York (1998)

Learning Coastal Upwelling Patterns from Wind Velocity via Interpretable Tree Models

Susana Nascimento[1]([✉]) [ID], Pedro Caldeirão[1] [ID], Paulo Relvas[2,3] [ID],
and Boris Mirkin[4,5] [ID]

[1] Department of Computer Science and NOVA LINCS, Faculdade de Ciências e
Tecnologia, Universidade Nova de Lisboa, Lisbon, Portugal
snt@fct.unl.pt
[2] Universidade do Algarve, Faro, Portugal
[3] Centre of Marine Sciences (CCMAR), Faro, Portugal
[4] Department of Data Analysis and Artificial Intelligence, National Research
University Higher School of Economics, Moscow, Russian Federation
[5] School of Computing and Mathematical Sciences, Birkbeck University of London,
London, UK

Abstract. Coastal upwelling systems are vital to ocean productivity
and regional climate regulation, yet quantifying the influence of wind
forcing on the persistence of upwelling remains a significant challenge.
This study presents a supervised learning framework to predict Upwelling
Stability Periods (USPs) by linking daily wind to Sea Surface Temperature (SST)-derived labels in the Canary Upwelling System. Building
on the Core-Shell clustering approach, which identifies USPs via unsupervised SST segmentation, we reformulate the problem as a multiclass
classification task. A fuzzification–defuzzification scheme is employed to
generate USP labels in a manner that reconciles the temporal resolution
mismatch between SST-based clustering and daily wind fields.

We construct three progressively enriched feature sets from wind and
SST data. Decision Trees (DTs) and Random Forests (RFs) are used to
model the relationship between wind and USPs. Over a 16-year period,
SST-enhanced features yield substantial gains in classification accuracy
(AUC > 0.94). DTs achieve strong predictive performance while maintaining interpretability through rule-based structures. RFs consistently
deliver robust performance reinforcing their role as a reliable benchmark
for classification.

Keywords: Multiclass Classification · Decision Trees · Fuzzy
Labeling · Wind–SST Modeling · Coastal Upwelling

1 Introduction

Coastal upwelling is a physical process in which the action of the wind on the
ocean causes nutrient rich cold water from the deeper layers to rise to the sur-

J. Valente de Oliveira et al. (Eds.): EPIA 2025, LNAI 16121, pp. 295–307, 2026.
https://doi.org/10.1007/978-3-032-05176-9_23

face, sustaining high biological productivity and influencing the regional climate. Accurate characterization of upwelling dynamics is critical to understanding ecosystem responses and improving ocean-atmosphere predictive models. Sea Surface Temperature (SST) and wind data are commonly used to monitor upwelling, often via statistical approaches to infer seasonal patterns and long-term trends [14,15]. Yet these methods, rooted in simplified linear assumptions and correlation-based analysis, struggle to capture nonlinear wind-ocean interactions that govern upwelling processes [18].

We introduced and developed the Core-Shell Clustering framework [12] which is a three-stage unsupervised clustering methodology that segments SST time series, derived from MODIS-Aqua satellite imagery, into spatially coherent intervals of persistent upwelling activity, termed *Upwelling Stability Periods* (USPs), observed throughout the upwelling seasons. While effective at delineating stable thermal structures in distinct geographic regions of the Canary Upwelling System (one of the major Eastern Upwelling Systems) [13] this approach did not take into account the contribution of wind fields to the onset or persistence of USPs.

This study addresses this critical gap by linking wind to SST-derived USPs in the Canary Upwelling System. Specifically, we investigate whether wind can predict USP labels associated with thermally stable periods in SST time series, thereby enabling the characterization of upwelling persistence via data-driven models based on physically informed features.

Geoscience problems pose unique machine learning challenges due to the spatiotemporal nature of the data, high dimensionality, and adherence to physical constraints [1,8]. A central difficulty lies in the choice of spatial and temporal resolution: geophysical systems span multiple scales and exhibit long-range dependencies, complicating both feature design and model generalization. Additionally, the scarcity or uncertainty of labeled data limits the direct application of conventional supervised learning methods. Establishing causal relationships is further hampered by confounding variables, spatial auto-correlation, and feedback dynamics intrinsic to Earth systems.

Here, we recast USP identification as a supervised classification task. We use wind-derived features to predict SST-based USP labels, thus probing the causal role of wind in upwelling persistence. The resulting classification problem is inherently multiclass and depends on spatially aggregated inputs, requiring models capable of capturing non-linear spatial dependencies. Fuzzification and defuzzification play a central role in our proposal, allowing crisp daily wind perturbation maps to be associated with graded USP memberships derived from SST-based unsupervised segmentation. We employ trapezoidal membership functions [9] due to their interpretability. To assign a single USP label per day, we apply the centroid defuzzification method [16], which offers a theoretically robust and stable mapping from fuzzy memberships to scalar class values. We use Decision Trees (DTs) for their interpretability, and Random Forests (RFs) as performance benchmarks. Both have proven effective in geoscientific prediction tasks [10,11,17].

The remainder of this paper is structured as follows. Section 2 reviews related work on machine learning approaches to upwelling analysis. Section 3 presents the proposed methodology. Section 4 reports and discusses the experimental results. Section 5 concludes with main findings and outlines future work.

2   Related Work on Machine Learning for Upwelling Persistence

In recent years, machine learning (ML) techniques have been increasingly applied to investigate coastal upwelling dynamics. Most of these studies, however, have focused on unsupervised clustering or regression-based methods, offering valuable insight into spatial variability and large-scale drivers of upwelling but falling short in modeling causal and temporal aspects, particularly the mechanistic influence of wind forcing on the persistence of upwelling regimes. However, supervised classification approaches especially those employing interpretable models such as tree-based classifiers, remain under-explored. The following works are recent attempts to explore interpretable supervised classification approaches within this context.

The work in [4] explored several ML regressors, including RFs, CART, and SVM, to examine seasonal SST and chlorophyll-a dynamics in the Satonda Island region using Landsat-8 satellite data. While the results highlight the effectiveness of RF regression for modeling SST-related variability, the study does not address event-level classification or upwelling persistence. In [3] it was developed a hybrid machine learning framework to reconstruct long-term trends in upwelling strength across the Eastern Boundary Upwelling Systems (EBUS). Self-Organizing Maps (SOMs) were used to extract dominant wind patterns from satellite data and back-project them onto reanalysis wind fields to estimate historical Ekman transport. Although effective for understanding decadal variability, this approach is unsupervised and does not aim to classify upwelling events or their persistence. Convolutional neural networks (CNNs) were applied in [2] to detect upwelling presence from SST imagery across major global coastal systems. While achieving high accuracy in image-based binary classification, this deep learning model does not incorporate wind forcing or temporal persistence—factors that are central to mechanistic understanding. Moreover, CNNs, while powerful, lack interpretability and require large labeled datasets, limiting their utility in operational settings with data constraints.

These studies demonstrate the growing interest in machine learning for upwelling analysis, yet reveal a consistent gap: the absence of interpretable, supervised classification frameworks that can link wind forcing to upwelling persistence. To the best of our knowledge, no previous study has formulated USP detection as a supervised multiclass classification task grounded in wind forcing. The present study proposes a novel wind-to-USP modeling framework that employs physically informed features and tree-based classifiers to capture the link between wind and the temporal persistence of upwelling.

3   Computational Methodology

We developed a computational framework to assess the extent to which wind data can predict USP labels associated with thermally stable upwelling periods. The process comprises the following stages:

Stage1 – Data Loading and Preprocessing

Two complementary data types spanning a continuous 16-year interval (2004–2019) were employed in this study: wind fields from the ERA5 reanalysis product [7], and SST grids from the OceanColor repository (https://oceancolor.gsfc.nasa.gov/). The wind data comprises hourly 10-meter zonal u (west-east) and meridional v (south-north) components at a spatial resolution of 25 km × 25 km, extracted from the ERA5 "Hourly data on single levels from 1940 to present" product. Two offshore coastal regions of Morocco are analyzed: the northern region (30°N–36°N; 5.5°W–16°W) and the southern region (20°N–27°N; 13°W–21.5°W). Each wind grid $W(I, J)$ contains vector tuples (u_{ij}, v_{ij}) over spatial coordinates (i, j), where $i \in I$ indexes latitude and $j \in J$ indexes longitude. The grid dimensions are 25 × 43 for the northern region and 33 × 35 for the southern region.

Hourly wind fields from the ERA5 reanalysis are processed into daily wind perturbation maps to reveal spatial patterns relevant for subsequent analysis. We define the Quadratic Wind Perturbation (QWP) at each grid point (i, j) as:

$$\phi_{ij} = (w_{ij} - \overline{w})^2, \tag{1}$$

where w_{ij} is the daily alongshore wind component at grid point (i, j), and $\overline{w}$ is the spatial mean of the wind component across the domain W.

This formulation emphasizes spatial variability by assigning higher values to regions where wind conditions deviate significantly from the domain-wide mean, thus enhancing the contrast of localized wind-driven upwelling patterns. As such, the QWP highlights regions of intensified or diminished wind forcing, offering a physically meaningful proxy for identifying spatial structures that may contribute to upwelling activity.

A five-stage preprocessing pipeline (Fig. 1) is employed to convert raw hourly wind fields into QWP maps:

- **Data Cleaning:** Wind vectors (u and v components) over land pixels are excluded to retain only oceanic grid points.
- **Temporal Aggregation:** Hourly wind maps are averaged over 24-hour periods to generate daily wind fields, as ocean responses to wind variability are typically assessed at this timescale.
- **Alongshore Wind Computation:** Wind vectors at each grid point are decomposed into alongshore and cross-shore components; the alongshore component—relevant for coastal upwelling—is retained.
- **Spatial Zooming:** To align spatial resolution with the SST grid, QWP maps are interpolated using a zoom factor computed from the ratio of grid dimensions. Interpolation is performed via SciPy's `zoom` function, facilitating wind vector overlays on SST data.

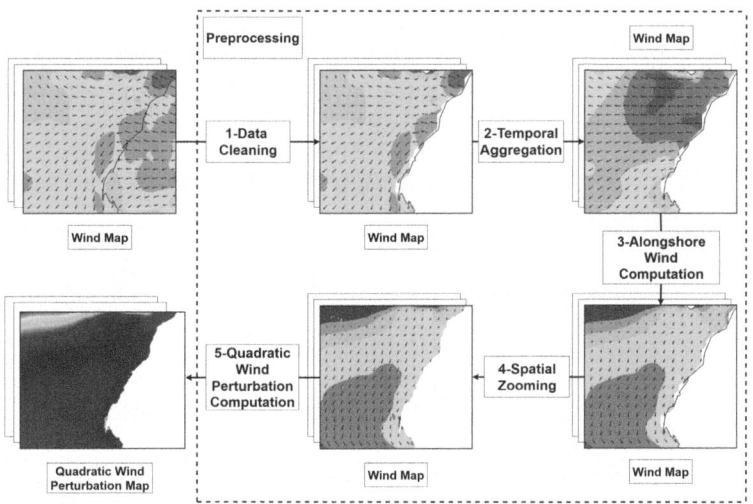

Fig. 1. Workflow illustrating preprocessing pipeline to transform wind maps into QWP maps.

- **Quadratic Wind Perturbation (QWP) Computation:** The final QWP value at each grid point (i, j) is computed by Eq. 1, resulting in daily QWP maps.

The SST data provides weekly SST fields at $2\,\text{km} \times 2\,\text{km}$ resolution, matching the spatial and temporal coverage of the wind dataset. Each SST grid $A(I, J)$ is defined by scalar temperature values a_{ij} (in °C). Northern region grids comprise 251×501 points, while southern grids contain 351×426 points. Its pre-processing pipeline is described in [12].

Stage2 – USP Label Generation via Fuzzyfication-Defuzzification

To assign USP class labels to daily QWP maps, we apply fuzzy membership functions to address the temporal overlap between daily wind observations and the defined upwelling stability periods (USPs). USPs are constructed from consecutive weekly SST instants, generated using a moving average filter with window size $W = 5$, which introduces overlapping intervals in the SST time series.

This overlap prevents a direct, one-to-one assignment of daily QWP maps to individual USPs. Instead, each day may belong to multiple USPs with varying degrees of membership. For example, a shared interval between USP-2 and USP-3 spanning days 168 to 199 includes boundary days that partially contribute to both classes. This soft association is modeled through fuzzy membership values, enabling a more nuanced and temporally consistent labeling approach. The use of fuzzy logic thus captures transitional dynamics between consecutive USPs while maintaining label interpretability for supervised learning.

To account for the temporal overlap among USPs, we adopt a fuzzy labeling scheme in which each day is assigned a graded membership across multiple periods. This is implemented using trapezoidal fuzzy membership functions [9,16], parameterized by four values a, b, c, and d, and defined as:

$$\mu(x) = \begin{cases} 0 & \text{if } x < a, \\ \frac{x-a}{b-a} & \text{if } a \leq x < b, \\ 1 & \text{if } b \leq x < c, \\ \frac{d-x}{d-c} & \text{if } c \leq x < d, \\ 0 & \text{if } x > d. \end{cases} \qquad (2)$$

Here, $[b, c]$ defines the *core* (full membership, $\mu(x) = 1$) and $[a, d]$ the *support* (partial membership, $\mu(x) > 0$).

For each USP, parameters a and d correspond to the start and end days of its *support*, defining the full range over which the USP has influence. Parameters b and c mark the beginning and end of the *core region*, where the membership value is 1. These are derived by subtracting the overlapping segments between adjacent USP supports, ensuring smooth, non-abrupt transitions.

Figure 2 illustrates this process for both USP 1 and USP 2 during the 2019 season in the South Morocco region. For USP 1, the trapezoidal parameters are: $a = 1$ (start of support), $b = 1$ (start of core), $c = 113$ (end of core), and $d = 144$ (end of support). Similarly, USP 2 starts overlapping on day 113 (end of USP 1's core) and spans until day 199. The trapezoid parameters for USP 2 are: $a = 113$, $b = 144$, $c = 168$ and $d = 199$, showing how transition regions are handled when USPs are temporally adjacent.

This parameterization ensures that membership transitions between USPs are continuous, allowing for more realistic modeling of gradual oceanographic shifts rather than abrupt categorical changes.

Each daily QWP map is then evaluated across all USP membership functions, and a unique label is assigned using a defuzzification rule based on the highest membership value. Two classical defuzzification functions are employed [16]: the Middle of Maxima (MOM), that returns the average of all values within the core; and Smallest of Maxima (SOM), corresponding to the smallest value in the core.

Stage3 – Dataset Construction and Feature Sets Extraction

Each QWP grid is partitioned into twelve zones arranged in a 3×4 layout, defined by latitude bands and proximity to the coastline, as illustrated in Fig. 3. This spatial division was empirically designed to strike balance between spatial resolution and interpretability ensuring that each zone is large enough to capture meaningful variability yet small enough to reflect localized wind forcing, enabling detection of mesoscale upwelling features without over-segmenting the domain. Land pixels (e.g., in zones 3 and 6) are excluded from all subsequent computations. Zones are overlaid onto the SST grid and indexed sequentially from 1 to 12, starting from the lower-left corner and proceeding row-wise.

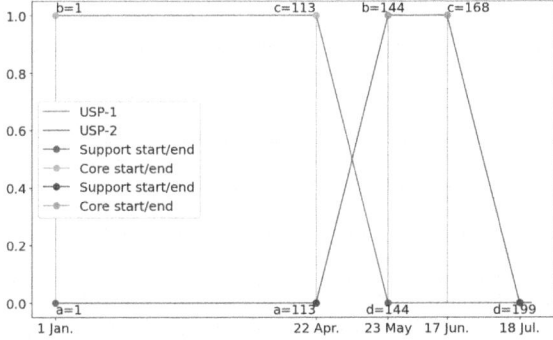

Fig. 2. Trapezoidal fuzzy membership function.

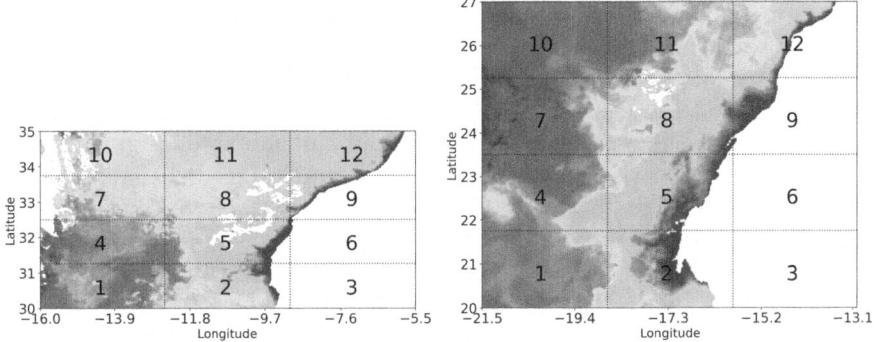

Fig. 3. Zonal division for the Northern (left) and Southern (right) Moroccan coast based on SST patterns.

From each of the 10 (excluding Land) predefined zones in the QWP and SST grids, three statistical features—minimum, average, and maximum—are extracted, yielding 30 features per variable type. To capture the cross-shore thermal structure relevant to upwelling dynamics, we compute zonal SST differences, defined as the average SST difference between nearshore latitudinal bands and their corresponding offshore zones. This yields a total of 64 features per daily sample: 30 derived from QWP, 30 from SST, and 4 additional features based on zonal SST differences. Table 1 summarizes the complete feature set.

Each annual dataset is structured as matrix of size 365×65 (or 366×65 for leap years), where each row corresponds to the daily 64-dimensional feature vector plus USP class label.

Following the fuzzyfication-defuzzification process (stage2), there were constructed labeled datasets for all combinations of two regions (North/South Morocco), sixteen years (2004–2019), and two defuzzification methods (MOM and SOM), resulting in a total of 64 datasets. Each of these yearly datasets

Table 1. Feature types and dimensions used in constructing input data for classification models.

Type	Statistics	# Features	Name Format ($n = 1, \ldots, 12$)
QWP	Min, Average, Max	30	`Min/Avg/Max_QWP_Zn`
SST	Min, Average, Max	30	`Min/Avg/Max_Temp_Zn`
SST diff	Average	4	`Zn_Zn+2_Diff`

was further represented by three distinct feature subsets: **DS1** contains only QWP features; **DS2** augments DS1 with inter-zonal SST difference features; and **DS3** incorporates the complete feature set, combining QWP and all SST-derived attributes.

Stage4 – Tree-based Classification Models

We employ DTs and RFs to model the relationship between QWP and SST-derived feature vectors and the USP class labels. To constrain Dts model search space and prioritize interpretability, we focus on hyperparameters that directly influence tree structure. Specifically, we tune the splitting criterion (`Gini`,`Entropy`), maximum tree depth, minimum number of samples required to split an internal node, and the minimum samples needed to define a leaf. For RF models, we additionally tune the number of trees in the ensemble.

We follow a standard three-stage protocol for the models construction: dataset partitioning, training–validation, and final evaluation. Initially, datasets are stratified to maintain class distribution, with 80% allocated for training and 20% for testing. A 10-fold stratified cross-validation procedure is used during training, applying grid search for hyperparameter optimization [6]. For DTs, the hyperparameters include maximum tree depth, minimum samples required for a split, and minimum samples per leaf. For RFs, the number of trees is additionally tuned. The optimal configuration is selected, retrained on the full training set, and evaluated on the held-out test set.

Performance is assessed using standard classification metrics: accuracy, precision, recall, and F1-score. To further evaluate model discrimination, we compute Receiver Operating Characteristic (ROC) curves and Area Under the Curve (AUC) scores [5]. Unlike point metrics, the AUC provides a robust, threshold-independent measure of separability between classes. Given the multiclass nature of the task, a One-vs-One (OvO) strategy is adopted to compute AUC values across all pairwise class comparisons. Final performance is summarized using the macro-averaged AUC, providing an aggregate measure of the model's discriminative capability.

4   Assessing Tree-Based Classifiers for Wind-Driven USP Prediction

We conducted a comprehensive empirical evaluation of tree-based models for predicting Upwelling Stability Periods (USPs) from wind-derived and SST-based features. The experimental analysis addresses three main objectives: (i) to evaluate the predictive capacity of QWP features alone for identifying USPs; (ii) to assess the added value of incorporating SST-based features in enhancing classification accuracy and model interpretability; and (iii) to compare the performance of DT and RF models across different feature sets and geographic regions (Northern vs. Southern Morocco), identifying configurations that best balance accuracy, complexity, and interpretability.

4.1 Experimental Setup

We begin by applying the Core-Shell clustering framework [12] to each of the 16 yearly SST datasets in both the northern and southern geographical regions, resulting in the identification of USPs.

Our methodology is applied to characterize and predict USPs, using the previously identified USP labels as ground truth. The mapping process is executed independently for each *year-region* combination, yielding the labeling of all 64 pre-constructed datasets. Each of the 64×3 labeled dataset is then used to train an optimal predictive model according to the procedure outlined at **Stage4**.

Hyperparameter tuning is performed via grid search to ensure reproducibility and comparability across datasets. For both Decision Trees (DT) and Random Forests (RF), the following configurations are explored: split criterion {Gini,Entropy}, maximum tree depth {3,4,5}, minimum samples required to split a node {2, . . . ,8}, and minimum samples per leaf {1,3,5}. For RF models, the number of estimators (trees) is additionally varied over {100,500,1000}.

To maintain interpretability, tree complexity is constrained by limiting depth to between 3 and 5 levels, as deeper trees often yield excessively complex rules. Only decision paths ending in leaf nodes with at least ten majority-class samples are retained to ensure rule reliability.

4.2 Classifying Upwelling Stability Periods

To investigate regional variation in model performance (Goal iii), we used the 16 years data from both North and South Morocco, and assess the classification accuracy and rule structures of models trained on the DS1, DS2, DS3 feature sets, thereby evaluating the influence of geographic region on predictive effectiveness.

Table 2 summarizes the classification performance of the optimal DT and RF models applied to all three feature configurations (DS1–DS3) for the NM region for the 16 years. The evaluation metrics were computed on both training-validation and test sets across different tree depths, and their averages and corresponding standard deviations were subsequently calculated.

Table 2. Classification metrics for DT and RF models in North Morocco.

Dataset	Depth	Train-Validation				
		Accuracy	Precision	Recall	F1	AUC
DT-DS1	3	0.40 ± 0.04	0.43 ± 0.07	0.40 ± 0.04	0.37 ± 0.05	0.62 ± 0.04
	4	0.40 ± 0.04	0.43 ± 0.05	0.40 ± 0.04	0.39 ± 0.04	0.62 ± 0.04
	5	0.40 ± 0.04	0.42 ± 0.05	0.40 ± 0.04	0.39 ± 0.04	0.62 ± 0.04
DT-DS2	3	0.81 ± 0.08	0.84 ± 0.08	0.81 ± 0.08	0.81 ± 0.08	0.94 ± 0.03
	4	0.87 ± 0.06	0.88 ± 0.05	0.87 ± 0.06	0.86 ± 0.06	0.97 ± 0.02
	5	0.91 ± 0.04	0.92 ± 0.03	0.91 ± 0.04	0.91 ± 0.04	0.97 ± 0.01
DT-DS3	3	0.95 ± 0.02	0.96 ± 0.02	0.95 ± 0.02	0.95 ± 0.02	0.99 ± 0.01
	4	0.97 ± 0.01	$0.97 \pm \pm 0.01$	0.97 ± 0.01	0.97 ± 0.01	0.99 ± 0.00
	5	0.97 ± 0.01	0.97 ± 0.01	0.97 ± 0.01	0.97 ± 0.01	0.99 ± 0.00
RF-DS1	-	0.45 ± 0.04	0.47 ± 0.04	0.45 ± 0.04	0.44 ± 0.04	0.70 ± 0.03
RF-DS2	-	0.90 ± 0.04	0.91 ± 0.03	0.90 ± 0.04	0.90 ± 0.04	0.99 ± 0.01
RF-DS3	-	0.98 ± 0.01	0.98 ± 0.01	0.98 ± 0.01	0.98 ± 0.01	1.00 ± 0.00
		Test set				
DT-DS1	3	0.36 ± 0.06	0.39 ± 0.13	0.36 ± 0.06	0.33 ± 0.07	0.58 ± 0.04
	4	0.39 ± 0.09	0.41 ± 0.12	0.39 ± 0.09	0.37 ± 0.10	0.59 ± 0.05
	5	0.38 ± 0.08	0.39 ± 0.10	0.38 ± 0.08	0.36 ± 0.09	0.59 ± 0.06
DT-DS2	3	0.80 ± 0.08	0.82 ± 0.10	0.80 ± 0.08	0.79 ± 0.09	0.94 ± 0.03
	4	0.85 ± 0.07	0.87 ± 0.06	0.85 ± 0.07	0.85 ± 0.08	0.97 ± 0.03
	5	0.90 ± 0.07	0.92 ± 0.06	0.90 ± 0.07	0.90 ± 0.07	0.98 ± 0.03
DT-DS3	3	0.95 ± 0.04	0.95 ± 0.04	0.95 ± 0.04	0.94 ± 0.04	0.99 ± 0.01
	4	0.97 ± 0.04	0.97 ± 0.03	0.97 ± 0.04	0.97 ± 0.04	0.99 ± 0.01
	5	0.97 ± 0.03	0.97 ± 0.02	0.97 ± 0.02	0.97 ± 0.04	0.99 ± 0.01
RF-DS1	-	0.43 ± 0.05	0.46 ± 0.08	0.43 ± 0.05	0.42 ± 0.06	0.68 ± 0.05
RF-DS2	-	0.90 ± 0.05	0.91 ± 0.05	0.90 ± 0.05	0.90 ± 0.05	0.98 ± 0.01
RF-DS3	-	0.98 ± 0.03	0.98 ± 0.02	0.98 ± 0.03	0.98 ± 0.03	1.00 ± 0.00

Models trained using the DS1 set, which includes only QWP-derived attributes, exhibit consistently weak predictive performance, with F1-scores $\leq$ 0.39 and AUC values not exceeding 0.62 in the Decision Tree (DT) models, and still limited performance in the Random Forest (RF) models (F1 $\approx$ 0.42, AUC $\approx$ 0.68). These results confirm that QWP features alone are insufficient for USP prediction. Incorporating SST-derived features, as done in DS2, leads to substantial gains in classification performance. DT models achieve F1-scores between 0.79 and 0.91 and AUC values up to 0.98, while RF models yield similarly strong results.

Across all configurations, RF models slightly outperform or match DT models. Moreover, RFs shown greater stability across tree depths and feature sets, reinforcing their role as a reliable performance benchmark. These findings support Goal (iii), highlighting the trade-offs between interpretability and accuracy in selecting between DT and RF classifiers.

Table 3 illustrates the interpretability of DT models via IF-THEN rules extracted from the optimal DT trained on the DS2 dataset for North Morocco (2012). The model, comprising seven rules and relying on eight features, demonstrates high interpretability, leveraging inter-zonal SST differences and quadratic wind perturbation (QWP)— standard indicators of upwelling intensity. Rules for USP 1 and USP 2 primarily depend on offshore-to-nearshore temperature gradients, established proxies for upwelling. In contrast, rules for USP 3 and USP 4, corresponding to peak upwelling season, emphasize wind-related variables, consistent with the known role of strong winds driving upwelling during these periods. The resulting classification accuracy is approximately 90.4%.

Table 3. Rule set from the optimal DT model (DT5) trained on DS2 for North Morocco region, 2012.

USP	Rule	Support
1	IF (Z7_Z9_Diff > 1.24) AND (Z4_Z5_Diff ≤ 1.24) AND (Z10_Z12_Diff > 0.48) THEN USP=1	**64**,0,0,0
2	IF (Z7_Z9_Diff ≤ 1.24) AND (Z1_Z2_Diff ≤ 0.83) AND (Z4_Z5_Diff > 0.22) AND (Z1_Z2_Diff > 0.38) THEN USP=2	0,**31**,0,0
3	IF (Z7_Z9_Diff ≤ 1.24) AND (Z1_Z2_Diff > 0.83) AND (Avg_QWP_Z12 > 0.02) AND (Z1_Z2_Diff > 1.61) THEN USP=3	0,0,**22**,0
	IF (Z7_Z9_Diff ≤ 1.24) AND (Z1_Z2_Diff > 0.83) AND (Avg_QWP_Z12 > 0.02) AND (Z1_Z2_Diff ≤ 1.61) AND (Z4_Z5_Diff ≤ 0.98) THEN USP=3	0,0,**19**,1
4	IF (Z7_Z9_Diff > 1.24) AND (Z4_Z5_Diff > 1.24) AND (Z7_Z9_Diff > 1.48) AND (Max_QWP_Z11 ≤ 43.82) THEN USP=4	0,0,0,**41**
	IF (Z7_Z9_Diff ≤ 1.24) AND (Z1_Z2_Diff > 0.83) AND (Avg_QWP_Z12 ≤ 0.02) AND (Avg_QWP_Z2 > 0.18) AND (Avg_QWP_Z7 > 0.16) THEN USP=4	0,0,0,**23**
	IF (Z7_Z9_Diff ≤ 1.24) AND (Z1_Z2_Diff > 0.83) AND (Avg_QWP_Z12 > 0.02) AND (Z1_Z2_Diff ≤ 1.61) AND (Z4_Z5_Diff > 0.98) THEN USP=4	0,13,9,**18**

The corresponding RF models largely reflect the patterns observed in the DTs. For DS2, the top-ranked features in the RF align with those used at the upper levels of the DT, confirming the predictive value and interpretability of SST-derived attributes over QWP-based ones. In contrast, the DS3 RF model shows weaker alignment: only two features (Z7_Z9_Diff and Avg_Temp_Z8) of its top five appear in the DT, both at deeper levels. This divergence likely results from the RFs broader feature integration, which enhances accuracy but disperses importance and reduces transparency.

As expected, RF models exhibit substantially higher training times than DTs, reflecting the computational cost of ensemble learning, emphasizing the efficiency advantage of simpler tree-based classifiers in resource-constrained scenarios.

5   Conclusion

This study extends the Core-Shell Clustering framework by introducing a supervised classification approach that links wind to SST-derived Upwelling Stability Periods in the Canary Upwelling System. By assigning USP labels to daily QWP maps via a fuzzification–defuzzification procedure and applying interpretable models such as DTs, we show that SST-enhanced features, particularly SST differences, significantly boost classification accuracy (AUC > 0.94) while remaining consistent with oceanographic understanding.

Although DS3-based DT models yield the highest classification accuracy, DS2-based DTs offer greater interpretability, aligning closely with RF feature importance rankings and supporting practical, expert-informed use. This framework enhances the Core-Shell method's explanatory power by enabling physically grounded inference from wind forcing to upwelling persistence.

Future work should incorporate additional atmospheric and oceanic predictors (e.g., wind curl, sea level anomalies), integrate uncertainty quantification, and generalize the method to other Eastern Boundary Upwelling Systems for broader comparative insights.

Acknowledgments. The authors are indebted to the reviewers for their helpful comments that allowed to improve the paper. S.N. and P.C. acknowledge the supported by UID/04516/NOVA Laboratory for Computer Science and Informatics (NOVA LINCS) with the financial support of FCT.IP, P.R. acknowledges the support through projects UIDB/04326/2020, UIDP/04326/2020 and LA/P/0101/2020, all funded by Portuguese national funds from FCT- Foundation for Science and Technology. B.M. gratefully acknowledges support from the Basic Research Program of the National Research University Higher School of Economics.

Disclosure of Interests. The authors have no competing interests to declare that are relevant to the content of this article.

References

1. Atluri, G., Karpatne, A., Kumar, V.: Spatio-temporal data mining: a survey of problems and methods. ACM Comput. Surv. (CSUR) **51**(4), 1–41 (2018). https://doi.org/10.1145/3161602
2. Belmajdoub, H., Minaoui, K., El Aouni, A., El Abidi, Z.: Monitoring upwelling regions in major coastal zones using deep learning and sea surface temperature images. Int. J. Remote Sens. **45**(14), 4553–4575 (2024). https://doi.org/10.1080/01431161.2024.2365811

3. Bustos, D.F., Narváez, D.A., Dewitte, B., Oerder, V., Vidal, M., Tapia, F.: Revisiting historical trends in the eastern boundary upwelling systems with a machine learning method. Front. Mar. Sci. **11**, 1446766 (2024). https://doi.org/10.3389/fmars.2024.1446766

4. Efriana, L., Nugroho, A.P., Rizal, S., Wibowo, D.A.: Decadal monitoring of upwelling dynamics in satonda island waters using landsat-8 and machine learning regression. Geosfera Indonesia **9**(2), 144–156 (2024). https://doi.org/10.19184/geosi.v9i2.47203

5. Fawcett, T.: An introduction to roc analysis. Pattern Recogn. Lett. **27**(8), 861–874 (2006). https://doi.org/10.1016/j.patrec.2005.10.010

6. Gomes Mantovani, R., Horváth, T., Rossi, A.L., Cerri, R., Barbon Junior, S., Vanschoren, J., Carvalho, A.C.D.: Better trees: an empirical study on hyperparameter tuning of classification decision tree induction algorithms. Data Mining Knowl. Discov. **38**(3), 1364–1416 (2024). https://doi.org/10.1007/s10618-024-01002-5

7. Hersbach, H., et al.: ERA5 hourly data on single levels from 1940 to present (2023). https://doi.org/10.24381/cds.adbb2d47. Accessed 18 Feb 2025

8. Karpatne, A., Ebert-Uphoff, I., Ravela, S., Babaie, H.A., Kumar, V.: Machine learning for the geosciences: challenges and opportunities. IEEE Trans. Knowl. Data Eng. **31**(8), 1544–1554 (2018). https://doi.org/10.1109/TKDE.2018.2861006

9. Klir, G., Yuan, B.: Fuzzy Sets and Fuzzy Logic, vol. 4. Prentice Hall, New Jersey (1995)

10. Liu, M., Liu, X., Liu, D., Ding, C., Jiang, J.: Multivariable integration method for estimating sea surface salinity in coastal waters from in situ data and remotely sensed data using random forest algorithm. Comput. Geosci. **75**, 44–56 (2015). https://doi.org/10.1016/j.cageo.2014.10.016

11. Mera, D., Cotos, J.M., Varela-Pet, J.G. Rodríguez, P., Caro, A.: Automatic decision support system based on SAR data for oil spill detection. Comput. Geosci. **72**, 184–191 (2014). https://doi.org/10.1016/j.cageo.2014.07.015

12. Nascimento, S., Martins, A., Relvas, P., Luís, J.F., Mirkin, B.: Core–shell clustering approach for detection and analysis of coastal upwelling. Comput. Geosci. **179**, 105421 (2023). https://doi.org/10.1016/j.cageo.2023.105421

13. Nascimento, S., Martins, A., Relvas, P., Luís, J.F., Mirkin, B.: Piece-wise constant cluster modelling of dynamics of upwelling patterns. Expert. Syst. **40**(10), e13446 (2023). https://doi.org/10.1111/exsy.13446

14. Ramanantsoa, J.D., Krug, M., Penven, P., Rouault, M., Gula, J.: Coastal upwelling south of Madagascar: temporal and spatial variability. J. Mar. Syst. **178**, 29–37 (2018). https://doi.org/10.1016/j.jmarsys.2017.10.005

15. Relvas, P., Luis, J., Santos, A.M.P.: Importance of the mesoscale in the decadal changes observed in the northern canary upwelling system. Geophys. Res. Lett. **36**(22) (2009). https://doi.org/10.1029/2009GL040504

16. Ross, T.J.: Fuzzy Logic with Engineering Applications. Wiley (2005)

17. Wei, C.L., Rowe, G.T., Escobar-Briones, E., Boetius, A., Soltwedel, T., et al.: Global patterns and predictions of seafloor biomass using random forests. PLoS ONE **5**(12), e15323 (2010). https://doi.org/10.1371/journal.pone.0015323

18. Yari, S., Mohrholz, V., Bordbar, M.H.: Wind variability across the north humboldt upwelling system. Front. Mar. Sci. **10**, 1087980 (2023). https://doi.org/10.3389/fmars.2023.1087980

Generative AI: Foundations and Applications (GenAI)

SynDocDis: A Metadata-Driven Framework for Generating Synthetic Physician Discussions Using Large Language Models

Beny Rubinstein[1] and Sérgio Matos[1,2]

[1] University of Aveiro, Aveiro, Portugal
{BenyR,aleixomatos}@ua.pt
[2] IEETA, DETI, LASI, University of Aveiro, Aveiro, Portugal

Abstract. Physician-physician discussions of patient cases represent a rich source of clinical knowledge and reasoning that could feed AI agents to enrich and even participate in subsequent interactions. However, privacy regulations and ethical considerations severely restrict access to such data. While synthetic data generation using Large Language Models offers a promising alternative, existing approaches primarily focus on patient-physician interactions or structured medical records, leaving a significant gap in physician-to-physician communication synthesis.

We present SynDocDis, a novel framework that combines structured prompting techniques with privacy-preserving de-identified case metadata to generate clinically accurate physician-to-physician dialogues. Evaluation by five practicing physicians in nine oncology and hepatology scenarios demonstrated exceptional communication effectiveness (mean 4.4/5) and strong medical content quality (mean 4.1/5), with substantial inter-rater reliability ($\kappa = 0.70$, 95% CI: 0.67–0.73). The framework achieved 91% clinical relevance ratings, while maintaining doctors' and patients' privacy. These results place SynDocDis as a promising framework for advancing medical AI research ethically and responsibly through privacy-compliant synthetic physician dialogue generation with direct applications in medical education and clinical decision support.

Keywords: Artificial intelligence · Natural language generation · Physician communication · Medical ethics · Synthetic data · Large language models

1 Introduction

The integration of Large Language Models (LLMs) into medicine represents a paradigm shift, moving beyond task automation to a synergistic partnership between artificial intelligence and human expertise. LLMs have surpassed previous Natural Language Processing (NLP) systems in medical question answering, summarization, text generation, and clinical decision support [9]; yet, an area

© The Author(s), under exclusive license to Springer Nature Switzerland AG 2026
J. Valente de Oliveira et al. (Eds.): EPIA 2025, LNAI 16121, pp. 311–323, 2026.
https://doi.org/10.1007/978-3-032-05176-9_24

where research is lagging behind is supporting physician-to-physician discussions of patient cases. Progress in this area requires access to real patient case discussions, which is challenging given the highly sensitive nature of patient data and strict privacy regulations, such as HIPAA in the United States and GDPR in the European Union. Furthermore, physician discussions remain sensitive even when de-identified, because of potential re-identification risks, and doctors are reluctant to share their decision-making processes due to fear of scrutiny and liability risks.

This study contributes to the assessment of synthetic clinical text generation for physician-physician discussions as a balanced approach that allows data sharing with researchers while minimizing privacy risks. We present a framework called SynDocDis, which focuses on generating synthetic physician-to-physician discussions using LLMs. Its primary goal is to create clinically accurate and privacy-preserving synthetic dialogues based on de-identified metadata extracted from real patient case discussions while maintaining both clinical accuracy and the natural communication patterns of discussions among physicians. This work is motivated by challenges in accessing real-world data for physician conversations due to privacy concerns, liability issues, and the sensitivity of de-identified discussions, and addresses two key research questions:

1. *Can general-purpose large language models generate high-fidelity physician-to-physician discussions using only de-identified metadata from real patient case discussions?*
2. *How do domain experts judge the quality of these synthetic discussions?*

The contributions of this study can be summarized as follows:

- We propose SynDocDis, a generic framework based on Context-Instructions-Details-Input (CIDI)[1] for generating physician discussions using metadata;
- We conduct a comprehensive evaluation of nine synthetic case discussions by practicing physicians from diverse specialties and geographical locations;
- We share a public package containing the prompts used, the synthetic medical dialogues, and expert ratings: https://github.com/aleixomatos/syndocdis

The remainder of this paper is organized as follows: Sect. 2 reviews related work on synthetic medical dialogue generation and LLMs in clinical settings. Section 3 describes the methods used to develop and evaluate the SynDocDis framework. Section 4 presents the evaluation results and discusses the findings, limitations, and future directions. Finally, Sect. 5 concludes the paper.

2   Related Work

Recent advances in clinician text-data generation have demonstrated significant potential for addressing data scarcity and privacy concerns in medical Artificial

---

[1] The CIDI framework is articulated in the LinkedIn course "Nano Tips for Using Chat GPT to 10x Your Productivity at Work with Gianluca Mauro".

Intelligence (AI) research. The current literature explores various facets of how LLMs can generate high-fidelity medical text, but there is limited direct evidence that they can reliably create authentic physician-to-physician discussions using only de-identified metadata from real patient-case discussions.

2.1   LLM Evolution in Clinical Text Generation

LLMs have rapidly advanced the generation of synthetic medical dialogue, particularly in tasks such as clinical text summarization (e.g., discharge summaries), medical question answering, and patient-provider communication. For example, Sufi [15] extracted features from synthetically generated patient discharge messages that correlated with the severity of patients' conditions. Moreover, research by Williams et al. [17] revealed that LLM-generated discharge summaries can meet quality and safety standards comparable to those written by human physicians, albeit with slightly higher error rates and lower comprehensiveness. Other studies have shown that LLM-generated text can outperform human responses in terms of quality, capturing nuanced communications that reflect both technical proficiency and empathy. Ayers et al. [1] highlighted that AI chatbots can generate responses that show quality and empathy for medical advice. This aligns with another study by Hartman et al. [4], which suggested that LLMs could streamline clinical tasks, such as emergency handoff notes, thus alleviating the burdens faced by health professionals and fostering effective communication between physicians. Their findings indicate the superiority of LLM-generated over physician-written notes in accuracy and detail, but show that they are marginally inferior in terms of usefulness and safety, suggesting that a physician-in-the-loop implementation design is necessary for safe adoption. Moreover, the clinical potential of LLMs in this context has been growing with their increasing capability to provide diagnostic support and reasoning explanations, which are crucial components of physician-to-physician dialogue. Spitzer et al. [14] note that LLMs can assist in generating explanatory content that clarifies the rationale behind clinical decisions, thereby enriching peer discussions and collaborative patient care. Such capabilities are central to creating more fluid communication between physicians. Although the implementation of LLMs in clinical settings is promising, several challenges remain. Small et al. [13] addressed concerns related to processing needs, model biases, and privacy, all of which hinder the deployment of LLM technology in clinical settings. Nonetheless, advancements in these models suggest that with continued refinement and resolution of these issues, LLM-based agents may complement and facilitate detailed and accurate case discussions.

2.2   Synthetic Medical Dialogue

The synthesis of medical dialogues represents a particularly challenging subset of medical data generation, which requires the preservation of both clinical accuracy and natural conversation flow. Existing research has primarily focused on patient-physician interactions; for example, a recent study indicated that although patients often express a preference for human doctors over AI, there is interest in hybrid models that incorporate AI assistance during consultations [10]. Recent literature also suggests that generative AI can transform the clinician-patient relationship into a triadic interaction that includes AI as a "third agent," ultimately guiding shared decision-making processes [2,7].

Previous studies have explored various aspects of medical dialogue generation, including record-centric narrative synthesis and privacy-preserving techniques for sharing healthcare data. Moser et al. [8] highlight the potential of LLMs to generate realistic medical dialogues, which is crucial for replicating natural conversational nuances in the clinical setting. This was complemented by Li et al. [5], who focused on semi-supervised variational reasoning for dialogue generation, which embodies strategies that could enhance the quality of inter-physician interactions by simulating inquiry and dialogue management, typical of clinical practice. In the context of dataset generation, Liu et al. [6] emphasized the importance of various medical conversational datasets aimed at enhancing dialogue agents that assist healthcare professionals. Similarly, Zeng et al. [18] introduced MedDialog, a dataset containing over three million turns of patient-doctor conversations in English and Chinese collected from online medical consultation platforms. This demonstrated that large-scale, privacy-preserved dialogue datasets can significantly improve the performance of medical dialogue systems, particularly in maintaining clinical accuracy and natural conversation flow.

While LLMs have made strides in synthesizing clinical text, such as discharge summaries or single-speaker clinical notes, there is a gap in research on their ability to create high-fidelity, authentic physician-to-physician dialogues based solely on de-identified metadata from real patient cases. This gap is due to the lack of conversational context, complexity of multispeaker interactions, and insufficient validation in this specific scenario. Multispeaker dialogue synthesis poses unique challenges related to conversational dynamics, speaker roles, and interaction contexts that are not present in standard clinical text summarization.

2.3   Gaps in Current Approaches

Despite the advances highlighted in the previous sections, several significant gaps remain, including:

– Limited focus on physician-to-physician communication: although substantial work exists on patient-provider dialogues, the synthesis of physician-to-physician discussions remains largely unexplored. This is particularly significant, given the unique characteristics of interprofessional medical communication, including specialized terminology and complex clinical reasoning;
– Privacy-utility trade-offs: existing approaches often sacrifice utility for privacy preservation, particularly when generating detailed clinical discussions. Giuffrè and Shung highlighted these challenges, but did not resolve them for dialogue generation [3];

– Evaluation metrics: while current evaluation approaches are adequate for structured data, they lack specific metrics for assessing the quality of synthetic medical dialogues, particularly in professional-to-professional communication.

Our approach builds upon existing work while addressing the unique challenges of synthetic physician-to-physician discussions, contributing to both the theoretical understanding and practical implementation of synthetic medical data generation. To our knowledge, our work is the first to (i) condition generation on shareable, de-identified metadata, (ii) create multi-speaker discussions with role tags and reference stubs, and (iii) evaluate them with practicing physicians from four specialties. In summary, the evidence suggests that general-purpose LLMs can generate high-fidelity physician-to-physician discussions by leveraging de-identified metadata from real patient cases.

3   Methods

We developed a new method for generating synthetic physician discussions, focusing on preserving the main characteristics of real-world medical conversations. We hypothesized that by carefully designing prompts to guide the models, we could create realistic and relevant discussions that protect privacy and are useful for developing AI tools to support physician discussions.

3.1   Study Design

Our approach focuses on three key aspects: (a) input: de-identified metadata extraction from real-world physician discussions; (b) setup: implementation of the CIDI framework for structured prompting; and (c) output evaluation: expert physician evaluation of synthetic data quality. The framework uses metadata from real-world physician discussions to generate synthetic expert discussions that maintain privacy while preserving clinical relevance and similar dynamics of medical discussions, which go through a structured human evaluation process (see Fig. 1). In addition, we aimed to generate diverse responses whenever possible because physicians value the variability of perspectives that are not always present in their real-world discussions, and also to include references to claims made in these simulated discussions about patient cases to ensure that they are evidence-based.

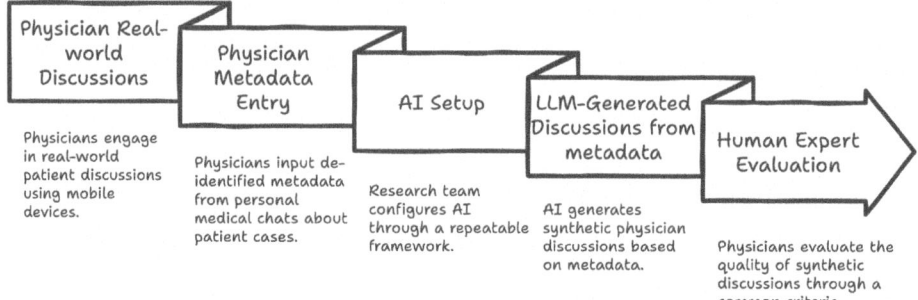

Fig. 1. Overview of study design and workflow.

3.2   Data Collection: Physician Input Through Metadata

We developed a data entry form and asked physicians to collect metadata describing real patient case discussions they were engaged in through their professional medical chat (PMC) groups (see Table 1). We then used these metadata as input to create high-fidelity synthetic data.

Table 1. Example of metadata provided from real-world physician discussions.

Metadata	Example
Chat Name	Pancreas ATM
Participant Doctors	52, 35, 6, 65, 46
Specialty of Participants	Head of Department in a large hospital; Head of Service in a peripheral hospital; Head of Unit in a large hospital; Head of Unit in a large hospital; Head of Unit in a large hospital
Patient Case	Male, age 69, PS1, Aug 2023 diagnosed with pancreatic adenocarcinoma, one lesion in pancreatic head and another in tail. Underwent total pancreatectomy, pathologic stage T2mN0M0, now is on adjuvant FOLFIRINOX. Genetic testing shows germinal mutation ATM C.103C>T heterozygote. The question is whether to give him maintenance PARP inhibitor
Number of responses	4
Are answers valuable?	Valuable. Standard of care
Variability in responses	All replied the same laconic- against PARP inhibitor. One added there is only evidence in BRCA mut

3.3   Synthetic Data Generation Framework

We applied the CIDI framework to structure the generation of synthetic physician discussions based on de-identified case metadata to establish a repeatable process and to enhance both the specificity and relevance of the AI-generated discussions (Fig. 2).

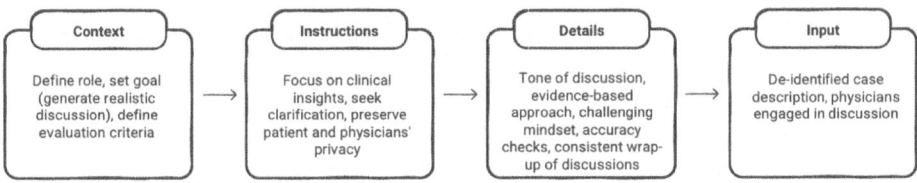

Fig. 2. Generation of synthetic physician discussions following the CIDI framework.

User Prompting. In addition to role-playing—asking the model to adopt a persona and act accordingly—we adopted a technique called emotion prompting, using capital letters to emphasize important aspects (see Fig. 3, top).

System Prompting. We applied prompting techniques such as role-playing to set up the context, and a hybrid prompting structure—mainly a zero-shot approach with a chain-of-thought technique—to instruct the LLM to approach the task step-by-step, followed by a definition of the expected output (Fig. 3) [12, 16].

Table 2. Evaluation criteria used to assess the synthetic discussions.

	Category	Description
Medical Content Quality	1.1 Clinical Accuracy	Assess whether the information shared is medically correct and up to date
	1.2 Evidence-Based	Evaluate if physicians are using evidence-based medicine principles in their discussion
	1.3 Relevance	Is the discussion directly applicable to the patient case at hand?
	1.4 Comprehensiveness	Check if all relevant aspects of the patient's condition are being addressed
Communication Effectiveness	2.1 Clarity & Coherence	Assess whether the discussion is clear, well-structured, and easy to follow
	2.2. Medical Terminology	Evaluate appropriate use of medical terms and explanations when necessary
	2.3 Active Listening	Observe if physicians are attentively listening to each other's input
	2.4 Variability/Diversity	Evaluate if physicians are challenging each other and exploring a diverse set of "schools of thought"

3.4   Evaluation Protocol

Our evaluation protocol for the quality of synthetic physician discussions employed a mixed-methods approach. Expert review remains the gold standard,

User Prompt: Act as an experienced and helpful physician and Head of a Unit/Department in a large hospital. With extensive experience and thousands of patient cases, you also moderate a WhatsApp group for oncologists with broad general medical knowledge. It is ESSENTIAL to create the discussion based on the provided INPUT which you will request from me, aiming for a thoughtful, high-value exchange among expert peers. Focus on enriching the conversation with clinical insights, expertise, and best practices in oncology and general medicine. Ensure that P0 (the 'Case owner') actively addresses relevant questions or contributions from other doctors as part of the patient case discussion.

System Prompt: You are a knowledgeable and experienced physician specializing in oncology. Your goal is to generate realistic discussions between physicians about patient cases based on the metadata that I will provide. Please maintain a professional, clear, and concise tone, with each doctor focusing on relevant clinical insights, differential diagnoses, and actionable next steps. Doctors will seek clarification, agree with, or build upon others' suggestions when appropriate.
Instructions: <begin>
• Step 1: Create a discussion that combines supportive, exploratory, and question-driven responses. Include occasional clarifications, agreements, challenges, or new and alternative suggestions to mirror real-life physician discussions. Ensure 'Case owner' participates by addressing questions, adding insights, asking clarifying questions, or responding to clarifications throughout the discussion as needed.
• Step 2: State the total number of unique physicians who participated in the discussion, counted once per doctor (and list their numbers). For example, if I enter 35, 10, 14 as input to <Physicians participating> then you should state "3 physicians engaged in the discussion: P35, P10, and P14"
• Step 3: Confirm the total number of replies (R) in the discussion, including all contributions from the 'Case owner' and other physicians as per the specified response count. For example, if 'Case owner' posted a case, and each of the additional two physicians responded twice, then R=2 physicians x 2 responses per physician (so R=4).
• Step 4: Cite relevant external references, such as research papers or medical guidelines, to enhance the clinical depth of the discussion when applicable. <end>"
Output: Begin the discussion with 'Case owner' presenting the case details and initial questions to peers. Conclude the conversation once all responses and follow-up from 'Case owner' have been addressed. Name each responding physician in the format "Doctor" followed by the number of the physician. Keep responses concise and relevant, each on a new line, ensuring they logically build on previous inputs. Adhere to the specified count for both unique physicians (P) and total responses (R).
Reward Criteria: An external physician will receive this guideline to assess output based on the following criteria:
1.Medical Content Quality Assessment
1.1 Clinical Accuracy: Assess whether the information shared is medically correct and up to date.
(...)
2.4 Variability of Responses: Evaluate if physicians are challenging each other and exploring a diverse set of "schools of thoughts."

Fig. 3. User and System prompts used to generate synthetic patient case discussions.

so the assessment of nine oncology and hepatology scenarios yielded 360 item-level judgments (nine dialogues × eight criteria × five raters). The evaluation was conducted by five practicing physicians from various specialties (intensive medicine (2), general surgery, oncology, ophthalmology) and geographical locations, who also provided additional commentary.

Each dialogue was evaluated across eight criteria, organized into two main categories: Medical Content Quality and Communication Effectiveness. The evaluators used a 5-point Likert scale for all criteria (5 = excellent, 4 = good, 3 = acceptable, 2 = limited, and 1 = does not meet the criteria). Although we did not use "LLM-as-a-Judge" as a prompting technique, we included the evaluation criteria (see Table 2) in the system prompt, noted as 'Reward Criteria', and asked the system to optimize the output.

4 Results and Discussion

The evaluation demonstrated strong performance across both assessment categories (Fig. 4). Communication effectiveness achieved a mean of 4.4/5, with over 98% of LLM-generated discussions rated "Excellent" (5) or "Good" for Clarity and Coherence, Use of Medical Terminology, and Active Listening. Medical content quality showed strong but less consistent results (mean = 4.1/5), with 91% and 78% of evaluations being "Excellent" (5) or "Good" (4) for Clinical Relevance and Clinical Accuracy, respectively.

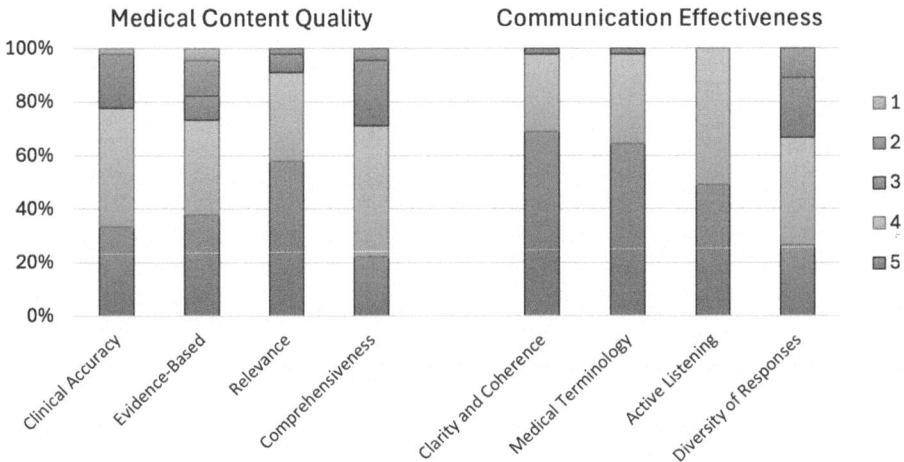

Fig. 4. Evaluation by medical experts (5 = Excellent; 3 = Adequate; 1 = Criteria not met).

To assess the agreement among physician evaluators, we employed the weighted Fleiss' κ using quadratic weights to penalize disagreements between distant categories (e.g., 1 vs. 5), and calculated 95% confidence intervals using bootstrap resampling with 1000 iterations. The results show substantial agreement among the physician evaluators overall ($\kappa = 0.70$, 95% CI: 0.67–0.73), with also substantial agreement for both medical content quality ($\kappa = 0.71$, 95% CI: 0.67–0.75) and communication effectiveness ($\kappa = 0.68$, 95% CI: 0.64–0.72).

Our study demonstrates that large language models, when guided by a structured metadata-driven approach, can generate high-quality synthetic physician-to-physician discussions while preserving privacy. The evaluation results reveal several significant findings that advance our understanding of synthetic medical data generation. The synthetic discussions achieved strong performance in clinical accuracy and relevance, with 91% of evaluations rated as "Excellent" or "Good" for Clinical Relevance. This suggests that metadata-driven generation can effectively capture the essential elements of physician-to-physician communication. However, the fact that 20% of the discussions were rated "Average" or below in clinical accuracy reinforces the ongoing challenge of maintaining consistently high clinical accuracy in synthetic data generation with general purpose large language models such as GPT-4.

The framework demonstrated exceptional performance in communication effectiveness, with a mean score of 4.4/5. Particularly noteworthy was the strong performance in clarity and coherence, and appropriate use of medical terminology, with over 98% of the evaluations rated as "Excellent" or "Good" in these areas. This suggests that the CIDI framework effectively structures synthetic medical discussions in a way that resembles real-world physician communication patterns.

Our metadata-driven approach successfully maintains privacy while generating clinically relevant discussions. By utilizing de-identified metadata rather than raw patient data as input, we address a critical challenge in AI research applied to physician-physician discussions: the need for real-world data that does not compromise patient or clinician confidentiality.

While the initial implementation of this study was conducted on proprietary LLM (GPT-4), which could potentially impact reproducibility, the CIDI framework is model-agnostic and can be implemented using various LLMs. We provide detailed prompting templates and metadata structures to enable reproduction using alternative models. Future work will explore open-source alternatives to improve accessibility and reproducibility, and/or specialized models such as MedGemma (released by Google in May 2025).

Evidence-Based Reasoning showed lower performance, with 18% of evaluations rated below adequate level. This suggests the need for better integration of additional data sources and/or external medical knowledge bases, together with Retrieval-Augmented Generation (RAG) and techniques such as self-reflection and chain-of-thought (CoT) to verify that the model outputs are grounded in scientific context, thus enhancing the quality of evidence-based discussions. Evaluators pointed out that while some of the references provided were somewhat outdated, it is a step forward towards augmenting discussions with relevant references, which are often unavailable in live discussions.

Moreover, although "Variability of Responses" had a mean of 3.8/5, this category received a rating of "2 -Limited diversity or challenge to established ideas" in 5 of the 45 evaluations. As some evaluators pointed out, this has been partially introduced by implementing the study with metadata mirroring exactly the real-world discussions, many of which had too few physicians engaged and/or not many responses (an evaluator also noted that not all discussions will or should lead to a wide diversity of opinions). Therefore, this can be addressed by not limiting the number of doctors participating in the discussion and/or the number of responses when providing metadata as input. This is an opportunity for further exploration of our framework, as increasing the variability and diversity of responses can create value for physicians and ultimately patients, as also suggested in a recent opinion paper [11].

5   Conclusion

The proposed SynDocDis framework uses a method based on metadata from real-world patient cases to generate realistic physician-to-physician dialogues, ensuring that the generated conversations are relevant to the context, clinically accurate, and reflective of the patterns and details found in real medical discussions. By combining structured prompting techniques with privacy-preserving de-identification strategies, SynDocDis demonstrates that large language models, when guided by a structured metadata-driven approach, can ethically generate physician-to-physician discussions that are both useful and privacy-preserving.

This study offers a pathway for future research that can leverage synthetic medical dialogues for training AI assistants, refining clinical guidelines, and augmenting medical education.

Acknowledgments. This work was partially funded by national funds through FCT - Foundation for Science and Technology, I.P., under project UID/00127. We acknowledge the contributions of Dr. Einat Shacham-Shmueli, MD (Senior Oncologist and Head of the Gastrointestinal Cancer Clinic at Sheba Medical Center). We also acknowledge the input and feedback from Adir C. Sommer, MD (Department of Ophthalmology, Rambam Health Care Campus, Rambam, Israel; Ruth and Bruce Rappaport Faculty of Medicine, Technion-Israel Institute of Technology, Haifa, Israel); Alon Botzer, PhD; Amir Sheik-Yousouf, MD, MBA; Bruno Gonçalves, MD, MSc, PhD (Hospital São Lucas Copacabana); Fabio Jung, MD, MBA; Limor Amit, MD; Ronen Tal-Botzer, PhD.

Disclosure of Interests. The authors have no competing interests to declare that are relevant to the content of this article.

References

1. Ayers, J.W., et al.: Comparing physician and artificial intelligence chatbot responses to patient questions posted to a public social media forum. JAMA Int. Med. **183**, 589 (2023). https://doi.org/10.1001/jamainternmed.2023.1838. https://jamanetwork.com/journals/jamainternalmedicine/fullarticle/2804309

2. Campos Jr., H., Wolfe, D., Luan, H., Sim, I.: Generative AI as third agent: LLMs and the transformation of the clinician-patient relationship. J. Participat. Med. (2025). https://doi.org/10.2196/68146

3. Giuffrè, M., Shung, D.L.: Harnessing the power of synthetic data in healthcare: innovation, application, and privacy. npj Dig. Med. **6**, 186 (2023). https://doi.org/10.1038/s41746-023-00927-3. https://www.nature.com/articles/s41746-023-00927-3

4. Hartman, V., et al.: Developing and evaluating large language model–generated emergency medicine handoff notes. JAMA Netw. Open **7**, e2448723 (2024). https://doi.org/10.1001/jamanetworkopen.2024.48723. https://jamanetwork.com/journals/jamanetworkopen/fullarticle/2827327

5. Li, D., Ren, Z., Ren, P., Chen, Z., Fan, M., Ma, J., de Rijke, M.: Semi-supervised variational reasoning for medical dialogue generation. In: Proceedings of the 44th International ACM SIGIR Conference on Research and Development in Information Retrieval, pp. 544–554. ACM (2021). https://doi.org/10.1145/3404835.3462921. https://dl.acm.org/doi/10.1145/3404835.3462921

6. Liu, W., Tang, J., Cheng, Y., Li, W., Zheng, Y., Liang, X.: Meddg: an entity-centric medical consultation dataset for entity-aware medical dialogue generation. In: Lu, W., Huang, S., Hong, Y., Zhou, X. (eds.) Natural Language Processing and Chinese Computing, pp. 447–459. Springer, Cham (2022). https://doi.org/10.1007/978-3-031-17120-8_35

7. Lorenzini, G., Ossa, L.A., Shaw, D.M., Elger, B.S.: Artificial intelligence and the doctor–patient relationship expanding the paradigm of shared decision making. Bioethics **37**, 424–429 (2023). https://doi.org/10.1111/bioe.13158. https://onlinelibrary.wiley.com/doi/10.1111/bioe.13158

8. Moser, D., Bender, M., Sariyar, M.: Generating Synthetic Healthcare Dialogues in Emergency Medicine Using Large Language Models. IOS Press (2024). https://doi.org/10.3233/SHTI241099. https://ebooks.iospress.nl/doi/10.3233/SHTI241099

9. Peng, C., et al.: A study of generative large language model for medical research and healthcare. npj Dig. Med. **6**, 210 (2023). https://doi.org/10.1038/s41746-023-00958-w. https://www.nature.com/articles/s41746-023-00958-w

10. Riedl, R., Hogeterp, S.A., Reuter, M.: Do patients prefer a human doctor, artificial intelligence, or a blend, and is this preference dependent on medical discipline? Empirical evidence and implications for medical practice. Front. Psychol. **15** (2024). https://doi.org/10.3389/fpsyg.2024.1422177. https://www.frontiersin.org/articles/10.3389/fpsyg.2024.1422177/full

11. Sarkar, A.: AI should challenge, not obey. Commun. ACM **67**, 18–21 (2024). https://doi.org/10.1145/3649404

12. Savage, T., Nayak, A., Gallo, R., Rangan, E., Chen, J.H.: Diagnostic reasoning prompts reveal the potential for large language model interpretability in medicine. npj Dig. Med. **7**, 20 (2024). https://doi.org/10.1038/s41746-024-01010-1

13. Small, W.R., et al.: Large language model–based responses to patients' in-basket messages. JAMA Netw. Open **7**, e2422399 (2024). https://doi.org/10.1001/jamanetworkopen.2024.22399. https://jamanetwork.com/journals/jamanetworkopen/fullarticle/2821167

14. Spitzer, P., et al.: The effect of medical explanations from large language models on diagnostic decisions in radiology (2025). https://doi.org/10.1101/2025.03.04.25323357. http://medrxiv.org/lookup/doi/10.1101/2025.03.04.25323357

15. Sufi, F.: Addressing data scarcity in the medical domain: a GPT-based approach for synthetic data generation and feature extraction. Information **15**,

264 (2024). https://doi.org/10.3390/info15050264. https://www.mdpi.com/2078-2489/15/5/264

16. Wei, J., et al.: Chain-of-thought prompting elicits reasoning in large language models. In: Koyejo, S., Mohamed, S., Agarwal, A., Belgrave, D., Cho, K., Oh, A. (eds.) Advances in Neural Information Processing Systems, vol. 35, pp. 24824–24837. Curran Associates, Inc. (2022). https://proceedings.neurips.cc/paper_files/paper/2022/file/9d5609613524ecf4f15af0f7b31abca4-Paper-Conference.pdf

17. Williams, C.Y.K., et al.: Physician- and large language model–generated hospital discharge summaries. JAMA Int. Med. (2025). https://doi.org/10.1001/jamainternmed.2025.0821

18. Zeng, G., et al.: MedDialog: large-scale medical dialogue datasets. In: Webber, B., Cohn, T., He, Y., Liu, Y. (eds.) Proceedings of the 2020 Conference on Empirical Methods in Natural Language Processing (EMNLP), pp. 9241–9250. Association for Computational Linguistics, Online (2020). https://doi.org/10.18653/v1/2020.emnlp-main.743. https://aclanthology.org/2020.emnlp-main.743/

Large Language Model Framework for Log Sequence Anomaly Detection

João Reis[1], Miguel Areias[2], and Jorge G. Barbosa[1]([⊠])

[1] LIACC, Faculty of Engineering, University of Porto, Porto, Portugal
jbarbosa@fe.up.pt
[2] INESC-TEC, Faculty of Science, University of Porto, Porto, Portugal

Abstract. Log analysis is fundamental to modern software observability systems, playing a key role in improving system reliability. Recently, there has been a growing adoption of Large Language Models (LLMs) for log anomaly detection, due to their ability to learn complex patterns. In this work, we propose a model-agnostic framework that allows seamless plug-and-play integration of different LLMs, making it easy to experiment with and select the model that fits specific needs. These models are first fine-tuned on normal log data, learning their patterns. During inference, the model predicts the most probable next tokens based on the preceding context in each sequence. Anomaly detection is performed using Top-K predictions, where sequences are flagged as anomalous if the actual log entry does not appear among the K most probable next tokens, with K determined using the validation dataset. The proposed framework is evaluated on three widely-used benchmark datasets—HDFS, BGL, and Thunderbird—where it consistently achieves competitive results, outperforming state-of-the-art methods in multiple scenarios. These results highlight the effectiveness of LLM-based log analysis and the importance of flexibility when selecting models for specific operational contexts.

Keywords: Log Analysis · Fault detection · Observability

1 Introduction

Logs record detailed information about the state and behavior of a system, making them a valuable resource for system monitoring, observability, and debugging. They can help detect and diagnose a wide range of issues early on, including security breaches, system malfunctions, and software bugs, which results in better system reliability.

Log analysis involves extracting insights and identifying patterns from structured log messages, enabling the detection of anomalies. This is achieved by learning the underlying patterns that distinguish normal behavior from abnormal. However, this task is challenging due to the complex and often long-range dependencies between log messages. As a result, a wide range of machine learning methods, ranging from traditional algorithms to deep learning approaches, have been explored [4–6].

© The Author(s), under exclusive license to Springer Nature Switzerland AG 2026
J. Valente de Oliveira et al. (Eds.): EPIA 2025, LNAI 16121, pp. 324–334, 2026.
https://doi.org/10.1007/978-3-032-05176-9_25

With the invention of the transformer architecture [18] and its widespread success across natural language processing (NLP) tasks, LLMs have been increasingly applied to the domain of log analysis. This has led to the development of frameworks that leverage LLMs for modeling log sequences and their patterns and detecting anomalies.

In this work, we introduce a novel and flexible framework that addresses a key limitation in existing LLM-based solutions: the lack of modularity and ease in switching between underlying LLMs. This is a significant issue, as the field of LLMs evolves at a rapid pace.

To tackle this, our framework leverages the open-source Unsloth library [10], which provides access to a wide range of popular LLMs. Our approach involves fine-tuning these models on sequences of normal logs so that they can learn the underlying structure and relationships within normal behavior. During inference, the model predicts the next token in a sequence. If the actual token is not among the Top-K most likely predictions, the sequence is flagged as anomalous.

We validate our approach through experiments using three widely used benchmark datasets in log anomaly detection. Our results show that the proposed framework outperforms state-of-the-art methods in many scenarios, demonstrating its effectiveness.

2   Related Work

Log anomaly detection involves identifying anomalies through the extraction of insights and identifying patterns from log messages. The primary goal is to monitor the system, detect and respond to potential issues, consequently improving its reliability and efficiency.

The field of log analysis has been significantly transformed by the rapid advancements in machine learning. Initially, traditional machine learning techniques such as Principal Component Analysis (PCA) [4], Isolation Forest [5], and one-class Support Vector Machines (SVMs) [6] were commonly employed. A subsequent wave of methodologies introduced Long Short-Term Memory (LSTM) Networks. These were successfully integrated into solutions like DeepLog [1] and LogAnomaly [2], marking a notable progression in the field.

In recent years, transformers [18] have driven significant advancements. Initially, models like BERT [19] were adapted for log analysis, notably in LogBERT [7]. Subsequently, the emergence of LLMs led to further attempts to apply them in this domain.

For instance, LogGPT [3] leverages GPT-2 [8] for log analysis and demonstrates impressive results. First, the Drain parser [9] is used to extract log templates from the raw log messages, with each template represented by a unique log key. These log keys are then used to construct log sequences. The model is trained exclusively on normal log data, sequences that do not contain any anomalies, and learns to predict the next log key based on the preceding keys in the sequence. To capture the inherent variability in normal log sequences, LogGPT employs Top-K prediction. This approach allows the model to consider a set of likely next log keys, rather than committing to a single prediction. This is crucial because multiple normal patterns may exist, and the Top-K strategy enables the model to accommodate this variability more effectively. The variable K is set to 50% of the total number of unique keys in the training dataset. Additionally, a reinforcement learning strategy is applied to further enhance anomaly detection performance. Specifically, the model is rewarded when the actual next log key appears within its Top-K predictions, encouraging it to capture a broader and more accurate representation of normal behavior.

Another example is the LogLLaMA framework [11], which follows a training approach similar to LogGPT. The model is trained to predict the next log key based on preceding keys and also incorporates a reinforcement learning strategy to further enhance anomaly detection performance. During inference, LogLLaMA likewise uses Top-K prediction, setting K to 50% of the total number of unique log keys in the training data. The main differences lie in the underlying model architecture and training data usage, where LogLLaMA utilizes Llama 2 instead of GPT-2 and adopts a proportional training strategy, using 10% of the dataset for training, as opposed to LogGPT, which consistently trains on a fixed sequence of 5,000 log lines regardless of the dataset size.

Recent advancements have showcased the versatility of modular LLM frameworks and their application to anomaly detection, highlighting a growing trend toward flexible, domain-agnostic LLM-based anomaly detection frameworks. For instance, recently Li et al. studied the problem of using LLMs to detect tabular anomalies [20]. LogiCode uses LLMs to autonomously generate code for detecting logical inconsistencies in industrial logs, and introduces a tailored benchmark for logical anomaly tasks [21]. ADALog is an unsupervised anomaly detection framework designed for modern software systems that generate extensive heterogeneous log data with dynamic formats, fragmented event sequences, and varying temporal patterns [22]. And finally, in the cybersecurity domain, APT-LLM embedding-based anomaly detection framework that integrates LLMs, BERT, ALBERT, DistilBERT, and RoBERTa, with autoencoder architectures to detect advanced persistent threats [23].

3   Proposed Framework

Our framework[1] depicted in Fig. 1, is designed to be model-agnostic, which sets it apart from most existing solutions that leverage LLMs for log anomaly detection. It is built on top of the Unsloth library [10], which abstracts away the underlying model architecture by providing a standardized interface for accessing and fine-tuning several open-source LLMs, such as Llama, Gemma, and Qwen [15–17].

The main motivation for adopting a model-agnostic framework lies in the fast-paced evolution of LLMs. New models are frequently released, each with different sizes and hardware requirements. In such a rapidly changing environment, the flexibility of our design enables seamless plug-and-play integration of

---

[1] Available   at   https://github.com/joaorr13/Model-Agnostic-Framework-Log-Sequence-Classification.

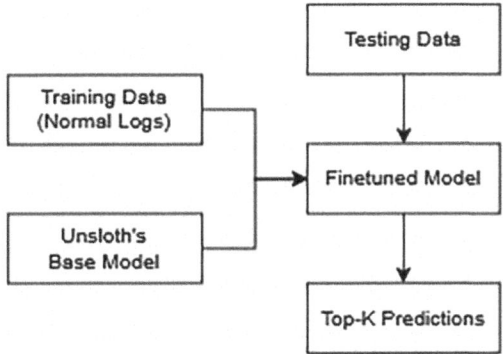

Fig. 1. Framework Overview.

any LLM supported by Unsloth, significantly reducing the engineering effort of experimenting with different architectures, and ensuring the long-term adaptability of the framework to the new computational challenges.

Rather than hardcoding support for a specific model architecture, our framework allows models to be loaded dynamically. Unsloth handles the necessary adaptations and integrations for each model internally. As a result, researchers can experiment with different LLMs by simply changing a configuration parameter, without needing to modify the training or inference code. This design makes the framework highly flexible and future-proof as new models become available.

The framework is composed of three main components: log parsing, model fine-tuning (training), and inference. Each of these components is fully decoupled from the specific model used, ensuring modularity.

In the log parsing phase, the Drain [9] parser is used to extract log templates from the raw log messages. This is followed by the training phase, which is inspired by the training process of LLMs, where the model is trained in normal log data, so it learns how to generate normal log sequences. Finally, the inference phase applies the Top-K prediction method to identify anomalies based on the model's output probabilities.

This stands in contrast to solutions such as LogGPT, which are tightly coupled to a specific model architecture—in this case, GPT-2. Adapting LogGPT to use a different model, such as Llama, would require significant changes to its codebase. Although LogLLaMA does not provide a codebase, there is no indication in the paper that such flexibility exists in its implementation at the time of writing.

Our framework avoids these limitations by design, offering a more flexible and extensible solution that enables broader experimentation and easier integration of new models.

3.1   Preprocessing

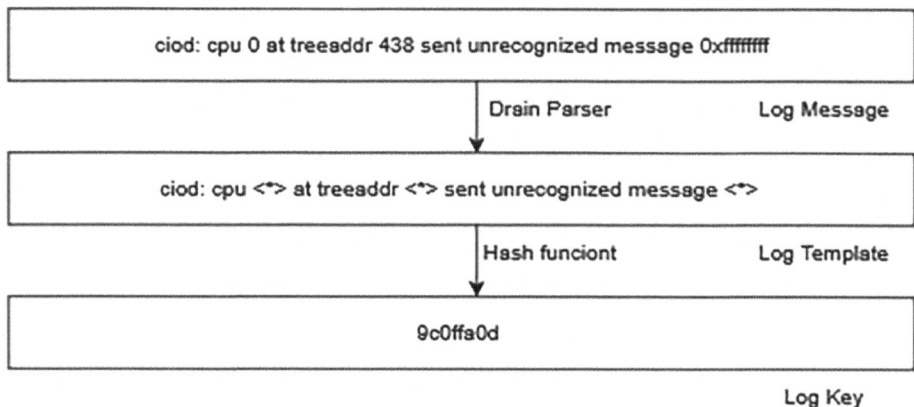

Fig. 2. Preprocessing stages.

Before training, an essential preprocessing phase is carried out that consists of log parsing, log key generation, and log sequence construction. For this, we reused the preprocessing code provided by LogGPT [3], and the process can be visualized in Fig. 2.

Log parsing is performed using the Drain algorithm [9], which constructs a fixed-depth parse tree to generate log templates. These templates group log messages of the same type. Each template is then passed through a hash function to generate a unique log key representing it. Specifically, we used the MD5 hash function and extracted the first 8 hexadecimal characters (i.e., the most significant bits) from the hash of the template string. This provides a compact and consistent identifier for each log template. Finally, these log keys are arranged in the order of the original log sequences to form log key sequences, which are used as input for training the model.

3.2   Model Training

In the fine-tuning phase, the model is fed with normal sequences of log keys. These types of model architecture enable them to learn patterns in the data, and with that information, they can generate normal log keys given as input a sequence of log keys. During training, we use the cross-entropy loss function, which can be defined as:

$$\mathcal{L}(\theta) = -\frac{1}{N} \sum_{i=1}^{N} \sum_{t=1}^{T_i - 1} \log p(k_{t+1}^i | k_{1:t}^i; \theta)$$

where θ is the model parameter, N is the number of training examples, T is the length of the current sequence, and $p(k_{t+1}^i | k_{1:t}^i)$ is the probability of the model correctly predicting k_{t+1}^i given the sequence $k_{1:t}^i$. This loss function is the same as stated in LogGPT [3].

3.3 Selecting K

For selecting K, we propose using the validation dataset. Specifically, we choose the smallest K such that, for every sequence in the validation set, the actual next log key appears within the model's Top-K predictions. In other words, we increment K until the model correctly includes the true next log key in the Top-K predictions for every step in every sequence. This mechanism provides a way to calibrate the model's confidence, such that expected behavior on regular sequences can be covered with high accuracy during the inference process.

4 Experiments

4.1 Datasets

To evaluate our framework, we selected three of the most commonly used datasets in the log anomaly detection field [12]. Using widely adopted datasets facilitates direct comparison with other state-of-the-art frameworks, which also rely on the same benchmarks. The datasets we used are: HDFS, BGL, and Thunderbird. Each is described below:

- **HDFS (Hadoop Distributed File System)**: This dataset consists of logs collected from the Hadoop Distributed File System, which is designed for storing and processing large-scale files. The logs were originally collected in 2008 [13] and were labeled by domain experts. Log messages are grouped into sequences based on session IDs.
- **BGL (BlueGene/L)**: This dataset contains logs from the BlueGene/L supercomputer at Lawrence Livermore National Laboratory, originally released in [14]. A sliding time window of 60 s is used to group log messages into sequences.
- **Thunderbird**: This dataset, also introduced in the same paper as BGL [14], was collected from systems at Sandia National Laboratories. To maintain consistency with other state-of-the-art frameworks, a subset of 20 million log messages were used. As in BGL, log sequences are created using a 60-second sliding window.

The dimensions of the datasets are shown in Table 1. We ensured they match those used in LogGPT [3], allowing for a fair and direct comparison with our framework.

330 J. Reis et al.

Table 1. Dimensions of the Datasets

Dataset	Training Data	Normal Testing Data	Anomalous Testing Data
HDFS	5,000	553,223	16,839
BGL	5,000	28,631	3,296
Thunderbird	5,000	67,039	40,920

4.2 Baselines

We compare our framework against two of the best existing solutions that leverage LLMs for log anomaly detection:

- **LogGPT** [3]: LogGPT utilizes GPT-2. The model is trained using the same loss function as in our framework, learning to generate normal log sequences. The value of K for Top-K prediction is set to half the number of unique log keys in the training dataset.
- **LogLLaMA** [11]: LogLLaMA employs Llama2 as its base model, although the specific version is not specified in the paper at the time of writing, and no code is provided to check it. Its training approach closely resembles that of LogGPT. A major difference lies in the amount of training data used: instead of the fixed 5,000 log lines, LogLLaMA uses 10% of the entire dataset for training, resulting in significantly larger training samples across all datasets.

4.3 Evaluation Metrics

These datasets are highly imbalanced, containing significantly more normal sequences than anomalous ones. This reflects the real-world nature of system logs, where abnormal events are rare. Therefore, like previous methods, we use Precision, Recall, and most importantly, the F1 Score to evaluate our model's performance.

The evaluation metrics are calculated as follows:

$$Precision = \frac{TP}{TP + FP} \tag{1}$$

$$Recall = \frac{TP}{TP + FN} \tag{2}$$

$$F1Score = 2 \times \frac{Precision * Recall}{Precision + Recall} \tag{3}$$

4.4   Implementation Details

To showcase the flexibility of our model-agnostic framework, we experimented with three different LLMs available through the Unsloth library [10]:

- **Gemma 3 with 1 billion parameters** [16]
- **Llama 3.2 with 1 billion parameters** [17]
- **Qwen 2.5 with 0.5 billion parameters** [15]

Gemma is a collection of lightweight, open-source models developed by Google DeepMind. We chose the smaller variant from the Gemma 3 family to ensure it can run on less powerful hardware. LLaMA 3.2, developed by Meta, is a collection of open-source compact models derived from the original LLaMA 3.1 family, specifically from the 8-billion-parameter version. Through pruning and distillation techniques, these models were reduced in size to form the lightweight LLaMA 3.2 collection, designed with mobile deployment in mind. Qwen 2.5 is a family of open-source models from Alibaba. We selected the smallest version, which is also optimized for lightweight applications, including potential use on mobile devices. In general, we focused our experiments on lightweight models that can run on most modern hardware. Although training these models benefits from more powerful hardware to reduce training time, running the trained versions should not pose a problem on most current systems.

All models were trained for a maximum of 100 epochs or until the validation loss did not improve for three consecutive epochs (early stoppage). The validation dataset, used for both early stopping and selecting the value of K, was consistently set to 20% of the training data. The learning rate used for the training is 2e-4.

4.5   Experimental Results

Table 2. Results in the HDFS, Thunderbird, and BGL Datasets.

	HDFS			BGL			Thunderbird		
	Precision	Recall	F1 score	Precision	Recall	F1 score	Precision	Recall	F1 score
LogGPT	0.884	0.921	0.901	0.940	0.977	0.958	**0.973**	**1.000**	**0.986**
LogLLaMA	**0.939**	0.852	0.894	0.927	**0.993**	0.959	0.957	0.992	0.974
Qwen 2.5	0.881	0.734	0.801	0.937	0.985	0.96	0.971	0.996	0.983
Gemma 3	0.905	0.919	0.912	**0.970**	0.984	**0.977**	0.971	0.997	0.984
Llama 3.2	0.883	**0.986**	**0.932**	0.933	0.987	0.959	0.971	0.996	0.983

Table 2 summarizes the performance of our framework using three different models, Qwen 2.5, Gemma 3, and Llama 3.2, while comparing them to two existing baselines, LogGPT and LogLLaMA, across three benchmark datasets: HDFS, BGL, and Thunderbird.

Our framework, when paired with either Gemma 3 or Llama 3.2, consistently outperforms the baselines on the HDFS and BGL datasets, achieving the highest F1 scores. Specifically, Gemma 3 shows outstanding performance on the BGL dataset, while Llama 3.2 achieves the best F1 score on the HDFS dataset. These results highlight the value of allowing users to select the most suitable model for their specific use case, as performance varies significantly depending on the underlying LLM and the dataset characteristics.

Although the Qwen 2.5 model achieves competitive results on the BGL and Thunderbird datasets, it struggles significantly on the HDFS dataset. In particular, its low recall suggests it fails to detect a large portion of anomalies, likely due to its limited capacity, as it has roughly half the parameters of the other models evaluated. This supports the intuition that smaller models may not capture complex relationships between log keys as effectively.

In the Thunderbird dataset, LogGPT slightly outperforms our framework in terms of F1 score. However, the margin is relatively small, and all models, including ours, achieve very high performance. This suggests that the Thunderbird dataset may be less challenging in terms of modeling log key dependencies, and existing solutions already generalize well.

Overall, our experiments demonstrate that Gemma 3 and Llama 3.2, when used with our flexible framework, deliver strong and reliable performance across all datasets. The results also emphasize the importance of model selection in log analysis, reinforcing the need for a model-agnostic framework that allows users to easily switch between different LLMs.

5   Conclusion

Log analysis plays a critical role in ensuring system reliability, and the application of LLMs has emerged as a promising strategy in this domain. In this work, we proposed a model-agnostic framework that allows users to easily experiment with different LLMs, enabling them to select the model that best fits the characteristics of their data.

Our experiments, conducted on three widely used benchmark datasets, HDFS, BGL, and Thunderbird, demonstrate that the proposed framework not only achieves competitive results but also outperforms existing state-of-the-art methods in multiple scenarios. These results reinforce the importance of flexibility and adaptability in modern log analysis solutions, especially as new and more capable language models continue to be released at a rapid pace. The work also demonstrates the practical relevance of incorporating modern AI techniques into enterprise observability pipelines, paving the way for more scalable, adaptable, and intelligent log analysis systems.

Despite its strengths, our framework does have some minor limitations. Fine-tuning multiple LLMs on large datasets can be computationally demanding, which may reduce accessibility for users with limited hardware resources.

As future work, we plan to deploy our framework in real-world operational environments to validate its practical effectiveness and robustness.

Disclosure of Interests. The authors have no competing interests to declare that are relevant to the content of this article.

References

1. Du, M., Li, F., Zheng, G., Srikumar, V.: DeepLog: anomaly detection and diagnosis from system logs through deep learning. In: Proceedings of the 2017 ACM SIGSAC Conference on Computer and Communications Security, pp. 1285–1298. Association for Computing Machinery, New York (2017). https://doi.org/10.1145/3133956.3134015
2. Meng, W., et al.: Loganomaly: unsupervised detection of sequential and quantitative anomalies in unstructured logs. In: Proceedings of the 28th International Joint Conference on Artificial Intelligence, pp. 4739–4745. AAAI Press, Macao, China (2019)
3. Han, X., Yuan, S., Trabelsi, M.: LogGPT: log anomaly detection via GPT. In: 2023 IEEE International Conference on Big Data (BigData), pp. 1117–1122. IEEE, Piscataway, NJ, USA (2023). https://doi.org/10.1109/BigData59044.2023.10386543
4. Xu, W., Huang, L., Fox, A., Patterson, D., Jordan, M.I.: Detecting large-scale system problems by mining console logs. In: Proceedings of the ACM SIGOPS 22nd Symposium on Operating Systems Principles, pp. 117–132. Association for Computing Machinery, New York (2009). https://doi.org/10.1145/1629575.1629587
5. Liu, F.T., Ting, K.M., Zhou, Z.H.: Isolation forest. In: 2008 Eighth IEEE International Conference on Data Mining, pp. 413–422. IEEE, Piscataway, NJ, USA (2008). https://doi.org/10.1109/ICDM.2008.17
6. Wang, Y., Wong, J., Miner, A.: Anomaly intrusion detection using one class SVM. In: Proceedings from the Fifth Annual IEEE SMC Information Assurance Workshop, 2004., pp. 358–364. IEEE, Piscataway, NJ, USA (2004). https://doi.org/10.1109/IAW.2004.1437839
7. Guo, H., Yuan, S., Wu, X.: LogBERT: Log Anomaly Detection via BERT. In: 2021 International Joint Conference on Neural Networks (IJCNN), pp. 1–8. IEEE, Piscataway, NJ, USA (2021). https://doi.org/10.1109/IJCNN52387.2021.9534113
8. Radford, A., Wu, J., Child, R., Luan, D., Amodei, D., Sutskever, I.: Language Models are Unsupervised Multitask Learners. OpenAI Technical Report (2019). https://openai.com/research/language-models-are-unsupervised-multitask-learners
9. He, P., Zhu, J., Zheng, Z., Lyu, M.R.: Drain: an online log parsing approach with fixed depth tree. In: 2017 IEEE International Conference on Web Services (ICWS), pp. 33–40. IEEE, Piscataway, NJ, USA (2017). https://doi.org/10.1109/ICWS.2017.13
10. Han, D., Han, M., Unsloth team: Unsloth. (2023). http://github.com/unslothai/unsloth Accessed 22 May 2025
11. Yang, Z., Harris, I.G.: LogLLaMA: Transformer-based log anomaly detection with LLaMA. arXiv preprint arXiv:2503.14849 (2025). https://arxiv.org/abs/2503.14849
12. Landauer, M., Skopik, F., Wurzenberger, M.: A critical review of common log data sets used for evaluation of sequence-based anomaly detection techniques. Proc. ACM Softw. Eng. **1**(FSE), Article 61 (2024). https://doi.org/10.1145/3660768

13. Xu, W., Huang, L., Fox, A., Patterson, D., Jordan, M.I.: Detecting large-scale system problems by mining console logs. In: Proceedings of the ACM SIGOPS 22nd Symposium on Operating Systems Principles, pp. 117–132. Association for Computing Machinery, New York, (2009). https://doi.org/10.1145/1629575.1629587

14. Oliner, A., Stearley, J.: What supercomputers say: a study of five system logs. In: Proceedings of the 37th Annual IEEE/IFIP International Conference on Dependable Systems and Networks, pp. 575–584. IEEE Computer Society, USA (2007). https://doi.org/10.1109/DSN.2007.103

15. Qwen, Team.: Qwen2.5: A Party of Foundation Models. (2024). https://qwenlm.github.io/blog/qwen2.5/Accessed 25 May 2025

16. Gemma, Team.: Gemma 3. Kaggle (2025). https://goo.gle/Gemma3Report, last accessed 2025/05/25

17. AI@Meta: Llama 3 Model Card. (2024). https://github.com/meta-llama/llama3/blob/main/MODEL_CARD.md Accessed 25 May 2025

18. Vaswani, A., et al.: Attention is all you need. In: Proceedings of the 31st International Conference on Neural Information Processing Systems, pp. 6000–6010. Curran Associates Inc., Red Hook, NY, USA (2017). https://doi.org/10.5555/3295222.3295349

19. Devlin, J., Chang, M.-W., Lee, K., Toutanova, K.: BERT: Pre-training of deep bidirectional transformers for language understanding. In: Proceedings of the 2019 Conference of the North American Chapter of the Association for Computational Linguistics: Human Language Technologies, Volume 1 (Long and Short Papers), pp. 4171–4186. Association for Computational Linguistics, Minneapolis, MN, USA (2019)

20. Li, A., et al.: Anomaly detection of tabular data using LLMs. arXiv preprint arXiv:2406.16308 (2024). https://arxiv.org/abs/2406.16308

21. Zhang, Y., Cao, Y., Xu, X., Shen, W.: LogiCode: an LLM-Driven framework for logical anomaly detection. IEEE Trans. Autom. Sci. Eng. **22**, 7712–7723 (2025). https://doi.org/10.1109/TASE.2024.3468464

22. Pospieszny, P., Mormul, W., Szyndler, K., Kumar, S.: ADALog: Adaptive Unsupervised Anomaly detection in Logs with Self-attention Masked Language Model. arXiv preprint arXiv:2505.13496 (2025). https://arxiv.org/abs/2505.13496

23. Benabderrahmane, S., Valtchev, P., Cheney, J., Rahwan, T.: APT-LLM: embedding-based anomaly detection of cyber advanced persistent threats using large language models. In: 2025 13th International Symposium on Digital Forensics and Security (ISDFS), pp. 1–6. IEEE, Piscataway, NJ, USA (2025). https://doi.org/10.1109/ISDFS65363.2025.11011912

LLM–Based Framework for Synthetic Data Generation in Portuguese Clinical NER

Luís Henriques[1]([⊠]) [iD], Nuno Guimarães[1,2] [iD], and Alípio Jorge[1,2] [iD]

[1] INESC TEC, Porto, Portugal
{luis.f.henriques,nuno.r.guimaraes}@inesctec.pt
[2] Faculdade de Ciências, Universidade do Porto, Porto, Portugal
amjorge@fc.up.pt

Abstract. The ever-increasing volume of data produced in Healthcare demands solutions capable of automatically extracting the relevant elements of their narratives. However, given privacy regulations, bureaucratic procedures, and annotation efforts, the development of said solutions via Natural Language Processing (NLP) systems becomes hindered due to training data scarcity. Such scarcity increases when we consider languages and language varieties with lower resource availability, such as European and Brazilian Portuguese. To address this problem, we propose a Large Language Model (LLM)-based **SDG** (**S**ynthetic **D**ata **G**eneration) framework to generate and annotate synthetic clinical texts for medical Named-Entity Recognition (NER). The SDG framework consists of a system/user prompt augmented with real examples, powered by GPT-4o. Our results show that, by feeding the framework few real clinical annotated texts, we can generate synthetic data capable of increasing the performance of NER models with respect to their non-augmented counterparts. In addition, the reduction of the BLEU scores in the generated texts indicates a decrease in the risk of privacy disclosure while ensuring greater lexical diversity. These results highlight the potential of synthetic data as a solution to overcome human annotation bottlenecks and privacy concerns, laying the groundwork for future research in clinical NLP across tasks, domains, and low-resource languages.

Keywords: Synthetic Data Generation · Clinical NER · Large Language Models

1 Introduction

NLP systems applied in healthcare have the potential to make use of Electronic Health Records (EHRs) to extract relevant data, allowing a more efficient and productive environment for healthcare professionals. Physicians can be overloaded with work, thus potentially increasing their error rate. As such, NLP systems can aid in the decision-making process by pinpointing and highlighting key data points. These NLP systems, particularly those with transformer-based Pre-trained Language Models (PLMs) encoders, have been proven useful [16,21,31,34].

Those NLP systems become better as more textual data is used to train and fine-tune them. However, given privacy regulations and bureaucratic procedures, access to

J. Valente de Oliveira et al. (Eds.): EPIA 2025, LNAI 16121, pp. 335–347, 2026.
https://doi.org/10.1007/978-3-032-05176-9_26

EHRs becomes a challenge for NLP developers and researchers. This problem worsens when we consider low- to medium-resource languages, such as European and Brazilian Portuguese. In the use cases of sequence tagging, particularly NER, having expert-level annotations can also be challenging [22]. Generative models, namely LLMs, have shown great advances in language understanding, processing long context windows, and solving tasks [6, 24]. These models could help overcome the challenges mentioned above by generating useful synthetic EHRs (SEHRs) that can extend existing data resources.

This work was carried out as part of the HealthFromPortugal (HfPT) project, aiming to address the limited access to large volumes of real EHRs, caused by privacy constraints. Our goal is to determine how synthetic data generated using LLMs, particularly GPT-4o, can improve the effectiveness of current NER approaches, namely transformer-based PLM encoders, for the Portuguese language. For that, we considered two use cases: one in Brazilian Portuguese and another in European Portuguese. The main contributions of this work are:

1. A framework to generate and annotate SEHRs to improve the performance of their baseline counterparts without data augmentation[1].
2. The annotated datasets generated via the SDG framework developed in this work.
3. The improved fine-tuned NER models for clinical data in Portuguese using SEHRs.

In Sect. 2 the related work is explored and summarized, namely on data generation and NER. Section 3 details the methodology followed while Sect. 4 showcases the exploratory analysis of the SEHRs generated. Section 5 dives into the NER results achieved, and finally Sect. 6 presents the conclusions and future works.

2   Related Work

In this section, we present the works related to the usage of LLMs as generators and annotators of textual data, as well as the applications of NER in the clinical domain in both European and Brazilian Portuguese.

2.1   Data Generation

In the current literature on the usage of LLMs for data generation and annotation, text classification is applied to PubMed20K, with ChatGPT being used to generate text samples semantically similar to one given to it [5]. After fine-tuning Bidirectional Encoder Representations from Transformers (BERT) [7] on real data, the model was further fine-tuned on synthetic data by adding contrastive learning to the loss function. This approach achieved the best results compared to using ChatGPT as a few-shot (FS) classifier. Other works show that LLM's zero-shot (ZS) performance could be higher than fine-tuning PLMs in certain tasks [20]. However, the overall results showed that models fine-tuned with real or synthetic data outperform ZS performance. ChatGPT was also used as a ZS data generator [37], showing better performance in three classification

---

[1] https://github.com/LIAAD/SDG_clinical_ner.

benchmarks relative to other approaches, including Few-Shot Learning (FSL), Easy Data Augmentation [38], BARTspan and BARTword [12].

In a different work, ChatGPT was instead used as a ZS annotator of real data [8]. It outperformed crowdsourced annotators from MTurk [4] regarding accuracy and even surpassed trained annotators in intercoder agreement, especially with temperature set to 0.2. This happens due to a more deterministic decoding. Similar conclusions were achieved with ChatGPT being used in a 2-stage approach [10]. First, ChatGPT was asked to generate Chains-of-Thought (CoT) for pre-existing annotations of real data instances. In stage 2, the authors combined FS demonstrations with their respective CoTs generated in stage 1 to annotate unlabeled data. Temperature was set to 0. The usage of CoT outperformed other In-Context Learning (ICL) approaches, with fine-tuning outperforming ICL.

The work most similar to ours was developed by Tang et al. [35]. Rather than using ChatGPT as annotator, they used local PLMs in a real-world setting. ChatGPT, instead, generated synthetic clinical data via FSL. That data was then used to fine-tune said PLMs. Results showed NER performance gains. Although PLMs fine-tuned with synthetic data outperformed ChatGPT in ZS, better overall performance was achieved with PLMs fine-tuned on real data.

Regarding the quality of synthetic data, some works used the cosine similarity between sentence embeddings [27] of real and synthetic samples [5,37]. Others mapped sentence embeddings into a 2-dimensional latent space using t-SNE [19], thus visualizing the semantic distribution of real and synthetic texts [35]. We call this resemblance. Another approach is to check for privacy disclosure risks in the synthetic data text, which none of the works cited so far have done. In non-LLM applications [1,9,14] metrics such as Bilingual Evaluation Understudy (BLEU) [25] and Recall-Oriented Understudy for Gisting Evaluation (ROUGE) [15] were employed towards this goal.

2.2 Named-Entity Recognition

As for the literature considered for NER, in Liu et al. [16], in addition to the use of the original BERT, the authors also used BioBERT [13], ClinicalBERT [11], and Blue-BERT [26] to identify classes such as chronic disease, BMI, cancer, and treatment. In [13], the original BERT was fine-tuned on biomedical domain corpora (PubMed abstracts and PMC full-text articles), thus developing BioBERT. This PLM outperformed several SOTA models on several NLP downstream tasks, such as NER. ClinicalBERT [11] was pre-trained in a large corpus of clinical texts. In Masked Language Modeling (MLM) there was an improvement from 0.495 to 0.857, and from 0.539 to 0.994 in Next Sentence Prediction (NSP). BlueBERT [26] was pre-trained by fine-tuning BERT-base and BERT-large on the MIMIC-III corpora and PubMed abstracts. BlueBERT achieved SOTA performance on several datasets, surpassing BioBERT [13].

Schneider et al. [31] developed three PLMs called BioBERTpt trained using transfer learning from BERT-Multilingual-Cased [7]. The training corpus for each of those PLMs comprised biomedical literature (bio), clinical notes from Brazilian hospitals (clin), and a combination of both (all). Another work also developed a BERT-based PLM trained in Brazilian Portuguese, called BERTimbau [34]. This PLM achieved

SOTA performance for NER against other approaches [3, 29, 30]. Nunes et al. [21] published a new family of PLMs in European Portuguese, called MediAlbertina. These models made further MLM pre-training based on the Albertina models [28] using electronic medical reports shared by the largest public hospital in Portugal. Two versions were made available: 900M and 1.5B parameters. MediAlbertina-900M achieved, for NER, F1-score (macro average) performance gains of more than 30% and 15% in a single model setting against BioBERTpt(all) [31] and BERTimbao [34], respectively. Those gains decreased in a multiple model setting.

For NER datasets, several works [18, 31] used the PortugueseClinicalNER dataset [17], consisting of 281 clinical texts from numbers 1 and 2 of Volume 17 published by the Portuguese Society of Neurology in the Synapse journal. SemClinBr [22], used in Schneider et al. [31] for fine-tuning, comprises 1,000 EHRs with 65,129 participants and 11,263 relations. Regarding the participants, these were annotated using 100 Unified Medical Language System (UMLS) [2] semantic types (STY) which were aggregated into 13 participant types.

There is a research gap regarding approaches to generate and annotate EHRs in both European and Brazilian Portuguese to improve NER performance. Considering the related works in this section and Sect. 2.1, the usage of LLMs with fine-tuned PLMs could be an effective approach to downstream NLP tasks. As such, our work aims to tackle this exact gap by developing a framework that generates and annotates clinical texts, in Portuguese, with enough quality so that better performance is achieved in NER tasks. We will also consider several data shortage scenarios to check the relative quality, or utility, of the synthetic data, as done in Møller et al. [20].

3   Methods

In this section, we detail the methods used for annotating SEHRs for both Brazilian and European Portuguese and describe our fine-tuning procedure, in particular, which PLMs were used and their hyperparameters.

3.1   SDG Pipeline

The SDG pipeline consists of an LLM-based framework that generates SEHRs together with their respective NER annotations. A system prompt was developed, after several adjustments to its structure (based on examples outside of the datasets used in the training and evaluation process), with details regarding each NER class definition, desired number of annotations per SEHR, file format for the generated output, and the language in which to write the SEHR's text. No structured data generation methodology, such as JSON-mode, was used. In addition to the system prompt, a user prompt template was also developed, which consists of a simple task description. We included an option to add a random disease or condition to the user's prompt based on a pre-defined finite set of UMLS concepts. We called this CONCEPT sampling. In addition, the LLM's context was also augmented with training examples using a tool mentioned next. These three components of the LLM's context were given to GPT-4o [23]. The training examples were fed to it using the Assistants API, more specifically using File Search, which, in our use case, poses as a retriever of context from the real EHRs.

Regarding the GPT-4o models hyperparameters, we chose 0.5 for both the temperature and the top-p threshold after several qualitative tests and observations. These values enabled a more consistent annotation decoding regarding the desired number of annotations defined in the system prompt and a more consistent EHR text length. The temperature allows to adjust the flexibility or creativity of the LLM. Values closer to zero make the LLM less stochastic. Top-p samples the most likely tokens to be generated next based on their cumulative probability. Values closer to zero make the sampling select more likely tokens. For example, a top-p threshold of 0.5 means sampling the next token from the set of most likely tokens with a cumulative probability of 50%.

This pipeline was developed using the SemClinBr dataset, which uses specific classes from UMLS, the STYs. In this work, STYs will refer to the NER classes, regardless of dataset used. We chose five STYs, given their annotation importance. We augmented the LLM's context with a total of four real EHRs from the SemClinBr's training data given the amount and variety of STYs annotated, and their textual variety in both content and format. We performed visual inspections to select them. The final SDG pipeline was developed only using this dataset. Thus, more comparisons and experiments were made, like choosing the GPT-4o snapshot and the usage (or not) of CONCEPT sampling.

To test the final SDG pipeline with an unbiased dataset and in European Portuguese, we chose PortugueseClinicalNER. As such, no comparisons or experiments were made. We chose STYs based on their respective fine-tuned baseline (no data augmentation) performance. We augmented said dataset by generating SEHRs considering the six STYs with the lowest baseline performance out of all STYs in the dataset. We augmented the LLM's context with a total of five real EHRs from the PortugueseClinicalNER's training data, following a similar selection procedure as with SemClinBr.

Regarding the SemClinBr dataset augmentation, we developed two synthetic datasets composed of 300 entries for each GPT-4o snapshot model used, gpt-4o-2024-05-13 and gpt-4o-2024-08-06. As for PortugueseClinicalNER, we built one synthetic dataset composed of 100 entries using the best GPT-4o snapshot model chosen from the SemClinBr experiments. We make an exploratory analysis of these datasets in Sect. 4, where we measure the resemblance and privacy disclosure risks of the SEHRs.

3.2   Fine-Tuning

To assess the importance of data augmentation in the training of NER models, we created three data shortage scenarios (600, 300, and 100 real EHRs available for training) to detect performance variations using SemClinBr. Regarding PortugueseClinicalNER, we considered only one scenario of 201 real EHRs. In the data shortage scenarios, the validation and test data didn't change: in SemClinBr, we considered 200 EHRs for validation and testing each, while in PortugueseClinicalNER that number was 40.

We selected two different PLMs to fine-tune with respect to each of the datasets. BioBERTpt(all) was used to achieve results for SemClinBr, while for PortugueseClinicalNER we considered MediAlbertina-900M. The PLM choice considered not only the use case and the specific Portuguese variant, but we also wanted an unbiased PLM for the test dataset. As mentioned in Sect. 3.1, SemClinBr was used to adjust the components of the SDG framework. As such, to check how the said framework performed in a different scenario, we changed not only the dataset, but also the PLM encoder. Given performance instability from the use of small datasets, we restarted model training 3 times, choosing to test the model with the highest strict F1 score [32] achieved on the validation data. This approach was similar to the one used for BERT [7]. For each restart, we used two model selection criteria and chose the best validation performance out of the two. The first criterion consists of simply choosing the model instance from the last epoch (one full cycle over the training data). The second was to select the model instance from the epoch with the lowest overfit, meaning the lowest difference between training loss and validation loss.

Regarding the hyperparameters for BioBERTpt(all), the optimizer and the learning rate scheduler remained the same as in Schneider et al. [31]. The weight decay regularization has a lambda of 0.1, a mini-batch size 32, a maximum sequence length of 256 (padded), and a learning rate of 3e-5. As for the epochs, a maximum of 4 was considered. For MediAlbertina-900M, the optimizer and the learning rate scheduler remained the same as with BioBERTpt(all). The weight decay regularization has a lambda of 0.5, a mini-batch size of 8, a maximum sequence length of 128 tokens (padded), and a learning rate 3e-5. As for the epochs, a maximum of 2 was considered.

4   Exploratory Data Analysis (EDA)

In this section, we present the EDA of the SEHRs generated, namely regarding the resemblance with their real counterparts and privacy disclosure risks, due to the replication of exact information from the real EHRs in the SEHRs.

4.1   Resemblance

An important aspect of assessing the quality of synthetic texts is measuring their semantic similarity with real samples. We mapped sentence embeddings from real EHRs (training data) and SEHRs, for both SemClinBr and PortugueseClinicalNER, into a 2-dimensional latent space using t-SNE [19]. Initial tests with BioBERTpt(all) showed that computing embeddings with our fine-tuned PLMs delivered better overlap. To do so, we removed the sequence tagging layer from the fine-tuned PLMs' architectures, enabling us to retrieve their sentence embeddings. So, we used BioBERTpt(all) and MediAlbertina-900M fine-tuned for SemClinBr and PortugueseClinicalNER.

●   Real sentences
●   Synthetic sentences

Fig. 1. Scatterplots showing the sentence embedding distribution of the real (training) and synthetic sentences using t-SNE for SemClinBr. The scatterplot on the left corresponds to gpt-4o-2024-05-13, while the one on the right corresponds to gpt-4o-2024-08-06.

The results achieved for the SemClinBr dataset, using gpt-4o-2024-05-13 and gpt-4o-2024-08-06 to generate SEHRs, can be seen in Fig. 1. The results achieved for the PortugueseClinicalNER dataset, using gpt-4o-2024-08-06 (the GPT-4o snapshot chosen for the final SDG pipeline) to generate SEHRs, can be seen in Fig. 2.

Comparing both LLMs for SemClinBr, a better overlap between real and synthetic sentences was achieved using gpt-4o-2024-08-06, indicating that it generated SEHRs with higher semantic similarity. Despite that, gpt-4o-2024-05-13 has statistically higher cosine similarity averages (p-value < 5%). Medians, of said averages, were 0.53 and 0.56 relative to gpt-4o-2024-08-06 and gpt-4o-2024-05-13, respectively. Thus, we hypothesize that similarity with no dimensionality reduction can lead to different conclusions with respect to the 2-dimensional ones.

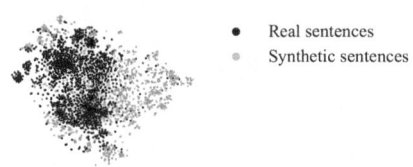

Fig. 2. Scatterplots showing the sentence embedding distribution of the real (training) and synthetic sentences using t-SNE for PortugueseClinicalNER. This scatterplot corresponds to gpt-4o-2024-05-13.

Regarding PortugueseClinicalNER, the real and synthetic sentence embeddings showed distinct distributions using t-SNE. Despite that, a cosine similarity average of 0.82 was achieved between real and synthetic sentence embeddings. Comparing the 2-dimensional mappings and cosine similarity statistics between SemClinBr and PortugueseClinicalNER, we can see a lower overlap but higher cosine similarities in the latter relative to the former. This further indicates how dimensionality reduction could lead to different conclusions relative to similarity measured with no reduction.

4.2 Privacy Disclosure

Another relevant analysis consists in the degree in which GPT-4o copied the text from the EHR examples. To do so, instead of measuring semantic similarity as in Sect. 4.1, we used BLEU scores to measure how n-grams from the EHR examples were mimicked by GPT-4o in the SEHRs it generated.

Regarding the SemClinBr dataset, we achieved lower BLEU scores using CONCEPT sampling compared to not using it, as shown in Fig. 3. By providing GPT-4o with a new disease or condition in the prompt, we were able to increase the variety of SEHRs and reduce the number of copied n-grams. Thus, by writing new EHRs with different words and n-grams, GPT-4o was able to reduce the risks of privacy disclosures.

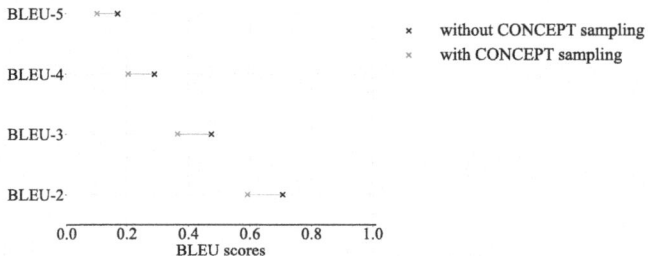

Fig. 3. Dumbbell plot of BLEU scores shows a decrease in privacy disclosure by opting for a prompt comprising CONCEPT sampling. Training EHRs used as references.

Considering we used real EHR examples to augment GPT-4o, we also measured BLEU scores with validation and test EHRs as references. Despite the same pattern, we achieved lower BLEU scores with those sets of real EHRs. This indicates that the validation and test EHRs are, up to a certain extent, more different than the training EHRs relative to the EHR examples given to GPT-4o.

Table 1. BLEU scores obtained, for PortugueseClinicalNER, considering as references the training, validation, and test EHRs. Only CONCEPT sampling was used.

BLEU score measures	Training refs	Val refs	Test refs
BLEU-2	0.6162	0.4554	0.4610
BLEU-3	0.4100	0.2560	0.2644
BLEU-4	0.2531	0.1276	0.1426
BLEU-5	0.1440	0.0607	0.0665

As for the PortugueseClinicalNER dataset, with the SDG pipeline developed and considering the results from Fig. 3, we only measured BLEU scores for this dataset using CONCEPT sampling. Results, considering real EHRs (training, validation, and test data) as references can be seen in Table 1. We achieved the lower BLEU scores using validation and test EHRs as references. This follows the same trend found for the SemClinBr dataset, further showing that, by providing GPT-4o with EHR examples from the training set, its respective BLEU scores increase.

5   Results

We used BioBERTpt(all) to individually fine-tune each STY in the SemClinBr dataset. We measured performance using strict F1 scores. We measured baseline performances (no data augmentation) across three real data shortage scenarios. Then, we compared them with the performance of augmenting those scenarios with two datasets with 300 SEHRs each, generated using gpt-4o-2024-05-13 and gpt-4o-2024-08-06. CONCEPT sampling was used in the prompts. The results are presented in Fig. 4.

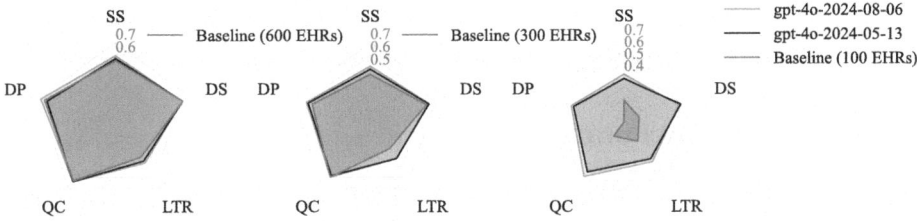

Fig. 4. Strict F1 scores achieved for sign or symptom (SS), disease or syndrome (DS), laboratory or test result (LTR), quantitative concept (QC) and diagnostic procedure (DP), for SemClinBr. The three data shortage scenarios consist of using 100, 300, and 600 real EHRs for fine-tuning.

Performance gains, comparing the baseline with the augmented performances, decrease as more real EHRs become available for training (right to left in Fig. 4) for SemClinBr. Overall, gpt-4o-2024-08-06 generated SEHRs capable of achieving the highest NER performance. Taking into account that LLM, we achieved average gains in the strict F1 scores of 32.7%, 4.5%, and 2.5% when using 100, 300, and 600 real EHRs for fine-tuning. This shows the impact of the real data from 100 to 300 EHRs. However, the average loss of augmenting 100 EHRs (right in blue) relative to using 300 EHRs with no augmentation (center in red) was 3.16%. This impact of the synthetic data relative to tripling the amount of real EHRs emphasizes the quality of the SEHRs.

We used MediAlbertina-900M for PortugueseClinicalNER in the same fashion as with SemClinBr. Considering this dataset was used to test the SDG pipeline, we only considered one data shortage scenario. The results can be seen in Fig. 5.

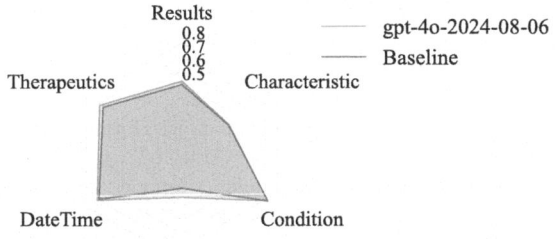

Fig. 5. Strict F1 scores achieved for characterization, condition, additional observations, datetime, therapeutics and results, for PortugueseClinicalNER. We considered one data shortage scenario with 201 real EHRs for fine-tuning.

The results show a performance gain for several STYs. That said, the only one with a considerable gain was Additional Observations, with a strict F1 performance increase of 6.7%. An average performance gain of 2.3% was achieved across all STYs. Considering the results for SemClinBr in Fig. 4, and despite PortugueseClinicalNER being used to test the SDG pipeline with European Portuguese EHRs, it could be expected a larger performance gain if we considered data shortage scenarios with less real EHRs.

6 Conclusions and Future Work

Recent works showed how LLMs can generate synthetic data or pose as annotators [8], thus comparing them to human annotations. In this work, we developed a framework capable of increasing NER performance by generating and annotating synthetic clinical texts using GPT-4o as generator and annotator. We fine-tuned the PLM encoders with real and synthetic samples. In addition, we also developed three synthetic datasets, two for the experiments with SemClinBr in Brazilian Portuguese and one with Portuguese-ClinicalNER in European Portuguese. Our results show how GPT-4o can augment clinical text datasets to improve NER performance of fine-tuned PLMs, thus tackling the research goals set for our research. In particular, our approach enables major performance gains as data scarcity increases. Our contributions can be further generalized by showing that balancing performance and privacy disclosure risks is possible.

In future works, we intend to extend our approach to other NLP tasks (such as relation extraction) in low-resource languages. In addition, we will experiment with the usage of CoT Prompting, either by manufacturing them manually or with LLMs [10], or using reasoning LLMs, such as DeepSeek-R1 [6], QwQ-32B [36], and o1 [24]. The usage of proprietary LLMs poses minimal computational costs, allowing the development of scalable solutions, being a great alternative to local deployment. However, local open-source models address concerns about the use of external APIs with sensitive data. Thus, we will shift our approach towards local and more private solutions for data generation. LLMs could also be used for classification tasks [8, 10]. However, fine-tuned PLMs are lighter and a local solution, making them better suited for clinical deployments as classifiers. Furthermore, we intend to improve the robustness of the privacy risk assessment with a more nuanced approach, such as membership inference [33].

Acknowledgments. This work is funded by national funds through FCT – Fundação para a Ciência e a Tecnologia, I.P., under the support UID/50014/2023 (https://doi.org/10.54499/UID/50014/2023). Luís Henriques also wants to acknowledge Component 5 - Capitalization and Business Innovation, integrated in the Resilience Dimension of the Recovery and Resilience Plan within the scope of the Recovery and Resilience Mechanism (MRR) of the European Union (EU), framed in the Next Generation EU, for the period 2021 - 2026, within project HfPT, with reference 41.

Disclosure of Interests. The authors have no competing interests to declare that are relevant to the content of this article.

References

1. Begoli, E., Brown, K., Srinivas, S., Tamang, S.: SynthNotes: a generator framework for high-volume, high-fidelity synthetic mental health notes. In: 2018 IEEE International Conference on Big Data (Big Data), Seattle, WA, USA, pp. 951–958 (2018). https://doi.org/10.1109/BigData.2018.8621981

2. Bodenreider, O.: The unified medical language system (UMLS): integrating biomedical terminology. Nucl. Acids Res. **32**(Database issue), D267–70 (2004)
3. Quinta de Castro, P.V., Félix Felipe da Silva, N., da Silva Soares, A.: Portuguese named entity recognition using LSTM-CRF. In: Villavicencio, A., et al. (eds.) PROPOR 2018. LNCS (LNAI), vol. 11122, pp. 83–92. Springer, Cham (2018). https://doi.org/10.1007/978-3-319-99722-3_9
4. Crowston, K.: Amazon mechanical turk: a research tool for organizations and information systems scholars. In: Bhattacherjee, A., Fitzgerald, B. (eds.) IS&O 2012. IAICT, vol. 389, pp. 210–221. Springer, Heidelberg (2012). https://doi.org/10.1007/978-3-642-35142-6_14
5. Dai, H., et al.: ChatAug: Leveraging ChatGPT for Text Data Augmentation. arXiv abs/2302.13007 (2023). https://doi.org/10.48550/arXiv.2302.13007
6. DeepSeek-AI: Deepseek-R1: Incentivizing Reasoning Capability in LLMs via Reinforcement Learning (2025). https://arxiv.org/abs/2501.12948
7. Devlin, J., Chang, M.W., Lee, K., Toutanova, K.: BERT: pre-training of deep bidirectional transformers for language understanding. In: Burstein, J., Doran, C., Solorio, T. (eds.) Proceedings of the 2019 Conference of the North American Chapter of the Association for Computational Linguistics: Human Language Technologies, Volume 1 (Long and Short Papers), Minneapolis, Minnesota, pp. 4171–4186. Association for Computational Linguistics (2019). https://doi.org/10.18653/v1/N19-1423. https://aclanthology.org/N19-1423
8. Gilardi, F., Alizadeh, M., Kubli, M.: ChatGPT outperforms crowd workers for text-annotation tasks. Proc. Natl. Acad. Sci. **120**(30), e2305016120 (2023)
9. Guan, J., Li, R., Yu, S., Zhang, X.: A method for generating synthetic electronic medical record text. IEEE/ACM Trans. Comput. Biol. Bioinf. **18**(1), 173–182 (2021). https://doi.org/10.1109/TCBB.2019.2948985
10. He, X., et al.: AnnoLLM: making large language models to be better crowdsourced annotators. In: Yang, Y., Davani, A., Sil, A., Kumar, A. (eds.) Proceedings of the 2024 Conference of the North American Chapter of the Association for Computational Linguistics: Human Language Technologies (Volume 6: Industry Track), Mexico City, Mexico, pp. 165–190. Association for Computational Linguistics (2024). https://aclanthology.org/2024.naacl-industry.15
11. Huang, K., Altosaar, J., Ranganath, R.: ClinicalBERT: Modeling Clinical Notes and Predicting Hospital Readmission. arXiv abs/1904.05342 (2019)
12. Kumar, V., Choudhary, A., Cho, E.: Data augmentation using pre-trained transformer models. In: Campbell, W.M., et al. (eds.) Proceedings of the 2nd Workshop on Life-long Learning for Spoken Language Systems, Suzhou, China, pp. 18–26. Association for Computational Linguistics (2020). https://doi.org/10.18653/v1/2020.lifelongnlp-1.3. https://aclanthology.org/2020.lifelongnlp-1.3/
13. Lee, J., et al.: BioBERT: a pre-trained biomedical language representation model for biomedical text mining. Bioinformatics **36**, 1234–1240 (2019). https://doi.org/10.1093/bioinformatics/btz682
14. Libbi, C.A., Trienes, J., Trieschnigg, D., Seifert, C.: Generating synthetic training data for supervised de-identification of electronic health records. Future Internet **13**(5) (2021). https://doi.org/10.3390/fi13050136. https://www.mdpi.com/1999-5903/13/5/136
15. Lin, C.Y.: ROUGE: a package for automatic evaluation of summaries. In: Text Summarization Branches Out, Barcelona, Spain, pp. 74–81. Association for Computational Linguistics (2004). https://aclanthology.org/W04-1013
16. Liu, X., Hersch, G.L., Khalil, I., Devarakonda, M.: Clinical trial information extraction with BERT. In: 2021 IEEE 9th International Conference on Healthcare Informatics (ICHI), Victoria, BC, Canada, pp. 505–506 (2021). https://doi.org/10.1109/ICHI52183.2021.00092

17. Lopes, F., Teixeira, C., Gonçalo Oliveira, H.: Contributions to clinical named entity recognition in Portuguese. In: Demner-Fushman, D., Cohen, K.B., Ananiadou, S., Tsujii, J. (eds.) Proceedings of the 18th BioNLP Workshop and Shared Task, Florence, Italy, pp. 223–233. Association for Computational Linguistics (2019). https://doi.org/10.18653/v1/W19-5024. https://aclanthology.org/W19-5024

18. Lopes, F., Teixeira, C., Gonçalo Oliveira, H.: Comparing different methods for named entity recognition in Portuguese neurology text. J. Med. Syst. **44**(4), 77 (2020)

19. van der Maaten, L., Hinton, G.: Visualizing data using t-SNE. J. Mach. Learn. Res. **9**(86), 2579–2605 (2008). http://jmlr.org/papers/v9/vandermaaten08a.html

20. Møller, A.G., Pera, A., Dalsgaard, J., Aiello, L.: The parrot dilemma: human-labeled vs. LLM-augmented data in classification tasks. In: Graham, Y., Purver, M. (eds.) Proceedings of the 18th Conference of the European Chapter of the Association for Computational Linguistics (Volume 2: Short Papers), St. Julian's, Malta, pp. 179–192. Association for Computational Linguistics (2024). https://aclanthology.org/2024.eacl-short.17

21. Nunes, M., BonÃ, J., Ferreira, J., Chaves, P., Elvas, L.: MediAlbertina: an European Portuguese medical language model. CBM **182** (2024). https://doi.org/10.1016/j.compbiomed.2024.109233

22. Oliveira, L.E.S.E., et al.: SemClinBr - a multi-institutional and multi-specialty semantically annotated corpus for Portuguese clinical NLP tasks. J. Biomed. Semant. **13**(1), 13 (2022)

23. OpenAI: GPT-4 Technical Report (2024). https://arxiv.org/abs/2303.08774

24. OpenAI: Openai O1 System Card (2024). https://arxiv.org/abs/2412.16720

25. Papineni, K., Roukos, S., Ward, T., Zhu, W.J.: BLEU: a method for automatic evaluation of machine translation. In: Proceedings of the 40th Annual Meeting on Association for Computational Linguistics, ACL 2002, pp. 311–318. Association for Computational Linguistics, USA (2002). https://doi.org/10.3115/1073083.1073135

26. Peng, Y., Yan, S., Lu, Z.: Transfer learning in biomedical natural language processing: an evaluation of BERT and ELMo on ten benchmarking datasets. In: Demner-Fushman, D., Cohen, K.B., Ananiadou, S., Tsujii, J. (eds.) Proceedings of the 18th BioNLP Workshop and Shared Task, Florence, Italy, pp. 58–65. Association for Computational Linguistics (2019). https://doi.org/10.18653/v1/W19-5006. https://aclanthology.org/W19-5006

27. Reimers, N., Gurevych, I.: Sentence-BERT: Sentence Embeddings using Siamese BERT-Networks (2019). https://arxiv.org/abs/1908.10084

28. Rodrigues, J., et al.: Advancing neural encoding of Portuguese with transformer Albertina PT-*, pp. 441–453. Springer (2023). https://doi.org/10.1007/978-3-031-49008-8_35

29. dos Santos, C., Guimarães, V.: Boosting named entity recognition with neural character embeddings. In: Duan, X., Banchs, R.E., Zhang, M., Li, H., Kumaran, A. (eds.) Proceedings of the Fifth Named Entity Workshop, Beijing, China, pp. 25–33. Association for Computational Linguistics (2015). https://doi.org/10.18653/v1/W15-3904. https://aclanthology.org/W15-3904/

30. Santos, J., Consoli, B., dos Santos, C., Terra, J., Collonini, S., Vieira, R.: Assessing the impact of contextual embeddings for Portuguese named entity recognition. In: 2019 8th Brazilian Conference on Intelligent Systems (BRACIS), pp. 437–442 (2019). https://doi.org/10.1109/BRACIS.2019.00083

31. Schneider, E.T.R., et al.: BioBERTpt - a Portuguese neural language model for clinical named entity recognition. In: Rumshisky, A., Roberts, K., Bethard, S., Naumann, T. (eds.) Proceedings of the 3rd Clinical Natural Language Processing Workshop, pp. 65–72. Association for Computational Linguistics, Online (2020). https://doi.org/10.18653/v1/2020.clinicalnlp-1.7. https://aclanthology.org/2020.clinicalnlp-1.7

32. Segura-Bedmar, I., Martínez, P., Herrero-Zazo, M.: SemEval-2013 task 9: extraction of drug-drug interactions from biomedical texts (DDIExtraction 2013). In: Manandhar, S., Yuret, D.

(eds.) Second Joint Conference on Lexical and Computational Semantics (*SEM), Volume 2: Proceedings of the Seventh International Workshop on Semantic Evaluation (SemEval 2013), Atlanta, Georgia, USA, pp. 341–350. Association for Computational Linguistics (2013). https://aclanthology.org/S13-2056

33. Shokri, R., Stronati, M., Song, C., Shmatikov, V.: Membership inference attacks against machine learning models. In: 2017 IEEE Symposium on Security and Privacy (SP), Los Alamitos, CA, USA, pp. 3–18. IEEE Computer Society (2017). https://doi.org/10.1109/SP.2017.41. https://doi.ieeecomputersociety.org/10.1109/SP.2017.41

34. Souza, F., Nogueira, R., Lotufo, R.: BERTimbau: pretrained BERT models for Brazilian Portuguese. In: Cerri, R., Prati, R.C. (eds.) BRACIS 2020. LNCS (LNAI), vol. 12319, pp. 403–417. Springer, Cham (2020). https://doi.org/10.1007/978-3-030-61377-8_28

35. Tang, R., Han, X., Jiang, X., Hu, X.: Does Synthetic Data Generation of LLMs Help Clinical Text Mining? arXiv abs/2303.04360 (2023). https://doi.org/10.48550/arXiv.2303.04360

36. Qwen Team: QwQ-32B: Embracing the Power of Reinforcement Learning (2025). https://qwenlm.github.io/blog/qwq-32b/

37. Ubani, S., Polat, S., Nielsen, R.D.: ZeroShotDataAug: Generating and Augmenting Training Data with ChatGPT. arXiv abs/2304.14334 (2023). https://doi.org/10.48550/arXiv.2304.14334

38. Wei, J., Zou, K.: EDA: easy data augmentation techniques for boosting performance on text classification tasks. In: Inui, K., Jiang, J., Ng, V., Wan, X. (eds.) Proceedings of the 2019 Conference on Empirical Methods in Natural Language Processing and the 9th International Joint Conference on Natural Language Processing (EMNLP-IJCNLP), Hong Kong, China, pp. 6382–6388. Association for Computational Linguistics (2019). https://doi.org/10.18653/v1/D19-1670. https://aclanthology.org/D19-1670/

RAG-EVO: Increasing the Reliability and Autonomy of LLMs via Iterative Recovery

Diego Rodrigues[1]([✉])(iD), Daniela Mascarenhas de Queiroz Trevisan[1](iD), Sílvia Araújo[2](iD), and David Nadler Prata[1](iD)

[1] Federal University of Tocantins (UFT), Palmas, Brazil
diego.rodrigues@ifto.edu.br, {danielatrevisan,ddnprata}@uft.edu.br
[2] University of Minho, Braga, Portugal
saraujo@elach.uminho.pt

Abstract. This article proposes RAG-EVO (Evolutionary, Self-Improving RAG Agent), an adaptive generation-enhanced retrieval architecture that incorporates heuristic introspection mechanisms, persistent vector memory and evolutionary learning through iterative logs. The technique was evaluated in a simulated scenario using real legal-epidemiological data and compared with approaches such as Self-RAG, HyDE, Multi-Query RAG, MMR, and ReAct. RAG-EVO showed superior performance in factual consistency and completeness, achieving a composite accuracy score of 92.6%. The architecture is particularly suitable for domains that require robustness in the accuracy of the answers generated through LLMs, traceability and continuous adaptation.

Keywords: LLM · RAG · Artificial Intelligence · Knowledge Retrieval

1 Introduction

In recent years, large language models (LLMs) have evolved significantly, becoming central tools in semantic search applications, question answering, report generation and automated assistance in various domains. However, these models face limitations when it comes to updating their internal knowledge, which compromises factual accuracy in contexts where information changes frequently or depends on specialized external databases. In this scenario, the Augmented Generation Retrieval (AGR) technique has emerged as a promising solution by allowing generative models to access external knowledge bases to enrich their answers with up-to-date and verifiable evidence [7].

Despite the progress made by RAG, its application in sensitive environments, such as government institutions, biomedical research centers or judicial systems, comes up against critical security, privacy and traceability restrictions [5]. Most of the available RAG implementations rely on commercial APIs or cloud solutions, which imposes vulnerabilities related to the exposure of confidential data,

© The Author(s), under exclusive license to Springer Nature Switzerland AG 2026
J. Valente de Oliveira et al. (Eds.): EPIA 2025, LNAI 16121, pp. 348–359, 2026.
https://doi.org/10.1007/978-3-032-05176-9_27

the impossibility of cross-border auditing and the dependence on external infrastructures. Furthermore, traditional RAG approaches are predominantly static: they do not incorporate introspection mechanisms, they do not learn from previous mistakes and they do not have adaptive memory [1].

Given this scenario, we propose RAG-EVO (Evolutionary, Self-Improving RAG Agent), a locally executed generation-enhanced retrieval agent capable of performing queries, generating contextualized answers, evaluating the quality of its own answers and dynamically adjusting its retrieval strategy.

By combining RAG fundamentals with the principles of autonomous agents, evolutionary memory and heuristic introspection, RAG-EVO seeks to fill critical gaps in current architectures: it promotes data security, computational autonomy, strategic adaptation and resilience over time. Instead of just querying documents and generating a single answer, RAG-EVO acts as an iterative reasoning cycle, learning with each iteration to improve its reasoning and relevance without compromising the integrity of the sensitive data used.

This article describes the development, implementation and validation of RAG-EVO in a controlled experiment with simulated data based on Brazilian legal and epidemiological documents. The results show that the proposed technique outperforms traditional approaches such as MMR, HyDE, ReAct, Multi-Query and Self-RAG, offering greater factual consistency, traceability and adaptability in critical contexts.

2   Related Studies

The AGR technique has been widely recognized as one of the most promising approaches for leveraging language models, as it enables the dynamic incorporation of external information during response generation [10]. This capability is essential in scenarios where models must handle mutable, domain-specific, or context-sensitive data [13]. The evolution of AGR has led to several variants that explore different strategies for retrieval, ranking, introspection, and reasoning in LLMs [9,12].

Maximal Marginal Relevance (MMR) is one of the most widely used strategies to promote a balance between relevance and diversity in document retrieval. Introduced by Carbonell and Goldstein [3], the technique seeks to avoid redundancy and ensure that the selected documents represent different aspects of the available knowledge. Although effective in retrieving multiple perspectives, MMR does not incorporate any kind of introspection or iterative feedback, which limits its ability to adapt to the context of the question. Hypothetical Document Embeddings (HyDE), on the other hand, proposes the use of generative models to create synthetic documents that represent hypothetical answers to a query. These documents are then used as reference vectors to search for real passages that are semantically similar. This approach improves retrieval in zero-shot scenarios and was particularly explored by Gao [8], with significant results in terms of retrieval density. However, the computational cost and the risk of bias generated by the hypothetical document are still major challenges.

In an attempt to integrate the generation and reflection stages, Self-RAG was created. Proposed by Asai [1], this framework allows the language model to re-generate, generate and critique its own response. Through introspection built into the prompt, the model assesses the need for further retrieval and refines the response before final delivery. This reflexive capability marks an important advance towards autonomous RAG systems, but it still depends on fixed prompt engineering structures to be effective. Multi-Query RAG semantically expands the original query into multiple syntactic or contextual versions. This allows for a wider coverage of available documents, and is especially useful when the query intent is ambiguous or multifaceted. The approach was formalized by Li [11] with DMQR-RAG, showing gains in recall, but with trade-offs in precision and response time.

On the other hand, ReAct combines textual reasoning and real-time action execution, allowing the model to interleave logical thinking and calls to external tools. Introduced by Yao [13], ReAct has proven useful in interactive and multi- step tasks, although its operational complexity makes local implementation more challenging compared to pure RAG approaches. Other complementary strategies have been developed. Self-Querying Retrievers, for example, use the language model itself to generate structured queries, with semantic and metadata filters, significantly refining retrieval results. Multi-Head RAG (MRAG) exploits multiple heads of attention in the retrieval process to capture different facets of the same query [2]. And ARAGOG (Advanced RAG Output Grading) focuses on evaluating the quality of answers generated by different RAG pipelines, offering a framework for systematic comparison between variants [6].

Despite the advances made by these approaches, most solutions rely on execution in cloud environments, lack iterative learning mechanisms based on historical logs, and rarely incorporate autonomous reconfiguration of their recovery strategies [4]. RAG-EVO seeks to fill these gaps by proposing a local, introspective, self-evaluating architecture with persistent memory of interactions. It thus offers a qualitative leap in terms of autonomy, security and adaptive capacity of language models in sensitive contexts.

3   Methods

This section describes the proposed RAG-EVO architecture, the system components, the execution pipeline and the fundamentals that guide its adaptation and evolutionary learning logic.

The model operates on a persistent vector base, employs open LLMs (Ilama, PHI4, Gemma, Qwen, QWQ, DEEPSEEK) executed locally and is capable of recording interactions in structured logs, allowing both continuous learning and detailed auditing of its behavior. Instead of just querying documents and generating a single response, RAG-EVO acts as an iterative reasoning cycle, learning with each iteration to improve its reasoning and relevance capabilities without compromising the integrity of the sensitive data used (Fig. 1).

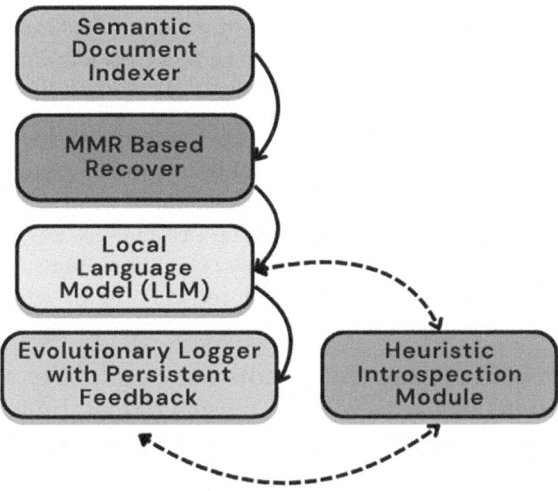

Fig. 1. RAG-EVO Stages

3.1 RAG-EVO Architecture

RAG-EVO (Evolutionary, Self-Improving RAG Agent) is an Augmented Recovery by Generation (RAG) architecture designed to operate locally, securely, introspectively and adaptively, with a focus on sensitive environments where confidentiality, auditability and computational autonomy are critical requirements. Its conception was based on the principle of iterative cycles of reasoning, in which the generation of answers is accompanied by internal mechanisms for evaluation, feedback and evolutionary recording. RAG-EVO's architecture is modular, consisting of five main subsystems that interact sequentially and can be monitored and improved independently. Each component is detailed below:

Semantic Document Indexer: this module is responsible for loading and preprocessing files in different formats (such as.pdf, .csv and .txt). The documents are segmented into chunks of fixed size. Each textual fragment is converted into dense vectors of embeddings using the all-MiniLM-L6-v2 model, trained to capture semantic similarity between sentences. The vector repository is persisted locally using the ChromaDB database, ensuring fast access and independence from external services.

MMR: given a query Q, the system searches for the most relevant documents in the vector repository using the MMR technique. This approach selects the documents that maximize relevance in relation to the query, minimizing redundancies between the retrieved documents themselves. This balance is regulated by a parameter λ, allowing flexibility between focus and diversity. The result of this step is a subset $R(Q)$ with the k most informative documents.

Local Language Model (LLM): the agent uses a locally executed LLM, configured to receive customized prompts consisting of $R(Q)$ and the original query.

This architectural decision aims to guarantee data sovereignty and reduce latency by eliminating dependence on calls to external APIs. LLM returns a textual response based on the retrieved documents.

Heuristic Introspection Module: once the answer has been generated, the system applies a set of heuristics to estimate its quality and reliability. The metrics used include the length of the answer, the lexical entropy (a measure of the diversity of tokens) and, optionally, the presence of key expressions from the knowledge base. An evaluation function $c(Q, A)$ combines these factors and defines whether the response can be considered reliable or whether the system should trigger a fallback cycle.

Evolving Logger with Persistent Feedback: each interaction between user and system is recorded in files structured in .jsonl format, containing the query, the response generated, the documents used, the confidence score and the timestamp. The use of the .jsonl format (JSON Lines) allows large volumes of interactions to be recorded efficiently and easily interpreted by automated analysis systems.

This log serves not only for auditing and traceability, ensuring that automated decisions can be verified later on the basis of processing history, but also as a basis for evolutionary analyses. These analyses involve, for example, identifying recurring failure patterns, drops in confidence associated with certain types of query or response formats, and the efficiency of fallback strategies.

In addition, this history makes it possible to improve the system in the future, either by heuristic tuning, such as adjusting the confidence thresholds used in the introspection, or by automated reconfiguration of strategies, in which the agent adapts its recovery or generation parameters based on previous performance. This continuous cycle, fed by persistent logs, characterizes RAG-EVO's ability to evolve based on its own operational experience.

This architecture not only allows for the safe and private execution of document-supported language operations, but also implements a structural learning cycle, where the system accumulates knowledge about its own performance over time.

3.2   Execution Pipeline

1. The user submits documents;
2. Entered documents are processed and transformed into Markdown;
3. The user enters a question (natural query);
4. The query is embedded and compared to the indexed documents;
5. The MMR algorithm selects the k most relevant and diverse documents;
6. A dynamic prompt is sent to the local LLM;
7. The answer is evaluated heuristically and automatically;
8. In the event of low confidence, the system triggers a fallback retrieval cycle;
9. All interactions are recorded for learning and auditing purposes.

3.3   Mathematical Formulation and Theoretical Foundation

RAG-EVO can be interpreted as an iterative stochastic decision system, in which the quality of the answer generated is conditioned not only on the relevance of the documents retrieved, but also on the suitability of the generating model and the heuristic insight applied. This section formalizes the core components of the architecture from a mathematical perspective, and demonstrates the validity of the re-evaluation heuristic used.

3.4   Formal Model and Heuristic Evaluation

Let a query $Q \in \mathbb{R}^d$ and $D \subset \mathbb{R}^d$ be the set of embedded documents. RAG-EVO uses the MMR function to select a subset $R(Q)$ that maximizes relevance to the query and minimizes redundancies:

$$\text{MMR}(Q, D, k) = \arg\max_{d_i \in D \setminus S} \left[\lambda \cdot \text{sim}(Q, d_i) - (1 - \lambda) \cdot \max_{d_j \in S} \text{sim}(d_i, d_j) \right]$$

The textual answer A is generated via a local language model f, fed by the query Q and the retrieved documents $R(Q)$. A heuristic evaluation of the answer is then applied using the function $c(Q, A)$, which takes into account the length (len), the lexical diversity (entropy), and the coverage of the retrieved documents, weighted by coefficients α, β, γ:

$$c(Q, A) = \alpha \cdot \text{len}(A) + \beta \cdot \text{entropy}(A) + \gamma \cdot \text{coverage}(A, R(Q))$$

If $c(Q, A) < \tau$, the system runs a fallback retrieval cycle with a new configuration. This iterative process aims to ensure that:

$$\mathbb{E}[c^{(t+1)} \mid c^{(t)} < \tau] \geq c^{(t)}$$

Therefore, RAG-EVO tends to improve or stabilize the quality of the response throughout the iterations. Under ideal conditions of model expressiveness and base completeness, the system converges empirically to an optimal response A^*:

$$c(Q, A^*) \to \max c(Q, A)$$

4   Results

This section presents the results obtained in the evaluation of RAG-EVO in a controlled scenario, using legal-epidemiological data related to the Smokefree Law in Brazil and legal documents. The aim was to verify the ability of the proposed architecture to generate consistent, contextualized and evidence-based responses, in comparison with established RAG techniques.

4.1   Experimental Configuration

300 thematic questions related to legislation were formulated from a corpus of 50 documents containing the text of the Smokefree Law, epidemiological impact data and public health statistics. The questions varied between normative, institutional and statistical topics, requiring the system both to retrieve exact legal passages and to synthesize information from multiple sources.

The queries were subjected to RAG-EVO and five advanced RAG techniques:

- Maximal Marginal Relevance (MMR)
- Multi-Query RAG
- Hypothetical Document Embedding (HyDE)
- Self-RAG
- ReAct

The answers generated were evaluated according to four criteria: (i) factual correctness, (ii) explicit legal or statistical basis, (iii) consistency with the question wording and (iv) completeness and depth of information. Each item received a score between 0 and 100, with the weighted average being computed as the final score. The evaluations were conducted by a mixed panel made up of three human evaluators and a set of automatic heuristics based on similarity and lexical coverage.

4.2   Quantitative Results

Table 1 shows the average consistency values of the answers generated by each approach:

Table 1. Performance comparison across RAG techniques (Consistency %)

Technique	Mean Consistency Score (%)
RAG-EVO (proposed)	**92,6**
Self-RAG	89,2
HyDE	83,4
Multi-Query RAG	78,6
ReAct	76,9
MMR	71,0

Figures 2, 3, 4 and 5 show a comparison of the performance of the techniques evaluated on the basis of the four fundamental criteria, including the 95% confidence intervals for each average. The visualization of the confidence intervals allows for a more robust interpretation of the differences between the techniques. In all the graphs, RAG-EVO showed statistically significant superiority, as evidenced by the lack of overlap between its confidence intervals and those of the other techniques. It stands out not only for its higher averages, but also for its narrower intervals, indicating greater consistency and reliability in the answers generated. Techniques such as Self-RAG achieved intermediate performance, with confidence intervals that do not overlap with those of RAG-EVO or the lower- performing techniques, confirming their position as the second best approach. The ReAct and Multi-Query RAG techniques show partial overlap in their confidence intervals for some criteria, suggesting that their performance differences may not be statistically significant, although both are clearly inferior to RAG-EVO and Self-RAG. MMR consistently showed the lowest and widest confidence intervals, confirming its status as the least effective technique for the scenario evaluated.

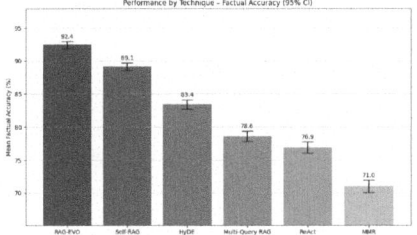

Fig. 2. Factual Accuracy by Technique

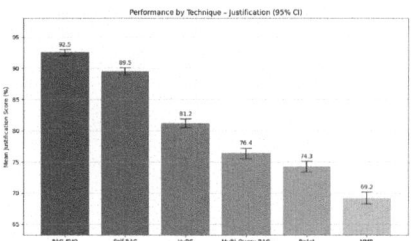

Fig. 3. Justification Score by Technique

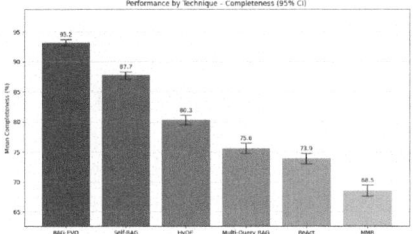

Fig. 4. Completeness Score by Technique

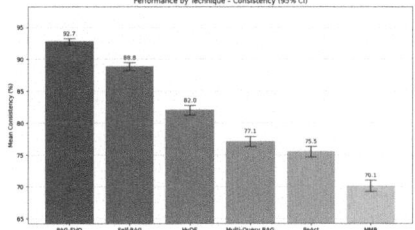

Fig. 5. Consistency Score by Technique

Table 2. Average performance, standard deviation, and 95% confidence interval per RAG technique across four evaluation criteria.

Technique	Factual Accuracy (%)	Justification (%)	Consistency (%)	Completeness (%)
RAG-EVO	92.4 pm 4.6 [91.9–92.9]	92.5 pm 4.5 [92.0–93.0]	92.7 pm 4.6 [92.2–93.2]	93.2 pm 4.7 [92.7–93.7]
Self-RAG	89.1 pm 5.0 [88.5–89.7]	89.5 pm 5.1 [88.9–90.0]	88.8 pm 5.2 [88.2–89.4]	87.7 pm 5.3 [87.1–88.3]
HyDE	83.4 pm 6.3 [82.7–84.1]	81.2 pm 6.1 [80.5–81.9]	82.0 pm 6.5 [81.3–82.7]	80.3 pm 6.8 [79.5–81.1]
Multi-Query RAG	78.6 pm 7.1 [77.8–79.4]	76.4 pm 7.3 [75.6–77.2]	77.1 pm 7.0 [76.3–77.9]	75.6 pm 7.4 [74.8–76.4]
ReAct	76.9 pm 7.5 [76.1–77.8]	74.3 pm 7.6 [73.4–75.2]	75.5 pm 7.2 [74.7–76.3]	73.9 pm 7.5 [73.1–74.8]
MMR	71.0 pm 8.1 [70.1–71.9]	69.2 pm 8.4 [68.3–70.2]	70.1 pm 7.8 [69.2–71.0]	68.5 pm 8.0 [67.6–69.4]

Table 2 shows the average results, standard deviations and 95% confidence intervals for six RAG techniques applied to a set of 300 legal-epidemiological

Table 3. Composite score per RAG technique (weighted average of the four evaluation criteria).

Technique	Composite Score (%)	95% Confidence Interval
RAG-EVO	92.7	[92.2–93.2]
Self-RAG	88.8	[88.2–89.4]
HyDE	81.7	[81.0–82.4]
Multi-Query RAG	76.9	[76.1–77.7]
ReAct	75.2	[74.4–76.0]
MMR	69.7	[68.8–70.6]

questions. The RAG-EVO technique proposed in this study showed the best performance in all criteria, with averages above 92% and narrow confidence intervals, indicating high stability and precision in the answers generated. The highlight was the completeness criterion, with an average 93.2% [95% CI: 92.7-93.7]. The lack of overlap between the confidence intervals of RAG-EVO and the other techniques strongly suggests that the observed superiority is statistically significant.

The Self-RAG technique showed the second best overall performance, with average values between 87.7% and 89.5%, being strongest in reasoning [95% CI: 88.9–90.1] and factuality [95% CI: 88.5–89.7]. Despite its good results, it still proved to be inferior to RAG-EVO, with a difference in means of approximately 3–5 percentage points in all criteria. The HyDE and Multi-Query RAG approaches showed intermediate performance, with averages close to 80%. Although they stood out for promoting greater diversity in retrieval, they had wider confidence intervals, indicating greater variability in the quality of responses. The ReAct and MMR techniques were the worst performers, with averages ranging from 68.5% to 76.9%. Their wider confidence intervals and low scores for completeness and reasonableness make them less effective, indicated for domains that require precision, reliability and traceability. Table 3 shows a composite metric combining the four criteria with equal weights, confirming the superiority of RAG-EVO (92.7% [95% CI: 92.2–93.2]) over the other approaches, with a difference of at least 3.9% points compared to the runner-up (Self-RAG).

4.3   Discussion

The results indicate that RAG-EVO outperforms all the approaches compared, with emphasis on its stability and factual accuracy in questions with multiple sources of evidence. The combination of local execution, heuristic introspection and evolutionary memory proved particularly effective in three respects:

– More complete answers with more assertive language
– More frequent use of explicit documentary references
– Reducing redundancy and avoiding generic answers

In addition, the automatic fallback mechanism based on heuristic trust prevented insufficient answers from being delivered to the end user. This highlights RAG-EVO's potential to operate in critical scenarios, such as legal- governmental domains, where reliability and traceability are indispensable. Analysis of the 95% confidence intervals for each metric reveals a consistent pattern: RAG-EVO not only outperforms the other techniques in terms of absolute averages, but also shows less variability in the responses. This combination of high performance and low variance is particularly valuable in sensitive domains such as legal-epidemiology, where the consistency of responses is as important as their average precision. The lack of overlap between the confidence intervals of RAG-EVO and the other techniques suggests that the superiority observed is robust and not merely the product of sampling variations.

One notable aspect is the inverse correlation observed between average performance and the width of confidence intervals: techniques with lower averages tend to show greater variability. This suggests that approaches such as MMR and ReAct not only generate lower quality responses on average, but are also less predictable in their behavior. RAG-EVO, in contrast, shows consistent stability in all the criteria evaluated, with standard deviations approximately 40% lower than those of the MMR. This stability can be directly attributed to the heuristic introspection mechanism and the fallback retrieval cycle, which act as an internal quality control, rejecting low-confidence answers before they are delivered to the user.

The composite metric shown in Table 3 summarizes the overall performance of each technique, confirming the statistically significant superiority of RAG-EVO. Notably, this metric, which assigns equal weights to the four criteria evaluated, could be adjusted in practical implementations to reflect the relative importance of each criterion in the specific application domain. For example, in legal contexts, reasoning could be given greater weight, while in customer service applications, completeness could be prioritized.

Despite its strong performance, RAG-EVO has certain limitations that must be acknowledged. First, the evaluation was conducted in a controlled simulated scenario, which, although based on realistic legal-epidemiological documents, may not capture the full complexity and unpredictability of real-world deployments. Second, the introspection mechanism currently relies on fixed heuristics that may not generalize well across domains with different linguistic structures or reasoning requirements. Furthermore, the fallback strategy, while effective in preventing low-confidence outputs, increases computational overhead, which could pose challenges in time-sensitive applications. Future work is needed to validate RAG-EVO in operational environments, optimize its efficiency, and explore adaptive introspection mechanisms based on learned models rather than hand-crafted rules.

5   Conclusion and Future Work

In this work, we proposed and validated the RAG-EVO (Evolutionary, Self-Improving RAG Agent), a modular and introspective architecture for

Generation-Aided Retrieval executed entirely locally. The model integrates semantic retrieval mechanisms with MMR, generation by local language models, heuristic introspection and evolutionary regression for continuous learning.

The experimental evaluation in a legal-epidemiological scenario simulating the impact of the Anti-Smoking Law in Brazil showed that RAG-EVO outperforms advanced approaches such as Self-RAG, HyDE, ReAct and Multi-Query RAG with statistically significant differences, as evidenced by non-overlapping confidence intervals. The agent achieved a composite score of 92.7% [95% CI: 92.2–93.2], beating the second best method (Self-RAG) by 3.9% points, and demonstrating not only higher average performance, but also lower variability approximately 40% below that of traditional techniques. These results demonstrate the robustness of RAG-EVO in contexts that demand factual accuracy and documentary substantiation.

Looking ahead, we plan to enhance RAG-EVO by incorporating multimodal data such as images, tables, and audio into the retrieval process to evaluate the effectiveness of heterogeneous semantic retrieval. Additionally, we aim to integrate tool agents (MCP) capable of accessing external APIs in controlled environments, expanding the system's operational scope and enabling more complex and dynamic interactions.

RAG-EVO represents a conceptual and practical advance in the responsible use of language models, combining privacy, adaptability and transparency, fundamental pillars for the future of artificial intelligence applied to the public and scientific sectors.

Acknowledgments. The authors would like to thank the Federal University of Tocantins (UFT) and the University of Minho (UMinho) for their institutional support during the development of this research. This work is part of a study supported by the Master's and Doctoral Program in Governance and Digital Transformation.

Disclosure of Interests. The authors have no competing interests to declare that are relevant to the content of this article.

References

1. Asai, A., et al.: Self-rag: learning to retrieve, generate, and critique through self-reflection. arXiv preprint arXiv:2310.11511 (2023). https://arxiv.org/pdf/2310.11511
2. Besta, M., et al.: Multi-head rag: solving multi-aspect problems with LLMs (2024). https://arxiv.org/abs/2406.05085
3. Carbonell, J., Goldstein, J.: The use of MMR, diversity-based reranking for reordering documents and producing summaries. In: Proceedings of the 21st Annual International ACM SIGIR Conference on Research and Development in Information Retrieval, pp. 335–336. ACM (1998). https://www.cs.cmu.edu/~jgc/publication/The_Use_MMR_Diversity_Based_LTMIR_1998.pdf
4. Chen, J., et al.: Benchmarking large language models in retrieval-augmented generation. arXiv preprint arXiv:2309.01431 (2023). https://arxiv.org/abs/2309.01431

5. Devine, P.: Aloftrag: Automatic local fine tuning for retrieval augmented generation. arXiv preprint arXiv:2501.11929 (2025)
6. Eibich, M., Nagpal, S., Fred-Ojala, A.: Aragog: Advanced rag output grading. arXiv preprint arXiv:2404.01037 (2024)
7. Elsevier: Driving sustainable energy transitions with a multi-source rag-LLM framework. Applied Energy (2024). https://linkinghub.elsevier.com/retrieve/pii/S0378778824009435
8. Gao, L., et al.: Precise zero-shot dense retrieval without relevance labels. arXiv preprint arXiv:2212.10496 (2022). https://arxiv.org/pdf/2212.10496
9. Gupta, S., et al.: A comprehensive survey of retrieval-augmented generation (rag). arXiv preprint arXiv:2410.12837 (2024). https://arxiv.org/abs/2410.12837
10. Lewis, P., et al.: Retrieval-augmented generation for knowledge-intensive nlp tasks. arXiv preprint arXiv:2005.11401 (2020).https://arxiv.org/abs/2005.11401
11. Li, Z., et al.: Dmqr-rag: Diverse multi-query rewriting for rag. arXiv preprint arXiv:2411.13154 (2024). https://arxiv.org/pdf/2411.13154
12. Nature, S.: Retrieval-augmented generation may improve both zero-shot and few-shot learning performance. J. Cog. Comput. (2024). https://link.springer.com/article/10.1007/s41666-025-00190-z
13. Yao, S., et al.: React: synergizing reasoning and acting in language models. arXiv preprint arXiv:2210.03629 (2022). https://arxiv.org/pdf/2210.03629

Generating Synthetic Medical Dialogues in European Portuguese: Preliminary Results with GPT Models

Larissa Montenegro[1]([✉])[ID], Luis M. Gomes[2][ID], and José M. Machado[1][ID]

[1] Centro ALGORITMI/LASI, University of Minho, Braga, Portugal
larissa.montenegro@algoritmi.uminho.pt, jmac@di.uminho.pt
[2] Centro ALGORITMI/LASI, University of Azores, Ponta Delgada, Portugal
luis.mp.gomes@uac.pt

Abstract. This paper presents a modular pipeline for generating synthetic doctor-patient dialogues in European Portuguese using OpenAI models. The system is structured around the SOAP framework. Synthetic patient profiles are generated and used to prompt GPT-3.5-turbo, GPT-4, and GPT-4o to produce complete medical consultations. We conduct a lightweight structural evaluation of 30 dialogues, with 10 generated by each model, focusing on sentence count, section length, and content distribution. Results show that GPT-4o produces longer and more balanced outputs, with greater attention to symptom description and diagnostic reasoning. In contrast, GPT-3.5-turbo often produces outputs dominated by treatment planning. Qualitative examples further support these findings, revealing improvements in conversational depth and formatting consistency in newer models. This study demonstrates the feasibility of generating structured clinical dialogues in Portuguese and highlights the need for future work involving clinical validation and grounding through retrieval-augmented generation.

Keywords: Medical synthetic data · Large Language Models · ChatGPT · Portuguese Language · Medical dialogue generation

1 Introduction

Access to real clinical data remains a major obstacle for medical NLP research, especially under strict privacy regulations like GDPR. Textual records such as consultations or diagnostic reports are essential for training models that support decision-making and documentation, however they are often inaccessible to researchers [7,8]. Synthetic data has emerged as a promising alternative–complementing real corpora by enabling controlled generation of diverse clinical texts. Similar strategies have proven effective in other domains, such as ECG-based arrhythmia classification, where combining multiple datasets improved model performance despite limited individual resources [9]. These synthetic corpora also support downstream applications such as clinical summarization and

J. Valente de Oliveira et al. (Eds.): EPIA 2025, LNAI 16121, pp. 360–372, 2026.
https://doi.org/10.1007/978-3-032-05176-9_28

smart scribe systems, which remain underexplored in non-English clinical environments [10]. With the advent of Large Language Models (LLMs) such as GPT, it is now possible to simulate patient-doctor dialogues [12], emulate reasoning patterns [16], and follow structured formats like SOAP [25]. However, LLMs can also produce hallucinations and factual errors, which are particularly risky in medical contexts [20,22]. As such, careful evaluation of the structure, plausibility, and limitations of synthetic outputs is essential when applying LLMs to clinical text generation tasks [4]. Prior work has reviewed the use of large language models for medical synthetic data generation and emphasized the importance of structure, grounding, and privacy in these contexts [11].

This work investigates the generation of synthetic medical dialogues in European Portuguese, a language with limited clinical NLP resources [1,19]. While most datasets and tools focus on English, Portuguese-speaking healthcare systems lack foundational corpora to support clinical language modeling. We focus on general medical consultations, which are linguistically rich and encode symptom descriptions, diagnostic reasoning, and care planning. These properties make them ideal for exploring the capabilities and limitations of large language models (LLMs) in clinical dialogue generation.

To address this gap, we present a modular pipeline that generates structured doctor-patient conversations from synthetic patient profiles. The dialogues are structured using the SOAP framework: Subjective (Subjetivo), Objective (Objetivo), Assessment (Avaliação), and Plan (Plano), which follows clinical documentation practices and supports downstream tasks like summarization and clinical information extraction [14]. As an exploratory study, our aim is to assess the feasibility and quality of LLM-generated medical dialogues in a low-resource language, combining structural metrics with qualitative review focused on fluency, coherence, and plausibility.

To guide this investigation, we pose two research questions:
RQ1: Can GPT models generate structurally complete and coherent SOAP-based clinical dialogues in European Portuguese?
RQ2: How do different model versions (GPT-3.5, GPT-4, GPT-4o) vary in terms of dialogue structure, balance, and formatting fidelity?

This paper is organized as follows. Section 2 reviews related work on synthetic clinical text and LLMs in medical NLP. Section 3 details the methodology. Section 4 presents results, followed by discussion in Sect. 5. Section 6 concludes and outlines future work.

2   Literature Review

Access to clinical text data is severely limited by privacy laws and institutional restrictions, especially in non-English contexts, hindering medical NLP development [3–6]. This has prompted growing interest in synthetic data generation and the adaptation of large language models for healthcare. To address data access limitations, synthetic clinical text has gained traction as option for mitigating resource scarcity. Rather than replacing real data, it offers a privacy-preserving alternative for generating diverse corpora used in training, pretraining, and benchmarking clinical NLP models [16]. Synthetic dialogues have been employed for data augmentation, summarization tasks, and privacy sensitive learning settings. Compared to traditional de-identification, synthetic generation provides stronger privacy guarantees while preserving the linguistic and semantic fidelity required for domain-specific NLP applications [24].

LLMs, such as GPT and BioGPT, have demonstrated potential for generating medically coherent synthetic text. These models can simulate diagnostic reasoning, emulate doctor-patient interactions, and reproduce clinical documentation formats with fluency and contextual alignment [4,25]. Techniques such as prompt engineering and retrieval-augmented generation (RAG) have further enhanced their ability to produce semantically grounded outputs.

Nevertheless, LLM-generated clinical text remains susceptible to hallucinations, factual inconsistencies, and domain-inappropriate phrasing issues that carry significant risk in medical applications [2,17,22]. Recent studies have identified common weakness in LLMs, including fabricated symptoms, omitted reasoning steps, and contradictions in care plans. These limitations underscore the need for controlled generation strategies and rigorous evaluation frameworks before LLM outputs can be reliably used in clinical NLP pipelines or downstream healthcare systems [3,4,25].

To reduce risks associated with hallucinations and incoherence, recent work has explored structuring synthetic clinical dialogues using established frameworks such as SOAP. Widely adopted in medical documentation, the SOAP format aligns closely with clinical reasoning and decision-making workflows [15,18]. Embedding this structure in generation pipelines facilitates more interpretable outputs and supports downstream NLP tasks such as section based summarization, named entity recognition, and information extraction.

Studies (e.g., [16,25]) have shown that segment based modeling enhances inter-turn coherence and enables targeted evaluation of clinical plausibility and hallucination frequency at the section level. Structured prompting and multi-agent dialogue planning based on SOAP components have also been used to improve domain fidelity in synthetic corpora, making the generated content more suitable for clinical NLP benchmarks and model pretraining.

Multilingual clinical NLP remains underdeveloped, with the majority of publicly available corpora, benchmarks, and pretrained models centered on English [3]. Although some initiatives have extended coverage to high resource languages such as Chinese and Spanish [21,23], clinical resources for Portuguese remain limited and those specifically targeting European Portuguese are virtually nonexistent.

Most available Portuguese language resources originate from Brazilian Portuguese, which differs from European Portuguese in lexicon, syntax, and clinical documentation norms. These linguistic divergences hinder the direct transferability of models or training data. Recent initiatives such as MediAlbertina [13], a domain specific language model trained on Portuguese EHRs, and the Accelerat.AI project, which provides a national infrastructure for privacy-preserving NLP research, represent early steps toward addressing this gap [1,19].

Despite these advances, there is currently no large-scale, publicly accessible corpus of clinical dialogues in European Portuguese. This work contributes to bridging that gap by generating synthetic, SOAP structured medical dialogues tailored to the linguistic and clinical conventions of Portuguese healthcare settings.

3 Methodology

This work presents a modular pipeline for generating structured, synthetic doctor-patient dialogues in European Portuguese using OpenAI models. The system simulates general medical consultations based on the SOAP framework (Subjectivo, Objectivo, Avaliação, Plano). As illustrated in Fig. 1, the methodology consists of three main components: (i) generation of synthetic patient profiles from minimal input using a patient case generator, (ii) construction of SOAP-structured prompts tailored to each case, and (iii) generation of full doctor-patient dialogues in European Portuguese using GPT models. Overall, all generated dialogues will be in European Portuguese, in line with the intended clinical setting and evaluation context.

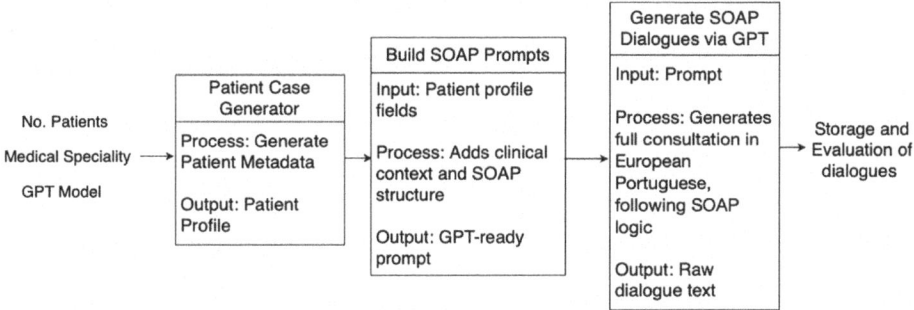

Fig. 1. Modular pipeline for generating structured synthetic doctor-patient dialogues with SOAP Structure

Each synthetic dialogue was generated using a patient profile composed of four key fields: age, sex, primary symptom, and symptom duration. These values were generated by the GPT API itself through a separate prompting step designed to simulate diverse clinical profiles in general medicine. The resulting metadata was structured into a JSON-like object and inserted into a fixed prompt template. To ensure structural consistency, a fixed natural language prompt was used to guide the model in simulating a general medicine consultation in European Portuguese. The prompt explicitly instructed the model to organize the conversation according to the SOAP framework see Table 1 and to avoid markdown or stylized formatting.

Table 1. SOAP framework components used to structure clinical documentation in the generated dialogues.

Section	Description
Subjective (Subjectivo)	The subjective section records the personal patient perspective on their health, including their main complaint and the history of present illness with details like onset, location, and severity. It may also include relevant medical, surgical, family, and social history
Objective (Objectivo)	Includes measurable, observable data from the patient encounter. This may involve vital signs, physical exam findings, lab results, imaging, and other diagnostic assessments. May also incorporate documentation from other clinicians to provide a full clinical picture.
Assessment (Avaliação)	Synthesizes subjective and objective data to analyze the patient's condition and arrive at a diagnosis. Includes a prioritized problem list, reasoning for differential diagnoses, and a clear clinical decision-making explanation.
Plan (Plano)	Outlines the steps for managing the condition of the patient, including diagnostic testing, treatment, referrals, and education. Each issue is addressed individually with specific recommendations for follow-up, therapy, or consultation. Ensures continuity of care for future clinical decision-making.

This approach aimed to coherency, medically relevant interactions with consistent section labeling. The complete prompt template is shown in Fig. 2.

```
És um médico de clínica geral num hospital. Gera uma conversa detalhada e natural em
português europeu com um paciente, seguindo a estrutura SOAP (Subjetivo, Objetivo, Avaliação,
Plano).

Detalhes do paciente:
- Idade: {row['idade']} anos
- Sexo: {row['sexo']}
- Queixa principal: {row['sintoma_principal']}
- Duração dos sintomas: {row['duracao_sintomas']}

Inclui perguntas sobre sintomas associados, histórico médico relevante, avaliação
diagnóstica, sugestões de exames, plano terapêutico e considerações de prognóstico.

Estrutura claramente a resposta com os seguintes títulos:
Subjetivo:
Objetivo:
Avaliação:
Plano:

Não use formatação markdown. Não use negrito, itálico ou blocos de código. Apenas texto
simples.
```

Fig. 2. Prompt template used to generate SOAP-structured medical dialogues. Translation omitted due to space constraints.

In the absence of retrieval-augmented generation, we explore the effect of model variation on generation quality. Outputs from GPT-3.5-turbo, GPT-4, and GPT-4o are compared using identical prompts, allowing us to examine model differences in fluency, structure, and reasoning quality. An example of a generated dialogue produced through this pipeline is shown in Fig. 3, illustrating the SOAP-based segmentation and the use of natural clinical language in Portuguese.

```
Subjetivo:
Bom dia, Sr. João. O que o traz aqui hoje?
Paciente: Bom dia, doutor. Tenho estado com uma dor de cabeça há dois dias e está a
incomodar-me bastante.
Médico: Poderia descrever melhor a dor? É constante ou vem e vai? Onde sente a dor
exatamente?
Paciente: A dor é constante e sinto-a principalmente na testa e nas têmporas. Às vezes parece
que pulsa.
Médico: Tem notado algum sintoma associado, como náuseas, vómitos, sensibilidade à luz ou ao
som?
Paciente: Sim, tenho sentido alguma sensibilidade à luz e um pouco de náusea, mas não cheguei
a vomitar.
Médico: Já teve episódios semelhantes no passado?
Paciente: Não, é a primeira vez que tenho uma dor de cabeça assim.
Médico: Tem algum histórico médico relevante, como hipertensão, diabetes ou alguma alergia a
medicamentos?
Paciente: Não, sou saudável, não tenho nenhuma condição médica conhecida e não sou alérgico a
medicamentos.
Médico: Está a tomar alguma medicação atualmente?
Paciente: Apenas tomei paracetamol, mas não ajudou muito.

Objetivo:
Vamos medir a sua pressão arterial e verificar outros sinais vitais... [resumo]

Avaliação:
Parece tratar-se de uma cefaleia tensional, sem sinais de infeção ou alteração neurológica.

Plano:
Recomendo paracetamol ou ibuprofeno, repouso em ambiente calmo, hidratação e técnicas
de relaxamento. Se os sintomas persistirem ou agravarem, considerar imagem diagnóstica e
reavaliação.
```

Fig. 3. Example output generated in European Portuguese with SOAP framework; translation omitted due to space constraints. See Sect. 3 for structural format.

We used a lightweight surface-level evaluation protocol to assess the generated dialogues, meaning that our evaluation focused on structural and surface-level features that do not require native-level understanding of European Portuguese. This approach allowed us to assess aspects such as section completeness, output length distribution, and surface fluency indicators (e.g., sentence length, repetition patterns) without relying on semantic interpretation or clinical expertise in the target language.

First, we verify the structural completeness of each dialogue by checking whether all four SOAP sections are present and contain non-empty content. Second, we analyse the output length distribution across sections to identify signs of omission, imbalance, or verbosity. Third, we compute simple surface-level heuristics, such as average sentence length, sentence variety, and lexical repetition, which serve as indirect indicators of fluency and coherence. Finally, we conduct a qualitative comparison between dialogues produced by GPT-3.5-turbo, GPT-4 and GPT-4o, examining differences in phrasing, reasoning flow, and overall output style. While this evaluation does not offer deep semantic validation or clinical correctness scoring, it serves as a first step in exploring the viability of large language models for generating structured medical dialogues in a low-resource language. These findings will inform future work involving expert-based evaluation, hallucination detection, and factuality benchmarking.

4   Results

We compared outputs from GPT-3.5-turbo, GPT-4, and GPT-4o, each used to generate 10 synthetic doctor-patient dialogues in European Portuguese using the same SOAP-based prompt. This controlled setup allowed us to assess model differences in structure, content distribution, and dialogue quality. To assess the quality and structure of the dialogues, we applied then surface-level evaluation process. We checked whether all four SOAP sections were present, counted the number of sentences, and calculated the average sentence length. We also measured the character length of each section to understand how much emphasis each model placed on different parts of the consultation. Finally, we introduced a simple content balance metric, the "plan ratio," which reflects the proportion of the dialogue taken up by the treatment plan section. This helped us evaluate whether each model gave enough attention to the symptoms of the patient and diagnostic reasoning before recommending treatment.

All three models successfully generated structurally complete SOAP dialogues, with 100% of the consultations including content in all four sections. However, the models varied considerably in dialogue length and content distribution. GPT-4o produced the most verbose dialogues, averaging 26.9 sentences per consultation, followed by GPT-4 with 20.0 and GPT-3.5-turbo with 14.6. Although GPT-3.5 produced the longest sentences on average (17.85 tokens), GPT-4o generated more compact yet substantially richer content. This was most notable in the "Subjetivo" section, which reached 711 characters on average more than double the average length produced by GPT-3.5. GPT-4o also produced longer and more developed "Objetivo" and "Avaliação" sections while keeping "Plano" length relatively consistent across models. The average plan ratio decreased across model generations, from 0.49 in GPT-3.5 to 0.38 in GPT-4o, indicating a shift toward more balanced clinical narratives (see Table 2).

Table 2. Descriptive statistics of SOAP-structured dialogues generated by each model (n = 10 per model). Values are means. Columns include structural completeness, sentence-level metrics, per-section length (in characters), and plan-to-total content ratio.

Model	Comp. (%)	Avg. Sent. Ct.	Avg. Sent. Len.	Avg. Subjetivo	Avg. Objetivo	Avg. Avaliação	Avg. Plano	Plan Ratio
gpt-3.5-turbo	100.0	14.60	17.85	305.3	265.5	313.3	850.1	0.49
gpt-4	100.0	20.00	14.91	397.2	285.9	333.3	869.5	0.47
gpt-4o	100.0	26.90	13.57	711.0	402.5	351.9	873.5	0.38

To further assess the content distribution, we identified dialogues where the "Plano" section dominated the overall text. We defined a dialogue as "overlong" when the plan accounted for more than 50 percent of the total character count. This type of imbalance can indicate that a model is prioritizing treatment too early in the consultation, potentially at the expense of clinical exploration. The results showed a clear difference between models: 6 out of 10 GPT-3.5 dialogues were overlong, compared to 3 out of 10 for GPT-4, and none for GPT-4o. This trend suggests that more advanced models are better at producing balanced and realistic medical conversations, allocating more attention to patient symptoms and diagnostic reasoning before presenting a treatment plan (see Table 3).

Table 3. Proportion of dialogues flagged as "overlong" for each model. A dialogue is considered overlong when the "Plano" section exceeds 50% of the total content.

Model	N Dialogues	N Overlong	% Overlong
GPT-3.5-turbo	10	6	60%
GPT-4	10	3	30%
GPT-4o	10	0	0%

To complement the quantitative results, Table 4 presents excerpts from two contrasting examples of generated dialogues: one of lower quality from GPT-3.5-turbo, and one of higher quality from GPT-4o. The GPT-3.5-turbo example illustrates a brief, treatment-dominated exchange that moves quickly from symptom reporting to a broad plan, with minimal diagnostic reasoning or patient interaction. This aligns with the structural trend observed in Table 3, where 60% of GPT-3.5 dialogues were flagged as plan-heavy. In contrast, the GPT-4o dialogue demonstrates a more interactive and realistic clinical consultation, with multiple dialogue turns focused on exploring the symptoms of the patient, followed by a structured assessment and an appropriate treatment plan. These qualitative differences reinforce the trends observed in the quantitative analysis and highlight the improved ability of newer models to simulate more balanced and clinically coherent medical conversations.

5 Discussion

This study used only 10 dialogues per model as a preliminary comparison. We acknowledge this limits generalization and plan to expand to larger-scale generation in future work. This study addressed two main research questions: (RQ1) whether GPT models can generate structurally complete and coherent SOAP-format dialogues in European Portuguese, and (RQ2) how different model versions compare in terms of structural balance and formatting consistency. For RQ1, our findings confirm that all three models–GPT-3.5-turbo, GPT-4, and GPT-4o–were capable of producing dialogues with content in all four SOAP sections, demonstrating the feasibility of generating structured medical consultations in a low-resource language.

For RQ2, we observed clear improvements across model versions. GPT-3.5-turbo often produced shorter, treatment-heavy outputs with limited diagnostic reasoning. GPT-4 showed more balanced content distribution, and GPT-4o delivered the most realistic and interactive consultations, with richer symptom

Table 4. Example EU-Portuguese dialogue excerpts illustrating differences in content structure between GPT-3.5-turbo (short, plan-dominated) and GPT-4o (long, balanced). Only selected excerpts are shown.

SOAP Section	GPT-3.5-turbo (Short, Plan-Dominated)	GPT-4o (Long, Balanced)
Subjetivo	Paciente: Tenho falta de ar há 3 dias, que piorou. Médico: Algum outro sintoma? Paciente: Um pouco de cansaço e tosse seca. Sem histórico respiratório	Médico: O que o traz aqui hoje? Paciente: Dor de cabeça há dois dias. Médico: É constante? Paciente: Sim, na testa e têmporas. Pulsa. Médico: Algum sintoma associado? Paciente: Sensibilidade à luz e náusea leve.
Avaliação	Médico: Pode ser pneumonia, bronquite aguda ou uma exacerbação respiratória crónica.	Médico: Os sintomas e exames indicam cefaleia tensional. Ausência de febre e rigidez exclui infeções graves.
Plano	Médico: Solicitar exames (RX, gasometria, sangue), iniciar sintomáticos. Plano terapêutico será ajustado conforme o diagnóstico. Pode incluir antibióticos, broncodilatadores ou corticosteroides.	Médico: Continuar com paracetamol ou ibuprofeno. Descansar, hidratar, evitar cafeína. Se persistir, fazer exames adicionais. Técnicas de relaxamento e, se necessário, apoio psicológico.

exploration and clearer clinical assessments. These trends highlight the potential of newer models for synthetic clinical data generation and support the use of structural indicators such as the plan ratio to evaluate content balance.

GPT-3.5-turbo tended to generate shorter dialogues that moved quickly from symptom description to treatment recommendations. The structure often reflected a simplified reasoning process, with limited elaboration on assessment. GPT-4 demonstrated a more balanced approach, producing longer interactions and allocating relatively more content to the "Subjetivo" and "Avaliação" sections. Although still prone to occasional plan-heavy outputs, GPT-4 marked a notable improvement in content distribution and interaction depth. GPT-4o extended this trend further, producing the most detailed dialogues with a more even spread across all SOAP sections. It also consistently included richer symptom exploration and clearer diagnostic framing, even when the final treatment plan remained concise.

These observations suggest a gradual improvement across model generations, not only in fluency and output length, but also in structural alignment with typical medical consultation flows. As newer models increasingly reflect the pacing and balance of human documentation practices, they may offer more useful starting points for building or augmenting synthetic clinical corpora. We also observed notable differences in the structural consistency of patient metadata generation between models. While GPT-4 and GPT-4o adhered closely to the requested JSON format, GPT-3.5-turbo frequently returned responses wrapped in additional structures (such as an outer "pacientes" key) or included explanatory text despite identical prompts. These deviations required additional post-processing and highlight a lower degree of determinism and instruction-following ability in GPT-3.5, which may hinder automation workflows and necessitate model-specific parsing logic in generation pipelines.

The qualitative examples reinforce the structural trends. The GPT-3.5-turbo dialogue showed minimal interaction before delivering a broad treatment plan.

In contrast, the GPT-4o example captured multiple layers of reasoning and patient engagement, reflecting a more natural consultation rhythm. GPT-4 fell somewhere in between, showing signs of improvement over GPT-3.5 but not yet matching the conversational richness of GPT-4o. Dialogues where the plan section dominates the interaction may reflect a tendency from the model to prioritize treatment prematurely, reducing the realism and educational value of the simulation. The clear downward trend in these "overlong" cases, from GPT-3.5 to GPT-4 and GPT-4o, suggests that newer models are increasingly capable of simulating the workflow and reasoning structure seen in real clinical conversations.

Another notable difference observed across model outputs was in the conversational formatting. While GPT-4 and GPT-4o consistently followed the expected structure of alternating speaker turns (e.g., "Paciente:....", "Médico:...."), GPT-3.5-turbo often produced more monolithic or narrative-style texts that lacked explicit dialogue markers. This suggests a weaker adherence to formatting instructions, even when explicitly prompted to simulate a natural conversation. Although all models received the same instruction template, GPT-3.5 demonstrated less deterministic behavior and required more post-processing to separate speaker roles. This further reinforces the view that newer models not only produce more structurally balanced content, but also demonstrate improved control over generation style and formatting fidelity. While synthetic data presents an accessible alternative to real clinical records, it tends to exhibit reduced variability and lacks the ambiguity, omissions, and conflicting evidence found in real-world clinical narratives. This predictability limit the transferability of models trained exclusively on synthetic data.

It is important to emphasize, however, that references to "balanced" or "realistic" output in this study are limited to surface-level properties such as section length and structural coherence. These terms do not imply that the generated content is clinically correct, safe, or contextually appropriate. The outputs were not reviewed by medical professionals, and no semantic validation was performed to assess the factual accuracy of symptoms, diagnoses, or treatments. As such, this analysis should be viewed as a first step in evaluating dialogue structure rather than clinical validity.

6   Conclusions and Future Work

This study presented a preliminary comparison of synthetic medical dialogues generated by three versions of OpenAI models, structured using the SOAP framework and written in European Portuguese. The proposed pipeline that combines automatic patient profile generation, SOAP-based prompt structuring, and dialogue synthesis, demonstrates a practical and extensible approach to controlled medical text generation in an under-resourced language. The inclusion of the SOAP framework as a semantic scaffold promotes structured, interpretable outputs that better reflect clinical reasoning flows.

Our results show that while all models produced technically complete dialogues, newer versions such as GPT-4 and GPT-4o achieved longer, more balanced, and diagnostically coherent outputs. The proposed "plan ratio" metric offered a simple but effective lens for quantifying section imbalance, highlighting improvements in structural fidelity across model generations. A key limitation of this study is the use of a single model to simulate both doctor and patient roles, which may lead to reduced variability and overly structured interactions.

Future work will explore multi-agent generation strategies, assigning different models to each speaker to better reflect the spontaneity and complexity of real clinical conversations. We also plan to integrate retrieval-augmented generation and structured prompting techniques, such as SOAP-aware or few-shot prompting, to improve factual grounding and reduce hallucinations. Enhancing validation will involve embedding-based evaluation metrics like BERTScore and entity-level F1, along with automated fact-checking methods and clinical knowledge sources such as UMLS or medQuAD. To increase generalizability, future work will also expand the dataset size, assess inter-turn coherence, explore additional clinical specialties, and address ethical considerations related to the use of synthetic text in healthcare contexts.

Disclosure of Interests. The authors have no competing interests to declare that are relevant to the content of this article.

References

1. Abad, A., Ribeiro, E., Batista, F.: Accelerat.ai: multimodal conversational agents for less-resourced languages with application to european portuguese. In: Proceedings of IberSPEECH 2024 (2024). https://doi.org/10.21437/IberSPEECH.2024-5
2. Ghanadian, H., Nejadgholi, I., Al Osman, H.: Socially aware synthetic data generation for suicidal ideation detection using large language models. IEEE Access **12**, 3358206 (2024).https://doi.org/10.1109/ACCESS.2024.3358206
3. Ghebrehiwet, I., Zaki, N., Damseh, R., Mohamad, M.S.: Revolutionizing personalized medicine with generative AI: A systematic review. Artif. Intell. Rev. **57**, 128 (2024). https://doi.org/10.1007/s10462-024-10768-5
4. Guo, Y., Qiu, W., Leroy, G., Wang, S., Cohen, T.: Retrieval augmentation of large language models for lay language generation. J. Biomed. Inf. **149**, 104580 (2024).https://doi.org/10.1016/j.jbi.2023.104580
5. Javaid, M., Haleem, A., Singh, R.P.: ChatGPT for healthcare services: an emerging stage for an innovative perspective. BenchCouncil Trans. Benchmarks Stan. Evaluations **3**, 100105 (2023). https://doi.org/10.1016/j.tbench.2023.100105
6. Johnson, R., Madden, S., Cafarella, M.: Datasynth: generating synthetic data using declarative constraints. Proc. VLDB Endowment **13**(11),pp. 2071–2083 (2022). https://doi.org/10.14778/3402755.3402785, https://dl.acm.org/doi/10.14778/3402755.3402785
7. Kalkman, S., Mostert, M., Gerlinger, C., van Delden, J.J.M., van Thiel, G.J.M.W.: What prevents us from reusing medical real-world data in research. Sci. Data **10**(1), 1–5 (2023)

8. Lund, J.A., Burman, J., Woldaregay, A.Z., Jenssen, R., Mikalsen, K.Ã.: Instruction-guided deidentification with synthetic test cases for norwegian clinical text. In: Proceedings of the 5th Northern Lights Deep Learning Conference (NLDL) (2024). https://doi.org/10.1007/s10462-024-05912-6
9. Montenegro, L., Abreu, M., Fred, A., Machado, J.M.: Human-assisted vs. deep learning feature extraction: an evaluation of ECG features extraction methods for arrhythmia classification using machine learning. Appl. Sci. **12**(15), 7404 (2022https://doi.org/10.3390/app12157404
10. Montenegro, L., Gomes, L.M., Machado, J.M.: Ai-based medical scribe to support clinical consultations: A proposed system architecture. In: Moniz, N., Vale, Z., Cascalho, J., Silva, C., Sebastião, R. (eds.) Progress in Artificial Intelligence. EPIA 2023. Lecture Notes in Computer Science, vol. 14116. Springer, Cham (2023). https://doi.org/10.1007/978-3-031-49011-8_22
11. Montenegro, L., Gomes, L.M., Machado, J.M.: What we know about the role of large language models for medical synthetic dataset generation. AI **6**(6), 109 (2025). https://doi.org/10.3390/ai6060109
12. Moser, D., Bender, M., Sariyar, M.: Generating synthetic healthcare dialogues in emergency medicine using large language models. Stud. Health Technol. Inf. **321**, 235–239 (2024). https://doi.org/10.3233/SHTI241099. PMID: 39575815
13. Nunes, R., Fialho, P., Oliveira, H.G.: Medialbertina: the first european portuguese medical language model. Comput. Biol. Med. **167**, 107535 (2024). https://doi.org/10.1016/j.compbiomed.2024.107535
14. Podder, V., Lew, V., Ghassemzadeh, S.: Soap notes. StatPearls [Internet] (2023)
15. Podder, V., Lew, V., Ghassemzadeh, S.H.: The soap note: use and misuse. StatPearls [Internet] (2023). https://www.ncbi.nlm.nih.gov/books/NBK482263/, originally published 2004, continuously updated
16. Schlegel, V., et al.: Pulsar at mediqa-sum 2023: large language models augmented by synthetic dialogue convert patient dialogues to medical records. CEUR Workshop Proc. **ISSN 1613-0073** (2023). https://github.com/yuping-wu/PULSAR
17. Serbetçi, G., Leser, U.: Challenges and solutions in multilingual clinical data analysis. J. Glob. Health Inf. **15**(2), 210–222 (2023). https://doi.org/10.1007/s10462-023-05812-6
18. Silverman, J., Kurtz, S., Draper, J.: Skills for communicating with patients. Radcliffe Publishing, 2nd edn. (2005)
19. Sousa, D., Antunes, A., Coheur, L.: Tradutor: A variety-specific translation model for european portuguese. In: Proceedings of the AAAI Conference on Artificial Intelligence (2025). https://arxiv.org/abs/2501.10541
20. Thorp, H.H., Krumholz, H.M., Ross, J.S.: Hallucination rates and reference accuracy of ChatGPT and bard large language models: Cross-sectional study. J. Med. Internet Res. **26**, e53164 (2024)
21. Tian, Y., Gan, R., Song, Y., Zhang, J., Zhang, Y.: Chimed-GPT: a chinese medical large language model with full training regime and better alignment to human preferences. arXiv preprint **2311.06025** (2024).https://github.com/synlp/ChiMed-GPT
22. Xu, R., et al.: Knowledge-infused prompting: assessing and advancing clinical text data generation with large language models. In: Proceedings of the 2024 Conference on Empirical Methods in Natural Language Processing (EMNLP), pp. 321–339 (2024).https://doi.org/10.18653/v1/EMNLP-2024-341
23. Zafar, A., Sahoo, S.K., Bhardawaj, H., Das, A., Ekbal, A.: Ki-mag: A knowledge-infused abstractive question answering system in the medical domain. Neurocomputing **571**, 127141 (2024). https://doi.org/10.1016/j.neucom.2023.127141

24. Zecevic, A., et al.: Privacy-preserving synthetic text generation using differentially private fine-tuning of biogpt. Artif. Intell. Med. **150**, 102649 (2024).https://doi.org/10.1016/j.artmed.2023.102649

25. Zhang, X., et al.: Data-augmented large language models for medical record generation. Appl. Intell. **55**, 88 (2025).https://doi.org/10.1007/s10489-024-05934-9

Artificial Intelligence: Theory, Methods, and Applications (AITMA)

Convolutional Spiking Neural Networks with Molecular Fingerprints for Drug Discovery

Dinu Bosîi[✉], Luis H. M. Torres, Joel P. Arrais, and Bernardete Ribeiro

CISUC/LASI – Centre for Informatics and Systems of the University of Coimbra,
Department of Informatics Engineering, University of Coimbra, Coimbra, Portugal
dinubosii@student.dei.uc.pt, {luistorres,jpa,bribeiro}@dei.uc.pt

Abstract. Molecular property prediction is a critical task in drug discovery, aiding in the differentiation between promising and ineffective *drug-like* compounds. While machine learning (ML) methods have been employed to predict the biological activity of drug candidates, capturing more complex and highly discriminative features from molecular data has led to the adoption of advanced deep learning (DL) techniques. In this work, we propose a deep convolutional Spiking Neural Network (SNN) architecture, fpCSNN, that utilizes molecular fingerprints to encode the chemical structure of compounds as binary vectors for molecular property prediction. By converting molecular fingerprints into spike trains, SNNs are able to process the molecular data in a temporal encoded format. This approach enables the extraction of local dependencies from neural spike signals to predict molecular properties, such as chemical toxicity and potential drug side effects. We validate fpCSNN's accuracy and robustness through experiments on benchmark datasets, including Tox21 and SIDER, outperforming standard ML baselines. Future work explores additional spiking models, hyperparameter optimization, and more datasets. Data and code are available at: https://github.com/Dinu-Bosii/fpCSNN.

Keywords: Deep Learning · Drug Discovery · Molecular Property Prediction · Molecular Fingerprints · Spiking Neural Networks

1 Introduction

Drug discovery is the multi-stage process in which new drug candidates for the treatment of a specific disease are identified. It focuses on finding and optimizing chemical compounds that are later tested and refined in the drug development stage. This process is extremely costly and time-consuming, often taking up to 10 years to complete and over 1 billion USD to discover and develop a potential drug until final approval and market release. This is due to efficiency limitations of the experimental methods used and the high attrition rates and unexpected toxicity observed across the drug discovery and development pipeline [1].

© The Author(s), under exclusive license to Springer Nature Switzerland AG 2026
J. Valente de Oliveira et al. (Eds.): EPIA 2025, LNAI 16121, pp. 375–387, 2026.
https://doi.org/10.1007/978-3-032-05176-9_29

Molecular property prediction is used to establish suitable quantitative structure-activity relationships (QSAR) in lead compounds. It's an essential step used to identify and optimize drug candidates that exhibit desirable activity properties by minimizing toxicity and drug side effects [2,3]. Recent advancements in artificial intelligence (AI) have proposed a set of deep learning (DL) methods to predict molecular properties and accelerate drug discovery, significantly outperforming traditional machine learning (ML) methods [4,5]. DL models require suitable representations to describe the structure of compounds. Simplified Molecular Input Line Entry System (SMILES) [6] strings have been commonly used to store molecular data and, although they provide a simple and powerful representation, they can be converted into more complex representations such as molecular fingerprints, which encode the molecular data as a binary vector based on the main substructures and functional groups of the molecule [7].

Spiking Neural Networks (SNNs), often referred to as the third generation of deep neural networks, are inspired by the biological mechanisms in the human brain to learn from complex representations to obtain efficient and explainable predictions. These DL networks rely on spikes, small electrical impulses, to encode and transmit information between neurons. Hence, SNNs can use molecular fingerprints to predict the molecular properties of chemical compounds as they can be converted into spike trains used by these networks. SNNs can ultimately be implemented using neuromorphic hardware, designed to mimic the low-energy dynamics observed across neurons in the human brain [8–10].

In this study, we propose a convolutional SNN architecture, fpCSNN, to learn from molecular data using different types of molecular fingerprint representations of chemical compounds. The architecture predicts molecular properties by processing fingerprints in a temporal format through rate coding. We analyze the behavior of SNNs when applied to molecular fingerprints and conduct multiple experiments to address the challenge of molecular property prediction using benchmark datasets (Tox21, SIDER) to compare fpCSNN with traditional ML methods used in this task. Moreover, we evaluate the statistical significance of the results and conduct an ablation study on the effectiveness of the convolutional operations of the proposed model.

2   Related Work

The advancements promoted by the computational power of recent DL architectures revolutionized the approach to drug discovery, enabling the adoption of powerful computer-aided drug design (CADD) methods [11] for molecular property prediction. Current approaches can be categorized into: structure-based drug design (SBDD) and ligand-based drug design (LBDD) [12,13]. The former leverages the 3-D shape and structure of proteins for the design of new drug candidates [14] while ligand-based approaches only require knowledge about the biological activity of molecules and known active binders. These methods can be used to predict the properties of compounds and their biological activity to accelerate the process of drug discovery [15]. DL models [16] have been commonly used to predict the biological activity of chemical compounds by screening large libraries of compounds against biological targets. Wang et al. [17] propose a semi-supervised Transformer-based model trained on SMILES strings to predict molecular properties by leveraging the natural language processing capabilities of Transformer networks. While these self-attention networks have shown promising results, they still face important limitations when trained on low-data and highly imbalanced chemical data [18]. ML, and particularly DL models, require high-discriminating molecular representations to predict molecular properties. Molecular fingerprints (MFs) provide a compact representation of molecules compatible with a wide range of ML models. These representations can map the characteristics and structural properties of molecules into binary vectors. They have diverse use cases in bioinformatics and drug discovery, notably for similarity searches and molecular property prediction [19, 20].

Spiking Neural Networks (SNNs) are DL methods based on the propagation of electrical impulses, denoted as spikes, observed in the human brain, which travel through synapses, the connections between presynaptic and postsynaptic neurons [21]. The sum of the electrical signals causes an increase in the potential of the post-synaptic neuron's membrane until a threshold is reached and a spike is transmitted. Thus, SNNs process information over discrete spike trains, through the timing or the frequency of spikes across spike trains [22]. Multiple spiking neurons with different degrees of biological plausibility have been theorized, with the Leaky Integrate-and-Fire (LIF) neuron [23] being the most widely used due to its computational viability and simplicity. The discrete nature of spiking neurons requires special attention to the training methods of derived networks. Supervised learning approaches have been adapted, such as spike-timing-dependent plasticity (STDP) [24] and backpropagation [25], and applied to classification tasks. Kim et al. [26] propose a SNN architecture combining convolutional operations with LIF neurons for object detection. Nascimben et al. [27] develop a shallow SNN architecture for the prediction of toxicity and other molecular properties, with rate-coded MACCS and ECFP molecular fingerprints as input.

3   Methodology

3.1   Molecular Fingerprints

Three types of molecular fingerprints are chosen to represent the input used for the models: Morgan [28], MACCS [29], and RDKitFP [30]. Each of these fingerprints uses a different approach for the encoding of molecular properties. The RDKit library is used to convert SMILES strings into molecular fingerprints. The Morgan fingerprint algorithm iterates over every atom in the molecule and, given a radius, retrieves all the substructures branching from the atom. These substructures are then hashed to give the identifier used to activate a bit in the resulting binary vector. Due to the properties of hash functions, the size of this vector can be manipulated, and more than one molecule can lead to the same fingerprint due to collisions in the hash function, which are more likely to happen for smaller vector sizes. The fingerprints are generated with a radius of 2 for a 1024-sized binary vector. The

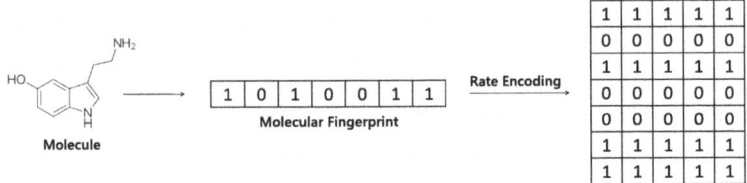

Fig. 1. Application of rate coding to molecular fingerprints.

MACCS (Molecular ACCess System) keys have a predetermined structure to their content, each bit being associated with a SMILES Arbitrary Target Specification (SMARTS) pattern. SMARTS expands on the SMILES representation to specify substructural patterns in molecules, providing a number of primitive symbols that describe atomic properties. The RDKitFP is a path-based fingerprint generated by the RDKit library. It generates hashes for paths, sequences of connected atoms and bonds, which are used as seeds for random number generators that return the indices to be activated in the fingerprint. As with Morgan fingerprints, the size of the fingerprint can be manipulated. Additionally, fingerprints are concatenated to increase the complexity of the molecular representation [31], integrating different feature extraction methods into a single binary vector while maintaining a consistent input size of 1024.

3.2   Input Encoding

SNNs require input in a suitable time-encoded format, with a fixed number of time steps. By representing data as spike trains, the network is able to capture complex patterns through neurons modeled by differential equations, while the usage of spikes allows the network to rely primarily on additions during inference, avoiding the computational cost of multiplications. Rate coding is commonly adopted for this purpose, encoding information in the frequency of spikes in the spike trains. The decoding of the output involves counting the number of spikes in the output neurons, where higher spike rates determine the class of the given sample. In Fig. 1, the application of the encoding algorithms to molecular fingerprints is illustrated. Given the binary nature of fingerprints, rate coding is equivalent to replicating the fingerprint over all the time steps, as each input feature is treated as the probability of firing a spike at each time step. A total of 10 time steps are considered to maintain low computational complexity while still ensuring a robust decoding of the output spike trains, as increasing this parameter does not improve the discriminative power of the input data.

3.3   Convolutional SNN Architecture

The Leaky Integrate-and-Fire (LIF) neuron is used for the implementation of the SNN. It is seen as a first-order model, given that it follows a first-order decay of

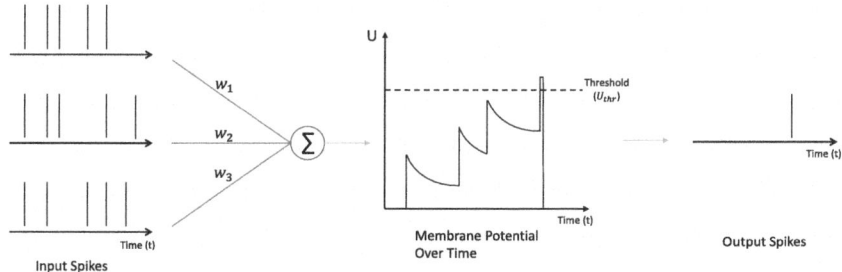

Fig. 2. Spike dynamics of the Leaky Integrate-and-Fire model.

the membrane potential, as expressed by the following mathematical equation:

$$U[t+1] = \beta U[t] + I_{\text{in}}[t+1] - S[t]U_{\text{thr}}$$

where $U[t]$ represents the membrane potential at time step t, and β represents the decay factor of the membrane potential over time. The term $I_{\text{in}}[t+1]$ represents the synaptic input, defined as $WX[t+1]$, W the learnable weights of the network, and $X[t+1]$ the input spike train at the time step $t+1$. The term $S[t]$ is the Heaviside equation used to determine the transmission of a spike. Additionally, it represents the reset mechanism for the membrane potential when coupled with U_{thr}, the threshold required to generate a spike. Based on the equation presented, the dynamics of the LIF neuron are illustrated in Fig. 2. The model workflow begins with the conversion of the SMILES representations into a molecular fingerprint using the RDKit Python package, which is then converted into spike trains with the rate coding method, serving as the input to the developed convolutional SNN model, fpCSNN. Here, convolutional operations are introduced to extract local dependencies from the fingerprints that assist in the prediction of molecular properties. The model consists of a 1-dimensional (1D) convolutional layer, followed by a max-pooling layer that is used to reduce the dimensionality of the filtered data. The data is passed through a LIF neuron layer, after the max-pooling operation, and flattened before passing through a linear layer at the end, with 2 output neurons used to compute the final prediction, as depicted in Fig. 3. Backpropagation Through Time (BPTT) is used to train the model, updating the weights at the end of the time steps, with cross-entropy loss applied to the accumulated spike count of the output neurons across all time steps.

4   Experimental Setup and Results

4.1   Datasets

To compare the performance of fpCSNN with ML baseline methods for molecular property prediction, benchmark datasets were chosen from MoleculeNet [32], a repository which compiles public datasets as well as multiple open-source tools to handle molecular data. All the datasets chosen use the SMILES format to

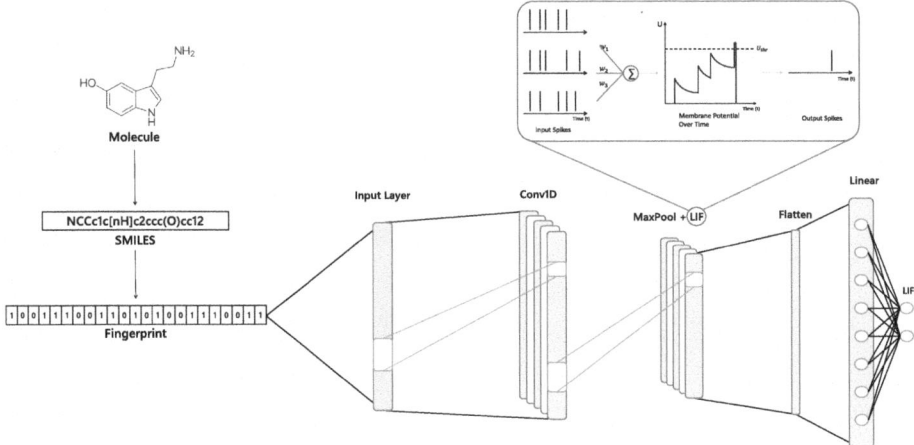

Fig. 3. Graphical depiction of the proposed convolutional SNN architecture (fpCSNN) for molecular property prediction.

represent each sample. Tox21, a highly imbalanced dataset with a total of 7832 samples and 12 targets, provides binary labels that indicate whether a compound shows activity for a particular toxicological pathway, grouped into Nuclear Receptors (NR) and Stress Response Pathways (SR). This work focuses on single class classification tasks, therefore, we select the target with the best balance between positive and negative classes, *SR-ARE*, containing 5832 compounds with a 1:6.19 positive to negative ratio. SIDER compiles compounds based on marketed medications and their recorded adverse drug reactions, grouped into 26 system organ classes. It contains 1427 samples, a significantly low amount that poses a challenge to the training of NNs. *Hepatobiliary Disorders* is chosen as a target as it exhibits the most balanced positive to negative ratio. The data is preprocessed to remove repeated or invalid samples and split in training, validation, and test sets in an 8:1:1 ratio using a random split, according to MoleculeNet specifications. Moreover, models are evaluated using the ROC-AUC score due to the class imbalance present in the data. The performance metrics are obtained over 30 runs, with fixed random seeds for all models, to allow the statistical evaluation of the results.

4.2   Hyperparameter Settings

In Table 1, we present the parameters subjected to experimentation for the training of the developed models. The experiments were conducted without the objective of extensive hyperparameter optimization for fpCSNN. The hyperparameters of the ML baselines are defined using a random hyperparameter search and following the same workflow as fpCSNN.

Table 1. Hyperparameters for the fpCSNN model.

Hyperparameter	Value
Input size	167, 1024
β	0.95
Activation function	arctan
No. of Conv layers	[1,2]
Conv kernel size	3
No. of kernels	8
Time steps	10
Batch size	16
Learning rate	$1e^{-4}$
Optimizer	Adam
Epochs	1000

4.3 Performance Results

Tables 2 and 3 showcase the results obtained by the baseline models and fpCSNN on the Tox21 and SIDER datasets, respectively. The best ROC-AUC values are highlighted in bold, and the performance difference of fpCSNN with the best baseline model is quantified in the last row. A more complex variant, fpCSNN (2), with two blocks of convolutional, max-pooling and LIF layers is considered for the SIDER dataset due to the underperformance observed with fpCSNN.

Table 2. ROC-AUC scores of fpCSNN and ML baselines on the Tox21 *SR-ARE* task. Results are reported as mean $\pm$ standard deviation and Δ represents the difference between the best baseline model and fpCSNN.

Model	Morgan	MACCS	RDKit	Morgan + MACCS	Morgan + RDKit
SVM	0.648 $\pm$ 0.029	**0.728 $\pm$ 0.026**	0.665 $\pm$ 0.030	0.687 $\pm$ 0.026	0.662 $\pm$ 0.029
RF	0.635 $\pm$ 0.020	0.655 $\pm$ 0.027	0.623 $\pm$ 0.027	0.614 $\pm$ 0.020	0.581 $\pm$ 0.016
XGB	0.578 $\pm$ 0.019	0.577 $\pm$ 0.018	0.586 $\pm$ 0.024	0.579 $\pm$ 0.018	0.571 $\pm$ 0.017
KNN	0.555 $\pm$ 0.041	0.611 $\pm$ 0.025	0.598 $\pm$ 0.023	0.587 $\pm$ 0.021	0.585 $\pm$ 0.021
MLP	0.642 $\pm$ 0.025	0.673 $\pm$ 0.030	0.671 $\pm$ 0.030	0.669 $\pm$ 0.027	0.663 $\pm$ 0.027
fpCSNN	**0.701 $\pm$ 0.026**	0.718 $\pm$ 0.021	**0.710 $\pm$ 0.024**	**0.723 $\pm$ 0.018**	**0.720 $\pm$ 0.023**
Improvement (Δ)	+0.053	-0.010	+0.039	+0.036	+0.057

4.4 Ablation Study

To understand the impact of the convolutional and max-pooling operations on feature extraction from spike data, we conduct an ablation study to evaluate the performance of SNNs without such operations, and compare those to the results

Table 3. ROC-AUC scores of fpCSNN and ML baselines on the SIDER *Hepatobiliary Disorders* task. Results are reported as mean ± standard deviation and Δ represents the difference in the mean between the best baseline model and the best fpCSNN model.

Model	Morgan	MACCS	RDKit	Morgan + MACCS	Morgan + RDKit
SVM	0.671 ± 0.035	0.673 ± 0.039	0.655 ± 0.035	0.682 ± 0.044	0.669 ± 0.037
RF	**0.699 ± 0.035**	0.683 ± 0.048	**0.696 ± 0.029**	0.691 ± 0.038	0.692 ± 0.036
XGB	0.642 ± 0.041	0.679 ± 0.037	0.672 ± 0.032	0.689 ± 0.033	0.693 ± 0.028
KNN	0.674 ± 0.032	0.664 ± 0.034	0.673 ± 0.032	0.683 ± 0.040	0.669 ± 0.024
MLP	0.662 ± 0.040	0.662 ± 0.042	0.646 ± 0.033	0.667 ± 0.041	0.658 ± 0.037
fpCSNN	0.678 ± 0.029	0.691 ± 0.037	0.694 ± 0.029	0.693 ± 0.032	**0.698 ± 0.032**
fpCSNN (2)	0.680 ± 0.025	**0.701 ± 0.029**	0.695 ± 0.023	**0.700 ± 0.026**	0.690 ± 0.026
Improvement (Δ)	−0.019	+0.018	−0.001	+0.009	+0.005

of fpCSNN. The modified architecture consists of a fully-connected SNN with a hidden layer of 512 neurons, while all other parameters remain unchanged. The results are presented for each dataset in Table 4.

Table 4. ROC-AUC scores with the fpCSNN and SNN models on the Tox21 *SR-ARE* and SIDER *Hepatobiliary Disorders* tasks. Results are reported as mean ± standard deviation, with the best scores highlighted in bold.

Dataset	Model	Morgan	MACCS	RDKit	Morgan + MACCS	Morgan + RDKit
Tox21	SNN	0.670 ± 0.027	0.716±0.019	**0.734 ± 0.026**	0.708 ± 0.019	**0.721 ± 0.025**
	fpCSNN	**0.701 ± 0.026**	**0.718 ± 0.021**	0.710 ± 0.024	**0.723 ± 0.018**	0.720 ± 0.023
SIDER	SNN	**0.693 ± 0.031**	**0.702 ± 0.033**	**0.712 ± 0.028**	**0.716 ± 0.034**	**0.712 ± 0.033**
	fpCSNN (2)	0.684 ± 0.029	0.701 ± 0.029	0.695 ± 0.023	0.700 ± 0.026	0.690 ± 0.026

4.5   Statistical Analysis

To assess whether the results of fpCSNN are statistically significant, we perform a statistical significance analysis with the Wilcoxon signed rank test [33], a non-parametric test for paired samples, on the ROC-AUC scores obtained with our model and the baseline ML models. The obtained p values for each dataset and baseline model are reported in Tables 5 and 6. If condition $p < 0.05$ is met, the null hypothesis is rejected and a statistically significant difference is assumed in the ROC-AUC scores between the models. The hypotheses are defined as:

H_0: There is no difference in ROC-AUC scores between fpCSNN and baseline models.

H_1: There is a difference in ROC-AUC scores between fpCSNN and baseline models.

Table 5. *p*-value results for the Tox21 *SR-ARE* task with the Wilcoxon signed-rank test on fpCSNN and each of the baseline models.

Model	Morgan	MACCS	RDKit	Morgan + MACCS	Morgan + RDKit
SVM	1.863e−08	7.612e−03	1.863e−08	1.863e−09	1.863e−09
RF	1.863e−09	1.863e−09	1.863e−09	1.863e−09	1.863e−09
XGB	1.863e−09	1.863e−09	1.863e−09	1.863e−09	1.863e−09
KNN	1.863e−09	1.863e−09	1.863e−09	1.863e−09	1.863e−09
MLP	3.725e−09	3.725e−09	1.192e−06	1.863e−09	3.725e−09

Table 6. *p*-value results for the SIDER *Hepatobiliary Disorders* task with the Wilcoxon signed-rank test on fpCSNN (2) and each of the baseline models.

Model	Morgan	MACCS	RDKit	Morgan + MACCS	Morgan + RDKit
SVM	3.285e−01	4.418e−04	6.918e−06	1.546e−02	6.232e−03
RF	3.707e−01	5.974e−06	1.583e−03	1.130e−02	2.987e−03
XGB	3.744e−03	3.643e−02	9.032e−01	1.981e−01	4.771e−01
KNN	6.287e−05	4.032e−03	3.450e−04	1.142e−01	5.699e−01
MLP	2.774e−02	4.657e−08	9.313e−09	7.057e−05	2.563e−04

Results should be interpreted with the consideration that the use of repeated random splits may introduce minor dependencies between samples.

5   Discussion

In this work, we propose a SNN architecture with convolutional operations for molecular property prediction, using molecular fingerprints. The ROC-AUC scores of these fpCSNN models is compared against more conventional ML models.

As shown in Table 2, fpCSNN significantly outperforms the baseline methods on the Tox21 *SR-ARE* task for four of the five fingerprint representations tested. This is supported by the statistical test showing significant differences for all data representations, as highlighted in Table 5, with all *p* values falling below 0.05. Notably, the fpCSNN model achieves the highest ROC-AUC when combining the Morgan fingerprint with other molecular fingerprints, particularly Morgan + MACCS (0.723). Furthermore, the standard deviation of the ROC-AUC with the Morgan + MACCS (0.018) representation is significantly lower compared to that of the other representations. This suggests that the combination of molecular fingerprints leads to a more comprehensive representation, which better captures the molecular dependencies needed for the prediction of the *SR-ARE* property.

The SIDER dataset includes a small number of compounds, which hinders the generalization capabilities of neural network models that struggle to effectively discriminate between positive and negative samples. In contrast, traditional ML methods perform better in this low-data scenario. This is illustrated by the performance results observed in Table 3, as the mean ROC-AUC score of fpCSNN with a single convolutional and max-pooling block is lower or comparable to the values obtained by the baseline models. This leads to the hypothesis that fpC-SNN's topology is not sufficient to deal with SIDER's limited data. Therefore, we increase the model's complexity to address this limitation by using two blocks of convolutional and max-pooling operations, each followed by a LIF layer. We observe higher and more consistent ROC-AUC values across 4 of the molecular representations, though not significantly outperforming all the baseline ML models, as observed in the p values presented in Table 6. However, the standard deviation is consistently higher for most of the baseline models tested, while the fpCSNN (2) model obtains more robust results with lower standard deviations across all molecular representations, showing more consistent and reliable predictions than the baseline models.

The ablation study conducted highlights fpCSNN 's struggle on the SIDER dataset, with consistently lower performance compared to the fully-connected SNN. On the Tox21 dataset, the SNN achieves a substantially higher ROC-AUC with the RDKit fingerprint, however, fpCSNN achieves competitive performance, outperforming the SNN on three of the data representations, despite having a considerably lower parameter count.

The results suggest that fpCSNN is better suited for complex and high-dimensional feature spaces, whereas the baseline ML models excel in discriminating between classes in low-dimensional feature spaces. This is evidenced by the highest mean ROC-AUC (0.728) achieved with the MACCS fingerprint by the SVM model that outperforms fpCSNN on the Tox21 task, whereas the rest of the traditional ML models perform poorly across all other data representations. Furthermore, the size of the dataset plays a critical role on the performance of the fpCSNN model as demonstrated by the lower performance on the SIDER task, despite the data being class-balanced. When compared to a fully-connected SNN, our model fpCSNN sees its advantages when applied to high-volume of data, with comprable performance despite the lower amount of parameters.

6   Conclusion

In this paper, we propose a deep convolutional spiking neural network, fpCSNN, for molecular property prediction using molecular fingerprints. This model is evaluated using different types of molecular fingerprints, and its performance is compared with baseline ML methods.

The results obtained demonstrate the viability of fpCSNN in learning from molecular fingerprint representations, as it outperforms the standard baseline methods on the *SR-ARE* task of Tox21 when using more complex representations such as Morgan + MACCS. The model achieves comparable performance to the baselines with respect to the SIDER data, while showing more robust and stable results across all molecular representations. However, fpCSNN is outperformed by a fully-connected SNN on the SIDER task. These findings highlight the effectiveness of using a convolutional SNN architecture to learn from molecular fingerprints in high-volume data but does not demonstrate a clear advantage over a non-convolutional SNN on smaller datasets such as SIDER.

For future work, the architecture can be extended to different types of spiking models to explore their impact on their effectiveness of learning from molecular fingerprints. Furthermore, a more systematic hyperparameter search can be carried out to maximize the performance and fully leverage the models' potential. The inclusion of other datasets and molecular representations in the experiments would better characterize the performance profile of the proposed fpCSNN model.

Acknowledgments. This research was supported by the Portuguese Recovery and Resilience Plan (PRR) through project C645008882-00000055, Center for Responsible AI (https://centerforresponsible.ai/.

Data Availibility Statement. The data and code supporting this article are available at: https://github.com/Dinu-Bosii/fpCSNN.

Disclosure of Interests. The authors declare that they have no competing interests.

References

1. Hughes, J.P., Rees, S.S., Kalindjian, S.B., Philpott, K.L.: Principles of early drug discovery. Br. J. Pharmacol. **162**(6), 1239–1249 (2011)
2. Lipinski, C.A.: Drug-like properties and the causes of poor solubility and poor permeability. J. Pharmacol. Toxicol. Methods **44**, 235–249 (2000)
3. Hopkins, A.L.: Network pharmacology: the next paradigm in drug discovery. Nat. Chem. Biol. **4**(11), 682–690 (2008)
4. Vijayan, R.S.K., Kihlberg, J., Cross, J.B., Poongavanam, V.: Enhancing preclinical drug discovery with artificial intelligence. Drug Discov. Today **27**, 967–984 (2022)
5. Chen, H., Engkvist, O., Wang, Y., Olivecrona, M., Blaschke, T.: The rise of deep learning in drug discovery. Drug Discov. Today **23**, 1241–1250 (2018)
6. Weininger, D.: Smiles, a chemical language and information system: 1: introduction to methodology and encoding rules. J. Chem. Inf. Comput. Sci. **28**, 31–36 (1988)
7. Yang, K., et al.: Analyzing learned molecular representations for property prediction. J. Chem. Inf. Model. **59**, 3370–3388 (2019)
8. Maass, W.: Networks of spiking neurons: the third generation of neural network models. Neural Netw. **10**, 1659–1671 (1997)
9. Taherkhani, A., Belatreche, A., Li, Y., Cosma, G., Maguire, L.P., McGinnity, T.M.: A review of learning in biologically plausible spiking neural networks. Neural Netw. **122**, 253–272 (2020)
10. Ribeiro, B., Antunes, F., Perdigão, D., Silva, C.: Convolutional spiking neural networks targeting learning and inference in highly imbalanced datasets. Pattern Recogn. Lett. **189**, 241–247 (2024)

11. Yu, W., Mackerell, A.D.: Computer-aided drug design methods. Methods Mol. Biol. (Clifton, N.J.) **1520**, 85 (2017)
12. Niazi, S.K., Mariam, Z.: Computer-aided drug design and drug discovery: a prospective analysis. Pharmaceuticals **17**, 22 (2023)
13. Leelananda, S.P., Lindert, S.: Computational methods in drug discovery. Beilstein J. Org. Chem. **12**, 2694–2718 (2016)
14. Batool, M., Ahmad, B., Choi, S.: A structure-based drug discovery paradigm. Int. J. Mol. Sci. **20** (2019)
15. Acharya, C., Coop, A., E Polli, J., D MacKerell, A.: Recent advances in ligand-based drug design: relevance and utility of the conformationally sampled pharmacophore approach. Curr. Comput.-Aided Drug Des. **7**, 10 (2011)
16. Tropsha, A., Isayev, O., Varnek, A., Schneider, G., Cherkasov, A.: Integrating QSAR modelling and deep learning in drug discovery: the emergence of deep QSAR. Nat. Rev. Drug Discov. **23**(2), 141–155 (2023)
17. Wang, S., Guo, Y., Wang, Y., Sun, H., Huang, J.: Smiles-BERT: large scale unsupervised pre-training for molecular property prediction. In: ACM-BCB 2019 - Proceedings of the 10th ACM International Conference on Bioinformatics, Computational Biology and Health Informatics, pp. 429–436. Association for Computing Machinery, Inc (2019)
18. Zhang, S., Fan, R., Liu, Y., Chen, S., Liu, Q., Zeng, W.: Applications of transformer-based language models in bioinformatics: a survey. Bioinf. Adv. **3** (2023)
19. Zagidullin, B., Wang, Z., Guan, Y., Pitkänen, E., Tang, J.: Comparative analysis of molecular fingerprints in prediction of drug combination effects. Brief. Bioinform. **22**, 1–15 (2021)
20. Cereto-Massagué, A., Ojeda, M.J., Valls, C., Mulero, M., Garcia-Vallvé, S., Pujadas, G.: Molecular fingerprint similarity search in virtual screening. Methods **71**, 58–63 (2015)
21. Yamazaki, K., Vo-Ho, V.K., Bulsara, D., Le, N.: Spiking neural networks and their applications: a review. Brain Sci. **12**, 863 (2022)
22. Kiselev, M.: Rate coding vs. temporal coding - is optimum between? In: Proceedings of the International Joint Conference on Neural Networks, pp. 1355–1359 (2016)
23. Dutta, S., Kumar, V., Shukla, A., Mohapatra, N.R., Ganguly, U.: Leaky integrate and fire neuron by charge-discharge dynamics in floating-body MOSFET. Sci. Rep. **7**(1), 1–7 (2017)
24. Diehl, P.U., Cook, M.: Unsupervised learning of digit recognition using spike-timing-dependent plasticity. Front. Comput. Neurosci. **9**, 149773 (2015)
25. Lee, J. H., Delbruck, T., Pfeiffer, M.: Training deep spiking neural networks using backpropagation. Front. Neurosci. **10**, 228000 (2016)
26. Kim, S., Park, S., Na, B., Yoon, S.: Spiking-YOLO: spiking neural network for energy-efficient object detection. In: AAAI 2020 - 34th AAAI Conference on Artificial Intelligence, pp. 11270–11277. AAAI press (2020)
27. Nascimben, M., Rimondini, L.: Molecular toxicity virtual screening applying a quantized computational SNN-based framework. Molecules **28**, 1342 (2023)
28. Rogers, D., Hahn, M.: Extended-connectivity fingerprints. J. Chem. Inf. Model. **50**, 742–754 (2010)
29. Durant, J.L., Leland, B.A., Henry, D.R., Nourse, J.G.: Reoptimization of mdl keys for use in drug discovery. J. Chem. Inf. Comput. Sci. **42**, 1273–1280 (2002)
30. RDKit. RDKit: open-source cheminformatics software (2020). Accessed 13 Jan 2025

31. Xie, L., Xu, L., Kong, R., Chang, S., Xu, X.: Improvement of prediction performance with conjoint molecular fingerprint in deep learning. Front. Pharmacol. **11** (2020)
32. Zhenqin, W., et al.: MoleculeNet: a benchmark for molecular machine learning (2018)
33. Rainio, O., Teuho, J., Klén, R.: Evaluation metrics and statistical tests for machine learning. Sci. Rep. **14** (2024)

Enhancing Privacy: Using Blurred Images with MobileNet SSD

Fernando Martins[1]([✉]) [iD], Karolina Baras[1] [iD], and Eduardo Marques[1,2] [iD]

[1] Universidade da Madeira, Caminho da Penteada, 9020-105 Funchal, Portugal
`2019414@student.uma.pt`
[2] CiTUR – Madeira, Rua dos Ferreiros, 9000-082 Funchal, Portugal

Abstract. People counting has numerous applications across various domains, from urban planning to crowd management. With advances in computer vision, the use of cameras for real-time video analysis has increased significantly. While camera-based people counting is an effective and versatile approach, particularly in outdoor environments, it raises significant privacy concerns. MobileNet SSD is a widely used computer vision algorithm for detecting and classifying people in images. However, its real-time functionality relies on processing clear pictures of individuals, which can compromise privacy. This study investigates whether applying a blurring technique to video streams can enhance privacy while maintaining accurate people counting. To evaluate this, a video recording of individuals walking was processed with different blur levels and the accuracy of people counting was analyzed across all versions. Notably, one blurred video maintained an accuracy of 76%, equivalent to the original unblurred footage. Additionally, face detection was applied to the frames where people were identified and counted, revealing significantly lower detection accuracy for blurred images compared to human-level recognition. These results suggest that blurring can improve privacy while still enabling accurate people counting.

Keywords: MobileNet SSD · People privacy · Computer vision · Outdoor envoiroments · People detection · Recognition

1 Introduction

People counting systems are used in many applications, such as security, surveillance, and traffic monitoring [1]. There are several technologies for implementing a people counting system such as biometric gaits [2], Bluetooth tracking [3], and camera-based counters [4]. Traditional people counters are based on sensors that can struggle in challenging environments [5]. The use of cameras for streaming and analyzing video footage with computer vision is a solution with proven results, demonstrating accuracy values of 97% [5,6].

The camera-based approach for people counting system is a cost-effective solution with the potential to prevent conflicts and even crowding in outdoor environments. However, it raises some ethical and privacy problems [7]. Society

J. Valente de Oliveira et al. (Eds.): EPIA 2025, LNAI 16121, pp. 388–399, 2026.
https://doi.org/10.1007/978-3-032-05176-9_30

is concerned about aggressive data retrieval, processing, and storage. This has led to the introduction of new regulations aimed at improving people's privacy [8].

European Union created the General Data Protection Regulation (GDPR) with the concept of privacy by design and default to protect people's data [9]. The Artificial inteligence (AI) Act regulation ensures Europeans can trust what AI has to offer. The act defines some unacceptable risks, such as creating or expanding facial recognition databases, and real-time remote biometric identification [10]. These policies affect the development of new technologies in society, with a significant impact on technologies based on computer vision [8]. The privacy of the images used by computer vision in closed systems, which do not report images, remains a concern for people, as they fear the system could be hacked and the images leaked [11]. To comply with the legislation, several approaches have been adopted, such as stripping a plastic on the lens [4], blurring, or pixelating images [8,13], resulting in unidentifiable people.

The MobileNet SSD is a computer vision algorithm capable of real-time identification, with a mean average precision of 72.7% for detecting objects [12,18]. This algorithm has been used in other works for detecting people in both private and public spaces, indoors and outdoors [1,5]. For counting people, the output of the MobileNet SSD is sent to a centroid tracking algorithm [12]. Counting people in real-time requires capturing live images to be processed by computer vision algorithms like MobileNet SSD. The capture of these images can raise privacy concerns, especially in outdoor environments.

In addition to using the MobileNet SSD an image segmentation could be considered has it is considered an essential component in multiple visual-based application, such as facial segmentation [14] and object detection [15]. Image segmentation requires the partitioning of the images or video frames into diverse objects to then apply a method for detection [16]. This approach can offer finer-grained localization, particularly in crowded scenes or when partial occlusion occurs due to the segmentation being more accurate and describing the appearance of models [17]. However, segmentation require more computational processing power, limiting their applicability in real-time or edge-computing scenarios, something required in this study [16].

Recently, researchers and open-source communities have made advances in facial recognition, achieving results that surpass human accuracy levels [19]. DeepFace is a face recognition and facial attribute analysis framework for Python, which include state-of-the-art models like VGG-Face, FaceNet, DeepFace, RetinaFace, and others [20]. RetinaFace is a deep learning-based facial detector with exceptional crowd face detection capabilities, demonstrating proven results in detecting faces even in small sizes [22]. Experiments within the framework indicate that humans achieve an accuracy of 97.53% in face detection. The models in this library have already exceded this level of human detection accuracy [19].

Concerning privacy issues, the need for a counting system in an outdoor environment, the lack of knowledge about the performance of MobileNet SSD on blurry person images, and advancements in facial recognition, two research questions emerged:

- RQ1: Can a specific AI technique ensure individual privacy while accurately counting people?
- RQ2: Can software techniques effectively blur individuals to prevent recognition while preserving essential visual information?

This study aims to determine whether a blurred video stream can improve privacy while maintaining accurate people counting, similar to an original video stream. Additionally, by analyzing the blurred video frames, the study aims to assess whether a computer vision approach and humans can still recognize faces, providing insight into people identification and privacy.

2   Methodology

The methodology section outlines the methods and processes used for data collection.

2.1   Study Design

The MobileNet SSD is capable of detecting people in multiple environments and conditions. This algorithm needs images that could compromise individuals' privacy. To address privacy concerns, this study proposes applying multiple blur parameters by adjusting the sigma values of the videos (Subsect. 2.2).

Next, both the blurred and original videos were used to count the number of people using the MobileNet SSD and Centroid Tracker algorithms. The retrieved data was then analyzed to determine whether the use of blurred videos introduces significant differences in people counting (Subsect. 2.3).

To assess privacy in blurred videos, the frames containing people were saved after the counting process. These frames were then analyzed by humans and a computer framework called DeepFace with the RetinaFace back-end, both to detect and count faces. These data helped to determine whether the framework, which includes models with accuracy surpassing human capabilities and human beings can still detect faces in blurred images, thus evaluating its effectiveness in preserving privacy (Subsect. 2.4).

2.2   Video Preparation

For this study, a video was recorded featuring volunteers walking in an outdoor environment. The volunteers followed a predefined script outlining their actions (e.g. walking near the camera, walking away from the camera, in groups) and were fully aware of the recording. Participants were selected using a convenience sampling method from an academic network, including students, teachers, and non-teaching staff. Informed consent was obtained from all participants, ensuring their voluntary participation in the study.

Different levels of blur were applied to the recorded (original) video, with sigma values set at 3, 5, 7, 10, and 15. To apply the blurring effect, the FFmpeg conversion tool was used [21]. This process generated five blurred videos with different sigma values. These varying levels of blur were applied to allow for a comparative analysis of the images.

2.3   People Counting and Analysis

From the recorded video of people passing by, a blurring effect with different sigma values was applied to protect individuals' privacy. To establish a comparison between the actual number of appearances in the video and the count generated by the computer vision system, a manual count was conducted.

Then, to detect people in the video frames, a pre-trained model of MobileNet SSD with a mean average precison of 72.7% was applied to the original video with a detection confidence threshold of 50%. Next, the detection data was sent to a Centroid Tracker algorithm to determine when the detected people passed a virtual line. The passage of the virtual line incremented the number of people counted. Afterward, the blurred videos were analyzed using the same process to collect the corresponding number of people.

During the people-counting process, both the original and blurred videos were duplicated and saved, with rectangles overlaid to highlight individuals detected by MobileNet SSD and subsequently counted by the Centroid Tracker.

From the video copies with rectangles, the time when people were counted were identified and recorded in a data table. Then, by comparing the original videos with their copies, the frames in which people were counted were matched. Using the FFmpeg tool, these frames were extracted from the original video and saved into a folder for further analysis (Subsect. 2.4).

2.4   Privacy Detection

As mentioned earlier, the frames from the videos containing detections and subsequent counting were saved. To assess the privacy of both the original and blurred videos, a face recognition process and manual visualization were performed.

The face recognition process utilized the DeepFace framework with the RetinaFace backend to extract and count all faces from the images. During face extraction, copies of the images were created with rectangles marking the positions of detected faces. Then, a person conducted a manual review to identify false positives. Finally, the number of false positives was compared with the total number of faces extracted to assess the accuracy of the detection process.

Finally, the people counting data and RetinaFace detection results were analyzed to determine an optimal level of video blurring that effectively protects individuals' privacy while maintaining accurate people counting.

3   Results

In this section, the results of the proposed methodology are presented. The first step in the methodology was to record a video of people passing by and then apply a blur effect with different sigma values. At a sigma value of 15, it was observed that the colors of the people began to blend with the background, making it more difficult to detect the individuals. Figure 1 illustrates an example of the original image content alongside its blurred counterparts. In the blurred videos, it is noticeable that from a sigma value of 5 onward, it becomes increasingly difficult for human observers to identify individuals by their faces.

Fig. 1. Illustration of an original image and its blurred versions with different sigma values. The top left displays the original image, followed by the blurred images in sequence with sigma values of 3, 5, 7, 10, and 15. To protect the participants privacy in the study, the authors used an example image, where the original image was taken by Mircea Iancu from Pixabay [23].

From the recorded video of people passing by, a manual count was conducted to determine the actual number of individuals. The manual count confirmed that 36 people moved from the top to the bottom of the video, while 40 people moved from the bottom to the top. In total, 76 people were counted in the video.

An analysis was conducted using the MobileNet SSD and Centroid Tracker algorithms to count the number of people passing in both the original and blurred videos with different sigma values. In the original video, 28 people were detected moving from the top to the bottom, while 30 were detected moving from the bottom to the top, totaling 58 people. The accuracy for the direction where people's faces were visible (top to bottom) was 78%.

The blurred videos with sigma values of 3 and 5 showed a 3% decrease in the accuracy of people counting when analyzing the side where faces were visible. The blurred video with sigma 7 exhibited a more significant decrease of 14% in accuracy for the same perspective. The sigma 10 and 15 videos produced the worst results, with almost no successful counts. More details can be observed in Table 1.

Table 1. People counting from different sources

Source	Count		Accuracy		
	Down[a]	Up[b]	Down	Up	Total[c]
Manual	36	40	–	–	–
Original video	28	30	78%	75%	76%
Blurred sigma 3	27	26	75%	65%	70%
5	27	31	75%	78%	76%
7	23	27	64%	68%	66%
10	5	3	14%	8%	11%
15	0	0	0%	0%	0%

[a]Down - People moving from the top to the bottom of the video.
[b]Up - People moving from the bottom to the top of the video.
[c]Total - The total made by people moving from top and down in the video.

Observing the total number of people counted from the blurred videos, the values for sigma 3 and 7 showed a difference of 6% and 10%, respectively, compared to the original video.

The blurred video with sigma 5 had the same total count as the original video. This was an unexpected performance trend since the video with sigma 3 had a lower accuracy than sigma 5. This counter-intuitive trend prompted a more detailed analysis of the object counting performance in videos blurred with sigma 3 and sigma 5.

Our investigation revealed a consistent misidentification issue in sigma 3 video: the centroid tracker frequently misidentified the center of individuals moving from the bottom to the top of the frame. Although the MobileNet-SSD algorithm accurately detected these individuals, the centroid tracker failed to maintain a consistent center position for the same person across consecutive frames. This inconsistency led to the creation of a new identifier for the same individual in subsequent frames, effectively treating them as a new person.

Figure 2 visually differentiates between a correctly placed center identification in the sigma 5 video and a misplaced one in the sigma 3 video. The authors hypothesize that the reduced sharpness and increased color similarity of the sigma 5 image contribute to this phenomenon, paradoxically enhancing the performance of the centroid tracker by making it less sensitive to minor changes in appearance.

As mentioned in the methodology section, the frames from detection and counting (with and without rectangles) were saved as images. By examining those images, it was possible to verify that the rectangles were correctly placed around people at the moment of counting. The images without rectangles were processed using RetinaFace to retrieve face detection and the corresponding

Sigma 5 – Before passing   Sigma 3 – Before passing   Sigma 5 – After passing   Sigma 3 – After passing

Fig. 2. Illustration of a person with a bag passing the virtual line on sigma values of 5 and 3. The sigma 5 images reveal a green dot in the center of the rectangle, correctly identifying the center of the person with the bag. The sigma 3 images reveal that the green dot is not identifying the center of the person correctly. (Color figure online)

count. The blurred videos with sigma 10 and 15 were ignored due to the low people count.

The RetinaFace results showed that the frames of the original video had an accuracy of 92.11% despite having two false positive detections. When analyzing the values of the blurred frames with different sigma levels, it was observed that they had a lower accuracy of face detection (sigma 3 - 87.23%, sigma 5 - 79.07%, and sigma 7 - 54.05%). A frame by frame analisys was made, more details about the original video and the blurred ones can be found in Table 2.

4 Discussion

From the results section, it was observed that blurring videos can make it more difficult for humans to identify people in images. In the study by Lupp et al. [4], a plastic strip was used to obscure facial visibility. That study used the sigma blur effect, similar to the approach in [8,13]. The Gaussian blur has been applied through FFmpeg due to the computational efficiency and wide support for multiple platforms. However, the authors acknowledge that others using other blurring techniques, with different trade-offs between visual distortion and detection performance, could provide different results, leaving these alternatives for future work. Based on the output images, it can be seen that with a sigma blur level above 5, people's privacy is slightly improved. Visually, this was an expected result.

The people counting had an accuracy of 78% in the original video when individuals faced the cameras. This accuracy was higher than the one reported in [12]. These results are superior to previous work because this study exclusively analyzed human figures, whereas [12] counted both people and other objects. In

Table 2. Face detection results using RetinaFace on video frames in the original video and blurred videos with sigma 3, 5, and 7. The table displays the manual total count for each video, and the RetinaFace total count and accuracy.

Frame	Manual Count				RetinaFace Count			
	Orginal	Sigma 3	Sigma 5	Sigma 7	Orginal	Sigma 3	Sigma 5	Sigma 7
1	1	1	1	1	1	1	1	1
2	2	-	2	2	2	-	2	2
3	3	-	-	3	3	-	-	2
4	-	3	3	3	-	3	3	2
5	3	3	4	4	2	3	1	1
6	3	-	-	-	3	-	-	-
7	-	3	3	3	-	3	3	3
8	1	-	-	-	1	-	-	-
9	-	2	2	1	-	0	0	0
10	1	-	1	-	1	-	1	-
11	2	1	1	2	2	1	1	2
13	2	1	1	2	2	0	0	0
14	-	6	-	6	-	5	-	3
15	2	-	6	-	2	-	6	-
16	6	6	-	2	5	6	-	1
17	-	-	6	-	-	-	6	-
18	6	4	-	1	6	4	-	1
19	-	3	2	1	-	2	1	0
20	1	-	-	-	1	-	-	-
21	-	4	4	4	-	4	4	2
22	2	1	1	1	1	1	1	0
23	-	4	-	1	-	3	-	0
24	1	-	4	-	1	-	3	-
25	1	4	-	-	1	4	-	-
26	0	-	1	-	-	-	0	-
27	0	1	1	-	1	1	1	-
28	1	-	-	-	1	-	-	-
Total	38	47	43	37	35	41	34	20
Accuracy					92.11 %	87.23%	79.07%	54.05%

a graph from [12], the mean average precision of person detection appears to be 79%, which is similar to the findings of this study.

People counting in the blurred videos surprised the authors of this study. They expected lower accuracy values, as the MobileNet SSD model is trained on

well-defined datasets (MS-COCO and VOC0712), which typically do not include
blurred images [18].

The accuracy of the blurred videos with sigma 3 and 5 was 6% lower compared
to the original video, while sigma 7 had 10% less accuracy. These accuracy values
are considered satisfactory, as they allow for improved privacy while still enabling
people counting. The results for sigmas 10 and 15 aligned with the authors'
expectations, as increased blurring should interfere with people detection and,
consequently, people counting.

Concerning the perception of people's privacy in the captured videos, facial
identification was performed using RetinaFace. The analysis of the original video
showed that accuracy was high (92.11%), according to the findings of [19]. The
accuracy for sigma 3 was 87.23%, representing a 4.88% reduction compared to
the original video. Similarly, the accuracy for sigma 5 was 79.07%, reflecting a
13.04% decrease.

The blurred video with sigma 7 had the lowest accuracy in face detection,
at 54.05%. In this case, the lower accuracy was beneficial, as it indicates that
privacy can be improved. This is particularly relevant since this study utilized a
face recognition framework with accuracy surpassing the human perception, as

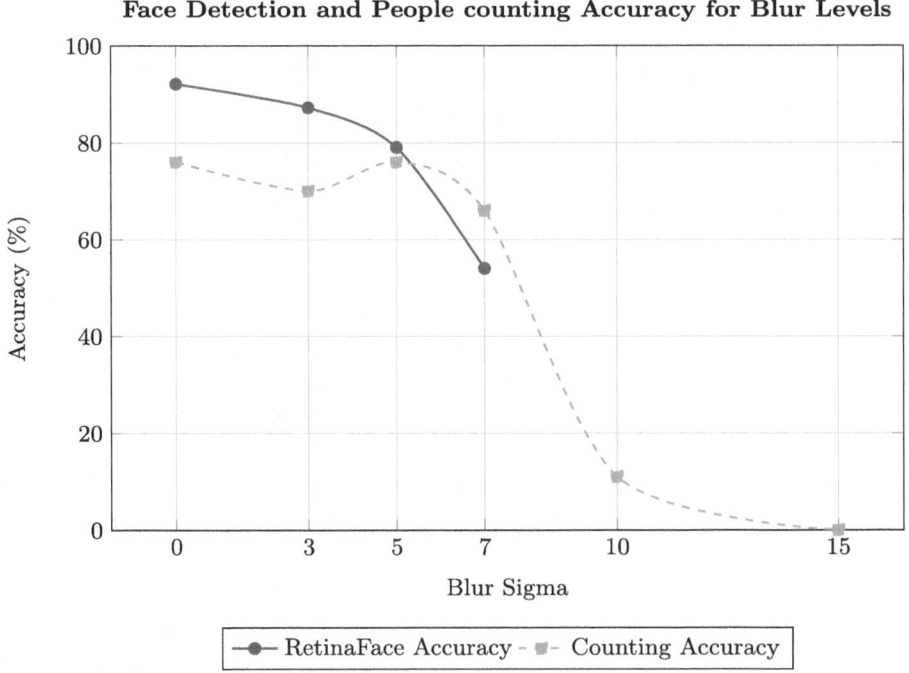

Fig. 3. Comparison of RetinaFace detection accuracy and people counting accuracy
under different levels of Gaussian blur (sigma).

noted in [19, 20]. Additionally, the blurred videos with sigmas 5 and 7 produced face and people visibility similar to the findings in [4, 8].

The blurred video with sigma 7 had lower face recognition accuracy, which was beneficial for improving people's privacy. When analyzing people counting, it was observed that despite the blurring effect, sigma 7 achieved an accuracy of 66%, which is 10% lower than the original video. Considering that the original video had no privacy protection and only achieved 76% accuracy, blurring the video proves to slightly improve privacy while maintaining a reliable number of people. Figure 3 illustrates a graph with two lines displaying the decrease of the accuracy for the face detection and the people counting when increasing the blur levels.

5   Conclusion

The purpose of this study was to determine whether blurred videos could effectively protect people's privacy while still allowing for accurate counting. A video was recorded featuring volunteers walking, and copies of the original video were created with different levels of blurring applied using various sigma values.

A manual count was performed on the original video to determine the number of people present. Then, a computer vision approach using MobileNet SSD and Centroid Tracker was applied to count people in both the original video and its blurred versions. The detected frames used for counting were saved for face identification using the DeepFace framework with RetinaFace backend.

The results of the people counting showed that the blurred videos with sigma 5 and 7 had accuracy values of 76% and 66%, respectively. These values were close to the accuracy of the original video analysis (76%). Additionally, processing the blurred images with DeepFace using the RetinaFace backend revealed that sigma 5 and 7 had lower face detection accuracy, indicating that people's privacy can be slightly improved.

Acknowledgments. The authors would like to thank all participants. Their voluntary participation was essential for collecting the data needed for this study.

Funded by national funds through FCT - Portuguese Science and Technology Foundation, within the project reference UIDB/04470/2023.

Disclosure of Interests. The authors have no competing interests to declare that are relevant to the content of this article.

Ethics and Data Protection. This study was approved by the Data Protection Officer of the University of Madeira as part of the research project "Controlo da afluência em trilhos na Ilha da Madeira", in compliance with the General Data Protection Regulation (GDPR).

Additionally, the study was approved by the Ethics Committee of the University of Madeira under the same research project, with the approved reference 73/CEUMA/2023.

References

1. Le, M., Le, M., Duong, M.: Vision-based people counting for attendance monitoring system. In: 2020 5th International Conference on Green Technology and Sustainable Development (GTSD), pp. 349–352 (2020)
2. Gafurov, D.: A survey of biometric gait recognition: approaches, security and challenges (2007)
3. Shoval, N., Ahas, R.: The use of tracking technologies in tourism research: the first decade. Tourism Geographies **18**, 587-606 (2016). https://doi.org/10.1080/14616688.2016.1214977
4. Lupp, G., et al.: Visitor counting and monitoring in forests using camera traps: a case study from Bavaria (Southern Germany). Land **10**, 736 (2021). https://www.mdpi.com/2073-445X/10/7/736
5. Krishnachaithanya, N., et al.: People counting in public spaces using deep learning-based object detection and tracking techniques. In: 2023 International Conference On Computational Intelligence and Sustainable Engineering Solutions (CISES), pp. 784–788 (2023)
6. Chato, P., Chipantasi, D., Velasco, N., Rea, S., Hallo, V., Constante, P.: Image processing and artificial neural network for counting people inside public transport. In: 2018 IEEE Third Ecuador Technical Chapters Meeting (ETCM), pp. 1–5 (2018)
7. Staab, J., Udas, E., Mayer, M., Taubenböck, H., Job, H.: Comparing established visitor monitoring approaches with triggered trail camera images and machine learning based computer vision. J. Outdoor Recreation Tourism **35**, 100387 (2021). https://linkinghub.elsevier.com/retrieve/pii/S2213078021000232
8. Climent-Pérez, P., Florez-Revuelta, F.: Protection of visual privacy in videos acquired with RGB cameras for active and assisted living applications. Multimedia Tools Appl. **80**(15), 23649–23664 (2021). https://doi.org/10.1007/s11042-020-10249-1
9. Official Journal of the European Union, Official Journal, L 119, 4 May 2016 (OJ L 119 04.05.2016)
10. Comissão Europeia, U. Regulamento Inteligência Artificial | Shaping Europe's digital future (2025). https://digital-strategy.ec.europa.eu/pt/policies/regulatory-framework-ai
11. Griffiths, E., Assana, S., Whitehouse, K.: Privacy-preserving image processing with binocular thermal cameras. In: Proceedings of the ACM on Interactive, Mobile, Wearable and Ubiquitous Technologies **1**, 1–25 (2018). https://doi.org/10.1145/3161198
12. Heredia, A., Barros-Gavilanes, G.: Video processing inside embedded devices using SSD-MobileNet to count mobility actors. In: 2019 IEEE Colombian Conference on Applications in Computational Intelligence (ColCACI), pp. 1–6 (2019)
13. Coste, S.: Crowd analysis on edge devices: a comparative study of neural networks on blurred images (2022)
14. Yoon, Y., Jeon, H., Yoo, D., Lee, J., So Kweon, I.: Learning a deep convolutional network for light-field image super-resolution (2015)
15. Saito, S., Li, T., Li, H.: Real-time facial segmentation and performance capture from RGB input. In: Leibe, B., Matas, J., Sebe, N., Welling, M. (eds.) ECCV 2016. LNCS, vol. 9912, pp. 244–261. Springer, Cham (2016). https://doi.org/10.1007/978-3-319-46484-8_15
16. Ahmed, I., Ahmad, M., Khan, F., Asif, M.: Comparison of deep-learning-based segmentation models: using top view person images. IEEE Access **8**, 136361–136373 (2020). https://ieeexplore.ieee.ieee.org/abstract/document/9146648

17. Lin, Z., Davis, L.: Shape-based human detection and segmentation via hierarchical part-template matching. IEEE Trans. Pattern Anal. Mach. Intell. **32**, 604–618 (2010). https://ieeexplore.ieee.org/abstract/document/5374413
18. Chuanqi305 MobileNet-SSD (2018). https://github.com/chuanqi305/MobileNet-SSD
19. Serengil, S., Ozpinar, A.: A benchmark of facial recognition pipelines and co-usability performances of modules. Bilişim Teknolojileri Dergisi **17**, 95–107 (2024)
20. Serengil GitHub - serengil/deepface: A Lightweight Face Recognition and Facial Attribute Analysis (Age, Gender, Emotion and Race) Library for Python. GitHub. https://github.com/serengil/deepface/tree/master?tab=readme-ov-file
21. Newmarch, J. FFmpeg/Libav. Linux Sound Programming, pp. 227–234 (2017). https://doi.org/10.1007/978-1-4842-2496-0_12
22. Serengil, S. serengil/retinaface (2025). https://github.com/serengil/retinaface. original-date: 2021-04-25T20:34:22Z
23. Iancu, M.: Couple young casual - free photo on Pixabay. https://pixabay.com/photos/couple-young-casual-walking-9380130/

From Homeostatic Principles to Discrete Emotions in an Agent Architecture – The HOmeostatic Regulation Architecture (HORA)

Hélder Bastos[1,2]([✉])(iD) and Luís Correia[1](iD)

[1] LASIGE, Faculdade de Ciências da Universidade de Lisboa, Lisbon, Portugal
helder.bastos@isel.pt, luis.correia@ciencias.ulisboa.pt
[2] Instituto Superior de Engenharia de Lisboa, Lisbon, Portugal

Abstract. This paper presents an innovative homeostatic agent architecture, which we named HOmeostatic Regulation Architecture (HORA), that redefines multi-dimensional homeostatic regulation as a cornerstone for adaptive decision-making and behaviour in autonomous systems. Unlike conventional frameworks focusing on a narrow range of low-level physiological parameters, our approach integrates a broader range of perceptual dimensions into a cohesive homeostatic space. The architecture facilitates agents in assessing their states against established setpoints and guiding behaviour through internal adaptations based on comprehensive homeostatic signals. Notably, the architecture enables the emergence of emotional behaviour as natural action tendencies, fostering adaptive and context-sensitive behaviours.

The proposed model is experimentally validated through a foraging agent simulation in a grid world, demonstrating the agent's ability to balance energy consumption, food storage, and response to harmful stimuli. This work proposes a novel view of homeostatic principles and their relationship with emotions in agent design, presenting a scalable framework that enhances the development of robust, autonomous systems.

Keywords: Autonomous Agents · Behaviour · Homeostasis · Emotion

1 Introduction

To achieve Artificial General Intelligence, researchers must study independent self-regulated control mechanisms that can efficiently or sufficiently adapt to any level of information. The current homeostatic control mechanisms [1,31,32] manage in a self-regulatory way several agents' relevant variables, which often rely on embodied information such as interoceptive signals. These self-regulatory mechanisms enable efficient behaviour in simpler cases, but are not easily scalable to complex problems.

Homeostatic control models usually follow the drive reduction theory [22], which maps specific *homeostatic* variables according to the agent's internal and

J. Valente de Oliveira et al. (Eds.): EPIA 2025, LNAI 16121, pp. 400–412, 2026.
https://doi.org/10.1007/978-3-032-05176-9_31

external conditions. The behaviour will reduce tensions on these homeostatic variables caused by unmet needs [7,9,10,16,17,40]. Not only is this view challenged in biology [1], but it also challenges computational models since it reduces the information space to generally very low-level spaces, not taking advantage of all available information for decision-making. We point out this factor as a possible limiting choke point for the scalability of homeostatic models, which we intend to address in this paper.

On the other hand, we have Damasio's perspective of the relationship between behaviour and homeostasis, stating that every behavioural level searches for homeostatic stability in its corresponding level, highlighting a hierarchical homeostatic formulation [12]. Moreover, each level of homeostatic formulation opens up a new set of available emotional phenomena, providing the living being a new set of tools to manage its cognitive limitations better [11,12,38]. The assertion that emotions derive from homeostatic processes to preserve an organism's internal equilibrium provides a compelling framework to construct emotionally intelligent machines.

This paper proposes the HOmeostatic Regulation Architecture (HORA), an agent architecture designed to be scalable for more complex agent architectures. The primary goal is to investigate the homeostatic principles in complex architectures, as observed in human behaviour, according to Damásio and other authors. Under this purpose, HORA operates according to homeostatic principles in a multi-level homeostatic space by directly mapping relevant perception dimensions. All the homeostatic properties apply to this mapping: setpoints assume the core of the agent's motivational aspect, gravitating around the setpoint by managing endogenous and exogenous forces within different homeostatic balances in a coordinated manner, through what can be considered emotions to guide the agent's behaviour. This integration between homeostasis and emotion aims to move research towards General AI by providing one more step towards integrating emotional behaviour into agents and enabling agents that better integrate with humans.

To validate HORA as a control mechanism, we implement it in an architecture for a foraging agent that needs energy to operate, eating and storing food when possible, enabling the formation of action tendencies [11,12,14], an emotional phenomenon showing that is possible to elicit emotional properties from homeostatic grounding.

1.1 Homeostasis

Homeostatic principles have been unfolded since their initial proposal by Cannon in 1926 [3]. There is an agreement that homeostasis is the maintenance of really constant conditions in the internal environment, despite controversy about whether this maintenance is due only to physiological attributes [18,33] or applies to other degrees of attributes [12,21,30].

The literature is rich in approaches for homeostatic agents and models; most, if not all, are closely related to control theory. For example, Ashby's homeostat consists of interconnected units with adjustable parameters that self-regulate to achieve equilibrium [2]. Maturana and Varela, on the other hand, became influential in designing adaptive, self-regulating artificial systems with their idea of homeostasis by autopoiesis - the process by which an entity continuously regenerates and maintains itself [29]. Carver and Scheier [4–6] developed agents with reference values (setpoints) for different variables that minimise deviations from these setpoints, maintaining homeostasis through continuous feedback and adjustment. Several authors also propose homeostatic hormonal architectures [13,23,34,36] where specific perceptual information secrets hormones and the agent aims to stabilise the hormonal secretion via homeostatic principles. The TOMASys [8,37] is a modern approach to homeostatic agents, which integrates homeostatic control with modules that monitor and regulate internal states. On the other hand, Yoshida [39] addresses homeostasis as a geometrical space that defines a reward value for Reinforcement Learning problems. Although interesting, TOMASys approach conveys something similar to the drive reduction theory, while Yoshida's work lacks a proper model and architecture to support his ideas.

All the mentioned architectures share one thing in common: the reduçal of perceptual information into a short set of features, all internal simulation of biological features, to later produce behaviour. Even though efficient behaviour is enabled, there is an information loss that can be relevant to behaviour. Moreover, the aforementioned architectures that also address emotions do it only under the drive reduction theory [23,34,36], or develop emotion through other processes rather than homeostasis [13].

1.2   Emotional Architectures Derived from Homeostasis

The Reinforcement Learning framework is a common framework for studying the relationship between emotion and homeostasis. Researchers primarily focus on exploring the elicitation of emotions as an outcome of internal variable regulation. For example, [10,17,20] uses homeostatic variables to set emotional cues to generate the reinforcement signal and action filtering mechanisms (which we can relate to action tendencies) from a set of homeostatic variables. Another explored path is the definition of well-being as an emotion and its relationship with homeostatic variables [9,15,35]:

$$W_t = K - D_t = K - \sum_{i=1}^{N} \theta_i \left| h_i^* - h_{i,t} \right| \tag{1}$$

In this formulation, W_t indicates the state of well-being at time t, where K serves as a reference or baseline value to which individuals aspire. The term D_t quantifies the distance at instant t between every dimension (i) of the setpoint (h_i^*) and the current situation ($h_{i,t}$). Other approaches [25] define emotions as homeostatic variables, able to regulate through behaviour.

1.3   Motivation

Despite the many available homeostatic architectures and models, very few position homeostasis as a widespread phenomenon that encompasses all layers of decision processes. The trend in homeostatic agent architectures is that a conversion layer transforms the agent's general situation into a smaller signal space representing the agent's most fundamental homeostatic variables (energy, food, or integrity). The resulting point is a homeostatic evaluation, further used to generate or bias behaviour. This informational conversion is not necessarily bad, since it provides a simplification, given that different homeostatic variables may have a specific influence on specific behaviours. However, although theoretically logical, research evidence suggests the difficulty in applying these concepts for complex behaviour, with the conversion of perception to homeostatic variables only applied to survival behaviour, in some rare cases to fundamental goals, and some limited emotional characterisation aimed at Human-Computer Interaction (HCI).

Reducing perception for behaviour reduces a rich signal, losing important information without generating anything new. Moreover, when emotion elicitation is a research goal, this homeostatic signal is reduced to an emotional tag, which is even more limited in influencing the agent's internal functioning. We understand that this view is practical, for example, in HCI because it enables the agent (or robot) to display emotional cues; however, it does not take advantage of all emotional properties that enrich emotional phenomena, as Damásio proposes.

Our proposed HOmeostatic Regulation Architecture (HORA) implements the previous idea in an agent architecture that uses multidimensional homeostatic signals to produce internal adaptations. This enables control mechanisms based on homeostatic principles, which we show demonstrate - as Damásio upholds - are a possible genesis for emotional behaviour.

2   The HOmeostatic Regulation Architecture (HORA)

The ideas that Damásio maintains [12], where homeostatic principles core all behavioural levels (from reflexes to social level), enable an agent with multiple behavioural levels that share the same structure and control principles: evaluating the current situation against a setpoint (the desired condition) and gravitating around the setpoint through behaviour. Setpoints define the desired internal and external conditions on their abstraction level, and behaviour operates under its abstraction scope. Therefore, an agent implementing HORA can have several behavioural layers, each operating independently under this perspective. Five processes compose each behavioural layer (Fig. 1).

1. Perception: describes the agent's internal and external stance.
2. Homeostasis: compares the perceptual information against a setpoint in the Homeostatic Space. The result is the Homeostatic Signal.

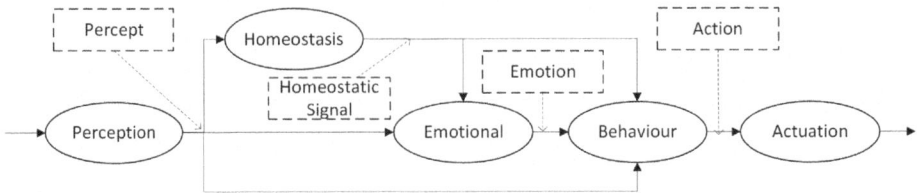

Fig. 1. The HOmeostatic Regulation Architecture. Solid arrows mean a connection, ellipses identify processes, and dashed boxes and arrows indicate the type of information and where it flows.

3. Emotional: defines the changes in the behavioural process for the latter to cope with the Homeostatic Signal.
4. Behaviour: produces regulatory behaviour of any abstraction level, like reactive, adaptive, deliberative, social, and meta-cognitive, among others.
5. Actuation: performs the behaviour in the environment or internally.

To better understand how emotions derive from the Homeostatic Signal, we now focus on the Homeostatic Space, which supports the Homeostatic Signal.

2.1   The Homeostatic Space

The homeostatic space (Φ) supports characterising the agent's situation. The proposed one is similar to the Agent Flow Model [28] that ultimately follows Gardenfors' ideas [19]. It is a space defined by a set of K dimensions $\Phi = \{\phi_1, \phi_2, \ldots, \phi_K\}$ with $K \in N$ in such a way that enables the computation of distances, velocities and accelerations between points. The number of dimensions depends on the complexity of the layer. For instance, a reactive layer might represent straightforward sensor information. In contrast, a deliberative or social layer uses a composition of signals derived from other cognitive processes, like memory or inferences, to capture the nuances of its environment. The homeostatic space supports the following types of elements:

1. Observations are points in the homeostatic space characterising the agent's situation. Each observation is a vector of intensities for each dimension.

$$O = \langle o_1, o_2, \ldots, o_K \rangle \tag{2}$$

2. Setpoints are points in the homeostatic space that identify a desirable situation—the motivation—where the agent will gravitate. Each setpoint is a vector of intensities for each dimension.

$$S = \langle s_1, s_2, \ldots, s_K \rangle \tag{3}$$

3. Homeostatic Signals (H) characterise the quality of the agent's stance regarding one setpoint. For simplicity, under the scope of this paper, we propose

the Homeostatic signal as a tuple (η_0) of distances between the observation and a setpoint resembling the drive definition of aforementioned works [27]. The Homeostatic signal has as many dimensions as the homeostatic space and is normalised in all dimensions to enable comparison between features with different domains:

$$\eta_0 = (S - O)/S \tag{4}$$

The Homeostatic Signal works as the foundational information to elicit emotions.

2.2   Emotions

Each agent embodies Behavioural Parameters (M), a set of behavioural variables μ which, in turn, comprise the internal agent dynamics that result in adaptive behaviour.

$$M = \langle \mu_1, \mu_2, \ldots, \mu_L \rangle, \tag{5}$$

where L represents the total number of behavioural parameters.

Emotions are instances of Behavioural Patterns - resembling somatic markers [12] - that the agent exhibits under specific homeostatic conditions. They can operate under natural or real domains, depending on the abstraction level and the model of M. The emotional process maps each homeostatic signal (H) into an emotion (E).

This formulation for Emotion provides the flexibility needed for agents to rapidly shift between behavioural configurations based on survival and goal context, promoting immediate survival and long-term homeostatic balance.

3   Tests and Validation: Foraging Agent

To test and validate HORA's homeostatic adaptation and emotional elicitation capabilities, we focus on a foraging task in a grid world with a base to store food and randomly appearing food elements to be consumed or stored by the agent. There is also an adverse stimulus, static, which the agent seeks to avoid.

The agent's internal energy ranges between $[0, 1]$ and obtains 0.5 units of energy for each eaten food unit and loses 0.01 or 0.005 units of energy at each time step if it is carrying or not a load of food, respectively. The environment is a 5×20 grid environment with a base at position $(0, 2)$, an adverse stimulus at position $(17, 2)$, and the agent begins at the base. Initially, there is no food in the environment, and one new food element appears in an environment's random position at every N simulation steps. The agent can only carry one unit of food each time.

The agent's homeostatic space is $\Phi = \{\phi_1, \phi_2, \phi_3\}$: the amount of energy the agent has (ϕ_1), the amount of food on base (ϕ_2), and the distance to the adverse stimulus (ϕ_3). Moreover, ϕ_1 and ϕ_2 are attractive setpoints while ϕ_3 is a lower threshold.

The agent's homeostatic setpoint is $S = \{1, 10, 3\}$, which means that the ideal situation for the agent is to have full energy (1), have 10 food elements stored at the base (10), and be at least 3 cells away from the adverse stimulus. To note the distance between the agent's setpoint and the first observation in simulation $O = \{1, 0, 17\}$ and the fact that the agent will seek to approach values in dimensions one and two and increase distance to adverse stimulus beyond value in dimension three.

Table 1. Agent Action Tendencies and Dimensions

Dimension Affected	Action Tendency
ϕ_1	*eat loaded food, eat stored food, load, walk to food, walk to a loaded base*
ϕ_2	*unload, walk to base, load, walk to food*
ϕ_3	*walk from adverse stimulus*

In this simulation, the agent commits to the actions described in Table 1 - to which we refer as action tendencies. Each action tendency pursues a specific homeostatic dimension (ϕ), chosen by the homeostatic control as the most relevant to pursue, that is, the most distant dimension between setpoint and observation.

When the action tendencies are received, the control mechanism chooses the action based on the available ones in their hierarchical order according to their triggering conditions, as seen in Table 2.

Table 2. Triggering conditions for each action

Action	Triggering Conditions
eat loaded food	The agent is currently carrying food (loaded)
eat stored food	The agent is not loaded with food and is on the base
load	The agent is loaded with food and is currently at a food location
unload	The agent is loaded with food and is on the base
walk from adverse stimulus	True
walk to base	The agent is loaded with food and there is a base
walk to food	There is food in the environment and the agent is not loaded with food
walk to loaded base	There is a base and the base has food stored

We use homeostatic distress (D), the sum of the normalised differences in each dimension between the setpoint and the current observation, as the evaluation metric of agent performance. The higher the sum of the distress along the simulation, the lower the performance.

Figure 2 shows the results of three simulations varying from the available food amount: $N = [5, 15, 30]$ ran on 1000 time steps. When the agent has plenty

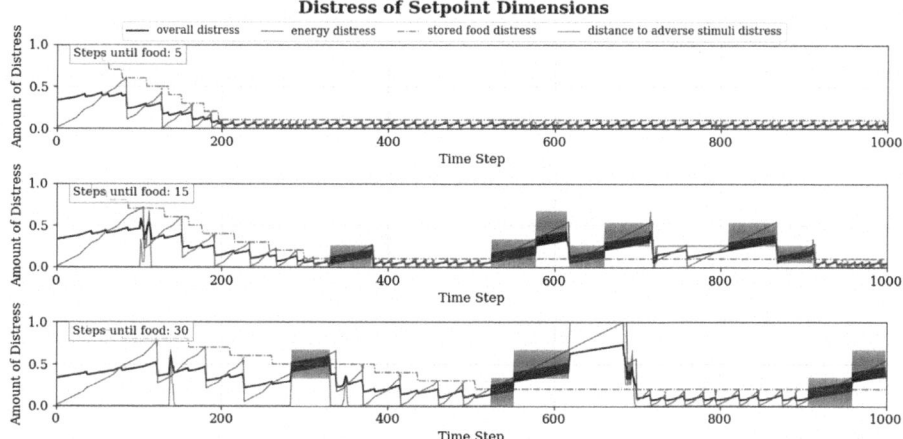

Fig. 2. Results of the overall and individual stress of the homeostatic dimensions along three simulations that differ from the value of N - the number of steps required for a food sample appear.

of food available ($N = 5$), the overall distress quickly stabilises in values close to 0. The agent can maintain energy and store food at their highest levels while complying with the minimum distance from adverse stimuli. In the remaining simulations, there are more intense and frequent peaks of distress directly proportional to food scarcity, observed in the distress of the agent on approaching the harmful stimulus.

It is also possible to note some of the inefficiencies of the reactive architecture. Between steps 500 and 700 of the second and third simulations Âă($N = 15$ and $N = 30$), it becomes evident that the agent prioritises pursuing food in the environment over consuming food already stored at the base, even when doing so requires approaching the adverse stimulus. This behaviour is visible through the high-frequency variation of adverse stimulus distress. It highlights that in the resulting behaviour of this architecture, action selection is heavily biased towards immediate external stimuli, even at the cost of increased homeostatic distress.

When the base has not yet reached full or near full capacity, the agent tolerates lower energy levels for storing food, as observed in the simulations' first cycles. Conversely, when the base is complete or nearly full, the agent exhibits greedy behaviour, consuming food even when its energy levels are high.

Moreover, when energy levels are stable, the agent successfully avoids adverse stimuli. However, when operating under reduced energy or storage levels, and a food element is next to an adverse stimulus, the agent oscillates back and forth in behavioural indecision until a further decrease in energy levels. This phenomenon is due to the motivational dynamics of the setpoint pursuit, which pursues the most distance dimension between the setpoint and observation. This effect occurs in an oscillating loop, moving between the distress caused by proximity to the

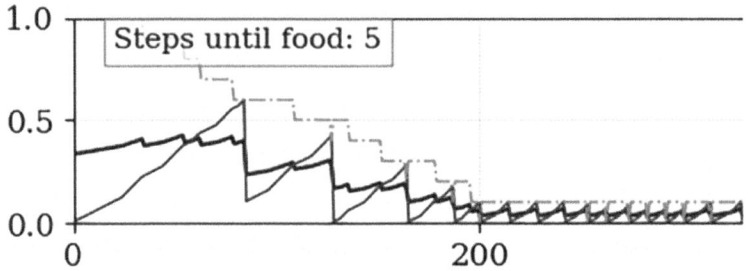

Fig. 3. Zoom of the first 350 steps of the first simulation of Fig. 2.

harmful stimulus and energy distress during several steps. This oscillation ends when the energy distress increases to exceed the distress caused by the distance to the harmful stimulus, to the extent that it enables the agent to approach or even bypass the adverse stimulus to access food. This behaviour explicitly evidences a fearful or cautious emotion that takes precedence until another homeostatic dynamic, such as hunger, dominates it due to low energy levels, making the agent relegate avoiding the harmful stimulus to a secondary plan. Therefore, our architecture generates emotional behaviour from homeostatic regulation to better control the overall behaviour of the agent.

Another behaviour worth mentioning is eating stored food only when no food is available in the environment. This is observable in Fig. 3, a zoom of the first 350 steps of the first simulation of Fig. 2. Around step 120, we notice a decrease in the stored food distress, which is immediately topped by the energy distress, making the agent consume the food load it had just stored (small downward spike in the red dotted line). This means that the agent is carrying food and arrives at the base and stores it, but immediately, the energy distress surpasses the stored food distress, and the agent opts to eat the food just stored, zeroing the energy distress. In the same figure, around step 250, we observe repeated cycles of the zeroing of the food store distress to go up immediately, meaning the agent stored the food at the base, but as soon it does it, the energy distress goes up, and the agent eats a loaded food.

Further, we developed another set of four simulations to address the architecture's robustness. Simulation one varies the setpoint value of dimension one $S = \{0.5, 10, 3\}$; the second simulation varies the setpoint value of dimension two $S = \{1, 5, 3\}$, and the third, the setpoint value of dimension one $S = \{1, 10, 9\}$. Notice that in all simulations, the initial conditions are distant from the setpoint. A final simulation tests the agent architecture against a situation that starts in a stable stance $0 = S = \{1, 10, 3\}$.

In simulations one and two, the agent achieves overall stability of the homeostatic distress, which means it can self-regulate around the setpoint. On the remaining ones, the agent stabilises its level of distress, although it may experience periodic peaks due to different factors. In the third simulation $(S = \{1, 10, 9\})$, the minimum distance to the harmful stimulus encompasses nearly half the environment, forcing the agent to distress when approaching the harmful stimulus to capture food. Moreover, in the fourth simulation, despite starting in equilibrium, the lack of enough food in the safe zone of the environment also presents a challenge to food and harmful distance distress. Simulations one and two have a less strict agent that excels with half the energy capacity and five elements of food stored (in contrast with ten on all the remaining ones), respectively. From a goal achievement perspective, the previous dynamics show that two agents with the same features except the setpoint, the agent with a more strict setpoint, can achieve more at the cost of a more unstable and distressed homeostatic condition.

In all the experiments, the HORA exhibits robustness since it performs under a significant variety of environmental contexts without any change in the parameterisation of the architecture components.

4 Conclusions

This paper highlights homeostasis as a control mechanism for autonomous agents at any level of behavioural abstraction, from the reactive to the most cognitive levels, in such a way that elicits emotions. For the effect, we propose the Homeostatic Regulation Architecture (HORA), an agent architecture agnostic to the behavioural level that focuses on homeostatic principles applied to a broad set of dimensions to enable emotions.

To test our model, we created a simulation in which a foraging agent, set with HORA, reactive architectures, and action tendencies, eats, stores food, and avoids danger. Several simulations under different environmental and agent configurations evidenced two things: (i) HORA is an effective control architecture and robust since it was able to perform under several different environmental configurations without any change in the agent parameters; (ii) it is possible to elicit emotions using homeostatic principles.

HORA differs from Gadanho's model [15] by explicitly using multidimensional perceptual inputs directly as homeostatic signals rather than relying solely on physiological-like variables. Also, HORA employs emotions as immediate action tendencies, enhancing real-time adaptive behavioural responses without learning-dependent delays. On the other hand, HORA contrasts with Salichs and Malfaz [35] by directly integrating emotions as action tendencies rather than emotional states merely modulating decisions. Using comprehensive multidimensional perceptual inputs in HORA expands emotional elicitation capabilities, facilitating rapid and contextually richer behavioural adaptation beyond basic survival mechanisms. Finally, unlike Cos et al. [9], HORA directly derives emotions from comprehensive homeostatic signals instead of hedonic-based motivational evaluations. HORA also emphasises immediate adaptive behaviours, leveraging a broad range of perceptual dimensions to create flexible, context-sensitive emotional responses.

We recognise that HORA lacks optimality since opportunistic behaviour is absent. For example, the agent does not catch a nearby food element when moving away from the adverse stimuli. Other types of inefficient behaviour include pursuing food in an undesired environment zone, even when the base has plenty of food. We also acknowledge that emotions are in a subdued form since we used a reactive architecture; however, we propose future work on more complex agents with additional cognitive behavioural layers, as this could manifest emotions more distinctly.

This paper suggests several future research avenues. A consistent model for the action tendencies and their triggers is lacking. For the action tendencies model, we propose exploring action as forces related to goals [24, 26]. Furthermore, we could investigate how adding weights to the computation of η_0 could shift priorities among its dimensions or employ non-linear functions to measure the distance between observations and setpoints.

Another potential area of research involves expanding the emotional changes to Perception, Homeostasis, and Actuation. For instance, this could mean providing additional energy to actuators or developing an attentional mechanism to select the relevant homeostatic variables to operate.

Acknowledgments. This work was supported by FCT through the LASIGE Research Unit, UID/00408/2025 - LASIGE.

Disclosure of Interests. The authors have no competing interests.

References

1. Arias, C.F., Acosta, F.J., Bertocchini, F., Fernández-Arias, C.: A functional approach to homeostatic regulation. Biol. Direct **19**(1), 134 (2024)
2. Ashby, W.R.: The Homeostat, pp. 100–121. Springer (1960)
3. Cannon, W.B.: Physiological regulation of normal states: some tentative postulates concerning biological homeostatics. Ses Amis, ses Colleges, ses Eleves (1926)
4. Carver, C.S., Scheier, M.F.: Control theory: a useful conceptual framework for personality–social, clinical, and health psychology. Psychol. Bull. **92**, 111 (1982)
5. Carver, C.S., Scheier, M.F.: On the structure of behavioral self-regulation, pp. 41–84. Elsevier (2000)
6. Carver, C.S., Scheier, M.F.: On the Self-Regulation of Behavior. Cambridge University Press (2001)
7. Cañamero, L.: Emotion understanding from the perspective of autonomous robots research. Neural Netw. **18**, 445–455 (2005)
8. Corbato, C.H.: Model-based self-awareness patterns for autonomy. Ph.d. thesis, Universidad Politécnica de Madrid (2013)
9. Cos, I., Cañamero, L., Hayes, G.M., Gillies, A.: Hedonic value: enhancing adaptation for motivated agents. Adapt. Behav. **21**, 465–483 (2013)
10. Coutinho, E., Miranda, E.R., Cangelosi, A.: Towards a model for embodied emotions. In: 2005 Portuguese Conference on Artificial Intelligence, pp. 54–63. IEEE (2005). https://doi.org/10.1109/EPIA.2005.341264
11. Damasio, A.R.: Descartes' Error. Random House (2006)
12. Damasio, A.R.: The strange order of things: life, feeling, and the making of cultures. Vintage (2018)

13. Dias, J., Mascarenhas, S., Paiva, A.: Fatima modular: towards an agent architecture with a generic appraisal framework. In: Emotion Modeling: Towards Pragmatic Computational Models of Affective Processes, pp. 44–56 (2014)
14. Frijda, N.H.: Emotion, cognitive structure, and action tendency. Cogn. Emot. **1**, 115–143 (1987). https://doi.org/10.1080/02699938708408043
15. Gadanho, S.C.: Learning behavior-selection by emotions and cognition in a multi-goal robot task. J. Mach. Learn. Res. **4**(Jul), 385–412 (2003)
16. Gadanho, S.C., Hallam, J.: Emotion-triggered learning in autonomous robot control. Cybern. Syst. **32**, 531–559 (2001)
17. Gadanho, S.C., Hallam, J.: Robot learning driven by emotions. Adapt. Behav. **9** (2001). https://doi.org/10.1177/105971230200900102
18. Guyton, A.C., et al.: Textbook of Medical Physiology, vol. 548. Saunders Philadelphia (1986)
19. Gärdenfors, P.: Conceptual Spaces: The Geometry of Thought. MIT Press (2004)
20. Haugwitz, R.V., Kitamura, Y., Takashima, K.: Modulating reinforcement-learning parameters using agent emotions. In: The 6th International Conference on Soft Computing and Intelligent Systems, and The 13th International Symposium on Advanced Intelligence Systems, pp. 1281–1285 (2012)
21. Hsu, F.L.K.: Psychosocial homeostasis and Jen: conceptual tools for advancing psychological anthropology. Am. Anthropol. **73**, 23–44 (1971)
22. Hull, C.L.: Principles of Behavior: An Introduction to Behavior Theory. D. Appleton-Century Company, New York (1943)
23. Jimenez-Rodriguez, A., Prescott, T.J., Schmidt, R., Wilson, S.: A framework for resolving motivational conflict via attractor dynamics. In: Conference on Biomimetic and Biohybrid Systems, pp. 192–203. Springer (2020)
24. Johnson, M.: The Body in the Mind: The Bodily Basis of Meaning, Imagination, and Reason. University of Chicago press (2013)
25. Kelkar, A.: Cognitive homeostatic agents. arXiv preprint: arXiv:2103.03359 (2021)
26. Leonard, T.: Force dynamics in language and thought. Cogn. Sci. **12** (1988)
27. Moerland, T.M., Broekens, J., Jonker, C.M.: Emotion in reinforcement learning agents and robots: a survey. Mach. Learn. **107**, 443–480 (2018)
28. Morgado, L., Gaspar, G.: A signal based approach to artificial agent modeling. In: European Conference on Artificial Life, pp. 1050–1059 (2007)
29. Mugerauer, B.: Maturana and Varela: From Autopoiesis to Systems Applications, pp. 158–178. Routledge (2013)
30. Parker, P.M., Tavassoli, N.T.: Homeostasis and consumer behavior across cultures. Int. J. Res. Mark. **17**, 33–53 (2000)
31. Peña, J.U.L., Morales, F.S., Carlos, J.C., Fossion, R.: Parallels between homeostatic regulation and control theory. In: AIP Conference Proceedings, vol. 2348. AIP Publishing (2021)
32. Petzschner, F.H., Garfinkel, S.N., Paulus, M.P., Koch, C., Khalsa, S.S.: Computational models of interoception and body regulation. Trends Neurosci. **44**(1), 63–76 (2021)
33. Ravichandran, N.B.: Modelling homeostatic regulation in multi-objective decision-making (2018)
34. Rosado, O.G., Amil, A.F., Freire, I.T., Verschure, P.F.: Drive competition underlies effective allostatic orchestration. Front. Robot. AI **9**, 1052998 (2022)
35. Salichs, M.A., Malfaz, M.: A new approach to modeling emotions and their use on a decision-making system for artificial agents. IEEE Trans. Affect. Comput. **3**(1), 56–68 (2011)

36. Schmickl, T., Hamann, H., Crailsheim, K.: Modelling a hormone-inspired controller for individual-and multi-modular robotic systems. Math. Comput. Model. Dyn. Syst. **17**(3), 221–242 (2011)
37. Silva, G.R., et al.: MROS: a framework for robot self-adaptation. In: 2023 IEEE/ACM 45th International Conference on Software Engineering: Companion Proceedings (ICSE-Companion), pp. 151–155 (2023)
38. Simon, H.A.: Theories of bounded rationality. Dec. Organ. **1**(1), 161–176 (1972)
39. Yoshida, N.: Homeostatic agent for general environment. J. Artif. Gen Intell. **8**, 1 (2017)
40. Yoshida, N., Daikoku, T., Nagai, Y., Kuniyoshi, Y.: Emergence of integrated behaviors through direct optimization for homeostasis. Neural Netw. **177**, 106379 (2024). https://doi.org/10.1016/j.neunet.2024.106379

Multi-Objective Reinforcement Learning Algorithm for Irregular Spatial Clusters Detection

Dênis Oliveira[1] , Anderson Duarte[3] , André Ottoni[2] ,
and Gladston Moreira[2](✉)

[1] Postgraduate Program in Computer Science, Federal University of Ouro Preto,
Ouro Preto, MG, Brazil
[2] Computing Department, Federal University of Ouro Preto, Ouro Preto, MG, Brazil
gladston@ufop.edu.br
[3] Statistics Department, Federal University of Ouro Preto, Ouro Preto, MG, Brazil

Abstract. Methods for detecting irregular spatial clusters encompass a wide range of practical applications, establishing themselves as valuable tools for analyzing disease outbreaks and other phenomena. However, spatial scan statistics, widely adopted as a methodology in these analyses, require the support of strategies to mitigate the overestimation of candidate clusters. To address this challenge, multi-objective optimization techniques have been introduced, which optimize the scan statistic simultaneously with a penalty function applied to the shape or structure of candidate clusters. We propose an innovative method based on a Multi-Objective Reinforcement Learning (MORL) paradigm with a specialized Multi-Objective Markov Decision Process (MOMDP). Our approach centers on a novel Pareto Q-Learning Scan (PQL-SCAN) algorithm that dynamically learns an efficient policy set. This method generates candidate clusters by optimizing a reward vector defined by two conflicting objectives: maximizing the spatial scan statistic and minimizing the dispersion penalty function. Comprehensive computational experiments were initially conducted on a synthetic dataset map with artificial clusters, followed by evaluations on a real-world disease map. The results demonstrate the high efficiency, robustness, and adaptability of the PQL-SCAN in accurately detecting complex irregular clusters.

Keywords: Multi-Objective optimization · Reinforcement Learning · Irregular Spatial Cluster Detection

1 Introduction

Cluster detection methods have been developed for both aggregated data and point processes while addressing problems involving spatial, temporal, or spatiotemporal information. In practical applications, these approaches are critical across diverse fields, including public health [5,7], disease outbreaks [1,12], criminology [9, 18], ecology [23], urban traffic [8], among others. One major challenge in the spatial domain arises from the size of the candidate cluster search space. An exhaustive analysis of a map composed of m areas, considers $2^m - 1$ non-empty subsets of areas. This order of magnitude makes full-search-based approaches computationally infeasible with current technology.

The analysis for candidate clusters by combining the component areas of a map can be formulated as a combinatorial optimization problem. Among the various approaches designed, the spatial scan statistic [11] is a widely adopted strategy in optimization methods. However, solely maximizing the scan statistic may yield overestimated clusters that encompass too many map areas. To address this, several studies have introduced multi-objective optimization techniques [2, 3, 14, 15] that simultaneously optimize the scan statistic and apply additional criteria such as penalty functions to constrain the shape of candidate clusters.

Reinforcement learning (RL) is a machine learning paradigm [19] that excels in developing strategies for a wide range of challenges, including combinatorial optimization problems [13]. At its core, RL utilizes the Markov Decision Process (MDP) framework, which formalizes the interaction between an intelligent agent and its environment [19]. In this framework, the agent interacts with the environment by observing states, performing actions that alter the environment's perception, and observing a numerical reward signal as feedback. Throughout this cycle of experience collection, the agent strives to learn an optimal policy by mapping state-action pairs to maximize the total discounted accumulated rewards. Multi-objective Reinforcement Learning (MORL) extends traditional single-objective RL by simultaneously considering several objectives [6, 20, 22]. In MORL, the reward is represented as a vector, with each component corresponding to a distinct objective that the agent seeks to optimize. This approach enables the balancing of competing goals within a single coherent framework.

Single-objective RL algorithms have been applied to irregular cluster detection processes [16]. However, methodologies employing MORL remain noticeably absent from the literature. To address this gap, we propose a novel approach based on the MORL paradigm. Our algorithm, Pareto Q-Learning Scan (PQL-SCAN), iteratively learns and maintains a diverse set of efficient policies throughout the experience collection process. Each policy is optimized over a numerical reward vector that balances two competing objectives: maximizing scan statistics [11] and minimizing the dispersion penalty function [15]. As a result, the PQL-SCAN learning process generates a comprehensive collection of candidate spatial clusters, each representing a distinct trade-off between the likelihood maximization and the structure of compact clusters.

This study is organized as follows. In Sect. 2, we review key concepts related to spatial cluster detection. Next, we introduce the objective functions considered in our multi-objective PQL-SCAN algorithm: the Kulldorff spatial scan statistic and the dispersion penalty function. Subsection 2.3 then provides an overview of the MORL paradigm. Section 3 presents our novel MORL approach, including the specialized MOMDP and a description of the PQL-SCAN algorithm. We detail the computational experiments in Sect. 4. Finally, Sect. 5 presents the study's findings and potential topics for future research.

2 Background

In the spatial cluster detection process, for a study map divided into m areas, denoted by $u_1, u_2, \ldots, u_m$, the cases of a phenomenon of interest are distributed as $c_1, c_2, \ldots, c_m$. This structure can be applied to analyzing occurrences of any phenomenon, such as a disease outbreak. In addition, the target population of susceptible individuals is distributed as $p_1, p_2, \ldots, p_m$ in each map area. Therefore, we have $P = \sum_{i=1}^{m} p_i$ as the total target population, and $C = \sum_{i=1}^{m} c_i$ as the total number of observed cases for the phenomenon of interest in the map under study.

A zone z is defined as any non-empty subset of areas on the map under study. The definition of a zone is crucial for analyses related to spatial cluster detection. It's essential to emphasize that, in this study, the regularity of the shape and the connection or disconnection of the areas within the zone establish considerable heterogeneity among the possible zones under investigation. The primary objective of the methodologies developed for detecting spatial clusters is to identify the most likely zone z^* among the set of all investigated zones.

A *spatial cluster* is defined as a zone z^* on the map under study whose relative risk for the phenomenon's cases is considered statistically discrepant, either very high or very low, but statistically significant in relation to the dataset under analysis. Establishing what is statistically significant requires conducting a hypothesis test; this is the role of the spatial scan statistic proposed by [11], as described in Sect. 2.1, which performs this task through a likelihood ratio test.

2.1 Kulldorff's Spatial Scan Statistics

Let Z be the set of all zones z that will be evaluated, and let $z \in Z$ represent any zone under study. Let c_z and p_z denote the number of cases and the target population associated with the zone z. A hypothesis test is proposed where, under the null hypothesis, no zone z has a statistically significant number of cases. On the other hand, the alternative hypothesis assumes that at least one zone z^* on the map under study has a statistically significant number of cases. The function $L(z)$ represents the likelihood function under the alternative hypothesis, while the function L_0 represents the likelihood function under the null hypothesis.

This study examines statistical discrepancies where the number of cases in the study area is significantly higher than expected. However, it can be extended to account for discrepancies below the expected average. Under the null hypothesis, it is typically assumed that the number of cases for a zone z follows a Poisson distribution with a rate μ_z proportional to the population distribution, i.e., $\mu_z = C(p_z/P)$. Therefore, consider the relative risk inside a zone z, which is a candidate for the definition of a spatial cluster, defined by $I_z = c_z/\mu_z$. The relative risk outside this candidate zone is represented by $O_z = (C - c_z)/(C - \mu_z)$. The logarithm of the likelihood ratio test statistic is given by:

$$\Lambda(z) = \begin{cases} c_z \log(I_z) + (C - c_z) \log(O_z) \,, & \text{if } I_z > 1 \\ 0 & , \text{ otherwise.} \end{cases} \tag{1}$$

The search strategy for the most likely zone on the map under study involves maximizing the function $\Lambda(z)$ concerning the set Z of zones z under analysis. Consequently, the spatial scan statistic [11] is defined as follows:

$$T = \max_{z \in Z} \Lambda(z). \tag{2}$$

2.2 Dispersion Penalty Function

The dispersion function is designed to prioritize candidate zones that are spatially smaller or compact. It is computed by analyzing the two-dimensional distribution of the centroid coordinates corresponding to the areas within a candidate zone. The function calculates the harmonic mean of the distances between the centroids of the border areas in a zone. Given a study map composed of m spatial areas $\{a_1, a_2, \ldots, a_m\}$, where each area a_i has an internal point of coordinates $c_i(x, y)$ called the centroid. Consider a zone z formed by n_z spatial areas, the corresponding centroids of z are $(x_1, y_1), \ldots, (x_{n_z}, y_{n_z})$, with $1 \leq n_z \leq m$. Define $\overline{x} = \max\{x_i\}$ and $\underline{x} = \min\{x_i\}$, where $i \in \{1, \ldots, n_z\}$, and calculate $d_1 = \overline{x} - \underline{x}$. Similarly, define $d_2 = \overline{y} - \underline{y}$. The dispersion penalty [15] for z is expressed in Eq. 3:

$$\mathbb{DP}(z) = \frac{2(d_1 d_2)}{d_1 + d_2}. \tag{3}$$

2.3 Multi-Objective Reinforcement Learning

Multi-Objective Reinforcement Learning (MORL) enhances classical RL by integrating multiple objectives into the decision-making process [6]. Unlike classical RL, which relies on a single scalar reward, MORL employs a numerical reward vector. This allows the framework to manage several competing objectives. MORL retains the foundational RL components: an intelligent agent, its environment, a state space, and a set of actions, but redefines them under a multi-dimensional reward system. This approach is formalized using the Multi-Objective Markov Decision Process (MOMDP) framework, which is specifically designed to address sequential decision-making problems with multiple objectives [22]. The Diagram in Fig. 1 illustrates the fundamental components and highlights their interrelationships in the context of a MOMDP.

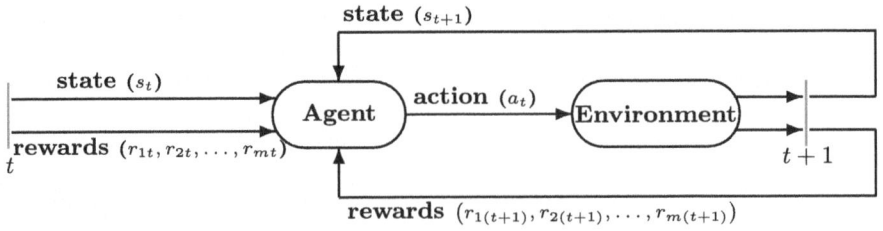

Fig. 1. Diagram of the interaction process between the learning agent and the environment in the MOMDP's context.

At each timestep t, the learning agent observes the current state s_t and selects an action a_t that changes the environment's perception. Following this interaction, the agent receives an m-dimensional reward vector $(r_{1t}, r_{2t}, \ldots, r_{mt})$, where each element corresponds to a specific optimization objective. The process then advances to the subsequent timestep $t + 1$: the agent observes a new state s_{t+1}, executes an action a_{t+1}, and obtains the updated reward vector $(r_{1(t+1)}, r_{2(t+1)}, \ldots, r_{m(t+1)})$. This cycle continues until a predefined stopping criterion is reached.

The MOMDP elements can be characterized as a tuple $M = \langle S, A, R, T, \gamma, H \rangle$:

- S is the set of states such that $s_t \in S$;
- A is the set of actions such that $a_t \in A(s_t)$;
- $R : S \times A \to \mathbb{R}^m$ is a vector reward function defined by a m-dimensional vector where each component corresponds to a distinct objective in a multi-objective setting.
- T is the transition function that reports the dynamics of the change from some specific state, $s_t \in S$, to a subsequent state, $s_{t+1} \in S$, with a response to execution simultaneous action $a_t \in A(s_t)$.
- $\gamma \in [0, 1]$ is the scalar discount rate used to balance current and future rewards;
- H is the horizon that determines the duration of an episode, the upper limit of iterations in an episode is usually established by defining a stopping criterion.

In single-objective RL, a unique optimal value function V^* exists, although several optimal policies π^* may achieve this value. The objective is to learn one of these optimal policies. In contrast, MORL operates in environments with multiple objectives, where different policies can be optimal or efficient concerning individual objectives, reflecting the inherent trade-offs in complex decision-making scenarios [20]. The Pareto dominance relation is employed as an optimality criterion in multi-objective optimization. Given two policies, π_x and π_y, with their respective value functions V^{π_x} and V^{π_y}, we say that π_x strictly dominates π_y, denoted as $\pi_y \prec \pi_x$, if every objective in V^{π_x} is not strictly less than the corresponding objective in V^{π_y}, with at least one objective being strictly higher. On the other hand, if V^{π_x} strictly improves V^{π_y} in one objective, while V^{π_y} strictly improves V^{π_x} in another, the two policies are considered incomparable. A policy π^* is considered Pareto efficient if no other policy strictly dominates it; that is, V^{π^*} either strictly dominates or is incomparable with the value functions of all other policies. The collection of such efficient policies is known as the Pareto front.

3   MORL for Irregular Spatial Cluster Detection

The novel MORL approach for detecting irregular spatial clusters extends the single-objective reinforcement learning methodology [16]. At its core, the method incorporates a specialized MOMDP framework, seamlessly integrated into the learning algorithm. This tailored framework guides the multi-objective process during training, enabling the identification of diverse, efficient policies. Through an iterative experience collection process, these policies yield candidate spatial clusters that are defined without conventional geometric constraints.

In the specialized MOMDP framework, the agent interacts with multiple environments by observing states, performing actions, and receiving a discounted reward vector whose dimensions correspond to two key objectives: maximizing spatial scan statistics and minimizing the dispersion penalty function. Concurrently, the agent learns and maintains a set of efficient policies. Each environment in this set is represented by a construction zone paired with the relevant study map data, providing a structured yet flexible context for learning.

To adapt the problem for the MORL approach, consider a map partitioned into m areas. A submap is defined for each area comprising the k nearest neighboring areas determined by the Euclidean distance between their centroids. This results in m submaps, each containing k areas. Every submap i with $i \in 1, \ldots, m$ is represented by a tuple $M_i = \langle S_i, A, R, T, \gamma, H \rangle$ which groups the core elements of the specialized MOMDP. These elements are defined as follows:

- The set of states S_i is defined by all the areas of the submap i, which means each state $s_t \in S_i$, $t \in \{1, \ldots, k\}$, corresponds to an area of the respective submap;
- The set of actions is given by $A = \{0, 1\}$ with 1 indicating the inclusion of a certain area in the zone and 0 indicating the non-inclusion of that area;
- The reward vector R is defined by the dimensions corresponding to the scan statistic (see (2)) and the dispersion function (see (3)), based on the resulting zone of new perceptions;
- The transition function T reports the dynamics of change of the rate μ_z proportional to the population distribution between the initial state s_t and the $k - 1$ subsequent states $s_{t+1}, s_{t+2}, \ldots, s_{t+k}$ observed by the agent;
- The scalar rate γ is determined in the refinement procedure of the most efficient tuning hyperparameters;
- The horizon H (episode) is associated with the number of states k that define the submap.

Our MORL approach comprises a novel Pareto Q-Learning Scan (PQL-SCAN) algorithm, designed to learn a set of efficient policies considering two conflicting objectives in the context of specialized MOMPD. We implement an adapted version of the Pareto Q-Learning temporal difference algorithm [20], an extension of the Q-Learning algorithm [21], which operates in multi-objective environments. Classical Q-learning enables an agent to learn an optimal policy by continuously interacting with its environment. The agent estimates $\hat{Q}$-values, representing the quality of specific actions in particular states. These estimates are stored in a matrix of $s \times a$ dimensions, where s denotes the number of states within the environment and a refers to the possible actions. Otherwise, Pareto Q-*Learning* accommodates multi-objective environments by computing multiple $\hat{Q}$-values for each objective. These $\hat{Q}$-values are then grouped into a set called the $\hat{Q}_{set}$, which enables the learning of a range of Pareto efficient policies.

3.1 PQL-SCAN Algorithm

The PQL-SCAN algorithm learns and maintains a collection of efficient policies to generate candidate spatial clusters. Initially, a policy set Π is defined to store the efficient policies. For every submap of the study map, the action-value $\hat{Q}_{set}(s, a)$ is initialized as an empty set. At the beginning of each episode, the agent observes the initial state s and selects an action a based on the hypervolume indicator (HVI) derived from the policies in $\hat{Q}_{set}(s, a)$. The chosen action is executed, leading the agent to transition to a new state s' and receive a corresponding reward vector r. Next, the algorithm retrieves the current non-dominated policies $nd_t(s, a)$ for each action in state s'. The average immediate reward $\bar{r}(s, a)$ for each objective is updated using the new reward vector r along with the action count $n(s, a)$. Following this, $\hat{Q}_{set}(s, a)$ is updated according to Eq. 4; at the end of the episodes, the efficient policy set Π is updated. Finally, candidate spatial clusters corresponding to the policies maintained in Π are retrieved.

$$\hat{Q}_{set}(s, a) \leftarrow \bar{r}(s, a) \oplus \gamma[nd_t(s, a)] \tag{4}$$

In PQL-SCAN, the HVI was used as a metric within the action selection strategy to assess the quality of the efficient policies stored in $\hat{Q}_{set}(s, a)$. The hypervolume values guide action selection in a process similar to the ϵ-greedy method. Specifically, for the parameter $\epsilon \in [0, 1]$, an action is chosen uniformly at random with probability ϵ, while with probability $1 - \epsilon$, the action corresponding to the policy set with the highest HVI is selected.

We define a tuning range for hyperparameters (γ, ϵ) in PQL-SCAN based on empirical observations of the highest HVI measure at the end of episodes. For the discount factor γ, we consider values in the interval $[0, 1]$. Starting at an initial value of 0.0001 and increasing in increments of 0.0500, the set for γ is given by: $\{0.0001, 0.0500, 0.1000, \dots, 1.0000\}$. Similarly, for the parameter ϵ, we explore the interval $[0, 0.2]$. Beginning with an initial value of 0.0001 and increasing in steps of 0.0025, the resulting set for ϵ is: $\{0.0001, 0.00025, 0.0050, \dots, 0.2000\}$. The hyperparameter tuning procedure is performed for each tested dataset. In the algorithm, 10 episodes were defined as sufficient for convergence.

4 Experimental Results

The experiments were conducted in an execution environment featuring a 10th Gen Intel® Core™ i9-10900 processor with 10 physical cores (20 threads) operating at 2.80 GHz and equipped with 128 GB of RAM. The system ran on Linux Mint version 21.3 (64-bit). The algorithms were implemented in Java. All codes are available upon request for research and educational purposes.

The experiments were initially conducted using a synthetic dataset designed to evaluate the performance of the algorithms. Next, a real-world dataset map containing information on occurrences of diabetes cases in the population of Minas Gerais, Brazil, was employed. We employed three performance measures for analyzing the synthetic dataset: detection power, accuracy, and the F_1 score.

The detection power is evaluated by the proportion of efficient solutions in multi-objective algorithms that include at least one solution positioned to the right of the significance isoline of p-value $= 0.05$, as determined by the attainment function procedure (see 4.1). The accuracy and F_1 score performance measures were employed to evaluate the quality of the cluster detection algorithms. In the accuracy and F_1 score metrics, $Pop_{(dc)}$ and $\overline{Pop_{(dc)}}$ represent the population within the detected cluster and the population outside the detected cluster, respectively. Similarly, $Pop_{(ac)}$ and $\overline{Pop_{(ac)}}$ denote the population within the artificial cluster and the population outside the artificial cluster, respectively. The accuracy and F_1 score measures are defined as follows:

$$Accuracy = \frac{Pop_{(dc)} \cap Pop_{(ac)} + \overline{Pop_{(dc)}} \cap \overline{Pop_{(ac)}}}{Pop_{(all\ map)}},$$

$$F_1 score = 2 * \frac{precision * sensitivity}{precision + sensitivity},$$

where $Precision = \dfrac{Pop_{(dc)} \cap Pop_{(ac)}}{Pop_{(dc)}}$ and $Sensitivity = \dfrac{Pop_{(dc)} \cap Pop_{(ac)}}{Pop_{(ac)}}$.

The performance of the PQL-SCAN was compared against the classical Scan Elliptic algorithm (ELL-SCAN) introduced by [10]. ELL-SCAN detects candidate clusters by scanning the map with adjustable elliptical windows that overlap the study areas. The windows are parameterized by maximum window size, eccentricity, and rotation angles, which allow the algorithm to refine its search for clusters. The method identifies the most likely cluster by maximizing the scan statistic. In our experiments, the parameter values were the maximum window size, the values for variations in eccentricity $\{1, 1.5, 2, 3, 4\}$, and the values for variations in rotation angle $\{\pi, \pi/4, \pi/6, \pi/9, \pi/12\}$. In this implementation, the set of non-dominated solutions identified from the solutions generated in the algorithm's search process is reported. For a rigorous comparison, both PQL-SCAN and ELL-SCAN are evaluated using only connected cluster solutions.

4.1   Attainment Function

The attainment function [4] is a concept used to evaluate the significance of the solutions produced by the multi-objective algorithms. Given a multi-objective optimization problem, with the pair of functions f_1 and f_2 to be maximized, and $\mathbb{O}$ representing the set of efficient solutions in the objective space from a single execution of the multi-objective algorithm, the set $\mathbb{O}$ is associated with a frontier that divides the objective space into two regions, R_1 and R_0. R_1 is the region of points that are dominated by, or equal to, at least one point in $\mathbb{O}$, whereas R_0 is the region of points that are not dominated by any point in $\mathbb{O}$. A solution x that is dominated by at least one solution in $\mathbb{O}$ is said to be attained by $\mathbb{O}$. Therefore, any solution located in the region R_1 is attained by $\mathbb{O}$. After n runs of the multi-objective algorithm, each producing distinct outcomes, the objective space can be split into $n+1$ types of regions based on the frequency at which these regions are attained. The boundaries of these regions are called attainment surfaces. In practice, by considering n outcome sets $O_1, \ldots, O_n$, approximations of the p-value isolines for every $p = i/(n+1), i = 1, \ldots, n$, can be constructed through the estimated attainment surfaces. For more details, see [4] and [3]. The attainment surfaces are a natural extension of the p-value concept to multi-objective problems, as they preserve the dependence between points within the same Pareto set for all Pareto sets obtained by the Monte Carlo simulation.

4.2   Synthetic Dataset Map with Artificial Clusters

The first dataset consists of a synthetic map composed of 90 regular hexagons. This map represents a total population of 180,000, distributed across the areas using a multinomial distribution. For areas 16, 22, 28, 34, 40, 46, 52, 58, 64, and 70, the population proportions were doubled, aiming to create a scenario where a specific subset of areas would exhibit higher population density. This map established a prevalence of 0.005 for case occurrence within the population, amounting to 900 cases. On this map, eight artificial clusters (labeled A, B, C, D, E, F, G, and H) were projected, as illustrated in Fig. 2.

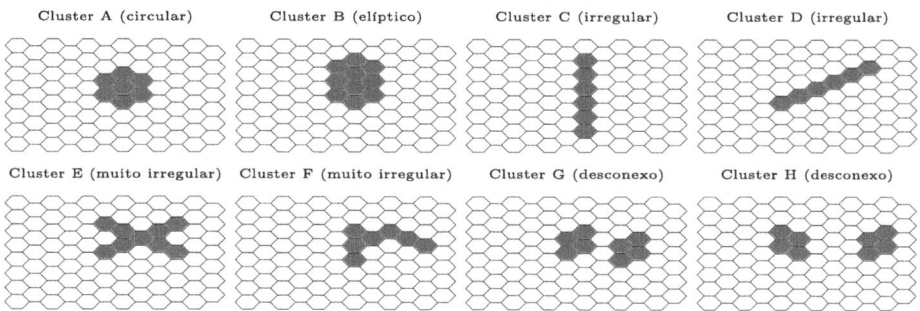

Fig. 2. Artificial clusters projected onto the regular hexagons map.

The clusters were designed with varying shapes to provide a robust and comparative testing for the evaluated algorithms. For each of the eight alternative hypotheses, 5,000 simulations were performed using multi-objective algorithms, resulting in the most efficient set of solutions. These solutions were then compared to the significance level defined by the 0.05 p-value isoline, derived from the attainment function based on 10,000 Monte Carlo simulations under the null hypothesis through a Poisson distribution. The experiments were conducted in zones with a 20% maximum size of the number of map areas. In the hyperparameter tuning, the best settings for PQL-SCAN were $(\gamma, \epsilon) = (0.6500, 0.1275)$.

Table 1 shows a comparative overview of the average and the standard error (s.e.) for the performance measures obtained from simulations under the alternative hypothesis, by the PQL-SCAN and ELL-SCAN algorithms across eight artificial clusters on the synthetic dataset map. The quality measures reflect the averages of the significant solutions in the detected efficient sets. In power, PQL-SCAN was superior in six clusters (B, D-H), while ELL-SCAN showed superiority in cluster C. In accuracy, PQL-SCAN obtained better results in five clusters (B, E-H). At the same time, ELL-SCAN demonstrated an advantage in clusters C and D. Both algorithms yielded comparable performance in cluster A on these metrics. Furthermore, in F_1 Score, PQL-SCAN attained higher values in six clusters (A, B, E-H), with ELL-SCAN performing better in C and D. For CPU runtime, the average results indicate that PQL-SCAN was more efficient, recording 0.061 s, while ELL-SCAN ran in 0.099 s. Overall, these results highlight the effectiveness and applicability of the PQL-SCAN algorithm in detecting irregular spatial clusters.

Table 1. Average and the Standard Error (s.e.) of the Performance Measures for the Algorithms in Artificial Clusters (Best Results in **Bold**).

Cluster	Power (s.e.)		Accuracy (s.e.)		F_1 score (s.e.)	
	PQL-SCAN	ELL-SCAN	PQL-SCAN	ELL-SCAN	PQL-SCAN	ELL-SCAN
A	**0.955 (2.9E-3)**	**0.955 (2.9E-3)**	**0.942 (2E-4)**	**0.942 (3E-4)**	**0.711 (1.4E-3)**	0.710 (1.5E-3)
B	**0.965 (2.6E-3)**	0.960 (2.8E-3)	**0.919 (3E-4)**	0.916 (3E-4)	**0.685 (1.4E-3)**	0.679 (1.5E-3)
C	0.955 (2.9E-3)	**0.969 (2.5E-3)**	0.947 (4E-4)	**0.974 (4E-4)**	0.742 (2.0E-3)	**0.881 (1.7E-3)**
D	**0.908 (4.1E-3)**	0.906 (4.1E-3)	0.944 (3E-4)	**0.953 (3E-4)**	0.605 (1.7E-3)	**0.648 (2.0E-3)**
E	**0.919 (3.9E-3)**	0.890 (4.4E-3)	**0.929 (3E-4)**	0.923 (4E-4)	**0.630 (1.7E-3)**	0.598 (1.9E-3)
F	**0.942 (3.3E-3)**	0.914 (4.0E-3)	**0.940 (3E-4)**	0.928 (3E-4)	**0.684 (1.7E-3)**	0.628 (1.8E-3)
G	**0.911 (4.0E-3)**	0.855 (5.0E-3)	**0.934 (3E-4)**	0.913 (3E-4)	**0.608 (1.7E-3)**	0.500 (1.6E-3)
H	**0.864 (4.8E-3)**	0.842 (5.2E-3)	**0.930 (3E-4)**	0.927 (3E-4)	**0.448 (1.3E-3)**	0.420 (1.2E-3)

4.3   Real-World Disease Dataset Map

The real-world dataset employed examines the occurrences of diabetes in the population of the state of Minas Gerais, Brazil, and was previously used in the study conducted by [17]. The Minas Gerais state comprises 853 municipalities. For this dataset, a target population of 7,033,712 individuals was counted, among which 28,039 confirmed cases of diabetes were recorded. In the experiments, 1,000 runs were performed for each tested algorithm. One run was conducted under the alternative hypothesis, and 999 simulations were performed under the null hypothesis. In the alternative hypothesis, the non-dominated solutions detected by the multi-objective algorithms were evaluated and considered significant according to the significance level defined by the isoline of p-value = 0.05. The best hyperparameters settings for PQL-SCAN were $(\gamma, \epsilon) = (0.8500, 0.0575)$.

Figure 3 displays the Pareto fronts in the objective space, which represent the sets of efficient solutions generated by the PQL-SCAN and ELL-SCAN algorithms on the diabetes dataset. While PQL-SCAN achieved 245 solutions, ELL-SCAN generated only 59. Moreover, the results show that the solution set from PQL-SCAN provides a more comprehensive coverage of the objective space, dominating most of the solutions detected by ELL-SCAN. Thus, for this dataset, the superiority of PQL-SCAN is evident in both quantitative and qualitative terms, showcasing greater diversity and a more extensive exploration of the objective space.

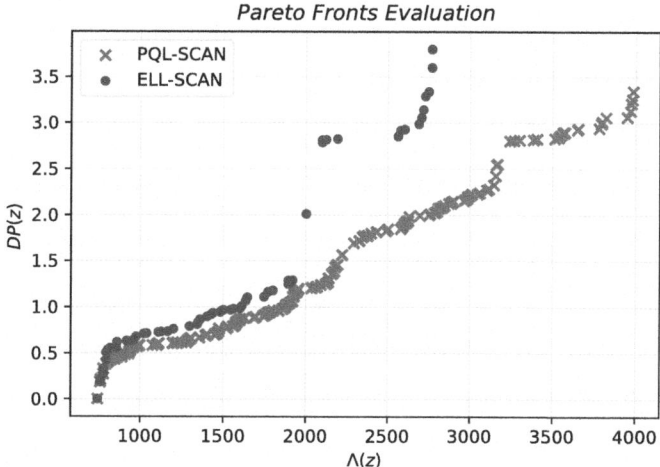

Fig. 3. Pareto Front generated by the PQL-SCAN (×) and ELL-SCAN (•) algorithms on the diabetes dataset from Minas Gerais.

5   Conclusions

We present a novel approach based on the MORL paradigm for detecting and inferring irregular spatial clusters. In our work, we detail the specialized components of a MOMDP framework and introduce the new PQL-SCAN algorithm. The algorithm iteratively learns a set of effective policies by observing states, taking actions that modify the environment's perception, and receiving a numerical reward vector for each environment. Each reward vector dimension corresponds to a conflicting objective: one that aims to maximize the spatial scan statistic and another that seeks to minimize the dispersion penalty function. The resulting set of efficient policies is then used to generate an efficient collection of candidate spatial clusters.

We conducted a comprehensive set of computational experiments using a synthetic dataset with irregularly shaped artificial clusters to evaluate the cluster detection algorithms rigorously. The performance of our PQL-SCAN algorithm was benchmarked against Elliptic Scan, traditionally used for irregular cluster detection, with PQL-SCAN demonstrating superiority in the majority of settings. Furthermore, additional experiments on a real-world dataset validated the practical applicability of our proposed approach in realistic scenarios. In future tasks, we plan to drive continuous improvements in the algorithm, such as evaluating different penalty functions. Additionally, a key aspect to be improved is the development of efficient optimization strategies focused on tuning the algorithm's hyperparameters.

Acknowledgments. The authors would like to thank the Fundação de Amparo a Pesquisa do Estado de Minas Gerais (FAPEMIG, grant APQ-01647-22), Conselho Nacional de Desenvolvimento Científico e Tecnológico (CNPq, grants 307151/2022-0),

Coordenação de Aperfeiçoamento de Pessoal de Nível Superior (CAPES), and Universidade Federal de Ouro Preto (PROPPI/UFOP) for supporting the development of this study.

Disclosure of Interests. The authors have no competing interests to declare that are relevant to the content of this article.

References

1. Abolhassani, A., Prates, M.O., Mahmoodi, S.: Irregular shaped small nodule detection using a robust scan statistic. Stat. Biosci. **15**(1), 141–162 (2023)
2. Bodevan, E.C., Duczmal, L.H., Duarte, A.R., Silva, P.H.L., Moreira, G.J.P.: Multi-objective approach for multiple clusters detection in data points events. Commun. Stat. - Simul. Comput. **51**(3), 1313–1332 (2020)
3. Cançado, A.L., Duarte, A.R., Duczmal, L.H., Ferreira, S.J., Fonseca, C.M., Gontijo, E.C.: Penalized likelihood and multi-objective spatial scans for the detection and inference of irregular clusters. Int. J. Health Geogr. **9**(1), 55 (2010)
4. Fonseca, C.M., Da Fonseca, V.G., Paquete, L.: Exploring the performance of stochastic multiobjective optimisers with the second-order attainment function. In: International Conference on Evolutionary Multi-Criterion Optimization, pp. 250–264. Springer (2005)
5. Fonseca-Rodríguez, O., Gustafsson, P.E., San Sebastián, M., Connolly, A.M.F.: Spatial clustering and contextual factors associated with hospitalisation and deaths due to COVID-19 in Sweden: a geospatial nationwide ecological study. BMJ Global Health **6**(7), e006247 (2021)
6. Hayes, C.F., et al.: A practical guide to multi-objective reinforcement learning and planning. Auton. Agent. Multi-Agent Syst. **36**(1), 1–59 (2022). https://doi.org/10.1007/s10458-022-09552-y
7. Hu, T., Huang, L., Xu, J., Tiwari, R.: Spatial-cluster signal detection in medical devices using likelihood ratio test method. Ther. Innov. Regul. Sci. **55**, 56–64 (2021)
8. Inoue, R., Shiode, S., Shiode, N.: Detection of irregular-shaped clusters on a network by controlling the shape compactness with a penalty function. GeoJournal **88**(4), 3817–3832 (2023)
9. Jiang, C., Liu, L., Qin, X., Zhou, S., Liu, K.: Discovering spatial-temporal indication of crime association (STICA). ISPRS Int. J. Geo Inf. **10**(2), 67 (2021)
10. Kulldorff, M., Huang, L., Pickle, L., Duczmal, L.: An elliptic spatial scan statistic. Stat. Med. **26**, 3929–3943 (2006)
11. Kulldorff, M.: A spatial scan statistic. Commun. Stat. - Theory Methods **26**(6), 1481–1496 (1997)
12. Lee, S., Moon, J., Jung, I.: Optimizing the maximum reported cluster size in the spatial scan statistic for survival data. Int. J. Health Geogr. **20**, 1–14 (2021)
13. Mazyavkina, N., Sviridov, S., Ivanov, S., Burnaev, E.: Reinforcement learning for combinatorial optimization: a survey. Comput. Oper. Res. **134**, 105400 (2021)
14. Moreira, G.J., Paquete, L., Duczmal, L.H., Menotti, D., Takahashi, R.H.: Multi-objective dynamic programming for spatial cluster detection. Environ. Ecol. Stat. **22**, 369–391 (2015)
15. de Oliveira, D.R.X., Moreira, G., Duarte, A.R., Cançado, A., Luz, E.: Spatial cluster analysis using particle swarm optimization and dispersion function. Commun. Stat.-Simul. Comput. **50**(8), 2368–2385 (2021)

16. Oliveira, D.R., Moreira, G.J., Duarte, A.R.: Arbitrarily shaped spatial cluster detection via reinforcement learning algorithms. Environ. Ecol. Stat., 1–23 (2025)
17. Oliveira, F.L., Cançado, A.L., Duczmal, L.H., Duarte, A.R.: Assessing the outline uncertainty of spatial disease clusters. InTech (2012)
18. Smith, T.B., Mao, R., Korotchenko, S., Krohn, M.D.: Partners in criminology: machine learning and network science reveal missed opportunities and inequalities in the study of crime. J. Quant. Criminol. **40**(2), 421–443 (2024)
19. Sutton, R.S., Barto, A.G.: Reinforcement Learning: An Introduction. MIT Ppress (2018)
20. Van Moffaert, K., Nowé, A.: Multi-objective reinforcement learning using sets of pareto dominating policies. J. Mach. Learn. Res. **15**(1), 3483–3512 (2014)
21. Watkins, C.J.C.H.: Learning from delayed rewards. Ph.D. thesis, University of Cambridge, England (1989)
22. Zhang, L., Qi, Z., Shi, Y.: Multi-objective reinforcement learning-concept, approaches and applications. Procedia Comput. Sci. **221**, 526–532 (2023)
23. Zhang, M., et al.: Spatiotemporal patterns and driving force of urbanization and its impact on urban ecology. Remote Sens. **14**(5), 1160 (2022)

Exploring the Early Universe with Deep Learning

Emmanuel de Salis[1]([✉]) [iD], Massimo De Santis[1] [iD], Davide Piras[2] [iD],
Sambit K. Giri[3] [iD], Michele Bianco[4] [iD], Nicolas Cerardi[5] [iD], Philipp Denzel[6] [iD],
Merve Selcuk-Simsek[7] [iD], Kelley M. Hess[8] [iD], M. Carmen Toribio[8] [iD],
Franz Kirsten[8] [iD], and Hatem Ghorbel[1] [iD]

[1] Haute Ecole Arc Ingénierie, University of Applied Sciences and Arts Western
Switzerland (HES-SO), Saint-Imier, Switzerland
emmanuel.desalis@he-arc.ch
[2] Département de Physique Théorique and Centre Universitaire d'Informatique,
Université de Genève, Genève, Switzerland
[3] Nordita, KTH Royal Institute of Technology and Stockholm University, Hannes
Alfvéns väg 12, 106 91 Stockholm, Sweden
[4] Institute for Particle Physics and Astrophysics, ETH Zurich,
Wolfgang-Pauli-Str 27, 8093 Zurich, Switzerland
[5] Laboratoire d'Astrophysique, Ecole Polytechnique Federale de Lausanne EPFL,
Observatoire de Sauverny, Versoix 1290, Switzerland
[6] Centre for Artificial Intelligence, ZHAW Zurich University of Applied Sciences,
Technikumstrasse 71, 8400 Winterthur, Switzerland
[7] Institute for Data Science, FHNW University of Applied Sciences and Arts
Northwestern Switzerland, Bahnhofstrasse 6, 5210 Windisch, Switzerland
[8] Department of Space, Earth and Environment, Onsala Space Observatory,
Chalmers University of Technology, 43992 Onsala, Sweden

Abstract. Hydrogen is the most abundant element in our Universe. The
first generation of stars and galaxies produced photons that ionized hydrogen gas, driving a cosmological event known as the Epoch of Reionization (EoR). The upcoming Square Kilometre Array Observatory (SKAO)
will map the distribution of neutral hydrogen during this era, aiding in
the study of the properties of these first-generation objects. Extracting
astrophysical information will be challenging, as SKAO will produce a
tremendous amount of data where the hydrogen signal will be contaminated with undesired foreground contamination and instrumental systematics. To address this, we develop some of the latest deep learning techniques to extract information from the 2D power spectra of the hydrogen
signal expected from SKAO. We apply a series of neural network models
to these measurements and quantify their ability to predict the history of
cosmic hydrogen reionization, which is connected to the increasing number
and efficiency of early photon sources. We show that the study of the early
Universe benefits from modern deep learning technology. In particular, we
demonstrate that dedicated machine learning algorithms can achieve more
than a $0.95\ R^2$ score on average in recovering the reionization history. This
enables accurate and precise cosmological and astrophysical inference of
structure formation in the early Universe.

© The Author(s), under exclusive license to Springer Nature Switzerland AG 2026
J. Valente de Oliveira et al. (Eds.): EPIA 2025, LNAI 16121, pp. 426–438, 2026.
https://doi.org/10.1007/978-3-032-05176-9_33

Keywords: Machine Learning · Simulation-based inference · CNN · Epoch of Reionization · 21-cm signal · Cosmology & Astrophysics

1 Introduction

The Epoch of Reionization (EoR) marks a pivotal yet poorly understood phase in the early Universe, occurring within the first billion years after the Big Bang— less than 10% of its current estimated age of 13.8 billion years [1]. During this time, ultraviolet photons from the first stars, galaxies, and quasars gradually reionized the cold, neutral hydrogen in the intergalactic medium (IGM), completing a major phase transition in the Universe's thermal and ionization history over approximately 500 million years [9]. A key probe of this process and the presence of these primordial sources is the 21-cm signal, arising from the hyperfine transition in neutral hydrogen (HI), which emits or absorbs radiation at a rest-frame wavelength of 21-cm and frequency of 1.42 GHz [9].

To detect this faint signal, the world's largest radio telescope – Square Kilometre Array Observatory (SKAO)[1] – is under-construction and aims to observe the redshifted 21-cm emission from neutral hydrogen across cosmic timescales ranging from approximately 150 million to a few billion years after the Big Bang [18]. Due to the expansion of the Universe, the original 21-cm wavelength is stretched (redshifted), shifting the signal into lower radio frequencies over time. This effect enables three-dimensional mapping of the neutral hydrogen distribution across different cosmic epochs, a technique known as 21-cm tomography. With its unprecedented sensitivity and resolution, SKAO's low frequency component (SKA-Low) is expected to measure the 21-cm signal from the EoR [10].

Current radio experiments, such as the Low-Frequency Array (LOFAR), already generate terabytes of data in their efforts to detect the 21-cm signal [25]. The SKA will take this even further, producing petabytes of data [19], posing significant challenges for manual analysis and interpretation. Extracting meaningful physical constraints on the early Universe from such large datasets will require automated, scalable approaches. In this work, we explore and compare several machine learning methods for analysing simulated 21-cm signals, focusing on their effectiveness in recovering key physical parameters. These developments are essential for building a robust data analysis pipeline capable of handling the enormous data volumes expected from SKA-Low.

2 Related Work

Machine learning techniques have shown significant potential in extracting the 21-cm signal and inferring parameters of the EoR, owing to their ability to process complex, high-dimensional data.

Convolutional neural network (CNN) architectures are particularly suited to analyse spatial patterns within tomographic maps and spectrograms [12,23],

---

[1] www.skao.int.

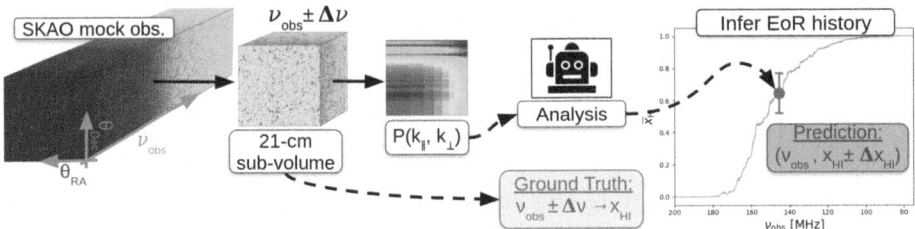

Fig. 1. Schematic representation of our inference pipeline for one of the three frequency ranges, $\nu_{\mathrm{obs}} \pm \Delta\nu$ as explained in Subsect. 3.1.

and have shown effective results in closely related tasks [3,4]. Artificial neural networks (ANN), including multilayer perceptron (MLP)-based models, also showed notable results in similar applications [15], while autoencoders, particularly variational autoencoders (VAEs), have been successfully applied to extract signal parameters with high accuracy, even under challenging conditions [33]. Other techniques to perform robust inference include simulation-based inference (SBI), which has found extensive applications across multiple disciplines, including astrophysics [34], seismology [27], chemistry [6], and more. Recent studies have demonstrated that SBI is a powerful tool for extracting the 21-cm signal [26], particularly in scenarios with intractable or non-Gaussian likelihoods. SBI leverages neural networks to approximate posterior distributions directly from simulations, bypassing the need for explicit likelihood formulations.

3 Methods

3.1 Dataset Generation

We produce a training set of expected data from the SKA-Low to develop machine learning methods. Radio interferometry-based telescopes, such as the SKAO, can reconstruct fluctuations in the differential brightness temperature δT_{b} at a given position on the sky $\mathbf{r}$ and the frequency at which it is observed ν_{obs}, thus $\delta T_{\mathrm{b}}(\mathbf{r}, \nu_{\mathrm{obs}}) \propto x_{\mathrm{HI}}(\mathbf{r}, \nu_{\mathrm{obs}})$ [9]. This three-dimensional data is referred to as tomographic 21-cm signal data, where the values of ν_{obs} corresponds to different cosmic time. This data is sensitive to the spatial and temporal evolution of x_{HI}, quantifying the fraction of neutral hydrogen (HI) in the IGM during the EoR, which depends on the properties of the primordial source of radiation.

We employ the `21cmFAST` code [21] to simulate the 21-cm signal measurement, δT_{b}, between frequencies 200 and 70 MHz. We create a dataset with 15'945 samples by varying the cosmic initial conditions and six astrophysical parameters to obtain different reionization histories. The dataset is split into 12'000 samples for training (75.3%), 2'000 for validation (12.5%) and 1'945 for testing (12.2%). These astrophysical parameters define the efficiency of the formation of luminous sources and the production rate of ionising photons; we treat them as nuisance parameters, namely, they do not constitute the main target of our inference process (see [24] for a detailed description).

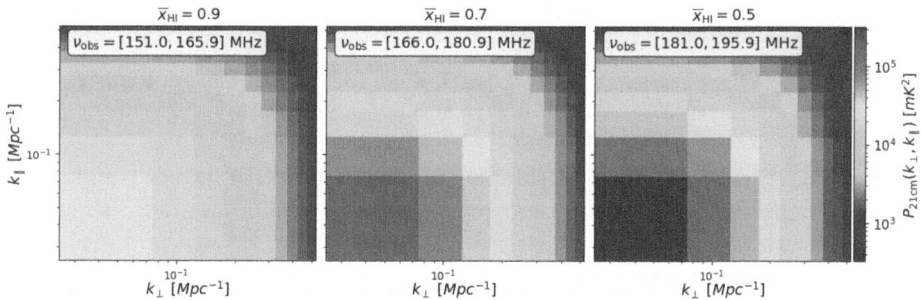

Fig. 2. 2D power spectra of the cosmological 21-cm signal measured at the three different observed frequency ranges for one model in our dataset. On top of each panel, we show the corresponding volume-averaged neutral fraction, $\bar{x}_{\mathrm{HI}}$.

Radio telescopes measure the 21-cm signal in Fourier space, proportional to the fluctuations in δT_{b}, providing observations in terms of spatial frequency components. The primary observable from the initial SKA-Low datasets will be the 2D power spectrum, $P(k_\perp, k_\parallel)$, where $k_\perp$ and $k_\parallel$ represent the transverse and line-of-sight wave numbers, respectively. To simulate this, we divide each realisation into three sub-volumes corresponding to frequency ranges [151, 165.9] MHz, [166, 180.9] MHz, and [181, 195.9] MHz. For each range, we compute $P(k_\perp, k_\parallel)$ using the `tools21cm` package [11]. This quantity retains sensitivity to the underlying IGM ionization state: $P(k_\perp, k_\parallel) \propto \bar{x}_{\mathrm{HI}}^2$ [9], where $\bar{x}_{\mathrm{HI}}$ is the volume-averaged neutral fraction within the observed frequency range.

In Fig. 1, we show an example of the inference pipeline for this paper. From each realisation of δT_{b} 3D SKAO mock observation data, we select three sub-volumes for the above frequency range and calculate the 2D power spectra, $P(k_\perp, k_\parallel)$. This 2D power spectra data is analysed to infer the EoR history ($\bar{x}_{\mathrm{HI}}$). In Fig. 2, we show the computed 2D power spectra of the model at the three observed frequency ranges. These 10×10 images constitute the input of our machine learning approaches, while the corresponding average neutral fraction, $\bar{x}_{\mathrm{HI}}$, at the observed frequency range is the target.

3.2   Evaluation Methodology

We employ two metrics to quantify the regression performed by the different deep learning methods. The first metric is the coefficient of determination, R^2, defined as:

$$R^2(y, \hat{y}) = 1 - \frac{\sum_i (y_i - \hat{y}_i)^2}{\sum_i (y_i - \bar{y})^2} . \tag{1}$$

Here $\hat{y}$ is the prediction and y is the ground truth, while $\bar{y} = \frac{1}{N} \sum_i y_i$ is the average over the test dataset at a given frequency range. The second metric is the root-mean-square error, $RMSE$, defined as:

$$RMSE(y, \hat{y}) = \sqrt{\frac{1}{N} \sum_i (y_i - \hat{y}_i)^2} . \tag{2}$$

In our case, N is the number of samples for the test set. In Tables 1 and 2, we compare the score on the test set for different deep learning methods. To ensure a fair comparison, all models presented in this paper are trained and evaluated on the same dataset, see Subsect. 3.1.

3.3   Deep Learning Models

In this section, we present the models implemented to solve this challenge. We implemented and evaluated a broad selection of promising models highlighted by the literature and models that yielded high-performing results for similar tasks.

Generative Flow Network. The GLOW (Generative Flow) architecture [16] builds upon one of the most widely employed architectures [17], i.e., coupling flows. Each layer comprises three invertible transformations: an activation normalization (Act-Norm), a 1×1 invertible convolution, and an affine coupling operation.

Normalizing Flow (NF) networks learn a mapping between a complex data distribution $\hat{p}_Y$ and a simple base distribution p_Z for the target and random variables, $\mathbf{Y}, \mathbf{Z} \in \mathbb{R}^D$, respectively. A bijection function defines the mapping, $f : \mathbb{R}^D \to \mathbb{R}^D$, between the target random variable $\mathbf{Y} = f^{-1}(\mathbf{Z})$ and the random distribution. The mapping is composed of N invertible transformations $f^{-1}(\mathbf{z}) = f_N^{-1} \circ f_{N-1}^{-1} \circ \cdots \circ f_1^{-1}(\mathbf{z})$ referred as the coupling flow. We then consider a disjoint partition that splits the input in half $x^A, x^B \in \mathbb{R}^{D/2}$. The first part is processed by the coupling flow, $y^A = f^{-1}(x^A)$ while x^B is processed by the 1×1 invertible convolution, Θ, $y^B = f^{-1}(\Theta(x^B))$. The result is then concatenated and processed by the next layer. This approach gradually introduces dimension in the flow generative process, reducing computational cost while capturing the multi-scale structure of the high-dimensional distribution [7].

The network is optimized by training and learning the parameters, $W \in \mathbb{R}^{D \times D}$, of the transformations f such that the total likelihood of the observed data is maximized.

SE-CNN. The SE-CNN proposed architecture is a convolutional neural network augmented with Squeeze-and-Excitation (SE) blocks [14]. These blocks allow the network to adaptively recalibrate channel-wise feature responses, helping the model to emphasize informative features and suppress less useful ones. After each convolutional layer, an SE block is inserted to dynamically modulate feature importance across channels.

This mechanism enhances the network's representational capacity by guiding attention toward the most relevant activations. In their study on hyperspectral image classification, [2] showed that such channel-wise attention mechanisms improve classification performance on hyperspectral data, where channel relevance varies across samples. In our case, this selective emphasis may reduce overfitting and improve generalization.

Model Summary:

- Input: $10 \times 10 \times 1$ grayscale image
- Two Conv2D layers, each followed by:
  - Batch normalization
  - ReLU activation
  - Max pooling
  - Squeeze-and-Excitation block
- Fully connected layers (2) with dropout
- Final output: scalar regression head.

SE-CNN Ensemble-10. The SE-CNN Ensemble-10 is composed of ten independently trained instances of the SE-CNN architecture described in Subsect. 3.3. Each model shares the same structure but is initialized with a different random seed, encouraging diversity among the learned representations.

At inference time, the ensemble's predictions are obtained by averaging the outputs from all ten models. This approach aims to reduce model variance and increase prediction stability, leveraging the complementary strengths of individual learners. Prior work has shown that deep ensembles offer reliable uncertainty estimation and improved generalization in regression settings [20].

Model Summary:

- Architecture: 10 independent SE-CNN models (see Subsect. 3.3)
- Training: Each model trained with a different random seed
- Inference: Prediction obtained by averaging outputs from all models

MLP-Mixer. The MLP-Mixer is a neural network architecture that entirely replaces convolution and attention mechanisms with multilayer perceptrons (MLPs), separately applied for spatial (token) and channel-wise mixing [31]. It processes the input as a sequence of tokens and performs global mixing through stacked MLPs.

Our implementation receives a 10×10 image, reshaped into a sequence of 100 tokens. Each token is projected into a higher-dimensional space before being processed by a series of Mixer blocks. Each block consists of two stages: a token-mixing MLP to model spatial relationships, and a channel-mixing MLP to capture cross-feature interactions. These operations are interleaved with residual connections, GELU activations [13], and layer normalization. After the mixer

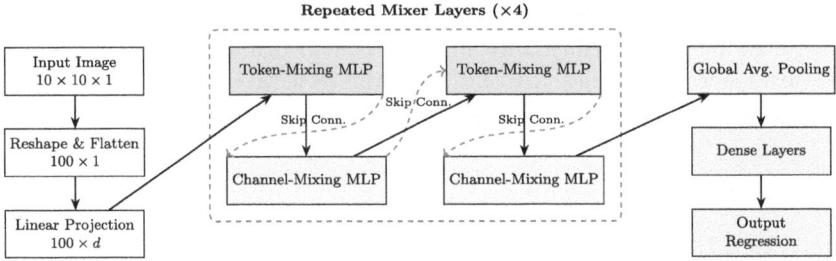

Fig. 3. MLP-Mixer architecture adapted for 2D input, see Subsect. 3.3. The model processes flattened image patches through repeated Mixer layers, each combining token-mixing and channel-mixing MLPs with skip connections. The final output is obtained via global average pooling and dense layers.

layers, the output is aggregated using global average pooling and passed through fully connected layers for scalar regression.

The architecture's simplicity, lack of convolutions or attention, and competitive performance highlight the potential of pure MLP designs even for small-scale, structured scientific data. A schematic representation is provided in Fig. 3, illustrating the flow from token reshaping to regression output.

Residual connections, layer normalization, and GELU [13] activations are used throughout. After the mixer layers, the output is globally averaged, passed through two fully connected layers with dropout, and finally mapped to a scalar output for regression.

MiniViT. MiniViT is a compact Vision Transformer (ViT) architecture tailored to the small input size of our cosmological data maps (10×10 pixels). Our proposed architecture adapts the ViT framework [8] by simplifying the transformer depth and tokenization strategy to suit low-resolution inputs and reduce computational complexity.

The input image is first reshaped into a sequence of 100 tokens (one per pixel), and each token is linearly projected into a higher-dimensional embedding space. A learnable positional encoding is added to each token to retain spatial information. The sequence is then passed through several transformer encoder blocks, each consisting of a multi-head self-attention mechanism followed by a feed-forward MLP, with GELU activations [13], residual connections, and layer normalization.

This lightweight ViT design preserves key transformer properties such as global receptive fields and dynamic attention while remaining computationally feasible for small-scale data. Prior work has shown that such compact ViT variants can offer favorable efficiency-performance tradeoffs even when the input resolution is low [28].

Model Summary:

– Input: $10 \times 10 \times 1$ grayscale image
– Reshape to 100 tokens and linearly project to hidden dimension
– Learnable positional encodings added to each token
– Transformer encoder stack:
  • Multi-head self-attention layer with dropout
  • Feed-forward MLP with GELU activations
  • Residual connections and layer normalization throughout
– Global average pooling
– Dense layers for regression

Frequency-Aware CNN. We implemented a custom convolutional neural network designed to explicitly condition on the observational frequency band. This approach allows the model to leverage auxiliary frequency information to adapt its predictions to different spectral regimes, which may exhibit varying signal characteristics.

Conditioning is performed by encoding the input frequency as a categorical variable. The scalar frequency index is one-hot encoded into a $1 \times 1 \times 3$ tensor, then upsampled to the spatial resolution of the input image (10×10). The result is concatenated along the channel axis with the $10 \times 10 \times 1$ input image, forming a $10 \times 10 \times 4$ tensor. This allows the network to process both spatial and contextual information jointly from the first convolutional layer.

This technique has been previously used in other architectures such as conditional GANs [22], where auxiliary information is injected by expanding low-dimensional vectors to match the input dimensionality. In our setting, it provides a simple yet powerful mechanism for frequency-aware learning, enabling the model to adapt to frequency-specific features without requiring separate networks for each case.

Model Summary:

– Inputs:
  • $10 \times 10 \times 1$ image
  • Scalar frequency category (as integer index)
– Frequency conditioning:
  • One-hot encoding and reshape to $1 \times 1 \times 3$
  • Upsample to $10 \times 10 \times 3$ and concatenate $\rightarrow 10 \times 10 \times 4$
– Convolutional backbone:
  • Two Conv2D layers with ReLU activation
  • Batch normalization and max pooling
– Fully connected layers with dropout
– Final output: scalar regression head

Simulation-Based Inference. The physical processes underlying the EoR are inherently complex, and approximations like the Gaussian likelihood typically assumed in Bayesian analyses could significantly bias the final inference. SBI recently emerged as a principled framework to actually learn the likelihood (or analogous quantities following Bayes' theorem) from a set of fiducial simulations [5], as those described in Sect. 3.1. We therefore develop an SBI pipeline to learn the posterior distribution $p(\theta|\mathbf{d})$ from our set of simulations; in this case, the SBI task is usually dubbed neural posterior estimation (NPE). We employ the publicly available sbi package [30], which provides the infrastructure required to train a NF to learn the posterior distribution and apply it using the same data splits as in the previous sections. We consider two distinct SBI approaches: the *marginal* prediction of each individual $\bar{x}_{\mathrm{HI}}$ (at different frequencies) together with the astrophysical parameters; and the *joint* prediction of $\bar{x}_{\mathrm{HI}}$ at different frequencies but from the same simulation, ignoring the nuisance astrophysical parameters. In the latter case, the input of the NF consists of the stacked power spectra for each frequency. In principle, this provides more information to disentangle the effect of the simulation parameters from the EoR history.

4   Results and Discussion

Table 1 shows the overall performance of each implemented model on the full test dataset, while Table 2 shows the measured metric for three observed frequency ranges, see Subsect. 3.1.

Table 1. Performance comparison of different models on the test dataset.

Model	R^2 [%] ↑	RMSE ↓
GLOW	98.09	3.72×10^{-2}
SBI (marginal)	88.04	9.31×10^{-2}
SBI (joint)	97.44	4.23×10^{-2}
SE-CNN	98.06	3.75×10^{-2}
SE-CNN Ens.-10	**98.61**	$\mathbf{3.18 \times 10^{-2}}$
MLP-Mixer	98.58	3.21×10^{-2}
MiniViT	95.55	5.67×10^{-2}
Freq.-Aware CNN	98.43	3.37×10^{-2}

Table 2. Summary of the metrics on the test dataset for the different methods, split by frequency range.

Model	[151, 166] MHz R^2 [%] ↑	RMSE ↓	[166, 181] MHz R^2 [%] ↑	RMSE ↓	[181, 196] MHz R^2 [%] ↑	RMSE ↓
GLOW	95.76	3.87×10^{-2}	97.75	3.65×10^{-2}	98.41	3.62×10^{-2}
SBI (marginal)	88.08	6.50×10^{-2}	78.03	11.42×10^{-2}	89.40	9.37×10^{-2}
SBI (joint)	94.50	4.17×10^{-2}	96.53	4.40×10^{-2}	97.93	4.10×10^{-2}
SE-CNN	97.69	2.84×10^{-2}	97.84	3.57×10^{-2}	97.98	4.08×10^{-2}
SE-CNN Ens.-10	97.96	2.68×10^{-2}	98.10	3.36×10^{-2}	**98.47**	$\mathbf{3.56 \times 10^{-2}}$
MLP-Mixer	**98.41**	$\mathbf{2.37 \times 10^{-2}}$	**98.30**	$\mathbf{3.17 \times 10^{-2}}$	98.25	3.80×10^{-2}
MiniViT	92.94	4.97×10^{-2}	94.37	5.77×10^{-2}	94.31	6.82×10^{-2}
Freq.-Aware CNN	98.11	2.55×10^{-2}	97.82	3.59×10^{-2}	97.98	4.07×10^{-2}

Our benchmark study across multiple deep learning architectures reveals consistently high performance in predicting the neutral hydrogen fraction from 2D 21-cm power spectra. Among the models, the SE-CNN Ensemble-10 achieves the highest overall performance on the test set, benefiting from the variance reduction and robustness typically provided by deep ensembles. However, when evaluating performance across individual frequency ranges, the MLP-Mixer slightly outperforms the ensemble in two out of three bands and shows remarkably stable results throughout. Despite being the second-best model in terms of global metrics ($R^2 = 98.58\%$), its consistency across observational conditions highlights its strong generalization capabilities. This divergence between aggregate and group-wise results is reminiscent of Simpson's paradox [29], where trends observed in subgroups can be masked when data is pooled. Together, these results suggest that the MLP-Mixer is an exceptionally reliable architecture under varying data regimes and may benefit further from ensemble strategies.

Notably, the Frequency-Aware CNN, a custom model explicitly conditioned on the frequency band via one-hot encoded inputs, performs nearly on par with ensemble and attention-based models. This shows that integrating frequency context can be just as effective as channel attention mechanisms like SE blocks.

By contrast, the MiniViT architecture underperforms, with R^2 scores consistently below 96%. During training, this model exhibited slow convergence and high variance, likely reflecting the known data inefficiency of transformer-based models, which generally require large-scale datasets and extensive pretraining to reach optimal performance [8,32]. This underscores a key limitation of applying ViT-style models directly on small cosmological datasets without tailored adaptations.

The GLOW architecture shows an increasing accuracy for increasing frequency, starting from the low frequency range at $R^2 \approx 95\%$ and $RMSE \simeq 3.8 \times 10^{-2}$ up/down to $R^2 \approx 98\%$ and $RMSE \simeq 3.6 \times 10^{-2}$. This trend follows the signal evolution in the input data (the 2D power spectra) as shown in Fig. 2, indicating that the network is sensitive to the fluctuations of the 21-cm signal. If not accounted for, we expect instrumental noise to decrease the accuracy of the network, as systematics will increase the signal-to-noise ratio and break the signal evolution.

Regarding SBI, the joint model outperforms the marginal approach. This is the consequence of more information being provided to the network and demonstrates the importance of including all frequencies together to break degeneracies between $\bar{x}_{HI}$ and the astrophysical parameters of the simulations. It is noteworthy that the joint model performs nearly on par with several CNN-based architectures. In contrast, the SBI model does not take advantage of the 2D nature of the data, since the input is flattened.

5   Conclusion

In this paper, we implemented a broad selection of various Deep Learning models in the hope of progressing the 21-cm signal extraction, a complex task that traditional approaches struggle with. Our models were tested on a dataset we generated according to the SKA specifications. Several models performed quite well, especially the ensemble CNN method and MLP-Mixer, with a maximum R^2 score of 98.61%. Our approaches could be used and tested on real data when the SKAO will be operational in the coming years.

In the meantime, other models such as Kolmogorov-Arnold Networks (KANs) showed promising results recently and could be an interesting addition to this problem. Lastly, our approach could be challenged with the introduction of instrumental noise and real contamination to fully validate the models' usefulness in an observational context.

Acknowledgments. The authors acknowledge access to Piz Daint at the Swiss National Supercomputing Centre, Switzerland, under the SKA share with the project ID sk014. The authors acknowledge support from the Sweden SKA Regional Center (sweSRC) node operated by Onsala Space Observatory in collaboration with Chalmers e-Commons. The Onsala Space Observatory national research infrastructure is funded through Swedish Research Council grant No 2019-00208. The authors acknowledge funding from the Spark grant CRSK-2_228671 from the Swiss National Science Foundation.

Disclosure of Interests. The authors have no competing interests to declare that are relevant to the content of this article.

References

1. Aghanim, N., et al.: Planck 2018 results. A&A **641**, A6 (2020)
2. Asker, M.E., Güngür, M.: A hybrid approach consisting of 3D depthwise separable convolution and depthwise squeeze-and-excitation network for hyperspectral image classification. Earth Sci. Inf. (2024). https://doi.org/10.1007/s12145-024-01469-2

3. Bianco, M., Giri, S.K., Iliev, I.T., Mellema, G.: Deep learning approach for identification of H ii regions during reionization in 21-cm observations. MNRAS **505**(3), 3982–3997 (2021). https://doi.org/10.1093/mnras/stab1518

4. Bianco, M., et al.: Deep learning approach for identification of H II regions during reionization in 21-cm observations - II. Foreground contamination. MNRAS **528**(3), 5212–5230 (2024). https://doi.org/10.1093/mnras/stae257

5. Cranmer, K., Brehmer, J., Louppe, G.: The frontier of simulation-based inference. Proc. Natl. Acad. Sci. **117**(48), 30055–30062 (2020)

6. Dingeldein, L., Cossio, P., Covino, R.: Simulation-based inference of single-molecule experiments. arXiv e-prints: arXiv:2410.15896 (2024)

7. Dinh, L., Sohl-Dickstein, J., Bengio, S.: Density estimation using real NVP (2017). https://arxiv.org/abs/1605.08803

8. Dosovitskiy, A., et al.: An image is worth 16x16 words: transformers for image recognition at scale (2020). https://arxiv.org/abs/2010.11929

9. Furlanetto, S.R., Oh, S.P., Briggs, F.H.: Cosmology at low frequencies: the 21 cm transition and the high-redshift Universe. Phys. Rep. **433**, 181–301 (2006). https://doi.org/10.1016/j.physrep.2006.08.002

10. Giri, S.K., Mellema, G., Ghara, R.: Optimal identification of H II regions during reionization in 21-cm observations. MNRAS **479**(4), 5596–5611 (2018). https://doi.org/10.1093/mnras/sty1786, https://academic.oup.com/mnras/article/479/4/5596/5050068

11. Giri, S.K., Mellema, G., Jensen, H.: Tools21cm: A python package to analyse the large-scale 21-cm signal from the epoch of reionization and cosmic dawn. J. Open Source Softw. **5**(52), 2363 (2020). https://doi.org/10.21105/joss.02363

12. Hassan, S., Liu, A., Kohn, S., La Plante, P.: Identifying reionization sources from 21 cm maps using convolutional neural networks. Mon. Not. R. Astron. Soc. **483**(2), 2524–2537 (2019)

13. Hendrycks, D., Gimpel, K.: Gaussian Error Linear Units (GELUS). arXiv (Cornell University) (2016). https://doi.org/10.48550/arxiv.1606.08415

14. Hu, J., Shen, L., Sun, G.: Squeeze-and-excitation networks. In: 2018 IEEE/CVF Conference on Computer Vision and Pattern Recognition, pp. 7132–7141 (2018). https://doi.org/10.1109/CVPR.2018.00745

15. Jennings, W., Watkinson, C., Abdalla, F.: Analysing the epoch of reionization with three-point correlation functions and machine learning techniques. Mon. Not. R. Astron. Soc. **498**(3), 4518–4532 (2020)

16. Kingma, D.P., Dhariwal, P.: Glow: generative flow with invertible 1x1 convolutions (2018). https://arxiv.org/abs/1807.03039

17. Kobyzev, I., Prince, S.J., Brubaker, M.A.: Normalizing flows: an introduction and review of current methods. IEEE Trans. Pattern Anal. Mach. Intell. **43**(11), 3964–3979 (2021)

18. Koopmans, L.V.E., et al.: The cosmic dawn and epoch of reionization with the square Kilometre array. PoS **AASKA14**, 001 (2015). https://doi.org/10.22323/1.215.0001

19. Lahav, O.: Deep machine learning in cosmology: evolution or revolution? arXiv preprint: arXiv:2302.04324 (2023)

20. Lakshminarayanan, B., Pritzel, A., Blundell, C.: Simple and scalable predictive uncertainty estimation using deep ensembles (2016). https://arxiv.org/abs/1612.01474

21. Mesinger, A., Furlanetto, S., Cen, R.: 21cmFAST: a fast, seminumerical simulation of the high-redshift 21-cm signal. MNRAS **411**(2), 955–972 (2011). https://doi.org/10.1111/j.1365-2966.2010.17731.x

22. Mirza, M., Osindero, S.: Conditional generative adversarial Nets (2014). https://arxiv.org/abs/1411.1784

23. Murakami, K., Kadota, K., Nishizawa, A.J., Nagamine, K., Shimizu, I.: Differentiating warm dark matter models through 21-cm line intensity mapping: a convolutional neural network approach. Phys. Rev. D **110**(2), 023526 (2024)

24. Park, J., Mesinger, A., Greig, B., Gillet, N.: Inferring the astrophysics of reionization and cosmic dawn from galaxy luminosity functions and the 21-cm signal. MNRAS **484**(1), 933–949 (2019). https://doi.org/10.1093/mnras/stz032, https://academic.oup.com/mnras/article/484/1/933/5281299

25. Patil, A.H., et al.: Upper limits on the 21 cm epoch of reionization power spectrum from one night with LOFAR. Astrophys. J. **838**(1), 65 (2017). https://doi.org/10.3847/1538-4357/aa63e7

26. Prelogović, D., Mesinger, A.: Exploring the likelihood of the 21-cm power spectrum with simulation-based inference. Mon. Not. R. Astron. Soc. **524**(3), 4239–4255 (2023)

27. Saoulis, A.A., Piras, D., Spurio Mancini, A., Joachimi, B., Ferreira, A.M.G.: Full-waveform earthquake source inversion using simulation-based inference. Geophys. J. Int. **241**(3), 1741–1762 (2025). https://doi.org/10.1093/gji/ggaf112

28. Si, H., Wan, Y., Do, M., Vasisht, D., Zhao, H., Hamann, H.F.: Towards scalable foundation model for multi-modal and hyperspectral geospatial data (2025). https://arxiv.org/abs/2503.12843

29. Simpson, E.H.: The interpretation of interaction in contingency tables. J. Roy. Stat. Soc.: Ser. B (Methodol.) **13**(2), 238–241 (1951)

30. Tejero-Cantero, A., et al.: SBI – a toolkit for simulation-based inference (2020). https://arxiv.org/abs/2007.09114

31. Tolstikhin, I., et al.: MLP-Mixer: an all-MLP architecture for vision (2021). https://arxiv.org/abs/2105.01601

32. Touvron, H., Cord, M., Douze, M., Massa, F., Sablayrolles, A., Jégou, H.: Training data-efficient image transformers & distillation through attention (2021). https://arxiv.org/abs/2012.12877

33. Tripathi, A., Datta, A., Choudhury, M., Majumdar, S.: Extracting the global 21-cm signal from cosmic dawn and epoch of reionization in the presence of foreground and ionosphere. Mon. Not. R. Astron. Soc. **528**(2), 1945–1964 (2024)

34. von Wietersheim-Kramsta, M., et al.: KiDS-SBI: simulation-based inference analysis of kids-1000 cosmic shear. Astron. Astrophys. **694**, A223 (2025)

Improved Complex-Valued Kolmogorov–Arnold Networks with Theoretical Support

Rui Che$^{(\boxtimes)}$ ⓘ, Ludvig af Klinteberg ⓘ, and Masood Aryapoor ⓘ

Division of Mathematics and Physics, Mälardalen University, Västerås, Sweden
{rui.che,ludvig.af.klinteberg,masood.aryapoor}@mdu.se

Abstract. In the field of artificial neural networks, the Kolmogorov–Arnold Network (KAN), which is inspired by the Kolmogorov–Arnold representation Theorem (KAT), has demonstrated outstanding performance in function fitting. Complex-Valued Kolmogorov–Arnold Network (CVKAN) transfers KAN into the complex domain, providing superior capabilities in complex-valued function fitting. In this paper, we formulate a complex-valued KAT that provides theoretical support for this transformation. Also, given the high suitability of modulus-based activation functions in complex-valued Neural Networks, we propose a ModELU-based CVKAN, which replaces the $\mathbb{C}$SiLU residual function in CVKAN with the ModELU function. Experiments demonstrate that our method outperforms CVKAN in function fitting in terms of accuracy and stability. Furthermore, we adopt RBFs with learnable shape parameters in ModELU-based CVKAN, replacing the previous fixed ones. This replacement enhances the model's performance in function fitting.

Keywords: Kolmogorov–Arnold Networks · Complex-Valued Neural Networks · Radial Basis Functions · Deep Learning

1 Introduction

The Kolmogorov–Arnold representation Theorem (KAT) [10] states that every multivariate continuous function can be represented as a composition of continuous single-variable functions. Inspired by this theorem, Liu et al. [13] proposed the Kolmogorov–Arnold Network (KAN) by adopting learnable single-variable activation functions on edges. KAN approximates multivariate functions by learning these activation functions, which are parameterized using B-splines augmented with a Sigmoid Linear Unit (SiLU) residual function.

The Complex-Valued Kolmogorov–Arnold Network (CVKAN) [24], which integrates KAN with Complex-Valued Neural Networks (CVNNs) [2], aims to deal with complex-valued function fitting tasks. By considering FastKAN [12], which replaces B-splines in KAN with Radial Basis Functions (RBFs) to accelerate training, CVKAN employs complex-valued RBFs to transfer KAN into

© The Author(s), under exclusive license to Springer Nature Switzerland AG 2026
J. Valente de Oliveira et al. (Eds.): EPIA 2025, LNAI 16121, pp. 439–451, 2026.
https://doi.org/10.1007/978-3-032-05176-9_34

the complex domain. For the residual function SiLU, a complex-valued variant ℂSiLU is also proposed [24] for CVKAN. Experiments in [24] show that CVKAN exhibits better performance compared to KAN in complex-valued function fitting.

Although CVKAN has shown promise in achieving more accurate complex-valued representations, it does not demonstrate whether KAT, the theoretical foundation of KAN, can work in the complex domain. Moreover, the split-type residual function ℂSiLU will pose significant challenges. The reason is that ℂSiLU deals with the real part and the imaginary part of the complex-valued input separately using the real-valued SiLU [24]. Such a design ignores the internal connection between the two parts, which is vital to modeling complex-valued behavior. Therefore, it is necessary to explore alternative complex-type residual functions that can preserve and utilize this connection. In addition, the shape parameter of the RBFs plays a crucial role in their performance [16]. Although CVKAN employs RBFs for function fitting, it adopts a fixed RBF shape parameter without further discussion. This may lead to suboptimal results.

To address these problems, we formulate a complex-valued version of KAT to provide theoretical support for CVKAN. We also propose a ModELU-based CVKAN that adopts ModELU [7] as the residual function. Unlike ℂSiLU, ModELU preserves the internal connection of complex-valued inputs by preserving their phases and only modulating the amplitudes [7]. This characteristic enables the function to perform well in the complex domain and CVNNs. Additionally, we make the RBF shape parameters learnable rather than fixed in our model, to improve its adaptability. In summary, our contributions are as follows:

- We formulate the complex-valued KAT to demonstrate the applicability of KAT in the complex domain. This provides theoretical support for CVKAN.
- We propose a ModELU-based CVKAN by replacing ℂSiLU in CVKAN with ModELU. Compared with CVKAN, our model not only achieves higher accuracy in function fitting, but also improves stability.
- We introduce learnable RBF shape parameters into ModELU-based CVKAN. By assigning a learnable RBF shape parameter to each edge in the network, the model achieves better performance compared to ModELU-based CVKAN and CVKAN with fixed RBF shape parameters.

The remainder of this paper is organized as follows. Section 2 provides a review of KAT, KAN and CVKAN. Section 3 formulates the complex-valued KAT and provides a proof. Section 4 presents a description of the proposed ModELU-based CVKAN and introduces the learnable RBF shape parameters. Section 5 presents the experiments and analysis. Section 6 provides a brief conclusion.

2   Background

2.1   Kolmogorov–Arnold Representation Theorem

The fundamental principle of the Kolmogorov–Arnold representation Theorem (KAT) [10,18] is that a multivariate continuous function $f : [0,1]^n \to \mathbb{R}$ admits a representation as a combination of single-variable functions and sums. More specifically, given a function $f(x_1, \cdots, x_n)$, it can be expressed as:

$$f(x_1, \cdots, x_n) = \sum_{q=1}^{2n+1} \Phi_q \left(\sum_{p=1}^{n} \phi_{q,p}(x_p) \right), \tag{1}$$

where $p = 1, \cdots, n$ and $q = 1, \cdots, 2n + 1$. The function $\phi_{q,p} : [0,1] \to \mathbb{R}$ refers to an inner function, and $\Phi_q : \mathbb{R} \to \mathbb{R}$ refers to an outer function.

Further research can be divided into improving the representation [14,20] and deepening the proof [3,10,22]. In addition, a variety of works have been done to discover the connection between KAT and neural networks [8,17,21].

2.2   Kolmogorov–Arnold Networks

Rooted in the KAT, the Kolmogorov–Arnold Network (KAN) proposed by Liu et al. [13] differentiates itself from traditional neural networks by employing learnable activation functions on edges instead of fixed ones on nodes. KAN leverages the KAT by considering the outer and inner functions as these learnable activation functions. Therefore, (1) was transferred to a three-layer neural network. The inner functions represent the activation functions on the edges that connect the input layer and the hidden layer, while the outer functions represent the activation functions on the edges that connect the hidden layer and the output layer. The paper also extended this shallow structure to a deeper network by defining a KAN layer represented by a matrix $\Phi = \{\phi_{q,p}\}$, where $\quad p = 1, \ldots, n_{\text{in}}$ and $q = 1, \ldots, n_{\text{out}}$. Thus, in the notation of [13], the architecture of a KAN with L layers takes the form

$$\text{KAN}(\mathbf{x}) = (\Phi_{L-1} \circ \Phi_{L-2} \circ \cdots \circ \Phi_1 \circ \Phi_0)\,\mathbf{x}. \tag{2}$$

To learn these activation functions, they are parametrized using a spline function coupled with a residual function, with their weights w_b and w_s separately,

$$\phi(x) = w_s \text{spline}(x) + w_b b(x), \tag{3}$$

where the spline function is defined as a linear combination of B-splines [1],

$$\text{spline}(x) = \sum_i c_i B_i(x), \tag{4}$$

and the residual function is represented by the SiLU function,

$$b(x) = \text{SiLU}(x) = x/(1 + e^{-x}). \tag{5}$$

2.3   Complex-Valued Kolmogorov–Arnold Network

Radial Basis Functions and FastKAN. To speed up the training of KAN, Li proposed the FastKAN [12], which replaces the spline function in (3) with Radial Basis Functions (RBFs),

$$\phi(x) = w_s \text{RBF}(x) + w_b b(x). \tag{6}$$

RBFs approximate a function using a weighted sum of radially symmetric functions centered at different points in the input domain [4],

$$\text{RBF}(x) = \sum_{i=1}^{N} w_i \varphi(|x - c_i|), \tag{7}$$

where w_i is the adjustable weight, $|x - c_i|$ denotes the distance between the input x and a center c_i, and N refers to the number of centers. The function φ represents the radial basis function which is chosen as Gaussian type [12,25],

$$\varphi(r) = \exp(-r^2/\sigma^2), \tag{8}$$

where σ is the shape parameter [16] controlling the width of the function. Since they are radially symmetric, RBFs are trivial to implement in higher dimensions. This makes them a good choice for complex approximation.

Complex-Valued Kolmogorov–Arnold Network (CVKAN). The Complex-Valued Kolmogorov–Arnold Network (CVKAN) was proposed in [24] based on KAN and FastKAN, while also incorporating the concepts of CVNNs [7, 11]. In CVKAN, the residual function SiLU of (5) was transformed to a complex-valued equivalent type $\mathbb{C}$SiLU which can be applied in the complex domain,

$$b_{\mathbb{C}}(z) = \mathbb{C}\text{SiLU}(z) = \text{SiLU}(\text{Re}(z)) + i\text{SiLU}(\text{Im}(z)), \tag{9}$$

where $\text{Re}(z)$ and $\text{Im}(z)$ represent the real part and imaginary part of z separately. Similarly, the RBF(x) in (6) and (7) was also transformed to the complex-valued type [5,19], making it applicable for complex-valued input,

$$\text{RBF}_{\mathbb{C}}(z) = \sum_{i=1}^{N} w_i \varphi(|z - c_i|) \in \mathbb{C}, \tag{10}$$

where $c_i \in \mathbb{C}$ denotes the center, $\varphi(|z - c_i|) \in \mathbb{R}$ represents the Gaussian radial basis function and $w_i \in \mathbb{C}$ refers to its weight. Thus, in CVKAN, the representation of ϕ in (6) is given as follows, where $\beta \in \mathbb{C}$ is a bias of $b_{\mathbb{C}}(z)$

$$\phi(z) = w_s \text{RBF}_{\mathbb{C}}(z) + w_b b_{\mathbb{C}}(z) + \beta. \tag{11}$$

3   Complex-Valued Kolmogorov–Arnold Representation Theorem

In this section, we formulate the complex-valued KAT and provide a proof. The structure of the proof is as follows: First we formulate and prove the vector-valued KAT, then we show that the complex-valued KAT is a special case of the vector-valued KAT.

3.1   Vector-Valued Kolmogorov–Arnold Representation Theorem

Theorem 1. *Let $k, n \geq 1$ be integers and set $E_k = [0,1]^k$. There exist continuous functions $\phi_{q,p}^k : E_k \to \mathbb{R}^k$, where $q = 1, \ldots, 2kn+1$ and $p = 1, \ldots, n$, such that every continuous function $f : E_k^n \to \mathbb{R}^k$ can be written as*

$$f(v_1, \ldots, v_n) = \sum_{q=1}^{2kn+1} \Phi_q^k \left(\sum_{p=1}^{n} \phi_{q,p}^k(v_p) \right),$$

for some continuous functions $\Phi_q^k : \mathbb{R}^k \to \mathbb{R}^k$.

Proof. Let $f : E_k^n \to \mathbb{R}^k$ be a continuous function, which has k components,

$$f(v_1, \ldots, v_n) = (f_1(v_1, \ldots, v_n), \ldots, f_k(v_1, \ldots, v_n)),$$

where each component $f_i : E_k^n \to \mathbb{R}$ is continuous and $v_i = (v_i^1, \cdots, v_i^k)$.

By applying the KAT to each $f_i : [0,1]^{kn} \to \mathbb{R}$, there exist continuous functions $\phi_{q,p,l}^{(i)} : [0,1] \to \mathbb{R}$ and $\Phi_{q,i} : \mathbb{R} \to \mathbb{R}$ such that

$$f_i(v_1, \ldots, v_n) = \sum_{q=1}^{2kn+1} \Phi_{q,i} \left(\sum_{p=1}^{n} \sum_{l=1}^{k} \phi_{q,p,l}^{(i)}(v_p^l) \right).$$

Define $\phi_{q,p}^k(v_p) : E_k \to \mathbb{R}^k$, such that

$$\phi_{q,p}^k(v_p) := \left(\sum_{l=1}^{k} \phi_{q,p,l}^{(1)}(v_p^l), \cdots, \sum_{l=1}^{k} \phi_{q,p,l}^{(k)}(v_p^l) \right).$$

Then, define $\Phi_q^k : \mathbb{R}^k \to \mathbb{R}^k$ as

$$\Phi_q^k(v) := \left(\Phi_{q,1}(v^1), \ldots, \Phi_{q,k}(v^k) \right),$$

where $v = (v^1, \cdots, v^k) \in \mathbb{R}^k$. Therefore, the function f can be expressed as

$$f(v_1, \ldots, v_n) = \sum_{q=1}^{2kn+1} \Phi_q^k \left(\sum_{p=1}^{n} \phi_{q,p}^k(v_p) \right).$$

Since each $\phi_{q,p,l}^{(i)}$ is continuous, the sum $\sum_{l=1}^{k} \phi_{q,p,l}^{(i)}(v_p^l)$ is continuous. Therefore, the function $\phi_{q,p}^k(v_p)$ is continuous because it is a vector of continuous functions.

Similarly, since each $\Phi_{q,i}$ is continuous, the function $\Phi_q^k(v)$ is also continuous. Hence, both $\phi_{q,p}^k$ and Φ_q^k are continuous functions, completing the proof of the theorem.

3.2   Complex-Valued Kolmogorov–Arnold Representation Theorem

Since $\mathbb{C} \cong \mathbb{R}^2$, the complex-valued KAT is a corollary of Theorem 1 when $k = 2$:

Theorem 2. *Let $n \geq 1$ be an integer and let $E_{\mathbb{C}} = [0,1] + i[0,1]$. Then every continuous function $f : E_{\mathbb{C}}^n \to \mathbb{C}$ can be written as*

$$f(z_1, \ldots, z_n) = \sum_{q=1}^{4n+1} \Phi_q^{\mathbb{C}} \left(\sum_{p=1}^{n} \phi_{q,p}^{\mathbb{C}}(z_p) \right),$$

where $\phi_{q,p}^{\mathbb{C}} : E_{\mathbb{C}} \to \mathbb{C}$ and $\Phi_q^{\mathbb{C}} : \mathbb{C} \to \mathbb{C}$ are continuous functions.

Proof. We identify $\mathbb{C}$ with $\mathbb{R}^2$ using the assignment $x + iy \mapsto (x, y)$, such that $E_{\mathbb{C}} = [0,1] + i[0,1]$ can be viewed as $E_2 = [0,1]^2$, which makes $E_{\mathbb{C}}^n$ can be viewed as E_2^n. Under this identification, the function f can be regarded as $f : E_2^n \to \mathbb{R}^2$. Therefore, we can apply Theorem 1 when $k = 2$ to f, which proves the desired formula.

Remark 1. Note that this implies nearly twice the number of nodes in the hidden layer compared to the real-valued KAT. This was not discussed in CVKAN.

4   Proposed Model

The primary challenge of CVKAN is that the $\mathbb{C}$SiLU residual function in (9) may negatively affect the performance of the model. This is because the function only deals with the real part and the imaginary part of the complex-valued input separately, while ignoring their connection. Additionally, the fixed RBF shape parameter σ in (8) also reduces the adaptability of the model.

To address these challenges, we propose ModELU-based CVKAN. By replacing the $\mathbb{C}$SiLU residual function with the ModELU function, the internal relation of the complex-valued input can be preserved, which will improve the performance of the model. In addition, we assign a learnable σ to each edge in ModELU-based CVKAN to improve the flexibility and accuracy of the model.

In this section, we first introduce ModELU-based CVKAN, and then we will investigate the model that employs learnable RBF shape parameters at each edge.

4.1   ModELU-Based CVKAN

Modulus-based activation functions can enhance the performance and stability of CVNNs by modulating the amplitude of the input while preserving the phase [7]. ModSiLU [7] and ModReLU [23] are two representative functions of this category:

$$\text{ModSiLU}(z) = \frac{|z|}{1 + e^{-|z|+b}} \frac{z}{|z|}, \text{ModReLU}(z) = \begin{cases} \left(\frac{|z|+b}{|z|} \right) z, & |z| + b \geq 0 \\ 0, & |z| + b < 0 \end{cases} \quad (12)$$

The Modulus-based Exponential Linear Unit (ModELU) [6,7] also falls into this type, which is defined as:

$$\text{ModELU}(z) = \begin{cases} (|z| - b)\frac{z}{|z|}, & |z| < b \\ \alpha\left(e^{|z|-b} - 1\right)\frac{z}{|z|}, & \text{otherwise} \end{cases} \tag{13}$$

where $b \geq 0$ is a shift parameter. This function combines linear and exponential terms. When $|z| < b$, it adjusts the amplitude by adding $-b$ to $|z|$. Otherwise, it employs an exponential transformation modulated by α. ModELU adjusts the amplitude while maintaining the phase, preserving the real-imaginary relationship and leading to superior performance for CVNNs.

Here, we propose to replace the $\mathbb{C}$SiLU residual function of (9) in CVKAN with ModELU, which yields the formula $b_{\text{ModELU}}(z) = \text{ModELU}(z)$. Thus, the function $\phi(z)$ in (11) is replaced by:

$$\phi(z) = w_s\text{RBF}_{\mathbb{C}}(z) + w_b b_{\text{ModELU}}(z) + \beta \tag{14}$$

We refer to CVKAN employing this expression for approximation as ModELU-based CVKAN. An example structure of this model is illustrated in Fig. 1.

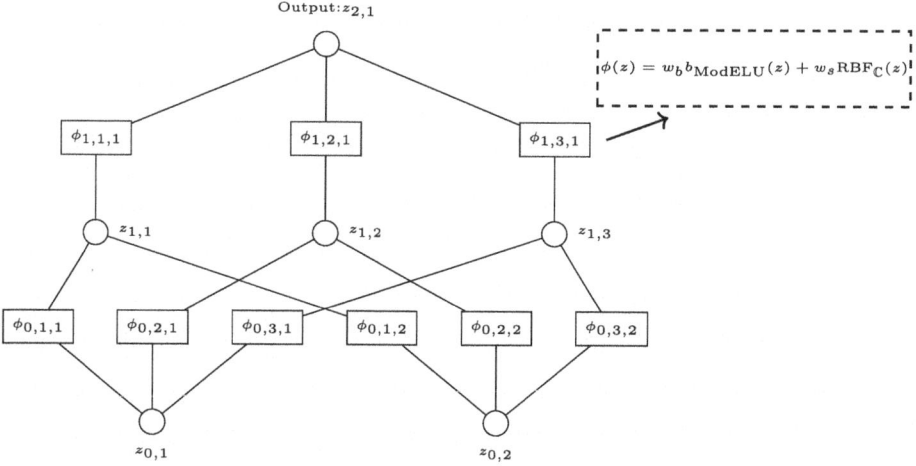

Fig. 1. Illustration of ModELU-based CVKAN with size $[2, 3, 1]$.

4.2   ModELU-Based CVKAN with Learnable Shape Parameters

Different values of the RBF shape parameter σ in (8) result in different approximation performances [16]. CVKAN [24] adopts RBFs with a fixed σ, which may limit the model to achieve optimal performance. Soares et al. [19] made σ learnable in the RBF network and proposed updating it using the steepest descent algorithm.

We adopt this idea and propose that each edge in ModELU-based CVKAN is assigned its own learnable σ. As a result, each ϕ defined on an edge has a distinct σ. For example, in a ModELU-based CVKAN network of size $[2, 3, 1]$ shown in Fig. 1, there are a total of nine learnable RBF shape parameters σ, each belonging to an edge in the network. Then these σ are updated separately using AdamW [15], which applies the weight decay in Adam [9]:

$$\sigma[n + 1] = \sigma[n] - \eta_\sigma \left(\frac{\hat{m}_t}{\sqrt{\hat{v}_t} + \epsilon} + \lambda \sigma[n] \right), \tag{15}$$

where $\hat{m}_t$ and $\hat{v}_t$ represent two bias-corrected moments estimates, and λ is the weight decay coefficient. In our experiments in Sect. 5.2, we will study the performance of ModELU-based CVKAN with learnable σ.

5   Experiments

To compare our ModELU-based CVKAN with CVKAN, and to study the impact of learnable RBF shape parameters, we conducted two experiments:

- Experiment 1: We analyze the performance of our ModELU-based CVKAN model by comparing it with CVKAN and several models which employ other modulus-based activations as the residual function.
- Experiment 2: We apply learnable RBF shape parameters to ModELU-based CVKAN and compare its performance with ModELU-based CVKAN and the original CVKAN adopting fixed RBF shape parameters.

We used the same datasets as in the experiments of [24] to ensure a convincing comparison. We also adopted the same experimental settings: the input range is $[-2, 2] + i[-2, 2]$, the number of RBF centers in (10) is 8, the value of the fixed RBF shape parameter σ is 1 in Experiment 1, which is also used as the initial values for all the learnable σ of ModELU-based CVKAN in Experiment 2. Optimization is performed using AdamW, combined with a StepLR scheduler which decreases the learning rate by a factor of 0.6 every 10 epochs. All training processes are carried out for 1000 iterations. 5-fold cross validation and Mean Square Error (MSE) are employed to evaluate the function fitting performance.

For each dataset, we selected several network sizes used in [24]. Additionally, according to Theorem 2, the complex-valued KAT constructs a network of size $[n, 4n+1, 1]$. Thus, we also employed this size for each dataset in our experiments, where n denotes the number of variables in the function.

5.1   Experiment 1: Performance of ModELU-Based CVKAN

In this part, we compared ModELU-based CVKAN with CVKAN. To better verify the effects of ModELU as residual function, we chose two other variants of CVKAN for comparison: ModSiLU-based CVKAN and ModReLU-based CVKAN, each replaces ℂSiLU by ModSiLU and ModReLU separately.

Function Fitting. Among the four complex-valued functions in Table 1, we made comparisons for the four models mentioned above. Each dataset has 5000 training points and 1000 test points. The results are shown in Table 1. Additionally, Table 1 also presents the values of α and b of ModELU (12) employed in our ModELU-based CVKAN across all datasets and sizes.

Table 1. Results of different models on simple functions for function fitting.

Dataset	Model	Size	Test MSE	Size	Test MSE
z^2	ModELU-based CVKAN	[1, 2, 1]	**0.011** ± 0.002	[1, 5, 1]	0.010 ± 0.001
	CVKAN		0.018 ± 0.004		0.011 ± 0.004
	ModSiLU-based CVKAN	$\alpha = 1$	0.017 ± 0.004	$\alpha = 0.5$	**0.009** ± 0.001
	ModReLU-based CVKAN	$b = 0$	0.016 ± 0.005	$b = 0.4$	0.011 ± 0.001
$\sin(z)$	ModELU-based CVKAN	[1, 2, 1]	0.008 ± 0.002	[1, 5, 1]	0.005 ± 0.0004
	CVKAN		0.010 ± 0.001		0.005 ± 0.0006
	ModSiLU-based CVKAN	$\alpha = 1$	0.010 ± 0.002	$\alpha = 0.1$	0.004 ± 0.0004
	ModReLU-based CVKAN	$b = 0.5$	0.008 ± 0.002	$b = 0.4$	0.005 ± 0.0006
$z_1 z_2$	ModELU-based CVKAN	[2 ,4, 2, 1]	0.044 ± 0.008	[2, 9, 1]	0.036 ± 0.006
	CVKAN		0.065 ± 0.038		0.042 ± 0.007
	ModSiLU-based CVKAN	$\alpha = 0.5$	**0.040** ± 0.024	$\alpha = 0.5$	**0.031** ± 0.003
	ModReLU-based CVKAN	$b = 1$	0.050 ± 0.023	$b = 0.5$	0.036 ± 0.008
$(z_1^2 + z_2^2)^2$	ModELU-based CVKAN	[2, 4, 2, 1]	**7.631** ± 1.002	[2, 9, 1]	**7.691** ± 1.318
	CVKAN		8.027 ± 3.432		9.057 ± 1.679
	ModSiLU-based CVKAN	$\alpha = 0.001$	10.047 ± 5.492	$\alpha = 0.001$	9.363 ± 1.707
	ModReLU-based CVKAN	$b = 1$	11.466 ± 5.057	$b = 0.5$	9.749 ± 2.316

Table 1 shows that ModELU-based CVKAN achieves lower test MSE than CVKAN across all datasets and sizes. It also exhibits lower standard deviations across all cases, except for $\sin(z)$ with size [1 ,2, 1], where the difference between two models is only 0.001. These results demonstrate that ModELU-based CVKAN consistently surpasses CVKAN in function fitting in terms of accuracy and stability. Furthermore, although ModSiLU-based CVKAN attains the best performance in certain cases, it cannot outperform CVKAN consistently.

Physical Equations. Consider the following two meaningful physical formulas used in the experiments of [24]. The first formula is holography, where the hologram intensity H is formed by three complex-valued wave components E_R, E_0 and $\hat{E}_R$:

$$H = \hat{E}_R \cdot |E_R + E_0|^2. \tag{16}$$

The second formula is circuit, where the complex-valued voltage $\underline{U}_{R_L}$ is generated by real-valued components R_G, R_L, ω, C and L, as well as the complex-valued component $\underline{U}_G$:

$$\underline{U}_{R_L} = \frac{U_G}{1 + \frac{R_G}{R_L} - \omega^2 \cdot L \cdot C + i\omega \cdot (\frac{L}{R_L} + R_G \cdot C)}. \tag{17}$$

We chose these formulas to generate datasets for function fitting, each containing 100000 training points and 1000 test points. The results and associated values of α and b for ModELU are shown in Table 2.

Table 2. Results of different models on physical equations for function fitting.

Dataset	Model	Size	Test MSE	Size	Test MSE
Holo-graphy	ModELU-based CVKAN	[3, 1, 1]	**37.272** ± 1.417	[3, 3, 1]	**0.202** ± 0.064
	CVKAN		37.323 ± 1.719		7.197 ± 1.173
	ModSiLU-based CVKAN	$\alpha = 1$	38.466 ± 2.354	$\alpha = 1$	8.172 ± 2.515
	ModReLU-based CVKAN	$b = 0$	37.342 ± 3.208	$b = 0$	6.445 ± 0.480
	ModELU-based CVKAN	[3, 10, 1]	**0.239** ± 0.025	[3, 13, 1]	0.315 ± 0.055
	CVKAN		0.258 ± 0.030		0.320 ± 0.072
	ModSiLU-based CVKAN	$\alpha = 1$	0.304 ± 0.041	$\alpha = 0.1$	**0.281** ± 0.026
	ModReLU-based CVKAN	$b = 0.4$	0.335 ± 0.057	$b = 0.5$	0.332 ± 0.037
Circuit	ModELU-based CVKAN	[6, 1, 1]	5.478 ± 0.041	[6, 3, 1]	**5.730** ± 0.073
	CVKAN		5.498 ± 0.072		5.834 ± 0.134
	ModSiLU-based CVKAN	$\alpha = 2$	5.469 ± 0.085	$\alpha = 2$	5.835 ± 0.134
	ModReLU-based CVKAN	$b = 2$	**5.455** ± 0.037	$b = 2$	5.746 ± 0.136
	ModELU-based CVKAN	[6, 10, 1]	**5.486** ± 0.105	[6, 25, 1]	3.460 ± 0.092
	CVKAN		5.515 ± 0.055		3.476 ± 0.124
	ModSiLU-based CVKAN	$\alpha = 0.5$	5.571 ± 0.034	$\alpha = 0.001$	3.380 ± 0.055
	ModReLU-based CVKAN	$b = 0.4$	5.490 ± 0.025	$b = 0.5$	**3.371** ± 0.056

As observed in Table 2, ModELU-based CVKAN achieves lower test MSE and standard deviation than CVKAN on the holography dataset across all four sizes of the network. Especially in size [3, 3, 1], it exhibits a significantly better performance compared to CVKAN. Thus, ModELU-based CVKAN consistently outperforms CVKAN on the holography dataset. Although ModSiLU-based CVKAN obtains the lowest test MSE in size [3, 13, 1], it performs worse than CVKAN in other sizes.

Furthermore, both ModELU-based CVKAN and ModReLU-based CVKAN show a slight improvement in test MSE on the circuit dataset across all sizes of the network compared to CVKAN. However, the performance differences among all these four models within the same size are minimal. One reason is that the circuit function is not continuous due to the presence of singularities in the range of $[-2, 2] + i[-2, 2]$, which conflicts with the requirement of the complex-valued KAT that the function for approximation be continuous. Therefore, CVKAN and its variants are not suitable for approximating the circuit function, which results in similar performance when using different residual functions in CVKAN.

5.2 Experiment 2: Evaluating the Performance of ModELU-Based CVKAN with Learnable RBF Shape Parameters

In this part, we will study the performance of ModELU-based CVKAN applying learnable RBF shape parameters σ. In ModELU-based CVKAN, we assign a learnable σ to each edge of the network. We set these parameters the same initial value 1 and they update separately during training. We compare the performance of the model with those of ModELU-based CVKAN and CVKAN with fixed σ using the same functions from Experiment 1 for function fitting. Each dataset is trained using the same number of training and test points as in Experiment 1. The results and corresponding values of α and b in ModELU for each case are shown in Table 3.

Table 3. Results of ModELU-based CVKAN with learnable shape parameters.

Dataset	Model	Size	Test MSE	Size	Test MSE
z^2	ModELU-based CVKAN	[1, 3, 1]	0.010 ± 0.003	[1, 5, 1]	0.010 ± 0.001
	Model with learnable σ	$\alpha = 1$	$\mathbf{0.009} \pm 0.003$	$\alpha = 0.5$	$\mathbf{0.009} \pm 0.001$
	CVKAN	$b = 0$	0.019 ± 0.014	$b = 0.4$	0.010 ± 0.002
$\sin(z)$	ModELU-based CVKAN	[1, 3, 1]	0.0060 ± 0.001	[1, 5, 1]	0.0055 ± 0.001
	Model with learnable σ	$\alpha = 0.1$	$\mathbf{0.0057} \pm 0.002$	$\alpha = 0.1$	$\mathbf{0.0049} \pm 0.001$
	CVKAN	$b = 0.4$	0.0070 ± 0.001	$b = 0.4$	0.0051 ± 0.001
$z_1 z_2$	ModELU-based CVKAN	[2, 5, 1]	0.033 ± 0.006	[2, 9, 1]	0.041 ± 0.004
	Model with learnable σ	$\alpha = 0.5$	$\mathbf{0.029} \pm 0.005$	$\alpha = 0.5$	$\mathbf{0.031} \pm 0.004$
	CVKAN	$b = 0.5$	0.046 ± 0.006	$b = 0.5$	0.041 ± 0.003
$(z_1^2 + z_2^2)^2$	ModELU-based CVKAN	[2, 5, 1]	15.114 ± 3.933	[2, 9, 1]	7.772 ± 1.412
	Model with learnable σ	$\alpha = 0.001$	$\mathbf{13.759} \pm 6.178$	$\alpha = 0.001$	$\mathbf{7.355} \pm 1.782$
	CVKAN	$b = 0.5$	15.729 ± 2.974	$b = 0.5$	8.912 ± 2.085
Holo-graphy	ModELU-based CVKAN	[3, 7, 1]	0.216 ± 0.029	[3, 13, 1]	0.254 ± 0.025
	Model with learnable σ	$\alpha = 1$	$\mathbf{0.166} \pm 0.029$	$\alpha = 0.01$	$\mathbf{0.242} \pm 0.057$
	CVKAN	$b = 0$	0.380 ± 0.150	$b = 0.5$	0.301 ± 0.045
Circuit	ModELU-based CVKAN	[6, 13, 1]	5.314 ± 0.060	[6, 25, 1]	5.405 ± 0.073
	Model with learnable σ	$\alpha = 0.1$	$\mathbf{5.284} \pm 0.034$	$\alpha = 0.01$	$\mathbf{5.397} \pm 0.050$
	CVKAN	$b = 0.5$	5.322 ± 0.085	$b = 0.5$	5.401 ± 0.072

As shown in Table 3, ModELU-based CVKAN with learnable σ achieves the lowest test MSE among three models across all datasets and sizes. The results suggest that making the RBF shape parameters learnable can enhance its performance in function fitting.

6 Conclusion

We have formulated the complex-valued KAT with a proof. It provides theoretical support for CVKAN that transforms KAN into the complex domain. We have also proposed ModELU-based CVKAN which replaces the residual function from CSiLU to ModELU. Our experiments demonstrate that ModELU-based CVKAN performs better in function fitting compared to CVKAN, in terms of both precision and stability. Additionally, we have studied the effects of making the shape parameters of RBFs learnable in ModELU-based CVKAN. Experiments reveal that ModELU-based CVKAN with learnable RBF shape parameters outperforms the model employing fixed shape parameter in function fitting.

Despite the promising results, one major constraint of our study is that we need to manually select the optimal values of α and b in ModELU used in ModELU-based CVKAN for each dataset and size. This process may cause errors that do not yield the best settings of the hyperparameters in ModELU for each case, which will negatively influence the model's performance. In addition, the learnable RBF shape parameters in ModELU-based CVKAN are easily stuck in non-optimal values around the initial value, which may prevent the model from achieving the best possible outcomes. Future research could explore making α and b of ModELU learnable in our model, to avoid manual errors and achieve better performance. Furthermore, we aim to develop better strategies for training learnable RBF shape parameters, which will lead them to the global optimum.

Disclosure of Interests. The authors have no competing interests to declare that are relevant to the content of this article.

References

1. Basina, D., Vishal, J.R., Choudhary, A., Chakravarthi, B.: KAT to KANs: a review of Kolmogorov-Arnold networks and the neural leap forward. arXiv preprint arXiv:2411.10622 (2024)
2. Bassey, J., Qian, L., Li, X.: A survey of complex-valued neural networks. arXiv preprint arXiv:2101.12249 (2021)
3. Braun, J., Griebel, M.: On a constructive proof of Kolmogorov's superposition theorem. Constr. Approx. **30**, 653–675 (2009). https://doi.org/10.1007/s00365-009-9054-2
4. Buhmann, M.D.: Radial basis functions. Acta Numerica **9**, 1–38 (2000). https://doi.org/10.1017/S0962492900000015
5. Chen, S., McLaughlin, S., Mulgrew, B.: Complex-valued radial basic function network, part i: network architecture and learning algorithms. Signal Process. **35**(1), 19–31 (1994). https://doi.org/10.1016/0165-1684(94)90187-2
6. Clevert, D.A., Unterthiner, T., Hochreiter, S.: Fast and accurate deep network learning by exponential linear units (elus). arXiv preprint arXiv:1511.07289 (2015)
7. Hammad, M.: Comprehensive survey of complex-valued neural networks: insights into backpropagation and activation functions. arXiv preprint arXiv:2407.19258 (2024)
8. Hecht-Nielsen, R.: Kolmogorov's mapping neural network existence theorem. In: Proceedings of the International Conference on Neural Networks, vol. 3, pp. 11–14. IEEE Press, New York (1987)
9. Kingma, D.P., Ba, J.: Adam: a method for stochastic optimization. arXiv preprint arXiv:1412.6980 (2014)

10. Kolmogorov, A.N.: On the representations of continuous functions of many variables by superposition of continuous functions of one variable and addition. In: Dokl. Akad. Nauk USSR, vol. 114, pp. 953–956 (1957)

11. Lee, C., Hasegawa, H., Gao, S.: Complex-valued neural networks: a comprehensive survey. IEEE/CAA J. Automatica Sinica **9**(8), 1406–1426 (2022). https://doi.org/10.1109/JAS.2022.105743

12. Li, Z.: Kolmogorov-Arnold networks are radial basis function networks. arXiv preprint arXiv:2405.06721 (2024)

13. Liu, Z., et al.: KAN: Kolmogorov-Arnold networks. arXiv preprint arXiv:2404.19756 (2024)

14. Lorentz, G.: Approximation of Functions.-Holt, Rinehart and Wilson. Inc., New York (1966)

15. Loshchilov, I., Hutter, F.: Decoupled weight decay regularization. arXiv preprint arXiv:1711.05101 (2017)

16. Mongillo, M., et al.: Choosing basis functions and shape parameters for radial basis function methods. SIAM Undergraduate Res. Online **4**(190–209), 2–6 (2011)

17. Montanelli, H., Yang, H.: Error bounds for deep relu networks using the Kolmogorov-Arnold superposition theorem. Neural Netw. **129**, 1–6 (2020). https://doi.org/10.1016/j.neunet.2019.12.013

18. Schmidt-Hieber, J.: The Kolmogorov-Arnold representation theorem revisited. Neural Netw. **137**, 119–126 (2021). https://doi.org/10.1016/j.neunet.2021.01.020

19. Soares, J.A., Luiz, V.H., Arantes, D.S., Mayer, K.S.: Deep complex-valued radial basis function neural networks and parameter selection. In: 2024 19th International Symposium on Wireless Communication Systems (ISWCS), pp. 1–6. IEEE (2024). https://doi.org/10.1109/ISWCS61526.2024.10639101

20. Sprecher, D.A.: On the structure of continuous functions of several variables. Trans. Am. Math. Soc. **115**, 340–355 (1965). https://doi.org/10.1090/S0002-9947-1965-0210852-X

21. Sprecher, D.A.: A universal mapping for Kolmogorov's superposition theorem. Neural Netw. **6**(8), 1089–1094 (1993). https://doi.org/10.1016/S0893-6080(09)80020-8

22. Sprecher, D.A.: A numerical implementation of Kolmogorov's superpositions. Neural Netw. **9**(5), 765–772 (1996). https://doi.org/10.1016/0893-6080(95)00081-X

23. Trabelsi, C., et al.: Deep complex networks. arXiv preprint arXiv:1705.09792 (2017)

24. Wolff, M., Eilers, F., Jiang, X.: CVKAN: complex-valued Kolmogorov-Arnold networks. arXiv preprint arXiv:2502.02417 (2025)

25. Wu, Y., Wang, H., Zhang, B., Du, K.L.: Using radial basis function networks for function approximation and classification. Int. Scholarly Res. Not. **2012**(1), 324194 (2012). https://doi.org/10.5402/2012/324194

From Execution to Representation: Capturing Metaheuristic Behaviour via Graph-Derived Meta-features

José Carlos Souza Pacheco Júnior[1], Enrico Uchoa da Silva Leal[1],
Nicolly Carvalho Cutrim[1], Guilherme Alberto Sousa Ribeiro[2],
Bruno Feres de Souza[1], and Alexandre César Muniz de Oliveira[1](✉)

[1] Universidade Federal do Maranhão, São Luís, MA 65080-805, Brazil
{jose.cspj,enrico.uchoa,nicolly.cutrim}@discente.ufma.br,
{bruno.feres,alexandre.cesar}@ufma.br
[2] Hospital Israelita Albert Einstein, São Paulo, SP 05652-900, Brazil
guilherme.asr@einstein.br

Abstract. This work proposes a new methodology for extracting meta-features from graphs representing the behaviour of metaheuristic algorithms for meta-learning applications. In contrast to traditional approaches that rely on problem-specific or program-specific tailored meta-features, the goal is to represent the dynamic behaviour of stochastic algorithms, such as metaheuristics, during their execution, generating a more robust and informative representation for meta-learning applications. The primary motivation is to fill a gap in the literature regarding the construction of generalizable and descriptive meta-representations, which can enrich the knowledge base for automatic selection and configuration of optimisation algorithms. As a case study, five metaheuristic variants were applied to the Travelling Salesman Problem (TSP), with parametrised variations in their components. For each run, behaviour graphs were generated based on their search behaviours. These graphs extracted structural and topological meta-features like connectivity, centrality, and entropy measures. Visualization and analysis tools were used to investigate the expressiveness and quality of these representations. The results indicate that the graph-based approach is promising for separating algorithms in the meta-feature space, enabling the construction of more representative meta-bases and supporting advancements in algorithm recommendation for unseen problems based on behaviour similarity.

Keywords: Meta-learning · Program analysis · Meta-heuristics

1 Introduction

Graph representations are exciting, as we can use the vast machinery of Graph Theory to extract meta-features. Selecting a *powerful* graph representation is also

J. Valente de Oliveira et al. (Eds.): EPIA 2025, LNAI 16121, pp. 452–463, 2026.
https://doi.org/10.1007/978-3-032-05176-9_35

essential: different ways of representing problem instances as graphs can generate meta-features with different predictive powers. Previous work has investigated meta-learning applied to optimisation problems with meta-features generated by problem-specific graph representation [20].

In general, descriptive metrics are calculated over meta-features extracted from graphs. These metrics are expected to capture structural information about the analysed problem. The graph-based representation can encode local neighbourhood relations, as well as the global characteristics associated with spatiality and density of the structural elements of the problem instance [21].

In traditional meta-learning, features of problems are learned to recommend algorithms, rather than the other way around. Programs or algorithms have been described via features extracted from their structure, behaviour, or performance profiles. Similar algorithms, in the feature space, are assumed to perform similarly on the same instances [32]. In recommendation systems, it is new to learn features of algorithms to understand what problems they can solve. The focus on the algorithm rather than the problem space is the first point of novelty of this work.

Algorithm similarity modelling enables an understanding of the algorithm and facilitates generalization to unseen (or new) problems through analogy. A reduced dependence on problem-specific features is especially useful when problem instances are too complex or raise concerns about data privacy. Additionally, the new approach can facilitate knowledge transfer from existing algorithms to new ones without necessitating extensive re-evaluation.

In the literature, features have been commonly used to describe algorithms [6]. For example, structural features, type (e.g., greedy, evolutionary, heuristic search, ML-based), complexity (big-O estimates if known), number of hyperparameters, randomness (deterministic vs. stochastic), runtime distributions, code-level, number of loops/branches, exploration or exploitation profile, etc.

Graph representations have been widely employed to describe algorithms statically by linking fine-grained components, facilitating applications in cybersecurity, program classification, and software engineering [18]. However, graph representation to describe dynamic behavioural features has not been explored yet.

This study introduces a novel methodology for extracting meta-features from graphs that represent the behaviour of metaheuristic algorithms for meta-learning applications. Our approach generates graph representations from parametrized stochastic executions of the target metaheuristics applied to a selected Travelling Salesman Problem (TSP) instance. The graph represents the probabilistic traversal of the key heuristic components or logic conditions extracted from the optimization algorithm taxonomy, such as generating neighbours and accepting or rejecting candidate solutions.

This paper is organized as follows: Sect. 2 presents the background of optimisation, metaheuristics, meta-learning, and graph representation devoted to program analysis. Section 3 describes the proposal as a methodology for meta-features based on behaviour graphs. Section 4 presents the computational results, and Sect. 5 highlights the main findings and outlines future research directions.

2   Background and Related Work

Optimization Problems. Optimization problems are applicable in various fields, including engineering, economics, logistics, and computer science [3]. Fundamentally, an optimization problem aims to identify the best solution among the possible alternatives, defining this solution based on one or more criteria [5]. The complexity of these problems ranges from simple formulations with analytical solutions to more complex problems that require advanced computational techniques [22]. In practice, many optimization problems encountered in real-world contexts are classified as NP-hard, indicating that no efficient algorithm is known to solve all instances of these problems in polynomial time [23].

Optimization problems have unique characteristics and relevance in their respective application areas [14]. Among the most studied problems in the literature is the Travelling Salesman Problem (TSP) [10], which aims to find the shortest route for a set of cities, visiting each city exactly once and returning to the origin. The Miller-Tucker-Zemlin (MTZ) formulation applies integer linear programming to solve TSP, ensuring an optimal solution by preventing subcycles [9].

Pursuing approximate or heuristic solutions becomes a relevant area of investigation [4,8]. Thus, various heuristic approaches, such as genetic algorithms, tabu search, and machine learning techniques, have been developed and refined over the years to address the complexity of these problems [28]. Each approach presents specific advantages and challenges, chosen based on the characteristics of the problem and the operational constraints involved [2]. Meta-heuristics and meta-learning techniques effectively adapt to the problem's specificities, enhancing the solution's resilience and versatility.

Metaheuristics. The process of optimization plays a crucial role in improving efficiency, reducing costs, and enhancing performance across various domains. Many problems across different scientific and engineering fields can be modelled as numerical optimization problems, such as structural design, financial modelling, and control system configuration [24].

The heuristic approach, more flexible and primarily based on evaluating the objective function, offers practical alternatives for exploring complex and high-dimensional search spaces while making minimal assumptions in real-world problems. Metaheuristics, for example, are powerful tools that guide the search for optimal solutions by mimicking natural or social processes to build a probabilistic model of the search space, where candidate solutions are spread [12].

Metaheuristics can be broadly classified based on their search strategies and problem assumptions. Population-based metaheuristics, such as Genetic Algorithms (GA) and Particle Swarm Optimization (PSO), explore the search space using a set of candidate solutions simultaneously, promoting diversity and parallelism. In contrast, trajectory-based metaheuristics, such as Simulated Annealing

(SA) and Iterated Local Search (ILS), follow a single solution path, refining it iteratively. Blackboard optimizers, as Ant Colony Optimisation (ACO) and Estimation of Distribution Algorithm (EDA), are used to build explicit probabilistic models that locate expected high-quality solutions [27].

Meta-learning Concepts and Mechanisms. Meta-learning offers a promising approach for multi-problem scenarios, allowing models to adapt to various optimization tasks with distinct characteristics by transferring knowledge among them [30]. Instead of being restricted to a specific task, meta-learning systems generalize previous experiences to improve performance in new contexts [13]. This method excels in complex applications that require flexibility, where conventional models struggle to adapt to various optimization problems [15].

Meta-features are crucial for the success of meta-learning in multi-problem scenarios, as they describe key properties of datasets and tasks, enabling the model to adapt to the specificities of each problem [7]. These features include attributes such as the number of samples, the amount of noise, and the complexity of the patterns to be learned, providing the model with valuable information to select and adjust the most appropriate learning strategies for each new context [31].

Graph Representation. For each problem, mathematical modelling is developed, allowing the formulation of linear or integer optimization models according to the specific nature of each case [34]. Following this formulation, the datasets are converted into individualized graphical representations [11], generating a graph for each instance. These directed graphs provide a comprehensive structural overview of the problems, where the nodes represent variables and constraints, and the edges indicate dependencies between them. The graph representation offers an intuitive perspective on the interactions among different parts of the model, facilitating the identification of patterns and relationships that may influence the solution [17]. Thus, each graph comprehensively captures the internal structure and interactions between variables and constraints.

Program Analysis. Algorithm portfolios have been successfully applied to select the best solvers or classifiers, such as SATzilla [33] or Auto-WEKA [29]; however, they utilize only problem features and lack an understanding of the relationships between algorithms. Abstract Syntax Tree (AST) and Control Flow Graph (CFG) are program code representations based on graphs widely used for static analysis with good potential to feed Graph Neural Networks to extract robust meta-features [25].

Once a dataset is generated, clustering or embedding techniques, such as T-distributed Stochastic Neighbors Embedding (t-SNE) and Uniform Manifold Approximation and Projection (UMAP) [19], or Graph Neural Network (GNNs), are used [1] can be used to visualize algorithm similarity. At last, classifiers like k-NN or others can predict which algorithm might work well on a new instance based on algorithm similarity[16].

The current research challenges rely on a) normalization and extracting meaningful, generalizable features from heterogeneous algorithms, b) Trade-off between static (code-based) vs. dynamic (run-based) features, c) building a fine-tuned performance space to evaluate the algorithms' behaviour for each problem instance robustly, and d) scalability to large algorithm libraries.

Our approach addresses most of these challenges, providing a convergent taxonomy that enables the extraction of meaningful and generalizable features from heterogeneous algorithms using only dynamic behavioural graphs, also allowing for scaling to a comprehensive metaheuristic library.

3   Proposed Approach

This section outlines the methodological guidelines for characterizing metaheuristic behaviour using graph-based meta-features, including construction rules for node labelling and edge direction setting. The method also involves calculating the graph metrics to achieve the final dataset.

Behaviour Graphs. The behaviour graph is capable of capturing all transitions in a macro sense, in which each internal heuristic procedure that composes a given metaheuristic is traced at runtime. Each algorithm is then instrumented to record its internal behaviour, printing nodes and edges. Nodes represent standardized procedures and logic conditions of the search process, and edges represent the normalised number of transitions between procedures.

Heuristic Dictionary. To ensure consistent and robust behavioural graphs, a unified English-language naming convention was adopted for graph nodes. Heuristic procedures are catalogued in a dictionary of general or specific taxonomic terms that become graph vertices. Some examples of standard node names are: *select parents, select individuals, update velocity, update current, update the best, local search*, and so on. Remarkably, this dictionary is under construction, and as new metaheuristics are incorporated, new terms are added, while others are updated to enhance consistency and robustness.

Capturing Stochastic Transitions. Since metaheuristics are stochastic algorithms, experiments require a significant number of executions under the same set of parameters for a given problem instance. Notably, the parameters often need to be tuned to achieve success, requiring a time-consuming experiment. Examining the resulting meta-feature space, variant algorithms may be equivalent to others that are not supposed to be similar, making the graph analysis problem more challenging.

Meta-feature Extraction. We utilize the vast machinery of Graph Theory to extract meta-features, such as the number of nodes and edges, the sum and average of weights, the standard deviation, centrality, and connectivity degrees, among others. Notably, algorithm meta-features are the same for problems, as detailed in the meta-learning application in [20].

Meta-feature Space and Further Application. The meta-feature space is composed of $n-$dimensional vectors displayed in $\mathbb{R}^n$ representing meta-instances (or algorithms). After the construction of the feature space, each meta-instance can be labelled with the list of optimization problem instances that it can solve well (or that are state-of-the-art). The resulting multi-class, multi-label classification problem can then be leveraged to design a comprehensive recommendation system, allowing for the prediction of the problem and the corresponding algorithm.

4   Experimental Results

4.1   Dataset Description

The dataset used in this work was constructed by extracting structural and statistical features from the graphs generated during the experiment. Each dataset instance corresponds to an individual graph, represented by a vector of numerical attributes that describe its topological structure and weighted properties. The extracted features include:

- **Number of nodes (*n_ nodes*) and edges (*n_ edges*)**: measure the structural size of the graph.
- **Total sum of weights (sum_weight), average edge weight (avg_w_edges), standard deviation of weights (std_w), maximum weight (max_w), and minimum weight (min_w)**: describe the statistical distribution of the edge weights.
- **Weighted density (*density_ w*)**: represents the graph density considering the weights of the connections.
- **Average weighted degree (*avg_ degree_ w*)**: computes the average of the weighted degrees of all nodes in the graph.
- **Average degree centrality (*degree_ centrality_ avg*)**: evaluates the average centrality of the nodes based on their connections.
- **Weight entropy (*entropy_ w*) and relative weight variation (*variation_ w*)**: capture the complexity and dispersion of the weight distribution.
- **Graph density (*density_ g*)**: measures the proportion of existing connections relative to the total possible, considering the graph as unweighted.

These and other metrics were selected for their ability to reflect relevant aspects of graph topology, as detailed in Table 1.

4.2   Algorithms and Parameters

This work evaluates five optimization algorithms from the class of metaheuristics: *Genetic Algorithm* (GA), *Particle Swarm Optimization* (PSO), *Iterated Local Search* (ILS), *Simulated Annealing* (SA), and *Stochastic Hill Climbing* (SHC). The algorithms are chosen due to their popularity and to enable the exploration of graph possibilities for different types of strategies: population, single-solution, and swarm. Each algorithm was adapted to make the procedure tracing under the same problem configuration (a 100-city instance of the Travelling Salesman Problem). The following summarizes the parameters used for each method:

Table 1. Features extracted from graphs generated by SA and PSO.

nnodes	nedges	sumweight	avgw edges	stdw	maxw	minw	densityw	avgdegree w	degreecentrality avg	entropyw	variationw	densityg
Simulated Annealing												
4	6	2016	336.0	461.08	996	4	168.0	1008.0	1.0	0.8004	1.3722	0.5
4	6	2017	336.17	457.06	991	9	168.08	1008.5	1.0	0.8294	1.3596	0.5
4	6	2021	336.83	458.05	995	5	168.41	1010.5	1.0	0.8253	1.3598	0.5
Particle Swarm Optimization												
6	8	120016	15002	14788.42	30000	16	4000.53	40005.33	0.5333	1.42497	0.98576	0.26667
6	8	120012	15001.5	14760.38	30000	12	4000.40	40004.00	0.5333	1.42866	0.98393	0.26667
6	8	120008	15001	14776.16	30000	8	4000.27	40002.67	0.5333	1.42611	0.98501	0.26667

- **Genetic Algorithm (GA)**: Crossover probability of 90%, mutation probability of 10%, population size of 50, and a maximum of 1,000 generations.
- **Particle Swarm Optimization (PSO)**: Inertia weight $w = 0.5$, cognitive coefficient $c_1 = 1.5$, social coefficient $c_2 = 1.5$, particle population size of 30, and a maximum of 1000 iterations.
- **Iterated Local Search (ILS)**: Maximum of 1,000 iterations.
- **Simulated Annealing (SA)**: Maximum of 1,000 iterations.
- **Stochastic Hill Climbing (SHC)**: Maximum of 1,000 iterations.

After that, graphs were generated from each execution to capture the algorithm's behaviour. At last, the meta-feature space was evaluated by applying techniques of visualization and quantitative assessment (Table 2).

Table 2. Standardized node nomenclature used in algorithm behaviour graphs.

Node Name	Description
Update Current	Updates the best point found locally
Update Global Best	Updates the best point found globally
Don't Update Current	No local update (solution worse than previous ones)
Local Search	Execution of a local search phase
Perturbation	Perturbation phase of the current solution
Select Individual	Selection of an individual for evaluation (PSO)
Update <attribute>	Update of an individual's attribute (e.g., velocity in PSO)
Mutate	Mutation applied to an individual (GA)
Select Parents	Selection of individuals for parents (GA)
Crossover	Crossover operation between individuals (GA)
New Population	Generation of a new population (GA)

4.3   Execution Graph Visualization

Figures 1 and 2 present the graphs generated during the execution of each algorithm. Nodes represent standardized algorithm steps, while edges reflect the flow of solutions through these steps during execution. GA begins by creating a random population (`New Population`). The procedure *Select Parents* occurs in all transitions, but with 90.32% undergoing crossover, 0.996% mutation only, and 0.188% both. After mutation, in 9.998% transitions the local best is improved, and in 0.432% the global best is updated.

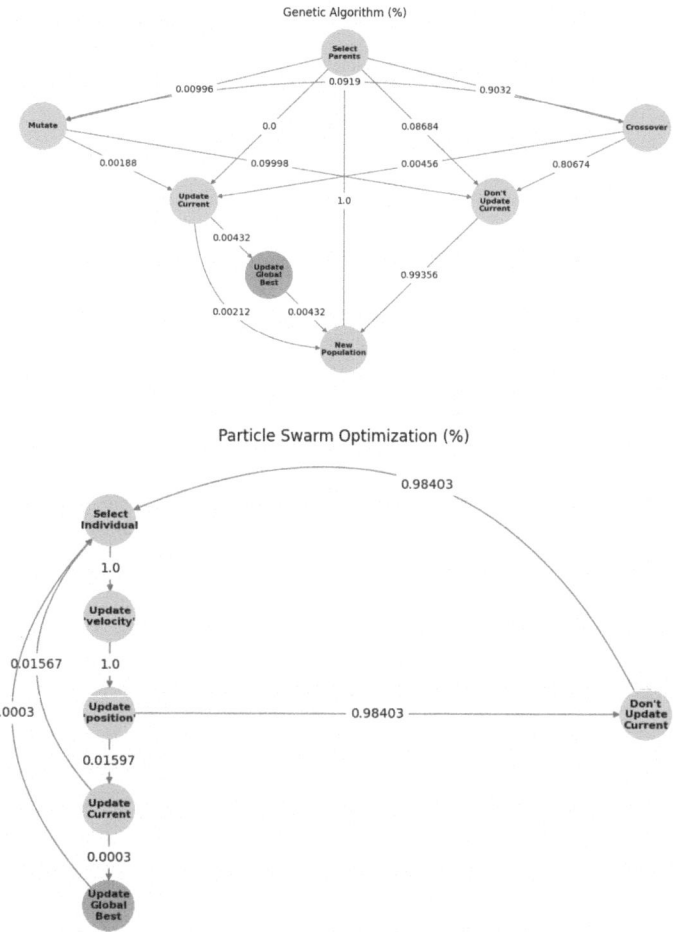

Fig. 1. Graphs generated during the execution of population metaheuristics GA and PSO: nodes represent standardized procedures or conditions, coloured differently if initial (cyan) or final procedures (orange). (Color figure online)

PSO updates one individual at a time, modifying its velocity and position. After movement, 1.597% transitions are improved locally, 0.03% update the global best, while 98.403% show no improvement at all. ILS starts with a perturbation, followed by local search. In 80.9% of cases, the local best is updated; 16.7% of these also improve the global best. Only 2.5% of transitions result in no improvement. The cycle restarts with a new perturbation. SA performs a local search in every iteration. The candidate replaces the current solution in 99.5% of cases, with 1.4% improving the global best. Even non-improving moves are accepted probabilistically (98.1%), considering the current temperature.

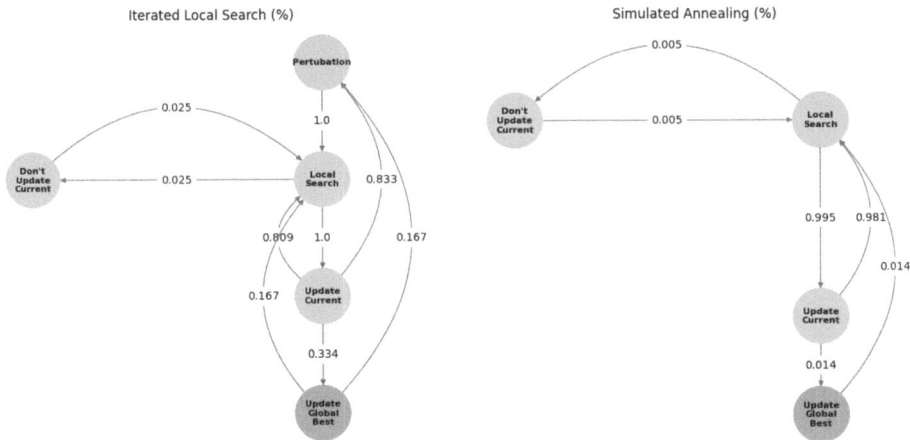

Fig. 2. Graphs generated during the execution of single-solution algorithms ILS, and SA: edge weights represent transition probabilities, computed based on the number of occurrences during an execution.

4.4 Dimensionality Reduction for Visualization

To visualize the meta-feature space and assess the structure of the data generated by the algorithms, we used the t-SNE (t-distributed Stochastic Neighbors Embedding) technique. t-SNE is a popular unsupervised, non-linear dimensionality reduction method for exploring and visualizing high-dimensional data, providing intuitive insights into structural relationships that extend beyond three dimensions. Figures 3a and 3b show the visualization of meta-features using t-SNE for 2D and 3D representations. Notably, the visualization corroborates the understanding that the feature vectors effectively express the behaviour of the five metaheuristics evaluated in this work. Apparently, in this case, there is no close relationship between population algorithms (GA, PSO) and trajectory algorithms (SA, SHC, ILS).

The silhouette score indicates which objects lie well within their cluster and which ones are merely located somewhere in between clusters. The tightness

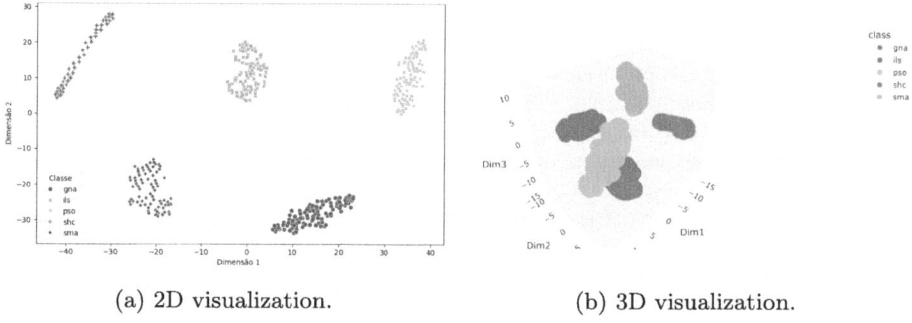

(a) 2D visualization.   (b) 3D visualization.

Fig. 3. Visualization of meta-features extracted from graphs generated during the execution of GA, PSO, ILS, SHC and SA, using t-SNE.

and separation are used to estimate the relative quality of the clusters, taking values between -1 and 1, where values close to 1 indicate that the data is well clustered and separated [26]. In this dataset, the silhouette score obtained is 0.9943, demonstrating strong intra-cluster cohesion and inter-cluster separation.

5   Conclusion

In this paper, we introduce a graph-based approach for characterizing the dynamic behaviour of stochastic metaheuristics. By tracing internal heuristic transitions during optimization, recorded using a standardized nomenclature (e.g., Update Current, Local Search, Mutate), we construct behaviour graphs that encode algorithmic dynamics as structural meta-features, such as node degree distributions, edge weights, and entropy measures. Unlike traditional performance-based metrics, these features capture how an algorithm explores the search space, not just its final output.

We validate our method on five metaheuristics (GA, PSO, ILS, SA, and SHC) applied to a 100-city TSP instance. Dimensionality reduction (t-SNE) and clustering analyses (using the silhouette score) reveal a clear separation between algorithms in the meta-feature space, indicating that these graphs effectively fingerprint heuristic behaviour. As such, we provide evidence that meta-feature extraction can move from problem-oriented features to algorithm-centric, behaviour-driven representations.

Future work will explore: (i) extending the taxonomy of heuristic procedures and enriching the heuristic dictionary to cover a broader spectrum of metaheuristics; (ii) evaluating the approach on diverse problem domains beyond TSP, and (iii) investigating the sensitivity of meta-features to parameter settings and execution budgets.

Disclosure of Interests. The authors have no competing interests to declare that are relevant to the content of this article.

References

1. Allamanis, M.: Graph Neural Networks in Program Analysis, pp. 483–497. Springer, Singapore (2022)
2. Barnhart, C., Jiang, H., Marla, L.: Optimization approaches to airline industry challenges: airline schedule planning and recovery. In: Models and Algorithms for Optimization in Logistics (2009)
3. Bazaraa, M.S., Sherali, H.D., Shetty, C.M.: Nonlinear Programming: Theory and Algorithms. Wiley, Hoboken (2006)
4. Binh, H.T.T., Bang, B.H., Thai, N.D., Ha, P.B., et al.: A multi-population multi-tasking variable neighborhood search algorithm with diversity enhancements for inter-domain path computation problem. Swarm Evol. Comput. **86**, 101501 (2024)
5. Boyd, S., Vandenberghe, L.: Convex Optimization. Cambridge University Press, Cambridge (2004)
6. Brazdil, P., Giraud-Carrier, C., Soares, C., Vilalta, R.: Metalearning: Applications to Data Mining, 1st edn. Springer, Cham (2008)
7. Brazdil, P., et al.: Metalearning: Applications to Data Mining. Springer, Cham (2008)
8. Buriol, L.S., Figueiredo, C., Resende, M.G., Uchoa, E.: The guide to NP-completeness is 40 years old: an homage to David S. Johnson. Oper. Res. **40**, e236329 (2020)
9. Campuzano, G., Obreque, C., Aguayo, M.M.: Accelerating the Miller-Tucker-Zemlin model for the asymmetric traveling salesman problem. Expert Syst. Appl. **148**, 113229 (2020)
10. Dahiya, C., Sangwan, S.: Literature review on travelling salesman problem. Int. J. Res. **5**(16), 1152–1155 (2018)
11. Dulebenets, M.A.: A diffused memetic optimizer for reactive berth allocation and scheduling at marine container terminals in response to disruptions. Swarm Evol. Comput. **80**, 101334 (2023)
12. Eiben, A., Smith, J.: From evolutionary computation to the evolution of things. Nature **521**, 476–482 (2015). https://doi.org/10.1038/nature14544
13. Finn, C., Abbeel, P., Levine, S.: Model-agnostic meta-learning for fast adaptation of deep networks. In: International Conference on Machine Learning, pp. 1126–1135. PMLR (2017)
14. Ghasemi, A., Heavey, C., Laipple, G.: A review of simulation-optimization methods with applications to semiconductor operational problems. In: 2018 Winter Simulation Conference (WSC), pp. 3672–3683 (2018)
15. Hospedales, T., Antoniou, A., Micaelli, P., Storkey, A.: Meta-learning in neural networks: a survey. IEEE Trans. Pattern Anal. Mach. Intell. **44**(9), 5149–5169 (2021)
16. Kong, D., Su, X., Wu, S., Wang, T., Ma, P.: Detect functionally equivalent code fragments via k-nearest neighbor algorithm. In: 2012 IEEE Fifth International Conference on Advanced Computational Intelligence (ICACI), pp. 94–98. IEEE (2012)
17. Kraus, B., Matzke, S., Kirchner, E.: Utilizing a graph data structure to model physical effects and dependencies between different physical variables for the systematic identification of sensory effects in design elements. In: DS 119: Proceedings of the 33rd Symposium Design for X (DFX2022) (2022)
18. Maarleveld, J., Guo, J., Feitosa, D.: A systematic mapping study on graph machine learning for static source code analysis. Inf. Softw. Technol. **183**, 107722

(2025). https://doi.org/10.1016/j.infsof.2025.107722. https://www.sciencedirect.com/science/article/pii/S0950584925000618

19. Van der Maaten, L., Hinton, G.: Visualizing data using t-SNE. J. Mach. Learn. Res. **9**(11), 2579–2605 (2008)

20. Miranda, E.S., Fabris, F., Nascimento, C.G.M., Freitas, A.A., Oliveira, A.C.M.: Meta-learning for recommending metaheuristics for the maxsat problem. In: 2018 7th Brazilian Conference on Intelligent Systems (BRACIS), pp. 169–174 (2018). https://doi.org/10.1109/BRACIS.2018.00037

21. Morais, G., Prati, R.C.: Complex network measures for data set characterization. In: Brazilian Conference on Intelligent Systems (BRACIS), pp. 12–18. IEEE (2013)

22. Nocedal, J., Wright, S.J.: Numerical Optimization. Springer Series in Operations Research, Springer, Cham (2006)

23. Papadimitriou, C.H., Steiglitz, K.: Combinatorial Optimization: Algorithms and Complexity. Courier Corporation (2013)

24. Pardalos, P.M., Resende, M.G.C.: Handbook of Applied Optimization. Oxford University Press (2002)

25. Putra, I.S., Rukmono, S.A., Perdana, R.S.: Abstract syntax tree (AST) and control flow graph (CFG) construction of Notasi algoritmik. In: 2021 International Conference on Data and Software Engineering (ICoDSE), pp. 1–6 (2021)

26. Rousseeuw, P.J.: Silhouettes: a graphical aid to the interpretation and validation of cluster analysis. J. Comput. Appl. Math. **20**, 53–65 (1987). https://doi.org/10.1016/0377-0427(87)90125-7. https://www.sciencedirect.com/science/article/pii/0377042787901257

27. Talbi, E.G.: Metaheuristics: From Design to Implementation, vol. 74. Wiley, Hoboken (2009)

28. Talbi, E.G.: Machine learning into metaheuristics: a survey and taxonomy. ACM Comput. Surv. **54**(6), 1–32 (2021)

29. Thornton, C., Hutter, F., Hoos, H.H., Leyton-Brown, K.: Auto-weka: combined selection and hyperparameter optimization of classification algorithms. In: Proceedings of the 19th ACM SIGKDD International Conference on Knowledge Discovery and Data Mining, pp. 847–855 (2013)

30. Vanschoren, J.: Meta-learning: The Springer Series on Challenges in Machine Learning. Springer, Cham (2019)

31. Vettoruzzo, A., Bouguelia, M.R., Vanschoren, J., Rognvaldsson, T., Santosh, K.: Advances and challenges in meta-learning: a technical review. IEEE Trans. Pattern Anal. Mach. Intell. **46**(7), 4763–4779 (2024)

32. Wistuba, M., Schilling, N., Schmidt-Thieme, L.: Learning hyperparameter optimization initializations. In: 2015 IEEE International Conference on Data Science and Advanced Analytics (DSAA), pp. 1–10 (2015). https://doi.org/10.1109/DSAA.2015.7344817

33. Xu, L., Hutter, F., Hoos, H.H., Leyton-Brown, K.: Satzilla: portfolio-based algorithm selection for SAT. J. Artif. Intell. Res. **32**, 565–606 (2008)

34. Zhang, Z.Q., Qian, B., Hu, R., Jin, H.P., Wang, L.: A matrix-cube-based estimation of distribution algorithm for the distributed assembly permutation flow-shop scheduling problem. Swarm Evol. Comput. **60**, 100785 (2021)

A New Proposal of Layer Insertion in Stacked Autoencoder Neural Networks

Francisco dos Santos Viana[1]([⊠]) [iD], Bianca Valéria Lopes Pereira[2] [iD],
Moisés Santos[4] [iD], Carlos Soares[3] [iD], and Areolino de Almeida Neto[1] [iD]

[1] Federal University of Maranhão, São Luís, Brazil
`francisco.santos@discente.ufma.br, areolino.neto@ufma.br`
[2] Weduu Data Analytics Solutions LTDA, São Paulo, Brazil
[3] Fraunhofer AICOS Portugal, Lab. AI and CS (LIACC), Faculty of Engineering of
Porto, University of Porto, Porto, Portugal
`mrsantos@fe.up.pt`
[4] Faculty of Engineering of Porto, University of Porto, Porto, Portugal
`csoares@fe.up.pt`

Abstract. One strategy for constructing an artificial neural network with multiple hidden layers is to insert layers incrementally in stages. However, for this approach to be effective, each newly added layer must be properly aligned with the previous layers to avoid degradation of the network output and preserve the already learned knowledge. Ideally, inserting new layers should expand the network's search space, enabling it to explore more complex representations and ultimately improve overall performance. In this work, we present a novel method for layer insertion in stacked autoencoder networks. The method developed maintains the learning obtained before the layer insertion and allows the acquisition of new knowledge; therefore, it is denoted collaborative. This approach allows this kind of neural network to evolve and learn effectively, while significantly reducing the design time. Unlike traditional methods, it addresses the common challenges associated with manually defining the number of layers and the number of neurons in each layer. By automating this aspect of network design, the proposed method promotes scalability and adaptability between tasks. The effectiveness of the approach was validated on multiple binary classification datasets using neural networks initialized with various architectures. The experimental results demonstrate that the method maintains performance while streamlining the architectural design process.

Keywords: Deep Learning · Stacked Autoencoder Networks · Collaborative Insertion · Accumulative Learning

1 Introduction

A central area of artificial intelligence is machine learning, where computers learn from examples, often inspired by human learning [18]. In machine learn-

J. Valente de Oliveira et al. (Eds.): EPIA 2025, LNAI 16121, pp. 464–476, 2026.
https://doi.org/10.1007/978-3-032-05176-9_36

ing, a model is built and iteratively refined based on input data, with its learning behavior dictated by the specific type of learning employed (e.g., supervised, unsupervised, or reinforcement learning). Among the computational models used in this domain, artificial neural networks (ANNs) stand out for their ability to approximate complex nonlinear functions and model high-dimensional input-output relationships. Their success is largely attributed to their universal approximation capability and their flexibility in adapting to a wide range of tasks [21].

To achieve high performance, ANNs require careful configuration before training, a process known as hyperparameter tuning. This includes determining the number of hidden layers, neurons per layer, learning rate, dropout rate, activation functions, momentum, number of epochs, batch size, among others [8,16,20]. Selecting these hyperparameters is often manual and time-consuming, typically involving a labor-intensive trial-and-error approach [7,19].

One of the most critical and challenging hyperparameters is the network depth, i.e., the number of hidden layers. This choice often depends heavily on the designer's experience and intuition [9,10]. If too few layers are used, the network may lack the capacity to model complex patterns (underfitting); if too many are used, it may become unnecessarily large, overfit the data, or waste computational resources [2]. Poorly chosen architectures not only degrade model quality but also lead to inefficient use of time and processing power. Consequently, there is a clear need for methods that can automatically and efficiently determine the optimal number of layers.

Defining the network topology—that is, the overall structure and arrangement of neurons—is a non-trivial task. When incrementally adding layers to deep neural networks, especially in stacked autoencoder architectures, a critical challenge arises: preserving the knowledge acquired by previously trained layers while ensuring that the new layers contribute meaningfully to the overall network performance. Traditional approaches that simultaneously train all layers often suffer from issues such as the vanishing gradient problem and the accumulation of estimation errors during backpropagation through many layers [12]. Furthermore, stacking multiple layers sequentially may lead to the overweighting of the original input data in the deeper layers, limiting the ability of the network to extract higher-level abstractions. The lack of systematic methods for topology selection often results in tedious and suboptimal designs, discouraging exploration, and slowing development cycles. In response to this challenge, this work proposes a new collaborative approach for building stacked autoencoder neural networks. In this approach, each new layer is generated independently as a parallel branch, which is later integrated and transformed into a cohesive network layer. This strategy aims to reduce manual intervention, streamline architecture design, and improve the adaptability and performance of the resulting neural networks.

This article is organized into sections. Section 2 presents a literature review. Section 3 describes the proposed collaborative approach. Section 4 presents the materials and setup of the experiments. The obtained results are depicted and discussed in Sect. 5. Finally, Sect. 6 presents the conclusions and further steps.

2   Literature Review

An adequate neural network topology depends on the selection of multiple hyper-parameters, such as learning rate, network depth, layer width, and activation function. To address this challenge, [16] employed Bayesian optimization to identify optimal hyperparameter configurations in physics-guided neural networks. Their method leveraged the loss function history as a predictive guide to explore the hyperparameter search space more efficiently, enabling the selection of high-performance combinations without exhaustive manual tuning.

The studies by [13] and [5] converge in their pursuit of effective hyperparameter optimization strategies for neural networks, although they adopt different approaches. [13] explores various deep recurrent neural network architectures, focusing on hyperparameter tuning and performance comparison with other machine learning techniques. In contrast, [5] employs bio-inspired optimization methods—specifically, the genetic algorithm and particle swarm optimization—to search the hyperparameter space of a multilayer perceptron neural network. Both works report promising results, highlighting the relevance of efficient optimization techniques for enhancing neural network performance across different applications.

The study by [4] investigated the joint construction of Stacked Autoencoder neural networks and the optimization of hyperparameters, demonstrating that the proposed models can compete with and, in some cases, outperform existing approaches in the literature. Similarly, [17] proposed a hyperparameter optimization method based on particle swarm optimization applied to Stacked Autoencoders. Their results show that the proposed algorithm achieves competitive classification accuracy while reducing computational complexity, highlighting the effectiveness of bio-inspired optimization techniques in enhancing stacked architectures.

An improved cascade correlation neural network based on single-objective and multi-objective intelligent group optimization algorithms was proposed by [6]. Compared to the original model, this approach reduced both the required number of hidden units and the network depth. Similarly, [11] introduced a dynamic neural network structure algorithm called CCG-DLNN, which integrates features of the cascade correlation algorithm by inserting new neurons into the hidden layer of an already trained network, allowing incremental growth.

Addressing hyperparameter selection during training, [1] conducted a comparative study of different optimization methods—grid search, Bayesian optimization, and genetic algorithms—to identify the most effective technique for hyperparameter tuning.

3   Collaborative Layer Insertion

The proposed method for collaboratively inserting new hidden layers into a stacked autoencoder network is based on a novel branching architecture designed to preserve learned knowledge while effectively expanding the network's representational capacity. This method is schematically depicted in Fig. 1, which illustrates the integration of a new hidden layer branch alongside an additional branch that directly connects the network's original input to the newly inserted layer. The initial network (solid black lines) is trained using the backpropagation algorithm, and its weights are then kept fixed. A second branch is created and trained with three types of connections: randomly initialized intra-branch connections (blue dashed lines), inter-branch connections connecting both branches (red dashed lines), and connections initialized with zero weights (black dashed lines).

When adding new layers to deep neural networks, especially stacked autoencoders, the main challenge is preserving previously learned knowledge while ensuring the new layers add value. Training all layers simultaneously often causes vanishing gradients and error accumulation [14]. Sequential stacking can overweight the original input in deeper layers, limiting higher-level feature extraction. To solve this, the approach adds new layers as parallel branches, allowing complementary learning without disrupting prior knowledge. An extra branch connects the original input directly to the new layer, balancing the influence of old and new representations and improving incremental learning.

The original input to the network is denoted as $X = (x_1, x_2, \ldots, x_n)$ where n is the number of input neurons. The output of the first hidden layer of the original branch (branch 1) is represented by $H_1 = (h_{11}, h_{12}, \ldots, h_{1m})$, and is computed via a nonlinear activation function (f) applied to the weighted sum of inputs plus biases, according to Eq. 1

$$H_1 = f(W_1^1 X + b_1^1) \tag{1}$$

where W_1^1 is the weight matrix connecting the input layer to the first hidden layer, and b_1^1 is the bias vector for that layer. Simultaneously, the output layer of the original branch produces $O_1 = (o_{11}, o_{12}, \ldots, o_{1n})$, which represents the network's learned representation or prediction at the current stage, representation by the matamaic process of Eq. 2. Ther W_1^2 is the weight matrix that connects the hidden layer to the output and b_1^2 is the bias vector for that layer.

$$O_1 = f(W_1^2 H_2 + b_1^2) \tag{2}$$

The newly inserted extra branch $E = (e_1, e_2, \ldots, e_p)$ computes its output as shown in Eq. 3, where the original input data is passed through a nonlinear transformation.

$$E = f(W_1^e X + b_1^e) \tag{3}$$

where W_1^e and b_1^e are the weights and biases that directly connect the input layer to the extra branch neurons. This direct linkage ensures that raw input

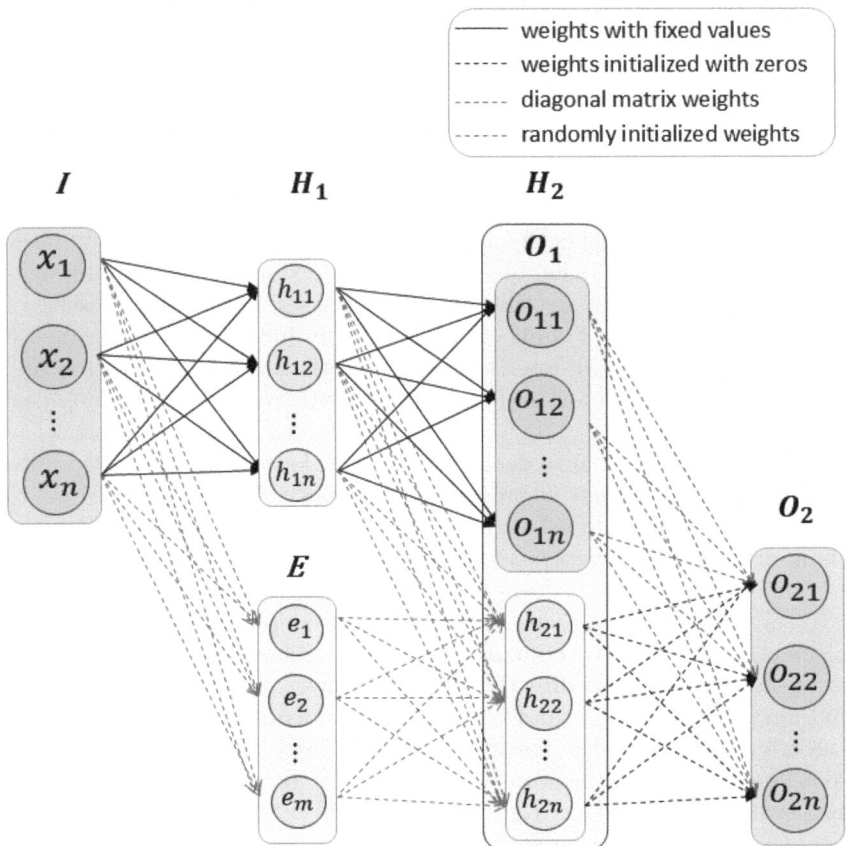

Fig. 1. Schematic of collaborative insertion with creation of hidden layer and extra branch.

information is preserved and can influence the new hidden layer independently of the learned representations from previous layers.

The new hidden layer branch (branch 2) receives inputs from two sources:
- The output of the original hidden layer H_1, - The output of the extra branch E, - The output layer of the original branch O_1.

The combined input to the new hidden layer is formulated in Eq. 4.

$$H_2 = [f(W_2^1 H_1 + W_2^e E + b_2^1) \ O_1]^T \tag{4}$$

W_2^1 and W_2^e are the respective weight matrices connecting H_1 and E to the new hidden layer, and b_2^1 is the bias vector. The hidden layer of the new branch is concatenated with the previous output O_1, ensuring that the prior knowledge is explicitly integrated into the input space of the new layer.

The weights w_2^2, represent the connections between the newly added hidden layer and the output layer of the second branch. This initialization ensures that the new neurons do not interfere with the network's previously acquired knowledge at the start of training.

The output layer of the new branch (branch 2) receives inputs from two distinct sources: (i) the hidden layer of the same branch and (ii) the output layer of the previous branch (branch 1). The connections originating from the hidden layer of the new branch are represented by the weight vector w_2^2, which is initially set to zero to avoid interfering with the prior learning stage. On the other hand, the direct contribution of the previous branch's output to the final output is controlled through a diagonal weight matrix $I_k(n)$, where each element on the main diagonal has a fixed gain value k. This matrix maintains the influence of the previously trained branch during the training of the new hidden layer.

These two components are concatenated horizontally to form the complete weight matrix W_2^2, as shown in Eq. 5. This matrix defines the weights between the concatenated representation of the previous output and the new hidden layer (vector H_2) and the output layer of the second branch:

$$W_2^2 = [I_k(n) \ \ w_2^2]_{n \times (n+m)} \tag{5}$$

where n corresponds to the number of output neurons (same as in branch 1), and m is the number of neurons in the newly added hidden layer. The resulting matrix W_2^2 is of dimension $n \times (n + m)$, ensuring that each output neuron has access to both the original predictions from branch 1 (scaled by k) and the new latent features from the additional hidden layer.

This structure ensures a collaborative training process, in which the new hidden layer complements rather than overrides the contributions of the earlier network. Initially, only the newly added connections (i.e., w_2^2) are subject to updates during backpropagation, while the contributions from the original network remain unchanged through the fixed values in $I_k(n)$.

In parallel, the matrix $I_k(n)$ represents a fixed identity-like diagonal connection between the output of the first branch and the final output layer of the network. Each element on the main diagonal of this matrix has a fixed value k, which defines the strength of the direct contribution from the first branch's output to the final output.

Together, w_2^2 and $I_k(n)$ are horizontally concatenated to form the complete weight matrix W_2^2, which determines the final output of the model after the second branch is added. The structure of W_2^2 is illustrated below, where the red-highlighted elements (k) represent the fixed diagonal values from the previous branch, and the remaining elements (initialized to zero) correspond to the new connections yet to be trained:

$$W_2^2 = \begin{bmatrix} k & 0 & \cdots & 0 & 0 & 0 & \cdots & 0 \\ 0 & k & \cdots & 0 & 0 & 0 & \cdots & 0 \\ \vdots & \vdots & \ddots & \vdots & \vdots & \vdots & \ddots & \vdots \\ 0 & 0 & \cdots & k & 0 & 0 & \cdots & 0 \end{bmatrix}_{n \times (n+m)}$$

This way of initializing the weights ensures that the output of the new branch does not lead to an increase in the training error of the network. Thus, initially, the final output layer of the neural network continues to reflect the behavior of the previous configuration (branch 1), while at the same time providing room for improvement through training the newly added connections in w_2^2.

Finally, the output of branch 2 is computed by applying the activation function (f) to the weighted sum of the new hidden layer activations plus biases:

$$O_2 = f(W_2^2 H_2 + b_2^2) \tag{6}$$

where W_2^2 and b_2^2 correspond to the weights and biases from the new hidden layer to its output layer.

The activation function of the output layer of the new branch should initially be linear to avoid interference with existing learned knowledge. However, we explore the feasibility of mutating this function during the training process of the new branch to evaluate possible improvements.

4   Experimental Set-Up

The algorithms were developed using the Python programming language and computational resources provided by Google Colab [15]. The system used the OpenML CC18 database, selecting data sets with between 500 and 1000 instances, 20 to 25 features, and exactly 2 classes, making a total of 4 datasets [3].

The mean squared error (MSE), defined in Eq. 7, was used to optimize the network parameters during training using the backpropagation algorithm.

$$J_{MSE}(\theta_f) = \frac{1}{n} \sum_{i=1}^{n} L_{MSE}(O_i, O_i') = \frac{1}{n} \sum_{i=1}^{n} \left(\frac{1}{2} ||O_i - O_i'||^2 \right) \tag{7}$$

To validate the functioning of the proposed model, we used the same validation metrics chosen in many studies in this area: accuracy, precision, sensitivity, specificity, F1-score, and AUC - which measure the area under the Receiver Operating Characteristic (ROC) curve and indicate the model's ability to discriminate between positive and negative classes.

The networks started with an input layer, a first hidden layer with 100 neurons, and a single-neuron output layer. A learning rate of 10^{-5} was used for both input-to-hidden and hidden-to-output connections. Hidden layers employed the hyperbolic tangent (tanh) activation function; the output layer used a linear activation. Each procedure of inserting a new branch was executed for up to 500 epochs.

For each layer insertion method in the stacked autoencoder network, four additional hidden layers were incrementally inserted. After all insertions, the architecture consisted of one input layer, five hidden layers, and one output layer. The impact of mutating the output layer's activation function from linear (*Normal*) to nonlinear was analyzed. This mutation was applied in two scenarios:

while the layer still functioned as an output layer (*ChangeOut*), and after it had been transformed into a hidden layer (*ChangeHidden*).

In the experiments, different types of growth of stacked autoencoder collaborative networks were evaluated, which means, the number of neurons in the new hidden layer, related to previous ones, could be the same (constant), increasing, decreasing, and random number. In addition to the number of neurons, the adjustment of the weight k (the connection between the hidden layer of the new branch and the output layer of the old branch) was evaluated. To mitigate the overweighting of the original data at each inserted layer, the use of the extra branch was evaluated. With this, the following conventions were created:

- M1: constant k weight and no extra branch (no connection to layer E in Fig. 1)
- M2: adjustable k weight and no extra branch
- M3: constant k weight with extra branch (with connection to layer E)
- M4: adjustable k weight with extra branch

5   Results

Figure 2 presents the average accuracy as new layers are added, considering the method types used across datasets and the presence or absence of mutation in the activation function of the branch output layer. Thus, *ChangeHidden* achieves the highest accuracy, reaching approximately 0.765 at layers four and five. *ChangeOut* performs slightly below *ChangeHidden* but surpasses *Normal* after layer two. The *Normal* configuration plateaus around 0.755 starting from layer three. In method M2, *ChangeOut* attains the highest accuracy, about 0.785 at layer five. *ChangeHidden* also shows steady improvement but remains marginally behind *ChangeOut*. Meanwhile, *Normal* saturates early at around 0.745 and stays flat from layer two onward. For the method M3, all configurations show accuracy gains with additional layers. *ChangeOut* and *ChangeHidden* perform comparably and outperform *Normal*, which exhibits modest growth and plateaus near 0.75. In the M4, *ChangeOut* and *ChangeHidden* rapidly increase accuracy, reaching around 0.80 at layers four and five. Conversely, *Normal* grows more slowly and stabilizes below 0.75.

ChangeOut and *ChangeHidden* consistently outperform the *Normal* training strategy as network depth increases. The most pronounced gains in accuracy are observed between layers one and three, indicating that the modified training strategies are particularly effective during early-stage deepening. Among the two, *ChangeHidden* tends to be either competitive with or superior to *ChangeOut*, especially in deeper architectures. In contrast, the *Normal* strategy yields the lowest accuracy across all configurations and exhibits minimal responsiveness to increasing depth, underscoring its limited scalability in deeper models.

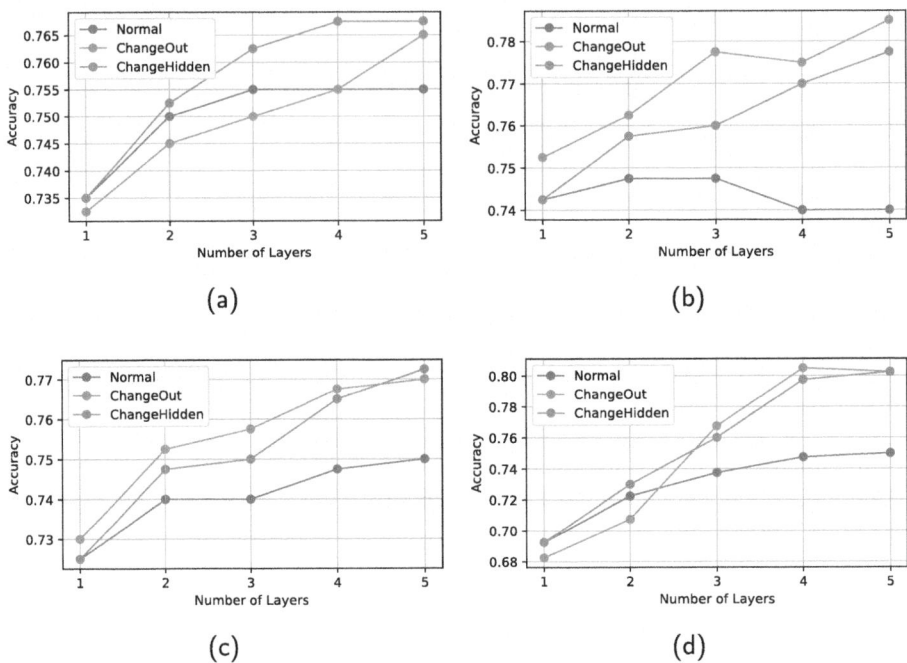

Fig. 2. Average accuracy as a function of the number of layers inserted: (a) Method M1. (b) Method M2. (c) Method M3. (d) Method M4.

These results highlight how each training strategy leverages increased network depth. *ChangeOut* and *ChangeHidden* consistently outperform the *Normal* strategy, particularly during the early stages of deepening (layers one to three), where most accuracy gains are observed. This suggests that the proposed strategies integrate additional layers more effectively. Among them, *ChangeHidden* shows superior performance across different methods. In contrast, the *Normal* strategy saturates quickly, with minimal improvement beyond layer two, indicating poor scalability. Although there is slight variation across datasets (M1–M4), the overall trend remains consistent, reinforcing the generalizability of the findings. These results indicate that the proposed modifications are not only beneficial but also better suited for deeper network configurations.

The boxplots in Fig. 3 compare test accuracy across three output layer activation function scenarios: *Normal*, *ChangeOut*, and *ChangeHidden*. Each subplot presents the mean, standard deviation, minimum, and maximum accuracy values for each condition.

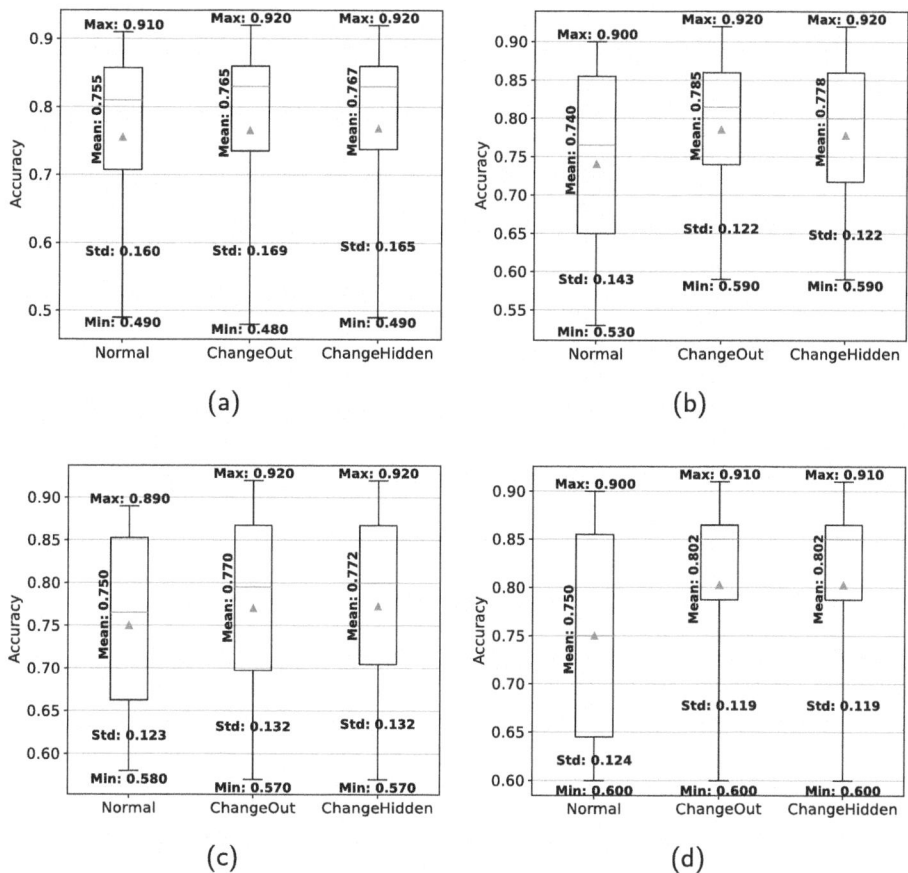

Fig. 3. Evolution of the calculation according to the number of layers inserted (a) Method M1. (b) Method M2. (c) Method M3. (d) Method M4.

In subplot (a), mean accuracy is similar for *Normal* and *ChangeOut* (both 0.775), while *ChangeHidden* has a slightly lower mean (0.747). Variability, measured by standard deviation, is greatest for *ChangeHidden* (0.185), followed by *ChangeOut* (0.169) and *Normal* (0.160). This shows that despite stable mean accuracy, the modified scenarios—especially *ChangeHidden*—display higher variability. In subplot (b), both *ChangeOut* and *ChangeHidden* surpass *Normal* in mean accuracy (0.765 and 0.766 vs. 0.740) and exhibit lower variability (standard deviations 0.122 vs. 0.143), indicating improved performance and greater consistency. The subplot (c), mean accuracy increases for both modifications (0.770 for *ChangeOut* and *ChangeHidden* against 0.750 for *Normal*), but *ChangeOut* exhibits the highest variability (standard deviation of 0.157), followed by *ChangeHidden* (0.132) and *Normal* (0.123). Finally, subplot (d) shows the highest mean accuracies for *ChangeOut* and *ChangeHidden* (both 0.802), with lower standard deviations (0.119) compared to *Normal* (0.124). Thus, *ChangeOut* and *ChangeHidden* significantly improve prediction accuracy and stability, with *ChangeHidden* having an advantage over the *Normal* strategy.

Table 1 summarizes the mean ± standard deviation of key performance metrics for three training paradigms: *Normal*, *ChangeOut*, and *ChangeHidden*. Os valores foram obtidos a partir da mídia dos resultados obtidos nos conjuntos de dados usados, independentemente do tipo de crescimento e do método. Both *ChangeOut* and *ChangeHidden* demonstrate notable improvements in classification accuracy (0.778 and 0.777, respectively) and specificity (0.830 for both) relative to the *Normal* strategy (accuracy: 0.705; specificity: 0.747). Despite these gains, a substantial reduction in sensitivity is observed (0.180 vs. 0.273 with *Normal*), indicating a diminished capacity to correctly identify positive instances. Precision and F1-score exhibit minimal variation across the methods. We intend to expand the analysis to include more datasets to verify if the observed low AUC values persist. This aims to better understand the robustness and generalization capacity of the models across diverse data.

Table 1. Performance metrics for each training strategy

Strategy	Accuracy	Sensitivity	Specificity	Precision	F1-score	AUC
Normal	0.705	0.273 ± 0.252	0.747 ± 0.261	0.279 ± 0.279	0.242 ± 0.230	0.512
ChangeOut	0.778	0.182 ± 0.281	0.829 ± 0.282	0.267 ± 0.338	0.187 ± 0.268	0.536
ChangeHide	0.777	0.177 ± 0.268	0.835 ± 0.265	0.275 ± 0.335	0.188 ± 0.264	0.533

The *ChangeOut* and *ChangeHidden* strategies outperformed the *Normal* method across key metrics, with more consistent accuracy and higher specificity. Both also achieved better AUC values, indicating improved class separability. Precision was slightly better with *ChangeHidden*, reflecting enhanced accuracy in predicting positive cases. Even with lower sensitivity and F1-score, strategies that perform activation function mutation demonstrated clear improvements in robustness and overall performance.

6   Conclusion

The proposed approach demonstrates that employing a collaborative branching strategy to insert new hidden layers into stacked autoencoders offers significant advantages in both performance and scalability. The experimental results indicate that the ChangeOut and ChangeHidden configurations consistently outperform the standard model, particularly in terms of accuracy and specificity, while also preserving or enhancing other critical metrics such as precision. Although sensitivity remained relatively low across all tested configurations, the overall balanced performance suggests that the collaborative mechanism effectively maintains useful learned representations and significantly improves the network's ability to extract, integrate, and combine relevant features.

This approach's core strength lies in its ability to preserve previously acquired knowledge while increasing the model's representational capacity through direct input pathways and modular training processes. By enabling the insertion of new layers without requiring complete retraining, the system fosters a more stable and flexible learning environment, reducing the risks of catastrophic forgetting. Consequently, the network can progressively deepen, adapt, and evolve in response to new data or tasks, all while maintaining efficiency.

Furthermore, this modular design facilitates easier experimentation and customization, as different branches can be trained or fine-tuned independently before integration. This not only reduces computational overhead but also opens pathways for transfer learning and incremental updates in real-world applications. Taken together, these benefits establish the collaborative branching strategy as a promising and practical framework for developing deeper, more adaptive, and resource-efficient neural models that can tackle increasingly complex problems. Future work will focus on extending this method to larger architectures, comparing it against baselines in other tasks, and improving sensitivity performance through targeted optimization techniques, including cost function adjustments and class reweighting.

Acknowledgments. We thank IFMA, UFMA, and FEUP for institutional support. This work was supported by the Coordination for the Improvement of Higher Education Personnel (CAPES) – Brazil, under Financing Code 001. It was also partially funded by FCT through the 2020–2023 plurianual funding of LIACC (UIDB/00027/2020 and UIDP/00027/2020). Computational resources were provided by Google Cloud Platform under the project CPCA-IAC/AF/594904/2023.

Disclosure of Interests. The authors declare no competing interests relevant to this article.

References

1. Alibrahim, H., Ludwig, S.A.: Hyperparameter optimization: comparing genetic algorithm against grid search and Bayesian optimization. In: 2021 IEEE Congress on Evolutionary Computation (CEC), pp. 1551–1559 (2021). https://doi.org/10.1109/CEC45853.2021.9504761
2. Bejani, M.M., Ghatee, M.: A systematic review on overfitting control in shallow and deep neural networks. Artif. Intell. Rev. **54**(8), 6391–6438 (2021). https://doi.org/10.1007/s10462-021-09975-1
3. Bischl, B., et al.: OpenML benchmarking suites. arXiv:1708.03731v2 [stat.ML] (2019)
4. Brunner, C., Kő, A., Fodor, S.: An autoencoder-enhanced stacking neural network model for increasing the performance of intrusion detection. J. Artif. Intell. Soft Comput. Res. **12**(2), 149–163 (2021)
5. Buarque, T.M.T., Marinho, M.B.L., Junior, F.M.B.: Genetic algorithm and PSO applied to the choice of hyperparameters of an MLP neural network for non-functional requirements classification. Res. Soc. Dev. **11**(3), e55411326984 (2022)

6. Deng, J., Li, Q., Wei, W.: Improved cascade correlation neural network model based on group intelligence optimization algorithm. Axioms **12**(2), 164 (2023). https://doi.org/10.3390/axioms12020164

7. Hammad, M.M.: Artificial neural network and deep learning: fundamentals and theory. arXiv preprint arXiv:2408.16002 (2024)

8. Hansen, L.D., Stokholm-Bjerregaard, M., Durdevic, P.: Modeling phosphorous dynamics in a wastewater treatment process using Bayesian optimized LSTM. Comput. Chem. Eng. **160**, 107738 (2022)

9. Liao, L., Li, H., Shang, W., Ma, L.: An empirical study of the impact of hyper-parameter tuning and model optimization on the performance properties of deep neural networks. ACM Trans. Softw. Eng. Methodol. (TOSEM) **31**(3), 1–40 (2022)

10. Mienye, I.D., Swart, T.G.: A comprehensive review of deep learning: architectures, recent advances, and applications. Information **15**(12) (2024). https://doi.org/10. 3390/info15120755. https://www.mdpi.com/2078-2489/15/12/755

11. Mohamed, S.A.E.M., Mohamed, M.H., Farghally, M.F.: A new cascade-correlation growing deep learning neural network algorithm. Algorithms **14**(5), 158 (2021). https://doi.org/10.3390/a14050158

12. Montesinos López, O.A., Montesinos López, A., Crossa, J.: Fundamentals of artificial neural networks and deep learning. In: Multivariate Statistical Machine Learning Methods for Genomic Prediction, pp. 379–425. Springer, Cham (2022). https://doi.org/10.1007/978-3-030-89010-0_10

13. Morteza, A., Yahyaeian, A.A., Mirzaeibonehkhater, M., Sadeghi, S., Mohaimeni, A., Taheri, S.: Deep learning hyperparameter optimization: application to electricity and heat demand prediction for buildings. Energy Build. **289**, 113036 (2023)

14. Ravikumar, A., Sriraman, H.: Mitigating vanishing gradient in SGD optimization in neural networks. In: International Conference on Information, Communication and Computing Technology, pp. 1–11. Springer, Cham (2023)

15. dos Santos Viana, F., Pereira, B.V.L., Santos, M., Soares, C., de Almeida Neto, A.: Algorithm for layer insertion in stacked autoencoder neural networks with activation function change (2025). https://github.com/frahncky/RNAStacked-learning

16. Silva, R.E., Camata, J.J.: Hyperparameter optimization of physics-guided neural networks in convective-diffusive problems. In: Simpósio em Sistemas Computacionais de Alto Desempenho (SSCAD), pp. 137–144. SBC (2024). https://doi.org/ 10.5753/sscad_estendido.2024.244373

17. Sun, Y., Xue, B., Zhang, M., Yen, G.G.: An experimental study on hyper-parameter optimization for stacked auto-encoders. In: 2018 IEEE Congress on Evolutionary Computation (CEC), pp. 1–8. IEEE (2018)

18. Taye, M.M.: Understanding of machine learning with deep learning: architectures, workflow, applications and future directions. Computers **12**(5), 91 (2023)

19. Ünal, H.T., Başçiftçi, F.: Evolutionary design of neural network architectures: a review of three decades of research. Artif. Intell. Rev. **55**(3), 1723–1802 (2022). https://doi.org/10.1007/s10462-021-10049-5

20. Yu, T., Zhu, H.: Hyper-parameter optimization: a review of algorithms and applications. arXiv preprint arXiv:2003.05689 (2020)

21. Zhang, A., Lipton, Z.C., Li, M., Smola, A.J.: Dive into Deep Learning. Cambridge University Press, Cambridge (2023)

Ethics and Responsibility in AI (ERAI)

Evaluating Coreset Selection with Coverage and Density: A Data Quality Perspective

Bárbara Capelo[1,2]([✉]) [iD], Maria Russo[2] [iD], André Carreiro[2] [iD],
Hugo Gamboa[1,2] [iD], and Duarte Folgado[2] [iD]

[1] LIBPhys (Laboratory for Instrumentation, Biomedical Engineering and Radiation Physics), Lisbon, Portugal
[2] Fraunhofer Portugal AICOS, Porto, Portugal
barbara.capelo@aicos.fraunhofer.pt

Abstract. Coreset selection aims to identify small, informative subsets of data that retain the essential characteristics of the full dataset, enabling efficient model training. However, the quality of these subsets is typically evaluated solely based on downstream performance metrics such as accuracy, leaving open questions about what makes a good subset beyond predictive performance. In this paper, we revisit two data quality measures used for evaluating synthetic data (coverage and density) and study how they can be applied to evaluate coreset selection methods. Coverage measures how well the coreset spans the full dataset, while density captures how concentrated the subset samples are within regions densely populated by the full dataset. We evaluate four coreset selection strategies (Uniform sampling, Entropy-based selection, Contextual Diversity, and Graph Cut) on the CIFAR-10 dataset using a ResNet-18 model. Our results show that coverage and density offer valuable insights into the behavior of coreset selection methods, explain performance differences, and highlight trade-offs between exploration and exploitation. Our findings suggest that incorporating coverage and density into the evaluation of coreset selection can inform the design of more effective coreset algorithms and serve as complementary benchmarks for the community to assess and compare dataset quality beyond accuracy alone.

Keywords: Coreset Selection · Responsible AI · Data Quality · Density · Coverage · CIFAR-10

1 Introduction

Deep Learning (DL) has achieved remarkable success in recent years, enabled by advances in computational hardware and the availability of large-scale datasets. However, as neural network architectures and training datasets grow in size, so do the demands on memory, computing, and energy consumption. This raises practical and environmental concerns, particularly for researchers and practitioners with limited computational resources. *Coreset selection* has emerged as

J. Valente de Oliveira et al. (Eds.): EPIA 2025, LNAI 16121, pp. 479–491, 2026.
https://doi.org/10.1007/978-3-032-05176-9_37

a compelling approach to mitigate these issues, focusing on identifying a compact subset S of the most informative examples from a larger training dataset T, thereby reducing the overall training computational burden.

Training a model on a carefully curated, smaller dataset offers several advantages: (1) it enables cost savings and accelerates research iterations by facilitating a more efficient exploration of hypotheses through manual and automated experimentation; (2) it lowers computational demands, directly reducing the carbon footprint associated with energy-intensive hardware; and (3) it democratizes access to state-of-the-art models by allowing a broader community to train high-performance algorithms on more widely available computational resources.

Numerous coreset selection strategies have been proposed, including importance sampling [8], herding [14], k-center selection [17], and gradient-based subset selection [9]. Guo et al., [5] conducted a large experiment evaluating 15 coreset selection methods. The results suggest that, although various methods have advantages in certain experimental settings, random selection remains a surprisingly strong baseline. These methods are typically evaluated based on their downstream performance, most often measured by test accuracy, across varying subset sizes.

Although various coreset selection strategies have been extensively evaluated for their predictive performance, the representational fidelity of these subsets remains inadequately understood. Motivated by this gap, our study addresses the need for a more comprehensive evaluation of coreset selection using data quality metrics. We draw inspiration from metrics developed in the context of evaluating synthetic data. These metrics quantify the similarity between real and generated data distributions, making them also well-suited to evaluate how faithfully a coreset approximates the full dataset. Although such metrics have gained traction in synthetic data evaluation [13], their application to coreset selection remains underexplored.

In this study, we examine whether metrics originally designed to assess the fidelity and diversity of synthetic data can provide complementary insights into the representativeness of coresets. Specifically, we reinterpret these metrics to compare a coreset against the full dataset, thereby assessing how well the subset selected for a given coreset selection method preserves the structural properties of the original data distribution. The main contributions of this work are as follows:

1. We adapt and formalize existing data quality metrics for evaluating coreset fidelity and diversity.
2. We present an empirical evaluation of coreset methods using these metrics on an image classification task, showing how they capture properties not reflected in accuracy alone.
3. We provide empirical evidence addressing *why* random selection remains a robust baseline by highlighting its inherent representational properties.

This work contributes to Responsible Artificial Intelligence (AI) by introducing a more transparent and interpretable evaluation framework for coreset selection. By leveraging data quality metrics beyond accuracy, we enable practitioners to assess how well a subset performs and how faithfully it represents the original data distribution. This contributes to fairness and robustness auditing by highlighting potential underrepresentation of rare or diverse patterns in training subsets. Additionally, the selection of smaller yet representative datasets promotes sustainability by reducing computational costs and energy consumption in model training and evaluation.

The remainder of the paper is structured as follows. Section 2 defines the data quality metrics and their adaptation to coreset evaluation. Section 3 outlines the experimental setup. Section 4 presents and discusses the results, followed by a broader discussion in Sect. 5, and concluding remarks in Sect. 6.

2   Preliminaries

In this section, we begin by formally defining the coreset selection problem. We then describe three representative coreset selection methods employed in our experiments. Finally, we revisit data quality measures originally proposed for evaluating synthetic data and clarify how they can be interpreted in the context of coreset selection to compare a given subset with the full dataset.

2.1   Problem Formulation

Given a supervised learning task, a large training set $\mathcal{T} := \{(x_i, y_i)\}_{i=1}^{|\mathcal{T}|}$, where each input x_i belongs to the input space $\mathcal{X}$ and each corresponding label y_i belongs to the output space $\mathcal{Y}$. The objective of coreset selection is to identify a smaller, yet highly informative subset $\mathcal{S} := \{(s_i, y_i)\}_{i=1}^{|\mathcal{S}|}$, where $\mathcal{S} \subset \mathcal{T}$, such that $|\mathcal{S}| \ll |\mathcal{T}|$, and training a model $\theta_{\mathcal{S}}$ on this subset yields comparable generalization performance to training the model $\theta_{\mathcal{T}}$ on the full training dataset.

2.2   Coreset Selection Methods

Uncertainty-Based Selection. Uncertainty-based selection operates under the assumption that samples the model is less confident about can contribute more significantly to learning during optimization than those it classifies with high confidence. As such, these uncertain samples are prioritized when constructing the coreset. Given a classification problem with C classes, the uncertainty of a sample x_i is quantified using the entropy of the predicted class distribution:

$$\mathcal{H}(p(\hat{y} \mid x_i)) = -\sum_{i=1}^{C} p(\hat{y} = i \mid x_i) \log p(\hat{y} = i \mid x_i). \tag{1}$$

Samples are ranked based on these scores and selected in decreasing order.

Contextual Diversity. Contextual Diversity [1] emphasizes the selection of samples that exhibit diverse contextual relationships within the model's output space. Unlike other methods focusing solely on uncertainty or feature-space diversity, Contextual Diversity leverages the observation that the predicted probability vectors of a Convolutional Neural Network (CNN) encapsulate information from a broader receptive field, reflecting spatial co-occurrence patterns. By analyzing these probability distributions, the method identifies samples that introduce novel contextual variations, thereby enhancing the representational richness of the training set. This approach is particularly effective in capturing the nuances of spatial context, which are often overlooked by conventional selection criteria.

Graph Cut Submodular Function. Graph Cut [7] is a submodularity-based method that selects informative examples by maximizing a submodular objective that balances representativeness and diversity. The training set is modeled as a fully connected graph, where each node corresponds to a sample and edges represent pairwise similarities, measured using a similarity kernel $d(\cdot, \cdot)$, such as the cosine similarity computed in the model's embedding space. The selection criterion is defined as:

$$f(S) = \lambda \sum_{i \in \mathcal{T}} \sum_{s \in \mathcal{S}} d_{is} - \sum_{s_1, s_2 \in \mathcal{S}} d_{s_1 s_2}, \tag{2}$$

where $\mathcal{T}$ is the full training set, $\mathcal{S}$ is the selected subset, and λ captures the trade-off between diversity and representativeness. The first term favors subsets $\mathcal{S}$ that are highly connected to the entire dataset $\mathcal{T}$, while the second penalizes internal redundancy within $\mathcal{S}$. Thus, Graph Cut tends to select representative and diverse examples, often favoring samples from regions of the feature space that are well-connected to the rest of the dataset, which may include dense areas, while avoiding redundancy among selected samples.

2.3   Data Quality Measures

Naeem et al. [13] introduced *Density* and *Coverage* for evaluating *fidelity* and *diversity*, respectively, in the synthetic image generation task. Fidelity refers to the degree to which the generated samples resemble the real ones. Diversity measures whether the generated samples cover the full variability of the real samples. Although initially proposed for evaluating synthetic data, we argue that these metrics extend naturally to assessing coreset selection methods.

Both metrics count the number of samples within manifolds of the full training set data distributions. Let $B(x, r) \subset \mathbb{R}^D$ denote the closed ball of radius r centered at point $x \in \mathbb{R}^D$ of D features. We define $\mathrm{NND}_k(x_i)$ as the distance from $x_i \in \mathcal{T}$ to its k-th nearest neighbor in $\mathcal{T} \setminus \{x_i\}$.

Density. In the context of coreset selection, *density* quantifies how concentrated the subset samples are within regions densely populated by the full dataset.

$$\text{Density} := \frac{1}{k \cdot |\mathcal{S}|} \sum_{j=1}^{|\mathcal{S}|} \sum_{i=1}^{|\mathcal{T}|} \mathbf{1}_{s_j \in B(x_i, \mathrm{NND}_k(x_i))}, \tag{3}$$

where k is the k-nearest neighbors. Density reflects the expected overlap of the coreset samples with high-density regions of the full dataset manifold. It is not upper-bounded by 1 and may exceed 1 in densely packed regions of $\mathcal{T}$.

Coverage. The *coverage* metric captures how well the coreset spans the full dataset. Intuitively, it measures the proportion of samples in the full dataset $\mathcal{T}$ that are "covered" by the coreset $\mathcal{S}$. i.e., whose local neighborhood contains at least one coreset point. Coverage is formally defined as:

$$\text{Coverage} := \frac{1}{|\mathcal{T}|} \sum_{i=1}^{|\mathcal{T}|} 1_{\exists j \text{ s.t. } s_j \in B(x_i, \text{NND}_k(x_i))}. \tag{4}$$

This metric lies in the interval $[0, 1]$ and reflects the proportion of the full dataset locally represented by the coreset. Higher coverage indicates that the coreset touches more regions of the original data manifold.

3 Experimental Setup

Dataset. We use the CIFAR-10 dataset, a standard benchmark for image classification and coreset selection, comprising 60,000 color images (32×32 pixels) across 10 classes [10]. Our experiments follow the standard data splitting strategy, using 50,000 images for training and 10,000 for testing.

Model. We used a ResNet-18 as the backbone architecture for all experiments [6]. All models were trained using stochastic gradient descent (SGD) with a batch size of 128, an initial learning rate of 0.1, and a cosine annealing learning rate scheduler. We set the momentum to 0.9 and applied a weight decay of 5×10^{-4}. Each model was trained for 200 epochs.

Workflow. We used the DeepCore library [5] to perform coreset selection using three methods: ENTROPY, CONTEXTUAL DIVERSITY, and GRAPH CUT. For the GRAPH CUT, we set $\lambda = 1$. As a baseline, we included uniform RANDOM sampling. For each method, we generated class-balanced subsets of varying sizes, ranging from 0.1% to 90% of the full training set, ensuring an equal number of samples per class. All experiments were repeated five times with different random seeds to account for variability in the selection process. For each run, the subsets were constructed incrementally, with the smaller ones fully contained in the larger. In total, we evaluated $13 \times 4 \times 5 = 260$ subsets.

For each selected subset, we trained a model using only the subset and evaluated its accuracy on the held-out test set. In addition, we computed coverage and density to compare the subset with the full training dataset. These metrics were computed using the pyMDMA library [2], with Euclidean distance as the underlying metric. For coverage, we used $k = 1$, and for density $k = 5$.

All reported values for accuracy, coverage, and density are averages over five independent runs.

To qualitatively assess the selected subsets across different fractions, we projected the feature embeddings from the global average pooling layer of a pre-trained ResNet-18 into two dimensions using Uniform Manifold Approximation and Projection (UMAP) [12]. We visualized the results for a representative random seed and estimated the sample density over the embedded space by fitting a Gaussian Kernel Density Estimation (KDE) model to the UMAP-transformed data. These visualizations allowed us to observe how the spatial distribution of selected samples evolves across different fraction sizes and selection strategies.

4   Results

4.1   Quantitative Evaluation

Figure 1 shows the accuracy, density, and coverage of the different methods across several subsets with varying fraction size. The accuracy curve obtained aligns with the reported results from Guo et al. [5].

RANDOM sampling achieves the highest value of accuracy in early fractions ($\geq 10\%$ and $\leq 30\%$). RANDOM sampling has higher coverage than all the other methods and has an approximate constant density for fractions higher than 5%. This behavior is likely due to its broad, unbiased selection. It quickly spans the manifold by capturing a diverse initial subset of samples (high coverage) without overfocusing on dense regions (moderate density).

ENTROPY and CONTEXTUAL DIVERSITY initially focus on low-density regions, leading to lower early-stage coverage and lower redundancy. While this downgrades accuracy in early fractions ($\leq 30\%$), their later-stage sampling spans the data manifold more effectively, resulting in higher accuracy for the later fractions. Entropy-based selection targets ambiguous or low-confidence samples, which the model finds difficult to classify. In CIFAR-10, such samples are not necessarily located near class boundaries; instead, they may represent atypical examples within each class that lie in sparser areas of the feature space. Similarly, CONTEXTUAL DIVERSITY emphasizes semantic diversity[1] and initially selects peripheral samples, leading to similarly low early coverage and density. As a result, both methods tend to avoid densely populated, confidently classified regions in the early stages, which slows coverage and density growth. Although these uncertain points are often informative, they do not broadly represent the dataset's structure, which limits generalization in the early stages and contributes to the lower accuracy observed for smaller subsets.

GRAPH CUT shows better accuracy in small fractions between 0.1%–5%. However, as the fraction size increases, its performance degrades, yielding lower

---

[1] Semantic diversity captures variation in class predictions across samples, accounting for differences in object categories and their surrounding spatial context. For example, two images may both contain a pedestrian, but one in front of a fence and another beside a bicycle. Though visually similar, their differing contextual backgrounds induce distinct prediction patterns in the model [1].

accuracy compared to alternative methods in the 20%–60% range. In terms of density, GRAPH CUT selects subsets with higher density for fraction sizes up to 50%; beyond this point, the density falls below that of RANDOM selection. This behavior reflects the diminishing returns of submodular optimization: in small fractions, GRAPH CUT prioritizes highly connected, dense points. As the fraction size increases, most representative regions have already been covered, and additional selections increasingly consist of peripheral, less connected points, causing a drop in average density. GRAPH CUT consistently prioritizes representative samples from dense regions while preserving sufficient diversity to minimize redundancy. While effective at small fraction sizes, this focus leads to diminishing marginal gains as the fraction increases, ultimately resulting in lower accuracy compared to alternative methods in the 20%–60% range.

4.2   Qualitative Evaluation

Figure 2 presents UMAP visualizations of the feature embeddings from selected subsets at different fraction sizes and under the selection strategies. These visualizations complement the quantitative analysis by offering additional insights into how each method explores the structure of the data manifold.

The RANDOM method shows a broad and even spread of samples across the embedding space from the outset, consistently covering both dense and sparse regions. In contrast, ENTROPY and CONTEXTUAL DIVERSITY initially start in lower-density regions of the data manifold, often corresponding to ambiguous or high-uncertainty zones. This behavior is especially pronounced at lower selection fractions, where these methods avoid the densely populated clusters, yet locally differentiated, prioritized by GRAPH CUT and indirectly by RANDOM selection.

As selection size increases, ENTROPY and CONTEXTUAL DIVERSITY expand and progressively incorporate more central and denser regions. Notably, ENTROPY tends to focus on uncertain examples near class boundaries, resulting in early selections that are informative but localized. On the other hand, CONTEXTUAL DIVERSITY prioritizes semantically diverse yet often peripheral samples, gradually shifting toward denser and more representative areas as the subset grows.

The GRAPH CUT method exhibits a distinct pattern: selected samples concentrate in high-density regions from early fractions. This leads to subsets composed of samples that are likely related in feature space. As the selection fraction increases, GRAPH CUT remains focused on these dense areas during the early stages, before gradually expanding coverage.

The visual qualitative evaluation agrees with the insights previously described in the quantitative evaluation. We can observe two distinct patterns: ENTROPY and CONTEXTUAL DIVERSITY initially target sparse, uncertain, and low-density regions and later expand more broadly across the embedding space. GRAPH CUT initially selects samples from medium- to high-density regions, showing limited spatial variation at early selection fractions. As the selection fraction increases, the selected samples gradually spread across the embedding space, reflecting broader coverage.

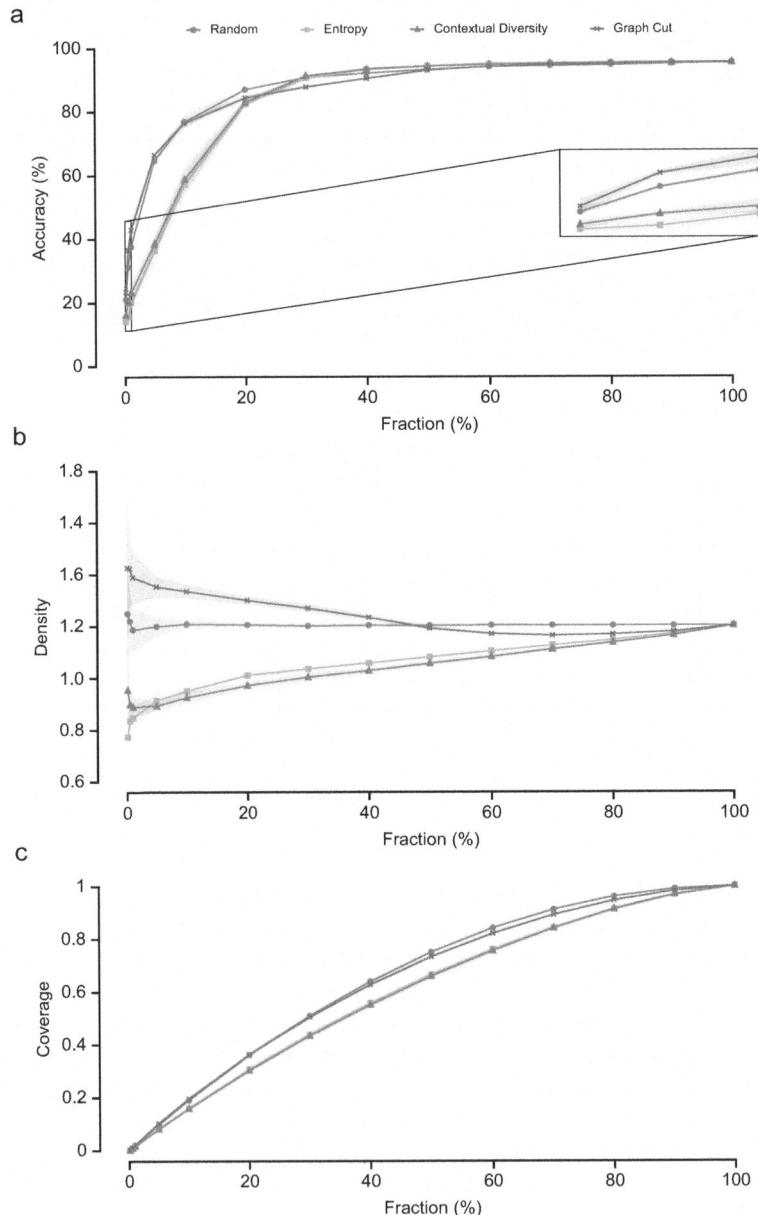

Fig. 1. Evaluation of utility and data quality metrics across subsets of varying fraction sizes selected from CIFAR-10. Each subplot reports the mean and standard deviation (shaded region) over five random seeds for four selection strategies: RANDOM, ENTROPY (Uncertainty), CONTEXTUAL DIVERSITY, and GRAPH CUT.

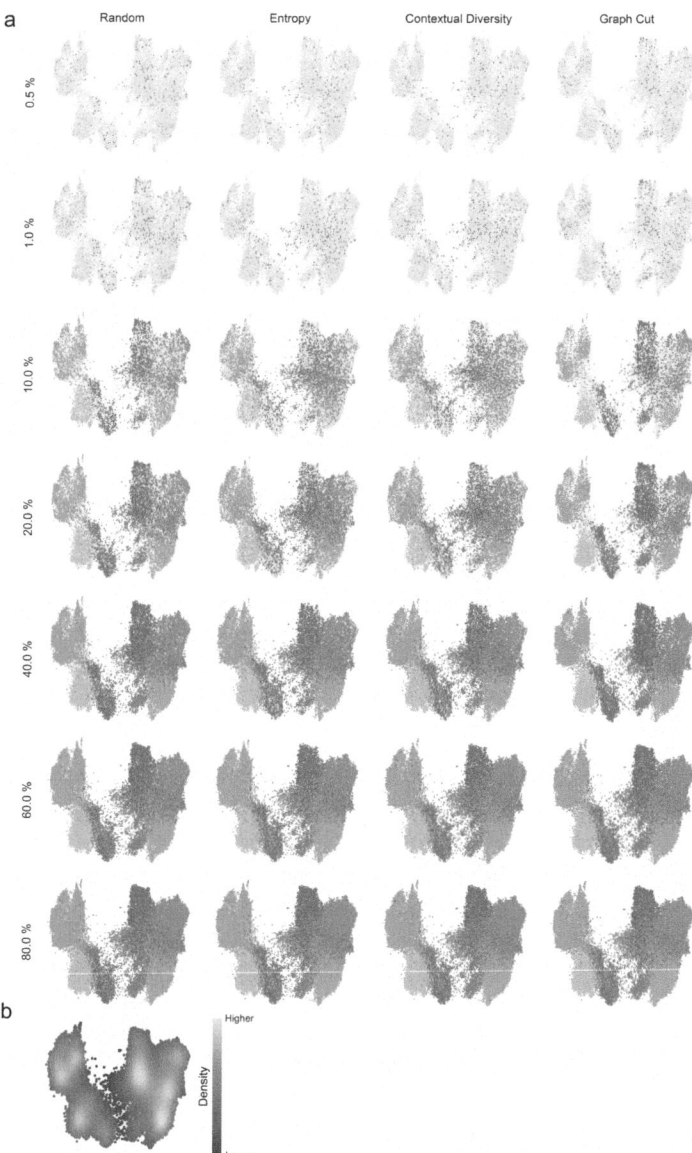

Fig. 2. UMAP visualization of CIFAR-10 using pre-trained ResNet-18. **a**: Embeddings across different coreset methods and selection fractions. Each row corresponds to a selection fraction, and each column to a coreset selection strategy: RANDOM, ENTROPY (Uncertainty), CONTEXTUAL DIVERSITY, GRAPH CUT. Each color corresponds to a different class label **b**: KDE Density estimate of the embedding.

5 Discussion

Our findings demonstrate that data quality metrics such as coverage and density offer valuable complementary insights into the behavior of coreset selection methods. Moving beyond the individual interpretation of each method previously described, we believe our observations can also be interpreted more broadly in the context of *exploration* and *exploitation*. Exploration is characterized by low density and growing coverage, indicating that a given coreset selection method seeks samples across diverse or peripheral regions of the manifold, rather than concentrating on known, frequent examples. ENTROPY and CONTEXTUAL DIVERSITY demonstrate exploratory behavior in early fractions by selecting atypical or uncertain samples across the manifold. Exploitation, in contrast, is marked by selecting subsets from high-density regions and likely pointing out that a given selection method is focusing on central regions, often reinforcing what is already well-represented. GRAPH CUT exemplifies early-stage exploitation by sampling mainly from the dense areas with the manifold.

While evaluating coreset selection methods across a full range of fraction sizes is informative for analysis, real-world deployments typically operate under practical constraints. In the context of training large models, coreset integration strategies may include: (i) selecting a coreset within a fixed data budget or narrow range, (ii) pretraining on the full dataset followed by fine-tuning on the coreset to accelerate convergence, and (iii) dynamically adjusting the coreset size during training, either by growing it incrementally or shrinking it to focus on the most informative samples.

Comparison with Related Work. Some works already include data quality metrics for selecting coresets, with methods that leverage representativeness, diversity, and fidelity (e.g., Contributing Dimensions Structure [20], FaceCoresetNet [18], SubPIE [19], and DENSITY [15]). However, the literature remains fragmented and lacks standardization. In contrast, coreset evaluation, i.e., after subset selection, is largely restricted to downstream metrics such as accuracy [5], loss, or ROC AUC [11], especially in classification, overlooking more intrinsic measures of data quality. Some recent exceptions explore alternative tasks, such as representation similarity in interpretation models [3] or clustering distortion heuristics [16]. This gap reveals a key opportunity to revisit well-established quality metrics from synthetic data and generative model evaluation, which are widely adopted but have never been systematically applied to evaluating coreset selection.

Random Selection as a Strong Baseline Explained by Data Quality Metrics. Our experiments reinforce the observation that random uniform sampling remains a surprisingly strong baseline in coreset selection. Using data quality metrics, we show that random sampling achieves consistently high coverage across all subset sizes. This broad and unbiased selection enables it to span diverse regions of the data manifold quickly, capturing representative samples without overfocusing on dense or uncertain areas. Although it does not actively prioritize high-uncertainty or semantically diverse examples, its high coverage and stable density help explain its strong classification accuracy, especially in small to mid-sized subsets.

Implications for Designing Future Coreset Selection Methods. These results also point to interesting notes for research in new coreset selection methods. For early fractions, practitioners should favor high coverage with moderate density, i.e., broad but not overly conservative sampling. Later and higher fraction sizes benefit from complete coverage and well-placed reinforcement in dense regions, which supports model refinement.

Limitations. In this exploratory work, we used only the CIFAR-10 dataset and the ResNet-18 architecture. While CIFAR-10 is a widely used benchmark in coreset selection and image classification, its small size, balanced class distribution, and low resolution limit the generalizability of our findings. Its controlled nature may overlook challenges in more complex, real-world datasets, such as class imbalance, high intra-class variability, and domain-specific noise. The proposed metrics should be further evaluated on a broader range of datasets to assess the generalizability of our findings. This includes other coreset benchmarks, such as CIFAR-100 and ImageNet [4], as well as biomedical datasets from the MedMNIST collection [21], which have also been considered in related studies. In addition, future work should include class-specific evaluations to assess whether certain classes are underrepresented in the subset selection.

Our evaluation relies on embeddings from ResNet-18, meaning that coverage and density reflect the structure of this particular feature space. Although the absolute values of these metrics may vary when computed in the embedding spaces of other architectures, we expect their conceptual meaning to remain valid. Evaluating the consistency of these metrics across different model representations is an important direction for future work.

6   Conclusions

In this work, we explored how data quality metrics offer complementary insights to traditional performance metrics when evaluating coreset selection methods. While accuracy remains the standard benchmark, it often overlooks structural properties of the selected subsets. By adapting metrics from synthetic data evaluation, we introduced a principled way to assess the fidelity and diversity of coresets.

Our empirical study on CIFAR-10 revealed that these metrics uncover meaningful behavioral differences between coreset selection strategies. These insights help to explain the trade-offs between generalization and representational fidelity across coreset sizes.

Beyond benchmarking, our findings provide actionable guidance for designing new coreset algorithms. We advocate for balancing exploration and exploitation according to the target fraction size. Furthermore, this work contributes to responsible AI by enabling a more transparent and interpretable evaluation of data selection practices.

Acknowledgments. This work was supported by European funds through the Recovery and Resilience Plan, under the project "Center for Responsible AI" (C645008882-00000055), and by the European Union's Horizon Europe research and innovation programme under Grant Agreement No. 101189689.

Disclosure of Interests. The authors have no competing interests to declare that are relevant to the content of this article.

References

1. Agarwal, S., Arora, H., Anand, S., Arora, C.: Contextual diversity for active learning. In: Vedaldi, A., Bischof, H., Brox, T., Frahm, J.-M. (eds.) ECCV 2020. LNCS, vol. 12361, pp. 137–153. Springer, Cham (2020). https://doi.org/10.1007/978-3-030-58517-4_9
2. AICOS, F.: pyMDMA: Multimodal Data Metrics for Auditing real and synthetic datasets (2024). https://github.com/fraunhoferportugal/pymdma
3. Behzadi-Khormouji, H., Oramas, J.: Deep model interpretation with limited data: a coreset-based approach. arXiv preprint arXiv:2410.00524 (2024)
4. Deng, J., Dong, W., Socher, R., Li, L.J., Li, K., Fei-Fei, L.: ImageNet: a large-scale hierarchical image database. In: 2009 IEEE Conference on Computer Vision and Pattern Recognition. IEEE, Miami, FL (2009). https://doi.org/10.1109/cvpr.2009.5206848
5. Guo, C., Zhao, B., Bai, Y.: DeepCore: a comprehensive library for coreset selection in deep learning. In: Strauss, C., Cuzzocrea, A., Kotsis, G., Tjoa, A.M., Khalil, I. (eds.) Database and Expert Systems Applications. DEXA 2022. LNCS, vol. 13426, pp. 181–195. Springer, Cham (2022). https://doi.org/10.1007/978-3-031-12423-5_14
6. He, K., Zhang, X., Ren, S., Sun, J.: Deep residual learning for image recognition. In: Proceedings of the IEEE Conference on Computer Vision and Pattern Recognition, pp. 770–778 (2016)
7. Iyer, R., Khargoankar, N., Bilmes, J., Asanani, H.: Submodular combinatorial information measures with applications in machine learning. In: Algorithmic Learning Theory, pp. 722–754. PMLR (2021)
8. Katharopoulos, A., Fleuret, F.: Not all samples are created equal: Deep learning with importance sampling. In: International Conference on Machine Learning, pp. 2525–2534. PMLR (2018)
9. Killamsetty, K., Paria, B., Golovin, D., Mirzasoleiman, B., Goyal, N.: Gradmatch: gradient matching based data subset selection for efficient learning. In: International Conference on Machine Learning (ICML) (2021)
10. Krizhevsky, A., Hinton, G., et al.: Learning multiple layers of features from tiny images (2009)
11. Lu, F., Raff, E., Holt, J.: A coreset learning reality check. In: Proceedings of the AAAI Conference on Artificial Intelligence, vol. 37, pp. 8940–8948 (2023)

12. McInnes, L., Healy, J., Melville, J.: Umap: Uniform Manifold Approximation and Projection for Dimension Reduction. arXiv preprint arXiv:1802.03426 (2018)

13. Naeem, M.F., Oh, S.J., Uh, Y., Choi, Y., Yoo, J.: Reliable fidelity and diversity metrics for generative models. In: International Conference on Machine Learning, pp. 7176–7185. PMLR (2020)

14. Rebuffi, S.A., Kolesnikov, A., Sperl, G., Lampert, C.H.: ICARL: incremental classifier and representation learning. In: Proceedings of the IEEE conference on Computer Vision and Pattern Recognition, pp. 2001–2010 (2017)

15. Sachdeva, N., et al.: How to train data-efficient llms. arXiv preprint arXiv:2402.09668 (2024)

16. Schwiegelshohn, C., Sheikh-Omar, O.A.: An empirical evaluation of k-means coresets. arXiv preprint arXiv:2207.00966 (2022)

17. Sener, O., Savarese, S.: Active learning for convolutional neural networks: a coreset approach. In: International Conference on Learning Representations (ICLR) (2018)

18. Shapira, G., Keller, Y.: Facecoresetnet: differentiable coresets for face set recognition. In: Proceedings of the AAAI Conference on Artificial Intelligence, vol. 38, pp. 4748–4756 (2024)

19. Song, H., Xiang, Q., Shu, J.: Leave no stone unturned: optimizing subpattern information entropy for coreset selection. In: ICASSP 2025-2025 IEEE International Conference on Acoustics, Speech and Signal Processing (ICASSP), pp. 1–5. IEEE (2025)

20. Wan, Z., Wang, Z., Wang, Y., Wang, Z., Zhu, H., Satoh, S.: Contributing dimension structure of deep feature for coreset selection. In: Proceedings of the AAAI Conference on Artificial Intelligence, vol. 38, pp. 9080–9088 (2024)

21. Yang, J., Shi, R., Wei, D., Liu, Z., Zhao, L., Ke, B., Pfister, H., Ni, B.: MedMNIST v2 - a large-scale lightweight benchmark for 2D and 3D biomedical image classification. Sci. Data **10**(1) (2023). https://doi.org/10.1038/s41597-022-01721-8

Invisible Citizens, Visible Futures: Rethinking Inclusivity in Urban Digital Twins

Delia Maria Coluccino[1,2,3], Beatrice Balzola[1,4], Simone Vagnoni[1,5(✉)],
Lucas Ramon Ciutat[1,4], and Andrea Filippo Ferraris[1,6]

[1] LAST-JD, Alma AI, Alma Mater Studiorum - University of Bologna (UNIBO),
Bologna, Italy
{deliamaria.coluccin2,beatrice.balzola,simone.vagnoni3,
lucas.ramonciutat,andrea.ferraris3}@unibo.it
[2] Artificial Intelligence Research Institute (IIIA), CSIC, Barcelona, Spain
[3] Law Department, Universitat Autònoma de Barcelona (UAB), Barcelona, Spain
[4] Centre for IT and IP Law (CiTiP), KU Leuven (KUL), Leuven, Belgium
[5] OEG, Universidad Politécnica de Madrid (UPM), Madrid, Spain
[6] DIKE, Law Department, Vrije Universiteit Brussel (VUB), Brussels, Belgium

Abstract. Urban Digital Twins (UDTs) are fast becoming integral
to municipal governance, furnishing planners with dynamic, data-rich
environments for scenario testing and public engagement. Yet early
evidence indicates that the benefits of UDTs accrue unevenly, reinforcing pre-existing digital and social divides. This article interro-
gates the twin hypotheses that (i) limited digital skills and (ii) structural access barriers—such as documentation requirements or inaccessible interfaces—systematically exclude already-vulnerable groups from
UDTs, conceived as platforms where citizens can participate in the
hybrid physical-digital public sphere. Drawing on a multidisciplinary
review of European pilot projects, relevant EU regulations (GDPR, Data
Governance Act, European Accessibility Act, AI Act) and an intersectional vulnerability framework, we map how these technologies currently
privilege a "participatory elite" while marginalising citizens with low
digital literacy, persons with disabilities, undocumented migrants, the
unhoused and other precarious communities. We then analyse design
choices and governance practices—co-design workshops, flexible identity models, accessibility-by-default guidelines and equity audits—that
can mitigate exclusion without compromising legal certainty or system
security. Our findings reveal a regulatory lacuna: EU hard-law instruments ensure privacy and basic accessibility but impose no affirmative
duty on cities to involve marginalised subjects in the modelling loop.
We conclude that vulnerability must be treated as an explicit design
and governance variable. Embedding participatory obligations, intersectional equity metrics and adaptive identification mechanisms in future
EU regulatory frameworks would enable UDTs to illuminate rather than
obscure Europe's invisible citizens, transforming Digital Twins into genuinely democratic urban commons.

J. Valente de Oliveira et al. (Eds.): EPIA 2025, LNAI 16121, pp. 492–504, 2026.
https://doi.org/10.1007/978-3-032-05176-9_38

Keywords: Smart Cities · Urban Digital Twins · Digital Divide · Accessibility · Participatory Design · Social Vulnerability · Digital Governance

1   Introduction

Urban Digital Twins (UDTs) are rapidly moving from experimental pilots to core components of municipal governance across Europe and beyond, enabling planners to test policy options and communicate complex scenarios through interactive, data-rich interfaces [13, 26]. Since these platforms knit together real-time sensor streams, predictive simulations and citizen-facing dashboards, they can be conceived as a new kind of digital public squares - a space where people can see, debate and even co-create the futures of their cities [12].

Yet empirical studies already show that the benefits of UDTs accrue unevenly. People with low digital literacy, persons with disabilities and communities facing legal or socio-economic precarity are consistently underrepresented among active users, while well-connected citizens emerge as the primary interlocutors of municipal twin projects [11, 31, 33]. Without deliberate safeguards, the same technology promising inclusive, data-driven governance can thus reproduce a "participatory elite" and deepen existing urban inequalities [1].

This article argues that vulnerability must be treated as a design and governance variable if UDTs are to fulfil their democratic promise. Focusing on two cross-cutting layers of exclusion, namely limited digital skills and structural barriers, we argue how ill-considered twins could amplify disadvantage, whereas thoughtfully structured systems may help to bridge it. Crucially, the legal frameworks most often invoked in European smart-city debates—the General Data Protection Regulation (GDPR), the Data Governance Act (DGA) and the European Accessibility Act (EAA)—provide essential passive protections but impose no affirmative duty on cities to involve marginalised residents in the modelling loop. Bridging this gap requires active measures, from co-design workshops and flexible identity models to equity audits tied to EU funding streams [30, 37, 51].

The discussion unfolds in six parts. Section 2 reviews UDTs spread and the transformative claims accompanying them. Section 3 dissects the relevant EU policy landscape, highlighting where hard-law instruments fall short of their inclusion goals. Section 4 examines how digital-literacy deficits and structural constraints translate into concrete barriers to UDTs-enabled policy-making, while Sect. 6 explores the feedback loop between vulnerabilities and the broader digital transformation of public services. The concluding section synthesises our findings and underscores the importance of ensuring that UDTs illuminate, rather than obscure, the invisible citizens of Europe.

2   Theoretical Background on Urban Digital Twins

Cities are increasingly turning smart by digitising access to public services, with the goal of enabling more efficient resource management able to connect data, people and infrastructures. Although there is no universally agreed-upon definition of a smart city, it is commonly understood as an urban environment that leverages ICT to enhance the intelligence and efficiency of its systems and services—i.e. administration, education, and transportation [52]. Within the European Union (EU) context, the smart city concept has come to embody a civic dimension, where the pursuit of efficiency is intended to benefit not just businesses but also enhance the quality of life for broad city users.[1]

UDTs represent a facet of this digital revolution aimed at turning cities smart by easing data collection and data processing, thereby supporting smarter decision making. More broadly, Digital Twins (DTs) [29] consist of a physical object, its digital replica, and a continuous flow of data between the two, allowing the digital counterpart to adapt in real time to changes occurring in the physical domain.

The technology behind them relies on three layers: (a) The Internet of Things (IoT), namely sensors embedded in the physical object that enable data collection; (b) The Edge, where data are temporarily processed to generate predictions; (c) The Cloud or a supercomputer, where data are stored in the long term.

Although primarily adopted in the industrial sector in the early 2000s [50] to optimise machinery lifecycles and workflows, DTs have since found application in various other fields, including agriculture, healthcare [53], and urban studies—where they are increasingly used to support spatial planning and design practice [6].

Indeed, cities both across and beyond the EU are investing in Urban DTs [43] to optimise resource management and improve operational efficiency [7]. As mentioned, an ambitious challenge lies in their prediction capabilities: by processing large volumes of data, they can provide municipalities with valuable insights, ultimately supporting urban planning and inspiring better policy-making.

UDTs are commonly employed by organisations and administrations to collect urban data and use it to enhance the efficiency and performance in city environments [4,13]. More specifically, they can contribute to enrich urban datasets [40], improve disaster response and emergency services [6], shape municipal policies [43], and model future scenarios [8], also through predictive analyses.

Several cities already exemplify these uses: Antwerp employs DT technology to optimise port operations [44]; Barcelona utilises predictive models to foster sustainable urban mobility [15]; and Singapore has developed a dynamic 3D city model integrating more than twenty datasets [43]. Sometimes, the drive for optimisation is accompanied by citizen-engagement intent. As a result, these UDTs are designed as participatory tools allowing laypeople to more actively join the civic sphere by easily accessing and sharing data and, possibly, by influencing policy decisions. Examples include Herrenberg [13], Ghent [40], and the Bologna DT project [5]. Here, the DTs integrate resource-optimisation tools with participatory ones, such as petition-based initiatives and decision-making platforms, allowing cities to envision a more horizontal and inclusive governance model.

---

[1] https://commission.europa.eu/eu-regional-and-urban-development/topics/cities-and-urban-development/city-initiatives/smart-cities_en.

These UDTs aim to promote citizen participation, particularly among marginalised and historically excluded communities. Conceiving UDTs as digital, public squares where city-users and stakeholders can not only access data but also interact with it meaningfully, designing them as user-friendly platforms promoting individual and collective participation in decision-making, and granting equitable access to the platforms are all key aspects of the effort to democratise their impact [35].

However, social and digital inequalities pose significant challenges to these ambitions by affecting the access to digital technologies and limiting meaningful participation on platforms, therefore marginalising already invisible communities. Gender, cultural backgrounds and socio-economic disparities are only some of the factors hindering effective use of digital technologies. If not addressed, they may likely lead to unequal opportunities for representation, participation and knowledge-sharing, thus perpetuating already existing social disparities [46]. A well-designed UDT should prevent digital illiteracy from becoming a further exclusionary force, actively addressing these barriers to avoid the risk of reinforcing existing social divides, privileging some while further marginalising others.

At the EU level, a mix of regulatory frameworks and soft-law instruments help govern the implementation of UDTs, address their implications, and harness the realisation of their benefits. The following paragraph provides an overview of these tools, outlining their scope and limitations.

3   Policy Context Surrounding Urban Digital Twins

EU policy frames UDTs as engines for greener, more participatory cities. Flagship agendas—the EU Data Strategy [22], European Green Deal [21], and Digital Decade Targets 2030 [23]—urge municipalities to mine large-scale urban data for real-time optimisation and citizen engagement. Complementary programmes such as the New European Bauhaus and Living-in.EU anchor this push in inclusive design, ethical AI, and civic tech.

Interoperable, open data ecosystems championed by the EU Data Strategy bolster UDT predictive power, while the Green Deal links digitalisation to climate resilience. Yet the hard-law instruments that accompany these ambitions still privilege a "participatory elite." The GDPR secures privacy but says nothing about involving seniors, migrants, or persons with disabilities in UDT design and oversight. The Data Governance Act (DGA) streamlines public-sector data sharing but likewise omits participatory duties.

Accessibility rules narrow, rather than close, the gap. The European Accessibility Act (EAA) requires public-facing digital services to be usable by all, but enforcement lags and the Act offers scant guidance for complex, data-rich platforms. The forthcoming AI Act (AIA) will regulate "high-risk" systems, yet UDTs often fall outside that category unless they directly automate essential services. Even when they do, the AIA targets bias mitigation, not inclusive governance.

Consequently, EU policy rhetoric outpaces regulatory reality: sustainability, ethical AI, and digital inclusion are celebrated, but local authorities receive no binding mandate—or resources—to embed marginalised voices in the UDT "modelling loop" [28,34,54]. The result is a fragmented regime where cities must protect data and ensure basic accessibility without clear directives for co-design, outreach, or capacity-building—conditions that can entrench existing divides.

Bridging this lacuna requires affirmative obligations. Future reforms could make EU funding contingent on early accessibility audits, documented engagement with underserved groups, and sustained digital-literacy support [47]. Protection alone (privacy and anti-discrimination safeguards) is insufficient; active co-creation is needed to foster genuine civic agency. Until participatory and intersectional equity duties are codified, UDTs will continue to illuminate city systems while leaving Europe's most vulnerable citizens in the shadows.

4   Vulnerable Subjects and the Digital City

4.1   Conceptualising Vulnerability in the Digital City

Theorisations of vulnerability have been characterised by a multidisciplinary approach, encompassing fields such as gender studies, political philosophy or law and ethics, expanding all the way to policy making [39]. A pivotal concept within this discourse is intersectionality [9], which refers to the interconnected nature of social categorisations such as race, gender, class, and others as they apply to a given individual or group, creating overlapping and interdependent systems of discrimination or disadvantage.

Intersectionality serves as a fundamental aspect of Luna's [36] theorisations of vulnerability, which stand out for their approach based on "layers" rather than "labels". According to Luna, layers of vulnerability are not fixed attributes of specific individuals or groups but are features constructed by status, time and location. This layered model mirrors Crenshaw's argument by emphasising how multiple, intersecting social positions can produce compounded forms of disadvantage. In this sense, Luna's framework stresses the cumulative and transitory potential of vulnerability: all individuals are vulnerable, but some individuals have more layers of vulnerability than others [38]. Such layers can take different forms and the intersectionality between them - meaning the ways in which different axes of identity and structural disadvantage interact to produce distinct experiences of marginalisation - constitutes the conceptual foundation from which this paper stems.

As claimed by Friemel [27], the diffusion of new digital technologies is neither a random nor egalitarian process. Instead, patterns of access and participation within digital infrastructures are profoundly shaped by existing sociodemographic stratifications and structural inequalities [20]. Empirical studies consistently demonstrate that variables such as income level, educational attainment, gender, age, and migratory status determine both the availability of digital resources and the capacity to engage meaningfully with them [16,46]. These disparities are not incidental. Instead, they seem to reflect known social, economic and cultural relationships of the offline world, including inequalities [14]. As such, far from serving as a neutral platform for equal participation, digital technologies often function as amplifiers of existing socio-economic hierarchies, reinforcing digital divides along intersecting axes of marginality [46].

4.2 Vulnerable Populations and UDTs

As observed over our analysis, UDTs are a promising tool for transforming public administration by inspiring decision-making, facilitating access to public services and potentially opening new avenues for civic participation and engagement. As key elements of the ongoing digital transformation, they aim to make public services easier to access, smarter and less demanding in terms of time and effort. But who are they intended for, and who are they designed to serve?

This section wants to shed light on the complex intertwining between UDT-driven digital transformation and selected forms of vulnerability—particularly those related to physical, educational, socio-economic and age-related dimensions. As the following analysis argues, deploying UDTs may have both amplifying and mitigating effects on vulnerabilities. Indeed, depending on the type and characteristics of the vulnerability in question, UDTs may either widen the gap between vulnerable and less-vulnerable subjects or, conversely, eliminate existing barriers by shifting to digitised access. The following subsection will elaborate further on this issue.

Digital Literacy. The digitalisation process has allowed for greater and easier participation in society, whether for social, political, or educational reasons. However, despite its simplification effects, undesirable consequences persist due to the lack of digital knowledge encompassing part of the population. Indeed, digital literacy has become one of the basic competencies for humans, alongside literacy and numeracy [32]. EU institutions recognise its essential role, together with internet access, for both personal and professional life [25], yet approximately 32% of the European population still lacks basic digital skills [24].

The reasons for this digital divide are multiple, with age being one of the most impactful determinants. The grey divide [42] highlights the inequalities between older members of society and their younger counterparts. A study showed that only 30% of old seniors (+75) are likely to use the internet, either for motivational indifference (perceived uselessness of the information the internet can provide) or deficient knowledge [27].

In this sense, when designing participatory UDTs, one cannot overlook the difficulties the elderly have when accessing digital technologies. Devices with big buttons and fonts, simplified designs, or step-by-step guidance tutorials might be an initial attempt to lower this divide. Providing information on the usefulness and goals of UDT platforms through communications systems most used by the elderly could also have a positive impact: televisions and radios could also play a role in the involvement of the seniors.

However, age is not the only determinant of digital literacy. Incarcerated persons and ex-convicts are often overlooked in the discussion on access and participation. Inadequate digital knowledge not only affects inmates in general, but specifically those with longer sentences and disadvantaged backgrounds [45]. Because of the fear of inmates breaching secure internet connections or conducting illegal activities on computers and other devices, digital classes and access to technology are banned in the majority of detention institutions [2, 3, 48].

The consequences of this lack of education affect ex-convicts when re-entering society [48]. Social reintegration is a critical phase for ex-convicts, as the ultimate aim of the prison system is not merely punitive but rehabilitative, enabling individuals to successfully reintegrate into society. However, the rapid advancement of digital technologies has transformed everyday life at an unprecedented pace, making the digital divide faced by ex-convicts a significant disadvantage [45], further marginalising an already vulnerable population. Indeed, once inmates step outside of prison gates, they become more or less invisible - barring, of course, reoffence [19]. If limiting exclusion is an important goal of UDTs, taking into account the barriers faced by ex-convicts might be helpful to fulfill it.

Structural Barriers. In the offline – as much as the online – world, structural barriers can prevent people in different situations and environments from accessing and participating. While digitisation has frequently been portrayed as a tool for eliminating barriers and discrimination, a closer examination of participation within UDT platforms could reveal valid concerns. Indeed, allowing access to services from the comfort of one's home might very well benefit people with physical disabilities, or allow neurodivergent people to prefer interactions with a machine instead of a human [18].

However, disabilities are heterogeneous and multifaced, and if not sufficiently explored, digitisation may fall short of becoming the inclusive tool it promises to be. Digital structural barriers may range from technical obstacles - such as the lack of screen reader support for a blind person -, to physical obstacles - such as the need for documents or citizenships to access a platform for people without documents.

Notably, while cellphone ownership among homeless adults has increased compared to previous years [49], signaling a partial narrowing of the primary digital divide, the frequent change of residence or the absence of a permanent address continues to present significant obstacles to digital participation. Moreover, the lack of identity documents - or documents not recognised by the country developing the DT - may further marginalise parts of the territory's population.

The requirement to upload state-issued identity documents for accessing governmental digital services is typically justified by legal certainty and administrative security. Reliable digital identification safeguards public resources and ensures user traceability within e-governance frameworks. Yet, this simultaneously produces exclusionary effects, disproportionately affecting undocumented migrants, asylum seekers, and those awaiting citizenship. To address this, user account systems could be designed to avoid mandatory ID uploads or offer alternative identification methods to broaden participation.

People with disabilities should not be regarded as one homogeneous population [32] for disabilities vary widely, encompassing physical, sensory, cognitive, and neurological impairments, which differently impact access and use of digital technologies. A study conducted in the USA [17] found that people with hearing or walking impairments are more likely to use the Internet than other types of disabilities. For this reason, the tools and design chosen to create an accessible and participating environment should be built taking into consideration all forms disability may have, whether temporary or permanent, congenital or acquired, visible or not.

For our discussion, disabilities can be grouped into five categories: a) visual impairments; b) hearing impairments; c) motor disabilities; d) cognitive and learning disabilities; and e) speech impairments. Each requires tailored strategies for accessible platform design. Visual impairments, ranging from blindness to color blindness, make inadequate contrast, small text, or lack of screen reader support significant barriers. Likewise, hearing impairments demand alternatives to audio-only alerts and video content, such as captions, transcripts, or sign language translation.

UDT platforms should also ensure that people with motor disabilities can easily navigate the platform. Limited dexterity, tremors, or mobility impairments may raise difficulties if the interface requires the sole use of the mouse, clicking small buttons or dragging maps. In this sense, it is important that keyboard navigation with shortcuts is supported, alongside voice command alternatives and compatibility with alternative input devices such as eye-tracking systems, switch control, or adaptive joysticks.

Cognitive and learning disabilities require different tools, as impairments can range from dyslexia and ADHD to dementia and intellectual disabilities. Overly complex interfaces, dense text, or fast-changing visuals may be overwhelming. Readable, adjustable fonts, step-by-step guidance, and visual cues could improve accessibility. Similarly, speech impairments make voice-based platforms difficult to use; here, chatbots, predictive text, and autocomplete features can help mitigate digital exclusion.

4.3 Carrying Biases in the Digital City Design

The vulnerabilities discussed in the previous sections—digital literacy gaps and structural barriers—do not operate in isolation but are deeply embedded within the broader socio-political contexts that shape UDT design and implementation. Pre-existing social, economic, and cultural biases become integrated in digital infrastructure when designers fail to critically examine their assumptions about users and their capabilities. As De Cindio and Trentini [10] highlight in their "Rainbow of Digital Citizenship" framework, participatory technologies cannot achieve their democratic potential when fundamental inequalities remain unaddressed.

The digital translation of urban governance systems inherits systemic biases that have historically marginalised certain populations in non-digital contexts. Mirzoev et al. [41] underscore this dynamic when they explain that social exclusion is driven by "unequal power relationships interacting across four dimensions (economic, political, social and cultural)" that operate across multiple societal levels.

To function as genuinely participatory tools, UDTs must be designed with explicit recognition of diverse user capabilities, resources, and needs— accounting, among others, for diversity in digital literacy, access patterns, cognitive processing, language preferences, and cultural contexts. Without deliberately inclusive design principles, UDTs risk amplifying rather than mitigating existing inequalities, potentially excluding precisely those voices that traditional urban planning processes have already marginalised. This points to the necessity of embedding equity considerations throughout the entire UDT development cycle, from initial conceptualisation through implementation and evaluation, rather than treating inclusion as a separate or supplementary concern.

5   Final Considerations

By locating UDTs within the broader smart cities phenomenon and as a facet of the ongoing digital shift in cities design and governance, the paper approached this technology in its declination as a public and participative tool, highlighting both its issues and promises for civic engagement.

It did so by emphasising UDTs capacity to enable more intelligent management and governance of public resources and services, and by illustrating how vulnerable subjects may be inadvertently left out—not only from accessing digital tools and related services, but also from participating in digital public agoras and engaging with civic processes.

After introducing UDTs, the paper examined the applicable regulatory framework, pointing out its shortcomings and advocating for a more holistic approach able to embed ethical considerations in UDTs design. The fourth section shifted to concrete vulnerabilities, attempting to reconstruct the intricate relationship between digital transformation and exclusionary dynamics. After providing a conceptual framework, the paragraph emphasised the ambivalence of digitisation —sometimes acting as a vector for social exclusion, and at others, as a tool for inclusion.

Throughout our analysis, we have argued that, despite their participatory aims, UDTs can reinforce social discrimination if they fail to address what hinders meaningful digital access; conversely, recognising these divides may help bringing marginalised individuals into visibility, creating a positive cycle that could help reduce social exclusion.

The following considerations emerge from this analysis and may inspire future research directions:

1. We advocate against oversimplifying the relation between digitisation and vulnerabilities. We believe in digitisation as a tool capable to transform cities into intelligent and hyper-connected ecosystems where people, data, and services are effectively integrated. However, we also believe this is a distant ideal unless individuals and communities' specificities are fully acknowledged and adequately accounted for in the design of smart cities;

2a. Challenging the persistent neglect of already marginalised groups is an essential step towards democratising the physical and digital public space. Not only that: as UDTs promise to be effective tools for evaluating the impact of policies in urban contexts, ensuring accurate representation and active involvement of otherwise invisible subjects may significantly improve the quality of policy-making and predictive simulations. By bringing attention to these individuals and their challenges, subsequent research could inspire administrations and developers to design and implement more effective civic engagement strategies in the hybrid physical-digital sphere. In turn, this could create a positive loop by enhancing digital literacy, promoting meaningful use of technology, and contributing to broader social inclusion;

2b. Extensive and distributed civic participation could also be directly embedded into UDTs. Consider the Herrenberg's one: citizens were included in the town design process by complementing digital datasets with their lived experience, enriching the model with non-traditional data sources and enabling a more accurate representation of the city [13]. Similarly, UDTs that prioritise civic participation may benefit from the personal, social, racial heritage of the subjects involved, eventually building more resilient and inclusive cities deploying models of civic participation where each one is called to participate according to her needs, abilities and history.

Acknowledgment. We gratefully acknowledge Antonino Rotolo for his technical assistance and insightful suggestions.

Disclosure of Interests. Delia Maria Coluccino's scholarship is provided through PNRR funds. Simone Vagnoni's scholarship is provided in the framework of the research training projects "Territorio: Transizione tecnologica, culturale, economica e sociale verso la sostenibilità" (PR. FSE + 2021/2027–DGR n. 509 del 03/04/2023) - CUPJ33C23000610006 and with the support of the EU Commission funds within ERC HyperModeLex. Grant agreement ID: 101055185; and owns stock in TCS LAB SRL. The other authors have no competing interests to declare that are relevant to the content of this article.

References

1. Adade, S., de Vries, M.: Digital transformation and social exclusion in european cities. Cities **137**, 104321 (2025)
2. Antigone: In carcere è (finalmente) arrivata la tecnologia? xvii rapporto sulle condizioni carcerarie (2021). https://www.rapportoantigone.it/diciassettesimo-rapporto-sulle-condizioni-di-detenzione/tecnologie-e-diritti/
3. Azose, B.: Access to technology in the American carceral state (2021). https://techpolicy.press/access-to-technology-in-the-american-carceral-state/
4. Bauer, M., Cirillo, F., Furst, J., Solmaz, G., Kovacs, E.: A fiware-based model for urban digital twins. Automatisierungstechnik **69**(12), 1106–1115 (2021)
5. Benedetti, A., Costantino, C., Gulli, R., Predari, G.: The process of digitalization of the urban environment for the development of sustainable and circular cities: a case study of bologna, Italy. Sustainability **14**(21), 13740 (2022)

6. Biljecki, F., Stoter, J., Ledoux, H., Zlatanova, S., Çöltekin, A.: Applications of 3D city models: state of the art review. ISPRS Int. J. Geo Inf. **4**(4), 2842–2889 (2015)
7. Boccardo, P., La Riccia, L., Yadav, Y.: Urban echoes: exploring the dynamic realities of cities through digital twins. Land **13**(5), 635 (2024)
8. Brunner, P., Denk, F., Huber, W., Kates, R.: Virtual safety performance assessment for automated driving in complex urban traffic scenarios, pp. 679–685 (2019)
9. Crenshaw, K.: Demarginalizing the intersection of race and sex: a black feminist critique of antidiscrimination doctrine, feminist theory and antiracist politics. Univ. Chic. Leg. Forum **1989**(1), 139–167 (1989)
10. De Cindio, F., Trentini, A.: Dal Tecnocivismo alla Cittadinanza Digitale. Edizioni Themis (2024)
11. Dell'Era, C., Magistretti, S., Cautela, C., Verganti, R., Zurlo, F.: Urban digital twin challenges: a systematic review and perspectives for sustainable smart cities. Technol. Forecast. Soc. Chang. **176**, 121417 (2022)
12. Dembski, F., Wössner, U.: Urban digital twins and citizens: a systematic review. Cities **142**, 104544 (2024)
13. Dembski, F., Wössner, U., Letzgus, M., Ruddat, M., Yamu, C.: Urban digital twins for smart cities and citizens: the case study of Herrenberg, Germany. Sustainability **12**(6), 2307 (2020)
14. van Deursen, A.J.A.M., van Dijk, J.A.G.M.: The digital divide shifts to differences in usage. New Media Soc. **16**(3), 507–526 (2014). https://doi.org/10.1177/1461444813487959
15. Diaz-Sarachaga, J.M.: May urban digital twins spur the new urban agenda? The Spanish case study. Sustain. Cities Soc. **114**, 105788 (2024)
16. van Dijk, J.A.: The Digital Divide. John Wiley & Sons, Hoboken (2020)
17. Dobransky, K., Hargittai, E.: The disability divide in internet access and use. Inf. Commun. Soc. **9**(3), 313–334 (2006)
18. Dubois-Sage, M., Jacquet, B., Jamet, F., Baratgin, J.: People with autism spectrum disorder could interact more easily with a robot than with a human: Reasons and limits. Behav. Sci. **14**(2), 131 (2024)
19. Durnescu, I., Istrate, A.: Former prisoners between non-category and invisibility: the Romanian experience. Probat. J. **67**(4), 427–446 (2020). https://doi.org/10.1177/0264550520957541
20. Dutton, W.H., Reisdorf, B.C.: Cultural divides and digital inequalities: attitudes shaping internet and social media divides. Inf. Commun. Soc. **20**(10), 1463–1482 (2017)
21. European Commission: Communication from the commission to the European parliament, the European council, the council, the European economic and social committee and the committee of the regions: The European green deal (2019)
22. European Commission: Communication from the commission to the European parliament, the council, the European economic and social committee and the committee of the regions: A European strategy for data (2020)
23. European Commission: Communication from the commission to the European parliament, the council, the European economic and social committee and the committee of the regions: 2030 digital compass: the European way for the digital decade (2021)
24. European Commission: Report on the state of the digital decade 2023, shaping Europe's digital future (2023). Accessed 19 Feb 2025
25. European Union: Digital literacy in the eu: An overview (2023), european Data. Accessed 19 Feb 2025

26. Ferré-Bigorra, J., Casals, M., Gangolells, M.: Digital twins: a systematic literature review based on data analysis and topic modeling. Data Brief **42**, 108044 (2022)
27. Friemel, T.N.: The digital divide has grown old: determinants of a digital divide among seniors. New Media Soc. **18**(2), 313–331 (2016)
28. Garske, B., Holz, W., Ekardt, F.: Digital twins in sustainable transition: exploring the role of eu data governance. Front. Res. Metrics Anal. **9**, 1303024 (2024)
29. Grieves, M., Vickers, J.: Digital twin: mitigating unpredictable, undesirable emergent behavior in complex systems. In: Kahlen, F.-J., Flumerfelt, S., Alves, A. (eds.) Transdisciplinary Perspectives on Complex Systems, pp. 85–113. Springer, Cham (2017). https://doi.org/10.1007/978-3-319-38756-7_4
30. Hacker, P., Neyer, J.: Digital participation and vulnerable groups: towards inclusive smart city governance. Gov. Inf. Q. **40**(2), 101810 (2023)
31. Helsper, E.J., Reisdorf, B.C.: The digital divide and its implications for social capital and social mobility. New Media Soc. **19**(2), 157–175 (2016)
32. Johansson, S., Gulliksen, J., Gustavsson, C.: Disability digital divide: the use of the internet, smartphones, computers and tablets among people with disabilities in Sweden. Univ. Access Inf. Soc. **20**(1), 105–120 (2021)
33. Kebede, M., et al.: Digital divide and the COVID-19 pandemic: teachers' perspective on inequality in Irish post-primary schools. Comput. Educ. **180**, 104424 (2022)
34. Lopez Solano, J., de Souza, S., Martin, A., Taylor, L.: Governing data and artificial intelligence for all: Models for sustainable and just data governance. Technical report, European Parliament (2022)
35. Luca, M., Lepri, B., Gallotti, R., Paolazzi, S., Bigi, M., Pistore, M.: Towards civic digital twins: co-design the citizen-centric future of Bologna (2024). arXiv preprint arXiv:2412.06328
36. Luna, F.: Elucidating the concept of vulnerability: layers not labels. Int. J. Feminist Approaches Bioeth. **2**(1), 121–139 (2009)
37. Luoma, P., et al.: Participatory urban planning in the digital age: lessons from European cities. Urban Studies **61**(4), 789–807 (2024)
38. Malgieri, G.: Vulnerable data subjects. Comput. Law Secur. Rev. **37**, 105415 (2020)
39. Malgieri, G., Rebrean, M.L.: Vulnerability in the eu ai act: building an interpretation. SSRN Working Paper (2024). https://doi.org/10.2139/ssrn.5058591
40. Matthys, M., De Cock, L., Vermaut, J., Van de Weghe, N., De Maeyer, P.: An "animated spatial time machine" in co-creation: reconstructing history using gamification integrated into 3d city modelling, 4d web and transmedia storytelling. ISPRS Int. J. Geo Inf. **10**(7), 460 (2021)
41. Mirzoev, T., et al.: Systematic review of the role of social inclusion within sustainable urban developments. Int. J. Sustain. Dev. World Ecol. **29**(1), 3–17 (2021)
42. Morris, A., Brading, H.: E-literacy and the grey digital divide: a review with recommendations. J. Inf. Lit. **1**(3), 13–28 (2007)
43. Papyshev, G., Yarime, M.: Exploring city digital twins as policy tools: a task-based approach to generating synthetic data on urban mobility. Data Policy **3**, e16 (2021)
44. Paredis, R., Vangheluwe, H., Albertins, A.R.: Coock project smart port 2025 d3.2: variability in twinning architectures (2024)
45. Prison Learning Alliance: The digital divide: Lessons from prisons abroad (2020). https://prisonerlearningalliance.org.uk/wp-content/uploads/2020/07/The-Digital-Divide-Lessons-from-prisons-abroad.pdf
46. Ragnedda, M., Ruiu, M.L., Addeo, F.: The self-reinforcing effect of digital and social exclusion: the inequality loop. Telemat. Inform. **72**, 101852 (2022)

47. READJUST Consortium: Readjust: Just transition to a green and digital future for all (2024). Accessed 11 Feb 2025
48. Reisdorf, B.C., Rikard, R.V.: Digital rehabilitation: a model of reentry into the digital age. Am. Behav. Sci. **62**(9), 1273–1290 (2018)
49. Rhoades, H., Wenzel, S.L., Rice, E., Winetrobe, H., Henwood, B.: No digital divide? Technology use among homeless adults. J. Soc. Distress Homeless **26**(1), 73–77 (2017)
50. Saracco, R.: Digital twins: bridging physical space and cyberspace. Computer **52**(12), 58–64 (2019)
51. Wernick, A., et al.: Inclusive smart city development: a framework for equitable citizen participation. J. Urban Technol. **30**(3), 45–68 (2023)
52. Yin, C., Xiong, Z., Chen, H., Wang, J., Cooper, D., David, B.: A literature survey on smart cities. Sci. China Inf. Sci. **58**(10), 1–18 (2015)
53. Zhou, J., Zhang, S., Gu, M.: Revisiting digital twins: origins, fundamentals, and practices. Front. Eng. Manag. **9**(4), 668–676 (2022)
54. Zygmuntowski, J.J., Zoboli, L., Nemitz, P.F.: Embedding European values in data governance: a case for public data commons. Internet Policy Rev. **10**(3) (2021)

Subgroup Discovery Using Model Uncertainty: A Feasibility Study

Ana Cravidão Pereira[1]([✉])(iD), Duarte Folgado[1](iD), Marília Barandas[1](iD),
Carlos Soares[1,2,3](iD), and André Carreiro[1](iD)

[1] Fraunhofer Portugal AICOS, Porto, Portugal
ana.cravidao@aicos.fraunhofer.pt
[2] Faculdade de Engenharia da Universidade do Porto, Porto, Portugal
[3] Laboratory for Artificial Intelligence and Computer Science (LIACC),
Porto, Portugal

Abstract. Subgroup discovery aims to identify interpretable segments of a dataset where model behavior deviates from global trends. Traditionally, this involves uncovering patterns among data instances with respect to a target property, such as class labels or performance metrics. For example, classification accuracy can highlight subpopulations where models perform unusually well or poorly. While effective for model auditing and failure analysis, accuracy alone provides a limited view, as it does not reflect model confidence or sources of uncertainty. This work proposes a complementary approach: subgroup discovery using model uncertainty. Rather than identifying where the model fails, we focus on where it is systematically uncertain, even when predictions are correct. Such uncertainty may arise from intrinsic data ambiguity (aleatoric) or poor data representation in training (epistemic). It can highlight areas of the input space where the model's predictions are less robust or reliable. We evaluate the feasibility of this approach through controlled experiments on the classification of synthetic data and the Iris dataset. While our findings are exploratory and qualitative, they suggest that uncertainty-based subgroup discovery may uncover interpretable regions of interest, providing a promising direction for model auditing and analysis.

Keywords: Subgroup Discovery · Uncertainty Quantification · Responsible AI · Model Auditing · Robustness Evaluation

1 Introduction

Subgroup discovery refers to the task of identifying interpretable and sufficiently large subpopulations (i.e., subgroups) within a dataset that exhibit interesting behavior with respect to a target variable [2,17,20]. Subgroups are typically described by interpretable rules (e.g., conjunctions of feature conditions), representing patterns in the data corresponding to specific population segments [25].

J. Valente de Oliveira et al. (Eds.): EPIA 2025, LNAI 16121, pp. 505–517, 2026.
https://doi.org/10.1007/978-3-032-05176-9_39

A representative example of subgroup discovery in the context of the performance of a model for pneumonia diagnosis is: *While the model achieves an overall accuracy of 85%, it reaches 95% accuracy on patients under 60 years old with no prior lung conditions.* In this case, the subgroup comprises patients younger than 60 without a history of lung disease. The classification outcome pertains to the presence or absence of pneumonia, and the discovery insight is that the model performs substantially better on this subgroup compared to its overall performance, revealing a potentially important stratification in model behavior. Subgroup discovery has found applications in diverse domains including healthcare [12–14], finance [9,18], education [16,24], and algorithmic fairness [5,22].

Traditionally, subgroup discovery has been employed to identify regions within the input space where a predictive model performs significantly better or worse than expected, typically assessed through metrics such as accuracy, precision, or recall. Such analyses help expose biases, diagnose model failure modes, and understand generalization boundaries, particularly across demographic, geographic, or application-specific subpopulations [6]. By revealing segments where local performance deviates meaningfully from global averages, subgroup discovery contributes to Responsible Artificial Intelligence (AI) practices, helping to expose systematically misrepresented groups.

While accuracy remains a central metric for evaluating predictive performance, it provides only a partial view of model behavior. Treating predictions as strictly correct or incorrect overlooks the model's confidence in its decisions. This makes it insensitive to nuances such as high-confidence errors, low-confidence predictions, or areas where the model expresses epistemic uncertainty. In recent years, uncertainty quantification has emerged as a valuable complement to traditional metrics, offering a richer understanding of how models perform under ambiguity or data scarcity [3,4].

Given that subgroup discovery seeks interpretable deviations from global behavior and uncertainty reflects a different axis of model behavior, it is natural to ask whether subgroups characterized by systematic uncertainty may also yield meaningful insights. This could potentially reveal population strata where the model is systematically confident or uncertain, regardless of prediction correctness.

In this work, we ask: *Can we identify interesting behaviour concerning the uncertainty of model predictions using subgroup discovery?* We propose a novel perspective on subgroup discovery that shifts the focus from prediction accuracy to model uncertainty. Rather than identifying subgroups where the model is incorrect, we aim to uncover subgroups where its predictions are systematically uncertain, even when they are accurate. This uncertainty may arise from aleatoric sources (e.g., inherent noise or ambiguity in the data) or epistemic factors (e.g., a lack of knowledge due to insufficient or unrepresentative training data). Focusing on uncertainty opens up several important aspects of analysis. First, it enables the detection of hidden brittleness: a model may achieve high accuracy within a subgroup while still expressing high uncertainty, indicating weak generalization or underrepresentation during training. Second, it facilitates auditing model robustness by surfacing subgroups with consistently high uncertainty, which can guide targeted interventions such as data augmentation, calibration, or retraining.

The main contributions of this work are as follows:

1. We introduce a theoretical formalism for subgroup discovery based on model uncertainty, extending classical subgroup analysis to operate on model-derived uncertainty measures.
2. We present a proof-of-concept implementation, including a subgroup merging strategy based on effect size and quality prioritization in the discovered subgroups.
3. We present preliminary experimental results on synthetic datasets and the classical Iris dataset, demonstrating the feasibility and potential of the proposed approach for uncovering uncertainty-driven subgroup structures.

The rest of the paper is organized as follows: Sect. 2 introduces the preliminaries. Section 3 formally introduces our proposed method to incorporate model uncertainty into subgroup discovery. Section 4 describes our experimental setup. Section 5 reports the empirical results, discusses their implications, and outlines directions for future work. Finally, Sect. 6 summarizes our key findings.

2   Preliminaries

Let a dataset $D = \{x_1, x_2, \ldots, x_n\} \subseteq \mathbb{R}^m \cup \mathcal{V}^m$ consist of n samples, where each x_i is described by m features $A = \{a_1, a_2, \ldots, a_m\}$. Each feature a_j can be either numeric, with values in $\mathbb{R}$, or categorical, with values in a finite domain $\mathcal{V}_j$.

For categorical features, a selector (or basic pattern) is a Boolean condition of the form $a_j = v$, which evaluates to true for sample x_i if the value of feature a_j in x_i equals v. For numeric features, selectors are typically range conditions of the form $a_j \in I$, where $I \subseteq \mathbb{R}$ is an interval such as $[l, u]$ or unbounded variants like $[l, \infty)$, $(-\infty, u]$.

Let Σ denote the set of all such selectors. A subgroup pattern $P \subseteq \Sigma$ is defined as a conjunction of selectors:

$$P = \{\mathrm{sel}_1, \ldots, \mathrm{sel}_\ell\},$$

which evaluates to true for a sample x_i if all individual selectors hold:

$$P(x_i) = \mathrm{sel}_1(x_i) \wedge \cdots \wedge \mathrm{sel}_\ell(x_i).$$

The support set (or extension) of a pattern P is the subset of samples in the dataset that satisfy the pattern:

$$\mathrm{ext}(P) := \{x_i \in D \mid P(x_i) = \mathrm{true}\}.$$

3   Proposed Method

Model Uncertainty. Let $f : \mathbb{R}^m \to \Delta^C$ be a probabilistic classifier that outputs a predictive distribution over C classes for each input $x_i \in D$. That is,

$$f(x_i) = \hat{p}_i = (p_1^{(i)}, p_2^{(i)}, \ldots, p_C^{(i)}), \quad \text{with } \sum_{c=1}^{C} p_c^{(i)} = 1.$$

Here, $\hat{p}_i$ denotes the vector of predicted probabilities for input x_i, and each component $p_c^{(i)} \in [0,1]$ represents the probability assigned to class $c \in \{1, \ldots, C\}$.

Let $u : \Delta^C \to \mathbb{R}$ be a scalar uncertainty function that maps the model's predictive distribution to a real-valued score indicating its confidence or uncertainty. We denote the uncertainty score for sample x_i as:

$$u_i := u(\hat{p}_i).$$

Examples of uncertainty functions u include predictive entropy, margin (the difference between the top two class probabilities), or variance across an ensemble of models.

Subgroup Discovery on Model Uncertainty. Let $U := \{u_1, \ldots, u_n\}$ be the global distribution of uncertainty scores across the dataset. For a given subgroup pattern $P \subseteq \Sigma$, we define its associated uncertainty distribution:

$$U_P := \{u_i \mid x_i \in \text{ext}(P)\}.$$

The objective is to identify patterns P such that the local uncertainty U_P exhibits exceptional behavior relative to the global distribution U, revealing subpopulations where the model is systematically more confident or uncertain.

To systematically detect such deviations, we require a way to measure how "interesting" or exceptional a given subgroup is. For this purpose, we use a quality function widely adopted in numeric subgroup discovery. Formally, for a given subgroup S, the quality is computed as:

$$q(S) = \left(\frac{|S|}{|D|}\right)^{\alpha} |\mu_S - \mu_D|,$$

where $|S|$ is the number of samples in the subgroup, $|D|$ is the number of samples in the dataset, μ_S is the mean value of the target in the subgroup (in our case, the uncertainty score) and μ_D is the target's mean value of the dataset. Hence, the first factor corresponds to the relative size of the subgroup, and the second factor corresponds to the difference between the target's mean in the subgroup and the dataset. In all experiments, we use the absolute deviation $|\mu_S - \mu_D|$ to capture both unusually high and low values of the target variable relative to the dataset as a whole. The quality function $q(S)$ benefits larger subgroups whose mean differs significantly from the mean of the entire dataset, promoting more general groups with interesting characteristics. Furthermore, some subgroups may partially overlap, being prioritized the subgroup with the highest quality.

Subgroup Merging. The discovered subgroups are restricted to conditions where features are each compared to a fixed value using operators such as greater than, less than, or equal to. While this formulation enables interpretable rules, it inherently restricts the subgroup shapes to axis-aligned regions in the feature space. As a result, the method is limited in its ability to capture more complex structures, such as spatially disjoint clusters or curved decision boundaries. To address these limitations, we propose a post-processing step that merges closely related subgroups. While Friedman and Fisher have explored the concept of subgroup post-refinement [10], their approach applies only subtle changes to the subgroup boundaries, whereas our approach allows for more substantial restructuring, enabling the construction of higher-level groupings that may represent disconnected or irregularly shaped regions in the feature space. While this approach forms more general and semantically meaningful regions, reduces redundancy and improves interpretability, it does not overcome the limitation of not being able to model curved decision boundaries.

Let $\mathcal{S} = \{S_1, S_2, \ldots, S_N\}$ denote the set of support sets of discovered subgroup patterns, where each $S_i = \text{ext}(P_i) \subseteq D$ corresponds to a subgroup pattern $P_i \subseteq \Sigma$ as defined in Sect. 2. Each subgroup $S_i \subseteq D$ is associated with a scalar quality score $q(S_i) \in \mathbb{R}$, where q is the quality function which reflects its interestingness or relevance. To determine whether two subgroups S_i and S_j should be merged, we compute the effect size between their uncertainty score distributions using Cohen's d.[1] We merge subgroups S_i and S_j if Cohen's $d\,(S_i, S_j) < \tau$. If the previous condition is met, the subgroup with the lower quality score is absorbed into the one with the higher score.

$$q(S_i) > q(S_j) \quad \Rightarrow \quad S_j \hookrightarrow S_i.$$

Additionally, it is possible that subgroups overlap. Therefore, the quality value of the subgroup determines which overlapping subgroup persists. Let $q(S_i) > q(S_j) > q(S_k)$ and $S_j \cap S_k \neq \emptyset$. In the region where S_j and S_k overlap, S_j prevails due to its higher quality. If $S_k \hookrightarrow S_i$, that region is now assigned to S_i, since $q(S_i) > q(S_j)$.

4 Experimental Setup

4.1 Datasets

We created three synthetic datasets, each based on two features, as shown in Fig. 1a. These datasets represent simple scenarios with at least two class labels, which may or may not overlap, resulting in regions where the classes are not easily separable.

The first dataset, GaussianMixture, consists of two Gaussian distributions that partially overlap and correspond to different classes. The second dataset,

---

[1] We use Cohen's d as a measure of distributional "distance" between subgroups, based on the intuition that subgroups with similar uncertainty (i.e., low effect size) likely represent overlapping or redundant regions and can be meaningfully merged.

CHECKERBOARD, consists of four Gaussian distributions arranged in a checkerboard pattern (two at the top and two at the bottom). The top-left and bottomright distributions belong to one class, while the top-right and bottom-left distributions belong to another. The distributions overlap partially. The third synthetic dataset, TRIGAUSSIANMIXTURE, consists of three side-by-side Gaussian distributions that partially overlap. Each distribution corresponds to a different class, resulting in a total of three classes.

We also used the widely known Iris dataset [8] to incorporate a real-world example into our experiments. Although our proposed method works in an m-dimensional feature space, to simplify a qualitative analysis of the subgroups, two features were selected, *sepal length* and *petal length*.

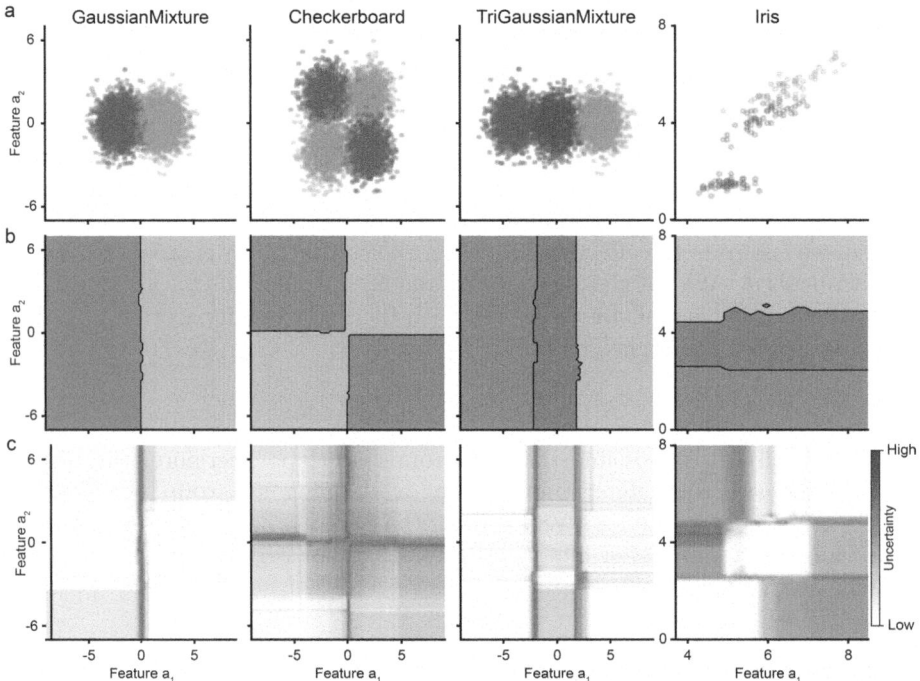

Fig. 1. The four datasets used in our experiments — GAUSSIANMIXTURE, CHECKERBOARD, TRIGAUSSIANMIXTURE and IRIS. **a**: Sample distributions across the feature space with colors indicating ground truth class labels. For the Iris dataset, a_1 corresponds to the *sepal length* and a_2 to *petal length*. **b**: Decision boundaries of a Random Forest classifier, with colors indicating predicted class labels (matching the groundtruth color scheme). **c**: Uncertainty per sample. (Color figure online)

4.2 Modeling

We trained a Random Forest classifier on each dataset. We used a maximum depth of 5 on the synthetic toy datasets and a maximum depth of 10 on the Iris dataset. All other remaining hyperparameters were set to their default values. The decision boundaries of each classifier are shown in Fig. 1b.

4.3 Instantiating the Uncertainty Measure

In this study, we instantiate the uncertainty function $u(\cdot)$ using the maximum class probability:

$$u(x_i) := 1 - \max_{c \in \{1,\dots,C\}} p_c^{(i)}, \tag{1}$$

interpreting higher values of $u(x_i)$ as greater predictive uncertainty. This choice is simple, model-agnostic, and widely used in prior work [11,19]. The results of $u(\cdot)$ on the datasets are presented in Fig. 1c.

4.4 Subgroup Discovery and Merging

We used the *pysubgroup* library for all our subgroup discovery experiments [21]. The library requires several key parameters: the dataset on which subgroups are to be discovered; the target, which will determine which characteristics of the data are relevant for subgroups; the search space, which defines which features of the data can be used to describe the subgroups; the number of selectors in a subgroup description and a quality function that evaluates the quality of the subgroups.

Regarding the target parameter, we explored two complementary approaches:

1. A baseline experiment of discovering subgroups on the data, providing the class of each sample as the target.
2. The discovery of subgroups that reflect the confidence of the model on its predictions, providing the uncertainty function $u(\cdot)$ as the target.

We set the maximum subgroup description depth to four selectors. Since the targets in both experiments are numeric, we used the STANDARDQFNUMERIC quality function from the *pysubgroup* library, with $\alpha = 1$, based on the formulation introduced in Sect. 3. The *pysubgroup* discovery algorithm returns a set of subgroups, each defined as a conjunction of selectors over the input features. To reduce redundancy and improve interpretability, we applied a subgroup merging procedure, with the overlap threshold τ empirically set to 0.8 for the toy datasets and 0.5 for the Iris dataset.

5 Results and Discussion

In this section, we report and discuss the results for the controlled toy datasets and the Iris dataset. The results of initial subgroup discovery and subgroup merging are shown in Fig. 2.

5.1 Synthetic Toy Datasets

For the GAUSSIANMIXTURE dataset (Fig. 2a), subgroup discovery based on class labels and model uncertainty yields similar structures prior to merging. Notably, the junction of the disjoint subgroups, due to the merging process, allows for the distinguishing of the two approaches. In both cases, the identified subgroups segment the feature space into regions where one class predominates and regions where both classes overlap. After merging, two distinct outcomes emerge. For the class label target, three final subgroups are identified, from left to right: dominance of class label 1, a region of overlapping labels, and dominance of label 2. In contrast, using model uncertainty as the target yields only two final subgroups: one representing regions where the model is highly confident in its predictions (the flanking subgroups), and the other capturing regions of higher uncertainty (the central subgroup). These outcomes are consistent with the patterns observed in model decision boundaries (Fig. 1b) and model uncertainty (Fig. 1c).

The subgroups identified for the other two datasets largely correspond to the intuition suggested by Fig. 1b and Fig. 1c.

For the CHECKERBOARD dataset, the benefits of applying the merging process are particularly evident in the class target label, as it enables the association of disjoint regions corresponding to the same label. A similar effect is observed in the confidence label, where the merging process effectively unifies the corner regions that exhibit highly similar confidence values. However, the subgroup corresponding to the horizontal bands on the right side does not correspond to the distribution of model uncertainty across the feature space (Fig. 1c). Instead, it was expected that these regions would be absorbed into the darker red subgroup. It is reasonable to assume that a more finely tuned merging threshold could have led to this outcome.

Focusing on the subgroups found in TRIGAUSSIANMIXTURE using uncertainty, one might have expected S_1, S_3 and S_5 to merge into the same subgroup, corresponding to a region of low uncertainty by the model, and S_2 and S_4 to merge into another subgroup, reflecting higher uncertainty by the model. Nevertheless, according to Fig. 1c, it is clear that the model is not as certain of its predictions in the S_3 region (where $a_1 = 0$) as it is on the S_1 and S_5 regions, validating the results.

5.2 Iris Dataset

The subgroups discovered in the Iris dataset using model uncertainty are shown in Fig. 3. There are two subgroups discovered as a result of the merging operation. There is also a gray region, which corresponds to a part of the feature space that is not covered by any of the discovered subgroups. The final subgroups align with regions where the model exhibits higher uncertainty (lighter red) and lower uncertainty (darker red). This segmentation is consistent with Fig. 1a, as the lighter red region corresponds to the area where class overlap occurs. However, according to Fig. 1c, there are two horizontal bands of higher

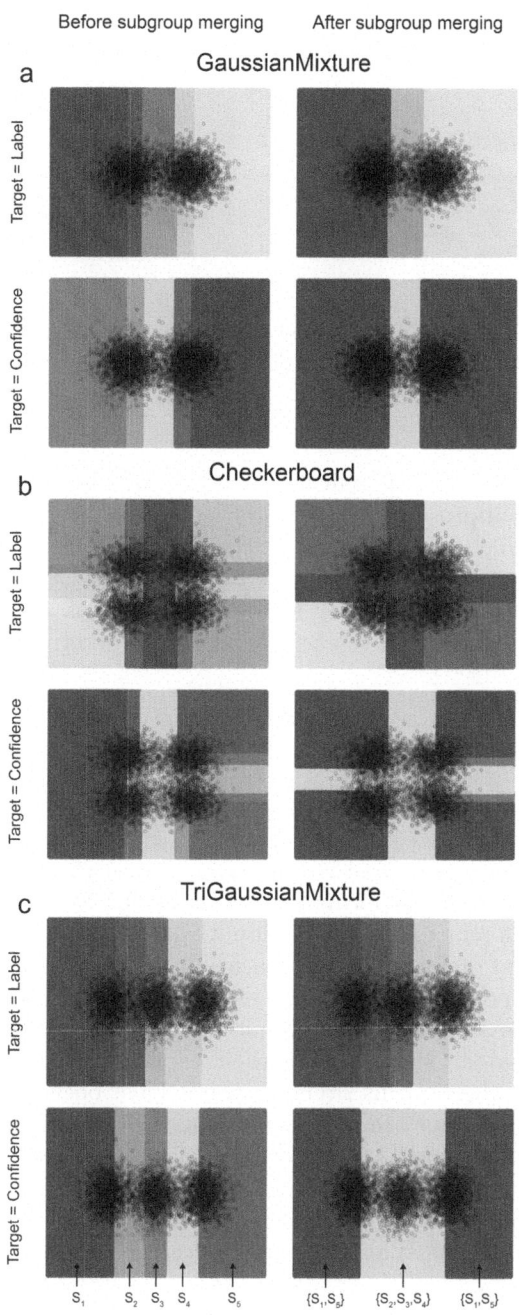

Fig. 2. a: GAUSSIANMIXTURE. **b**: CHECKERBOARD. **c**: TRIGAUSSIANMIXTURE. Top row: Subgroup discovery based on class labels. Bottom row: Subgroup discovery based on model uncertainty. Left column: All identified subgroups. Right column: Subgroups after merging. Color coding is consistent within each row. (Color figure online)

Before subgroup merging   After subgroup merging

Iris

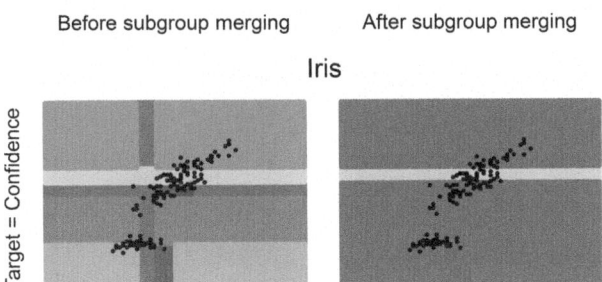

Fig. 3. Subgroup discovery based on model uncertainty in the Iris dataset. Subgroup color coding is consistent across both figures. Regions shown in gray are not assigned to any subgroup. (Color figure online)

uncertainty separating the different labels, which are also reflected in subgroups before the merging approach, as shown in Fig. 3. This discrepancy suggests that the merging threshold (τ) may be too brittle and could be refined to better preserve meaningful variation in model uncertainty. Nonetheless, given that a more conservative threshold was already selected for the Iris dataset compared to the synthetic datasets, further research is needed to determine optimal merging settings.

5.3   Related Work

He and Shaposhnik [15] formalize the notion of an *implicit trade-off* in model selection: two models with comparable overall performance may behave very differently across subpopulations, implicitly favoring certain feature regions over others. Scalar traditional performance measures fail to capture how a model performs across different regions of the input space. To mitigate this limitation, both qualitative and quantitative approaches have been proposed to reveal and interpret localized performance differences. Areosa et al. [1] proposed the *Error Dependence Plot*, a visualization technique designed to expose conditions under which regression models deviate from their expected global behavior. On the quantitative side, subgroup discovery methods have been applied to highlight systematic patterns in performance deviations. Prior work has explored these techniques in classification [7, 26] and regression settings [23], enabling more detailed assessments of model behavior across the feature space. Despite growing interest in understanding model behavior beyond global metrics, relatively few works have focused on analyzing *model uncertainty* across the feature space. Our work fills this gap in current model evaluation frameworks, particularly in settings where reliable confidence estimates are as important as accurate predictions.

5.4   Limitations and Future Work

While the proposed approach demonstrates promising results, it also presents several limitations that open directions for future research.

The discovered subgroups are defined by selectors, which are limited to axis-aligned, linear regions. This constraint significantly limits the algorithm's ability to capture more expressive subgroup shapes. While the merging procedure partially mitigates this limitation, it still fails to detect subgroups with curved or nonlinear boundaries.

Future research can explore a broader range of scenarios to allow for the discovery of non-linear or curved regions in subgroup discovery. It would also be valuable to expand the set of toy datasets, for instance, by including a Gaussian mixture with gradually increasing class overlap or a two-spiral dataset, and to evaluate the method across a wider variety of classifiers and other benchmark datasets. Finally, it is also important to extend the target of subgroup discovery to incorporate measures of aleatoric and epistemic uncertainty, thereby enabling a deeper understanding of the model's predictive behavior.

6   Conclusions

This study introduced a novel perspective on subgroup discovery using model uncertainty. Through controlled experiments on controlled synthetic datasets and the Iris dataset, we demonstrated the feasibility of identifying interpretable subgroups based on uncertainty. While preliminary, our results highlight the potential of uncertainty-driven subgroup discovery to reveal regions of systematic model uncertainty, complementing traditional performance-based analyses. These findings open promising directions for future work in Responsible AI, namely model auditing, interpretability, and robustness analysis.

Acknowledgments. This work was supported by European funds through the Recovery and Resilience Plan, project "Center for Responsible AI", project number C645008882-00000055.

Disclosure of Interests. The authors have no competing interests to declare that are relevant to the content of this article.

References

1. Areosa, I., Torgo, L.: Visual interpretation of regression error. Expert. Syst. **37**(6), e12621 (2020)
2. Atzmueller, M.: Subgroup discovery. Wiley Interdiscip. Rev. Data Min. Knowl. Discov. **5**(1), 35–49 (2015)
3. Barandas, M., et al.: Evaluation of uncertainty quantification methods in multi-label classification: a case study with automatic diagnosis of electrocardiogram. Inf. Fusion **101**, 101978 (2024). https://doi.org/10.1016/j.inffus.2023.101978

4. Barandas, M., Folgado, D., Santos, R., Simão, R., Gamboa, H.: Uncertainty-based rejection in machine learning: implications for model development and interpretability. Electronics **11**(3), 396 (2022). https://doi.org/10.3390/electronics11030396

5. Cabrera, A., Hohman, F., Lin, J., Chau, D.H.: Fairvis: visual analytics for discovering intersectional bias in machine learning. In: Proceedings of the 2019 IEEE Conference on Visualization (VIS), pp. 46–50. IEEE (2019)

6. Duivesteijn, W., Feelders, A., Knobbe, A.: Exceptional model mining. Data Min. Knowl. Disc. **30**(1), 47–98 (2016)

7. Duivesteijn, W., Thaele, J.: Understanding where your classifier does (not) work–the scape model class for EMM. In: 2014 IEEE International Conference on Data Mining, pp. 809–814. IEEE (2014)

8. Fisher, R.A.: Iris. UCI Machine Learning Repository (1936). https://doi.org/10.24432/C56C76

9. Flach, P.A., Gamberger, D., Lavrač, N.: Subgroup discovery in data mining and its application to marketing. In: Proceedings of the 13th IFIP TC12/WG 12.2 International Conference on Machine Learning: ECML 2001, pp. 445–446. Springer (2001)

10. Friedman, J.H., Fisher, N.I.: Bump hunting in high-dimensional data. Stat. Comput. **9**(2), 123–143 (1999). https://doi.org/10.1023/A:1008894516817

11. Gal, Y., Ghahramani, Z.: Dropout as a bayesian approximation: representing model uncertainty in deep learning. In: International Conference on Machine Learning (ICML) (2016)

12. Gamberger, D., Lavrač, N.: Expert-guided subgroup discovery: methodology and application. J. Artif. Intell. Res. **17**, 501–527 (2002)

13. Gamberger, D., Lavrač, N., Krstacic, G.: Characterization of patient groups with ischemic stroke using subgroup discovery method. J. Biomed. Inform. **40**(6), 679–685 (2007)

14. Gamberger, D., Lavrač, N., Srivatsa, S., Krstacic, G., Krstacic, A.: Induction of comprehensible models for gene expression datasets by subgroup discovery methodology. J. Biomed. Inform. **37**(4), 269–284 (2004)

15. He, Z., Shaposhnik, Y.: Visualizing the implicit model selection tradeoff. J. Artif. Intell. Res. **76**, 829–881 (2023)

16. Helal, S., Li, J., Liu, L., Ebrahimie, E., Dawson, S., Murray, D.J.: Identifying key factors of student academic performance by subgroup discovery. Int. J. Data Sci. Anal. **7**, 227–245 (2019)

17. Klösgen, W.: Explora: a multipattern and multistrategy discovery assistant. In: Advances in Knowledge Discovery and Data Mining, pp. 249–271 (1996)

18. Konijn, R., Duivesteijn, W., van Leeuwen, M., Knobbe, A.J.: Local subgroup discovery applied to fraud detection in health care. In: Proceedings of the 2013 IEEE 13th International Conference on Data Mining Workshops, pp. 856–863. IEEE (2013)

19. Lakshminarayanan, B., Pritzel, A., Blundell, C.: Simple and scalable predictive uncertainty estimation using deep ensembles. Adv. Neural Inf. Process. Syst. (NeurIPS) **30** (2017)

20. Lavrač, N., Gamberger, D., Todorovski, L., Džeroski, S.: Subgroup discovery with cn2-sd. J. Mach. Learn. Res. **5**, 153–188 (2004)

21. Lemmerich, F., Becker, M.: Pysubgroup: easy-to-use subgroup discovery in python. In: Joint European Conference on Machine Learning and Knowledge Discovery in Databases, pp. 658–662 (2018)

22. Piantek, S., Boudet, R., Vrain, C., Lenca, P.: Divexplorer: a tool for interactive and explainable biased subgroup discovery. In: Proceedings of the 30th ACM International Conference on Information and Knowledge Management (CIKM), pp. 2915–2918. ACM (2021)

23. Pimentel, J., Azevedo, P.J., Torgo, L.: Subgroup mining for performance analysis of regression models. Expert. Syst. **40**(1), e13118 (2023)

24. Romero, C., Ventura, S.: Educational data mining: a review of the state of the art. IEEE Trans. Syst. Man Cybern. Part C (Appl. Rev.) **40**(6), 601–618 (2010)

25. Siebes, A.: Data surveying: foundations of an inductive query language. In: KDD, pp. 269–274 (1995)

26. Torgo, L., Azevedo, P., Areosa, I.: Beyond average performance–exploring regions of deviating performance for black box classification models. arXiv preprint arXiv:2109.08216 (2021)

Author Index

J. Valente de Oliveira et al. (Eds.): EPIA 2025, LNAI 16121, pp. 519–522, 2026.
https://doi.org/10.1007/978-3-032-05176-9

The manufacturer's authorised representative in the EU is Springer
Nature Customer Service Centre GmbH, Europaplatz 3, 69115 Heidelberg,
Germany. If you have any concerns regarding our products, please
contact ProductSafety@springernature.com

Printed and bound by CPI Group (UK) Ltd, Croydon, CR0 4YY
29/04/2026
02099461-0019